Adventure Guide to Canada's Atlantic Provinces

Barbara Radcliffe Rogers
& Stillman Rogers

with additional birding and fishing notes by
Sara Godwin and Charles James

HUNTER

Hunter Publishing, Inc.
130 Campus Drive, Edison, NJ 08818
732 225 1900 / 800 255 0343 / Fax 732 417 1744
e-mail: hunterp@bellsouth.net

In Canada
1220 Nicholson Road, Newmarket, Ontario
Canada L3Y 7V1
800 399 6858 / Fax 800 363 2665

In the UK
Windsor Books International
The Boundary, Wheatley Road
Garsington
Oxford, OX44 9EJ England
01865-361122 / Fax 01865-361133

ISBN 1-55650-819-0

Visit our Web site at www.hunterpublishing.com

Cover: *Tiverton Lighthouse, Long Island, Bay of Fundy, NS*
Index Stock Photography, © Robert Houser

Back cover: *Flowerpot Rocks, The Rocks Provincial Park, Hopewell Cape, New Brunswick*
Courtesy Tourism New Brunswick

All other photos by authors, unless otherwise indicated.

Maps by Lissa K. Dailey, © 1999 Hunter Publishing, Inc.
Indexing by Nancy Wolff

2 3 4 5

Dedication

For Valerie – one of the best reasons we know for traveling in Atlantic Canada, if we could only stop laughing long enough to see where we're going.

A Word of Thanks

Where do we begin? With the many people who helped us arrange our travels? With the others who offered us their help and hospitality? With local people who were just being their natural, neighborly selves when they went out of their way to show us or take us to their favorite places? With those with whom we shared our often serendipitous adventures? With the sympathetic editor or with the next-door neighbor who, when deadline loomed, inspected the manuscript to be sure all the commas were in the right places? With our family, whose only reward for putting up with our long absences and periods of hibernation as we wrote was to get to share many of the adventures with us?

An alphabetical list would solve the problem, but not properly express our gratitude. Some sorting does seem to be in order, so we begin with the tourism representatives who have made our travels smoother in so many ways, answered our endless questions, ferreted out the little details only we would ask, and remained cheerful and hospitable all the while: Candee Treadway, Ralph Johansen, Valerie Kidney, Andrea Peddle, Kay Coxworthy, Randy Brooks, Carole Horn, Percy Mallet, Geraldine Beaton, Dorleen Sponagle, Nancy Lockerbie, Dick Griffiths and Melanie Coates.

Innkeepers and hosts at B&Bs are the greatest resource a writer or traveler can have in hunting for out-of-the-way places and local adventures, and we've been blessed with the best. So many in fact that we can't possibly name them all. But a few went so far beyond the call of even Canadian hospitality that we must mention them: Allan and Joan Redmond (who always save a serving of big, succulent scallops for Tim, even when we're late to dinner), Lynn Stephens (who not only sent us off with a delicious lunch, but included her silverware to eat it with), Lloyd Miller (who stayed up late to draw us maps and tell us of his outport hometown), Aiden Costello (who wouldn't let us leave hungry, even though his restaurant hadn't opened yet), Joan Semple (who pretends that she always reads way past midnight and isn't really staying up for us), Elizabeth Cooney (whose home is always such a welcome oasis to weary travelers), Katherine Van Weston (who held dinner on a back burner while her husband, Burt, took us to explore the then-unopened road into the Big Salmon River), Rudy and Kathy Zinn (whose elegant dinner party was the perfect conclusion to a long day of hiking), Leslie Langille (who shares, along with some of our pet peeves about travel books, a bounty of good stories), Larry and Ida Adair (who took the afternoon off to drive us to Martin Head and Quiddy Falls) and the Mullendores, who are always good company – and know all the best trails around Mabou.

Our gratitude, too, to those other friends whose latchstring is always out when we're on the road, most notably Nancy Sears and the Clowaters: Phoebe, Darla and Roger.

Thanks to Pamela Knight, and her parents at Budgel's in King's Point, and to Roy Richards, Pamela's uncle, who took part of his only day off to show us how to get through the Red Indian Lake route. And to all the other people who stopped whatever they were doing to give us directions, advice, a cup of tea, and sometimes lunch, dinner or a bed for the night, and otherwise helped us in our adventures. Hospitality is a way of life in Atlantic Canada, and we have been the beneficiaries of far more than our fair share of it.

Thanks to friends and fellow writers Tom Bross, who shared his files with us – the supreme act of generosity among travel writers – and Phyllis Vernon, whose knowledge of Canadian history, literature and art has brought so much more depth and meaning to our travels. And to Sara Godwin and Charles James, for their vital contributions on fishing and birding. Final thanks to Dixie Gurian, who reviewed each page with a sharp eye to the tiny details and to our patient editor Lissa Dailey, who insists that the stacked manuscript makes the best coffee table she's ever had in her office. All these people – and more whom we've left unnamed – have made this book a reality.

About the Authors

Tim and Barbara Rogers have been wandering around Canada since the very first days of their marriage, hiking its trails, camping in its parks, climbing its mountains, kayaking its waters and skiing its snow. Until recently, they saved the Atlantic Provinces for themselves, going there for family vacations while they wrote about other places in the world. Their books have covered such widespread locations as the Galapagos Islands of Ecuador, African safari parks, Portugal, New England and the rivers and seas of Europe. Their articles in magazines and newspapers have described their adventures on several continents, from climbing a volcano on the back of a camel to "driving" their own houseboat through the canals of England. Exotic, they insist, is simply a matter of perspective, and they find a lion in the bush no more exciting than being in the middle of an Avalon caribou herd or looking a Fundy whale straight in the eye.

The authors with dog team in Bathurst, New Brunswick

Authors' Foreword

Our adventures in Canada's four eastern provinces span several decades and evoke floods of happy memories. Our children learned how to dig for sweet tender clams in the red sands of PEI's north shore, and set upon their first deep-sea fishing voyages from the harbor at North Rustico. Before that, we caught our own first flounder and cod in the same waters. The Atlantic Provinces hold a lot of firsts for our entire family: we paddled our first kayaks along the rocky (and, we remember, windy) shore of Grand Manan, learned the delicate art of balancing on the icy runners of a dogsled in Bathurst, and sailed within reach of our first iceberg in Witless Bay. But each experience need not be a first to be an adventure. A trail we've hiked a dozen times – such as the shoreline at St. Andrews – is a new adventure each time, different in each season, each tide and each time of day.

These four provinces, so different in topography and geography, are a wonderland for the adventurous traveler. To us, the most exciting thing about these provinces is the way outdoor sports and activities blend with the natural environment. A challenging hike ends at a breathtaking gorge with a waterfall plummeting hundreds of feet into it. An afternoon of kayaking can take you around an iceberg, and puffins may swoop, dive and swim as they fish around your kayak. As you catch your breath in calm river waters after running exhilarating rapids, you may see a family of moose ahead, over the prow of your canoe. An afternoon's climb may take you across an almost plantless expanse of moon-like landscape. Or you can ride the tidal bore in a boat, skimming along the surface of the wall of water that pushes twice daily into the estuaries of the Bay of Fundy.

It's difficult to write about this land we love so much without our words sounding like a travel brochure. How, for example, does one describe the long white sweep of Kouchibouguac's barrier beach, or the impact of Western Brook Pond's half-mile vertical cliffs? We have set ourselves a limit of one use per chapter of the word "spectacular," and argue between ourselves over which view it should describe.

Not all the adventures we suggest have the adrenaline rush of canoeing the Main River Canyon. Many are quiet pastimes: watching birds at close range, learning a time-worn craft from a Native Canadian, sleeping in an historic lighthouse, inspecting a fossil-filled segment of a long-ago sea bed or watching a pitcher plant lunch on a mosquito. But nearly all require something of us, and all, we hope, give us much in return. Some require physical activity, others that we consider things we'd never thought about before. Some teach us about the world we live in and the creatures that inhabit it with us. All are more rewarding if we share ourselves with the local people whose home we explore. That very personal cultural exchange is the essence of both adventure and travel.

Barbara and Tim Rogers

Contents

Nova Scotia

MAPS

Introduction

IN THIS CHAPTER

- Geography
- History
- Getting Around
- Exchange Rate & Taxes
- About the Adventures
- Fauna & Flora
- Accommodation & Dining Price Key
- Information Sources

From the iceberg- and whale-filled waters of Newfoundland to the genteel historic streets of Fredericton is a land and coast filled with vast stretches of wilderness, herds of caribou, French country villages, miles of beaches, historical sites and reconstructions, and scenery ranging from sweeping river views and gently rolling farmlands to the most dramatic coastal cliffs and fjords on the continent. Dotted throughout are small cosmopolitan cities. Just as you think you know these four provinces, you discover another place, a new facet of their splendid diversity.

Much of the North America we know today began on this eastern seaboard. St. John's, Newfoundland, claims the continent's oldest main street, and in 1620 the Pilgrims stopped at a nearby fishing settlement to re-provision on their way to Plymouth. Historic sites are well-preserved and interpreted – the French Fortress of Louisbourg rivals any historic reconstruction in the world, and other villages interpret the lives of early Acadian, Scottish and English settlers.

Wherever you travel – New Brunswick's easygoing capital, along that province's Acadian coast to Caraquet, in lively British Halifax, among the Scottish towns of Cape Breton Island, cycling the new Confederation Trail across Prince Edward Island, in the remote north of Newfoundland or in a tiny outport reached only by boat – you will be welcomed with genuine hospitality and warmth. It's an almost legendary characteristic of Newfoundland, Canada's youngest province, where a quest for directions may lead to an invitation to a cup of tea or a drink of "screech," a fierce and fiery high-proof rum guaranteed to warm you to the toes of your woolly socks.

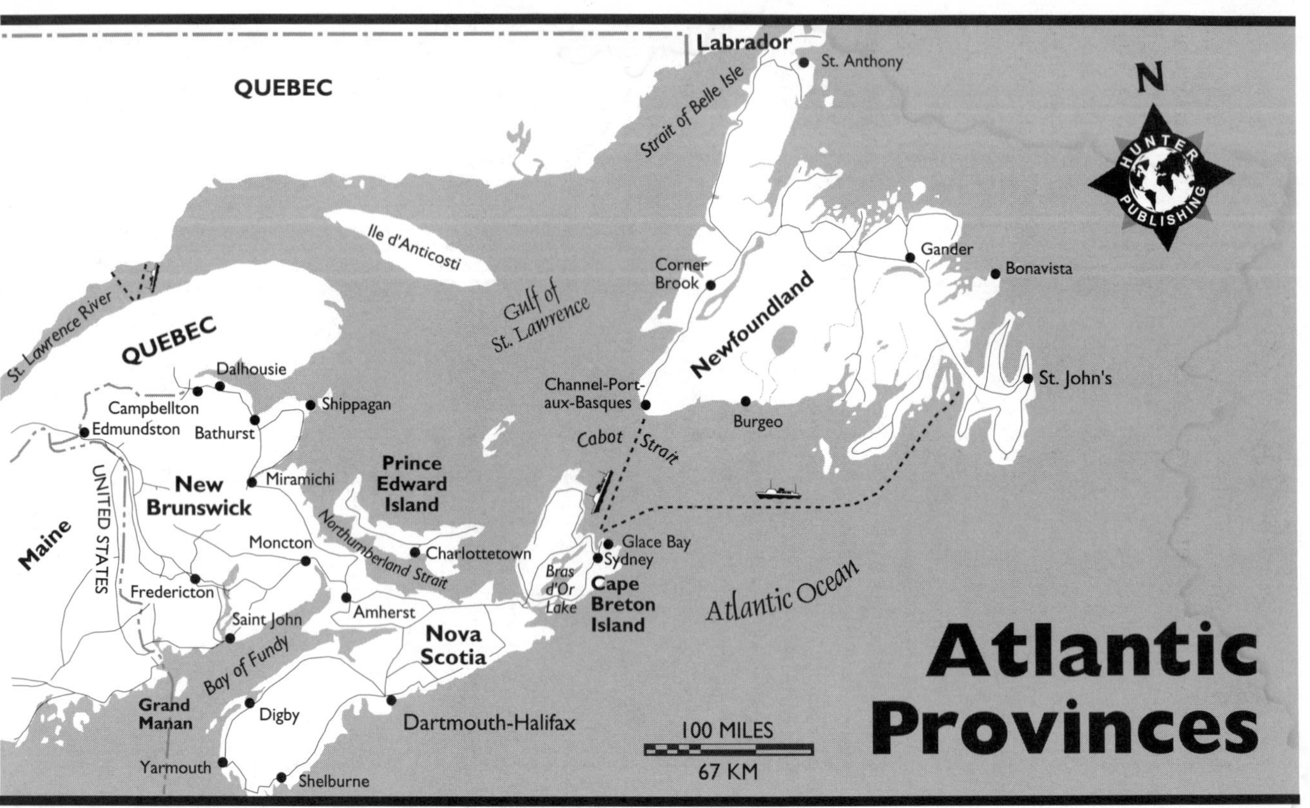
Atlantic Provinces
N
HUNTER PUBLISHING
QUEBEC
Labrador
St. Anthony
Strait of Belle Isle
Ile d'Anticosti
Gulf of St. Lawrence
St. Lawrence River
QUEBEC
Dalhousie
Campbellton
Edmundston
Bathurst
Shippagan
Corner Brook
Newfoundland
Gander
Bonavista
St. John's
Channel-Port-aux-Basques
Burgeo
Cabot Strait
Prince Edward Island
Miramichi
New Brunswick
UNITED STATES
Maine
Moncton
Northumberland Strait
Charlottetown
Glace Bay
Sydney
Bras d'Or Lake
Cape Breton Island
Atlantic Ocean
Fredericton
Amherst
Saint John
Nova Scotia
Bay of Fundy
Grand Manan
Digby
Dartmouth-Halifax
100 MILES
67 KM
Yarmouth
Shelburne

Geography

Border disputes have never been an issue among the four Atlantic provinces, where water separates them all (except for a tiny umbilical cord that holds Nova Scotia to New Brunswick). Although firmly attached to the continent on the west, where it borders both Maine and Quebec, New Brunswick has more coastal than land boundaries. In the three southern provinces, most of this coastline is bordered in beaches – miles of golden, red, gray, and white sands. The waters of the Northumberland Strait are warm – New Brunswick has the warmest saltwater swimming north of Virginia – and the beaches of Prince Edward Island and Nova Scotia are also pleasant and warm. What Newfoundland and Labrador lack in beaches (the water there is *not* warm), they more than make up in breathtaking coastal scenery.

Nova Scotia lies east and south of New Brunswick, with tiny **Prince Edward Island** off its northern shore, across the Northumberland Strait, which also separates it from New Brunswick. East and north of all these lies **Newfoundland**, an island of many peninsulas, separated from Quebec and Labrador on the mainland by the narrow Strait of Belle Isle. Its closest point to the other Atlantic provinces is **Cape Breton Island**, a five-hour ferry ride away. Cape Breton Island itself lies off the northeast end of Nova Scotia, attached to it since the 1950s by a causeway.

Grand Manan Island, New Brunswick

The other most noticeable geographical features are the **Bay of Fundy**, which nearly separates Nova Scotia from the mainland, and the **Gulf of St. Lawrence**, which cuts Newfoundland off from Quebec. Through New Brunswick's north run the **Appalachian Mountains**, which surface again in western Newfoundland. The rest of the terrain is gently rolling and fairly low, except for the northern part of Cape Breton Island, where the highlands rise to low, but rugged mountains. Prince Edward Island is fairly flat, its hills gentle and covered with a patchwork of green fields and meadows.

History

Descendants of the Maritime Archaic peoples, the first known in Newfoundland and Labrador, were Paleoeskimo peoples from the Arctic. They greeted and soon drove off the first Europeans to settle here: Vikings who explored the Labrador coast and established a small colony on the northern tip of Newfoundland about 1000 AD. There was no further recorded contact with the rest of the world for five centuries, when John Cabot, exploring on behalf of Britain, reached the shores of Newfoundland in 1497. The battle for land and the riches of the continent was on.

The first English settled in St. John's in the early 1500s, establishing a base from which to fish. Other Europeans followed, also attracted by the codfish of the Grand Banks, and the Dutch and French both set up supply bases in Newfoundland.

Meanwhile, the Micmac people fished along the shores and hunted the inland forests of what is now New Brunswick and Nova Scotia. In 1605 Samuel de Champlain established the first European colony at Port Royal, now Annapolis Royal, in Nova Scotia. Calling it Acadia, the French spread settlements along the west shore of Nova Scotia. As Scots were settling in eastern Nova Scotia and claiming it for England, the French established a settlement on Cape Breton Island, at Louisbourg. The French had already claimed Prince Edward Island in 1523 but didn't settle it until 1663, calling it Ile St-Jean.

Early contacts between the Europeans and the Native peoples were generally friendly. Europeans introduced more efficient tools and Natives taught the Europeans how to survive in the new environment, and traded them highly prized furs. But new settlers brought competition for land. European diseases, to which Native peoples had no immunities, wiped out complete villages, and in at least one case – the Beothuk of Newfoundland – entire peoples.

By the early 1600s, France was well ahead of Britain in the struggle to control the new territory. Adventurous French fur traders, explorers and missionaries had advanced into much of the eastern half of the continent, and their colonial empire – New France – included most of what is now the three southern provinces. The British controlled a number of areas, including Acadia, which France ceded to them in 1713 (although the French farmers remained on their land) and France kept Cape Breton Island.

Britain and France were, by 1750, rivals for colonial empires around the world: in India, the West Indies and North America. British colonies in Canada had grown faster than the French ones and had 30 times as many people. They provided stiff competition for New France's fur trade, and they brought armies and fleets from Europe. As skirmishes increased, the French made alliances with the Native peoples.

As the likelihood of war grew stronger, the British expelled the Acadian farmers that had remained in Nova Scotia after the French ceded it to Britain, fearing that they would side with the French and form the nucleus of an underground resistance. Many of these French settlers moved west into what is now New Brunswick; others fled to Louisiana.

In 1758 the English won a major battle against the French fort of Louisburg on Cape Breton Island. Gradually the French fell back and in 1759 they found themselves assailed on their major fronts. The decisive battle that sealed the fate of New France forever, took place in Quebec in 1759, where they were defeated. It was 1762 before the English secured their claim to Newfoundland by defeating the French at St. John's. France retained fishing rights off western Newfoundland and a base on the islands of St. Pierre and Miquelon, which are still part of France.

The capture of Quebec left Britain ruler of all of northern North America. To help recover the costs of the long war, the British government raised taxes on goods imported into the American colonies. The colonists rebelled, expecting the newly conquered French in the north to join them in revolution. But only a handful did, most fighting shoulder-to-shoulder with their British former enemies. Staunch Royalists and devout Catholics, they had little use for the "godless" Republicans from the south. After the War of 1812, Britain and the young United States agreed on a border between the United States and the group of colonies, by then known as Canada.

One of the side effects of the American Revolution was an influx of English-speaking immigrants from the American colonies: about 50,000 Loyalists settled, mostly in Nova Scotia and along the almost empty shores of what is now New Brunswick. These joined the Acadian refugees from Nova Scotia to become a separate colony, refusing an invitation to join their French neighbors as part of Quebec.

Borders made trade difficult between the Canadian colonies, and in 1864 representatives of each met in Charlottetown, Prince Edward Island (PEI), to discuss confederation. In 1867 the British Parliament created a federal union of Canada. Nova Scotia and New Brunswick hesitated over whether to remain separate, join the United States, or merge with Canada, but finally voted to merge. Remote Newfoundland hesitated longer, remaining a British colony until 1949, when it and Labrador became Canada's 10th province by a very narrow vote.

Getting Around

Eastern Canada is an easy place to reach. Travelers from the northeastern United States can drive through Maine and into New Brunswick, or they can take the mile-saving ferries from either Portland or Bar Harbor (both in Maine) to Yarmouth, Nova Scotia. Many people like to take the ferry one way and drive along the Quoddy and Fundy shores on the other, forming a circle of diverse land and seascapes. Flying is a faster way to get there, with most flights routed through the hub at Halifax, from which you can fly to all the other major cities and areas.

Rental Cars

Once in the Maritime Provinces (a designation which, you might be interested to know, includes the lower three, but not Newfoundland, which is part of the broader Atlantic Provinces group), you can move on to Newfoundland by ferry from Sydney, at the far end of Nova Scotia, or by air from Halifax. Before making that decision, do a lot of comparison shopping on car rental rates in Newfoundland, considering carefully the usual per-kilometer charge there. It might be less expensive to rent a car without a mileage add-on in another province and pay the ferry fare to take it there.

> **➲ CAR RENTAL TIP:** *When renting cars in Canada, don't forget to check the Canadian companies of* ***Tilden*** *(☎ 800/CAR-RENT in US or 800/387-4747 in Canada) and* ***Rent A Wreck*** *(☎ 800/327-9093 US or 800/327-0116 in Canada), whose rates and policies are traveler-friendly. They have locations in all four provinces.*

Driving in the Atlantic Provinces

As of 1997, you can drive to all three Maritime Provinces, with the opening of the whopping new Confederation Bridge linking New Brunswick to Prince Edward Island. To make a tidy circular route from New Brunwick to PEI and back to New Brunswick, you can use the bridge one way and the ferry from Wood Islands to Caribou, Nova Scotia, on the other.

Rules of the road are pretty much the same in Atlantic Canada as they are in the United States, with international road symbols in use most places. Distances on road signs and maps are shown in kilometers, and if you rent a car there, its odometer and speedometer will be also be in kilometers. (It's a bit startling to look down and realize you're tooling along at a cool 100.) When people tell you how far something is, they may use miles, especially in Newfoundland, where even young people who learned metric in school still think in miles.

The fastest conversion, if to-the-inch accuracy is not crucial, is two kilometers to a mile, plus a little. To translate longer distances, drop the last digit and multiply the rest by six. For example, change 100km to 10; 10x6=60 miles. We've used miles (because that's what our odometer measures in) and have given metric conversions only when the exact distance is crucial to your finding the right unmarked turn-off.

Going Metric?

To make your travels easier, we have provided the following chart showing metric equivalents for measurements you are familiar with.

1 km	=	.6124 miles
1 mile	=	1.6093 km
1 foot	=	.304 meters
1 inch	=	2.54 centimeters
1 square mile	=	2.59 square km
1 pound	=	.4536 kilograms
1 ounce	=	28.35 grams
1 imperial gallon	=	4.546 liters
1 US gallon	=	3.7854 liters
1 quart	=	.94635 liters

Exchange Rate & Taxes

$ We have the proverbial good news and bad news about money. The good news is very good indeed, for people from the United States traveling in Canada. The American dollar is worth about one-third more, so when you see a price tag of $10, you are really paying about $6.50-$7, depending on how and where you exchange your money.

Before you start planning how to spend all that extra money, hear the bad news. Federal and Provincial **sales taxes** in Canada, although they vary by province, are horrendous. A Value-Added Tax (the most regressive form of taxation ever dreamed up by a greedy government) eats up much of the exchange advantage, levying as much as 18% additional on everything, even postage stamps and parking tickets. Although there are ways to get some of it back – usually only on major purchases of actual goods, not services – these are awkward and return only a portion. To make matters worse, unless you leave Canada at a point with an instant rebate facility, the refund will arrive by Canadian check, which most banks charge you as much as $20 to process. (A friend of ours actually lost money trying to recover her taxes, since the refunds came in two checks – one from the Federal government and one from the province.)

A new HST (Harmonized Sales Tax) has replaced the old dual tax in New Brunswick, Nova Scotia and Newfoundland. This combined tax is sometimes included in quoted prices, printed on menus, lodging brochures, etc. PEI has not agreed to the new plan. Also, some small B&Bs are not subject to tax, so be sure to ask if a quoted price includes taxes.

Adventures

In the last decade or so the definition of adventure travel has moved from life threatening to life enriching. In this book, you'll find adventures of all sorts, none of them life-threatening unless you undertake them unprepared, ill-equipped or in a reckless manner. While Atlantic Canada has cliffs nearly a half-mile high that you could fall off the face of, we give our readers credit for recognizing such places as dangerous and not leaning over the edge.

Some suggestions may be helpful, however, especially if you've never tried a particular activity before, and we include them. Many of you will skip over them and get right on to the adventures. If you are already an experienced paddler, for example, you won't need our suggestions on taking your first strokes.

We hope this book will tempt you to try an adventure or an activity or a sport you've never done before. It needn't be rappelling, dogsledding, rafting the tidal bore, or paddling about in the ocean like an Inuit. It might be watching chimney swifts return home in the evening in a great cyclone-shaped whirl. Or it might be seeing your first puffin up close and personal, or driving through the middle of a herd of caribou. It could be riding on a sailboat in Passamaquoddy Bay, or going for a sleigh ride along the Miramichi, or watching salmon jump a falls, or learning to walk on snowshoes with a Micmac teacher. It might even be trying your hand – or eye – at spotting one of the local takes on Nessie, reputed to live here in at least two lakes.

Several types of adventures either require that you be able to read a topographical map or would be a lot easier or more interesting with one in hand. They are quite easy to read, and we suggest you study one – perhaps of an area you are already familiar with, such as your own neighborhood – before you need to use one in the woods.

READING A TOPOGRAPHICAL MAP

Each line represents a specific elevation, and wherever that line runs, the elevation will be the same. When the lines are close together it means the land rises (and falls) steeply. When they are widely spaced the land is nearly level. The interval between those levels varies with each map, and is written in the map key. When you see a lot of roughly concentric lines that form a group of sloppy circles, this usually indicates a mountain (elsewhere, this could indicate a crater, but not in Atlantic Canada). At its summit will be a dot with its elevation (if it's high enough).

Now for the interesting part. When you see a lot of lines close together forming a series of V-shapes, you have a ravine. You will usually see a blue river or stream line running through the points of the Vs, and you can tell which way it flows because the Vs will point upstream. Occasionally you may see a series of Vs without a river, which indicates a sharp, rising ridge. It is important to know, especially in Newfoundland, which is farther north, that these maps are oriented to true north (the North Pole), not to magnetic north. You will need to orient your map with your compass to make this adjustment, which can be off by more than 30° in northern Newfoundland.

Throughout the book you will see boxed segments attributed to **Sara Godwin and Charles James**. Both of them are consummate anglers, as well as birders. Sara writes about both subjects – she is the author of several fishing and wildlife books – and Chuck wields the camera. We were fortunate to have their expert input and are eternally grateful.

On Foot

Perhaps the most rewarding way to travel in Atlantic Canada is on foot, especially for those who love to watch for birds or woodland flowers. Trails lead through all sorts of environments, from highland bogs and moors to wave-swept seashores and beside wilderness lakes. Some are wide multi-purpose paths shared with cyclists, others rough and hard to find even with the help of trail blazes.

A few tips will make your hikes and walks safer, both for you and for the environment:

NATIONAL PARK PASSES: *If you plan to use several of the national parks during your visit to the Atlantic Provinces, consider buying a season pass good for either one person ($30) or a family ($75). Passes for children ages six-16 are $15; for seniors, $22.50. Since many of the best adventure activities are centered around these parks, this could be a good investment, equal to about three four-day passes or 10 single-day entrance fees. With one park on Prince Edward Island and two parks in each of the other three provinces, you have a lot of places and activities to choose from. If you plan to do any fishing, you can buy a fishing license at a national park that is good at any other national park.*

- Carry appropriate clothing and equipment for the time of year, but remember that weather in the Atlantic provinces is unpredictable and can change drastically within a few hours. Always be prepared for rain. Wear boots on rough trails or for long hikes and climbs.

- Plan a route and stick to it. Always tell someone your planned route and the approximate time you expect to return. If you do not have traveling companions other than those who will be on the trail with you, check in at the park headquarters, campground office or a local RCNP station, or tell your hosts at a hotel or inn.

- Know your own physical capabilities and those of others you hike with. Don't plan a trip that is beyond your limits. Investigate the difficulty of the trails and the steepness of the ascent before you take a trail.

- Carry plenty of water and enough food for the time you expect to be on the trail, plus a little extra in case of an unexpected delay. Don't drink water from streams, even in remote places.

- Carry basic first aid equipment on all overnight trips.

- Listen to a weather report for the time you expect to be on the trail. Check trail conditions locally, especially if there has been heavy rain recently.

- Read and obey trail warnings before you begin. During wet weather, trails which require fording rivers are sometimes closed due to deep water or heavy currents. Don't attempt to use these trails. During dry spells, woods may be closed to hikers as a forest fire prevention measure. It is your responsibility to check locally during times of drought.

- Be aware of the environment and your impact on it. Stay on trails, especially in steep areas where erosion is likely, to avoid damaging trailside plants. Carry litter out with you.

- Insects, especially mosquitoes are a fact of life in the northern woods, especially in the early summer, in wet or low places, and after rainy weather. Wear light-colored clothing and use a repellent designed for deep woods.

On Wheels

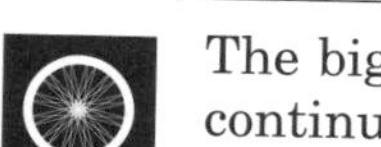

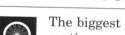

The biggest cycling news all across Canada is that work continues on the TransCanada Trail, with significant segments now open in the Atlantic Provinces. Much of the trail uses the abandoned CN rail lines and, while making it into an all-purpose trail may sound easy, it actually involves a lot of work and planning, not to mention money. Bridges are a primary problem, since the railroad bridges must be replaced with appropriate smaller crossings. The trailbed is level and usually fairly easy to reclaim, but needs resurfacing with foot- and wheel-friendly materials. Where the trail passes through long wilderness stretches, shelters are being constructed. Since the work is being done by local volunteer committees, these wilderness areas present the greatest obstacles, especially for Newfoundland, where population is more sparse and the economy is in such serious condition that little local money remains for anything. But the spirit of community volunteerism is particularly strong here, and they have completed several long trail sections.

When completed, it will be the longest trail in the world, stretching from sea to sea, and will be used by hikers, cyclists, skiers, horseback riders, and – in some areas – by snowmobilers. And, in some places, its location makes it useful as a canoe portage and access route. Its level, smooth surface makes it accessible to those in wheelchairs and others unable to travel on rough woodland trails.

It has, we think, the greatest appeal to cyclists, providing a traffic-free route with a dependable surface. If anything, it is usually **too** straight, and therefore less interesting than winding country roads, but it passes directly through towns, so cyclists have good access to services, including accommodations close to the trail. Local outfitters have quickly seen the potential for adventure travelers and in Edmundston, New Brunswick, you can bicycle north along the trail and return by canoe, with an outfitter meeting you at the far end to swap vehicles. In PEI you can cycle long distances while a cycle shop transfers your luggage between B&Bs along your route. A particularly scenic section has been completed across New Brunswick's Acadian Peninsula.

Those who enjoy biking on mountain trails will want a copy of **Mountain Bike! Atlantic Canada**, *by Sarah Hale and Jodi Bishop, published by Menasha Ridge Press.*

BRINGING YOUR BIKE BY AIR

Check with your airline if you plan to bring your own bicycle by air. Some require that it be boxed or bagged; some even provide a specially designed carton. Freewheeling Adventures of Hubbards, Nova Scotia, offers the following suggestions on how to disassemble and pack your bike:

- Remove both wheels and let air out of the tires.
- Remove front and rear mudguards, including stays.
- Lower saddle as far as it will go.

- Remove pedals and refit them into the inside of the cranks.
- Remove the rear derailleur without disconnecting the cable and, with an elastic band, attach it within the rear end of the frame. This will protect it from any knocks. As you do this, tie up the loose chain in a similar manner.
- Turn the handlebar and forks so they are aligned with the top tubes.
- Attach the mudguards to the wheels with elastic bands.
- Use bungee cords to attach each wheel to the side of the frame.
- Check this whole assembly for any protruding fragile parts and protect them in some way.

On Water

When you think of the collective name for these provinces – Atlantic Canada – you get a hint about the ratio of land to water: sea surrounds, for all practical purposes, three of the four provinces, and forms more than half the boundaries of the fourth. Rivers form a network across the land, and lakes and ponds dot it. There is a lot of water to play on here.

Canoeing

Although the same safety precautions that apply to canoeing anywhere apply in Atlantic Canada, in some places here they become more crucial. In Newfoundland, or the interior wilderness areas of other provinces, you may be miles from help in case something goes awry. The following makes a good mental checklist for any back country canoe trip:

- Watch the weather. Check the forecast ahead of time and remember that meteorology in coastal regions and islands – even very large ones – is an unreliable science. The weather can, and will, change almost instantly. It's as simple as a change in wind direction. No matter what the forecast, be prepared for bad weather, and high winds, which can turn a friendly lake into a raging sea.

➔ CLEARLY CANADIAN: *Canoes have been a part of Canada's heritage since long before there was a Canada. Their shape and form was developed by the First Peoples (as Canadians call their Native Americans) who built them of birchbark. In the virgin forests, birch trees sometimes grew so large that one tree's bark would sheath an entire canoe. They are not only part of the heritage, but also part of the unique Canadian mystique, right up there with the Mounties. As the writer Pierre Berton quipped: "A Canadian is someone who knows how to make love in a canoe."*

■ Plan ahead, and carefully, considering all the details. How will you get to your put-in? Where will you take out and how will you transport your canoe or car between the two?

■ Learn about the river or watershed system from a local who knows and who has canoed it recently. Better yet, take one along. A knowledgeable guide is not only good company, but can make your trip safer and more enjoyable.

■ Carry warm clothing, hiking boots, extra food and water, matches, first-aid supplies and bug repellent, all in a waterproof float bag.

■ Carry a healthy respect for the river, and scout ahead if you are in doubt of what's around the next bend. Know what the water levels are, and what hidden hazards may lurk at different levels. Know what water level makes the river navigable by canoe; some are passable only at high water, others are deadly then. Again, only someone with local knowledge can tell you.

■ Always wear a personal flotation device (PFD). Having one isn't enough: it needs to be on you, and properly secured. Your canoe should be wearing its safety gear, too, with painters (lines) on both bow and stern. Carry a spare paddle.

■ Be realistic about your own abilities, expertise and strength, and don't plan a trip that exceeds them.

■ Carry (and know how to read) topographical maps of every place you will go.

■ Leave a plan of your trip with someone who can get help if you fail to return when expected.

Kayaking

The variety of eastern Canada's coastlines is exceeded only by the variety of its weather. Both make sea kayaking interesting. So do whales and sea caves, and tides that think nothing of rising as much as 50 feet in a few hours.

Some of the challenges of kayaking in the sea are directly related to those features that make it the most interesting. Exploring sea caves, for example, can be very tempting, but remember that even at low tide, a sudden swell can bang your head against the roof. It is better to stay out of caves altogether, or at least wear a helmet. Enter one only on a falling tide and be extremely careful.

Likewise, kayaking around whales can be exciting, but dangerous. Stay away from whales that are engaged in any activity that makes them surface suddenly – breaching, lunge feeding – and if you find yourself too close to active whales, rap your paddle against the kayak sharply, making as much noise as you can, and leave the area quickly.

It pays to know a bit about icebergs if you will be paddling in Newfoundland in the early summer or spring. While the sides look straight from a distance, be aware of the shelf of ice that extends outward just below the surface of the water. This is very easy to bump into, and can damage your kayak. Also, when icebergs reach the "warm" waters off Newfoundland, they are well into their melt-down process, and always in danger of splitting in pieces or turning over suddenly. They are much larger than they appear – you've heard the phrase "it's just the tip of the iceberg" – and when they turn over or break apart, they cause tremendous disturbances in the water. You don't want to be there in a kayak.

What happens if you're a learning paddler and on the sea when a strong wind blows up? Your guide and instructor should have a tow line, and will simply attach it to your kayak and tow you inshore out of the wind, while you rest. If you are planning to paddle in exposed waters, ask your instructor about this. You'll feel better knowing there's a tow line available, even if you don't need it. And think twice before learning on open waters with someone who scoffs at the idea that you might need a tow. From Atlantic Canada, Ireland is the next stop.

IN A KAYAK BUILT FOR TWO

If you have never paddled a kayak and go to an outfitter for your first excursion, you may be given the choice of a single or a double kayak. The strong paddler – someone with good upper body strength and coordination – will probably prefer a single kayak, and rightly. But so should the weak paddler, if the purpose is to learn kayaking. You'll be better off in your own kayak, where you can get the feel of it, learn to use the rudder, and not constantly have to follow someone else's stroke rhythm. (This was stated by the weakest paddler on our team, who would never get into a double kayak unless she had one arm in a sling.)

Fishing

Atlantic Canada is a paradise for sportfishing, perhaps the world's greatest fishing hole. Thousands of lakes, rivers, and streams teem with all the major freshwater species, while the coast is home to striped bass, sharks, tuna and a plethora of deep-sea fish. As a general rule, the farther north you go, the better the fishing.

➔ **FISHING REGULATIONS:** *Each province has at least one special publication on fishing, giving the various laws, regulations and licensing information. You can get these by calling the toll-free numbers for the provincial tourist departments, found at the end of this chapter. You will note that in some places, for some rivers and some fish species, you will be required to fish with a guide unless you are a resident of the province. Those provinces can send you a list of licensed guides, with addresses.*

■ On Snow

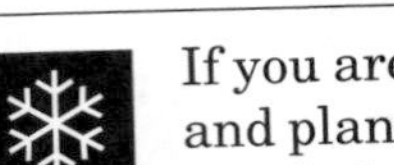

If you are planning a trip to eastern Canada in the winter and plan to engage in a lot of sports requiring snow, be advised that snow conditions become less reliable as you near the coast. The only coastal area where you can be almost sure of snow all winter (except in the rare mild or unusually dry winter), is along the Bay of Chaleur, which freezes over. The Bathurst area of New Brunswick has the highest snowfall in the province. Conversely, Prince Edward Island is the least likely to have dependable snow, although it very often has excellent cross-country skiing all winter. Coastal weather has a mind of its own.

SNOWMOBILE REGULATIONS & SAFETY

New Brunswick offers the following regulations and safety precautions, which are much the same everywhere in the Atlantic Provinces:

■ Don't operate a snowmobile within 25 feet of a highway, except for crossing, loading and unloading.

■ Come to a complete stop and look carefully before crossing a public road.

■ Keep lights on during the daytime, as well as at night. All machines must be equipped with working lights.

■ Drive on the right-hand side of the trail.

■ Wear a securely fastened helmet at all times (this is the law, in addition to common sense).

■ Watch for trail signs and obey them as you would traffic signs on highways.

■ The same rules prohibiting driving a car while under the influence of alcohol or drugs apply to operating a snow machine.

■ Always travel with other snowmobilers and be sure someone not on the trail knows where you are and your planned route.

■ Dress for the weather, with clothing to protect you in case of a change for the worse.

■ Stay on the trails for safety and to avoid trespassing on private property where permission has not been granted. Many trails cross private land with the generous permission of landowners; this access will not be renewed if the privilege is abused.

■ Carry everything out with you; avoid littering the trails.

■ When adding gas or oil, avoid spills; when these leak onto ice or snow, it spreads easily and is eventually washed into waterways where it damages fish and wildlife. Remember that one quart of oil can contaminate one million quarts of water.

You can bring your own snowmobile into Canada, just as you can bring in an automobile, and it will require the same documentation: your local registration and proof of liability insurance.

■ On Horseback

Throughout the provinces, although less so in Newfoundland, you will find riding stables where you can take trail rides, and often overnight adventures to a backcountry lodge, cabin or woodland campsite. But those who love horses will also find some different adventures, such as the chance to ride Icelandic ponies, descendants of those used by the Vikings, or the opportunity to meet the rare Newfoundland ponies. While most riding trails are through the woods, in some places you can ride along the beach – notably in Port-aux-Basques, Newfoundland and in Cheticamp, Nova Scotia, where you can explore the beaches on Icelandic ponies.

Cultural & Eco-Travel Experiences

The arts, from Acadian fiddling and stepdancing to Shakespeare, are alive and thriving in communities of all sizes: a town as small as Tyne Valley, on PEI, has a busy summer theater and artistry in traditional crafts is maintained by a full-credit college in Fredericton. Restored opera houses in Moncton and Saint John, both in New Brunswick, provide venues for an active symphony orchestra. Charlottetown, on Prince Edward Island, has a year-round center for the performing arts, home each summer to the Charlottetown Festival. Wolfville, Nova Scotia, has a repertory theater that has become a mecca for theater-goers throughout eastern Canada, and the tiny village of Lameque, New Brunswick, hosts an International Festival of Baroque Music each summer, with name musicians from all over the world.

Several towns and cities, most notably Trinity, Newfoundland, have open-air dramatic/historical performances. Each region's artistic expression reflects the history and background of the people. New Brunswick is especially rich in Francophone culture, with an entire village created around a dramatization of the novels of Antonine Maillet, while the haunting skirl of pipes in Cape Breton

Island and northern Nova Scotia is clearly Scottish. In New Brunswick and PEI, you will find Micmac bands and communities.

Scottish fiddler on Prince Edward Island.
(John Sylvester, © Tourism PEI)

Fauna & Flora

We don't have to tell adventure travelers to be careful with fire, but especially when you are camping in the wilderness, every spark is a potential disaster to you, the miles of forest around you, and all the creatures that call it home. This is not a place for cigarettes. Confine your campfires to existing fire rings and be sure the ground around them is completely cleared of grass, pine needles, leaves and anything else that could possibly burn. Make sure you have the required permits and that fires of any kind are actually allowed in the area. Keep the fire small, only large enough for essential cooking. Douse or bury your fire *completely* before going to sleep.

Wildlife

While your main interest may be in seeing the local wildlife, you will certainly want to keep these encounters friendly. Moose and bears are the biggest concern. Black

BEAR FACTS: *If you do encounter a black bear, avoid eye contact (threatening behavior in bear language) and back slowly away. We know this defies your instinct, which tells you to turn and run, but that is exactly what you should* ***not*** *do. Bears can outrun you easily, and are very likely to give chase. Talk calmly in a low voice as you retreat (right, that's easy for us to say, you're thinking) and don't play dead. Black bears eat dead mammals.*

bears will usually hear you coming and be long out of sight before you arrive, but they will be attracted to the smell of food. If you are camping, don't leave food in your tent in Newfoundland campgrounds or in the forest-surrounded parks anywhere. Keep it in the trunk of your car. In the back-country campsites in Newfoundland's national parks the rangers will provide you with "bear poles" to protect your food and campsite from ursine scavengers. Feeding the bears is not good for them (it makes them hang around and become dependent and surly) and not good for you either. Unleashed dogs invite trouble with bears and put them at their worst temper.

You're far more likely to see moose, and in Newfoundland you can almost expect it. If you see a moose when you are on foot and have no car or cabin to retreat to, don't try to get closer for a better picture. Move slowly and, if the moose moves toward you, move back slowly. Like bears, they can run quite fast (consider how long their legs are). Male moose are their most belligerent during the fall rutting season (you know how males are at times like that) and females are mean mammas when they are with young calves, which are born in late May, so that includes the early summer. If you think you are between a moose and her calf, move to the side, never toward either animal, no matter how good a picture that wobbly little moose would make. Don't let all this frighten you, but it pays to know what to do if the occasion should arise.

Insects

Far more annoying are a much smaller bit of Mother Nature's fauna: blackflies and mosquitoes. While, even in Newfoundland, these are smaller than moose – we've never actually seen one larger than a bald eagle, but we've heard fishermen talk – they can make being in the woods very unpleasant. Light-colored clothing attracts fewer insects than dark, and long sleeves and pants protect you better than any bug dope. Ask locals what they use, since each place has insects with different tastes. Our experience is that

Natrapel, Muskoll or any of several local brands work much better than the scented cosmetic company repellents. In the spring or in deep woods and moist places, a beekeeper's helmet is the only hope of escape.

> **FOR THAT SEVEN-YEAR ITCH:** *To stop the itch from insect bites, carry a package of meat tenderizer (we're serious; it contains papain, which breaks down the venom they inject into you) and mix a little with a drop or two of water to dab on bites. After you've traveled in the Newfoundland wilderness in May, you'll understand why the mosquito-eating pitcher plant is their official provincial flower.*

Sightseeing

All four provinces are filled with historic sites and restorations – after all, the history of European settlement in the New World began here. Forts and defensive positions remain from the early wars between Britain and France over who would own this part of North America, and include what we think ranks with the world's finest and most ambitious historical reconstructions: the Fortress of Louisbourg. Nearly every town has its little historical museum, and we like to take time to poke about in these little community attics. Some are beautifully restored period homes, such as a Loyalist's home in Saint John, New Brunswick, that give glimpses of how families lived in Canada's colonial days. Others, such as the wonderful Fisherman's Life museum on Nova Scotia's Marine Drive, show how very ordinary families worked and played and survived in this century.

Without trying to draw too fine a line between what is historical and what is cultural, we have arbitrarily put some of the historical villages into the *Cultural & Eco-Travel Experiences* sections, rather than in *Sightseeing*, and you may wonder why. Those that reflect and interpret a way of life in ways that are more cultural than historic, such as the Acadian Village in Caraquet, are put with *Cultural & Eco-Travel Experiences*, since you really do step into a different world there. Some examples are less clear, so if you are particularly interested in historical places, look in both sections. Other *Sightseeing* options are there because they are interesting, unusual, thought-provoking, or just plain fun. We think you'll find a good mix of places, whatever your interests.

Where To Stay & Eat

Here it is: the usual disclaimer that says "don't blame us." Places and prices will change, so will ownership. If you find that a place has changed notably, drop us a note. If you find a great place where the hosts know all the hiking trails and bike routes, share it with readers of the next edition. You can write to us in care of the publisher, whose address is on the back of the title page.

We have tried to include a good variety of dining and lodging styles, although we ourselves prefer small inns, and B&Bs in local family homes. For camping, you will notice that our preference is for quiet campgrounds with well-spaced campsites, preferably with tree cover, and without adjacent amusement parks.

Prices

To give you some idea of the prices to expect (and it is sometimes, in this changing world, only a rough idea) we have used a code of dollar signs. It is important to remember that these dollar signs are Canadian: All prices are in Canadian dollars unless they specify "US$" before the number.

> **TAKE NOTE:** *All prices given in this book are in* ***Canadian dollars****, except those clearly labeled "US$."*

For lodging, which includes a room for two people for one night, often (or always if we've designated "B&B") with breakfast. When the price includes dinner (known as MAP, or Modified American Plan), we've said so. Two ranges ($-$$, for example), can mean either that some rooms are in one range and some in another, or that the prevailing price is close to the edge of a price range. Remember that, at least for a while, you must add taxes to some prices. Be sure to ask when you reserve.

ACCOMMODATIONS KEY	
$	Under $50
$$	$50 to $100
$$$	$100 to $175
$$$$	Over $175

For dining, the price represents the average cost of dinner entrées on the regular and daily special menu. When one or two dishes (usually lobster dinners) are much more expensive than the rest of the menu, we have disregarded these. You already know that you will have to pay extra for lobster. When a restaurant serves a meal that includes appetizer and dessert for a single price, we have tried to explain this. If we missed this detail, you'll be happily surprised. Remember that we usually slide into a restaurant for dinner just as someone is walking toward the door with the "closed" sign in their hand, so you'll forgive us if our notes are a little hard to read by then. Fortunately, we are never too tired to enjoy a good meal, or to remember the important little details of how it was prepared.

DINING KEY	
Reflects the price of one dinner entrée.	
$	Under $10
$$	$10-$20
$$$	Over $20

Local Foods

We, like Napoleon's army, march on our stomach. Figuratively, of course, but we do like good food, and will drive (or walk) miles out of our way to find it. We particularly enjoy well-prepared fresh seafood.

While we like chefs who create innovative and unique dishes, we don't applaud the trend toward putting together any weird combination just to be different, and we are happy to see that chefs in these provinces haven't been tempted by this wave of silliness. So when we describe a menu as "innovative" we don't mean trendy. We mean that a thoughtful chef has experimented successfully.

We think that local chefs anywhere do their best job with local ingredients, and we look for restaurants that take advantage of farm-fresh produce and native berries as they ripen. Newfoundland chefs are particularly adept at using **partridgeberries** (like a tiny cranberry) and others in tarts and pies. **Cloudberries**, a rare treat that grows in hard-to-reach places like bogs, are rarer in restaurants, but worth seeking out. In the summer, any New Brunswick menu worth reading will feature **raspberry pie**. The use of **blueberries** with meats, which you may find in Nova Scotia and elsewhere, is not nouvelle cuisine; it was a combination used by the Micmacs long before *nouvelle* became *au courant*. For restaurants in Nova Scotia that use primarily fresh local products, pick up a copy of the free *Taste of Nova Scotia* directory, which also has detailed accounts of the restaurants listed.

Baked goods, whether wild berry pies or hot scones, tend to be good everywhere, and reflect the local ethnic traditions. In Scottish areas of Nova Scotia and PEI, look for **oatcakes**, which can be anything from a scone-like biscuit to a rich shortbread cookie. The very best of the latter (and we'll hear no quibbling over this, please) are at Balmoral Grist Mill in Nova Scotia, where they grind wood-toasted oats on an original Scottish stone wheel.

New Brunswick is the world's primary source (sorry, Maine, but we have to face facts) of **fiddleheads**, the tightly curled new fronds of certain ferns. In the spring you will see these deep green vegetables piled high in farmers markets, and on the daily specials of nearly every restaurant. Fortunately they freeze well and appear throughout the year in soups, omelets, and other dishes. They are usually described as tasting like asparagus, and we suppose they do taste more like asparagus than like grapefruit, but the comparison doesn't hold far beyond their color.

Seafood is preserved in several ways, primarily smoking and salting. Salmon may be dry-smoked or in the form of lox, and other seafoods are smoked, too, including mackerel, mussels, oysters and eel. A delicious chowder is made by blending smoked and fresh fish. In some places you may find **finnan haddie**, a delectable dish made from smoked haddock. In Newfoundland a traditional dish called **fish and brewis** is made of salt-cod cooked with a very hard close-textured bread (the original was hardtack carried on board ships), which cooks to a texture of fine dumplings. It's served hot with a sprinkling of **scrunchions**, which are bits of rendered saltpork. Made right, it's delicious.

Acadian Specialties

We like good solid traditional foods, and have a particular weakness for the Acadian dishes we grew up with (which did not include *poutine* of any sort). The following Acadian dishes may be on menus, especially in New Brunswick, Cape Breton Island and western Nova Scotia.

- **Fricot** is a hearty chicken stew with – when properly made – whole chicken pieces and chunks of vegetables in a rich broth. It is a satisfying dish and usually one of the least expensive on the menu.

- **Poutine rapée** is a boiled dumpling with meat in the middle. Homemade, they can be excellent, but those who did not grow up eating them at *chez grandmère* often find them difficult to love.

- We draw the line at another dish, also called **poutine**, which is French fries with cheese melted over them, topped with gravy. Somewhat related, but a substantial meal is "**fries with the works**," a favorite of fast-food menus in Newfoundland. It is fries with a generous covering of hamburger in gravy, usually with peas and carrots.

■ **Tourtière** is a meat pie, that can, at its best, transcend all other forms of meat between crusts. Because we grew up with the best, made at home and served for breakfast, we may be snipey in our judgement of inferior examples, but it's usually a tasty, if rich, combination of ground pork (sometimes with beef), potato, onion and spices (our *Memere* uses allspice) baked in piecrust and served warm. You may find other versions of **meat pies**, however, which are like a hearty beef stew baked between crusts, more like a pot pie.

■ **Toutons** are disks of deep-fried bread dough, served hot and, at least in Newfoundland, usually with molasses. You can substitute rich tasty New Brunswick maple syrup (we never claimed we weren't prejudiced).

■ **Sugar pie** is very sweet, something like a southern pecan pie but without the nuts.

Information Sources

New Brunswick

■ **Department of Economic Development and Tourism**, PO Box 6000, Fredericton, NB E3B 5H1, ☎ 800/561-0123. Find New Brunswick on the Web at www.gov.nb.ca/tourism.

Newfoundland & Labrador

■ **Department of Tourism, Culture and Recreation**, PO Box 8730, St. John's, NF, A1B 4K2, ☎ 709/729-2830 or 800/563-6353.

■ Information on Labrador is available through **Destination Labrador**, 118 Humphrey Rd., Bruno Plaza, Labrador City, NF, A2V 2J8, ☎ 709/944-7788 or 800/563-6353. On the Web, find cultural and tourist information at www.wordplay.com.

Nova Scotia

■ **Nova Scotia Tourism**, PO Box 130, Halifax, NS, B3J 2M7, ☎ 800/565-0000 or 902/425-5781.

Prince Edward Island

■ **Tourism PEI**, PO Box 940, Charlottetown, PEI C1A 7M5, ☎ 800/463-4734 or 902/368-4444, Web site www.gov.pe.ca.

New Brunswick

Introduction

IN THIS CHAPTER

- The Quoddy Shore
- The Fundy Coast
- The Lower River Valley
- The Upper River Valley
- The Mountains
- The Acadian Coast
- The Miramichi
- The East Coast

New Brunswick is the most geographically diverse of the Atlantic provinces, with the broad river valley, the Fundy Coast and its islands, the Appalachian mountains that reach their highest Canadian point at Mt. Carleton (2,500 feet), the long Acadian peninsula dividing the Bay of Chaleurs from the Northumberland Strait and its long barrier islands. It is cut by rivers – two of world's most famous fishing rivers, the Miramichi and the Restigouche – and the broad, fertile St. John River valley, as well as the rolling farmlands of the Kennebecasis River's valley, which ends with lake-like inland bays.

The wide, winding valley carved by the St. John River has been a pathway of commerce since the First Peoples (as Canadians call their Native Americans) hunted and fished along its shores. Beside it stands the provincial capital, Fredericton, while two of the other three major cities are at either end, Saint John at the river's mouth where it flows into the Bay of Fundy, and Edmundston, close to its headwaters on the province's northwestern border with Quebec. The river forms, or runs close to, the western boundary with Maine, and seacoasts form the other three borders: the Bay of Chaleurs to the north, the Northumberland Strait to the east and the Bay of Fundy on the south.

The center is laced with a few unpaved roads and cut by the magical Miramichi River, beside which runs the only significant road through the middle of the province. Areas best known to visitors include the Miramichi Valley (a favorite for those who love to fish), the charming old resort town of St. Andrews (a center for whale-watching and other boat trips), and the eastern beaches and shore of Fundy National Park. Lesser-known, but equally attractive and interesting, is the Acadian Peninsula, where many of

New Brunswick

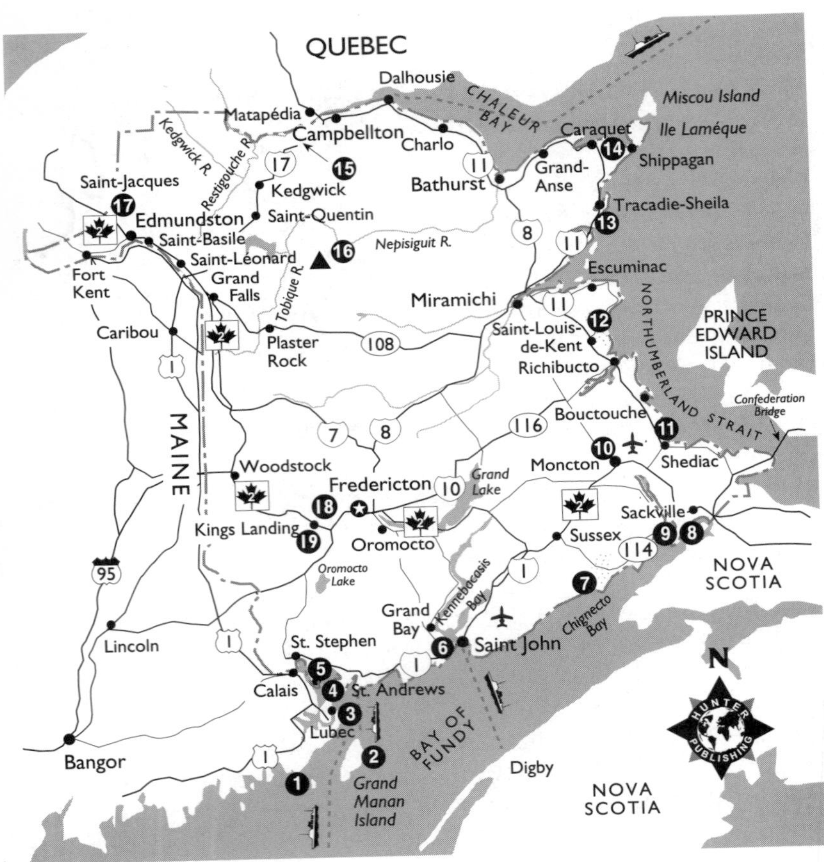

1. Machias Seal Island
2. Anchorage Provincial Park
3. Campobello Island; Roosevelt Campobello Int'l Park; Herring Cove Provincial Park
4. Deer Island
5. St. Andrews Nat'l Historic Site
6. Reversing Falls
7. Fundy National Park
8. Hopewell Rocks
9. The Rocks Provincial Park
10. Magnetic Hill Complex
11. Parlee Beach Provincial Park
12. Kouchibouguac National Park
13. Val-Comeau Provincial Park
14. Acadian Historical Village
15. Sugarloaf Provincial Park
16. Mount Carleton Provincial Park
17. Les Jardins Park Complex; Les Jardins Provincial Park
18. Mactaquac Provincial Park
19. Kings Landing Historical Settlement

the province's French-speaking people live, and a center for winter sports.

New Brunswick's position connecting northern Maine to Nova Scotia and Prince Edward Island has made it a well-used corridor, but too few stop to explore and savor its rural attractions – the riverboat inns, the quiet valleys with their covered bridges, the well-preserved historical homes and buildings, and the rugged islands of Passamaquoddy Bay.

Fewer still pause to enjoy the multitude of land and sea adventures it offers. It combines the best of all worlds for adventure-seeking travelers, with its abundant, but highly individual shorelines, and the inland pleasures of nearly pristine rivers and mountain forests. Because, unlike the other Atlantic provinces, it is a land-based province, not completely surrounded by sea, its winter weather supports heavy snowfall and accumulation necessary for skiing, snowmobiling and other snow sports. Even fishing continues into the winter with abundant smelt in the ice-covered Bay of Chaleurs and other ice fishing opportunities on bays and lakes across the province.

New Brunswick's Parks

■ **Fundy National Park**, on the southern coast, is one of Canada's best-known parks because of its phenomenon of the world's highest tides, as well as the uniquely carved coastal scenery they create. Its terrain is rugged, rising to headlands and highland bogs, giving great variety – and scenery – to its extensive trail network.

■ **Kouchibouguac National Park**, on its eastern shore, is lapped by the far more gentle waters of the Northumberland Strait, which separates it from Prince Edward Island. Its low, stunningly beautiful landscape and seascape of barrier beaches and white dunes, with lagoons, bogs and coastal forests, are easily reached by level walking trails and by waterways perfect for canoeing. The waters that play against its beaches are the warmest north of Virginia.

■ **Roosevelt Campobello International Park** is on an island accessible from Canada only by water. A bridge connects it to its neighboring mainland, which is in the United States. Smaller than the other two parks, and without their large campgrounds and outdoor recreation facilities, its primary purpose is to preserve the land and buildings of the summer home of the family of President Franklin Roosevelt, both as a memorial to him and as an example of the summer lifestyle of the wealthy of his era.

■ **Provincial parks** are scattered throughout New Brunswick, although they are not nearly as numerous as they were a few years ago, and the number appears to still be shrinking. With governmental belt-tightening, the province (and some other provinces as well) has decided to spin off the smaller parks, especially those which are mostly campgrounds or beaches. They have retained the park status of those which encompass important historical or natural attractions, such as Mount Carleton, but are getting out of the business of running campgrounds and purely recreational facilities.

Many of the beach and/or campground parks have been taken over by towns, others by private owners, concessionaires or community groups. As we write, most of these look much as they did when they were provincial parks, even retaining the distinctive sail-shaped signs, but with the word "provincial" painted out. Most have retained their original names, some their old telephone numbers. This will be somewhat of a jumble for a while, but from what we've seen, after the confusing (and often quite sudden) transition, the parks remain well-run. How well private owners will be able to maintain the grounds and facilities is still a question, and we expect the answer will vary with the park.

The plan is still a work-in-progress, so don't be surprised to find that a provincial park we mention has a new name and new owners when you arrive. One thing you need not – ever –worry about in New Brunswick: whoever owns or manages the park, you will be welcomed and everyone concerned will work very hard to make sure you have a good time as their guest. Hospitality is every New Brunswicker's middle name.

■ Day Adventures

New Brunswick has an innovative program of *Day Adventures*, which make it very easy for visitors to identify and participate in active experiences ranging from dogsledding and kayaking to learning a traditional craft of a century ago or traveling by boat through a Micmac reserve. Each adventure is described in the Travel Planner published each year by the tourism department, with details such as cost, time involved, season and exactly what is included in the package. You can sign up for one of these by calling the individual outfitter or facility, by visiting one of the **Adventure Centres** located in St. Andrews, St. George, and Caraquet, or making reservations in major provincial tourist offices throughout New Brunswick. Locally run tourist offices (as opposed to those operated by the province) can only make reservations for you if the outfitter has a toll-free or local number. It's just as easy to do it yourself, though, since you may want to ask questions.

The cost of these adventures may be as low as $5 for a two-hour personal tour of an open-air lumber camp museum in the wilds of the Restigouche, or more than $200 for a full day of snowmobiling with lessons, a guide, lunch, and the snowmobile and equipment all included. Multi-day adventures combine lodging, and often meals, with outdoor experiences. A day's skiing or snowmobiling might be paired with a night in a cozy log cabin or bicycling the scenic Madawaska River with a hotel room and meals in Edmundston.

These *Day Adventures* are especially designed to make it easy for travelers to try out a new sport in an inexpensive, safe, and non-threatening learning environment. If you have hesitated to try sea kayaking, rappelling or snowshoeing because you don't know the first thing about them, don't have the equipment and don't want to invest heavily in a sport you might not enjoy, this is your chance. If you find that you don't enjoy the activity, you'll still have a good time, see new scenery, meet new people and not spend a lot of money. It's a dabbler's dream. For a copy of the current catalog of adventures, call **New Brunswick's Dept. of Economic Development & Tourism**, ☎ 800/561-0123.

Another thing to remember about the *Day Adventures* program is that these businesses and outfitters usually offer a great many more options than the one or two they have listed as *Day Adventures*. A cycle shop, for example, may do multi-day trips in addition to the four-hour tour advertised, or a kayak center might have week-long coastal camping trips. Use the addresses and phone numbers as a starting point and ask about all the programs they offer. Complete mailing addresses, phone numbers, and often toll-free numbers are included in each listing.

Winter Day Adventures

The *Day Adventures* program has a separate catalog of winter activities, which include cozy romantic weekends in country inns, snowmobile trips, dogsledding, skiing and a variety of winter packages, many of which combine lodging with an outdoor adventure. Be sure to ask for the **White Gold Rush Catalogue** if you plan a winter trip, available from the **Dept. of Economic Development & Tourism**, ☎ 800/561-0123.

Snowmobiling in New Brunswick requires a trail permit if you use the province's network of 9,000 km of groomed trails – which you will certainly want to do (and would have trouble avoiding, even if you tried). You can get a permit from any of the 65 snowmobile clubs, and at some motels and gas stations along trails. If you bring your own machine, it must carry a valid registration from your own state or province, and you should also carry insurance from your own area to cover liability for any accidents. You will have to stop at the border and will be expected to produce the same sort of documentation for your snow machine as for your car. The most common local term for snowmobiles is "ski-doo"; in French look for *moto-neige*.

➲ **TIP:** *For trail conditions, a trail map and other information, contact the **New Brunswick Federation of Snowmobile Clubs** (NBFSC), Woodstock, NB E0J 2B0, ☎ 506/325-2625, fax 506/325-2627. You can also get a provincial trail map from **New Brunswick Tourism**, ☎ 800/561-0123.*

Fishing

Rivers with sea run salmon are *scheduled*, which means that nonresidents cannot fish in them without a licensed guide. Unlike most places in the United States, sections of river are owned by adjacent landowners, and the fishing rights belong to them. On some rivers, this means that nearly all the good fishing waters are closed to travelers. On other rivers, it means that fishing camps, lodges and outfitters own large segments of river, which are reserved for their guests. To fish these prime pools, you can book a fishing package at one of the lodges. If you hire a good guide, he will have permission of the appropriate land-owners – usually people who own camps but use them infrequently. Or, a guide will know which waters are public.

Information Sources

■ The central agency responsible for tourist information is the **Department of Economic Development and Tourism**, PO Box 6000, Fredericton, NB E3B 5H1, ☎ 800/561-0123. Local and regional information centers are listed under Getting Around in the beginning of each chapter. When you write or call for information, be sure to say what season you plan to travel in, since the *Day Adventure* guides are seasonal, and mention any specific interests, such as fishing, beaches, birding, cycling or snowmobiling, so the information officer will know to send you the appropriate special publications.

Recommended Reading

■ Those traveling on foot, whether on long hikes, wilderness camping trips, or just seeking out waterfalls or birding sites, should refer to ***A Hiking Guide to New Brunswick***, by Marianne Eiselt and H.A. Eiselt, available in bookstores throughout the province.

■ Mountain bikers need ***Mountain Bike! Atlantic Canada*** by Jodi Bishop and Sarah Hale, published by Menasha Ridge Press, available in outdoor shops and bookstores.

■ A general book about the province, half guidebook, half light-hearted and lively history and culture, but 100% well-written, is ***Roads to Remember***, by the popular Fredericton writer Colleen Whitney Thompson. She's a fine storyteller (of course, since her father's from the Miramichi) and brings the many characters, heroes, rogues and even ghosts of New Brunswick history and folklore to life as she meanders around the province. Her advice is good, and you'll certainly enjoy reading her book.

MOOSE WARNING

While you may be anxious to spot a moose during your trip, you don't want to spot it just as it jumps in front of your car. Accidents involving moose are serious, because of the tremendous weight of the animal and its height. When struck by a car, the moose's body is at windshield height and often crushes the roof or hits passengers at head level. Fatalities are fairly common in these accidents.

Moose are the undisputed kings of the wild, and with no predators they have no fear. A car is just another small animal to a moose, who expects the car to flee as other animals would. So the moose will either stand his ground or actually charge the car, with a rack of antlers that smashes right through windshields.

■ Keep a watch for moose appearing from the roadsides whenever you are traveling through wilderness areas, but particularly around dawn and dusk, or at night. If you must travel in remote areas at night, both driver and passengers should constantly scan the roadsides ahead for dark shapes or any sign of movement in the underbrush that might signal a moose about to cross the road.

■ If you see a moose in the road, stop and pull off to the side. At night, turn off your headlights so the moose will not be blinded by them and wait for the moose to leave the road. Under no circumstances should you get out of your car when a moose is near.

■ If you see moose near the roadside in daylight and want to photograph them, try to do it from the car. If you cannot, or if the moose are some distance away, get out of the car very slowly, and don't move too far from the car. Leave the engine running so you can get away quickly if the moose should suddenly head toward the road. Usually the moose will continue eating and ignore you, but if you have accidentally come between the parent and a young moose – which might be hidden in the brush on the opposite side of the road – the moose could charge with amazing speed. It is hard to believe how fast such a seemingly cumbersome and ungainly creature can run.

The Quoddy Shore

West of Saint John is a coastline of long peninsulas, deep coves, and rock-bound offshore islands. Connected in a circular route by ferries and a short drive through coastal Maine, the area abounds in water adventures, from kayaking under the cliffs of Grand Manan to watching the largest tidal whirlpool in North America. St. Andrews by the Sea is a summer holiday center for island exploration, seal watches, and birding, while inland lakes and rivers invite exploring by canoe.

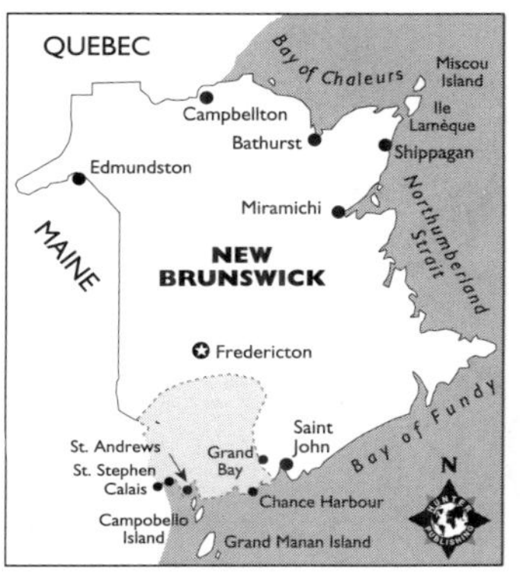

The *Day Adventure* program is at its busiest here, with centers in both St. George and St. Andrews, where you can literally shop from kiosk to kiosk, signing up for land and sea excursions. The choice of boat trips from St. Andrews is staggering.

Geography & History

Passamaquoddy Bay is almost enclosed by the St. George peninsula, Deer Island and a string of islets. While small in comparison to the giant Bay of Fundy, it holds a lot of water, much of which rushes in and out with the twice-daily Fundy tides. The shore is steep in places, with long narrow channels and dozens of small islands, as well as sand bars which appear and disappear with the tides. It is, as you might guess, a wonderland of sea adventures.

Although this region looks small on a map, it has an inordinate amount of coastline formed by a lot of smaller bays and inlets, with jutting peninsulas and abundant islands. One of the three largest, Campobello Island, is reached by bridge from Lubec, in Maine; all three are reached by ferry from the Canadian shore.

This is Loyalist country, largely founded by those who disapproved of the American Revolution and escaped to crown-held territory. Some brought their houses (you'll hear of this in Shelburne, Nova Scotia, too), disassembled beam by board and loaded on boats bound for St. Andrews, where you can still see some of the original homes brought from Castine, Maine.

But even when feelings ran strongest between residents of Maine and New Brunswick, those closest to the border, in the facing towns of St. Stephen, New Brunswick, and Calais, Maine, had a working relationship that neither government would have approved of. Commerce flowed back and forth as usual, and so many families were intermarried that sorting out loyalties was impossible. They were just a generation or so ahead of their times in international cooperation when the town of St. Stephen loaned the Americans gunpowder during the War of 1812 so they could have their July Fourth fireworks (which the Canadians enjoyed from their vantage point across the river). A favor or two among neighbors and cousins was none of the king's business, they reasoned.

Getting Around

From Saint John, take Rte. 1 through St. George to Rte. 127, which makes a loop south into St. Andrews and north again to rejoin Rte. 1 on its way to St. Stephen. Saint John to St. Andrews is 59 miles; it's 66 directly from Saint John to St. Stephen, 12 miles extra via St. Andrews. Either trip, to St. Andrews or St. Stephen, takes about an hour.

If you are arriving by air and don't plan to rent a car (which you can live without if you're staying in St. Andrews and taking day trips) a **shuttle service** takes guests between the **Algonquin Hotel** and the Saint John airport. (Call the hotel at ☎ 506/529-3101.) If you are not planning to stay at the Algonquin, check with your innkeeper to see if they have a similar service available or call **HMS Transportation**, ☎ 506/529-3371. They also rent cars.

Using the Deer Island ferries, the Lubec Bridge, and a stretch of Maine roads, you can explore the area by car on a route known as the **Quoddy Loop**, making a circle in either direction or using the ferries to cut off many miles of driving if you are entering or leaving New Brunswick from coastal Maine.

To begin this loop from New Brunswick, go to Letete, seven miles from St. George via Rte.772, to the free ferry. The ferry takes cars daily every half-hour from 7 am to 6 pm and hourly until 10 pm (July through August) and 7 am to 9 pm (September through June) to Deer Island, where another ferry takes them to Campobello Island. The first is government-run, the second is operated by **East Coast Ferries**, ☎ 506/747-2159. It makes seven round-trip crossings daily in July and August, six daily in June and September, weather permitting. (If the ferry isn't running, a sign at the dock will say so. Be sure you're in the right lane at Deer Island dock for the ferry to Campobello, because the ferry to Eastport, Maine, leaves from the same dock.) Cars cost $11 with driver, plus $2 per passenger, to a $16 maximum. From Campobello, a bridge crosses to Lubec, Maine, and connects via Rte. 189 to US Rte. 1, which goes north to the border at St. Stephen or south along the coast of Maine. Campobello Island is 243 miles from Portland, Maine.

Ferries to Grand Manan leave from Blacks Harbour, operated year-round by Coastal Transport Ltd., ☎ 506/662-3724. Six round trips run daily in July and August, three daily September through June, at $25.50 for automobiles, $8.50 for each adult, and $4.25 for children ages five-12. Reservations are accepted only for the first ferry leaving Grand Manan each morning; all other departures are on a wait-in-line basis.

Because getting to and from Grand Manan takes time (especially if the line is long and you have to wait for the next crossing), you will want to explore it all while you are there. To make planning your time there easier, we've sorted all the Grand Manan adventures into a separate sub-section, which is cross-referenced to each type of activity. So when you find kayaking, you will be reminded to check kayaking on Grand Manan.

Information Sources

Write ahead for tourist information from:

- **Tourism New Brunswick**, PO Box 12345, Fredericton, NB E3B 5C3, ☎ 506/453-3984 or 800/561-0123.
- **Quoddy Coastal Tourism Association**, PO Box 446, St. Andrews, NB E0G 2X0, ☎ 506/529-4677.
- **St. Andrews Chamber of Commerce**, PO Box 89, St. Andrews, NB E0G 2X0, ☎ 506/529-3555 or 800/563-7397.
- **Campobello Chamber of Commerce**, Welshpool, Campobello, NB E0G 3H0, ☎ 506/752-2233.

■ For information about Grand Manan, write or call **Grand Manan Tourism Association**, PO Box 193, North Head, NB E0G 2M0, ☎ 506/662-3442.

Once in the area you'll find ample information centers, the primary ones being:

■ **St. Andrews Welcome Centre**, 46 Reed Ave, St. Andrews, NB E0G 2X0, ☎ 506/529-3000, open daily 9 am to 8 pm in July and August, and 9 am to 6 pm in May, June and September.

■ The **Provincial Information Centre** at the International Bridge, open daily 9 am to 7 pm, May through mid-October, ☎ 506/752-7043.

■ **The Provincial Information Centre**, Rte. 1, St. Stephen, NB E3L 2W9, ☎ 506/466-7390, open daily 8 am to 9 pm from May through August, and 9 am to 7 pm, September through mid-October.

Note that there is no Visitors Center on Grand Manan, so you must get information in St. Andrews or at the Black's Harbour ferry landing before you cross, or from your hotel on the island.

■ For information on the coastal area east of St. Stephen, contact **Blacks Harbour Visitor Information Centre**, c/o Clarence Griffin, PO Box 90, Blacks Harbour, NB E0G 1H0, ☎ 506/456-4878. The information center is on the northern edge of town, and open daily, 9 am to 7 pm, in July and August.

Adventures

On the banks of the canal in St. George, a newly-built picnic grounds has a cluster of outdoor outfitters and an **Adventure Centre**, 13 Adventure Lane, ☎ 506/755-1023. Here you can sign up for *Day Adventures* in the local area or anywhere in the province. The tourist information office in St. Andrews has a *Day Adventure* centre and the Algonquin Hotel has another.

On Foot

Hiking

Herring Cove Provincial Park on Campobello Island has several nice hiking trails, one of which leads to the Roosevelt Cottage. The trail is well-marked with blue metal squares, and is about 4½ miles long for the whole loop. It's an easy walk, with no climbing. From a trailhead near the beach, you can walk another loop trail to the Rock of Gibraltar, a bit of hyperbole, but an impressive glacial erratic nonetheless. The trail goes along the beach for some distance, then joins a nature trail that crosses a bog on a boardwalk before entering the woods. You can climb to the top of the rock with the help of a rope secured to a tree growing out of its top (just don't think about where the roots of the tree are anchored as you are climbing). Ask at the park headquarters for a map of these trails.

Roosevelt Campobello International Park has 8½ miles of trails to walk, including one that leads along the shore from the international bridge, around Upper and Lower Duck Ponds (really coves), around Liberty Point and Owen Point to Raccoon Beach. You can follow these easily with the help of a map from the Visitors Centre at Roosevelt Cottage.

Also on Campobello, at Friar's Head, you can climb the hill to an observation deck, from which you can see over the bay to Eastport, Maine. Interpretive signs describe the view and the Bay of Fundy. A trail drops off to the left of the deck, through the woods, and joins a dirt road. Follow it to the right, then turn off to your left on another trail. Keep taking the left choice at forks and you will circle back around to climb Friar's Head again, completing the loop. The whole trail is less than a mile, but be prepared to climb a bit.

Scenic Walks

St. Andrews offers a number of places to walk, either along shore trails or on the streets of the town, interesting for their two centuries of architecture. From Katy's Cove, where there is a swimming beach, the old railway bed makes a level walking path along the shore, through beds of ferns and wildflowers.

St. Andrews fairly begs to be explored on foot, either wandering its streets randomly or with the map and information in A Guide to Historic St. Andrews, free at the Welcome Centre. That building and many others in town, are the work of the prominent turn-of-the-century architect and long-time summer resident, Edward S. Maxwell. The addresses of these and the two remaining homes brought from Castine, Maine, by fleeing Loyalists, are shown in the guide. If you have a particular interest in architecture, visit the Greenock Church (1824), on Montague St. to see the hand-carved pulpit of bird's-eye maple and mahogany and the maple pillars supporting the gallery.

Guided Walking & Hiking Tours

■ To explore the streets of St. Andrews with a live (and lively) guide who will share the town's many historical features with you, reserve a place in a walking tour by **Heritage Discovery Tours**, Town Wharf, ☎ 506/529-4011. The "Magical History Tour" introduces a healthy dose of local legend into its historical information, with tales of pirates, ghosts and buried treasure. In addition to their colorful history tours of the town, they conduct nature tours of the intertidal shore, exploring this unique world that appears when the tides recede. You'll need rubber boots or canvas shoes for this excursion, since saltwater might ruin leather shoes. (If you don't have appropriate shoes, tell them, as they can probably scout something up for you.) Tours are $15; half-price for children ages six-12.

■ At the *Day Adventure* Centre in St. George, you can join a guided hike along the Fundy coastline or climb Red Rock Mountain, overlooking the town, with **Outdoor Adventure Company**, ☎ 506/755-6415 or 800/667-2010.

■ **Path Less Travelled** at the Deer Island Point Campground, ☎ 506/747-2423, organizes interpretive hiking and walking tours on the island, visiting scenic coves and points, and coastal rock formations, including a stone arch worn by the high tides.

■ On Wheels

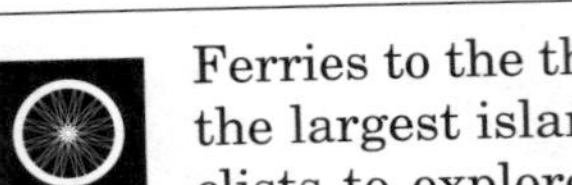

Ferries to the three major islands all carry bicycles. Even the largest island, Grand Manan, is small enough for cyclists to explore easily. Here cyclists will find roads uncrowded and traffic slow, with courteous drivers who treat bicycles with respect. Campobello Island is also a pleasure to travel by bicycle; it is only three miles wide by 10 miles long.

Bicycling Outfitters & Guided Tours

■ You can rent bikes on Grand Manan from **Adventure High**, ☎ 506/662-3563 or 800/732-5492. It's not a bad idea to reserve them ahead during the summer. You can also bring bicycles on board the ferry.

■ To explore Deer Island on wheels, you can rent bicycles from **Path Less Travelled** at the Deer Island Point Campground, ☎ 506/747-2423. Or bring your bicycle on board the free ferry from Letete on the mainland. You can rent bicycles at the **Granite Town Hotel** in St. George and their shuttle will take you and the bike to the free ferry in Letete, bound for Deer Island.

■ Bicycle tours of the Fundy Islands are led by **Outdoor Adventure Company**, ☎ 506/755-6415 or 800/667-2010. Three-day trips include meals and lodging in deluxe country inns, plus a support vehicle and all equipment, for $300. You'll see covered bridges, lighthouses, and beautiful shoreline scenery; sign up for these in St. George at the *Day Adventure* Centre, or reserve directly.

On Water

So many opportunities for water sports and excursions exist in the Quoddy region that we could easily fill this chapter with water activities alone. St. Andrews is a center for water-based adventures, but it doesn't have exclusive rights to Passamaquoddy Bay's wet resources. Just getting from island to island is a water-borne adventure, and from the ferries you may see porpoises, whales and the continent's largest whirlpool.

Swimming

You won't have trouble finding a place to swim. In St. Andrews, **Katy's Cove** has a bath house and snack bar at a beach in a bay protected from the cold Passamaquoddy tides; the **Algonquin's heated pool** is open to the public for a small fee. **Causeway Beach** in St. Stephen is a saltwater beach with lifeguards. On Campobello Island, **Herring Cove Provincial Park** has a mile-long sandy beach, unsupervised, but popular for swimming.

Canoeing & Kayaking

At the **Adventure Center**, 13 Adventure Lane in St. George, ☎ 506/755-1023, you can sign up for *Day Adventures* by canoe or kayak, or you can rent a kayak right there and paddle along the canal.

Explore the Magaguadavic River and the Bay of Fundy by canoe or kayak with **Piskahegan River Company** in St. George, ☎ 506/755-6269 or 800/640-8944. A three-to four-hour trip by canoe on the river or by kayak along the coast is $60, six-to seven-hour trips are $90. Coastal kayaking trips are in the protected waters among the many small islands, where kayakers share the water with seals, and eagles watch from the rocky isles. A sundown trip on the canal ends with dinner at the River House for $50. Longer trips through the islands, with overnight accommodations, begin at $245 for a couple.

Piskahegan also does whitewater kayaking trips down Class I and II rapids on the St. Croix River on Sundays and Fridays. Weekend trips on the St. Croix and Chiputneticook lakes explore the waterway that forms the US-Canadian border. These cost $200, and include canoes and meals. Guides and instructors are highly experienced, and all equipment is provided on their trips. Whitewater kayakers can challenge the Fundy tides at Lepreau Basin, where Rte. 790 crosses a tidal flat. An hour before high tide, water rushes through the narrows under the bridge to fill the basin, kayakers with it.

A full range of kayak experience and training is available from **Seascape Kayak Tours**, ☎ 506/529-4866. Guided trips with full instruction for beginners, are priced at $55 for 2½ hours on the water and $100 for 4-4½ hours. Sunset paddles circle Navy Island, then put ashore for a lobster bake. For a longer kayak experience, you can take a guided three-day kayaking and camping trip with all kayaking and camping equipment furnished, as well as meals and transportation to the launch-site from either St. Andrews or the islands. Routes include the Fundy shore along the mainland, Deer and Campobello Islands, or an excursion into the upper reaches of Passamaquoddy Bay, following an estuary and camping on islands. The cost of a three-day trip is $345 per person or $650 per couple. A family of four gets a 10% discount. Seascape also rents kayaks and runs courses in beginning kayaking, sea kayaking safety and coastal guide training.

Three-day guided adventures with camping or country inn accommodations are arranged by **Outdoor Adventure Company**,

☎ 506/755-6415 or 800/667-2010. Experienced guides will show you how, so even beginning kayakers can enjoy these trips. Rates begin at $300 per person. Full-day trips with lodging and three meals are $139. Their three-hour guided kayak or canoe trips, with instruction and lunch, are $45 per person; children under eight ride free.

Guests at **Loon Bay Lodge** in St. Stephen, ☎ 506/466-1240 or 888/LOON-BAY, have use of the lodge's canoes for outings on the St. Croix River, which flows below the property, forming the international boundary. Guests at **Bonny River House Bed & Breakfast** in St. George, ☎ 506/755-2248, can use the inn's canoes to explore the river which surrounds the point where the inn is located.

Sailing

A learn-to-sail package arrangement between Forest Lodge and **Prince Yacht Charters**, ☎ 506/529-4185, includes two days (more than 12 hours) of sailing instruction and hands-on experience on a 27-foot yacht and two nights lodging with breakfast and picnic lunches. You'll sail on the sheltered waters of Passamaquoddy Bay, among seals and porpoises, at a cost of $200-$225 per person.

Diving

Deer Island and Campobello offer outstanding diving, with 300-foot underwater cliffs, shipwrecks and a variety of sea life.

Certified divers can sign on for three hours of drift and wall dives in the waters off Deer Island with **Sparky Too Scuba Dive Charter**, Richardson, Deer Island, ☎ 506/747-2398, fax 747-2089, e-mail sparky@deerinet.nb.ca, Web site www.deerinet.nb.ca/sparky. Groups of five or six divers will explore an area rich in sealife and possibilities for underwater photography. a two-tank dive, about three hours, is $40. Tank and weight belt rentals are available.

Navy Island Dive Company teaches diving (PADI certified) to individuals and groups and offers dive charters aboard their 23-foot boat. Rates are $50 for a two-tank dive (plus air). Diving equipment is available for rent at $30 a day for a complete set and tank refills are $7. Contact them at 15 Williams St., St. Andrews, ☎ 506/529-4555.

Harbor & Bay Tours

A staggering assortment of boats leaves from St. Andrews, where you can choose at kiosks along Market Wharf or reserve through the Welcome Centre. If you have time, we suggest going to the wharf in the evening or in the morning to browse among the boats, most of which are docked there. You can talk to the captains and make reservations on the boat you like best. At the height of summer, it is, however, good to have a reservation ahead, especially if your time is limited, since many of the trips are filled.

> ➲ **SEA MONSTERS:** *Lake Utopia, close to St. George, has its own version of Nessie, a creature occasionally reported to have characteristics of both fish and reptile. To try your own luck at spotting the Lake Utopia Monster on a tour with* ***Natural Canal River Cruises*** *in St. George,* ☎ *506/755-0920.*

For cruises that are primarily concerned with whale, seal and bird viewing, see *Wildlife-Watching* under *Cultural & Eco-Travel Experiences* below. For boats leaving from Grand Manan, see that section.

The craft vary widely. A classic sailing yacht, the 72-foot gaff-rigged ***Cory***, ☎ 506/529-8116, takes passengers on three-hour cruises through Passamaquoddy Bay. Nature interpretation and a snack and beverage are included for $43 per adult, $25 under age 16 and $35 for seniors. Departures in the summer are three times a day, and passengers can do as much –hoist sails, take the helm – or as little as they please.

You can also trim sails or take a hand at the tiller of the sailing yacht *Miss T* with **Prince Yacht Charters**, ☎ 506/529-4185, as it sails around the island where Champlain wintered in 1604 on a three-hour bay cruise. Adults pay $40, youth $30, children $10. You are welcome to bring a picnic dinner for the sunset cruise (or they can provide one).

A high-speed catamaran takes a maximum of 12 for scenic and sunset cruises, nature tours, and aquaculture tours, operated by **Quoddy Link Marine**, ☎ 506/529-2600. A three-hour narrated cruise through the islands into the Bay of Fundy is $45, and includes hot chocolate and samples of local seafood. They also run a passenger ferry service to Campobello.

Fundy Tide Runners, ☎ 506/529-4481, fax 506/529-4933, explore the small islands on a high-speed rigid-hulled Zodiac to watch bird and marine life from a closer vantage point than larger craft can reach. Because of the high speed, you can get to outer reaches of the bay in a short time, then spend most of your trip among the wildlife. A two-hour trip, with flotation suits provided, is about $45, half-price for children.

Cline Marine offers whale-watches leaving Richardson, Deer Island, at 9:30 am and 12:30, 3:15 and 6:15 pm daily (if they have enough reservations), ☎ 506/529-4188 or 800/567-5880. Cruises are about $40 for adults, $20 for children.

Also leaving from Deer Island, which is very close to the whales' favorite feeding grounds, are boats run by **Lambert's Outer Island Tours,** ☎ 506/747-2426, fax 506/747-0886. Their two-hour tours include a snack of local seafood and are on a small six-passenger cruiser instead of a large tour boat. The cost is $35 for adults, $25 for children, or $95 for a whole family (up to four children, the boat's capacity).

A 24-foot pontoon boat explores the natural canal that circumvents the falls in St. George, on trips with **Natural Canal River Cruises,** ☎ 506/755-0920. This canal is the only one its kind in North America, and rare in the world. The boat leaves from the *Day Adventure* Centre and goes downstream to view the falls and gorge, then upstream to see beaver dams, birds, and possibly deer. A good seasoning of history adds spice to the nature-watching, as guides tell you about the days when St. George earned its nickname of Granite Town from the red granite taken from the quarries you will pass. Covered bridges and tales from the area's logging days add to the interest. Two-hour cruises cost $18 for adults, $10 for children.

Fishing

Deep-sea fishing trips are offered by **St. Andrews Bay Sport Fishing, Market Wharf,** ☎ 506/529-8196 or 888/808-FISH. They make three trips daily at $50 for adults and $30 for those under age 16. All gear and bait is furnished. They specialize in striped bass, but also fish for cod, pollock, wolffish and dogfish. A day's shark fishing – a 10-hour excursion – is $250 per person.

Interactive Outdoors in St. George, ☎ 506/755-2699 or 800/214-6906, has four-hour fishing trips for flounder, mackerel and cod at $40 for adults and $20 for children under 12. Or you can fish for trophy-sized striped bass, which run to 50 pounds. That boat accommodates four and costs $150 for half-day trips or $200 for full-day. They will also take you to their favorite fishing spot for small-mouth bass or fly-fishing for salmon.

■ On Snow

Because this region is so close to the moderating effect of the sea, snow is a variable that you can't always depend on. But the walking trails on the Fundy Islands and along the shore are used for cross-country skiing and showshoeing when the weather does cooperate. Ever the optimists, **Granite Town Hotel** in St. George, ☎ 506/755-6415 or 800/667-2010 offers special winter packages and sleigh rides. A two-hour ride and hot chocolate is $10 for adults, $6 for children.

The **Algonquin** (☎ 506/529-8823 or 800/563-4299) and the **Hiram Walker Estate** (☎ 506/529-4210 or 800/470-4088, fax 506/529-4311) are both open in the winter, warm and welcoming retreats offering special packages. Both offer luxury lodging, candlelight dinners, truffles and the kind of pampering and personal attention a cozy winter getaway deserves. Rates begin at about $200 a night.

■ Adventures On Grand Manan

Getting around this island is pretty simple: one main road runs its length, with a few side roads leading to coves and headlands. Grand Manan is about 15 miles long by five miles wide.

Grand Manan On Foot

More than 40 miles of hiking trails follow the rocky cliff-lined shore and crisscross the interior, often through low, almost stunted woods. The interior is mostly scrubby heath, bog and wetlands. This makes for wet trail conditions in some places, while the rocky nature of the coast makes other trails rough and uneven. Trails often skirt perilously close to precipitous cliff edges, made all the more uncertain when wet or after a rain when gullies and washouts remove portions of the trail.

At low tide you can walk along much of the shore, but be sure to check the tide schedules, available everywhere, to avoid being stranded by a rising tide. Remember that the exceptionally high Fundy tides mean that water levels change quickly. As anywhere else, it is important to let someone know where you will be hiking and when you expect to return.

Hole-in-the-Wall, an impressive arched rock, is reached by a shore trail beginning at the Angelical Church. It takes you to an overlook above Whale Cove, before turning along the shore to the

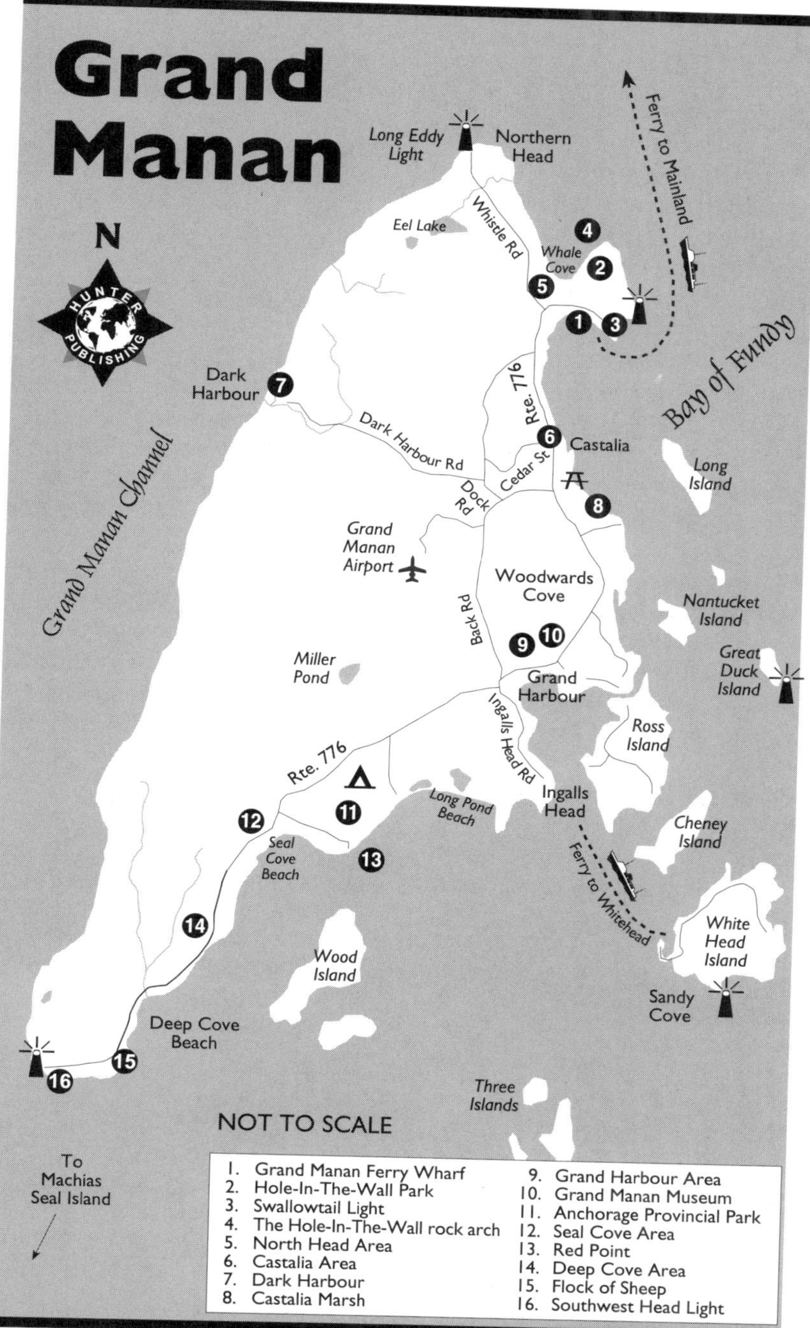

Grand Manan
Long Eddy Light
Northern Head
Ferry to Mainland
Eel Lake
Whistle Rd
Whale Cove
Dark Harbour
Rte. 776
Bay of Fundy
Dark Harbour Rd
Castalia
Cedar St
Dock Rd
Grand Manan Channel
Long Island
Grand Manan Airport
Woodwards Cove
Back Rd
Nantucket Island
Great Duck Island
Miller Pond
Grand Harbour
Ingalls Head Rd
Ross Island
Rte. 776
Long Pond Beach
Ingalls Head
Seal Cove Beach
Cheney Island
Ferry to Whitehead
White Head Island
Wood Island
Sandy Cove
Deep Cove Beach
Three Islands
NOT TO SCALE
To Machias Seal Island
1. Grand Manan Ferry Wharf
2. Hole-In-The-Wall Park
3. Swallowtail Light
4. The Hole-In-The-Wall rock arch
5. North Head Area
6. Castalia Area
7. Dark Harbour
8. Castalia Marsh
9. Grand Harbour Area
10. Grand Manan Museum
11. Anchorage Provincial Park
12. Seal Cove Area
13. Red Point
14. Deep Cove Area
15. Flock of Sheep
16. Southwest Head Light

rock formation. The trail is sometimes hard to find, so it is wise to get up-to-date directions from someone locally. You can also begin at Whale Cove, at the end of Swamp Rd., walking along the shore to join the trail at the far end of the cove.

> **STEP CAREFULLY:** *Watch where you put your feet, and be aware of what is underneath the trail when you are walking along cliffs.*

A shorter trail to Hole-in-the-Wall begins at the old airstrip inside **Hole-in-the-Wall Park**, a private campground and nature park that covers most of Fish Head. An admission fee of $3 allows you to use all the trails around the headland. The walk to Hole-in-the-Wall takes about 30 minutes. From there you can circle the entire head, all the way to Swallowtail Lighthouse, returning by the access road. Along the trail you will pass an old Indian pipestone quarry and a vein of barite that was once mined. A short **botanical walk** begins behind the reception office, passing through a grove of red spruce where fishermen once came to gather curving limbs perfect for building traps. Others, growing perfectly straight without knots, were used as weir stakes. Ask for the descriptive brochure as you enter.

Between the beach at Deep Cove and the Southwest Cove Lighthouse, where the road ends, you will see a trail on the coastal side of the road. The trail leads through a mossy wooded ravine

Hole-In-The-Wall Rock, Grand Manan

and along the coast to a series of ledges known as **Flock of Sheep**. The last glacier deposited some rounded white boulders, known as glacial erratics, along the ledges and fishermen thought they looked like sheep when viewed from the sea. The rock formations here are interesting, with vertical intrusions of harder rock that weathered more slowly. The ledges are punctuated with tidal pools caught in the uneven surface. You can follow the trail all the way to the lighthouse, returning along the road, or return the way you came. In August, the trail is lined with giant raspberries.

Another stretch of trail leads from Ingalls Point to **Red Point**, well-known to geologists as the fault where the two distinctly different geological regions of the island meet. Rock to the west of it is volcanic (dark gray), to the east sedimentary (reddish color). To reach the point, begin at Anchorage Provincial Park, parking at the beach and following the well-marked trail along the shore. It's about a mile to Red Point.

RECOMMENDED READING: *The best source of information and readable maps for the island's trails is a booklet entitled* Heritage Trails and Footpaths on Grand Manan, *available on the island or from Baldwin's Guest House in Seal Cove.*

Grand Manan On Wheels

Cyclists will find roads easy for bicycling, although some have steep hills and none are especially wide. Drivers are bike-friendly, however, and traffic is light and moves at a leisurely pace. Rent bikes from **Adventure High**, ☎ 506/662-3563 or 800/732-5492.

Grand Manan's Water Activities

To view Hole-in-the-Wall from every angle, and to explore other stretches of the cliff-lined shore, sign on for a kayak trip with **Adventure High Sea Kayaking**, North Head, ☎ 506/662-3563. Kayaking trips include full instruction for beginners. (We can testify to their quality, since we learned sea kayaking with them – and fell in love with the sport, despite an encounter with high winds on our very first venture.) A sunset paddle can include a lobster dinner prepared on the beach, with good conversation and fascinating local and Native American lore. Relaxing on the beach at twilight after an exhilarating paddle along the coast, while lobsters turn red in a pot over a beach fire, is quite possibly the most memorable of all Grand Manan experiences. Kayak trips and sunset excursions followed by dinner are available daily, May-October, for $35; $50 with a lobster dinner. It's worth adding that the mere $15 difference in price makes this the least expensive lobster dinner you're likely to find, not to mention the Camembert and smoked pollock appetizers and the potatoes cooked with dulse that go along with it.

"Introduction to Sea Kayaking" is an all-day program that includes instruction not only in handling a kayak, but in choosing one for your needs (several kinds will be there to try), as well as kayak safety. During the trip you will visit small islands in search of seals and birds. The all-day tour is $90. Longer trips include camping in secluded coves, with meals prepared over beach fires.

Island Wildlife-Watching

With more than 250 species of birds sighted on and around the island (including puffins) and the whales that swim regularly off its shores, Grand Manan is a favorite of birders and whale enthusiasts. Look for birds while exploring the shore by kayak or from the hiking trails that lead to secluded coves and along the rims of cliffs. John James Audubon first reported the exceptional variety of Grand Manan birdlife in the 1830s, and ornithologists have been visiting to see puffins, arctic terns, bald eagles and other birds ever since.

Atlantic puffin off Grand Manan.

The Marsh in Castalia is a good place to observe birds. When the tide is low, you can sometimes see 3,000-year-old tree stumps from a sunken forest. Look also for seals, either on the rocks at low tide or swimming offshore at high tide. You can observe birds from blinds at Long Pond and Great Pond in **Anchorage Provincial Park**. At **Bradford's Cove** on the west shore of the island you can often see bald eagles; it can be reached by an orange-blazed trail from Deep Cove (you can also reach it along the cliffs from Southwest Head, but the trail is overgrown, muddy and exasperating to follow.

You can sail among as many as eight species of whales aboard the schooner *D'Sonoqua* with **Sea-Land Adventures** in Castalia, ☎ 506/662-8997. Trips run daily and are $70 for a full day, including lunch. There is a naturalist aboard to identify whales and seabirds.

FOR SERIOUS BIRDERS

Located 10 miles off the southern tip of Grand Manan, **Machias Seal Island** is considerably more famous for its birds than for its seals. This is the place to see Atlantic puffins, razorbills, and other nesting seabirds from only a few feet away. The island is unique in that it is the only puffin colony in the Western Hemisphere where you can go ashore and watch the puffins from enclosed blinds – the puffins carry on with puffin business completely undisturbed. Other birds that nest on the island include common terns, Arctic terns, guillemots, and eider ducks.

Only 13 people are permitted ashore each day, so you must make reservations well in advance. Call **Sea Watch Tours**, ☎ 506/622-8552, fax 506/662-1081. Visitors land from a small dory, step onto wet, slippery rocks, and cross a plank bridge. The crew forms a human chain to hand you along from one to the next, so there's really no danger, but you do need to step carefully. Bring a bird book, binoculars, a camera and telephoto lens, and lots of film. Layer warmly (early mornings on the Atlantic tend be cold and damp) and wear rubber-soled shoes. Pack a hearty lunch, snacks, and a big thermos of something hot. The trip lasts about six hours and costs $60 per person.

You'll see seals at North Rock, near the island, where the colony features both gray seals (once thought to be extinct) and harbour seals. You may also spot whales – fin, humpback, minke, and the rare North Atlantic right whale are all possible during late July and August. Pelagic birds are frequently seen, also in late July and August, are greater, sooty, and Manx shearwaters, pomarine and parasitic jaegers, and both Wilson and Leach's petrels, as well as red and rednecked phalaropes, black-legged kittiwakes, and northern gannets.

Machias Seal Island is a rare and glorious experience. There is nothing else like this anywhere; don't miss the chance to see Atlantic puffins up close and personal. – *Sara Godwin and Charles James*

> **TIP:** *Although morning whale-watch trips normally leave at 7 am – usually too early to have breakfast at your inn – the waters are calmer then than they are at 12:30 pm when the afternoon trips leave.*

Several excursion boats operate whale-watches from the island. Ask your innkeeper's advice before reserving, since some operators cancel trips arbitrarily, too late for you to rebook with another operator. Like islanders elsewhere, the captains of Grand Manan vessels are an independent lot. Among those our innkeepers have suggested as reliable are **Island Coast Boat Tours**, ☎ 506/662-8181, fax 506/662-9904; **Surfside Boat Tours**, ☎ 506/662-8156; and Sea Watch Tours, ☎ 506/622-8552, fax 506/662-1081. Whale-watch rates are about $40, and the best months to see whales are August and September. **Ocean Search** offers a full day at sea with a marine biologist, ☎ 506/662-8488.

While the purpose is deep-sea fishing, you are likely to spot whales or porpoises on a fishing trip with **Big Fish Deep Sea Charters**, ☎ 506/662-5362, fax 506/662-8670. A three- to five-hour trip with instruction and all tackle and bait is $35 for adults and $20 for children. **Grand Island Deep Sea Fishing**, ☎ 506/662-8673, also runs deep-sea fishing trips.

Grand Manan's geology is just as fascinating and important to scientists as its birdlife. The island is formed from a combination of six-billion-year-old formations and much younger volcanic deposits. (See *Red Point*, page 49.)

Eco-Travel on Grand Manan

To learn more about the geology and birdlife of the island, visit the **Grand Manan Museum** in Grand Harbour, ☎ 506/662-3524. It's open Monday-Saturday, 10:30 am to 4:30 pm, and Sunday, 2 to 5 pm, from mid-June through September. Along with displays on the island's unique geology, it features its equally unique history, and has a collection of mounted bird species found on the island.

To learn about the creatures that live above, on and under the sea, stop at the **Grand Manan Whale and Seabird Research Station** at North Head, ☎ 506/662-3804. It's small, but you'll find exhibits that include everything from a whale skull to porpoise parasites.

Grand Manan's Culinary Delights

If you haven't already tried **dulse**, the seaweed gathered and dried throughout the area as a snack and as a flavoring, Grand Manan is the place to do it. Dark Harbour, the only settlement (a term we use loosely here) on the cliff-lined western shore, is the island's dulse-gathering center. Dulse is sold in snack-size bags, and locals munch it like potato chips. It's an acquired taste, and few people who didn't grow up eating it find it yummy.

Herring is the other local specialty from the sea, and you can often go out in the morning on a herring boat. Mackerel, herring, and salmon are turned into delicacies in island smokehouses, beginning late in July and continuing into fall and winter. You can buy these at the Saturday morning Farmers' Market in North Head, along with produce, preserves and island crafts, mid-June through September.

Cultural & Eco-Travel Experiences

The border town of St. Stephen still joins Calais, Maine, to celebrate their long-standing friendship with an **International Festival** the first week of August. The two bridges over the river that separates the two towns are busy as residents and tourists move back and forth for the music, parades and other activities, while officers at the two customs stations continue to check the papers of cars crossing the border. Canadian and American flags fly together in both towns.

In St. Andrews, gardeners and bird-lovers will want to visit **Steven Smith Designs and Crocker Hill Studios** at 45 King St., just off Water St., ☎ 506/529-4303. It's a charming shop in an historic 1834 brick building that was once the Registry of Deeds. Steven's bird paintings are well-known among art collectors, and he has moved his studio here from the beautiful hillside gardens he built in nearby St. Stephen. Providing the setting for Steven's art, the shop is filled with gardening suplies, books, and products. Look here for bird and wildflower guides, too. Garden lovers everywhere regret that Steven and Gail's Crocker Hill Gardens, which have been featured in nearly every garden magazine in Canada and the US, are no longer open to the public, but will enjoy the smaller scale garden surrounding the beautifully restored old brick building.

A newly landscaped and constructed arboretum and garden of more than 900 perennial varieties and nearly as many specimen trees is now open at **Kingsbrae Horticultural Garden**, at the head of King St. in St. Andrews, ☎ 506/529-3335, fax 506/529-4875, e-mail kinghort@nbnet.nb.ca. Kingsbrae, a 27-acre former private estate garden, has been fully renovated, with extensive collections of roses and daylilies, several fountains, a maze, and a labyrinth. A portion of the garden has been left natural, with trails winding through the wildflowers. The views of Ministers Island and Passamaquoddy Bay are superb.

Wild blueberries and balsam are at the heart of **Granite Town Farms** at 151 Brunswick Street in St. George, ☎ 506/755-6314. Jams, jellies and blueberry syrup are packed in boxes made from cedar grown on the farm. In the fall, the place is redolent with the sweet woodsy scents of their balsam wreaths.

Natural history and fine arts and crafts meet at the **Sunbury Shores Arts & Nature Centre** on Water St. in St. Andrews, ☎ 506/529-3386. In its galleries, open year-round, you'll find changing exhibits featuring art from all over Canada, but primarily from the local area and Atlantic provinces. Films, concerts, workshops and courses fill their schedule, with intensive one-week summer courses aimed at those in the area for short stays. These range from wildlife illustration and pottery to marine ecology. Art and nature workshops are designed especially for children, with a different theme each week, including whales, rocks, insects and using local plants.

Watch for the opening of **Green's Point Marine and Coastal Interpretive Centre** at Green's Point Light in Back Bay. This community facility is preserving the historic point of land and plans to include environmental, historical, maritime and archaeological interests in their displays and programs, while keeping the point and lighthouse open to the public.

Plan to be there at 11 am or 4 pm, when they feed the seals at the **Huntsman Aquarium Museum**, Brandy Cove Rd, St. Andrews, ☎ 506/529-1202. Visitors are invited to plunge their hands into the aquarium for a personal encounter with starfish, sea cucumbers, lobsters, and other marine life. Exhibits illustrate the work of marine biologists, whose work is the main reason for this facility (St. Andrews is a major center for marine biological research). The museum is open daily 10 am to 6 pm in July and August, 10 am to 4:30 pm in May and June, Wednesday-Sunday 10 am to 4:30 pm September and October. Admission is $3.50 adult, $2.50 child, $3 senior, $10 family.

This area has its share of phenomena caused by the Fundy tides, which rush in and out of Passamaquoddy Bay through a series of small islands that are set like teeth at the mouth of the bay. The tide pushing its way through these channels creates North America's largest whirlpool, second largest tidal whirlpool in the world, called **The Old Sow**. You will pass it on the ferry between Deer Island and Campobello, if the tide is right, or you can see it from the top of the hill at Deer Island Point Camping Park, where campers have a ringside seat.

The rocks of the Quoddy shores and islands are carved in fantastic shapes by the sea, including several natural arches – most notably those on Grand Manan and Deer Island, both known as **Hole-in-the-Wall**. Those interested in geology can find fossils and agates on the beaches of Back Bay near Letete, and mineral specimens, some of them semi-precious stones, in the old quarries at St. George. Along the shore of St. Andrews at low tide you can find quartz, peridotite, agate and both brown and red jasper. You can also find flint in yellow, brown, gray and black, but it is not a native stone. It was brought as ballast by ships sent to return full of timber and fish, and when they arrived they dumped the flint overboard. In the intervening centuries it has broken and been smoothed into pebbles by the tides. You may also find coral, also brought as ballast, this time by ships from the West Indies.

If, like us, you find bogs among the earth's most fascinating phenomena, you will be interested to know that about one-third of the **Roosevelt Campobello International Park's** 2,800 acres of natural area is composed of raised heath-covered bogs. The locations of these and a thorough description of their formation is given in a brochure appropriately entitled *The Bogs of Roosevelt Campobello International Park*, available free at the visitors' center.

Salmon Rule the Waves

You will meet the salmon wherever you go here, not just on menus and on your plate. But seldom will you meet this impressive fish eye-to-eye as you will at the **Atlantic Salmon Centre**, Rte. 127, St. Andrews, ☎ 506/529-1084. The viewing window is built into the water of Chamcook Creek, a natural spawning habitat for salmon. Displays inside the center show what this area looked like when Chamcook Creek was a thriving lumber and commercial center (the site of North America's first paper mill), and tell more about the life cycles of the salmon. On your way back to the park-

➲ **ON A RELATED SUBJECT...** *If you forget, as we did, to stop at the Brunswick factory on Grand Manan to purchase some canned sardines or smoked oysters, all is not lost. When you disembark from the ferry at Blacks Harbour, you can run into* ***Keith's Building Supplies*** *at 516 Main St. and pick up a couple of cases there. The prices are only a tad higher than at the factory itself, but still low (about 25¢ a can for sardines) compared to what we usually pay. When I suggested using a few cans as stocking stuffers for Christmas, Charles muttered things like "private reserve," "my stash," and "mine, all mine," so darkly, that I promised I'd never even consider such sacrilege again.* – Sara Godwin

ing lot, walk along the trail on the far side of the creek to see the various habitats in its pools, described by interpretive signs. The facility is open daily, 10 am to 6 pm, June through August, and Thursday-Monday, 10 am to 5 pm, in September. Admission is $1.

During the summer you can watch salmon jump the ladder at the falls in St. George. The dam prevented salmon from returning to their spawning pools, so the concrete **St. George Fishway** was built to get them upstream. South St. and Portage St. lead to the bridge below the falls, from which you get a good view of the gorge.

Learn how fish farming is helping save the Atlantic salmon, and why the waters here are the perfect habitat, on a **PC Fish Farm Tour** at Head Harbour Wharf at the northern tip of Campobello Island, ☎ 506/752-2296.

For another view of the salmon, visit **Oven Head Salmon Smokers**, Oven Head Rd., ☎ 506/755-8333. They are off Rte. 1 about four miles west of St. George near the junction with Rte.760. The turn is by Ossie's Restaurant. You can tour the small smokehouse and learn how they turn the bounty of the local waters into one of the most admired of all seafood products. You can also sample and buy their maple-smoked salmon here daily from 8 am until 9 pm.

Wildlife-Watching

Minkes, humpbacks, finbacks, right whales, dolphins, porpoises and seals all swim in the waters of Fundy and Passamaquoddy Bays. Grand Manan has a recorded total of over 250 bird species, and the entire area is prime birding country.

On Campobello Island, you can often see whales from the rocky promontory at **East Quoddy Head Lighthouse**, where you can have a picnic on the cliffs and watch whales in the channel. To go on a whale-watch trip by boat from Campobello, contact **Cline Marine**, ☎ 506/529-4188 or 800/567-5880. A boat leaves Head Harbour at 10 am and 3 pm, mid-June through September, with fares of $30 for adults and $15 for children. Cline Marine's five-hour whale-watches leave St. Andrews at 8:30 am and 2 pm daily.

Whale-watching tours are operated by **Interactive Outdoors** in St. George, ☎ 506/755-2699 or 800/214-6906. Trips on their 23-foot *Little Jenna* tour places where you're likely to spot whales, seals, porpoises, herring weirs and salmon farms. The cost is $40 per adult, and includes lunch. They depart at 9 am, 1 pm and 5 pm, June through September.

Roosevelt Campobello International Park lies on the Atlantic flyway, with 2,800 acres of habitat that includes bogs, saltwater and freshwater marshes, open fields, thickets, cliffs, ponds and several types of forest. From May, when the resident songbirds return, until October, when the largest waterbird movement occurs and the winter residents return, the park has a constant variety of bird activity. An excellent brochure, Birds of Campobello, free at the visitors center, has a map and descriptions of the 12 major habitats and observation areas, along with a checklist of the species seen there.

Sightseeing

Campobello Island is only about three miles long, but it's long on history and home of a rare international park, **Roosevelt Campobello International Park**, Rte. 774, ☎ 506/752-2922. President Franklin Roosevelt spent his childhood and early adult summers on Campobello Island, and it was at this 34-room cottage that he was stricken with polio. The cottage, for all its size (it was a big family, and they brought their staff with them), is rustic and quite unpretentious. Its gardens are beautiful. The Visitors Centre has family photographs on display, and there is an excellent 15-minute film, Beloved Island, about the family's summers here, which you should see before touring the cottage. Admission is free, and the cottage is open daily 10 am to 6 pm, May through mid-October, with the last cottage tour beginning at 4:45 pm. You can also tour the neighboring Hubbard Cottage, a more elegant and luxurious home with an unusual oval picture window

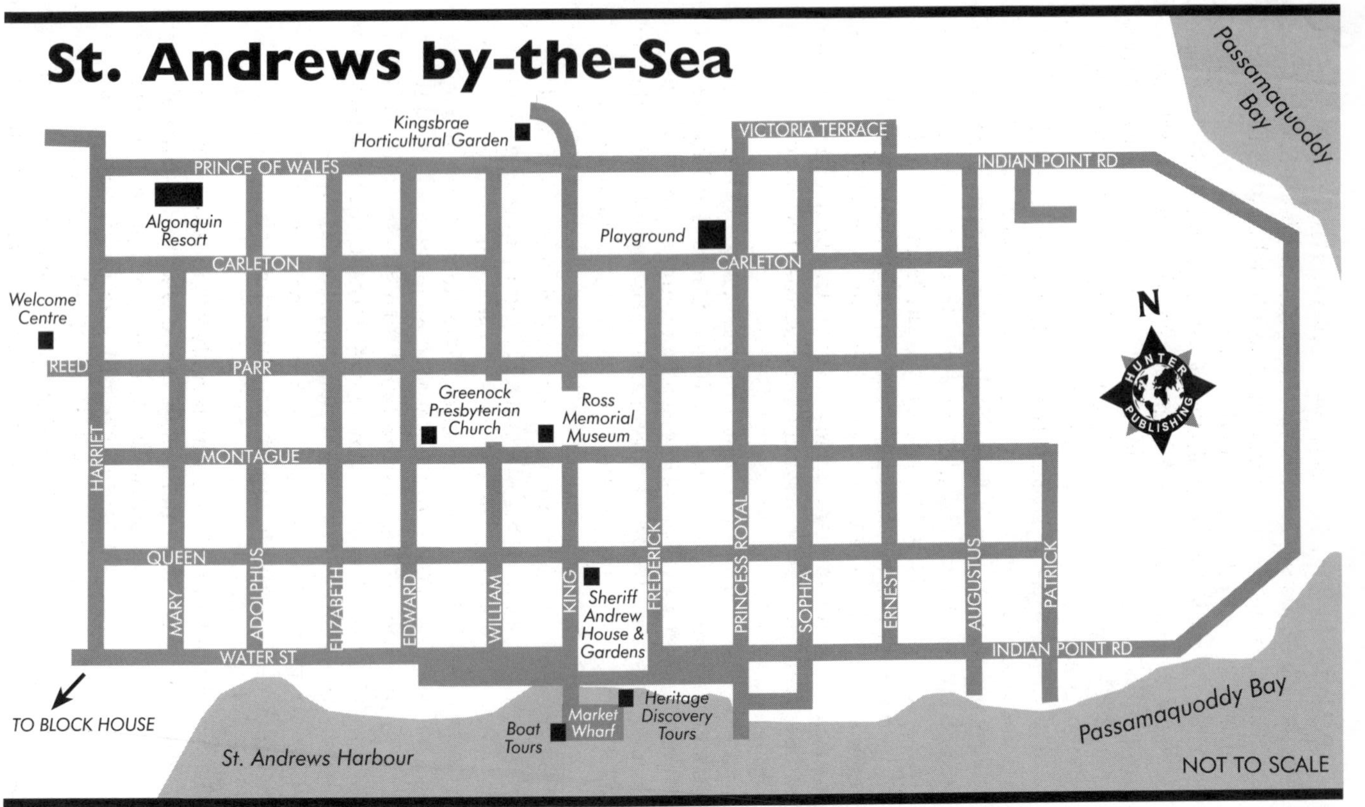
St. Andrews by-the-Sea
Kingsbrae Horticultural Garden
VICTORIA TERRACE
PRINCE OF WALES
INDIAN POINT RD
Passamaquoddy Bay
Algonquin Resort
Playground
CARLETON
CARLETON
Welcome Centre
N
HUNTER PUBLISHING
REED
PARR
Greenock Presbyterian Church
Ross Memorial Museum
HARRIET
MONTAGUE
QUEEN
MARY
ADOLPHUS
ELIZABETH
EDWARD
WILLIAM
KING
Sheriff Andrew House & Gardens
FREDERICK
PRINCESS ROYAL
SOPHIA
ERNEST
AUGUSTUS
PATRICK
WATER ST
INDIAN POINT RD
TO BLOCK HOUSE
Heritage Discovery Tours
Market Wharf
Boat Tours
Passamaquoddy Bay
St. Andrews Harbour
NOT TO SCALE

overlooking the bay. This cottage is open to the public in July and August when it's not in use. In 1960, the movie Sunrise at Campobello, starring Greer Garson and Ralph Bellamy as Eleanor and Franklin Roosevelt, was filmed here.

While you are on Campobello, drive to the far end of the island to see East Quoddy Head Lighthouse, the most photographed lighthouse in eastern Canada, and scramble over the rocky causeway to the lighthouse itself, if you are there at low tide. Watch for whales from the high cliffs here.

St. Andrews is a pleasure to stroll through, especially with the help of the booklet, *A Guide to Historic St. Andrews*, free at the Welcome Centre. Just admiring the architecture of three centuries lining its streets is a pleasant way to spend an afternoon.

St. Andrews Blockhouse National Historic Site on Water St. is open daily 9 am to 8 pm, June through August, and 9 am to 5 pm in early September. It is the lone survivor of 12 blockhouses built along the New Brunswick coast in the War of 1812. Admission is $1 for adults, free for children. Across the street is Centennial Park.

Two American summer residents of St. Andrews left their 1824 neoclassic house to the town as **Ross Memorial Museum**, 188 Montague St., ☎ 506/529-1824. The museum is filled with antique furnishings, paintings and decorative arts from their collections. Each year a different part of their collection is featured, so it's a place you can return to year after year. The museum is open Tuesday-Saturday, 10 am to 4 pm, and Sunday, 1:30 to 4 pm, in July and August; from late May through June and September through mid-October hours are Tuesday-Saturday, 10 am to 4:30 pm. Donations are requested. The Rosses' own home, Rossmount, is under *Where to Stay & Eat*, page 62.

To see period rooms restored and furnished in the style of the 1820s, visit the **Sheriff Andrews House**, King and Queen streets, ☎ 506/529-5080. Along with household equipment of the era, the house has a basement "keeping room" with beehive ovens. It's open daily, 9:30 am to 4:30 pm, July through mid-October; admission is free.

Sir William Van Horne was largely responsible for making St. Andrews into the summer resort of the wealthy, a turn of events that not only saved historic St. Andrews, but gave it its wealth of turn-of-the-century architecture. He was president of Canadian Pacific Railways and insisted on the line's extension to St. Andrews and the building of the Algonquin as a resort destination for its passengers. He built his own summer home, a complete operating farm that includes an enormous livestock barn, on an island accessible only at low tide, now open to the public as **Ministers Island Historic Site**, Bar Rd, ☎ 506/529-5081. You can only go there with a tour, although you drive your own car across the sandbar. Daily tours are scheduled for low tide, June through mid-October, and cost $5 adult, $2.50 ages 13-18. A tide schedule is posted at the bar, which is under 10 feet of seawater at high tide. The tour, which also includes Sir William's bathhouse with a tidal swimming pool, his windmill, and giant barn, takes about two hours.

Chocolate lovers – or anyone with a sweet tooth – should stop in St. Stephen at the **Ganong Chocolatier** company store, at 73 Milltown Blvd., near the US border, ☎ 506/465-5611. More than 80 kinds of chocolates are sold here; the best bargain are the seconds that had to be redipped. Ganong is open 9 am to 8 pm, Monday-Friday; 9 am to 5 pm, Saturday; and 11 am to 5 pm, Sunday.

Where To Stay & Eat

In St. Andrews

The **Algonquin Hotel** is one of Canada's premier resort hotels. Two golf courses, a heated outdoor pool, tennis, aerobics classes, lawn croquet and a health club keep guests busy at this famous landmark, set in its own hilltop park framed in stunning gardens. Rooms in the new wing all have air-conditioning and two queen-size beds; some also have kitchenettes. A bagpiper parades the front lawn at tea time, and non-guests are welcome to enjoy the music, too. Although the Algonquin is expensive, its facilities and the variety of special packages that include extras make it a good value. Its restaurant, the Passamaquoddy Veranda, serves a lunch buffet ($$) and Sunday brunch, as well as dinner ($$-$$$) nightly. Transport from the Saint John airport can be arranged at $35 per person, less for groups. *184 Adolphus St., St. Andrews, NB E0G 2X0, ☎ 506/529-8823, 800/563-4299 in the US, fax 506/529-4194 ($$$).*

Few inns or B&Bs can match the genuine warm hospitality of the **Hiram Walker Estate Heritage Inn**. When you sink into one of the sumptuous white sofas for afternoon tea in the elegant parlor, you really do feel like a house-guest in a private home. Possibly that's because its engaging owners have restored and decorated this showpiece mansion as their own family home. Rooms ar[e] luxurious and elegant without being frilly or overdone. (We like Room 6, but each one has its own appeal.) Do plan to eat dinner there at least once; it's by reservation only. Breakfast is a work of art, so you can imagine what dinner's like. *109 Reed Ave, St. Andrews, NB E0G 2X0, ☎ 506/529-4210, fax 506/529-4311 ($$-$$$).*

The Algonquin Hotel.

In the same upscale Algonquin neighborhood is **Pansy Patch**. A small B&B, it's in one of the town's many architecturally remarkable "cottages" of white stucco, with a round turret. Breakfast is served overlooking the gardens. Guests can use the Algonquin pool and spa. *59 Carleton St., St. Andrews, NB E0G 2X0, ☎ 506/529-3834, off-season 617/965-2601, fax 617/964-7115 ($$$).*

The town's third manor house inn sits in a stunning new horticultural garden: **Kingsbrae Arms**. It's luxury all the way, as well as pricey, with rooms that can only be described as grand and amenities to match. The get-away-from-it-all atmosphere of canopy beds, fireplaces, silk-covered easy chairs, soft robes and fresh flowers seems almost at odds with the state-of-the-art data ports and cable TVs in each room. *219 King St., St. Andrews, NB E0G 2X0, ☎ 506/529-1897, fax 506/529-1197 ($$$$$).*

…gings in this …ter the sum- …liage season, …e planning a winter … …ly spring trip consult the latest New Brunswick Travel Planner, which gives dates of operation for all the listed lodgings. Contact New Brunswick Tourism at ☎ 800/561-0123 to obtain a copy.

Another fine estate, on the slopes of Mt. Chamcook, has been transformed into a warm and welcoming hotel: **Rossmount Inn**. Built as the home of the wealthy Rosses (who furnished the Ross Memorial Museum with their priceless collections; see *Sightseeing* on page 59), its public rooms are furnished with antiques, many of which spill over into the guest rooms. Guests can take brisk walks on the trail to the summit, for the best view over the entire peninsula. *Rte. 127, St. Andrews, NB E0G 2X0, ☎ 506/529-3351, fax 506/529-1920, e-mail mackarch@nbnet.nb.ca, Web site www.sn2000.nb.ca/comp/rossmount-inn.*

In the center of town, you can stay in a recently restored historic waterfront home, the **Treadwell Inn**. Antiques furnish the rooms and the top-floor suite, which overlooks the harbor. *129 Water St., St. Andrews, NB E0G 2X0, ☎ 506/529-1011 ($$).*

The newest intown addition is a skillful restoration of a home built in 1798, furnished in distinguished examples of artistry and craftsmanship from the years 1780 to 1920, much of it by New Brunswick cabinetmakers. The **Windsor House** of St. Andrews, and its dining room serving classical French dishes, is not for the budget traveler, but it is a rare chance to stay among museum pieces. *132 Water St., St. Andrews, NB E0G2X0; ☎ 506/529-3330 or 888/890-9463; fax 506/529-4063 ($$$).*

Seaside Beach Resort is a homey, comfortable compound of waterfront apartments with kitchens, overlooking the harbor. Barbecues and picnic tables on the lawn, and rowboats at the shore are all for guests' use. The hosts really enjoy their guests, many of whom reserve each year for the following season. *339 Water St. (PO Box 310), St. Andrews, NB E0G 2X0, ☎ 506/529-3846 ($$).*

There's only one cottage, and anyone who's stayed there wants to come back, so call early to reserve the little shingled cottage at **Sea Garden**. The gardens in which it hides are breathtaking and set on the edge of the bay. *469 Water St., St. Andrews, NB E0G 2X0, ☎ 506/529-3225 ($-$$).*

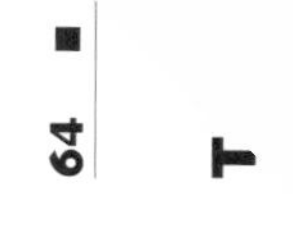

Opposite the Algonquin's golf course is the tidy **Motel**. Nothing fancy, but clean and comfortab have a two-burner stove, refrigerator and sink. *1 (PO Box 424), St. Andrews, NB E0G 2X0, ☎ 506 5*

For a complete change of pace – from any place you're likely to find in St. Andrews or elsewhere – stop at **Salty Towers**. Not only is the price refreshing, but the casual and decidedly quirky atmosphere contrasts sharply with the rest of the town. It has the air of a pre-World War II seaside guest house, but without the fussiness. Make your own breakfast in the cavernous kitchen and chat with the gregarious artist who keeps it all together. It's not for those who like a place for everything and everything in its place. *340 Water St., St. Andrews E0G 2X0, ☎ 506/529-4585 ($).*

Chef's Café is open June through August and claims to be Canada's oldest restaurant, which we've never heard disputed. Nor does anyone dispute the quality of the fish & chips they serve here. *180 Water St., ☎ 506/529-8888 ($$).*

For a view over the harbor and bay and well-prepared dishes made from its denizens, reserve a table at the **Lighthouse Restaurant**. Everyone raves about the fisherman's plate, abounding in haddock, scallops, and shrimp; it's the place of choice for a lobster dinner. Open daily for lunch and dinner. *Water St., ☎ 506/529-3082 ($$).*

L'Europe is continental with a German flavor. Rack of lamb and local seafood highlight the menu, and each dinner begins with the chef's own pâté and includes hearty German bread, salad and vegetables, so you don't need to order extras to make a complete meal. *48 King St., ☎ 506/529-3818 ($$-$$$).*

The Gables is noisy and casual, but a good choice for lobster roll, chowder, steamers or pasta, as well as fish cooked in a variety of ways. You can eat indoors or on the large patio overlooking the bay. *143 Water St., ☎ 506/529-3440 ($).*

In addition to its signature Bay of Fundy pickled herring, you can get grilled salmon, mussels steamed in wine, or a haddock and scallop chowder in the tavern atmosphere of **The Pickled Herring**. *211 Water St., ☎ 506/529-3766.*

The Mainland & Inner Islands

Blair House serves a full English breakfast. The atmosphere is warm and relaxed in this elegant Victorian home within walking distance of downtown St. Stephen. *38 Prince William St. (PO Box 112), St. Stephen, NB E3L 2W9, ☎ 506/466-2233, fax 506/466-2233 ($-$$).*

Located next to the Tourist Information Centre in St. Stephen is the **Grill & Griddle Restaurant**. The name tells you what to expect here, but doesn't tell you about the desserts, all baked in-house. *☎ 506/466-1814 ($).*

Bonny River House Bed & Breakfast sits on a point, surrounded by river on three sides. After a breakfast with homemade breads you can use the inn's canoes to explore the river. *RR 3, St. George, NB E0G 2Y0, ☎ 506/755-2248 ($-$$).*

Making St. George a center for outdoor adventure has been a long-time goal of the owners of the **Granite Town Hotel**. At their attractive modern hotel, which you can see from Rte. 1, they have a full-service adventure center, with everything from winter sleigh rides to kayak trips, as well as a restaurant. *15 Main St., St. George, NB E0G 2Y0, ☎ 506/755-6415, fax 506/755-6009 ($$).*

You'll find clams, fish & chips, roast pork, halibut or hot turkey sandwiches in the tidy green-and-white dining room at **Fred's River's End Restaurant**. *4 Wallace St, St. George, ☎ 506/755-1121 ($-$$).*

The setting doesn't get any better than at **Mariner's Inn**. It stands on an elevation above a wild stretch of shoreline; highly accommodating hosts are an added bonus. *Cove Rd. (Chance Harbour RR#2), Lepreau, NB E0G 2H0, ☎ 506/659-2619 or 888/783-2455, fax 506/659-1890.*

For a traditional sporting lodge atmosphere, spend an outdoorsy vacation in one of the upscale log cabins clustered around **Loon Bay Lodge**. It overlooks the St. Croix River, where you can catch your own dinner (they'll cook it for you) or use the lodge's canoes to explore. *Rte.745 (PO Box 101), St. Stephen, NB E3L 2W9, ☎ 506/466-1240 or 888/LOON-BAY, fax 506/466-4213 ($$).*

On Campobello Island, efficiency units are available at the well-kept **Friar's Bay Motor Lodge and Restaurant**. It's close to the international park and the beach. The restaurant ($-$$) s traditional home-style dishes. *Route 774, Welshpool,* ☎ *506/752-2056 ($).*

Owen House was built in the 1830s, with an enclosed sunporch overlooking the water. Bounteous breakfasts and homey, rather old-fashioned bedrooms are just right for its family summer cottage ambience. *Rte. 774, Welshpool, Campobello, NB E0G 3H0,* ☎ *506/752-2977 ($-$$).*

Inside the clubhouse at the Herring Cove Provincial Park's golf course, you can get seafood dinners at the **Herring Cove Restaurant**. *Herring Cove Provincial Park,* ☎ *506/752-1898 ($-$$).*

Halfway between the equator and North Pole is the **45th Parallel Motel and Restaurant**. The motel overlooks the Western Passage from a hilltop, and the restaurant specializes in seafood and home-style country cooking. *Deer Island,* ☎ *506/747-2231 ($-$$).*

On Grand Manan

You should reserve lodgings here before you arrive, because vacancies are few in the summer. It's also a good idea to make dinner reservations early. Places with a North Head address are closest to the ferry landing, probably the best choices for those arriving without wheels. Most inns are open May through October.

Shore Crest Lodge Country Inn is close to the landing, with bright, airy rooms and a wide front porch where you can watch the world go by. Their restaurant ($-$$) specializes in fresh seafood, prepared in a variety of interesting and traditional ways. *North Head, Grand Manan, NB E0G 2M0,* ☎ *506/662-3216 or (Nov-Apr) 410/247-8310 ($$).*

Aristotle's Lantern is a homey inn with good-humored hosts and a full restaurant. Go there in the afternoon for a real cream tea, served on fine china. *North Head, Grand Manan, NB E0G 2M0,* ☎ *506/662-3788 ($$).*

Compass Rose has comfortable rooms of varying size, some with sea views, in two old island homes. Its restaurant ($-$$) overlooks the water, and serves afternoon tea, as well as lunch and dinner. The chowder is thick, creamy, and filled with flaky chunks of fresh fish. *North Head, Grand Manan, NB E0G 2M0,* ☎ *506/662-8570 or (November-April) 514/458-2607 ($$).*

Marathon Inn is larger than most on the island, with 28 rooms, some with shared bath. It has tennis courts, hiking trails begin at its door, and the owners are helpful in advising about local outdoor activities. *North Head, Grand Manan, NB E0G 2M0, ☎ 506/662-8144 ($$).*

Some distance from the village in a lovely cove setting is The Inn at **Whale Cove Cottages**. Some rooms are in the inn, and there are two self-catering cottages, one of which, Orchardside, was used for many years by novelist Willa Cather. The dining room is outstanding, as are the lunches-to-go from Cove Cuisine, their food and catering shop. *North Head, Grand Manan, NB E0G 2M0, ☎ 506/662-3181.*

If you like the privacy of your own seaside cottage, try the brand new **Seaside Haven Cottages**. They are open year-round, have laundry facilities, and give discounts to seniors. *Grand Harbour, PO Box 45, Castalia, Grand Manan, NB E0G 1L0, ☎ 506/662-3377.*

On the southern end of the island, in the center of a highly scenic fishing village, sits **McLaughlin's Wharf Inn**. Its rooms, all of which share bathrooms, overlook the harbour. So does the attractive restaurant, where you can reserve ahead for a lobster dinner or order other entrées from the full menu. *Seal Cove, Grand Manan, NB E0G 2M0, ☎ 506/662-8760 ($$).*

The **Griff-Inn Restaurant** serves fresh seafood overlooking the waters where it was caught. Three meals a day are hearty and never ho-hum, from the morning porridge to the scallops and shrimp with anisette. *North Head, ☎ 506/662-8360 ($$).*

For live lobsters to cook yourself or fresh-boiled to eat on the dock, go to **Lindsays Lobsters**. *On the Public Landing at Grand Harbour, ☎ 506/662-3623.*

■ Camping

Tents and RVs fill a point overlooking the bay at **Passamaquoddy Park**. The Kiwanis Club, which owns and maintains it nicely, accepts reservations. *PO Box 116, St. Andrews, NB E0G 2X0, ☎ 506/529-3439.*

Deer Island Point Camping Park has open sites for tents and trailers and the island's best view of the whirlpool, The Old Sow. The wilderness campsites along the shoreline are more secluded and shaded by woods, but you must carry your gear there on foot. *Lord's Cove, Deer Island, NB E0G2J0, ☎ 506/747-2423.*

Herring Cove Provincial Park has a camping area with electrical hookups and tent sites, a nine-hole golf course, and a mile-long sandy beach (unsupervised). Inside the park is also a seafood restaurant. *Welshpool, Campobello Island, NB E0G 3H0, ☎ 506/752-7010.*

Those with a head for heights (and without small children) can camp along the clifftops overlooking the sea at **Hole in the Wall Park Campground** at North Head. Wooded sites away from the cliffs are better for those with children. The staff naturalist leads programs and walks exploring the scenic headland, which includes several interesting geological features and an ancient pipestone quarry. *North Head, Grand Manan, NB E0G 2M0, ☎ 506/662-3152, fax 506/662-3593.*

Also on Grand Manan, on the low eastern shore, is **Anchorage Provincial Park**. It has an unsupervised beach and encompasses a wildlife preserve. There are well-maintained tent sites and areas with trailer hook-ups. Fees are $20 for tent sites, $23 with hook-ups. *Rte. 776, ☎ 506/662-3215.*

The Fundy Coast

The Bay of Fundy has the highest tides in the world, creating a land- and seascape that changes dramatically twice each day. Broad bays and estuaries filled with water change suddenly to wide expanses of deep red mud, often carved into sculptured contours by the force of the tide. Rock formations are even more fantastic, with sea caves, soaring cliffs and bluffs and unusual offshore sea stacks that rise like giant

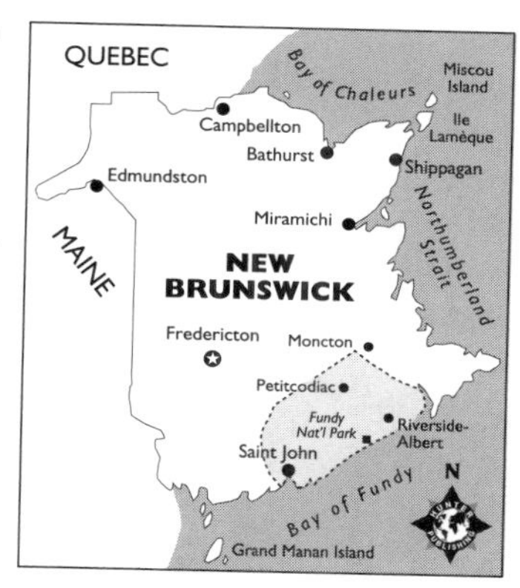

pointed fir trees. Other tide-related phenomena punctuate the area: reversing rapids, tidal bores,whirlpools and tremendous bird populations that thrive in the marshlands constantly fed with freshly arrived sea-borne food.

It is the part of Atlantic Canada through which the most travelers pass, but it is one of the least known and least explored. Most stop only to see the famous "Reversing Falls" and Hopewell Rocks, some use Fundy National Park as a stopover, but most hurry on to reach the ferry or road to somewhere else. Except for the busy Rte. 1, the roads of this beautiful area are left to the rest of us. Most of those who hurry past never know that they are passing the only wilderness remaining on the entire east coast of North America. They've never explored the sea caves in the lovely town of St. Martins, kayaked among the sea stacks and islands and under the soaring cliffs, looked down into the sea from the new road piercing the edge of the Big Salmon River's domain, or stayed in the elegant Victorian mansions that have become fine country inns. Nor have they explored the backroads of the inland valleys in search of covered bridges or spent a lazy week on a houseboat in its long scenic lakes.

Even when we plan a vacation to the beaches of Prince Edward Island or the highlands of Cape Breton, we save the first week to unwind in this surprising area and the only-slightly-better-known regions on either side of it. Sometimes we never get any farther.

Geography & History

Geography

Although county lines are of little concern to the casual traveler, it just happens that the borders we've drawn to delineate the Fundy region are exactly those shown on the provincial map as the borders of Saint John and King's counties. To those we've added the area south and west of Moncton, bordered on the west by the Petitcodiac River.

The map gives you a good idea of the land north of the city, where several long bays, which look more like lakes, bring the waters of the Kennebecasis and St. John rivers to meet at Grand Bay and flow through the narrow channel and to the Bay of Fundy. Rolling hills drop to lakeside towns; farther north, long valleys cut through more hills in a region of fertile farms.

But the map gives no clue at all to the dramatic Fundy coastline. Unless, of course, you are a very astute map reader and wonder why there are no towns or roads in most of the area between St. Martins and Fundy National Park. Only a relief map would explain this, for the Big Salmon River, Little Salmon River and several others flow through deep gorges, some so wide that the challenge of spanning them with a bridge has prevented the construction of a through road. This is a wilderness of steep slopes and dense forest, and a wall of rock hundreds of feet tall forms the precipitous shore along most of this section of the Bay of Fundy.

A scenic roadway with lookout points and steep trails leading down to the shore has just been constructed from St. Martins into a portion of this area, but it stops at Big Salmon River. Whether it will eventually go through, as is planned, to become a serious rival to Cape Breton Island's famous Cabot Trail is anyone's guess, but until it does, the spectacular sea cliffs beyond the Big Salmon River are accessible only by hiking long distances in from either side, camping along the trail. Many people – and we are among them – hope that this will be left as it is, the last and only real wilderness area south of Labrador on the entire east coast of North America. To ruin these stunning shores and their estuaries with highway bridges would be a grievous mistake for which future generations would never forgive the province and federal government, cohorts in the plan.

History

Saint John, the Fundy shore's principal city (in fact, it's the province's largest city), is older than Quebec, Montreal or Toronto. Founded by Samuel de Champlain in 1604, it was the site of a French fort built in 1631 for the fur trade and for defense against the English. The English conquered it, but it changed hands between English and French several more times before becoming an incorporated English city in 1785, after an influx of Loyalists arrived, fleeing the American Revolution.

These were not ordinary refugees. The thousands who fled, rather than join the rebels against the crown, were successful colonists, including many of New England's prominent leaders (not surprising, since they had the most to lose from a split with the crown) and they breathed new life into Saint John and the surrounding area, turning it into a major shipbuilding center and commercial port.

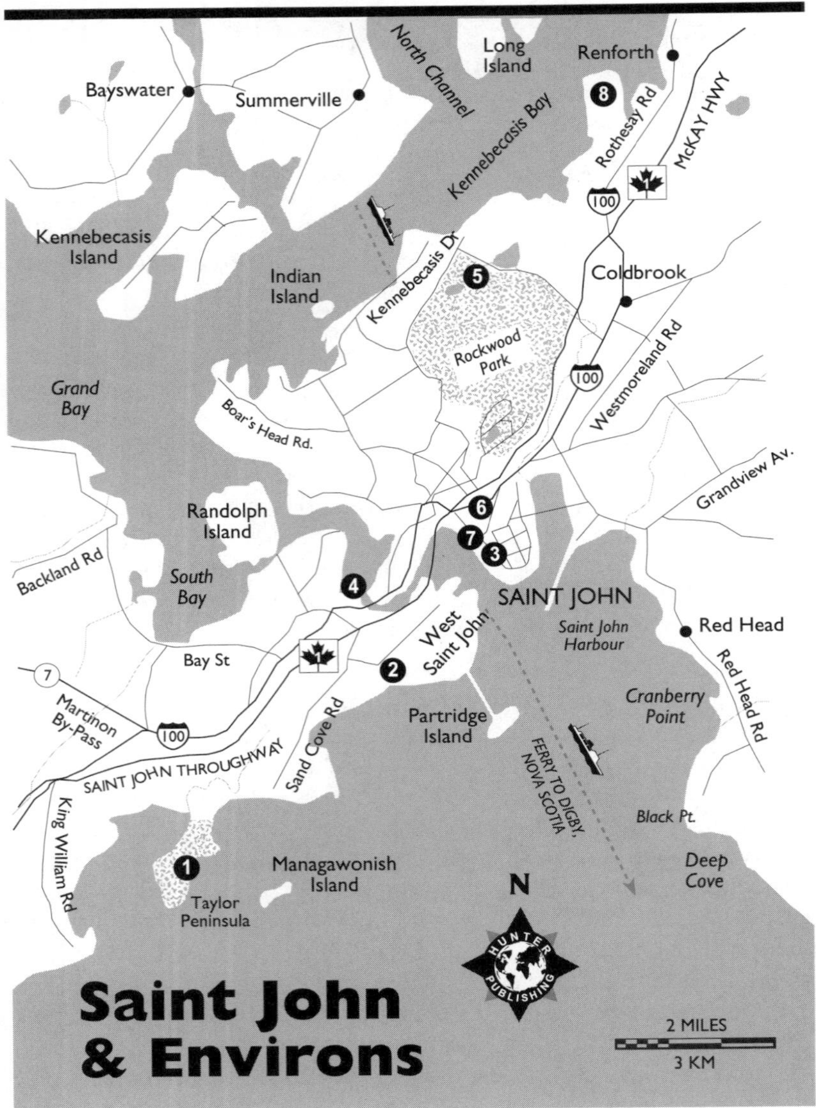

1. Irving Nature Park
2. Carleton Martello Tower
3. Loyalist Trail / Historic Area *(see map on page 77)*
4. Reversing Falls
5. Cherry Brook Zoo
6. Aitken Bicentennial Exhibition Centre; Sciencescape
7. Tourist Information Centre; Market Square; New Brunswick Museum
8. Kennebecasis Park

Getting Around

Saint John, the southern gateway to the Fundy Coast, is about an hour from the Maine/New Brunswick international boundary at Calais/St. Stephen. Driving north through Maine, the route numbers don't even change when you cross the border; US 1 becomes NB 1, and leads you to Saint John and on through the center of the region until it joins the East-West TransCanada Highway 2 at Sussex. A few miles east of this junction TransCanada-2 meets Rte. 114, which leads to Fundy National Park.

You have two choices if you are arriving from Nova Scotia: one by land, one by sea. When you enter from Nova Scotia at Aulac, you must go northward to Moncton before heading south into the Fundy Coast, since the wide tidal Petitcodiac River forms a natural barrier, unbridged until Moncton.

The sea route leads directly from Digby, on the western end of Nova Scotia, where Marine Atlantic's *MV Princess of Acadia* crosses the bay to Saint John three times daily in the summer, less often the rest of the year. The crossing takes about two hours and 45 minutes and carries both cars and foot passengers. One-way summer fares are $23 adult, $20.50 for seniors and $11.50 for children ages five to 12. These are reduced by $3-$5

➲ **IS IT SAINT JOHN OR ST. JOHN?** *You may not get a complete consensus on this question, but one thing is certain: when you are referring to the city in New Brunswick, it is always Saint John. The issue with the river is a little less clear. Generations of school children in the province have been taught to spell them the same, but the newer "official" spelling abbreviates the river to St. John. While not everyone agrees, we have gone with the new thinking, not because we are especially modern, but because we note that the river's first European explorer, Samuel de Champlain, who first named it in his journal, spelled it (in French, of course) St. Jean. If it was good enough for Sam, it's good enough for us. But either way, don't make the mistake of spelling – or pronouncing – either of them "St. John's." That's the capital of Newfoundland, a fact you need to remember if you are boarding a plane bound for either airport. And the Newfoundland city does not spell out "saint." So it's the St. John River, Saint John in New Brunswick, and St. John's in Newfoundland.*

> ➲ **TIP:** *When you arrive in the Saint John area, be sure to get a* ***tide table*** *(available at tourist information and visitor centers) so you can plan the best times to visit* ***Reversing Falls Rapids*** *and* ***Hopewell Rocks****, both of which are tide-dependent.*

off-season. Taking a car is $50 ($42.50 off season), and you should make a reservation. Call **Marine Atlantic** at ☎ 506/636-4048 in Saint John; in Digby, 902/245-2116; elsewhere, 800/341-7981.

Air Nova connects Saint John to Halifax, and from there to several US cities. You can rent a car at the airport in Saint John (be sure to reserve ahead); all the major companies have representatives there.

Information Sources

■ Saint John has four tourist information centers: at **Reversing Falls Bridge** on Route 100 (☎ 506/658-2937), **Market Square** at the downtown waterfront (☎ 506/658-2855), on **Rte. 1** west of the city (☎ 506/658-2940), and at the **airport**. The latter is open year-round, the others from mid-May to mid-Oct., from 9 am to 6 pm, with longer hours during July and August.

■ The **Visitor and Convention Bureau** on the 11th floor at City Hall (PO Box 1971), Saint John, NB E2L 4L1 (☎ 506/658-2990) is open weekdays year-round, 8:30 am to 4:30 pm.

■ The **Kings County Tourist Centre** on Maple Ave. in Sussex, at the junction of Rtes. 1 and 890, is staffed by the most helpful group of senior volunteers, who'll offer you coffee and tell you anything you want to know about their area. It's open 9 am until 9 pm, mid-May to mid-October, ☎ 506/433-2214. Be sure to get a copy of the covered bridge map. Or stop at the **in-town information center** at the old railway station on Broad St. (☎ 506/433-6602).

■ The **St. Martins Tourist Information Centre** is in a lighthouse-shaped building at the end of Main St. by the wharves, ☎ 506/833-2209.

Adventures

Fundy National Park is the area's centerpiece for hiking and several other outdoor activities, with 60 miles of hiking and walking trails providing views of its coastal cliffs, boreal forests and bogs. To enter the park you'll have to buy daily or four-day permits for each person. These cost about $3.50 for adults, half-price for children, or $7 for a family per day, and three times those fees for four-day passes. These permits entitle you to use the roads, trails, picnic areas, and facilities of the Visitor Centre. Swimming, camping and some other activities require an extra fee. So far, fees have only been levied between mid-May and mid-Oct, although the park is open year-round. Pick up a copy of the free guide Salt and Fir, available at the entrance, which describes park activities and attractions. The visitor centers in the park have shops with excellent reference books and pamphlets on various aspects of the park and its natural history. If you plan to do any hiking, be sure to buy a copy of the trail guide, which includes a topographical map. For information on the park, write to PO Box 40, Alma, NB E0A 1B0, ☎ 506/887-6000, fax 506/887-6008, e-mail Fundy_info@.gc.ca. The Visitor Centre and Information Centre each have *Day Adventure* information and voucher sales desks.

■ On Foot

Hiking

Fundy National Park has 60 miles of hiking trails, including a circuit of 30 miles of linked trails through all the park's biosystems. To hike it takes three or four days, so there are wilderness campsites along it. Be sure you have a copy of the park's trail guide, which includes a topographical map, before starting on any but the short self-guided nature trails.

Dickson Falls is reached by an easy 30- to 45-minute walk on a loop trail through the forest. The falls itself is viewed from a platform. The **Caribou Plain Trail** offers a boardwalk accessible to those in wheelchairs, and the entire two-mile hike is over gentle terrain on a smooth trail. It passes over northern bog landscape and through forests, passing a beaver dam. Be sure to take the side trail to an overlook with a good view of the bog; interpretive signs explain its formation and the plant life found there.

Third Vault Falls are the highest in the park at 53 feet, and the in-and-back trail is just over two miles each way. Although it is level most of the way, there is some climbing as you approach the falls. Like any waterfall, this is more impressive when water levels are high, but even in mid-summer it is well worth the hike.

Kinnie Brook Trail is a moderately strenuous hike, under two miles round-trip, but it passes some of the park's most interesting geological features, a gorge, large boulders, and a stream that flows through glacial formations, often disappearing completely. Interpretive signs explain the glaciation. Several small waterfalls near the end of the trail add to its appeal.

Different geological forces are at work in **Devil's Half Acre**, reached by a loop trail less than a mile in length. Layers of shale underneath the surface sandstone move as water seeps in and freezes. The splits and deep fissures in the rock change as the rock below is constantly shifting; movements of more than six inches a year have been recorded, uprooting trees and causing the area to look as though something had been tearing it apart, hence the name. Interpretive signs explain the geology.

East Branch Trail shows how human, instead of geologic, action has changed the face of the land. The entire loop is about 3½ miles, but the trail is easy and fairly level. About halfway you will come to an old logging dam and yard, where the logs were cut and stored before they were floated down the Point Wolfe River to the sawmill at its mouth. Interpretive signs tell of the logging days, but history is less certain on the strange earth mounds near the beginning of the trail. These were once believed to be native burial places, but more recent investigation suggests that they were not.

An interesting short walk near the mouth of the river completes the picture of what this area looked like in logging days. The half-mile **Ridge Trail**, off the end of Point Wolfe Rd., leads to the remains of a dam and the site of the sawmill where the logs were made into boards. Even if early industrial history doesn't interest you, the walk leads to some nice views of the coastal cliffs.

Geology and human activity combine in **Coppermine Trail**, an easy three-mile loop past a turn-of-the-century copper and gold mine. The trail skirts the bottom of the tailing pile, which you can climb to find the remains of mining equipment. Collectors may also want to look for minerals and traces of copper in the tailings. Although you can go either direction at the fork just after you cross the brook (this is the meeting point for the two ends of the loop), we suggest taking the right-hand option, since the grade is gentler; it's easier to go down the steeper places.

Dedicated hikers will want to follow the trail along the **Upper Salmon River** from the park headquarters in Alma. Although the whole trail is much longer, you can follow it for the first three miles to reach **Black Hole**, a large pool where salmon stop in the late summer and early fall, before continuing their journey upstream to spawn. Black Hole is also accessible from the other side via **Black Hole Trail**, a seven-mile moderate hike round-trip. If you have someone to pick you up at the other end, you can return via the Black Hole Trail instead of retracing your path.

The Upper Salmon River Trail continues to follow the river past its confluence with tributaries, then along Broad River to the beautiful **Broad River Falls**. From here, if you have someone to meet you at the other end, continue on the 1½-mile **Moosehorn Trail**, with a brief sidetrip to the right to see another waterfall. Those who just want to see this waterfall can hike Moosehorn Trail by itself, or combine it into a loop with the **Laverty Falls Trail**.

Or, if you want instant gratification without a lot of effort, take the easy 15-minute walk to **Shiphaven** for a fine view of the estuary and the interpretive signs that explain lumbering and its effects on the Atlantic salmon.

Guided walks exploring **Fundy Night Life** are held on Wednesday and Saturday evenings at the Caribou Plain Trail. The three-hour walks with a park naturalist cost $10 for adults, $7 for children and $30 for a family. Owls are usually a feature of these night adventures.

The continent's last **Atlantic coastal wilderness** south of Labrador is a vast stretch between St. Martins and Fundy National Park, where the Big Salmon River, Little Salmon River and several others cut into the soaring cliffs that meet the sea. All around it is woodland growing on an inhospitable terrain of deep gullies and ravines and steep mountainsides. Very few people have penetrated this area traversed only by trails, to walk along the rim or on the beaches beneath the 180-foot cliffs. While you can drive the newly built road or hike the nine-mile round-trip from the beginning of the multi-purpose trail to the banks of the Big Salmon River on your own – the trail is well-marked – you should have a guide to do any further exploring in this wilderness. And unless you are familiar with the area's natural history and flora, you'll find that a well-trained guide can make even that hike much more rewarding. The trail, which runs from St. Martins to the Big Salmon River, through the **Fundy Escarpment Provincial Park**, is a remarkable step toward making the area accessible to everyone. It is designed as a bicycle trail, eight feet wide, with its steeper sections fully paved and signage warning of curves and hills more complete than most automobile roads. It is fully wheelchair accessible, although the grades are long and steep in places. The views are often splendid, and side trails lead down to the shore at Melvin Beach. But many walkers will find it disappointing, for all its state-of-the-art construction. There is little sense of being in the wilderness, since it is within sight and earshot of the road for much of the way. The same views are visible from picnic pavilions and overlooks, which the trail and road share. Those who prefer less manicured trails through a not-so-parklike setting should consider driving to the Big Salmon River and begin their hike there, so they can see the upper, undeveloped reaches of this coastal wilderness.

Hiking Outfitters & Guided Tours

■ One outfitter who knows the Atlantic coastal wilderness area and its wildlife well is **Fundy Hiking and Nature Tours**, ☎ 800/56FUNDY or 506/833-2534. The cost of a guide and a hearty trail lunch is $40 a person for a full day. They can also provide trained guides to take you on less strenuous walks in the St. Martins area, including birding walks and natural history explorations, at the same price. (See *On Snow & Ice*, page 87, for winter explorations of the area.)

■ To explore the area for a longer trail-camping trip, reserve a guide from **Cape Enrage Adventures**, ☎ 506/887-2273. A minimum of four hikers is required, at $50 each per day.

Walking Tours

Several good walking routes lie within the city of Saint John, several of them in **Irving Nature Park** off Sand Cove Rd., ☎ 506/653-7367. (To get there from downtown, follow Rte. 1 west to Exit 107A; go over the bridge past the blinking light and up the hill, turning right onto Sand Cove Rd.) This 450-acre point is circled by a mile-long dirt road along the shore, and has picnic and parking areas. Four interconnected hiking trails range from just under a mile to four miles long, each leading along the shore, where you can see some of the 230 bird species that have been sighted here (including plover), as well as seals and porpoises. Maps are avail-

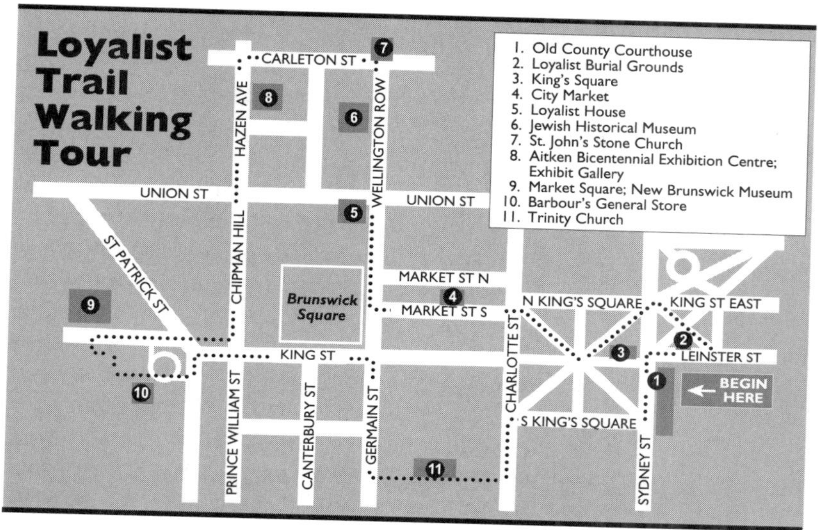

able at the entrance. The park is free and open daily from dawn-dusk. You can hike here year-round, but from December through May you have to leave vehicles at the gate.

In the heart of the city, **Saint John's Loyalist Trail** is lined by historical landmarks best explored on foot, with a map/brochure from the Tourist Information Centre. Begin at the **Old County Courthouse**, facing King's Square, and go inside to see its unsupported spiral staircase with each of its 49 steps a single piece of stone. Loyalist Burial Ground, just to the east of King's Square has headstones dating to 1784. As you walk through King's Square, with its elaborate Victorian bandstand, notice the Union Jack pattern of the walks. **St. John's Stone Church**, on Carleton St., is the city's oldest church building, from 1825, built of stone brought as ship ballast from England. Its 12-story steeple is topped by a six-foot gold salmon. In the summer guides will take you on a tour of this historic building. **Trinity Church** was built in 1880, after its predecessor was lost in the Great Fire of 1877. Be sure to notice the British royal arms over the west door; it has had several narrow escapes. First saved by Loyalists fleeing Boston, where it hung in the Boston Council Chamber, it was then rescued from the original church as it was burning.

The tourist office has maps describing two other self-guided walking tours. The **Victorian Stroll** explores the elegant 19th-century residential streets of downtown Saint John, noting the architecture of the fine old homes. **Prince William's Walk** follows the city's mercantile history.

Free 90-minute walking tours begin at **Barbour's Store** at 10 am and 2 pm in July and August; for information, ☎ 506/658-2939. The strong of heart can take ghost walks offered occasionally by the **Interpretation Center** in Rockwood Park, ☎ 506/658-2829.

The town of **Sussex** has several fine restored Victorian homes, identified with plaques and shown on the **walking tour map**, available free from local businesses or at the Tourist Centre. The tour begins at the Agricultural Museum. Be sure to stop and sample the waters at the **Mineral Spring Fountain** on Church Ave.

For scenery of an entirely different kind, join in exploring Hillsborough's **White Caves** with **Baymount Outdoor Adventures** in Hillsborough, ☎ 506/734-2660, fax 506/734-1980. A 2½-hour walking tour of the cave system with a naturalist guide includes helmet, gloves and headlamp; the cost is $40 for adult, $20 for children, or $80 for an entire family. If you've never been spelunking, this is a good chance to sample it safely and with knowledgeable guides.

Cape Enrage Adventures, on Rte. 915 about halfway between Alma and Riverside-Albert, offers rappelling instruction for both adults and older children. Basic instruction and full equipment for descents down the 145-foot vertical cliffs to a fossil beach on the Bay of Fundy are $40 per person or $120 for a family (up to 10 children included). Groups are limited in size so that everyone gets a maximum number of turns descending the cliffs. The center emphasizes safety while encouraging participants to try various styles in a highly controlled (but also very thrilling) environment. ☎ 506/887-2273 for information.

■ On Wheels

Bicycling

Cyclists of all energy levels will find good routes in this area, where the terrain varies from high headlands and rolling hills to low coastal plain and river valleys. If you are arriving from Nova Scotia by bicycle, you can bring it over on the ferry from Digby to Saint John for $11.25 in the summer, $7 off-season (mid-October-early June).

In **Fundy National Park**, six trails are open to mountain bikes. **Black Hole** is a seven-mile in-and-out trail on an old woods road, with an ascent of about 650 feet. **Marvin Lake Trail** runs 10 miles along an old cart road leading to two wilderness lakes, where you may see moose and beaver. It has an 800-foot ascent, quite steep in the first section. **Maple Grove** is a five-mile trail climbing continuously through open forest. **Bennett Brook Trail** is open to bikes only to the end of the logging road, where a trail begins the descent to the Point Wolfe River. The first half-mile of the **Goose River Trail** is a steep climb, as is the beginning of the return trip, when you must climb back up from the beach, but the coastal views are worth it. **East Branch Trail** is a loop for hikers, but bikes must go and return on the same trail. At the fork where the two routes split, take the one to the right.

The pastoral countryside and rolling hills of the Kennebecasis Valley are perfect for bicycling, and you can explore them on a five-hour guided tour with **Eastwind Cycle** in Sussex, ☎ 506/433-6439, fax 506/433-6439. You'll cycle through at least six covered bridges, learning about the cultural and natural history of the area as you ride. Quality bicycles are included, as is lunch at one of the area's best-known restaurants, the Broadway Café. The entire package is $45 per person. Or you can head into the coastal wilderness area of Martin Head for a full-day guided mountain bike tour. Martin Head is a small tidal island, isolated not only by the water, but by about an hour's drive from the nearest settlement. It's rugged country, with steep descents to beaches (and even steeper climbs back up). The day's adventure includes bicycle and helmet rental, van shuttle, a picnic lunch and the guide, for $60.

From St. Martins to the Big Salmon River, a wide, smooth all-purpose trail parallels the road through the **Fundy Escarpment Provincial Park**. Mountain bikers we talked to didn't care for its manicured surface, paved grades and highway-like signs, but it does offer miles of scenic off-road travel for cyclists (many of whom walk the steepest parts). The worst grade is at the very end, when the trail drops from the headlands to Big Salmon River in a series of very steep switchbacks. Since the trail runs close to the road from St. Martins to Big Salmon River, if you want to cycle shorter sections you can access it from any of the overlooks along the way.

Bicycle Outfitters & Guided Tours

■ **Florentine Manor**, RR 2, Albert, NB E0A 1A0, ☎ 506/882-2271 or 800/665-2271, only 20 minutes from the national park, has bicycles available for guests, as does **The Quaco Inn**, 16 Beech St., St. Martins, NB E0G 2Z0, ☎ 506/833-4772, fax 506/833-2531.

■ In Hampton, rent road or mountain bikes at **Darlings Island Bike Shop**, ☎ 506/832-0777. Mountain bikes are $10 per hour or $30 a day. They also repair bicycles, in case yours misbehaves.

■ For mountain biking, contact **Poley Mountain**, the ski area in Sussex, ☎ 506/433-3230. A three-hour guided excursion with mountain bike, helmet, and picnic lunch can begin at the top of the ski area or explore the trails of Fundy Model Forest, for $39 a person.

■ To tour on your own, ask for the free map and guide to biking trails in the Fundy area from **King's County Tourism Association**, ☎ 506/432-6116, or from **Fundy Model Forest**, ☎ 506/432-2806, which publishes this and two other maps with gradient diagrams and detailed directions with mileage. One gives seven road bike tours and the other details eight mountain bike routes, including ones to Little Salmon River and Martin Head.

Other Wheeled Excursions

For a different kind of experience on wheels, visit the **Salem & Hillsborough Railroad and Museum** in Hillsborough, ☎ 506/734-3195. One-hour rides on this vintage train are $7.50 for adults, $6.75 for seniors and $4 for children six-12. Weekend dinner runs of over three hours, during which passengers are served roast beef, turkey or a German buffet (in October), are $24. A three-hour fall foliage excursion into the Caledonian Highlands to see the brilliant foliage are $11, $10 and $5.50. The train operates from mid-June to mid-October; a museum at the station has a fine collection of rail memorabilia, open late-June-August, 10 am-8 pm, for an admission fee of $1.50.

Another wheeled excursion awaits you in St. Martins, where you can take a carriage ride with **Maple Miniatures**, 280 West Quaco Rd., ☎ 506/833-6240. Their gleaming, wine-colored open carriage was built for them in Ontario by Mennonites. The tour route leads from their farm along an unpaved lane to a lighthouse. The road is lined with wildflowers and offers views across meadows to the sea. We counted a dozen varieties of wildflowers in bloom during our ride one August evening, the colors of each highlighted by the rays of the early evening sun. Maple Miniatures also has miniature harness horses, which pull tiny carriages that can carry an adult and child. A cart ride is $10. Children can also take a saddle ride on one of these child-sized horses. Go in April and May to see the tiny foals, or just go to admire these unusual miniatures, whose ancestors were brought to Canada to work in the mines.

On Water

Swimming

Bennett Lake and **Wolfe Lake** in Fundy National Park each has a free unsupervised swimming beach, and the heated saltwater pool charges a daily fee of $1.75 for adults, $1.25 for children, or $4.50 for families who are camping or staying at chalets in the park. Those visiting on a day-entry pass must pay $3.25 for an adult, $2.25 for a child or $8 for a family to use the supervised pool.

The shore alternates between sea cliffs and sandy beaches: St. Martins offers miles of beaches that are surprisingly uncrowded, considering how close it is to Saint John. **Brown's Beach**, at the far end of West Quaco Rd. in St. Martin's, is a short walk from the small parking area. Here you will find a long beach enclosed by red sandstone cliffs, caves and rocks carved by the tides into convoluted shapes. There's hardly ever anyone on the beach.

Diving

Scuba divers can get equipment from **The Dive Shack** in Saint John, ☎ 506/634-8265. In addition, the shop offers entry level, advanced, master and rescue diving courses and a course on the local underwater environment. Their guided tours allow you to dive The Old Sow, one of the world's largest whirlpools.

Certified divers in the area for any length of time should contact **Tidal Divers**, ☎ 506/634-8265. The group dives year-round and sponsors events that include boat and shore diving, camping trips, scallop dives, night dives, whale-watching excursions and other non-diving activities.

Canoeing, Kayaking & Sailing

Fresh Air Adventures in Alma, ☎ 800/545-0020 or ☎/fax 506/887-2249, e-mail FreshAir@fox.nstn.ca, provides full-day, half-day and multi-day kayaking tours in the harbour and estuary and along the Fundy coast. They include instruction for beginners, as well as interpretive information about the natural environments explored. A *Day Adventure* package includes a three-hour guided trip, with kayaks and equipment, instruction and lunch, for $50 per adult, $30 per child or $150 for a family of four. You can choose from three destinations: the long inlet and harbor at Point Wolfe, the bird-filled tidal reaches of Long Marsh, or the sea caves and beaches of Fundy National Park's isolated stretches of coast. Two-hour tours at $35 explore either the estuary and harbor or the bay. Full-day trips, at $90, can explore even more of the coast, and include a hot meal. Multi-day kayak trips are scheduled throughout the summer, with all camping equipment except bedding supplied. Two-day overnight trips cost $230 per person, and three-day trips cost $340. These explore the coast of the park from Alma, or on a two-night trip travel the entire distance from Alma to St. Martin's, along a pristine coastal wilderness. Three-hour safety and rescue clinics are $60 per person.

Cape Enrage Adventures on Rte. 915 between Alma and Riverside-Albert, ☎ 506/887-2273, offers day trips by kayak and canoe. A four-hour guided trip with all equipment and a light lunch is $50 per canoe or kayak (double kayaks are available). You will explore salt water creeks that fill twice each day with the rush of Fundy tides, and saltwater lakes surrounded by wilderness. The best part is that, unlike river paddling, the current changes, so you can go in both directions with the current helping you. For those who have kayaked before – or for intrepid beginners –an optional rapids provides a little excitement.

Baymount Outdoor Adventures in Hillsborough, ☎ 506/734-2660, fax 506/734-1980, will take you on 1½-hour guided kayak excursions to Hopewell Rocks. The cost is $30 per adult, $25 for a child or $85 for a family, which includes instruction and all equipment. Trips are available from late June through August. Even if you have seen Hopewell Rocks from the beach below, you shouldn't miss this chance to paddle among them and view these amazing cliffs and caves from out at sea. The waters are placid and paddling is easy. You will get full instructions on land and in the water. Most of the kayaks are doubles, and are so stable that you can bring your camera (ask for a dry-bag to put it in). The photos you'll get of bright yellow kayaks drifting among the rocks (which become steep-sided islands) and through the arches and channels will be among the best of your trip. Trips are timed for the two hours preceding and following high tide, with two trips each day. Be sure to reserve a place, since the time schedule is a tight one. To reach Baymount, take the first road to your left after turning into the approach road for Hopewell Rocks.

In Fundy National Park you can rent sailboats, canoes and kayaks for about $7 an hour at Bennett Lake. To reserve, call **R&D Boat and Canoe Rentals**, ☎ 506/887-2115. No boats of any kind are allowed on Wolfe Lake.

You can rent canoes and kayaks in Saint John from **Eastern Outdoors** in Brunswick Square, ☎ 506/634-1530 or 800/565-2925. They also provide instruction and lead guided canoe and kayak tours.

Cove Boat Rentals in Quispamsis north of Saint John, ☎ 506/847-8046, rents canoes so you can explore the marshes and birding areas of Kennebecasis Bay. Just north of that, **River Marsh Tours** rents canoes and kayaks for $30 a half-day or $45 a full day, ☎ 506/832-1990.

Kayaking at Hopewell Rocks.

Harbor, Bay & River Tours

Two-hour cruises of the bay or the river begin at 1 and 7 pm daily in the summer with **Retreat Outfitters and Charters** in Saint John, ☎ 506/636-0130, fax 506/757-8062. The cost of either is $30 ($15 per child and $60 for a family of four), and you'll travel on board a custom-built New Brunswick cape-islander. The up-river cruise goes to Kennebecasis Island.

Nature and historical cruises on the Saint John River and Grand Bay to the old riverboat landing are offered by **NorthEast Yacht Charters**, ☎ 506/652-4220, fax 506/632-1698. The two-hour cruises on board the *MV Shamrock III* leave daily at 10am, mid-June through Sept. The rate is $28 adult and $12 child. They can meet you at your hotel.

Explore the marshes along the banks of the Kennebecasis River in Hampton on a trip with **River Marsh Tours**, ☎ 506/832-1990, fax 506/832-5292. The two-hour cruise includes information on the 100-plus wildlife species that live in one of New Brunswick's largest marshes (it covers more than 5,000 acres) plus local stories and folklore, and costs $25 for adults, $10 for children. Unlike some cruises, they do not require a minimum number; if you're the only one who reserves, you get a private trip.

AND IF YOU DON'T MIND GETTING WET...

Reversing Falls Jet Boat Ride, Fallsview Park, Saint John, ☎ 506/634-8987 ($20), purports to be an opportunity to observe at close hand the power and intensity of an astonishing natural phenomenon, Reversing Falls, where the tides of the Bay of Fundy force the Saint John River to run backward, thereby creating a cataract. It is, in fact, nothing of the sort. It is a chance to get thoroughly wet while laughing and shrieking as you tear across the water throwing huge rooster tails and splashing everything in sight. You could probably see the Reversing Falls if your glasses weren't wet and your hair weren't dripping water in your eyes, but at no time does that happen.

They plan to offer a new "dry ride" in addition to the "thrill ride," but, frankly, I'd skip it. The thrill ride may have no socially redeeming value, it may not be educational or a good nature experience, but it's an awful lot of fun. Call ahead to find out when the tide turns, and book a ride then, when it's most dramatic. Bring lots of towels and a change of dry clothes, shoes, and socks. Forget the camera, binoculars, and anything else that could be damaged by water. – *Sara Godwin and Charles James*

Rent your own houseboat to tour the lakes and bays at leisure for about $600 for two days or $1,000 for a full week from **Houseboat Vacations** in Sussex, ☎ 506/433-4801, fax 506/433-1609. Their boats sleep six and are very easy to handle. In Saint John contact **Bayshore Houseboat Vacations** at 506/763-2147.

Fishing

Misty Mountain U-Fish in Sussex, ☎ 506/433-4248, will teach you – and your children –how to cast and provide the equipment and bait for you to catch your own fish in their stocked waters. You keep the fish and can enjoy a hike and/or swim there, too, for $5 a person.

May and June bring speckled trout at its best, when guests at **Adair's Wilderness Lodge** (see pages 90 and 100) find them measuring 10-17 inches.

Deep-sea fishing on board a 40-foot New Brunswick-built boat, outfitted with a fly bridge and full cooking facilities, is available with **Retreat Outfitters and Charters** in Saint John, ☎ 506/636-0130, fax 506/757-8062. The cost of a full day, for any sized group is $800. The boat is fully Coast Guard certified and the crew is well-trained.

To try your hands at ice fishing, a tough thing to do unless you know someone with a bob-house, take advantage of a *Day Adventure* package that includes a heated hut, tackle and bait, the ready-cut hole in the ice and hot chocolate, for $60 a couple. You can reserve through the *Day Adventures* program or directly with **Retreat Outfitters and Charters** in Saint John, ☎ 506/636-0130, fax 506/757-8062. Rob Wilson, who runs these adventures, says he "keeps his ear to the ground" (or maybe the ice?) to find out where the fish are at any given time, and takes the portable hut to the best locations, so your chances of success are pretty good.

> **➔ FISHING PERMITS:** *A National Park Permit ($4.50 day, $14 season) is required for brook trout, which are in season from mid-May through mid-Sept. Salmon populations are quite low in the park and the inner bay rivers, so salmon fishing is not allowed here. Although you may keep five trout a day, the park encourages catch and release.*

■ On Snow & Ice

Winter sports are a Canadian specialty, and the Fundy Coast has its share. Natural snowfall, while not always predictable so close to the coast, is usually abundant enough to guarantee cross-country skiing and snow-covered trails for snowmobiling. The changing tides and cold temperatures combine to create unique and ever-changing ice sculptures along the bays and estuaries. Ice on the lakes and inner bays is substantial enough to support skating and ice fishing, which you can sample on a *Day Adventure* (see *Fishing*, above). In St. Martin's, where the changing tides leave long expanses of frozen beach, firm underfoot and free of snow, walking the beaches is a popular winter activity. These are bordered by carved and sculptured rock cliffs; be sure to check the tide schedules.

> **➲ WHAT'S A LOPPET?**
> *Cross-country skiers who want to join in some local fun can take part in loppets hosted by local ski clubs throughout the provinces. A loppet is defined, somewhat tongue-in-cheek, by a Miramichi ski newsletter as a "gathering of over-enthusiastic skiers who wish they could race, but can't, so they begin in a bunch at a starting line and go as fast as they want, trying to beat no one but themselves so they can have a big feed when they're finished...." We can't improve on that description, nor can we think of a better way to spend a day outdoors. Join one, and we promise you'll meet other skiers of your speed and interests along the way, whether you're 10 or 90, and whether you're the first to arrive at the finish or the last. You'll find loppets wherever there's snow, from Labrador to New Brunswick.*

Skiing

Fundy National Park has 30 miles of trails groomed for skiers in the winter. Some of these are along the coast, others explore the inland reaches of the park. The **Fundy Loppet** in February is a family day of cross-country skiing in a noncompetitive atmosphere. The park is open for winter camping and some of the accommodations in the town of Alma stay open year-round.

Skiing is always chancy to plan along the coast, because of the moderating effect of the Bay of Fundy on the winter weather. Some years cross-country skiing on the multipurpose trail into the Big Salmon River wilderness begins in mid-November, with excellent snow-cover lasting until spring. Other years the weather is warmer and the snow melts after each storm. But if you and the snow are both in the area at the same time, few trails provide skiers with more exhilarating views. For a guide – you definitely should not venture into this region very far alone in the winter – contact **Fundy Hiking and Nature Tours**, ☎ 800/56FUNDY or 506/833-2534. A full day's skiing with a hearty lunch will cost $40 per person, and with enough advance notice, they can usually provide you with skis and boots as well.

In Saint John you can ski through the 2,000 acres of **Rockwood Park** on Mount Pleasant Ave., north of downtown, ☎ 506/658-2883. Its trails are groomed, free and open 10 am to dusk daily.

Shepody Country Cottage on RR 2, Albert, NB E0A 1A0, ☎ 506/882-2667, fax 506/882-2625, has nine miles of groomed cross-country trails, a skating rink and plenty of trails for snowshoeing. Winter packages with meals and two-nights lodging are about $180 per person.

Although you might not plan a week's ski vacation at **Poley Mountain**, six miles from Sussex, it's nice to have it there if you're sampling all the other winter activities the area offers. The vertical drop of 660 feet allows space for 15 trails, a quad lift and a T-bar, plus a beginner slope and half-pipe. For $30 you can sign your kids (or yourself) up for a guaranteed learn-to-ski program; for $35 you can have a 90-minute lesson, all-day ticket for the beginner lift, ski or snowboard rental and lunch, through the *Day Adventure* program. Special activities include Family Night on Fridays and Steak Night on Thursdays. The area is lighted for night skiing Tuesday-Saturday evenings, ☎ 506/433-POLEY, fax 506/432-1009. For packages combining lift tickets with deluxe suites, complete with fireplaces in the sitting room, contact **Amsterdam Inn**, 143 Main St., Sussex, NB E0E 1P1, ☎ 506/432-5050 or 800/468-2828, fax 506/432-5069.

Snowmobiling

You can rent snowmobiles at **Broadleaf Guest Ranch**, Hopewell Hill, Albert County, NB E0A 1Z0, ☎ 506/882-2349 or 800/226-5405, located on Trail #22 of the New Brunswick network. Winter package weekends at the ranch, which has a full range of winter activities, are $100 per couple, in modern log cabins with fireplaces.

Sleigh Rides

Broadleaf Guest Ranch, Hopewell Hill, Albert County, NB E0A 1Z0, ☎ 506/882-2349 or 800/226-5405, offers sleigh rides through their woods and fields, behind a team of two or four horses. A package with a sleigh-ride to a hill-top lodge, where you have lunch and hot chocolate, is $40 a person, or take advantage of discounted family rates.

Maple Miniatures, 280 West Quaco Rd. in St. Martins, ☎ 506/833-6240, also offers sleigh rides in the winter. You can visit their miniature horses, which are table-top height and particularly gentle.

■ On Horseback

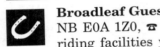

Broadleaf Guest Ranch, Hopewell Hill, Albert County, NB E0A 1Z0, ☎ 506/882-2349 or 800/226-5405, has full riding facilities year-round on a 1,500-acre cattle farm. Half a day's guided ride with instruction and a light trail lunch is $40 per person. Shorter rides are $15 an hour. Two-night packages include lodging in their new log cabin, a guided woodland ride with a picnic lunch, and instruction as needed, for $160 a person. You can ride through the woodland or across the Shepody marshlands, following Acadian dikes that hold back the Fundy tides. Summer riding camps for children provide well-rounded instruction at $275 a week, including lodging and meals. See their winter packages, under snowmobiling, above.

Fully guided trail rides with instructions and refreshments are the specialty of **Sheffield Stables Trail Rides** in Petitcodiac, ☎ 506/756-1110, fax 506/756-1110. Their trails travel through woodlands and open fields; the cost of a 2½-hour ride is $40, and there is no minimum number of people required. Or you can take a one-hour ride or an overnight camp-out, leaving the stables in mid-afternoon, pitching camp, enjoying a barbecue and campfire and returning the next morning.

Cultural & Eco-Travel Experiences

Festivals

Two festivals bring even more life to Saint John's already active streets, which all seem to flow down to the busy Market Square, on the waterfront. **Loyalist Days**, held the third week of July, sees residents in colonial costumes to re-enact the Loyalists' landing of 1784. The week is filled with historical programs, concerts, parades, and pageants.

In mid-August Saint John becomes a showplace for Canadian culture during the **Festival by the Sea**. Each of Canada's many cultures is represented through its performing arts, and you may see Nova Scotia Highland dancers, Acadian fiddling or Micmac drumming on the outdoor stage at Market Square.

Natural Areas

Cape Enrage Adventures, Rte. 915 halfway between Alma and Riverside-Albert, Cape Enrage, ☎ 506/887-2273, sponsors a variety of workshops and seminars, nature tours, and overnight trips. One-day workshop subjects may include photography, writing, watercolor painting, the ecology of a saltmarsh, fossils or working with stained glass. Outdoor activities range from water sports such as canoeing and kayaking, to rappelling, and wilderness hikes to explore caves, underground lakes, and waterfalls. The Interpretive Center includes a working lighthouse and fossil collection (both free). Week-long Adventure Camps for high school students feature science, fine arts or leadership training, with a full range of outdoor activities in each program, including kayaking, canoeing, caving, rappelling and hiking, for $250. Weekend programs include both adults and children; both require advance registration and include lodging in Chignecto House, the new adventure center. Off-season, contact Cape Enrage Adventures at Site 5-5, RR 1, Moncton, NB E1C 8J5, ☎ 506/856-6081.

Fundy Model Forest combines elements of a national park, private woodlots, industrial-owned, and public lands, covering in all about one million acres. You can explore the area on trips sponsored by the forest, following a variety of themes from coastline hikes and model forest tours to evening covered bridge tours. You can tour a sugar bush, create your own dried flower arrangement or build a shelf from locally harvested pine. You can fish for trout or photograph coastal scenery, all while learning about the many uses of the forest. All adventures begin from the historic train station in downtown Sussex, from which you will travel by van to the location. The level of activity varies from low to strenuous hiking; day trips begin at 9 am and end in mid-afternoon, including a meal or hearty snack. Prices vary, beginning at $25 for adults and $15 for children. For a current schedule of activities, call ☎ 506/433-1845 or 433-6602.

Accessible through lands managed by Fundy Model Forest is a spectacular and uninhabited coastline and inland hills cut by a number of rivers and only a few unpaved roads. This area lies between Fundy National Park and the town of St. Martins. A town once stood at the mouth of the Quiddy River, a wide sweep of cobble with a huge barrier beach and high tidal island at its tip. Now **Martin Head** is deserted, except for campers who arrive by four-wheel drive vehicles, mountain bikes and on foot. The road is passable to non-utility vehicles until the final approach to the coast, where it is badly washed out. To reach Martin Head, follow signs from Sussex to Poley Mountain and the town of Waterford. From there follow signs to Adair's Wilderness Lodge, where you should stop for further directions, since signage to Martin Head is of the home-made variety, and may or may not be in place. Ask also for directions to **Quiddy Falls**, a 15-minute hike from the road, not far from Adair's.

Among the many people who have fought to keep the Fundy shore free of the trappings of civilization – including eight-foot-wide paved trails and a scenic parkway with picnic pavilions and visitors centers, all part of several plans afoot – are Ida and Larry Adair, who have recently opened **Adair's Wilderness Lodge**. Larry grew up in these woods; his grandmother was born in a house just up the road from Larry and Ida's remote home on the shore of Walton Lake. When a parcel of William Randolph Hearst's property came on the market, Larry and Ida knew if they didn't buy it and build a good wilderness lodge, opening the land to responsible public use, someone else might do something far less appealing. The result is a comfortable, accommodating lodge and cabins, which have become a mecca for those who love the outdoors in all seasons. In the winter it is awash in snowmobiles; fishermen come in spring and fall; hikers and mountain bikers stop here in the summer. Their restaurant is open to the public. They take guests on hiking and nature tours, canoe adventures, and excursions to nearby natural attractions, including a moss-covered glacial erratic and the many waterfalls in the area. Adair's Wilderness Lodge is off (*way* off) Rte. 111, at 900 Creek Rd., Shepody, NB E4E 5R9, ☎ 506/432-6687, fax 432-9101, Web site www.discribe.ca/nb/resort/adair.

ALBERTITE

The area between Moncton and Fundy National Park has a long history of mining and stone quarrying. The mineral Albertite was discovered in Albert Mines in 1820, and the Canadian geologist Abraham Gesner invented a process for extracting kerosine from it. The streets of Boston were once lighted by kerosine from Albert. Quarries on Grindstone Island, in the Bay of Fundy off Marys Point, provided the stone to build Lord and Taylor's building in New York City.

The Fundy Tides at Work

Some of the most fascinating things to do and see here relate in some way to the Fundy tides, the highest in the world (as high as 50 feet), which ebb and flow twice each day. Tide-watching is an activity of its own, as is exploring the coastal phenomena this regular rush of water creates. With the tides come a daily supply of fresh food for whales and other sea life, and for the wide assortment of shore and waterfowl that inhabit the tidal marshes.

Alma Beach has a tide-viewing platform with a boardwalk and a measuring pole. At Herring Cove, and elsewhere in Fundy National Park, you can explore tidal pools when the water is at its lowest point. Herring Cove has a sea cave, as do St. Martins, Hopewell Cape and several other places.

Reversing Falls Rapids, under the bridge where Rte. 100 crosses the Saint John River, is a deep gorge with a rocky barrier in its bed. At low tide, with 450 miles of river emptying into the sea, the narrow gorge is filled and water rushes over the barrier heading east. As the tide rises, and the sea level exceeds that of the river, water is forced back upstream, again through the narrow passage and with all the force of ocean tides. When this happens twice a day, the rapids rushing over the barrier form a falls heading west. A viewing point above the falls has an information center, with a 20-minute film explaining the Bay of Fundy tides. Tide tables are available everywhere, so you can plan to be there at either high or low tide – or, for the full effect, at each. Watch from either side, but the best view is from Riverside Falls View Park, across the bridge.

The Rocks Provincial Park at Hopewell Cape off Hwy. 114, ☎ 506/734-2026, has perhaps one of the most familiar images of New Brunswick. Often called the "**flowerpot rocks**" (see the box on the next page for the story of how they are formed), they do look like giant flowerpots standing on the beach at low tide, with their clay-colored bases topped with clusters of green spruce trees. At high tide they look like wooded islands. When the tide is low, you can walk among these four-story rock formations and explore the sea caves that help the tides continue to create more flowerpots. At high tide, you can walk the nature trails along the top that lead into marshes and beaches and view the rocks up close from platforms. Park naturalists lead guided tours, pointing out examples of the process in action. For an even closer view, consider kayaking with **Baymount Outdoor Adventures** (see page 82).

The **St. Martins sea caves** are easy to visit at low tide, close to the road that passes through the covered bridge to your right as you approach the lighthouse-shaped Visitors Centre at the end of Main St. You can see them from the town's little harbor, large dark areas in the red sandstone cliffs, which you can walk to across a beach. At high tide you can explore them by kayak. The attractive park in which the Visitors Centre stands is on the site of the shipworks that made St. Martin's a prosperous shipbuilding center. Interpretive signs explain how the logs came down the river and were turned into ships. In the brick building beside the small dam is a fish-viewing room.

Birdwatching

The **Hampton Marsh** is one of the province's most productive wetlands, with more than 200 of its 5,000 acres under the care of Ducks Unlimited. The area is brood habitat for black ducks, blue-winged teal, wood ducks and other waterfowl, and nesting habitat for rails, bitterns and yellow-throats. Osprey and swallows forage here. You can travel through it by boat with **Rivermarsh Tours**, ☎ 506/832-1990.

Grey Brook Marsh in Hillsborough has walking trails through a marshland with a wide variety of birds. In Saint John, birders flock to **Red Head Marsh**, to see waterfowl and other species. Look here for piedbilled grebe, green-backed heron and least bittern. Also in the area is **Irving Nature Park**, off Sand Cove

Rd., which reports sightings of more than 230 bird species, including sharptailed sparrows and egrets. To get there from the city, take Rte. 1 west to Exit 107A; go over the overpass, and through the flashing light to the top of the hill, where you'll find Sand Cove Rd. Turn right to reach the park, ☎ 506/634-7135.

Although you may find loons elsewhere in the area, the best place to look is at **Wolfe Lake** in Fundy National Park. For almost certain sightings, visit **Walton Lake** near Adair's Wilderness Lodge outside of Sussex.

HOW THE FLOWERPOT ROCKS WERE FORMED

The story of these unusual sea stacks begins with the sand, silt, mud and rocks that eroded and washed down to the shore from inland mountains eons ago. The continuing deposits created such weight that they pressed the bottom layers into solid rock: The mud and sand became sandstone and the coarse rocky and pebbly layers, cemented together with mud, turned into a sedimentary rock called conglomerate.

As the earth's crust moved and tilted, this rock layer cracked into giant blocks, and the breaks between them began to collect water. The next phase of their development began as the water froze and expanded, enlarging the cracks and further eroding them. Glaciers, streams flowing through them, and the constant beating of the waves and 50-foot tides continued to wear these spaces larger and larger, washing away loosened sediment and separating the rocks even more. Sea caves were created as the tide wore away the softer sandstone more quickly than the harder conglomerate layers above it. Caves allow the tides to wear away the connecting land and eventually, some of the blocks became completely separate from the land around them, making it even easier for the tides to sculpt them into the round shapes you see today. The process continues, toppling old sea stacks as new ones are being formed. Geologists estimate that there is enough of the sedimentary stone left to keep forming flowerpots for another 100,000 years. So hang onto your pictures; when the last flowerpot topples, they will be valuable.

WATCHING THE SANDPIPERS

More than one million semi-palmated sandpipers migrate south through the upper Bay of Fundy, many of them stopping to feed and rest at the **Mary's Point Western Hemispheric Shorebird Reserve**. The greatest numbers of birds appear at Mary's Point in the first two weeks of July. Mixed flocks are common, and often include white-rumped sandpipers, least sandpipers, semi-palmated plovers, black-bellied plovers, and sanderlings.

The best time to see them is at high tide, so plan your timing carefully. Flocks of thousands upon thousands are common, skittering along the sand or wheeling against the sky. The semi-palmated sandpipers stay from 10 to 20 days, building the fat reserves necessary to fly 2,500 miles non-stop to Surinam in South America.

Benches on the beach make it easy to sit and watch the busily feeding flocks. Trained docents from the interpretive center cheerfully answer your questions and help with identification. Bring binoculars or a spotting scope, a bird guide, a windbreaker or warm jacket, and wear comfortable walking shoes. Trails and boardwalks lead you through the surrounding forests, fields, marshes, and sand beaches that make up the entire ecosystem. – *Sara Godwin and Charles James*

Courses in birding, along with similar programs on butterflies and wildflowers are taught by **Naturescape Inc.**, not far from the entrance to Irving Park in Saint John, ☎ 506/672-7722. Half-day courses begin with an indoor program on basic identification, then move to the field with an outdoor interpretive walk. Use of binoculars and field guide books are included. Naturescape also has a store with books, bird feeding supplies and optical equipment.

Serious birders should stop at **Birdwatchers Wild Bird Store** on Rte 114 at Edgett's Landing, between Hillsborough and Hopewell Rocks, ☎ 506/734-2473. Their outdoor feeder area attracts dozens of bird species, and you can "test-drive" state-of-the-art binoculars and telescopes there. They also carry a full range of bird guides and create custom bird carvings.

Seal- & Whale-Watching

One of the more unusual seal-watching opportunities is close to St. Martins at **West Quaco**. Take Rte. 137, the West Quaco Rd., watching for the flowerpot rocks along the coast to your left, and park at the Quaco Lighthouse. Follow the trail to the top of "the hump" (the trail crosses private property, but the owners are friendly about it). You can walk along the ridge and down to the area's only sandy beach. From this point, you can watch seals ride the race, when the tide is running. Then they'll swim around and do it again, and again, "like kids on a sliding hill," as our St. Martins friend, Nancy Sears, describes it.

Whale-watching cruises operate from Saint John with **Retreat Outfitters and Charters**, ☎ 506/636-0130, fax 506/757-8062. More than 20 species of whales have been sighted on these trips, including finback, minke, humpback and right.

Learn all about whales in a two-hour workshop given at the **New Brunswick Museum** at Market Square in Saint John, ☎ 506/643-2349. The museum has a particular interest in these mammals, since the Bay of Fundy has more varieties regularly seen than any other waters in the world. You'll learn why the bay attracts so many of these, and have your picture taken inside the jaws of the museum's whale. The $20 fee ($15 for children, $55 for a family) includes museum admission, so you can see the rest of the exhibits and use the Discovery Centre (see *Sightseeing*, page 98).

Other Wildlife

Cherry Brook Zoo in Saint John's Rockwood Park, ☎ 506/634-1440, has more than 100 animals, many of them endangered species. They are especially well-known for their breeding program with the brown lemur, golden lion tamarins and black wildebeest, and are credited with helping those species to survive. Along with seeing the animals – native and exotic – you can learn about the breeding and conservation programs. Saint John Transit buses go there June-September, and on weekends year-round. Admission is $6 for adults, $5 seniors, $4.50 ages 13-17 and $2.50 ages three-12. It's open daily all year, 10 am-4 pm.

Valley Farmlands

Covered bridges are plentiful in the area around Sussex, between Moncton and Saint John, and they fit perfectly into its rural, rolling landscape and small farming villages with their white churches. Pick up a free a map of the bridges from the Tourist Centre in Sussex; it gives a little of the history of each, as well as showing its location. The most famous is the **Oldfield Bridge**, shown on a Canadian quarter-dollar coin. Antique car buffs should come on the last weekend in Sept. for the Antique Car Covered Bridge Tour.

Sussex is in the center of farming country, so it's a fitting home for the **Agricultural Museum**, ☎ 506/433-6799. The museum shows how the farms developed, as well as tools and machinery used and skills that every farm family had to know. The museum, in Princess Louise Park, is open daily from mid-June to mid-September. Admission is $2 for adults, $1 for children, $5 for a family. Picnic grounds are available in the park, where a farmers' market is held on Friday mornings.

The summer's highlight for local farms is the **Westmoreland County Agricultural Fair**, held each year in early August in Petitcodiac, ☎ 506/756-8149. Also in Petitcodiac at the same time is the **New Brunswick Lumberjack Competition**, where you can watch old-time woodsmen's skills demonstrated, ☎ 506/453-2440. On Wednesdays you can visit the weekly **cattle auction** in Sussex, the dairy capital of the Maritimes. You are reminded of this fact by the 12-foot cow "Daisy" beside the road when you enter town on Rte. 1 from Saint John.

At **Armadale Farm** in Sussex (506/433-6031) they make fine Dutch Gouda cheeses, as well as Cheddar, Swiss, and butter. You can buy cheese at the spotless Dutch farm on weekdays, 6 am to 6 pm, or find it at the Sussex Farmers' Market on Friday mornings.

In Bloomfield, southwest of Sussex, you can tour **Ox-Bow Dairy Farm**, ☎ 506/832-4450. On a 1½-hour tour of this working dairy and beef farm you can feed the calves, meet a goat, milk a cow, and eat homemade strawberry shortcake with their own cream. Tours are $12 per person or $25 for an entire family. If you simply can't leave this idyllic 150-year-old farm with its panoramic view, you can spend the night – or the week – in the farm's B&B.

Honey Tree Farm in Petitcodiac, ☎ 506/756-2723, specializes in honey and beeswax crafts, and you can join a two-hour candle-making workshop there. All the materials are included, and you will make four different styles of candles. You can also learn to make the German-style wax Christmas ornaments. The cost is $25 for an adult, $20 for a child, and you will bring home your creations. Honey Tree Farm also has a shop.

Strawflower Ridge Dried Flower Farm on Darling's Island in Hampton, ☎ 506/832-4827, fax 506/847-4706, has three acres of flower and herb gardens. At workshops there you can learn about birds, botanical drawing, using native plants for healing, herbal cooking and herbal wreath-making. These classes range from $5 for birdwatching to $100 for a two-day course. "Create and Take" workshops, available only for a minimum of four people, include dried flower wreaths, topiary or centerpieces, for $12 a person, plus the cost of materials.

Jumping from agriculture to aquaculture, Albert is home to **IXOYE Aquaculture, Inc.** on Rte. 915, three miles from the Cape Enrage Rd. This experimental farm cultivates American and European oysters, blue mussels, and both bay and giant scallops, ☎ 506/882-2573, e-mail gebuhbaa@nbed.nb.ca.

Sightseeing

Barbour's General Store in Market Square next to the Tourist Information Centre, Saint John, ☎ 506/658-2939, is a restored general store with everything from salt cod to herbs to cure whatever ails you. Spats and corset stays are reminders of long-ago fashions. The fully stocked shelves are a museum and nothing is for sale, but they'll give you a packet of a local favorite food, dulse. This seaweed is gathered on the shore and dried to make a healthy snack, but most people find it an acquired taste. The store is open daily from May through October; admission is free.

Loyalist House, 120 Union St., Saint John, ☎ 506/652-3590, is the city's oldest unchanged building, dating from 1817, The architecture and furnishings are typical of the homes of Loyalists who built the city after fleeing from the American Revolution. Guided tours recount the history and importance of this home to the five generations that lived here. Open daily, June-Sept.

Aitken Bicentennial Exhibition Centre (ABEC), 20 Hazen Ave., Saint John, ☎ 506/633-4870, fax 506/648-4742, has changing exhibitions covering art, craft, photography, science, and history, as well as live performances and workshops. Sciencescape is a hands-on learning center for children. Ask at the tourist office for a current schedule. Admission to the galleries is free and the museum is open June-August, 10 am to 5 pm daily; Tuesday-Sunday afternoons the rest of the year.

Carleton Martello Tower, near Reversing Falls on Lancaster Ave. in Saint John (☎ 506/648-4011), is a rare remaining New World example of a round stone defensive tower common in the British Isles in the early 1800s. Inside, exhibits show the tower's history from its building to its use as a command post for World War II harbor defenses. A video explores its World War II role. Admission is $2.50 for adults, $2 for seniors and $1.50 for children; the tower is open daily, 9 am to 5 pm, June-Oct. 15.

The **Jewish Museum** at 29 Wellington Row, Saint John, ☎ 506/6331833, traces the long history of Saint John's small Jewish community, founded in 1858. It provides a fascinating look at the rich traditions of this ethnic community and their faith. Admission is free. The museum is open May to September, Monday-Friday, 10 am to 4 pm, and on Sunday from 1-4 pm in July and August.

New Brunswick Museum at Market Square, ☎ 506/643-2300, is in brand-new spacious quarters in the heart of town. The centerpiece is a 45-foot right whale, but you'll find exhibits on the age of sail, local shipbuilding, and a lumbering camp to walk through. Don't miss the original copy of *'Twas the Night Before Christmas*, written by Saint John native Clement Moore. Children will enjoy the Discovery Centre, filled with hands-on activities. The museum is open weekdays, 9 am to 9 pm; Saturday, 10 am to 6 pm; and Sunday, noon to 5 pm. Adult admission is $5.50, children $3, seniors $4.50, families $12. On Wednesday evenings it's free. See *Whale-Watching* on page 95 for the museum's whale workshops.

Located in a former jail, the **Albert County Museum**, Rte. 114 at Hopewell Cape, ☎ 506/7242003, still has the original cell block from its 1845 origins. Tools, household implements (look for the mechanical griddle that cooked eight pancakes at a time), dolls, needlework, ship models and period clothing fill its displays.

Those interested in historic needlework or quilts should stop at **Steeves House** on Mill St. in Hillsborough, ☎ 506/734-3102. The Grapevine Quilt in the master bedroom is recognized as one of Canada's finest examples of appliqued quilts. It is the original design of Maria Steeves, and was made about 1834 from fabrics she dyed using local plants. The well-restored home, completed in 1812, has another bedroom furnished in locally made false-grained cottage pieces. It is open in the summer from 10 am to 6 pm; admission is $1.50 for adults, 75¢ for children.

Where To Stay & Eat

Near Sussex and Fundy National Park

Florentine Manor is an 1860 stately home only 20 minutes from the national park. Two-night packages with candlelight dinners, picnic lunch, and bicycles are $370. A full hot breakfast, with choice of entrée, is served to guests at 8 am each morning. Dinners (which are memorable) are served to guests by reservation; the complete meal is $21.95. The home is rich in Victorian architectural detail and antiques. On our last visit, the room we stayed in had a complete matching suite of cottage Victorian, in perfect condition with original false graining and and painted designs. All rooms have quilts handmade by some of New Brunswick's best-known fabric artists. *RR 2, Albert, NB E0A 1A0, ☎ 506/882-2271 or 800/665-2271 ($$).*

Fundy Park Chalets, open mid-May through September, are inside the park near the Alma entrance. Each has a fully equipped kitchenette and a bedroom/living room with two double beds. Linens are provided. A large playground is across the road, as is a restaurant, a golf course and a heated saltwater pool are nearby. Credit cards are not accepted, but they will take your personal check. *Fundy National Park, PO Box 72, Alma, NB E0A 1B0, ☎ 506/887-2808 ($$).*

Captain's Inn is a 10-room inn at the entrance to the national park. *Main St., Alma, NB E0A 1B0, ☎ 506/887-2017, fax 506/887-2074 ($$).*

Rose Arbor B&B is in an 1860 home with Victorian decor and marble fireplaces. Save that bottle of wine for another night, however, since no alcohol is allowed on the premises. *244 Main St., Hillsborough, NB E0A 1X0, ☎ 506/734-2644 ($-$$).*

Peck Colonial B&B and Tea Room is a 1790s home set in wide lawns with gardens. Its three guest rooms are furnished in a blend of antiques and modern pieces. Breakfasts feature home-baked breads and the tearoom serves both lunch and dinner to the public. *Rte. 114, Hopewell Hill, NB E0A 1Z0, between Moncton and Fundy National Park, ☎ 506/882-2114 ($).*

Deluxe suites with fireplaces in the sitting rooms are found at **Amsterdam Inn**. They offer senior discounts and special ski packages with nearby Poley Mountain. *143 Main St., Sussex, NB E0E 1P1, ☎ 506/432-5050 or 800/468-2828, fax 506/432-5069.*

Adair's Wilderness Lodge, off Rte. 111 in Sussex, offers lodging in cabins. One of their cabins was built by William Randolph Hearst as a fishing camp, on the shores of an idyllic lake where loons nest and moose are an almost certain sight. For details on the lodge's nature tours, hiking and other activities, see page 90. Package rates of $175 a day include all meals, transportation, and activities such as canoeing, hiking and tours to natural points of interest in the area. The restaurant ($-$$), in a new log building that looks as though it grew there, serves three meals daily, from giant breakfasts to a dinner menu featuring steak, trout, ham and specials such as Atlantic char or lobster. *900 Creek Rd., Shepody, NB E4E 5R9, ☎ 506/432-6687, fax 506/432-9101 ($$).*

Apohaqui Inn Bed & Breakfast is in a stately home in a small riverside village. Nicely restored, its guest rooms feature canopy beds. *7 Foster Ave., Apohaqui, NB E0G 1A0, ☎ 506/433-4149 ($).*

Anderson's is a homey farmhouse with three guest bedrooms. Your full country breakfast will include eggs from the flock you meet in the barnyard. It's not "fancied up" to look like a decorator magazine; it's a real farm, and you'll be very comfortable in the midst of their warm hospitality. It's just like going to visit relatives on a working farm, and you're welcome to pat the sheep. *RR#2, Sussex, NB E0E 1P0, ☎ 506/433-3786 ($).*

Fundy National Park Hostel is set in a group of small, rustic cabins overlooking the Bay of Fundy in one of the park's loveliest areas. It has a kitchen and baggage storage for hikers. *General Delivery, Alma, NB E0A 1B0, ☎ 506/887-2216 ($).*

Broadway Café serves a varied menu ranging from hearty soups, quiches and whole grain sandwiches to a complete dinner menu on weekends, featuring curried scallops and steak in a creamy peppercorn brandy sauce. In the summer, don't leave without sampling their berry shortcake. Open Mon.-Thur. 9 am-3 pm, Fri. 9 am-9 pm, Sat. 10 am-9 pm. *73 Broad St. (opposite the railway station and information center), Sussex, ☎ 506/433-5414 ($-$$).*

Harbour View Grocery and Restaurant serves three home-style meals daily, from 7:30 am. *Main St., Alma,* ☎ *506/887-2450 ($).*

Collins Lobster, Ltd. in Alma sells local lobster live or cooked, along with other shellfish and fish. ☎ *506/887-2054.*

Kelly's Bake Shop is well-known even to non-locals as the home of the sticky bun. Along with these sweets you'll find fresh-baked bread, pies and picnic lunches. We have a friend from California who is described by his wife as "a connoisseur of nutritionally disastrous baked goods," and he rates the local attractions thus: "Alma's 50-foot tides are nice, the park is okay, the sticky buns are fabulous." *Main St., Alma,* ☎ *506/887-2460.*

The Old Shepody Mill Restaurant near Riverside-Albert serves dishes that lean heavily toward middle European, with a hearty Black Forest Plate (similar to a plowman's plate), emu-burgers, or bratwurst and potato salad for lunch, and a variety of schnitzels and emu filet mignon at dinner. The view over the marshlands to the sea is best from the upstairs dining room; in good weather you can have lunch on the terrace. They are open for dinner Tuesday through Sunday, for lunch Wednesday through Sunday, and only on weekends in the winter. *Rte. 114, Shepody, NB,* ☎ *506/882-2211 ($$).*

Seawinds, near the golf course in Fundy National Park, is a family restaurant specializing in seafood. ☎ *506/887-2808.*

The Keepers' Lunchroom at Cape Enrage Adventures serves a superb haddock chowder, sandwiches and soups in an original lighthouse keeper's quarters. It's open from 10 am to 7 pm, late May until mid-October. *Off Rte. 915 about halfway between Alma and Riverside-Albert,* ☎ *506/887-2273 ($).*

Gasthof Old Bavarian, like Anderson's Bed and Breakfast, is also set on a working farm. This flower-decked German chalet is just over the Oldfield covered bridge from Anderson's. Long wooden tables are set with red checkered tablecloths, surrounded by chairs of carved wood. From the minute you walk in and smell the heavenly aromas from the kitchen, you know this is the real thing. You can order Vienner schnitzel, Jaegerschnitzel, veal bratwurst, weisswurst, spaetzle, and all the classic German tortes, plus strudels. The Gasthof is open Friday-Sunday only, from noon until midnight. *RR#2, Sussex, NB E0E 1P0, ☎ 506/433-4735 ($-$$).*

If you long for a nice tearoom where you can have good fresh-baked biscuits or muffins, or a more sinful sweet, and a pot of tea or a cup of coffee, go to **Candlestick Tea Room**. It is open 10 am-5 pm, mid-June to mid-September, and has a crafts shop, too. Darla Clowater from Victoria Tea Room on the Miramichi led us here, and if anyone knows good baking when they taste it, the Clowaters do. *Rte. 695 in Stewarton, just west of Norton (between Sussex and Hampton). No phone.*

Saint John and the Bays

Manawagonish Bed & Breakfast is a private home in a nice residential neighborhood, open all year. *Rte. 100, Manawagonish Rd., Saint John, NB E2M 3X2, ☎ 506/572-5843 ($-$$).*

Delta Brunswick, a full-service chain hotel, is centrally located in Brunswick Square, a large shopping mall. It has an indoor swimming pool, whirlpool bath, saunas, exercise room, children's playroom and outdoor playground. *39 King St., Saint John, NB E2L 4W3, ☎ 506/648-1981 or 800/877-1133 in the US, ☎ 800/268-1133 in Canada, fax 506/658-0914 ($$-$$$).*

Saint John Hilton offers some good weekend rates and packages, especially in the summer. Children under 18 stay free and those under 12 also eat free in the hotel's restaurants. The only waterside hotel in the city, its location couldn't be better. For views of the ships coming and going, ask for a harbor-view room; all are decorated in furniture made of New Brunswick pine. Facilities include a small indoor swimming pool, Jacuzzi under a large skylight, saunas, exercise room, seven non-smoking floors. *One Market Square, Saint John, NB E2L 4Z6, ☎ 506/693-8484 or 800/445-8667 in the US, ☎ 800/561-8282 in Canada, fax 506/657-6610 ($-$$).*

Dufferin Inn has six guest rooms with soft duvets and deep armchairs. Antique features include the leaded-glass front door, paneled dining room, and stained-glass windows. Their Martello Dining Room ($$-$$$) has consistently been the area's best restaurant, where a European chef has free reign in his own kitchen. He uses fresh local ingredients when he can, and imports from

Europe when he must. Desserts are triumphant. You must reserve in advance. *357 Dufferin Row, Saint John, NB E2M 2J7, ☎ 506/635-5968, fax 506/674-2396 ($$).*

Parkerhouse Inn has nine beautifully decorated rooms in an elegant Victorian mansion close to the center of town and the renovated Imperial Theatre. Large private baths, lush linens with color-coordinated bathrobes, antiques and a fine-tuned sense of style characterize the rooms. A licensed dining room serves breakfast and dinner (5-9:30pm) to guests and the public. *71 Sydney St., Saint John, NB E2L 2L5, ☎ 506/652-5054, fax 506/636-8076 ($$).*

Inn on the Cove overlooks the water and Partridge Island, but is minutes from downtown. Five guest rooms are very nicely decorated; one has its own Jacuzzi by a window overlooking the bay. The dining room, open to guests and the public, is run by the host of a popular television cooking show, which is filmed here. Dining reservations should be made at least a day in advance. *1371 Sand Cove Rd. (less than a mile from Irving Nature Park), PO Box 3113 (Station B), Saint John, NB E2M 4X7, ☎ 506/672-7799, fax 506/635-5455 ($$-$$$).*

Red Rose Mansion has winter packages with two nights lodging, breakfasts, dinners (one at a highly rated restaurant), wine, and a sleigh ride, for $425 a couple. *112 Mount Pleasant Ave. North, Saint John, NB E2K 3V1, ☎ 506/649-0913 or 888/711-5151, fax 506/693-3233 ($$-$$$).*

Mahogany Manor has only three guest rooms that, combined with the magnetic personality of its host make it seem even more like you're a house-guest in a fine restored Victorian home. Guests can look out over the garden as they enjoy a full breakfast with home-baked muffins or breads. The inn is close to the center of town. *220 Germain St, Saint John, NB E2L 2G4, ☎ 506/636-8000 ($$).*

The Weslan Inn is a nicely restored Victorian sea captain's home with fine woodwork and large, bright guest rooms. (The bathrooms are larger than some hotel rooms we've stayed in.) An intimate dining room with a fireplace serves well-prepared

➔ LITTLE EXTRAS: *Either the Quaco or the Weslan inns can arrange for you to have a carriage ride along a country lane to a lighthouse for $30.*

local seafood (try the scallops) and other dishes, by reservation. Entrée prices ($19-22) include salad, dessert and tea or coffee. A winter package with dinner, champagne and other amenities (including a double whirlpool bath and fireplace) is about $200 for a couple. *45 Main St., St. Martins, NB E0G 2Z0, ☎ 506/833-2351, fax 506/833-1911 ($$).*

The Quaco Inn is a delightful Victorian mansion overlooking the water, with well-decorated rooms and good-humored hosts. Packages with two-nights' lodging, breakfasts and dinners, wine, a picnic lunch, a carriage ride and the use of bicycles, plus a hot-tub under the stars and a beach bonfire, cost $370 for a couple. The dining room there is excellent; expect fresh herbs, nice presentation, and elegant desserts. Entrée prices include soup (always interesting) or salad and dessert. *16 Beech St., St. Martins, NB E0G 2Z0, ☎ 506/833-4772, fax 506/833-2531 ($$).*

Shadow Lawn has nicely decorated and very comfortable rooms that retain the interesting architectural features of the house (we liked the big brick chimney passing through ours). It's only eight miles northeast of Saint John in historic Rothesay, whose streets are filled with equally elegant Victorian mansions, most built as summer homes. Much as we hate to spread gossip, we can't resist mentioning that the mansion's original owner was rumored to be the illegitimate son of King Edward VII. Dinner ($$) is served daily and it's wise to reserve a table when you reserve your room. Interesting entrées are beautifully prepared and stylishly presented. An appetizer of mussels was enough for a main course, and left just room enough for a bountiful serving of their splendid frozen lemon meringue torte. *3180 Rothesay Rd. (PO Box 41), Rothesay, NB E2E 5A3, ☎ 506/847-7539 or 800/561-1466, fax 506/849-9238 ($$-$$$).*

Grannan's Seafood Restaurant and Oyster Bar is on the lively waterfront where the action is, so reservations are important in the evening. It serves seafood in prodigious quantities, Mon-Sat 11:30 am-midnight, Sun 11:30 am-10 pm. The Captain's Platter would feed a platoon. Lighter lunch-time dishes include sandwiches, salads and, in summer, barbecue served on the patio. *Market Sq., Saint John, ☎ 506/634-1555 ($-$$$).*

At **Billy's Seafood Company Fish Market and Oyster Bar** lunch entrées ($) are available all day, and are substantial enough for a light dinner. The lobster roll is brimming with meaty chunks and all the fish is impeccably fresh and perfectly cooked. Open Monday-Thursday, 11 am-10 pm; Friday and Saturday, 11 am-11 pm; Sunday, 11 am-9 pm. *49-51 Charlotte St., Saint John; ☎ 506/672-3474 ($$).*

Beatty & the Beastro serves exceptional soups, salads, and sandwiches at remarkably low prices. One example: three-quarters of a pound of mussels steamed in garlic and white wine is $3.95. The dinner menu is intelligent and sophisticated, very like the chef herself, and prices are a bit higher than for lunch. Desserts, baked daily, are the stars here, if you have room – servings are very generous. *60 Charlotte Street at King Square, Saint John, ☎ 506/652-3888 ($-$$).*

Incredible Edibles Café, along with its café function, is a place to stop for a mid-afternoon or late evening espresso and a wedge of cheesecake (the source of their fame). Edibles serves lunch and dinner, Monday-Saturday, 11 am-10:30 pm. Substantial salads, pasta, pizza, and pita with hot or cold fillings are on the lunch menu. At night look for European favorites and fresh seafood dishes. *42 Princess St., Saint John, ☎ 506/633-7554 ($$).*

Our choice for lunch in Saint John is grazing through the historic **City Market** at King's Square on Charlotte St. Begin with chowder at **Lord's Lobster**, choose bread at **Vern's Bakery**, and fill it with cold cuts and cheese from **Jeremiah's** (or get a lobster roll). For a whopper salad, go to **Whale of a Café** and pick the ingredients – half-portions are probably enough – and pair it with souvlaki from **Yogel's**. Take the results to the park or waterfront, or eat it in the market's solarium. The market is open 7:30 am-6 pm Mon.-Thur., until 7 pm Fri. and 5 pm Sat.

A unique opportunity awaits at **Mount Hope Farm**. For $60 (including tax), you can enjoy an old-fashioned mussel feast, with 25 pounds of steamed mussels (enough for four-six people). If you don't have four people you can buy a single four-pound serving for $12. Butter is extra. You need to make reservations in advance for this or for their lobster dinners, which are $30 and include butter, plus mussels, cole slaw, potato salad, dinner rolls, dessert and tea or coffee. Meals are served at picnic tables on the lawn of an historic home, which you can tour before your meal. *690 Nerepsis Rd., Westfield, ☎ 506/757-8608.*

■ Camping

Four campgrounds and several wilderness sites along the trails of **Fundy National Park** provide more than 600 campsites, from full hook-ups ($16-$18) to unserviced tent sites ($9-$11). Reservations are accepted at some of these (☎ 800/213-PARK) and are required at all the wilderness sites (☎ 506/887-6000). But a lot of spaces are on a first-come-first-served basis, so it is a good idea to get to the park early in the day. Chignecto and Headquarters campgrounds have the most services and amenities, while Point Wolfe and Wolfe Lake are quieter and more primitive, usually favored by tenters and those who like camping the "old-fashioned" way. Neither of the latter has trailer sites. Wilderness sites cost $2.50 a night per person, plus the park entry fee. Some of these have fire pits, but the park encourages the use of backpacking stoves at all of them. These sites are in remote areas reached only by hiking trails.

Rockwood Park has camping facilities for tents ($13) and, in a separate area, trailers ($17). Hilltop tent sites have a splendid view over the bay, and the park provides all sorts of activities, from hiking and swimming to bumper-boats and water-golf. *Mount Pleasant Ave., Saint John, ☎ 506/658-2883.*

Lone Pine Park Campground, near Sussex, has a heated swimming pool, hiking trails and sites for both tents and RVs. *RR#1, Penobsquis, NB E0E 1L0, ☎ 506/432-4007.*

The Lower River Valley

Between Saint John and Fredericton lies a region broken by long bays and the meandering path of the lower St. John (the river is officially spelled with the abbreviated "Saint"). Once you leave its narrows at the Reversing Falls in the city, you can't cross by bridge until you reach Oromocto, almost to Fredericton. But a series of free ferries get you across the river at various points, in a much more interesting and scenic way than simply driving over a bridge.

The lower bays close to Saint John are covered under the Fundy Shore chapter, and if you have toured that region, the landscapes along the rest of the river will look familiar: patchwork fields, apple orchards, farmsteads and small villages with their white churches and clusters of homes.

Against the wide expanses of the river lies the peaceful old riverside settlement of Gagetown and the provincial capital of Fredericton, a lively, stately city with a decidedly English air.

Geography & History

Three hundred years ago the river was a highly prized fishing ground, its banks scattered with small settlements. In the late 1600s the French built a fort here at what is now Fredericton, which soon became a town. The British took it over in the mid-1700s, but, like Saint John, it was the Loyalists fleeing the American Revolution who shaped the city.

Kingston, on Rte. 845 north of Saint John, was one of the first areas in New Brunswick settled by these Loyalists, as you can see from its Anglican Church and Rectory, fine examples of late 1700s architecture. Three bodies of water surround the Kingston Peninsula – Long Reach (part of the Saint John River), its tributary the Kennebecasis, and Grand Bay.

Farther upstream, Gagetown was an important stop for the river steamers that were once the lifeblood of transportation here; to its north lies the huge Grand Lake, and several smaller lakes, which combine with the river and bays to give the whole area the feeling of floating on water.

Getting Around

To reach Fredericton directly from the Quoddy shore, follow Rte. 3 or Rte 127 to Rte. 3, which meets TransCanada-2 west of Fredericton. From Saint John, you have more choices, one of them fast and boring (Rte. 7), one slow and scenic as it follows the winding west

Fredericton

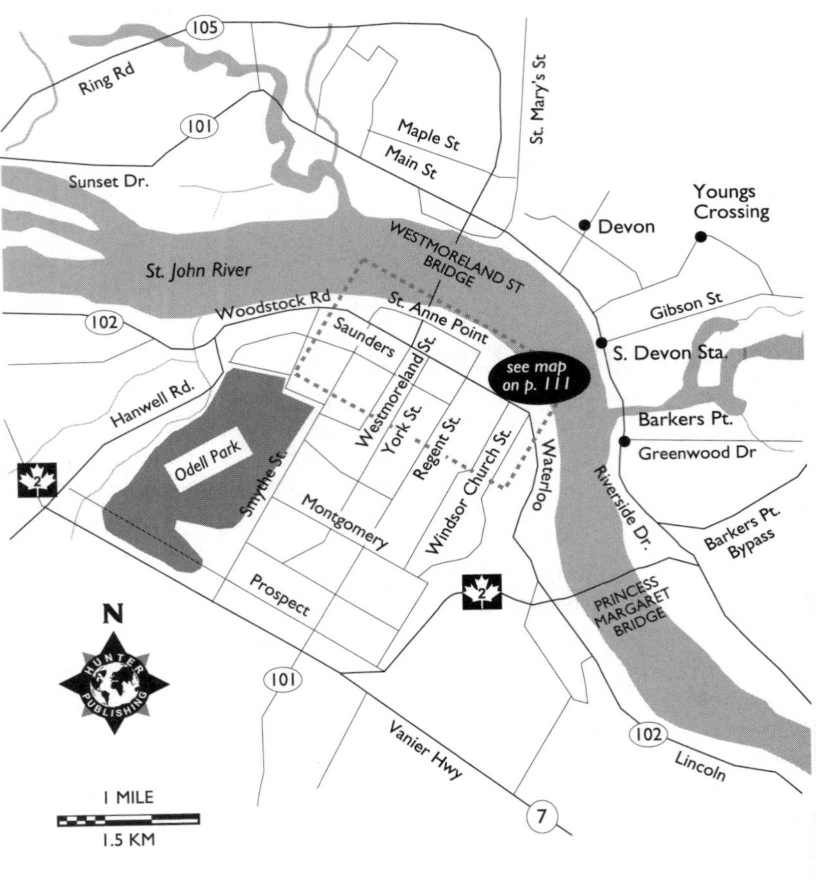

bank of the wide St. John River (Rte. 102), and a third even slower, but a great deal more fun. The latter crosses a series of long bays and narrow rolling peninsulas by free ferries, then crosses the main river and continue up its western bank through Gagetown to Fredericton.

Take Route 1 east from Saint John to Rothesay, then to Gondola Point via Rte. 100 to Rte. 119, following signs to the ferry.

Cross Kennebecasis Bay and take Rte. 845 east to Kingston, then Rte. 850 to another ferry, this one across Belleisle Bay. Rte. 124 takes you to the third ferry, and from Evandale you can follow Route 102 north to Gagetown. The ferries shuttle back and forth all day and it is rare to wait as much as 10 minutes for one. We look at these ferry trips as free boat tours.

If you are looking for an alternative route between Saint John and Fredericton, a bit more direct than the river or ferry route, but more interesting than the monotony of Rte. 7, take Rte. 101 to the west at Welsford, and follow it through Fredericton Junction to Fredericton. It's a rolling forested route, with little traffic, that passes a few farming communities and looks down on blue lakes with wooded shores.

Information Sources

■ For maps and details on opening hours and events, write or go to the **City Hall Visitor Information Centre**, 397 Queen St., at York Street, near the river, (PO Box 130), Fredericton, NB E3B 4Y7, ☎ 506/452-9508. Ask for the excellent *Fredericton Visitor Guide*, which has a good self-guided walking tour, and also for a free tourist parking pass that allows out-of-province visitors to park free at meters and in town lots. The office is open daily, 8 am to 8 pm, from mid-May-August; 8 am to 4:30 pm in September; and Monday-Friday, 8 am to 4:30 pm, the rest of the year.

■ On the highway approach to the city is another **Visitor Information Centre**, TransCanada-2 near Exit 289 (Hanwell Rd), ☎ 506/458-8331 or 506/458-8332. It's open daily, 8 am to 8 pm, in July and August; 9 am to 5 pm from mid-May through June and September through mid-October.

■ For advance information, you can also contact **Tourism New Brunswick**, PO Box 12345, Fredericton, NB E3B 5C3, ☎ 506/453-3984 or 800/561-0123.

Adventures

■ On Foot

Fredericton's streets are filled with historic buildings and sites, and the best way to see them is on a walking tour. Begin at **Officers' Square**, a park on Queen St. at Regent. It was once the city's military parade ground, and is bordered by quarters built in the early 1830s for officers of the British garrison.

Walk along Queen St., past the Soldiers Barracks, to the old **City Hall** (1876) at Phoenix Square, and see the Council Chamber's wool tapestries tracing the history of Fredericton. These were created by two local artists.

From there, head toward the river to walk along the **Riverfront Walkway**, which you can join anywhere downtown, as it follows the river for about three miles, from the Sheraton Hotel alongside the downtown streets. Follow the Walkway past the elegant **Waterloo Row** houses – a series of fine riverside mansions – to the remains of an old **Loyalist Cemetery**, with stones dating from 1783. The cemetery is just past Morell Park; follow the road beside the ball field. Return along Waterloo Row to the **Anglican Christ Church Cathedral** at the intersection of Brunswick and Church Streets (see *Sightseeing*). Walk along Brunswick St. past the Old York County Gaol to **The Old Burial Ground** at Regent St., in use from 1787 to 1878. Wander through it, looking for the graves of Loyalists families, and British soldiers. Turn up Carleton St., where you will see the distinctive white **Wilmot United Church** on the corner of King. Built in 1852, it's the only one remaining of the city's several large wooden churches that were built in the last century. The interior is decorated in hand-carved native woods. Guided tours are given on weekdays; ☎ 506/458-1066.

The *Fredericton Visitor Guide* includes a self-guided walking tour, or you can sign up for guided historical walking tours by costumed members of the theatrical group **Calithumpians**. Tours leave from the City Hall, Monday-Friday at 10 am or 2, 4 and 7 pm and on Saturday and Sunday at 10 am, 4 pm and 7 pm. Their lantern-lit "Haunted Hikes" through historic neighborhoods and graveyards are given on Tuesday and Thursday evenings at 9:15. ☎ 506/457-1975.

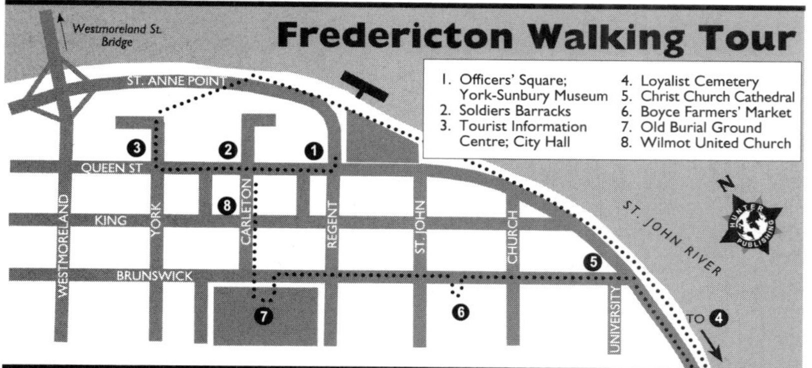

The arboretum of native trees is reached via two miles of walking trails through **Odell Park**, Rookwood Ave, ☎ 506/452-9500. It is free, and open daily 7 am to 10 pm. Interpretive signs describe the trees. In all, the park has 10 miles of walking trails, and the adjacent Fredericton Botanic Garden, on Prospect Street West, has nature trails.

Several miles of self-guided nature walks and hiking trails, including a one-mile wheelchair accessible trail around Beaver Pond, ramble through **Mactaquac Provincial Park** on Rte. 105, 15 miles west of Fredericton, ☎ 506/363-3011. Admission is $3.50 per car, and the park is open daily mid-May through mid-October, 8 am to dusk. The one-mile Jones Field Nature Trail and the Alex Creek Trail both explore a creek and an old farm site.

To see the fine 19th-century architecture that lines the streets of historic Gagetown with a knowledgeable guide, reserve a space on a Village of **Gagetown Walking Tour**, ☎ 506/488-2903.

■ On Wheels

The abandoned **CN railway line** extending from Rookwood Ave. about six miles west, is a multi-purpose path, good for cycling. It runs a distance along the banks of the river as far as McIntosh Brook. Since the trail is also used by walkers, they have the right-of-way.

You can rent bicycles in Fredericton at **Radical Edge** on Queen St., ☎ 506/459-3478, or from **Checker Charter River Cruises**, for $5 an hour or $25 a day. They're open every day from June through mid-October, at the Regent Street wharf, near the lighthouse, ☎ 506/451-0051.

You can also rent bikes in the park to explore the roads around **Mactaquac Provincial Park** on Rte. 105, 15 miles west of Fredericton, ☎ 506/363-3011. It is open mid-May through mid-October, daily 8 am to dusk, and admission is $3.50 per car.

■ On Water

The 50-mile-long headpond for the **Mactaquac Power Development Dam** is now part of Mactaquac Provincial Park, on Rte. 105, 15 miles west of Fredericton, ☎ 506/363-3011. It is open mid-May through mid-October, daily 8 am to dusk. Admission is $3.50 per car. Along with swimming and other activities along the shore, the pond is open for fishing, sailing, rowing, and waterskiing.

Woolastook Park, TransCanada-2, Upper Kinsclear, NB E3E 1P9, ☎ 506/363-5410, is open daily, 9 am to 9 pm, in July and August, 9 am to 5 pm, mid-May-June and September, has a beach (admission $2) and water slides, along with amusements and miniature golf.

Canoeing & Kayaking

In Fredericton you can rent kayaks or canoes to explore the river at **Small Craft Aquatic Centre**, Woodstock Rd, ☎ 506/462-6021. They conduct guided kayak tours and offer lessons in kayak and canoe handling and in rowing. You can also rent kayaks at **Heritage Outdoor Experience**, ☎ 506/454-2555, and from **Nashwaak Boat & Canoe**, ☎ 506/450-2628.

The gentle waters around Gagetown are perfect for canoes and kayaks, which are the best way to view some of the wide variety of birdlife that inhabits the river marshes. Inn guests are welcome to use the kayaks and canoes at the **Steamers Stop Inn** in Gagetown, ☎ 506/488-2903, fax 506/488-1116.

Lakeside Park, on Young's Cove Rd. in Waterborough, rents canoes for use on Grand Lake.

River Tours

One-hour cruises leave the Regent St. Wharf daily at 2, 4, 6 and 8 pm in the summer on board the ***Carleton***, a 25-passenger excursion boat. The cost is $5 for adults, $3 for children, ☎ 506/461-0633.

Fredericton's lovely riverfront mansions are only part of the scenery visible from river tours on the ***Bradside***, ☎ 506/461-0633.

Checker Charter River Cruises' (☎ 506/451-0051) two-hour trip visits the site of the Loyalists' first winter camp and includes stories about the city's long history. Tickets are $15 adults, $7.50 children. Five-hour "Oromocto River Adventures" are $50 adult, $25 for a school-age child, and follow the St. John River to Oromocto, with a barbecue and kite flying from the upper deck.

■ On Snow

In the winter, **Mactaquac Provincial Park** maintains cross-country ski trails, snowmobile and snowshoe trails, along with hills for tobogganing, and two lighted skating ponds. It's a popular place for ice fishing and you can take sleigh rides through the snow-covered forest and along the frozen pond, ☎ 506/363-3011 for reservations (Monday-Friday, 8 am to 5 pm).

Skiing

Seven miles of trails through the woods of Fredericton's **Odell Park**, entered from the end of Rookwood St., are groomed for cross-country skiing, as is the trail along the riverbank beside Sainte Anne Point Drive.

Mactaquac Provincial Park's cross-country ski trails include a half-mile beginner trail, a 1.5-mile intermediate trail and a three-mile advanced trail, all leaving from the lodge, ☎ 506/363-3011.

Downhill skiing is nearby at **Crabbe Mountain**; details are in the Upper St. John River section. Lodging packages are available with the **Mactaquac Inn** in Mactaquac Provincial Park, ☎ 506/363-5111 or 800/561/5111. For $160, a family of four can stay a night at the inn, have dinner, use the resort's indoor pool, and receive a discount on lift tickets at Crabbe Mountain.

Snowmobiling

A guided snowmobile trip, with machine and clothing included, as well as lunch, is $169 per person, with **Sports Experience Inc.** in Fredericton, ☎ 506/457-0872, fax 506/450-1172. The **Fredericton Snowmobile Club** maintains about 40 miles of trails, ☎ 506/452-0539. Mactaquac Provincial Park has 15 miles of marked groomed trails, fueling and food service. You can get a map of these from the park's lodge, ☎ 506/363-3011.

Sledding & Sleigh Rides

Dunbar Valley Adventures, in Durham Bridge off Rte. 8 north of Fredericton, ☎ 506/450-9612, offers guided dogsledding trips, with two hours on the trail, full instruction, and refreshments, for $60 a person. This same two-hour guided dogsledding trip, with instructions and refreshments, is part of a package with the **Sheraton Inn** in Fredericton, ☎ 506/457-7000 or 800/325-3535, fax 506/457-4000. The excursion, a room and breakfast is $239 for a couple.

In addition to sleigh rides at Mactaquac Provincial Park, they can be arranged with **Milton Price** in New Maryland (☎ 506/459-5780), **George Upshall** (☎ 506/446-4886), or **Newman & Creaser Horse & Carriage** (☎ 506/454-1554). Some offer meals or refreshments, such as hot chocolate, after the sleigh ride.

Sleigh rides are part of winter packages at **Pioneer Lodge and Log Cabins**, Cumberland Bay, NB E0E 1H0, ☎ 506/339-6458. They also furnish guests with toboggans for use on their hill.

■ On Horseback

A two-hour guided trail ride through the woods, including basic instruction for beginning riders, is available at **Royal Road Riding Stables** on Royal Rd. in Fredericton, ☎ 506/452-0040. The cost per person is $38 and you can sign up through the *Day Adventure* program or by calling directly. The stables also offers riding lessons and a summer riding camp.

Cultural & Eco-Travel Experiences

In Fredericton, the changing of the guard is re-enacted at **Officers Square** on Queen St., Tuesday through Saturday during July and August, at 11 am and 7 pm. The **Calithumpians** specialize in outdoor theatricals with an historic themes, which they perform free on Officers' Square, Monday-Friday 12:30 pm, and Saturday-Sunday at 2 pm, ☎ 506/452-9616. Maritime music concerts, also free, are held nearby, at the Lighthouse, and on Tuesday and Thursday at 7:30 pm, free band concerts at Officers' Square, may feature marching, military or bagpipe bands.

Fredericton is a city known for its encouragement of the arts, and near City Hall you can visit the **New Brunswick College of Craft and Design**, Canada's only college-level school for craftspeople and designers. The work of some of its pewtersmiths is in the Smithsonian, work of its potters, weavers and metalsmiths can be seen in frequent exhibits. Across from the Cathedral at 103 Church St., the **New Brunswick Crafts Council** sells high-quality weaving, pottery, needle arts, glassware, wood inlay and other work, ☎ 506/450-8989. On Saturday from 7 am to 1 pm the **Boyce Farmers' Market**, on George Street between Regent and St. John, has crafts along with fresh fruits and vegetables, farm cheeses, honey, sausages, preserves and baked goods.

The **Fredericton Botanic Garden**, begun in 1992, is well underway, and currently features a wildflower garden and walking trails. You can get a well-illustrated guide to the Woodland Fern Trail by writing the Botanic Garden Association at Box 57, Station A, Fredericton, NB E3B 4Y2. Enter the garden from Prospect St., next to the ball park.

Odell Park Arboretum is an outstanding collection of New Brunswick native trees, well-labeled and including some over four centuries old. An additional seven miles of walking trails through the woods are kept groomed in the winter for cross-country skiers. The park's entrance is at the end of Rookwood St. Odell Park is a good place to find songbirds, including the scarlet tanager.

Perhaps the most **unique birding experience** in Fredericton is the annual communal roosting of chimney swifts in late May and early June. Migrating flocks congregate in the air above chimneys, all flying in the same direction, and circle like a huge doughnut, then begin to drop in a swirl into the chimney. The best place to see this is at the chimney of the Incutech Building at the University of New Brunswick, which has been a roosting site for many years. The building is on MacKay Rd.; Follow York St. from Queen St., turning left on Kings College St. When it ends at the campus, follow the bird-symbol signs around the circular road, which becomes MacKay, until you reach the brick Incutech Building.

The **Fish Culture Station** at Mactaquac Provincial Park, gives guided tours of the fish hatchery in July and August or self-guided tours year round, where you may see live salmon being sorted for breeding and learn how they migrate into the rivers to spawn, ☎ 506/363-3021. At the Generating Station, across the dam, you can take a hard-hat-and-goggles tour to view the turbines at work. Tours are free, 9 am to 4 pm, mid-May to Labor Day, ☎ 506/363-3071.

The Farmers' Market in Fredericton.
(Photo by Charles James)

Plan to spend the whole day touring **King's Landing Historical Settlement**, Exit 259 from TransCanada-2, west of Fredericton, ☎ 506/363-5090 (or 506/363-5805 for recorded information). When plans for the Mactaquac Dam made it clear that miles and miles of riverside land would be flooded, and with it entire historic communities and many outstanding examples of the region's architectural, cultural and social heritage, the province decided to collect the best examples and group them into a living outdoor museum. Spanning the history of the riverside settlements from 1790 to 1910, the village includes working farms, grist and saw mills, village and country homes, a church and a Sash and Door Factory with 1909 machinery operated by a vintage motor.

The **Hagerman House** has furniture by a major Victorian cabinetmaker, the **Ingraham House** has fine New Brunswick pieces and a beautiful hedged garden, and the **Jones House** has good stenciled floors. Homes, farms and shops (including cooper and blacksmith shops) are all in use, by costumed interpreters who explain what they are doing as they work. You may find straw hats being braided, a bucket in progress, or a rug in the making. Things are not crowded together, so expect to do a lot of walking or take the wagon that makes the rounds of the main area. It's well worth going to the far end, beyond the schoolhouse, where you will see the modest cottage of a "recent" immigrant family.

Children may become "Visiting Cousins", living for five days as children lived 100 years ago, dressed in period costumes, attending school, playing period games, learning home and village arts, and eating meals with their "families." Tuition for five days, including lodging and meals is $280, and applications must be completed by mid-March for the following summer.

Workshops for adults concentrate on a specific subject, such as furniture stripping, open-hearth cooking, wool processing, tatting, chair caning or herbs. These last from 9:30 am to 1:30 pm, and cost $50. A one- or two-day wood-turning session is $175 a day, and includes a wooden bowl which each participant will make.

The museum is open daily 10 am to 5 pm, June-mid-October. Admission is $8.75 adult, $7.75 senior, $7.25 student over age 16, $5.50 ages six-16, $23 for an entire family.

Sightseeing

Fredericton history is well covered at the **Historical Society Museum**, Officers Square, ☎ 506/455-6041. It's open Monday-Saturday, 10 am to 6 pm, and Sunday, noon to 6 pm, May through early September. In July and August it stays open until 9 pm on Monday and Friday. Hours are shorter off-season. Admission is $1 for adults, $0.50 senior or child, $2.50 family. Under no circumstances should you miss seeing the 42-pound frog, once the pet of a local innkeeper.

The **Soldiers' Barracks and Guard House**, Queen and Carleton Streets, ☎ 506/453-3747, contains a military history museum. It is free, and open daily 10 am to 6 pm, June through August.

A benevolent native son built and endowed the **Beaverbrook Art Gallery**, 703 Queen St, ☎ 506/458-8545. Although it is best known for Salvador Dali's monumental "Santiago El Grande," it has other fine collections of paintings by Gainsborough, Reynolds, Constable, Turner, and Canadian artists, plus period rooms from the 1500s to the 1800s. It's open Monday-Friday 9 am to 6 pm, Saturday-Sunday 10 am to 5 pm in July and August, Tuesday-Friday 9 am to 5 pm, Saturday 10 am to 5 pm and Sunday noon to 5 pm, September through June. Admission is $3 adult, $2 senior, $1 child.

The first new cathedral founded on British soil since 1066 is **Christ Church Cathedral**, Brunswick St., ☎ 506/450-8500. The Cathedral offers visitors free tours. It's open Monday-Friday, 9 am to 8 pm; Saturday, 10 am to 5 pm; and Sunday, 1 to 5 pm. The building is an outstanding New World example of decorated Gothic architecture.

Waterford crystal chandeliers, portraits of King George III and Queen Charlotte, the Speaker's Chair and a spiral staircase at the end of the main hallway are the highlights in the **Legislative Assembly Building**, Queen St., ☎ 506/453-2527. Free tours are conducted every half-hour on weekdays.

You never know what special exhibit to expect in the **Fredericton National Exhibition Centre**, 503 Queen St. in Carleton, ☎ 506/453-3747. The subject can be anything from toys to technology, but will nearly always include interactive and hands-on features. It's free, and open May through August, Sunday-Thursday and Saturday 10 am to 5 pm, Friday 10 am to 9 pm. September through June it's open Tuesday-Friday noon to 4:30 pm, Saturday 10 am to 5 pm and Sunday 1 to 5 pm.

In Gagetown you'll learn about its colonial times and its later importance as a stop for river steamers, at **Queen's County Tilley House Museum**, ☎ 506/488-2966. It is open daily, 10 am to 5 pm, from mid-June through mid-September; Saturday and Sunday, 1 to 5 pm, from mid-September through mid-October. Admission is $1 adults, 25¢ children. The 1836 Queens County Courthouse is open the same hours, and free.

Look for gravestones of Loyalists and their slaves in the churchyard at **St. John's Anglican Church**, next to the Tilley museum in Gagetown. Like Fredericton, Gagetown is known for its craftsmen and artists, whose work you can see in local studios and galleries. Look especially for the tartans and handwoven clothing in the 1761 trading post, now **Loomscrofters**, ☎ 506/488-2400.

In Minto, west of Grand Lake, is a museum that preserves a unique bit of 20th-century history, **The New Brunswick Internment Camp Museum**, Municipal Building, Rte. 10, Minto, ☎ 506/327-3573. Although there were 26 World War II internment camps throughout Canada, this is the only one in the Atlantic provinces. The camp was erected here for its remote location and for the lumber that provided useful work for the internees. In the museum are about 400 artifacts and a scale model of the camp. Open weekdays and Saturday 10 am to 4 pm (later some days) and

Sunday noon to 6 pm, admission is free, but donations are appreciated.

Where To Stay & Eat

In and Near Fredericton

In the center of downtown, with rooms overlooking the river, is the **Lord Beaverbrook Hotel**. Guests can enjoy the indoor swimming pool, large Jacuzzi and sauna. All rooms have computer jacks. **The Terrace** ($-$$) is a reliably good place to eat, serving lamb chops, salmon and pasta dishes. The **Governor's Room** ($$$-$$$$), open for dinner only, has more trendy nouvelle fare and a more posh setting. *659 Queen St. (PO Box 545), Fredericton, NB E3B 5A6, ☎ 506/455-3371 or 800/561-7666, fax 506/455-1441 ($$-$$$).*

At the far end of the downtown area in a gleaming modern building you'll find the **Sheraton Inn**. The lobby opens onto a terrace and swimming pool overlooking the river; many rooms have river views, all have ironing boards, coffee makers, and voice-mail. Indoor and outdoor swimming pools, Jacuzzi and sauna, as you'd expect. **Bruno's** ($-$$$) offers outdoor riverside dining in the summer and a smart atmosphere indoors. They feature an innovative and international menu from which we've sampled salmon infused with ginger, shrimp cooked with sesame and tangerine, and a whopping chocolate and berries dessert called raspberry bash. *225 Woodstock Rd., Fredericton, NB E3B 2H8, ☎ 506/457-7000 or 800/325-3535, fax 506/457-4000 ($-$$$).*

For a comfortable B&B in an elegant old home, stay at **Carriage House Inn**. It's furnished in antiques and has a wide porch for watching the world go by on the tree-shaded street of fine Victorian homes. *230 University Ave., Fredericton, NB E3B 4H7, ☎ 506/452-9924 or 800/267-6068, fax 506/458-0799 ($$).*

Kilburn House is a B&B near the center of town. The shared bath has a whirlpool tub. *80 Northumberland St., Fredericton, NB E3B 3H8, ☎ 506/455-7078 ($-$$).*

For a location near TransCanada-2, try the **City Motel**. Rooms are nicely furnished in matched New Brunswick-made pieces. A seafood restaurant called **The Lobster Hut** ($-$$) is in the motel. *1216 Regent St., Fredericton, NB E3B 3Z4, ☎ 506/450-9900, fax 506/452-1915 ($).*

Town and Country Motel has several rooms with equipped kitchenettes. All rooms have air conditioning, although its airy riverside location (terraces face the shore) makes it mostly unnecessary. The hospitable owners are on-premises. *967 Woodstock Rd. (RR 3), Fredericton, NB E3B 4X4, ☎ 506/454-4223 ($-$$).*

Downtown and dormitory-style is the **York House Youth Hostel**. It's open only in July and August and has inexpensive meals as well. *193 York St, Fredericton, NB E3B 5A6, ☎ 506/454-1233 ($).*

The **University of New Brunswick** has dormitory rooms available in the summer. *PO Box 4400, Fredericton, NB E3B 5A3, ☎ 506/453-4891 ($).*

Chicadee Lodge is a log-built home with a bed and breakfast on a riverbank, with well-kept grounds. Guests are welcome to explore the river in the lodge's canoes. *Prince William, NB E0H 1S0, ☎ 506/363-2759 (May through November) or 506/363-2288 (December through April) ($-$$).*

Café du Monde serves seafood, pasta and lighter dishes, as well as breakfast, in a comfortable café atmosphere. The pastry is made in-house. *610 Queen St, ☎ 506/457-5534 ($-$$).*

The Barbecue Barn offers seafood and traditional French fare, and barbecue, of course. *540 Queen St, Fredericton, ☎ 506/455-2742 ($-$$).*

Schade's serves German and central European dishes in generous portions. Look here for hearty favorites such as Hungarian goulash, and for delicate veal schnitzel. *536 Queen St, Fredericton, ☎ 506/450-3340 ($-$$).*

The Diplomat is a combination of standard family dining and Chinese; they do a good job with both and serve a popular Chinese buffet at lunch and dinner. They are open 24 hours a day, and bake their pastries in-house. *253 Woodstock Rd, Fredericton, ☎ 506/454-2400 ($-$$).*

King's Head Inn in King's Landing Historical Settlement serves dishes appropriate to their historical setting: corn chowder, chicken pie and traditional favorites. *TransCanada-2, Exit 259, Prince William, ☎ 506/363-5090 ($$).*

Lower River & Grand Lake

Steamers Stop Inn has the easy peaceful ambience of its days as a stop for upper class riverboat passengers. Today it's a welcoming, nicely run inn, with antiques, river views, and a dock for guests, with kayaks and canoes for exploring the river. The dining room ($$) serves old-fashioned dishes (like gingerbread) and stylish modern entrées, mainly seafood, by reservation only. *Front St. (PO Box 155), Village of Gagetown, NB E0G 1V0, ☎ 506/488-2903, fax 506/488-1116 ($$).*

Tucked into a woodland setting on the northern shores of Grand Lake is **Pioneer Lodge and Log Cabins**. A big fieldstone fireplace in the lodge, candlelight dining, and homemade quilts in the log cabins make this place especially cozy for a winter getaway. *Cumberland Bay, NB E0E 1H0, ☎ 506/339-6458 ($-$$).*

If you take Rte. 101 between Saint John and Fredericton, places to eat are rare. But you can get a generous bowl of good chili or a sandwich at **The Hungry Farmer**. It's open 11 am to 9 pm on weekdays and from 8 am on weekends. On Saturday mornings you may find a country flea market there. *Rte. 101, Hoyt, NB, ☎ 506/687-1894 ($).*

Also south of Fredericton on the more traveled Rte. 3 is the unusual **Wanderer's Table**. Dishes typical to southern Africa are featured, including Malay curries. The restaurant, located in a small house in the middle of the village, is open for three meals a day, seven days a week in the summer; Friday-Sunday only in the winter, opening at 10 am on Sunday, 8 am on Friday and Saturday. *Harvey Station (just north of Harvey), ☎ 506/366-9013 ($-$$).*

Count on home-baked goodies at **Keswick Kitchen**. They're open all day, all year, and their scones are made in heaven. *Rte. 104 in Burtts Corner, just north of Fredericton, ☎ 506/363-5637.*

■ Camping

Mactaquac Provincial Park has 300 campsites for tents and trailers, some alongside the 18-hole golf course. *Rte. 105, 15 miles west of Fredericton on Route 105, off TransCanada-2,* ☎ *506/363-3011.*

Woolastook Park has a large campsite with a restaurant, beach, and amusement park. *TransCanada-2, Upper Kinsclear, NB E3E 1P9,* ☎ *506/363-5410.*

Grand Lake Park is large and busy, with a beach and other recreational facilities, including a boat launch and walking trails. Tent sites are $17, those with hookups are $19. *Princess Park, Grand Lake, NB* ☎ *506/385-2919.*

On the opposite side of Grand Lake is **Lakeside Park**. Wooded tent sites and pull-through sites with hookups are set back from the beach. Canoes and bicycles are available for rent. *Young's Cove Rd., Waterborough, NB* ☎ *506/488-2321.*

The Upper River Valley

For most of its course, the St. John River runs through gentle farmlands, in a region known for its potatoes and other crops. River settlements began with the early fishermen and traders, who were busy here as far back as the 1700s. Before that, the river was an important route for native peoples. It is one of the least touristed regions of New Brunswick, and visited mainly by those traveling from Quebec. It's a pleasant, scenic and pastoral area, with abundant opportunities for outdoor adventures.

Geography & History

The St. John River actually begins in Maine, and forms the border between Canada and the United States from several miles west of Saint-Francois-de-Madawaska to Grand Falls. From there it continues to flow south, parallel with the international boundary – or roughly so, since the border runs in a strait line and the river curves and winds its way – until it swings west at Meductic. For most of its course, the river is wide and mild mannered, but at Grand Falls, it drops suddenly over jagged rocks and into a steep-sided gorge. Before the building of the hydro-electric dam above the falls, it must have been a magnificent sight; even with the dam above it, constricting its flow, it is an impressive falls.

East of the river is mostly wilderness, cut by few roads. One of these leads to Plaster Rock, following the Tobique River just north of Perth-Andover, where it joins the St. John River. The road climbs up through dense forests, above one of the province's legendary fishing rivers.

Speaking of legends, the northern part of this region is alive with them. You will hear, wherever you go, references to the Republic of Madawaska, mythical as a republic, but a very real and beautiful land encompassing parts of two provinces and the state of Maine. It origins, like that of the Indian Stream Republic in Northern New Hampshire, were in a long-unsettled border dispute. The area between the headwaters of two rivers was claimed by Quebec, New Brunswick and Maine at various times, which so vexed its residents that they dreamed of its becoming an independent land of its own. The Webster-Ashburton Treaty in 1842 finally set the boundary, and the dream of independence melted into the mythic republic. Today it has a coat of arms and a council of "knights" which include the mayor of Edmundston and other leading people of the area.

Getting Around

From Fredericton, head west on TransCanada-2, toward Grand Falls, along the western bank of the river, which the highway crosses for a brief distance at Hartland. When the river becomes the international boundary between Maine and Canada at Grand Falls, you will cross it again. At Perth-Andover you can leave the river to make a loop through the highlands to Plaster Rock and

New Denmark, then rejoining TransCanada-2 at the river in Grand Falls.

Rte. 105 leaves Fredericton on the north side of the river, following the opposite bank from TransCanada-2. This is a slower route, only slightly more scenic as it follows closer to river level. You can alternate routes by crossing the many bridges along the way. You will see longer vistas from the higher TransCanada-2. From Fredericton to the Quebec border is 180 miles.

Information Sources

- For tourist information, contact **Tourism New Brunswick**, PO Box 12345, Fredericton, NB E3B 5C3, ☎ 506/453-3984 or 800/561-0123, or the **Visitors Centre**, 220 King St. (at the bridge), Woodstock, NB E7M 1Z8, ☎ 506/325-9049, open daily 9 am to 8 pm, late June through August.

- In the Tobique region you can get information at the **Tourist Park**, Box 129, Plaster Rock, NB E0J 1W0, ☎ 506/356-6077. It's open daily, 9 am to 8 pm, mid-June through August.

- For the far north, contact the **Tourist Information Centre**, Blvd. Hebert (TransCanada-2, Exit 18), Edmundston, NB E3V 1J6, ☎ 506/737-5064, open daily, 8 am to 8 pm, June through August.

- If you are entering the province from Quebec, stop at the beautiful **Tourist Information Centre** on TransCanada-2 at the border in Saint-Jacques, ☎ 506/735-2747. Their illuminated tourist maps of the different routes through the province are illustrated with highlights of each, and they show videos on the province.

Adventures

■ On Foot

Although the 90-mile stretch of the **Petit Temis Interprovincial Linear Park** between Edmundston and Rivier-du-Loup, Quebec is designed primarily for cyclists, walkers make good use of it, too. Rest stops every mile, access to the Botanical Garden (see *Cultural & Eco-Travel Experiences*, below) and the lakeside town of Cabano with its restored fort and rose gardens, make it a particularly attractive walking route.

The network of six trails in the **Forestry School's Experimental Forest** are free, or you can have a naturalist guide to go with you for $2 per person. Two of the trails have interpretive signs. The forest is located 25 miles from Edmundston, off Trans-Canada-2 in Ste-Anne-de-Madawaska, ☎ 506/737-5238.

Fraser Tree Nursery at Second Falls, has a 2.5-mile interpretive trail, ☎ 506/737-2220. A box at the trailhead has interpretive maps. The land is regenerating after a forest fire, and the trail passes through woods and along the edge of the nursery. Take a look inside the greenhouse you will pass toward the end of the trail to see spruce seedlings getting a start on life. To get there from Edmundston, take Victoria St. to Olivier Boucher Rd., about eight miles out of town.

A 20-mile walking trail along the St. John River, with many fine overlook views and benches, runs through the town of Hartland, and can be accessed from several points along Rte. 105. Centreville, near the international border west of Bristol on Rte. 110, has walking trails along the banks of the Presque Isle River.

A trail leading right from TransCanada-2 between Meductic and Woodstock has two attractions. It is an old Maliseet portage trail, well-used by Native Americans, and a side trail from it leads to a Hayes Falls, nearly 100 feet of cascades. About 3 miles north of Exit 212 is a large sign on the highway announcing the Maliseet Indian Trail, a short distance beyond. You can park on the road opposite the trailhead, on the east side of the highway. Blue markers with white stripes mark the trail, which is wide and well-maintained until you get to the fork leading to the falls, less than a mile from the highway. Turn right here (the second trail is not easy to spot, so watch for it), still following the striped markers. Nor far beyond, take another fork to the right, which leads down to the bottom of the falls.

■ On Wheels

Road Biking

Canada's first interprovincial cycling trail borders the Madawaska River and Temiscouata Lake, in Quebec, as it travels from Edmundston to Riviere-du-Loup, also in Quebec. **Motel Le Brayon**, 40 des Rochers, Saint-Basile, NB E7C

2J4, ☎ 506/263-5514, fax 506/263-5462, offers a package that solves the problem of returning on the same path. Two nights' lodgings, two breakfasts, a picnic lunch, a day's bicycle rental, a bicycling map and shuttle service to bring you back, costs $130 per person in the spring and fall, $150 in the summer.

Another shuttle service is operated by **Le Canotier**, ☎ 506/737-7173 or 506/735-0470. They offer the attractive flexibility of being able to combine rental and shuttle of bicycles and/or canoes and kayaks, so you can travel up the interprovincial linear park and return by water. Bicycle rentals are $20 a day or $7 per hour.

The lakeside town of **Cabano**, Quebec, is a good destination for a one-day round-trip, with a visit to its historic Fort Ingall and rose gardens. Lunch in one of its French restaurants or have espresso at Quai des Beumes Café Terrasse. The old railway station, right on the bicycle path, now operates as an inn called Auberge de la Gare, and houses the information center where you can get directions to the nearby fort and see menus from the restaurants.

Woodstock Cycle Centre on Lower Main St. in Woodstock, ☎ 506/324-8356, offers repairs and equipment, as well as bicycle rentals. Check there for information on their bicycle tours.

■ On Water

Baker Lake Provincial Park, about 20 miles from Edmundston, has a swimming beach and canoe rentals. Several campgrounds have small swimming beaches on lakes or the river.

Canoeing & Kayaking

The St. John, Madawaska and Tobique Rivers all offer fine paddling waters – the Tobique is canoeable for about 80 miles. Canoe and kayak rentals and shuttle service for the Madawaska and St. John Rivers are provided by **Le Canotier**, ☎ 506/737-7173 or 506/735-0470. Single kayak rental is $20 a day or $7 per hour, double $25 a day or $8 an hour. Canoe rental is $30 a day or $10 per hour. They also rent and shuttle bicycles, so you can combine a bike trip along interprovincial trail with a return by water.

Night kayaking in the quiet waters of Glazer Lake is offered by **Eagle Valley Adventures** in Edmundston, ☎ 506/992-2827 or 888/26-CANOE. The four-hour tour, which includes a stop for a snack, leaves from the Clair Historical Site, and will operate with as few as two people, at $50 each, including kayak, head lamps and a guide.

River Country Campground in Florenceville, ☎ 506/278-3700, rents canoes to campground guests and to the public.

River Tours

In Grand Falls you can take a boat tour of the gorge, signing up at the **La Rochelle Visitor Centre** in Centennial Park, ☎ 506/475-7788, between May and mid-October. The cost is $8 adult, $4 age five-12. If you have more than four in a group, the cost is $5 each.

Eagle Valley Adventures in Edmundston, ☎ 506/992-2827 or 888/26-CANOE, operates four-hour nature and historical tours of the Madawaska River in motorized cedar canoes, from June through Sept. for $60. These begin in Edmundston and go into Quebec; evening trips return to the city after dark for a unique night view. Full-day trips on the St. John River, at $120 ($50 for ages six-15) include hot lunches prepared by well-trained chefs and served along the riverbanks. Their "La Republicaine" trip weaves among the river islands between Edmundston and Clair, stopping for a tour of the historical site (see Sightseeing, below) and for a riverside lunch. You may see loons, eagles, ospreys, hawks and owls, along with flora unique to the river. The "American Colony Tour" travels the same route, with a stop in St. Clair, but focuses on history, both official and folklore, with stories about Prohibition days when rum-running was a profitable business on the river. It's a good-humored look at the history of a region largely ignored by history books.

The "Eagle's Run" tour begins at the St. Clair museum and goes through the narrow channel at The Ledges on the way to Crew Island for a hot lunch. Then the canoe continues up the St. Francis River to Glazier Lake. On the way back downstream, after a walking tour to explore the plant life of Kennedy Island, the canoe runs the rapids before returning to the take-out.

Tours of the Madawaska River by pontoon boat operated by **Le Canotier** from the Fraser Marina, include a guided tour of the New Brunswick Botanic Garden, and the rental of a bike for the return trip (or you can return by the pontoon boat), for $25. If you choose, you can return by canoe or kayak for $5 extra. You need to make reservations, ☎ 506/737-7173 or 506/735-0470. A two-hour tour of the Madawaska by pontoon boat, with a lunch that includes native fiddleheads and Brayonne meat pâté is also $25.

River Country Campground in Florenceville, ☎ 506/278-3700, offers river tours on their small excursion boat.

■ On Snow

Along with the usual northern winter outdoor pursuits, you can visit sugar houses in March and April to watch maple sap become syrup and sugar. In Saint-Andre, north of Grand Falls, stop at **Paradis de la Petite Montage** on Bourgoin Rd. to see this process, ☎ 506/473-6683.

Skiing

Mont Farlagne north of Edmundston, ☎ 506/735-8401, has 17 trails on a 600-foot vertical drop; the longest run is just over a mile. Six of the trails and the beginner slope are lighted for night skiing, and equipment rentals and ski lessons are available. It's a family-oriented area, with a lot of activities, including theme weekends and a winter carnival at the end of January.

Close to Fredericton, and with the highest vertical drop in the province (850 feet), is **Crabbe Mountain,** ☎ 506/463-8311. The mountain's longest run is 1.5 miles, and they offer glade skiing and a snowboard park. Night skiing is Wednesday through Sunday and they offer learn-to-ski packages. A one-hour beginner lesson, full-day pass for all lifts, ski or snowboard equipment rental and lunch are packaged together as a *Day Adventure* program for $37 per person or $135 for a family.

Cross-country trails abound, using abandoned rail lines and the numerous logging roads that web the area. The rail line from Plaster Rock to Perth-Amboy, along the Tobique River, is a multipurpose trail used by skiers in the winter. Three-hour guided ski tours, with an introduction to the basics for beginners, a hot drink and snack at a ski-hut, and an all-day trail pass so you can continue skiing on your own, is $25 per person ($10 for those under 12), with Tobique Nordic, in Plaster Rock, ☎ 506/356-8353, fax 506/356-8453. You can reserve directly or through the *Day Adventure* program.

Ten miles of marked trails in the **Experimental Forest** are available for cross-country skiers, as is the chalet. The forest is 25 miles from Edmundston, off TransCanada-2 in Ste-Anne-de-Madawaska, ☎ 506/ 737-5238.

Several cross-country ski clubs maintain trails in the area, many of which also have warming huts or chalets. In Edmundston contact **Republic Cross Country Club**, ☎ 506/735-6431. The **Tobique Cross Country Ski Club** is in Plaster Rock, with 20 miles of marked trails and a chalet, ☎ 506/356-8851 or 356-8503. **Perth Andover's Cross Country Ski Club** has six miles of trail with a chalet, ☎ 506/273-6829.

Snowmobiling

The river valley has one of the heaviest concentrations of Provincial snowmobile trails, with routes along both sides of the river in many places and an international twist to your snow travels as you cross and re-cross the US-Canadian border to make several loops. Trails continue on to Quebec, as well. A particularly scenic loop uses three trails to circle from Beechwood (north of Bristol) along the east bank of the river, through Perth Andover, up the Tobique River to Plaster Rock, westward through New Denmark to Grand Falls, then along the international boundary for a stretch before rejoining the river, this time on its west bank, to return to Beechwood. You can find lodging and services along this route at Beechwood, Grand Falls and Plaster Rock. For a slightly shorter loop, you can cut across below Grand Falls to meet the border trail.

The **Interprovincial Linear Park** is part of the multi-purpose trail which will eventually stretch from sea to sea across Canada, and the section between Edmundston and Riviere-du-Loupe, Quebec, is completed. Snowmobilers use the trail in the winter.

You can combine snowmobile rental with lodging in a *Day Adventure* package with **Joe Loue Tout** in Edmundston, ☎ 506/735-7122, fax 506/735-7122. A snowmobile, a night's accommodations, breakfast and snowmobile instruction for two people sharing a machine is $250 a couple, and includes 100 miles of travel. Expect to pay extra for more miles and for insurance. Or you can take a guided three-hour trip with the same outfitter, that includes a hearty trail lunch for $95 per machine, $20 extra for a second passenger.

Provincial Snowmobile Trail 19 runs through Edmundston, and several motels have connecting trails leading to it and

> **➔ LOCAL SNOWMOBILE INFORMATION:** *For more information about snowmobiling in the Upper River Valley, contact the local snowmobile clubs:* ***Woodstock Trailmakers****, ☎ 506/328-4469;* ***Twin River Snowmobile Club*** *in Perth-Andover, ☎ 506/273-6091; or* ***Northern Lights Trailblazers*** *in Hartland, ☎ 506/375-4061.*

New Brunswick

offer special packages for riders, including **Comfort Inn**, 5 Bateman Ave., Edmundston, NBE3V 3L1, ☎ 506/739-8361 or 800/228-5150, fax 506/737-8183. Lodging packages begin at $33 per person. **Motel Le Brayon**, 40 des Rochers, Saint-Basile, NB E7C 2J4, ☎ 506/263-5514, fax 506/263-5462, also has trail access, with rooms beginning at $45.

Provincial trails also run past **Crabbe Mountain**, ☎ 506/463-8311, where there is trail access to the main ski lodge, as well as facilities for refueling and snowmobile parking.

Sledding & Sleighrides

You can learn the art of mushing as you and your team explore the fabled Republic of Madawaska with an Acadian guide well-versed in its stories and folklore. "The Great Madawaska Husky Trek" is a half-day trip with instruction in using a sled and handling your team, and a stop for hot tea and a snack in an upland cabin warmed by a woodstove, operated by **Eagle Valley Adventures** in Clair, ☎ 506/992-2827 or 888/262-2663, fax 506/992-2827. The cost is $70 per person or $50 for a child under 12.

In February there are **dogsled races** in the town of Clair, on the St. John river a few miles upstream from Edmundston, ☎ 506/992-2181. A smaller racing event is held in nearby Sainte-Anne-de-Madawaska, on Quisibis Lake. For information, contact Club de Chien, ☎ 506/445-2749.

For an old-fashioned sledding party on new-fashioned sleds, reserve an air tube slide at **New Denmark Ski Lodge** in New Denmark, between Plaster Rock and Grand Falls, ☎ 506/473-2481. For $10 per person you can sled for three hours, enjoy a meal in the riverside lodge, and skate on their rink. The skate rental is not included. Without a meal, you can sled from noon to 3:30pm, 4 to 7:30 pm, or 8 to 11:30 pm. for $7 adult, $5 for ages 12 and under.

■ On Horseback

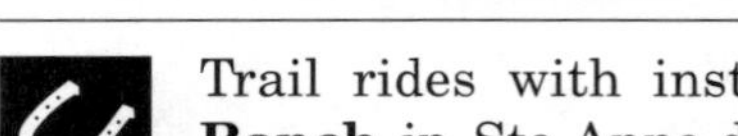

Trail rides with instruction are offered at **Nature's Ranch** in Ste-Anne-de-Madawaska, ☎ 506/445-3418 or 506/445-2605. Guided rides can be as short as half an hour or as long as five hours, which takes you to the experimental forest, where you stop for a lunch (included in the cost). Rates are $12 per person for one hour, $22 for two hours, or $10 per hour for longer trips. The ranch is open year-round. The trails are well-groomed and mostly through woodlands.

Cultural & Eco-Travel Experiences

Edmundston and the area around it are peopled by a rich cultural mix of French and English, but the French here are called Brayonne, and their traditions differ from those of the Acadians in the rest of New Brunswick. They celebrate these, and the special foods of their unique heritage, at the **Brayonne Festival** in early August, ☎ 506/739-6608.

Before either of the European groups came, peoples of the First Nation roamed the woodlands and fished the pristine waters of the rivers. Some of their descendants live at the **Negoot-Gook Maliseet Nation** near Perth-Andover, where you can find examples of their traditional crafts in the gift shop, ☎ 506/273-1140. On Labor Day weekend they hold the **Wabanaki Aboriginal Music Festival**. You can also buy native crafts in a shop at **Madawaska Maliseet First Nation Reservation** in Saint-Basile, the smallest in the province with a population of about 100.

You can learn more about the various peoples of the region as you explore it at the free **Musée du Madawaska**, with excellent displays of local history and culture, Blvd. Hebert (TransCanada-2, Exit 18), Edmundston NB E3V 1J6, ☎ 506/737-5064, open daily from 8 am to 8 pm, June through August.

To round out the ethnic stew, **New Denmark**, on Rte. 108 between Plaster Rock and Grand Falls, is home to the largest Danish community in North America. They have lived in the area for over 125 years, and a drive through their beautifully tended farmland is especially lovely when the fields are bordered in bright fall foliage.

The story of the first immigrants to Canada is told at **New Denmark Memorial Museum**, ☎ 506/553-6724. An immigrant's home and museum contain collections of household and farm implements, dolls and Danish porcelain. Its hours vary, but you're likely to find someone to let you in if you ask in town.

The best known natural attraction in the area is **Grand Falls**, dropping over jagged rocks in a mass of white before swirling through a narrow gorge with rock walls, where the rushing waters have worn giant potholes. Viewing platforms at two different interpretive centers look down into the turbulent waters, and a trail and stairs down to the potholes give even closer looks. A guided walking tour will help you understand the geology of the gorge and

➲ **LOCAL TREATS:** *Apart from its lumber and logging history, which is celebrated each year with a Woodsmen's Competition during Woodstock's Old Home Week in July, the area's best known wild product is the* ***fiddlehead fern****, a popular treat found in grocery stores, farmers markets and on restaurant menus all over the province each spring. Plaster Rock celebrates this bounty in its Fiddlehead Festival each July 1, on Canada Day.*

falls, as you descend the 253 steps to the rocks at water level, and see the holes sculpted by the rushing waters. The cost of the two-hour tour, which includes a pass to the stairway, is $10, or $30 for a family, ☎ 506/ 473-6013. It costs $2 ($1 for students, $5 for a family) to use the stairway and trails to the river. For a boat trip through the gorge, see *River Tours*, above.

In Saint-Jacques four miles north of Edmundston, don't miss **The New Brunswick Botanical Garden**, Trans-Canada-2, Exit 8, ☎ 506/735-3074. It is open daily 9 am to dusk, June through mid-October. Admission is $4.75 adult, $2.25 age seven-12. Gardens include collections of roses, lilies and alpine plants, themed plantings, vegetable, herb, alpine, bonsai, water and shade gardens. The rose gardens are particularly beautiful in early summer, but a good portion of the more than 80,000 plants and 30,000 annual bedding plants are in bloom all summer.

Nackawic's International Garden, on the town green, has more than 50 varieties of trees from around the world, ☎ 506/575-2241.

On a hillside above Saint-Jacques in the village of Moulin Morneault is **Ferme Aqua-Zoo**, ☎ 506/739-9149. Here you can see about 50 species of native and exotic animals, from deer and coyotes to yaks, wolves and buffalo. Along with a population of more than 80 large animals in the zoo, which is a family-run hobby-turned-business, there are 42 different kinds of chickens, including some very unusual exotic breeds. The four lakes on the large property are stocked with trout – some of them very large – and you can fish there, too. The zoo is open daily from mid-May to mid-September, from 10 am to dusk, and admission is $3.45 for adults and $1.75 for children.

Sightseeing

Rte. 103 follows the river bank closely through Woodstock, known for its Victorian buildings and The **Old Carleton County Court House**, 19 Court St, Upper Woodstock, ☎ 506/328-9706. Open daily 9 am to noon and 1-6 pm in July and Aug., it contains historic needlework and crafts.

Hartland Covered Bridge, the world's longest, is more than 1,000 feet long, about a fifth of a mile. You can cross it or photograph it from the center of Hartland, whose main street parallels the river.

Clair Historical Site is in the town of Clair, about 20 miles from Edmundston on the St. John River, ☎ 506/992-3637. Along with an historical house from 1848, the site contains a bunkhouse, cookhouse, church and barn, in which is a museum of agricultural tools. It is open mid-June through September, 9 am to 8 pm daily, at an admission fee of $2.

Adjacent to the Botanic Garden in Saint-Jacques is the **Antique Automobile Museum**, ☎ 506/735-2525. Gleaming examples of the greats in the history of automobiles – a 1905 REO touring car, a 1933 Rolls Royce Phantom – and unique vehicles, including a 1910 electrically-operated passenger coupe are displayed in a new facility built to house this private collection. It is open June-Aug., daily from 8 am to 9 pm.

Where to Stay & Eat

Woodstock to Perth-Andover

Stiles Motel and Hometown Restaurant has tidy rooms and a good home-style restaurant ($$) with a salad bar and known for fresh-baked breads and pies. The service is particularly friendly here. *827 Main St, Woodstock NB E0J 2B0, ☎ 506/328-6671, fax 506/328-3737 ($$).*

In one of the town's many fine Victorian homes is **The Queen Victoria Bed & Breakfast**, a period piece in Victorian antiques and decorations. *133 Chapel St, Woodstock, NB E0J 2B0, ☎ 506/328-8382 ($$).*

For a change of pace from the rest of the town's Victorian atmosphere, stay in a Swiss-style chalet at **Froehlich's**. It overlooks the river. *Rte. 105 (PO Box 1983), Woodstock, NB E0J 2B0, ☎ 506/328-6751 ($).*

If you are just passing through and want to stop along the highway without going into town (which would be a shame unless you'd already explored Woodstock on your way up-river), you'll find well-maintained, attractive rooms at **Atlantic Inns**. The dining room ($-$$) is reliable as well, serving home-style dishes like ham with pineapple, fisherman's platter, and fish & chips. *TransCanada-2 at Walker Mill Rd., Woodstock, NB E0J 2B0, ☎ 506/328-6688 ($-$$).*

For comfortable, homey rooms and beds covered with handmade quilts, stay in the farmhouse at **Campbell's Bed & Breakfast**. The pantry and refrigerator are filled with farm-fresh eggs, milk and other breakfast fixings, so you can prepare your own morning meal. The engaging hostess, who lives in the other house on the same farm, will keep you laughing with her stories after breakfast. *Rte. 105 (RR#1), Hartland, NB E0J 1N0, ☎ 506/375-4775 ($).*

Mary's Bakery serves light lunches and tea-time goodies, including pies made of whatever berry is in season. *On the riverside promenade in Perth-Andover, ☎ 506/273-2885.*

York's Dining Room, open daily May through mid-October, serves home-style meals, including lobster dinners. They are open for dinner daily, and for lunch every day except Saturday. Don't wait for the menu, because you won't get one. You'll get your choice of soup or lobster bisque and a green salad, then a hot corn fritter in maple syrup (think of this as dessert when you still have room for it). Then you have your choice of lobster (a good-sized one, at that) or any of several other entrée choices, then a smaller portion of another entrée, just so you can sample it. If you haven't slid under the table from the sheer weight of all this food, you can choose from a staggering list of desserts, from strawberry shortcake to their own mince pie. *West Riverside Drive in Perth-Andover, ☎ 506/273-2847 ($$).*

If you're looking for the action in Woodstock, stop at **JR's**. Downstairs is raucous and upstairs is far from sedate, but they have a large menu with everything from chili and fajitas to a fisherman's platter (under $10) and chicken teriyaki. The kids' menu is $1.99. *Off Rte. 103, south of the bridge, ☎ 506/328-9326 ($-$$).*

The Northern Valley

Nyborg's Bed & Breakfast is a good place to get a view of community life in the Danish settlement. *Foley Brook Rd (just off Rte. 108), New Denmark, NB E0J 1T0, ☎ 506/553-6490 ($).*

It would be a shame to be in Edmundston and miss staying and dining at **Auberge La Fief**. Rooms are warm, tasteful and inviting, and the dining room is as elegant as the classic French-with-a-Canadian-verve dinners they serve. We rank it among Atlantic Canada's best. *87 Church St, Edmundston, NB E3V 1J6, ☎ 506/735-0400, fax 506/735-0401 ($$).*

Comfort Inn has reliable lodging and offers reasonably priced packages. *5 Bateman Ave., Edmundston, NB E3V 3L1, ☎ 506/739-8361 or 800/228-5150, fax 506/737-8183 ($$).*

Motel Le Brayon has clean, tidy cabins and a restaurant with a terrace, on a lightly wooded hillside overlooking TransCanada-2. *40 des Rochers, Saint-Basile, NB E7C 2J4, ☎ 506/263-5514, fax 506/263-5462 ($-$$).*

Maple Bed & Breakfast has nicely decorated bedrooms, and their convenient location is within walking distance of the falls. *142 Main St., Grand Falls, NB E3Z 1E1, ☎ 506/473-1763 ($-$$).*

Settler's Inn has spacious modern cabins with full kitchens, screened porches, washing machines, tennis courts and free swimming at the adjacent park. A coffee shop serves light meals. *141 Main St., Plaster Rock, NB E0J 1W0, ☎ 506/356-9000 or toll free 888/356-273-4133, fax 506/356-8879 ($$)*

L'Oasis at The New Brunswick Botanical Garden serves budget lunches indoors and on a terrace above the gardens. *TCH-2 Exit 8 in Saint-Jacques, ☎ 506/735-3074 ($).*

Bel-Air has, like many restaurants in New Brunswick, a split personality. About half the menu is Chinese, the other half a mix of seafood, charcoal-grilled meats and Italian dishes. So if one of you hankers for Moo Goo Gai Pan when the other one wants pizza, you're in luck. *174 Victoria St., Edmundston, ☎ 506/735-3329 ($-$$).*

■ Camping

River Country Campground has tent and RV sites on a grassy riverbank lined by white birches. Sites are $15-17, and the park is open May through September. It has a beach, canoes rentals and river tours. *RR#2, Florenceville, NB E0J 1K0, ☎ 506/278-3700.*

Tourist Park, open mid-June through August, has campsites in an open pine forest for $12-$14, plus a pool, and trails around the small lake. Look for it at the crossroads at the bridge, behind the giant fiddlehead fern and the wooden lumberman in his canoe, both carved of wood. *Box 129, Plaster Rock, NB E0J 1W0, ☎ 506/356-6077.*

Crazy Inventor Campground is one of the many that used to be a provincial park. Private owners have kept its tidy appearance and spacious layout, with a beach, walking trails and separate picnic area. Sites with hookups are $17 ($14 for seniors), with rates dropping for multi-night stays. It's open June through early September, and you should at least stop to see some of the crazy inventions, such as a robot made of car parts. *470 Rte. 17, Saint-Leonard, NB E0L 1M0, ☎ 506/423-6815.*

The Mountains

The Appalachian Range provides eastern Canada's highest land, an area with very few roads, but uninterrupted miles of climbing, hiking, skiing and snowmobile trails. A downhill ski area and a long winter's ice cover for fishing add to the trails to make this a winter sports center. The Tobique River winds through scenic miles, with just enough whitewater to make canoeing an adventure. The Restigouche River, which shares its name with the county encompassing this region, is so legendary a fishing stream (a 90-pound salmon was caught – and released – here not long ago) that unless you know

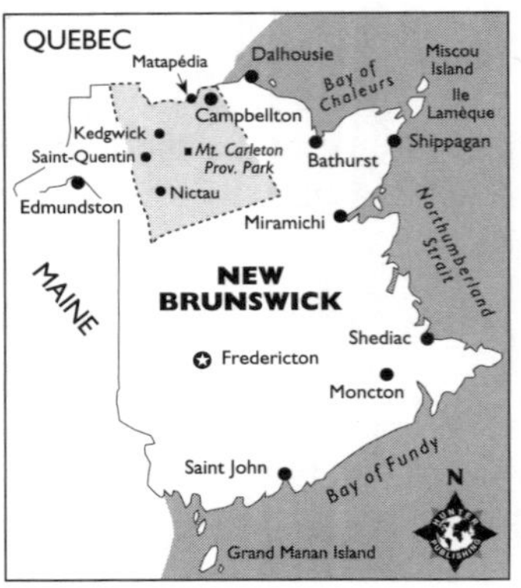

somebody who owns one of its pools it's hard to find a place to fish in it.

Geography & History

The region known as the **Restigouche** is largely wilderness, stretching west from Rte 17 to the Quebec border for about 50 miles without encountering a road or a town, and east even farther, as far as Bathurst, with only the tenuous dotted line of the seasonal Rte. 180 across it. It's rough terrain, with the Appalachian Mountains rising to more than 2,500-foot altitude at Mount Carleton.

This peak and the lakes surrounding it are part of Mount Carleton Provincial Park, a green spot in the center of a virtually empty expanse of map.

To the north the area is bounded by the Bay of Chaleurs, which begins west of Campbellton at Tide Head, and the mouth of the Restigouche River. South of Mount Carleton are more peaks and more rivers, all headwaters and tributaries of the Miramichi.

Much of the region's history can be summed up in one word: timber. It was logging country almost from the earliest days of its European settlement, and vast areas are still owned by timber companies. The Restigouche was a major transportation route for the Micmacs, and later for the logs that raced to the bay on its spring freshets. With the last of the spring log runs past, and because so few roads reach the Restigouche River, and only one town – Kedgwick River –is on it, the river is almost the sole domain of the salmon and those wealthy enough to own a piece of their spawning route.

The Battle of Restigouche, in 1760, was the last naval encounter in the Seven Years' War between the French and the British as they struggled for control of what would be eastern Canada. The French had begun their first settlement of the area in 1685, and the next wave of immigration was by Acadians expelled from Nova Scotia, who later moved on to Quebec. In the early 1800s Scottish settlers arrived, followed by more Acadians, who stayed to work on the railroads and in the growing lumber industry, which was a mainstay of the region's economy by mid-century.

Getting Around

You can approach this region from the upper St. John River Valley, either through Plaster Rock on Rte. 385 or from Saint-Leonard on Rte. 17. The latter is the more direct route if you are going straight to Campbellton, the former leads along a scenic, winding mountain road and past the entrance to Mount Carleton Provincial Park.

Campbellton, the northern gateway to this region, is also easy to reach from the east coast, via Bathurst on Rte. 11. A more direct route from Bathurst directly to Saint-Quentin, passing very close to Mount Carleton, is under construction (and has been for some time).

Plaster Rock, south of this region, but on one of only two roads that reach it from the south, is a center for fishing and other outdoor activities to its north, and a good source of information on the area between the town and Mount Carleton.

Information Sources

- Stop at the **Tourist Park**, Box 129, Plaster Rock NB E0J 1W0, ☎ 506/356-6077, open daily 9 am to 8 pm, mid-June-August.

- The information center at the northern entrance to this region is in a replica railway station at **Salmon Plaza**, Box 639, Campbellton, NB E3N 3H1, ☎ 506/789-2700, fax 506/789-7403.

- Another well-stocked center for information is at the **Sugarloaf Mountain** base lodge in Campbellton, ☎ 506/789-2367.

Adventures

Adventure and the great outdoors is what this area is all about, with its mountain peaks, legendary rivers, and miles and miles of forest untouched by road or settlement.

On Foot

Hiking In Mount Carleton Provincial Park

Mount Carleton Provincial Park has 39 miles of hiking trails, in 10 routes that range from short walks to a waterfall to climbs to the peak of the mountain itself. Before taking any trail, sign in at the park headquarters, which allows the rangers to respond more quickly to emergencies. The easiest trails are to **William's Falls** and **Pine Point**, the former a 15-minute walk through the forest and the second a one-mile trail around a point in the lake, where waterfowl are plentiful. The point is covered in a stand of red pines, regenerated after a forest fire in the early 1930s.

A little more demanding, the **Caribou Brook Trail** follows the old Indian portage between the two lakes, which connected the headwaters of the Nepisiguit and Tobique rivers, the only break in the water route that cut across the province from Bathurst to the St. John River valley. The **Mount Bailey Trail** is about four miles long, and climbs steadily through the hardwood forest along the shoulder of the mountain, where a one-mile (round trip) side trail leads to the rocky summit.

Dry Brook Trail, also classed as intermediate, crosses the divide between the waters that flow east to the Bay of Chaleurs and west, then south, to the Bay of Fundy via the St. John River. On the trail are several waterfalls, including one 30-feet high.

Two trails lead to the top of **Mount Carleton**, the easiest and shortest (2.5 miles) is from the east. It leads past an old fire tower to a ridge that leads to the open rocky summit, where you should be prepared for chilling winds on even the warmest of days. This is the highest peak in the Maritime provinces, with a view of several lakes and other mountains.

Hiking at Sugarloaf Mountain

You can also climb Sugarloaf Mountain in Campbellton, which has an elevation of almost 1,000 feet and views of the Bay of Chaleurs and Restigouche Valley. (The summit is less rewarding than some for climbers, since it has a viewing platform reached by a chairlift.) A two-mile trail circles the base of the mountain and another slightly shorter trail circles Pritchard Lake. Altogether there are 12 miles of hiking trails in Sugarloaf Park.

On Wheels

Road Biking

The back roads of this area are so sparsely trafficked that cyclists could easily mistake them for wide bike paths. One tip: if you plan to cycle along the shore of the Bay of Chaleurs, traveling from west to east will put the wind at your back, since the prevailing winds blow from the west.

Cyclists have to love a town named **Flatlands**, especially when it's in mountain country. Rte. 134 leads from Campbellton, along the mouth of the Restigouche, through Flatlands, and along the river. You can cross the bridge over the Restigouche and return on the Quebec side of the river for a double dose of good scenery.

BIKING MAP: *The province has published a very useful pamphlet with maps and detailed directions for touring this area by bicycle on public roads and streets with little through traffic. Suggested routes are described and shown on a map. For a copy of the* **Bicycle Tour Map and Guide**, *contact New Brunswick Tourism at ☎ 800/561-0123.*

At **Mount Carleton Provincial Park** is a road closed to cars but open to bicycling. It extends from the road along the shore of Lake Bathurst, passing Lake Teneriffe and Moose Bogan to the shores of Lake Nepisiguit. Another leaves from the group camping area near the entrance gate, and a trail on which bicycles are allowed makes a loop through the woods from the park headquarters. Bicycles are allowed on any of the park's roads or cross-country ski trails, but not on the hiking trails.

Mountain Biking

Mountain biking trails descend the slopes of **Sugarloaf**, where you can rent tandem mountain bikes, ☎ 506/789-2366. They also have organized mountain bike tours.

Bicycle Outfitters & Guided Tours

■ **Velo Restigouche** in Campbellton, ☎ 506/753-6194, rents bicycles for $8 an hour or $30 for eight hours. Guided tours range in price from $12 for one person for one hour to $20 each for two to five persons for a full-day trip. Tours include a support vehicle. Experienced cyclists might opt for their 35-mile ride along the abandoned rail line from Kedgwick to Campbellton, which crosses 19 brooks on the way.

■ On Water

Some of the first people to travel through this region came on water, by canoe. Long before Europeans arrived, Native Americans followed the Nepisiguit and Tobique rivers across this vast mountain wilderness. Today, you can paddle the same waters.

Canoeing & Kayaking

More than 200 miles of canoeable waters are accessible on and from the Restigouche River. The river runs through dense forests of cedar, spruce and balsam interspersed with white birch; beaver and mallards, plus an occasional osprey are common sights from the river. To run the river from Kedgwick Bridge to the Bay of Chaleurs, a 57-mile stretch which includes some whitewater rapids, takes two or three days. You can camp almost anywhere on its sandy banks.

Anyone who enjoys canoeing – or who admires fine craftsmanship – should stop in Nictau on Rte. 385 at **Miller Canoes**, ☎ 506/356-2409. In a workshop on the hill behind the house you are likely to find third-generation canoe-maker Bill Miller building fine custom canoes. You can watch as he patiently fits each piece of wood in place and see the tools with which he bends the frames and planes the sheathing for some of the most beautiful craft that ever ran a river. The sign is hard to see, so look for a mailbox with a little canoe on top, about 6 miles north of the road with a sign pointing to Tobique River Tours, and about 20 miles south of the Mount Carleton park entrance.

Centre Echo Restigouche on Rte. 265 in Kedgwick River, ☎ 506/284-2022, fax 506/284-2927, is on the banks of the Restigouche, where they rent canoes and run organized canoe trips for groups as small as four persons. Accommodations in their modern log cabins are included in some packages, camping along the river is included in others. All packages include meals. One day canoeing with lunch is $75 per person; with three meals and lodging the price is $100 per person. They also rent camping equipment. Their longer trips (four days, $200 per person) explore the waters of the Nepisiguit River, which has its headwaters in Mount Carleton

Provincial Park. Multi- , full- and half-day guided canoe excursions all require advance reservations.

Tobique River Tours in Riley Brook, ☎ 506/356-2111, rents Old Town canoes and kayaks, and provides a shuttle service on the Tobique River. They have carrying trailers, or they will meet you at your take-out with your own vehicle. Half-day canoe rentals are $17.50, full-day $30. Kayaks are $10 for half-day and $20 full-day. Most shuttle transport in the local area is $10. Those who have canoed in wilderness waters in mosquito season (which is anytime from spring thaw to the first snow) will be happy to hear that this outfitter will provide smudgepots at no charge.

Petit-Gadoo River Runs, in Nigadoo (farther along the Chaleurs coast toward Bathurst), ☎ 506/783-4553, 506/783-3649 or 506/547-4554, offers guided canoe trips on the Tobique and Restigouche rivers, as well as canoe rentals and shuttle service. A three-day excursion on the Restigouche, camping along the river is $50 per person (you provide the food) or $85 with meals and a guide. A three-day excursion on the Tobique, which runs through Plaster Rock, with a guide and food included, is $95 per person. All include transportation from Nigadoo.

Restigouche Frontier in Campbellton, ☎ 506/759-8677, fax 506/546-3739, does two- and three-day guided canoe trips on the Restigouche, including canoes, meals and camping equipment, staying at tent sites along the river, beginning at $190 per person.

Centre de Plein Air du Vieux Moulin in Saint-Quentin, ☎ 506/235-1110, also runs guided trips by canoe and kayak.

Tobique & Serpentine Camps on Rte. 385 at Riley Brook, ☎ 506/356-8351, rent canoes from their attractive cottages and the **Kedgwick Canoe and Kayak Club**, ☎ 506/284-2201, rents canoes and kayaks. In Campbellton you can rent canoes from **LeBlanc Rentals** on Boucher St., ☎ 506/753-6080.

Harbor & Bay Tours

You can explore Campbellton and the western end of the bay from the water on board ***Chaleur Phantom***, which leaves from the Dalhousie Marina, ☎ 506/684-4722 or 600/277-0688. Narrated nature cruises take you to Heron Island, Miquasha Point (a rock formation on the Gaspe coast), Arch Rock and Bon Ami Rock, covered with seabirds. The boat departs at 9 am and at 2 and 7 pm, daily from mid-May to the end of September, rain or shine; the fare is $10 for adults, $6 for children.

Fishing

Public access to salmon fishing on the Restigouche is limited to the section between Montgomery Bridge and the mouth of Jardin Brook, and on two other "Crown Reserve" sections. Daily permits are sold to both residents and non-residents.

■ On Snow

Both **Mount Carleton Provincial Park** and **Sugarloaf Park** are open in the winter for snowmobile, cross-country and snowshoeing. Real winter enthusiasts can camp at Mount Carleton. At Sugarloaf, a 1.5-mile trail beginning at the entrance to the campground is reserved for snowshoeing. A hill for tobogganing and a natural pond, lighted and groomed for ice skating, round out the park's winter sports.

Skiing

Both cross-country and downhill skiing are available at **Sugarloaf Park** in Campbellton, where some trails are lighted for night skiing. Eight alpine trails, with a maximum run of 3,500 feet, are served by a double chairlift and two T-bars. They also have a snowboard park. The 18 miles of groomed cross-country trails are mostly concentrated around the cross-country ski lodge, but one longer one circles Pritchard Lake.

Mount Carleton Provincial Park has groomed trails ranging in length from half a mile to four miles, all beginning at a heated warm-up cabin. Or you can ski on any of the 30 miles of roads, which you will be sharing with snowmobilers.

Les Montagnards Cross Country Ski Club in Campbellton, ☎ 506/759-9722, and **Club de ski de fond Husky** in Sainte-Quentin, ☎ 506/235-3253, are good sources of local cross-country ski information.

Centre de Plein Air du Vieux Moulin in Saint-Quentin, ☎ 506/235-1110, has cross-country ski trails, skating and cabin rental.

Snowmobiling

Mount Carleton Provincial Park and **Sugarloaf Park** are open in the winter for snowmobiling, with their own trails, in addition to access to the provincial trail network. Provincial trail #23 passes through the length of Mount Carleton, connecting on the east to the main trail between Bathurst and Miramichi, and on the west, via Riley Brook, to Plaster Rock and the upper St. John River valley. The 30 miles of roads inside the park are used by snowmobilers. Trails in **Sugarloaf Park** circle the base of the mountain (about two miles) and the perimeter of the park, with a total of 20 miles.

Centre Echo Restigouche in Kedgwick River, ☎ 506/284-2022, fax 506/284-2927, has year-round log cabins (with kitchens) on the banks of the Restigouche. The cabins have direct access to NB snowmobile trail #17, linking to the entire trail network.

New World Adventures in Dalhousie offers full-day snowmobile expeditions that cover trails in Quebec's Gaspe, the Restigouche River, the Appalachian Range and the Acadian coast in one day's travels. Snowmobile suits, machines and other equipment are included, along with lunch, at $260 per person, ☎ 506/684-1020, fax 506/684-5340.

For a package that includes a night's lodging with breakfast, a trail lunch, dinner, and snowmobile rental, call the **Best Western Manoir Adelaide** in Dalhousie, ☎ 506/684-1020, fax 506/684-5340. The cost, based on double occupancy, is $135 per person. A guided trip, or snowmobile suit rentals are available separately.

The local group is the **Restigouche Snowmobile Club** in Campbellton, ☎ 506/753-7956.

Dogsledding

Dogsled races are held in Nictau Village each year, and you can usually arrange to go dogsledding with the owners of **Black's Cabins** in Riley Brook. To find out about either, call Rita Black, ☎ 506/356-2429.

Cultural & Eco-Travel Experiences

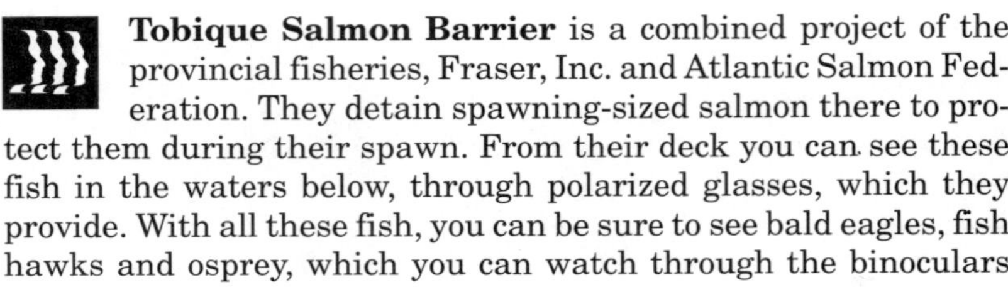

Tobique Salmon Barrier is a combined project of the provincial fisheries, Fraser, Inc. and Atlantic Salmon Federation. They detain spawning-sized salmon there to protect them during their spawn. From their deck you can see these fish in the waters below, through polarized glasses, which they provide. With all these fish, you can be sure to see bald eagles, fish hawks and osprey, which you can watch through the binoculars they also provide. The facility is free, about a mile north of Miller Canoes and 17 miles south of Mt. Carleton Provincial Park.

A rare chance to learn firsthand the crafts and traditions of the ancient Maliseet peoples, is offered as a *Day Adventure* by **Bodin's Native Crafts and Supplies** in Tobique, ☎ 506/273-4066. A two-hour workshop includes instruction and all materials for you to make your own necklace, basket or dreamcatcher. A traditional snack and beverage will be served. The program is available Tuesday-Thursday, year-round, and costs $50 per person.

One of our favorite places to visit in the Restigouche is the lumber camp at the **Kedgwick Forestry Museum** in Kedgwick, ☎ 506/284-3138. The artifacts and buildings show life in the days when crews of lumbermen worked all winter in the woods to cut the logs that would float down the Restigouche on the spring floods. An excellent audio-visual show introduces the open-air museum, a combination of early film footage and interviews with people who worked in the camps. Outside are bunkhouses, a blacksmith shop, office, storage sheds, cookhouse and a trapper's cabin, all filled with the tools and equipment used by the lumbermen, but what brings it all to life for us is that the guide is someone who remembers the camps. Rejean Bergeron's mother was a camp cook, and he worked in the camps. He was on the last log drive on the Restigouche when he was 16, in the 1960s. The museum is open in the summer, 10 am to 6 pm on weekends, 9 am to 6 pm weekdays, and costs $5 for adults, $3 over age 50, $2 for children. A campground is also on the property.

The park headquarters building at **Mount Carleton Provincial Park** has some very interesting exhibits on the Maliseets, showing how they hunted moose with a birchbark calling horn and how they speared salmon by luring them with torches at night. Other displays concern fiddlehead ferns, Maliseet basketmaking, and the origin of snowshoes. You don't have to pay park admission fees to see these; the headquarters building is close to Rte. 385, at the entrance gate, and open until 10 pm daily.

Sightseeing

New Brunswick towns tend toward giant replicas of their most famous product, from the **big cow** that welcomes you to Sussex to the **world's largest ax** in Nackawick. While all these are great fun, not all are works of art. One exception is the giant stainless steel salmon, nicknamed **Restigouche**

Campbellton's giant salmon.

Sam, on the waterfront in Campbellton. The fish seems arrested in mid-jump, its scales shimmering in the water jets from the fountain below it. The design and construction are excellent, and it would be a prized sculpture at the entrance to any art museum. It's also a handy landmark, and people in Campbellton are likely to give you directions beginning from "the fish."

To learn the story of the Restigouche area, visit the **Restigouche Regional Museum** at Adelaide and George streets in Dalhousie, ☎ 506/684-7490. Its permanent and temporary exhibits trace the development of the Micmac, Acadian, Scottish, British and Irish cultures. It's free, and open daily in the summer, with shorter hours the rest of the year.

Oliver's Museum in Saint-Jean-Baptiste-de-Restigouche focuses on the early Europeans who settled here, and features the contents of an old store, ☎ 506/284-2444.

Where To Stay & Eat

Many of the lodging and dining facilities in the area are seasonal, so it's wise to call for a reservation at any time of year and check before driving any distance to a restaurant.

Along the Chaleurs Coast

Journey's End motel, reached from Exit 415 off Highway 11, is just past the Sugarloaf Mall. *3 Sugarloaf St. West, Campbellton, NB E3N 3G9, ☎ 506/753-4121, or 800/668-4200 ($$).*

Aylesford Inn B&B is open year-round, with six comfortable rooms in a distinguished Victorian home. Homegrown vegetables highlight the fine meals served here. *8 McMillan Ave, Campbellton, NB E3N 1E9, ☎ 506/759-7672 ($$).*

Best Western Manoir Adelaide is a full-service hotel with a restaurant. *385 Adelaide St., Dalhousie, NB E0K 1B0, ☎ 506/684-1020, fax 506/684-5340 ($$).*

Campbellton Lighthouse Youth Hostel is Canada's only youth hostel in a lighthouse (but not the only lodging in one; see *PEI*, page 449), and centrally located at the waterfront. It's open in July and August, and features equipment storage, laundry facilities and on-site parking. *1 Ritchie St., Campbellton, NB E3N 3G1, ☎ 506/759-7044 ($).*

➔ *A useful feature at the Visitors Centre in Campbellton is the alcove with local menus. You can browse through these to see exactly what you'll find in nearly all the area's restaurants, from fast-food take-outs to the most elegant dining rooms.*

Sanfar Cottages & Country Kettle Dining Room serves salmon (since Tide Head is at the mouth of the Restigouche, it's only right) wrapped in parchment, and scallops on the half-shell. The tidy cottages ($) have kitchenettes, and continental breakfast is free to guests in July and August. *Rte. 134 west of Campbellton in Tide Head, ☎ 506/753-4287 ($$).*

Something Else Restaurant serves pan-fried trout, which is not so surprising, but the mango and jalepeño it's flavored with are not typical local fare. Neither are the chicken medallions with artichoke hearts and Bernaise. The menu's creative, but you can still find a hearty, satisfying clam chowder here. *City Centre Mall, in Campbellton, ☎ 506/753-2510 ($-$$).*

In the Heart of the Restigouche

Tobique River Tours has a nice log lodge, with one private room with bath upstairs and three smaller rooms with bunks and shared bath downstairs. The rate is $25 per person for either. A common room has kitchen facilities. They run canoe trips (see section on canoeing, above). *In Riley Brook, RR#1, Plaster Rock, NB E0J 1W0, ☎ 506/356-2111, fax 506/633-0706 ($).*

Tobique & Serpentine Camps have attractive rustic cabins which you can rent by the night, week or month. They sleep up to six people, in single beds; weekly rates are $300 per cottage. They are open year round. *On Rte. 385 at Riley Brook, ☎ 506/356-8351 ($-$$).*

Mount Carleton Wilderness Camps offers lakeside cottages, some with cooking facilities. Some provide bedding, some have kitchens, others are quite basic with beds where you bring your own linens. They sleep from two to 10 persons and cost from $30 to $150 a night, depending on the facilities and the size. Some share an adjacent common bath and shower room. For a booklet describing each cabin's facilities, write to Partners for Youth, Inc., 125 Hanwell Rd., Fredericton, NB E3B 2P9 or fax 506/462-0328. You will need to reserve these well ahead. *In Mount Carleton Provincial Park, ☎ 506/453-1443.*

Le Marinier serves seafood dishes. *Saint-Quentin, ☎ 506/235-3033.*

For ice cream cones, stop at **Noyes Country Store**. They sell a little bit of everything, and have since their founding in 1908. Campers can buy ice here. Open Monday-Saturday, 9 am to 5 pm. *Rte. 17 in Robinsonville.*

Centre Echo Restigouche is one of the few places you can stay on the banks of the Restigouche. Modern log cabins, with fully equipped kitchens, sleep eight people and are open year round. They rent canoes, run canoe trips, and have access to the NB snowmobile trail network. *Rte. 265 (PO Box 362), Kedgwick River, NB E0K 1C0, ☎ 506/284-2022, fax 506/284-2927 ($-$$).*

■ Camping

Mount Carleton Provincial Park has nicely maintained campgrounds and four wilderness sites along the trails. The main campground at Armstrong Brook has hookups for RVs as well as showers and a kitchen shelter, while two smaller areas of eight and nine sites respectively have no facilities except toilets. Reservations are not accepted at any of these. If you camp here, be sure to bring everything you need, since the nearest source of anything, including automobile fuel, is in Saint-Quentin, 25 miles away. The park office and entrance gates are open 7 am to 10 pm daily in the summer. *☎ 506/235-2025.*

Sugarloaf Mountain has 76 well-spaced, mowed campsites carved into the woods, most with hookups, separated from the busy heavy-use areas of the park. You can reserve some sites, but the park is usually not too crowded except during the last two weeks of July. A number of recreation facilities are available, including alpine slides, tennis and inline skating. An activities program schedules walks, crafts and events for children throughout the summer. Tent sites are $15, or $14 for seniors; fully-serviced sites are $20, $17 for seniors. Monthly rates are $200-$325. *Campbellton, ☎ 506/789-2366 or 506/789-2386.*

Kedgwick Park has serviced and unserviced campsites, as well as attractive cottages. An outdoor center provides guides for canoe trips on the Restigouche and other activities. *At the Kedgwick Forestry Museum, Rte. 17 (PO Box 224), Kedgwick, NB E0K 1C0, ☎ 506/284-3138.*

The Acadian Coast

Golden beaches and clear waters warm enough for comfortable swimming mark the Acadian summers. Marshes and miles of uninterrupted bog provide nesting sites and migration stops for waterfowl and songbirds and the rivers run with fish. In winter the landscape is covered with the province's highest snowfalls, and the Bay of Chaleurs freezes to extend the white world across to the shores of Quebec's Gaspe Peninsula. Snowmobiles seem as common as cars, dogsleds travel through white forests, and you can buy fresh smelt caught through the ice on the Bay.

Geography & History

The Bay of Chaleurs separates New Brunswick from the Gaspe Peninsula, and along the western end its southern shore lie a string of beaches, backed by a narrow strip of settlement before the vast northern interior wilderness begins. Beaches continue east of Bathurst, where the Acadian Peninsula starts, sweeping upward between the Bay and the Gulf of St. Lawrence until it ends in Miscou Island. South of Miscou, the shore is protected by a ribbon of barrier islands as it drops to Miramichi Bay, at the mouth of the Miramichi River.

The character of this coastal area is distinctly French. For the most part they are not the French of nearby Quebec, but are descendants of the Acadians who were expelled from their farms in Nova Scotia in 1755. They moved here to begin anew, fishing, farming, and harvesting the peat that forms deep layers throughout much of the region. Signs, menus and conversation are likely to be in French, but this is bi-lingual New Brunswick, where the word "bi-lingual" means not that two different languages are spoken by the different people, but that both languages are taught in school and used in everyday life. If *merci* is the limit of your French, don't worry. They can change to English here in mid-sentence – and without making you feel language-disadvantaged.

Getting Around

You can reach the area from the north by Rte. 11, a continuation of Quebec Rte. 132 from Mont-Joli to the border near Campbellton, and from northwestern New Brunswick, by Rte. 17, which leaves TransCanada-2 south of Edmundston and also goes to Campbellton. Most visitors arrive from the south, either from Fredericton via Rte. 8 along the Miramichi, or from Moncton and the Nova Scotia border by Rte. 11.

Once in the region, you can follow Rte. 11 along the coast of the peninsula or cut across the sparsely-settled interior on Rte. 8, by far the fastest way to reach the north coast. Most arrive by car, except in the winter, when many visit the area on the vast network of snowmobile trails. Hotels and cabins are connected to the main trails by their own access trails; one, the Atlantic Host in Bathurst, lies right on the main trail, at its intersection with Rtes. 8 and 11.

Information Sources

■ Information is available from **Association Touristique de la Peninsule Acadienne**, Case Postale 5626, Caraquet, NB E1W 1B7, ☎ 506/727-6622.

■ The **Tourist Information Center** is on Rte. 11 (boulevard St-Pierre) and open daily in the summer from 10 am to 8 pm.

■ For information on the Chaleurs coast, contact **Tourisme Chaleur**, CP 89, Pointe-Verte, NB E0B 2H0, ☎ 506/783-1973.

■ You will find other local information offices, clearly marked from the main roads, in **Neguac** (☎ 506/776-8907), **Bathurst** (☎ 506/548-0418), and **Shippagan** (☎ 506/336-3013), and at Atlas Park in **Pointe-Verte**.

Adventures

On Foot

More than 100 km of walking trails have been created from former CN railway routes, stretching uninterrupted from Tracadie-Sheila to Grand Anse, with a side trail to the tip of Miscou Island. The trails intersect at Inkerman Ferry. In the summer a Trail Patrol is on hand to answer questions and insure safety for trail users, who include cyclists as well as walkers. Rest areas, picnic tables and signs interpreting local history and wildlife are in process. Because of the terrain, some stretches of trail between Shippagan and Miscou are along the edge of the road.

Overlooking Bathurst from across the bay, **Daley Point Reserve** is a low waterside area with five walking trails through its 100 acres of fields, low woods and marshes, and an observation deck where you can see birds in the saltmarshes below. Names of the trails give a clue to their habitats: the Field Trail explores former farmland in the process of reverting to forest, the Saltmarsh Trail is a boardwalk for most of its length, and the Warbler Trail passes through alders and willows filled with songbirds. The most demanding is the White Pine Path, through a woodland of early stage woodlands, with birch, spruce, cedar and poplar along with white pine. Thousands of Canada geese stop here during their fall migration. Daley Point is one of only four saltmarshes in the world with the rare Maritime ringlet butterfly. The reserve's less attractive (except to the birds, who find them quite tasty) winged wildlife are its abundant mosquitoes, so be prepared. From Caraquet, leave Route 11 in Janeville and Promenade Carron along the shore. From Bathurst, turn left onto Promenade Carron from Bridge St. Signs point the way.

Another area rich in birdlife is **Miscou Island**, beyond Lamèque at the easternmost end of the region. The bogs and hundreds of lakes on the island were left by the retreating glacier, and attract resident birds to nest and migrating waterfowl to stop en route. The entire island is a stopover, with over 250 breeding and migratory species reported.

One of the bogs has a boardwalk with interpretive signs explaining the natural history of the island and the life of a bog. Climb **Miscou Lighthouse**, built in 1856, for a wide-ranging view before walking along the beach to the point to see the waters of the Bay of Chaleurs meet those of the Northumberland Strait. The sandy beach becomes a shingle of rounded stones washed here by the tides, but the walking is not difficult.

Ile-aux-Foins, off the east coast at Neguac, has hiking trails and boardwalks across the marsh, which is also a bird sanctuary. Follow rue Joseph from rue Principale (Rte. 11) to reach this island, where a municipal park also provides swimming and picnic facilities.

At **Beresford**, the newly opened **municipal park** includes a boardwalk over the saltmarsh with other trails and an observation tower for viewing 54 bird species and the butterflies that frequent the marshes. An interpretation center explains the environment.

■ On Wheels

Sentiers Peninsule Acadienne is an association created to reclaim the abandoned CN railway routes, creating three separate level paths for bicycling and walking between Tracadie-Sheila, Grand Anse and Miscou Island. The trails intersect at Inkerman Ferry, where a rest area provides picnic tables and information. Some stretches of trail between Shippagan and Miscou are along the edge of the road, but the rest of the route passes through woods, fields, farmland, saltmarshes and bogs. For information, or to join the Trail Club, contact Sentiers Peninsule Acadienne at ☎ 506/727-4199.

A bridge has replaced the poky little red cable ferry that until very recently took cars to Miscou Island, beyond Lamèque off the eastern tip of the peninsula, but the island roads are still uncrowded by cars. The island is flat and perfect for bicycling, but be sure to bring a lunch, since eateries are few.

➲ **BICYCLE TOURING INFORMATION:** *The province has published an excellent pamphlet with maps and detailed directions for touring this area by bicycle using public streets and roads that have minimal through traffic. Suggested routes include a 31 km circle around the Maisonnette Peninsula near Caraquet, beginning at the Acadian Historical Village, and a circle tour of Lamèque Island. For a copy of the* Bicycle Tour Map and Guide, *contact New Brunswick Tourism at ☎ 800/561-0123.*

Guided Bicycle Tours

■ For a guided bicycle tour of Caraquet, including bike and helmet rental and a snack, contact **T.F. Sport Impact**, 270 boul. St-Pierre Ouest, Caraquet, ☎ 506/727-2811. Tours are $25 per person and begin daily, from mid-June through August, at the Carrefour de la Mer, the local center for the province's *Day Adventure* program, through which you can reserve by calling 800/704-3966. The tour will feature local history, folklore and Caraquet's relation with the sea. T.F. Sport Impact also rents bicycles from its shop.

■ **Padek** at Camping Shippagan, ☎ 506/336-3960, can arrange bicycle tours throughout the area.

On Water

Beaches & Swimming

Miscou Island has some of the province's finest beaches, and even with the new bridge to speed up access, these natural beaches and dunes are seldom crowded. To find one, follow any road with "Beach" in its title, or go to the lighthouse at the far end. Adrien Gionet Beach, on Rte. 113, has changing facilities and a snack bar.

To enjoy the waters of the Bay of Chaleurs for swimming, look for **Youngall Beach Park** on Youngall Drive, off Rt. 134, 3 miles north of Bathurst. The park is free and has changing facilities. Youngall is pronounced like the rental trucks: U-Haul. Beaches line both the north shore along the Bay and the east shore along the Northumberland Strait. **Jacquet River Park** sits on a bluff above a sand and gravel beach, where there are full swimming facilities and a small campground. Between there and Belledune are

> **LOCAL LORE:** *Perhaps the most unique experience on the waters of the Bay of Chaleurs is one you can't plan ahead: seeing the ghost ship of* Chaleurs, *a phantom ship in flames, so real that those who see its fiery masts and sails report it to the Coast Guard as a burning ship. This phenomenon, probably caused by reflected heat waves, is said to be the ghost of a French ship burned and sunk in the Battle of Restigouche in 1760. Another version says it's a pirate ship that went aground off the rocks here. Take your pick. Reports of the ship come from the entire length of the shore from Campbellton to Bathurst. It doesn't happen frequently, so we suggest a window table at La Fine Grobe sur-mer (see* Where To Stay & Eat, *below) as a good place to wait.*

sand dunes, and **Eel River Bar**, near Charlo, is a mile-long barrier sandbar with freshwater swimming on one side and saltwater on the other. **Beresford Beach** is backed by a long sand dune. A fine beach, but often almost deserted, is at **Anse Bleue** just off Rte. 11 on Rte. 303 near Caraquet. Or follow Rte. 303 farther to the protected beach at **Maisonnettte Park**. Youngall is the only beach on the north shore with a lifeguard; most require a modest parking or admission fee.

If the calm waters of the Bay of Chaleurs aren't exciting enough for you, head for the eastern coast, where the more open waters of the Gulf of St. Lawrence create bigger waves. Beaches at **Val-Comeau** and **Neguac** are two of the largest on the east coast, with a full mile of dune-backed white sand at **Val Comeau Provincial Park** and some fine birding habitats to explore both there and at **Neguac Park**, which is also known for its excellent windsurfing.

Canoeing & Kayaking

The **Nepisiguit River** is a favorite place for paddling, with wooded banks and salmon swimming under the canoe, but lakes and even the bay provide good canoeing waters, too. **Petit-Gadoo River Runs** in Nigadoo, ☎ 506/783-4553, 506/783-3649 or 506/547-4554, offers a variety of guided canoe trips, as well as canoe rentals and shuttle service. A three-hour excursion on a wilderness lake, with guide, instruction, transportation, canoe and equipment is $30 per person. A full day guided trip on the Nepisiguit River, with all equipment, instruction, transport and a seafood lunch is $55; two days is $75.

If you would like to try a canoe in saltwater, Petit-Gadoo guides can also take you to Bathurst Harbour to explore the littoral of the Bay of Chaleurs in protected waters. Plan to begin your day there with the splendid sunrise views from the water. The bay trip is two hours and costs $20. Rentals of Old Town canoes begin at $10 for an evening; half day rentals are $20, full-day is $30. Rental and shuttle for two days on a river starts at $45 per person.

For a kayaking trip on the Bay of Chaleurs, contact **Inch Arran Expeditions** in Dalhousie, ☎ 506/684-7363. A 2½-hour paddle at $25 per adult, $15 for a child, includes instruction, all equipment, and explanations of the environment you'll be paddling through. Trips explore the sandy shore, with historic sites and a Micmac Reserve at Eel River. Dalhousie is at the point where the bay narrows, and the scenic coast of the Gaspe, in Quebec, is only a short distance away.

Shippagan sits inside a deep protected bay, with islands you can explore in a handmade Inuit-style kayak. **Padek** at Camping Shippagan, ☎ 506/336-3960, takes you through the Chaleur Islands after instruction on handling these ancestors of the modern kayak. You'll also learn about the bird and plant life of the shores you explore, and stop for a snack on one of the islands. Three-hour paddles are $40, or you can take an overnight trip.

At Caraquet you can rent kayaks from **Tours Kayaket**, at 51 boul. St-Pierre Est, ☎ 506/727-6309. A single kayak is $12 an hour, $30 a half-day and $45 a day. Doubles are double the price. Or you can join a group for a guided tour with a snack stop for $45.

Harbor & Bay Tours

From Caraquet you can go on whale-watching trips aboard 12-passenger rigid-hulled boats originally designed for sea rescues. These are comfortable and protect passengers from the waves at the high speeds these boats travel. The most commonly seen whale is the humpback, but blue whales, nearly twice the size of humpbacks, are found here, along with minke, fin and pilot whales. Three-hour trips with **Une-Mer-d'Adventures!**, ☎ 800/704-3966 or 506/727-2727, are $50 for adults, $30 for children under 12. You can tour the Gaspe shore to Perce Rock or take an evening cruise along the Acadian coast with them as well. Boats are in the water from mid-June to mid-September.

La Rose des Vents sails the schooner *Marquise* from the same quai in Caraquet. Passengers on this 56-foot sailing vessel will learn how sails work with the wind to propel a ship, and can help hoist the sails. Four-hour cruises, including lunch on board, cost $55 for adults and $28 for children, and leave at 10 am daily from mid-June to mid-September, ☎ 506/727-3841 or 800/704-3966.

To explore the western end of the bay, take a cruise on ***Chaleur Phantom*** from the Dalhousie Marina, ☎ 506/684-4722 or 600/277-0688. Named for the legendary ghost ship, this very real boat specializes in narrated nature cruises to Heron Island, Miquasha Point (a rock formation on the Gaspe coast), Arch Rock and Bon Ami Rock, interesting for its seabirds. Heron Island and the Chaleur shore are particularly rich in birdlife. The boat departs at 9 am and at 2 and 7 pm, daily from mid-May to the end of September, rain or shine; the fare is $10 adult, $6 for children.

Diving

Atlas Park on Rte. 134 in Pointe-Verte, ☎ 506/783-3717, offers scuba diving in crystal clear water of a 100-foot deep quarry. On a Sunday in mid-July the park presents an Introduction to Scuba Diving program. The park is open weekend afternoons from mid-May to mid-June, and daily 10 am to 10 pm from mid-June through August. In the winter, the park offers scuba diving under the ice.

Le Club des Plongeurs les Oursins (Diving Club les Oursins) at Anse-Bleue, ☎ 506/732-5238, has programs for experienced divers and for those with no experience at all. Two shipwrecks off the coast provide interesting dive sites, and a boat can take you out to a diving bell for underwater observation. The club sponsors a diving jamboree in mid July.

In nearby Caraquet, Hurricane boats at **Une-Mer-d'Adventures!** are equipped to take divers, ☎ 800/704-3966 or 506/727-2727.

Fishing

The Nepisiguit River flows northeast to its mouth in the Bay of Chaleurs at Bathurst, and is another success story for the salmon enhancement program. It is now a scheduled salmon river, so you'll need a guide from **Petit-Gadoo River Runs** in Nigadoo, ☎ 506/783-4553, 506/783-3649 or 506/547-4554.

The lake at **Atlas Park** on Rte. 134 in Point-Verte, ☎ 506/783-3717, is stocked with trout, and you can fish there with your equipment or theirs. A special package program includes fishing for trout (all equipment is provided), a paddleboat excursion, and a trout dinner, where you can enjoy the fruits of your fishing experience. The package cost is $15 per adult, $10 per child. The park is open weekend afternoons from mid-May to mid-June, and daily 10 am to 10 pm from mid-June through August.

Ile Caramer, a 45-foot diesel-powered boat, takes passengers fishing for cod and mackerel (with equipment provided) or on sunset tours along the Caraquet coast. Three fishing trips a day leave at 11 am, 1 pm and 3 pm from June through mid-September. These trips are shorter than deep-sea fishing excursions, but give a taste of the saltwater fishing experience. Boats leave from the *Day Adventure* Centre at Carrefours de la Mer in Caraquet, ☎ 506/727-0813 or 800/704-3966.

For a fishing tour on the high seas, you can travel on the 40-foot boat of **Albain Landry**, which leaves from the quai in Anse-Bleue just west of Caraquet, ☎ 506/732-5232.

Chaleur Phantom at the Dalhousie Marina, ☎ 506/684-4722 or 600/277-0688, takes passengers on deep-sea fishing trips in the morning, with tackle and bait supplied, at $15 each or $20 per couple.

■ On Snow & Ice

This is winter carnival country, with a schedule that begins at the Beresford Groundhog Festival in late January and early February, where you'll see elaborate ice sculptures. The next weekend is Pointe-Verte's ***Carnaval des Moules*** (Mussels Festival), followed by **Snowarama** and finishing with Bathurst's **Snowbear Winter Carnival** the last weekend in February.

Atlas Park in Pointe-Verte is open Friday and Saturday evenings and Saturday and Sunday afternoons in the winter, offering a variety of winter outdoor sports. On Friday and Saturday evenings their licensed snack bar serves steamed mussels. A day pass for use of any of their facilities is $2.50 for an adult, $1.50 for a child, ☎ 506/783-3717.

Auberge D'Anjou in Petit-Rocher, ☎ 506/783-0587 (see also *Where To Stay & Eat*, below), offers a winter outdoor weekend package that includes two nights lodging, breakfasts, a boxed lunch, and dinner in their restaurant (very nice to come home to), plus your choice of snowshoeing, ice fishing, a sleigh ride, cross-country skiing, skating of sledding – the Acadian Coast has it all.

Skiing & Snowshoeing

Cross-country ski clubs make sure that trails are well-maintained in this region of heavy and frequent snowfalls. In Bathurst, the **Snow Bear Cross-Country Ski Club**, Golf St., ☎ 506/548-0437 (548-0410 out of season), has four trails with a total of 23 km; **Rough Waters Cross-Country Ski Club** on Rough Waters Drive, ☎ 506/546-9693, has 15 km. Both have canteens and organized activities. In Pointe-Verte, Atlas Park has a six-km cross-country trail. Open Friday and Saturday evenings, and Saturday and Sunday afternoons, they provide free portable lights for cross-country skiers. Ski rentals are $5 a day.

Auberge Les Amis de la Nature in nearby Robertville, ☎ 506/783-4797 or 800/327-9999, offers winter packages that include two nights lodging, breakfasts, dinner with wine (they specialize in organic foods from their own farm) and cross-country skiing for $249 a couple.

La Fine Grobe sur Mer in Nigadoo combines fine dining with a chance to work off some of the calories by skiing the cross-country trails by the river or walking along the shore of the Bay of Chaleurs. The package, at $170 per person, includes two nights lodging, breakfasts, fondue and a full dinner in chef George Frachon's memorable dining room overlooking the frozen bay. You'll also get a discount on your wine (the list is excellent and moderately priced) and a chance to relax and talk with this fascinating chef/artist as you toast your toes in front of the fireplace, ☎ 506/783-3138, fax 506/783-4071.

Learn about the ancient peoples of this area as you showshoe on their trails with Micmac folklorist and historian Gilbert Sewell. In a half-day adventure divided between a snowshoe walk and a program of drumming and chanting, you will learn winter survival skills practiced here for thousands of years, and have a chance to sample traditional foods. The cost is $25 ($10 for those under age 16), and you can reserve through the *Day Adventures* program or directly with **Mui'n Adventures** in Pabineau Falls, near Bathurst, ☎ 506/548-1017.

Snowmobiling

In the heart of a network of 450 km of well-groomed trails, and with the province's highest snowfall, Bathurst is a center for snowmobiling. **Atlantic Host Inn** (☎ 506/548-3335 or 800/898-9292) is the province's only hotel located directly on the trail network. Its owner, Keith DeGrace, is an avid snowmobile enthusiast himself.

On/off loading ramps, a fueling area, heated repair bays, pressure wash, electric plug-ins, and equipment and machine rentals make the Atlantic Host a popular headquarters for this sport.

When we were there during a March blizzard, we were particularly impressed by the concern of the entire staff for the safety of those still on the trails. The owner himself left the motel at the height of the storm, about 10 pm, and was out looking for guests who had not checked in as expected. When he returned several hours later, having found the missing riders safe in a cabin along the trail, the entire place – guests, staff and locals in the busy lounge – heaved a sigh of relief and went to bed. At daybreak, with the storm finally subsided, the owner was in the lobby giving trail directions and advice to departing guests.

Atlantic Host offers snowmobile packages that include lodging, use of the snowmobilers' hospitality suite, storage and maintenance facilities, and trail breakdown assistance, for $62 a night for a double room. A guided three-hour trip with snowmobile and equipment, as well as lunch on the trail, is $85 per person from **Canada East Tours**, located at the Atlantic Host Inn, ☎ 506/548-3335 or 800/898-9292.

Danny's Inn and Conference Center has lodging packages for snowmobilers at about $65 a couple. Danny's maintains a groomed trail connecting the hotel to the provincial trail network. They are on Peters Ave (PO Box 180), Bathurst, NB E2A 3Z2, ☎ 506/546-6621.

Visiting snowmobilers may want to contact **Nepisiguit Sport Lodge** south of Bathurst, ☎ 506/548-9174. This very active snowmobile club maintains 350 miles of trails and organizes events throughout the winter, including the Snowarama and the Atlantic CAN-AM Challenge, the main racing event in the Maritime provinces.

In other parts of the region, lodging packages for snowmobilers are offered by **Manoir Adelaide**, Adelaide St., Dalhousie, NB E0K 1B0, ☎ 506/684-5681; **Heron's Nest Cottages**, Box 50, Charlo, NB E0B 1M0, ☎ 506/684-3766, fax 506/684-3850; **Motel Boudreau**, PO Box 3359, **Tracadie-Sheila**, NB E1X 1G5, ☎ 506/395-2244 or 800/563-2242; and **Motel Beauséjour** and **Chez Raymond Restaurant**, PO Box 74, Neguac, NB E03 1S0, ☎ 506/776-8718, fax 506/776-5462.

Sport Action 2000 in Caraquet (☎ 506/727-5567) offers a package that includes one night's lodging with breakfast, a snowmobile, equipment and insurance, instruction and a guided tour of the Acadian coast and forests at $295 per couple sharing a snowmobile, $260 each with two machines. Or you can combine snowmobiling with ice fishing on a full day 60-mile excursion, stopping to cook the catch of the day for lunch. Depending on the season, this will be smelt or trout, but either way, nothing tastes as good as lunch you've caught fresh and cooked outdoors.

New World Adventures in Dalhousie offers full-day snowmobile expeditions that combine Quebec's Gaspe, the Restigouche River, the Appalachian Range and the Acadian coast into one jam-packed experience. Snowmobile suits, machines and other equipment are included, as well as lunch, for $260 per person, ☎ 506/684-1020, fax 506/684-5340.

Dogsledding

With all this snow, Bathurst is also a prime center for dogsledding, and two outfitters maintain kennels and sleds for guided excursions. You will drive your own team, but with plenty of help and instruction from the upbeat and enthusiastic owners of these teams of huskies, which can hardly contain themselves to do what they enjoy most – running through the snowy woods with a sled in tow.

Part of the team at Teagues Lake Dogsledding.

Rather than duplicate each other's programs, the two outfitters below offer different experiences. We can't decide between them, so we schedule a trip with each whenever we're in Bathurst in the winter.

Frank Vienneau at **Northeast Outfitters** gives everybody their own space on the trail. He is usually just out of sight ahead, the support snowmobile well out of earshot behind, so all you see or hear is your own team and the pristine snow-filled woods. Halfway through the trip the teams get a rest (although they don't seem to want to stop running) at a cozy cabin in the woods where Frank also takes guests on overnight dogsledding excursions. A thermos of hot coffee and a tin of the world's best cookies, baked by Frank's wife, appear and quickly disappear. To sled with Frank Vienneau, call Northeast Outfitters at ☎ 506/545-6394.

To drive a team of Malamutes, call Bob and Ann Metzler of **Teagues Lake Dogsledding**, ☎ 506/548-9136, fax 506/548-9757. The Metzlers' destination is a wilderness lake, where you stop for a warming bowl of soup and Ann's home-baked blueberry muffins around a roaring outdoor campfire. On the trail, they keep the sleds in sight of one another. With either outfitter, expect to pay from $65 for a half-day trip to $150 for a full day.

GOING TO THE DOGS: *Although each winter is different, dogsledding season usually lasts from mid-December to mid-April. Dog teams and onlookers from all over gather in the area when the Bathurst Mushers Club has its annual Dog Sled Race in late January.*

ON-THE-TRAIL LEARNING

The enthusiasm of five handsome huskies, literally jumping up and down in place in their excitement to be off and running, would have been more contagious if we'd been more evenly matched. They knew where they were going and how to get there in the fastest, most exciting way possible. This was, I feared (and rightly), at top speed, with or without me hanging on and trying to remain upright. *I*, on the other mittened hand, had never actually driven my own sled. I'd been a happy passenger once, in Finland, sitting on the sled at ground level, wrapped in woolly blankets while someone who spoke the same language as the dogs did the mushing.

The differences were apparent at once. First, of course, was the view – the old saying is right: unless you're the lead husky, the view's pretty much the same. The view was better standing up. How to stay standing up turned out to be the problem, as I released my tether and my team and I took off at just slightly under mach-1. I think we were going through a low pine forest, but the trees were moving so fast they could have been a herd of moose for all I could see. On the back of the sled, where I was, there's no platform to stand on; each boot is, supposedly, planted firmly on a runner, which allows the musher to steer by shifting weight from one to the other. But when you're having trouble keeping boots on two narrow slippery sticks, balance and steering are little niceties easily lost.

The answer seemed to be to slow the team down, but using the brake required lifting one foot. That changed my already precarious balance and that of the sled, and caused it to go sliding off the trail at an alarming angle which made keeping the other foot on its runner almost impossible. Forget that. Meanwhile I yelled things to my dogs, who clearly spoke only French and misinterpreted anything I said to mean "mush" or "can't you guys move it any faster?" They yipped back agreeably and sped up. When I finally decided that this had to stop – or I would just fall off and be left there in the snow by a team that would continue on happily right across the frozen Bay of Chaleurs and into Quebec without me, I did the only possible thing. I hung on for dear life and jumped on the brake with both feet.

Bad move. The sled stopped and, being tied to the sled, the dogs stopped. I didn't, and narrowly missed becoming lead dog myself.

A few tips ahead of time may save you a similar ignominy. First, if, like me, you don't love high speeds, mention it to your outfitter. And second, tell him how much you weigh. These nice New Brunswick gentlemen would never ask a lady's weight, especially one who's wrapped in so many layers of down and insulation that she looks like the broad side of a barn. So if you're a tall lightweight like me, they'll over-estimate. I had, it turned out, one dog too many for my combined weight and ineptitude. One husky fewer and a reminder about how to slow down by dragging my heels, and I was off and running at a kinder, gentler pace. I could actually identify trees as I passed. – *Barbara Radcliffe Rogers*

Sliding Hills & Sleigh Rides

Sliding hills are maintained by **Snow Bear** (☎ 506/548-0437) and **Les Joyeux Copains** (☎ 506/783-2959), cross-country ski clubs in Bathurst and Petit-Rocher respectively; Atlas Park has a sliding hill as well. If you prefer to have a horse, instead of gravity, pulling your sled, sleigh rides are offered in Pointe-Verte by **Remi Guitard**, ☎ 506/783-8985.

Skating, Diving & Ice Fishing

The frozen pond at **Atlas Park** becomes a giant skating rink in the winter and both **Snowbear** (☎ 506/548-0437) and **Les Joyeux Copains** (☎ 506/783-2959) cross-country clubs have lighted skating rinks at their chalets. Indoor skating is available at the rinks in the **K.C. Irving Regional Centre in Bathurst**, ☎ 506/547-0410. Family skating on Sunday afternoons and Thursday evenings is $2 each with a maximum of $5 per family; adult skating Wednesday and Sunday evenings is $3, teen skating on Saturday evening is $2, children's skating on Saturday afternoon is $2 and senior skating on Monday, Wednesday and Friday mornings is $1. Noon-hour skating on Monday, Wednesday and Friday is open to adults only, at $3 each.

If you enjoy watching ice sports, the Centre also has figure skating competitions, ice shows, hockey, and the Scottish sport of curling. The **Groundhog Carnival** in Beresford includes a curling tournament.

If being under the ice sounds like fun, go to **Atlas Park**, where you can scuba dive in the quarry hole for $6 a day. See *On Water*, above. To try your luck at ice fishing, join **Sport Action 2000** for a guided snowmobile and fishing trip. See *Snowmobiling*, page 159, for their contact information.

■ On Horseback

Les Ecuries Blanchard, in the village of Blanchard near Caraquet, ☎ 506/727-6803, offers horseback riding excursions with guides. To reserve a mount, contact Les Ecuries office, open between 9 am and 7 pm daily.

Cultural & Eco-Travel Experiences

A great part of the cultural attraction of the area stems from its rich Acadian French past – and present. Caraquet is 97% Francophone, and you can join in celebrating the town's French-ness at its annual Acadian Festival in mid-August, highlighted by the Blessing of the Fleet. Caraquet's harbor is still active, and even more colorful than usual on this occasion.

Nearby Shippagan's waterfront is even larger, with an active fishing fleet which, from early May until mid-summer, returns each day to unload (and sell to those who meet them at the wharves) their catch of crabs. The **Blessing of the Fleet** is on the third Sunday of July, and as lively as Caraquet's.

Smaller **fishing wharves** at Pointe-Verte, Petit-Rocher, Salmon Beach and Stonehaven are good places to buy fresh seafood, too. Look for lobster during May and June, scallops from May through October, and mussels in the winter. You will also see signs for fresh smelt, although you can't buy them at the wharves during the winter, when local people catch them through the ice. Check at the wharves for a fishing boat willing to take you out for a day to watch them at work. It's much more fun – and more interesting – than a tour on a cruise boat.

For more views of local fishing, take Rte. 113 from Shippagan to the islands of Lamèque and Miscou. At Pigeon Cove, on the eastern side, you'll find a small fishing harbor filled with brightly painted boats. Just before you get to the harbor, in the town itself, stop to look at the old capstans that used to haul boats ashore. Where the road makes an elbow turn to the left, follow the lane straight ahead, past the fence. Nearer the harbor, you'll see peat being harvested.

With the decline of the ocean fisheries, the Atlantic provinces have looked to cultivating their own seafood, especially salmon and shellfish. Caraquet has become a center of oyster farming, and the Caraquet oyster is recognized as one of the best, for its white flesh and delicate flavor. The **Centre d'Interpretation de l'Industrie Huîtrière** in Caraquet has a program explaining their culture.

The tiny wooden **Chapel of Sainte-Anne-du-Bocage**, west of Caraquet on Rte. 11, has only six pews and was founded in memory of the Acadian settlers. The Source is a water fountain where local people go for a drink at sunset. The chapel is open daily 9 am to 9 pm, and is the site of a pilgrimage on the third week of July each year. On August 15, you may find special religious observances in French areas for the **Feast of the Assumption**, the national fête of Acadians.

For an enjoyable immersion in the world of the early Acadian settlers, visit **Village Historique Acadien**, on Rte. 11 west of Caraquet, ☎ 506/727-3467. This living museum of 42 buildings features interpreters in period costumes going about the daily activities, trades, and traditional amusements of Acadia's town and home life in the 1800s. The village is a good place to see how the clever system of gated dikes was used by Acadians to farm tidal lands here and in Nova Scotia. The Village Restaurant serves Acadian specialties. In July, ***Chez Ti-Toine*** is a dinner theater that combines a meal of Acadian dishes with song and dance (expect audience participation) for $35. You'll catch the humor and enjoy the music even if you don't speak French. Reserve ahead by calling the museum directly.

> ➔ **FOR CHILDREN:** *The children's program at Village Historique Acadien allows visiting youngsters to become part of a village "family" for a day, dressed in a traditional costume; the $16 fee includes lunch, an authentic Acadian meal that the children help prepare. English speakers are introduced as a "cousin from the States." Although parents do not take part in the program, most enjoy following the activities during the day (from 9 am to 4 pm) to photograph their children in costume as they play old-fashioned games or learn traditional crafts and skills. Reserve a place for your child – ages eight-16 – by calling the museum or through the* Day Adventures *program.*

The village is open daily, June through early September, 10 am to 6 pm; after that, through early October, 10 am to 5 pm daily. Admission is $8 for adults, $4.50 for children ages six-18, $6 for students over 18 and seniors; half-price from early September through early October.

For a more traditional museum view of early Acadian life, visit the **Musée Acadien**, 15 boul. St-Pierre Est, PO Box 292, Caraquet, NB E1W 1B7, ☎ 506/727-1713. Two floors of exhibits show the daily lives of Acadians from their arrival in 1755 until the early 1900s. An interactive computer helps interpret the exhibits. As at the Acadian Village, most of the artifacts in the museum were donated by local families – often valued heirlooms – in order to create a record of their ancestors' lives for the whole community to share. Admission is $3 for adults and $2 for seniors; children are free. Open Sunday-Friday noon to 5 pm, Saturday 10 am to 5 pm.

The First Nation at Eel River Bar near Dalhousie is in the process of creating an **Aboriginal Heritage Garden,** with examples of plants used by the Micmacs and others for medicine, food, textiles and ceremonial uses. The garden's purpose is to help modern Indians and others understand the deep relationship between the native peoples and the native plants, as well as to record and research the traditional uses of plants while the knowledge is still alive. Interactive displays are planned and visitors are welcome during the garden's development. The garden is at 11 Main St., Eel River Bar First Nation, ☎ 800/3-WIGWAMS or fax 506/684-6238.

Lamèque, an island east of Shippagan, is the scene of a major **International Festival of Baroque Music** in mid-July, with artists from all over the world performing. For a schedule and tickets, contact the festival at C.P. 644, Lamèque, NB E0B 1V0, ☎ 506/344-2296.

The **Aquarium and Marine Centre**, Route 113, Shippagan, ☎ 506/336-3013, mixes the human and natural history of the sea in a nicely presented series of displays and interactive exhibits. You can stand in the wheelhouse of a state-of-the-art fishing boat and learn about fishing rivalries that began in the 11th century, or watch fascinating native fish species in giant tanks. Smaller tanks present small species of fish and other sea life up close. At 11 am and 4 pm the seals have lunch and dinner, a show you're sure to enjoy. Admission is $5.50 for adults; $2.25 for children ages six-18; family, $10.70. The center is open daily, 10 am to 6 pm, May through September.

Pokeshaw Provincial Park has a dramatic sea stack, a giant piece of shoreline that was cut off and made into an island by the sea's constant abuse. From the lookout you can see the thousands of cormorants that cover the entire crown of the stack. You can see even the fledglings clearly with binoculars. From the far left end of the fence you can see a point with a round hole worn through the rock by the sea. At low tide you can walk to the base of the sea stack from the beach below the observation point. The park is open for picnics 9 am to 9 pm daily; go at sunset for fine views of the stack silhouetted against the evening sky.

To see blue herons, scan the marshlands along Rte. 134 between Jacquet River and Charlo, or take a boat to **Heron Island**, where many other species nest or rest.

As rivers drop from the inland mountains, you'll find two waterfalls near Bathurst. Follow Rte. 430 about seven miles to find **Pabineau Falls**, where the Nepisiguit River cuts through a bed of dark rock, with fractures so geometrical they almost look like large building stones. Look for salmon jumping from level to level in the fall. You're likely to meet local families picnicking on the flat rocks.

Heading east from Bathurst on Rte. 180 for about four miles (seven km), you'll find **Tetagouche Falls** in South Tetagouche. A higher waterfall than Pabineau, this one drops into a gorge through walls of ragged rock. A picnic area at the falls has tables.

Bathurst has a City **Farmers' Market** on Saturday mornings year-round at 150 Main St., ☎ 506/546-2162. Look for local produce, honey, syrup, jams, jellies and pickles, as well as crafts, both here and at the Bathurst Farmers' Market, near the Exhibition Building next to Coronation Park. It's also open Saturday mornings, but only from May to November, ☎ 506/548-4733.

To get closer to the farm life of the region, visit **Sunnyside Farms**, where they raise pigs naturally, and also have barn dances, pig roasts, horse-drawn wagon rides and farm tours. The farm is in Sunnyside at Nash Creek, just west of Jacquet River, ☎ 506/237-9885.

Or take a tour of a goat farm and see how cheese is made from their milk (with samples, of course). The only operation of its type in northern New Brunswick, **Les Blancs d'Arcadie** offers children a chance to pet baby goats, foals and bunnies, and to ride in pony carts. Tours are daily at 10 am and 1 and 6:30 pm from May through October and cost $6. Find them at 340A boul. St-Pierre Est, Caraquet, ☎ 506/727-5952, fax 506/727-7379.

Sightseeing

The entire area is Roman Catholic, as you will guess from the number of churches and shrines you see. The **Musée de Papes**, or Popes Museum, on Rte. 11 in Grande-Anse (☎ 506/732-3003), covers the religion in general and the popes in particular. Among the displays is a large model of St. Peter's Basilica in Rome and exhibits on the religious orders that served in the area, as well as collections of church plates and vestments. It's open from early May to early September.

Mining of the minerals and metals discovered along the Acadian shore brought a mining boom that has evolved into a mainstay of the local economy. **Mining World** on Rte. 134 in Petit-Rocher (☎ 506/783-0824), teaches about the process of locating and extracting minerals from the earth and refining them for commercial use. Children enjoy the elevator, which simulates a descent into a mineshaft 2,800 feet below the surface. Mining World is open daily June through August, 10 am to 6 pm.

Where To Stay & Eat

The North Coast

Atlantic Host Inn is located directly on the provincial snowmobile trail network, with loading ramps, a fueling area, heated repair bays, and other special facilities for snowmobilers in the winter. But it's just as nice a place to stay in the summer, with an indoor pool, sauna, recreation room, and courtesy bicycles for guests' use. The Brass Horn Lounge is a lively gathering place, and Ambiance ($-$$), the attractive dining room, is reliably good and reasonably priced. It is open for three meals every day, and serves a popular $2.99 breakfast (that's $2 in US dollars). *Vanier Blvd. at Rte. 11, Bathurst, NB E2A 4H7, ☎ 506/548-3335 or 800/898-9292 ($$).*

Danny's Inn and Conference Center off Rte. 134 north of downtown Bathurst, is a full-service hotel with a heated pool, tennis courts, playground, and dining room ($-$$). *Peters Ave (PO Box 180), Bathurst, NB E2A 3Z2, ☎ 506/546-6621 ($$).*

La Fine Grobe sur Mer is toward the shore in Nigadoo, immediately west of the Nigadoo River bridge. We always laughed as we translated this as "Good Grub by the Sea" until we learned from its live-wire owner that "Grobe" is French lumber-camp slang for chow, and is the origin of the word grub. We were righter than we knew. And you'll be making the right choice if you plan to dine here. The view over the bay is beautiful as the sky and water change colors in the evening, and the food is magnifique. The chef/owner uses the freshest and most wholesome ingredients, some of which he grows in his little seaside garden; he bakes the bread in a traditional clay oven behind the restaurant. This is such a warm, romantic place; we counted three couples leaning over their tables to kiss while we were lingering over our espresso and raspberry cobbler. Daily from 11:30 am to 10 pm. Six simple rooms over the restaurant comprise the B&B, with private and shared baths, priced under $50. *Rte. 134 (PO Box 219), Nigadoo, NB E0B 2A0, ☎ 506/783-3138 ($$-$$$).*

Auberge D'Anjou has six stylish bath-en-suite rooms in the main house, including a Victorian bridal suite and another designed for families, with two baths. A former convent adjacent to the inn has been renovated to add 10 more rooms, more simply appointed, and some sharing baths. Guests in the main house have a full served breakfast, those in the convent a continental breakfast. In the attractive dining room ($$-$$$), the seafood is impeccably prepared and presented – the bouillabaisse is bountiful, and the Atlantic pot pie is filled with shellfish and has a crust so tender you know it can't possibly be good for you. Open for dinner daily mid-June through September, and Saturday only in spring and fall; lunch is served Monday-Friday year round. *587 rue Principal (Rte. 134), Petit-Rocher, NB E0B 2E0, ☎ 506/783-0587, fax 506/783-5587 ($-$$).*

Auberge Les Amis de la Nature is not just a place to stay, but a 46-acre nature center with trails for walking, skiing or snowshoeing, and places to watch birds and stars. Meals are prepared from the fruits of their own organic garden, including naturally raised chickens. *Chemin Lincour, Robertville, NB ☎ 506/783-4797 or 800/327-9999 ($-$$).*

Heron's Nest Cottages are located on the beach and include equipped kitchens. *6 Rue Chaleur, Box 50, Charlo, NB E0B 1M0, ☎ 506/684-3766, fax 506/684-3850 ($$-$$$).*

Brochetterie Le Vieux Moulin serves charcoal-grilled fish, other seafood dishes, and steaks in what was the area's first grain mill, built in 1850. It is the region's only Greek restaurant. *Rte. 134, Nigadoo, ☎ 506/783-3632 ($$).*

Au Café Gourmet is a bright French café with aromas of fresh-baked croissants and breads. Their sandwiches are thick and tasty, their soups hearty, their coffee worth traveling through a blizzard for. When the weather's good, enjoy an afternoon strawberry tart with your coffee on their sidewalk terrace. *210 King Ave., Bathurst, ☎ 506/545-6754.*

On The Peninsula

Like everyone else who travels a lot, we have our own short list of favorite places to lay our heads after a day on the road. **Hotel Paulin** is on it. We like to sink into the big white sofa in the parlor with glasses of good French wine in hand and watch the dinner guests arrive, while our appetites grow for the huge plates of succulent mussels we always begin with (although the pâté is tempting, too). The dining room is small – only six tables – and has the easy atmosphere and crisp linens of a French village auberge. It was built as a hotel by the owner's grandfather, and updated recently to add modern private baths without losing a bit of its historic charm. After dinner ($-$$), walk through the back yard to the little cove and watch the lights twinkling along the Gaspe shore. Breakfast is served daily from 7:30 to 10 am, dinner from 5:30 to 10 pm. The hotel is open from June through October. *143 boul. St-Pierre Ouest, Caraquet, NB E0B 1K0, ☎ 506/727-9981 ($$).*

Maison Touristique Dugas has guest rooms in the main house with shared baths, and two suites with kitchens in a separate building. Rustic cabins also have kitchens, and they have a campground, too. You're welcome to picnic at tables set among the wildflowers that decorate the well-tended grounds. Guests may use the private beach at the end of a dirt road. *683 boul. St-Pierre Ouest, Caraquet, NB E1W 1A1, ☎ 506/727-3195 ($).*

l'Auberge Le Pionnier is a bit inland, but a short drive to beaches. It's a friendly place with a reliable restaurant and comfortable rooms. *1093 rue du Parc, Paquetville, NB E0B 2B0, ☎ 506/357-8424 ($-$$).*

Auberge de Jeunesse offers two bunk rooms with five and 10 beds respectively, sharing two showers and a bright cheerful kitchen. *577 bd. St-Pierre ouest, Caraquet, NB E0B 1K0, ☎ 506/727-2345 ($).*

At **Jardin de la Mer** seafood is king, especially shellfish. It's a modern restaurant near the wharves, where the freshest crabs arrive each day. Snow crab, scallops, and mussels highlight the menu, and they are famous for their chowder. Open daily, 9 am to 10 pm, July through August; 9 am to 9 pm, May through June and September through December. *Pavillon Aquatuque (next to the Aquarium), Shippagan, ☎ 506/336-8454 ($-$$).*

Au Mariner is not toney, but the seafood is excellent. They are also open for breakfast, serving bountiful plates of pancakes drenched in maple syrup. *Rte. 11 in the center of Shippagan, ☎ 506/336-8240 ($-$$).*

Restaurant la Pantrie offers a daily table d'hôte at $15, which includes three courses and coffee or tea. They also serve à la carte, specializing in local seafood and traditional Acadian dishes. Their $7 Sunday brunch, served 10 am to 1 pm, is very popular with locals. *170 boul. des Acadiens, in Bertrand (near Caraquet), ☎ 506/764-3019 ($-$$).*

Carey's By-the-Sea, a local favorite, serves seafood. *Salmon Beach,* ☎ *506/546-6801.*

Along the East Coast

Motel Boudreau is a family-owned, modern motel with a reliable restaurant, Le Deux Rivierres ($-$$) open daily from 6:30 am to 11 pm, specializing in seafood. *PO Box 3359, Tracadie-Sheila, NB E1X 1G5,* ☎ *506/395-2244 or 800/563-2242 ($$).*

Motel Beauséjour, which also houses Chez Raymond Restaurant, is a comfortable motel open year-round. *PO Box 74, Neguac, NB E03 1S0,* ☎ *506/776-8718, fax 506/776-5462 ($-$$).*

Maison de la Fondue offers many other dishes in addition to their fondues, which include traditional Swiss cheese as well as beef, chicken and a delectable one with shellfish. Open Tuesday-Sunday for dinner only. *3613 rue Luce, Tracadie-Sheila,* ☎ *506/393-1100 ($$).*

■ Camping

Camping Shippagan, four miles west of town, has tent and trailer sites with a beach, playground and boat ramp. Expect to pay $22 a day for a fully serviced site, $17 for semi-serviced. *200 Hotel De Ville Ave, Shippagan, NB E0B 2P0,* ☎ *506/363-3690.*

Maison Touristique Dugas charges $8 to pitch your tent, $16 for a trailer site. You can join the B&B guests for breakfast for about $5. *683 boul. St.-Pierre Ouest, Caraquet, NB E1W 1A1,* ☎ *506/727-3195.*

Motel Camping Hache has a heated swimming pool; serviced and semi-serviced sites are $15-18. *rue Principal, Nigadoo,* ☎ *506/783-3739.*

Jacquet River Park, formerly a provincial park, is now operated by the Village of Belledune. Its 31 campsites are open only June through August. Fees are $16 with electricity, $13 without. Be sure to reserve early for July 1, Canada Day, when the park is the scene of the local observations, ending with fireworks in the evening. *931 Main St., Belledune, NB E0G 1G0,* ☎ *506/237-2826, off-season, 506/522-5613.*

The Miramichi

White pines more than 350 years old tower beside the trail to a waterfall, salmon jump above the sparkling waters, huskies pull a sled along the banks of the frozen river in February, and the forest floor is scattered with edible mushrooms in the summer. The Miramichi is more than a river, more than a region, it's a state of mind and a way of life, and the people who live there have a culture and language all their own. But once you sort out their strings of double negatives, it's easy to understand – after a few days of casting your butterfly into the dinges with devillywit, we don't suppose you won't have to conjuberate long to know this is the best in the dear world, eh?

Geography & History

When we say that the Miramichi is more than a river, we mean it literally. It's a whole system of rivers in a watershed so complex that even locals don't try to sort out its source from among the multiple headwaters. If you look at a map in the geographical heart of New Brunswick, north of Stanley, you'll see a number of blue lines. These rivers and streams have a variety of names, some of them with "Miramichi" in them, and they begin to converge into the Southwest Miramichi River. But don't think you've found it all. Look almost due west of the new city of Miramichi, on the east coast, and you'll find another Southwest Miramichi River, this one's components with a varied string of qualifiers which grow longer and longer until they reach the world's record river name: Lower North Branch Little Southwest Miramichi River. Then there's the Northwest Miramichi River....

All the tributaries aren't named Miramichi. There's the Renous, a river well-known to anglers, the Cains, and others. Altogether, they form one of the most famous salmon-fishing river systems in the world, and all the greats have fished here. You can too, quite easily, but you'll need a guide and a salmon license.

> ➲ **SAYING IT RIGHT:** *In order to ask directions to the Miramichi, you should know how to pronounce it. The accent is always on the last syllable. Locals are about evenly divided, according to their ethnic heritage, between Murry-mi-SHEE and Merry-mi-SHEE. You'll do fine with either, but at all costs avoid the standard mistake of calling it the Mary-mitchie.*

Logging, fishing and shipbuilding built the Miramichi. The first commercial salmon fishery began in the mid 1700s, along with a thriving trade in the tall, straight first-growth trees for ship masts. In 1825 the Great Miramichi Fire, fanned and spread by gale-force winds, destroyed 400 square miles along the river, with other scattered fires destroying thousands more. Along with the towns (Newcastle was reduced to a dozen buildings), the once great forests were destroyed. But towns and forests grew back, and lumber again became the backbone of the economy. The Cunard brothers, of the Cunard Lines family, established a shipyard in Chatham in the early 1800s, which thrived until iron ships took over the market at mid-century. But wood was always in demand, and huge timbering operations thrived here into recent memory.

Getting Around

The best way to reach this region is by car, although most fishing lodges will meet you at the airport in the city of Miramichi. From your lodge you can arrange most activities to include transportation. For the non-angler, or the traveler who wants to sample a little bit of everything this rich area offers, a car is much easier, and offers more flexibility.

As you travel, you may be puzzled by the inconsistent names for the cluster of eleven communities that include Chatham, Newcastle, Loggieville, Douglastown and several others. These previously separate towns were grouped, by order of the Canadian government, into one city in 1995. It was an administrative move not entirely favored by local residents, who still use the old town names. They don't do this to be stubborn or to confuse you; it actually makes your life much easier, since the old names tell you where to look for something in this rather sprawling new city. Chatham (now Miramichi East), Nelson, and Loggieville addresses are on the southeast bank of the river, Douglastown and Newcastle (now Miramichi West) on the northwest. The provincial highway map shows locations of the separate towns. We, too, shall use the older, more precise designations to make finding your way easier.

Information Sources

- The **Tourist Information Office** (☎ 506/622-9100) is in the lighthouse at Ritchie Wharf; it's open daily, 9 am to 9 pm, from mid-May through early September.

Adventures

If your heart doesn't sing in tune with the birds, or if you think the only place for fish is on your plate, or if green isn't your favorite color, perhaps you'd better bypass the Miramichi. It's a place for those who love the outdoors in all its moods and seasons. The best way to see and appreciate the river is from a canoe; the only way to see most of the land between its tributaries is on foot – or with the help of a dog team or horse. In the winter, many of the roads are open only to snowmobiles. In the spring you can be born through the woods in chariots pulled by mosquitoes the size of mastodons.

■ On Foot

Trails crisscross the entire area, some following old rail spurs and lines, others logging roads. Some of these are still in active use, others overgrown and used by hunters, anglers and others who use four-wheel-drive vehicles. Some are badly eroded by heavy use, others grassy pathways through the woods. Many are used by snowmobilers in the winter, and the local clubs keep them cleared of brush and fallen trees.

Because of the network of old roads and trails, it is often difficult to give accurate directions, so be sure to have a local with you or to get thorough instructions and a map before setting out on the back country trails. You are heading into a vast wilderness in almost any direction, so be sure you're prepared for surprises and be sure someone knows where you are going and when you expect to return. The woods are lovely, but they can swallow you up in minutes. The following trails are well-marked and easy to locate and follow.

➲ **MAPS:** *For maps of the area showing trails and access roads in the more remote areas, stop at the* ***Ranger Station****, 80 Pleasant St, Newcastle,* ☎ *506/622-2636, where they can also give you information on trail conditions. For trails on the abandoned rail line, see* On Wheels, *below.*

Sheephouse Falls Nature Trail (also known as the Pulp and Paper Nature Trail) leads through part of a 300-acre reserve, about 30 miles northwest of Miramichi. Access is from the Fraser-Burchill Road, off Rte. 430. About six miles from the intersection, turn left onto Little Sheephouse Road, and left at the fork. The trail begins at the picnic area just before the bridge. Interpretive signs along the well-groomed brookside trail describe the natural environment, and on the way to the 40-foot waterfall you'll pass another smaller one. The larger falls is in a deep gorge, where a bridge crosses the stream.

Middle Island Trail is a 1½-mile walk on cleared grass, circling Middle Island Park. It's an easy trail with nice views of the river and the island, which curiously is the same size and shape as a nearby lake. This has given rise to a number of legends about the land being scooped out and dropped into the river. The park has an unsupervised beach.

French Fort Cove lies between the Newcastle and Douglastown areas of Miramichi, and a two-mile trail circles the cove where the French built a fort in 1755. The easy trail begins at the intersection of Cove Road and Rte. 8, and takes about 90 minutes to walk. Scenic lookouts give views over the water, and you'll see the work of beavers (or the animals themselves if you go in the early morning or evening). Along the way you'll pass a gorge and some cliffs. Watch out for the headless nun who haunts the area and for the chests of gold buried by pirates at the north side of the bridge, both persistent legends you're likely to hear around the campfire. To book a place on the daily "Headless Nun Tour" of French Fort Cove, call ☎ 800/459-3131. We haven't, so you're on your own; we're not sure if the guide appears without a head, or has any other bad habits.

Strawberry Marsh Trail is shorter, about a mile, and has a gravel surface. It starts opposite Country Inn & Suites, on Rte. 8 in Newcastle, traveling along the river through a landscape of marsh grass alive with waterfowl. In the river is Beaubear Island, where if you keep a sharp watch you may see a bald eagle.

FALLS BROOK FALLS: *One of the province's most spectacular sights is the 130-foot Falls Brook Falls, located near the Miramichi River in Boiestown. It is on private land, so you will need a guide, which* ***Clearwater Hollow Expeditions*** *(☎ 800/563-TRAIL) can provide, along with lunch, transportation to the trailhead and nature interpretation along the trail. In the deep woods beside the river you'll see wildflowers, especially in the spring (when you should shower in the strongest local bug-dope you can buy at McClosky's General Store). The falls is its most impressive in the spring or early summer, particularly after a good rain.*

Guided Hiking Tours

- **Upper Oxbow Outdoor Adventures**, Sillikers, NB ☎ 888/227-6100 or 506/622-8834, offers guided hikes in the Little Southwest Miramichi area near Newcastle. These hikes include transportation to the trailhead, nature interpretation and lunch, at about $50 per person. Debbie Norton will take groups as small as two on these hikes.

On Wheels

Several good bike routes use the recently refurbished abandoned rail lines along the river. One four-mile stretch connects Loggieville to Chatham, beginning at the corner of Wellington and Water streets. Its surface is covered in crushed rock. Birds and wildflowers thrive in the low woodland, which opens to frequent views over the river. Since these trails are multi-use areas, cyclists must give way to walkers and joggers.

Another good section, the **Whooper Trail**, follows the river along the route of the old train, named for the ghostly Dungarvon Whooper, between Doaktown and McNamee. Its gravel surface is usually in good condition, except in early spring when there may be occasional washouts. You can continue on to Boiestown, emerging at the Woodmen's Museum, a good point if someone is meeting you to save you the return trip. **Clearwater Hollow** (☎ 800/563-TRAIL) rents mountain bikes and provides shuttle service, as well as guided bicycling excursions.

On Water

At least once, step into a canoe and learn why people use terms like "magical" and "mystical" to describe this river. Gliding silently downstream through water dappled with splashes of sunlight and the dark shadows of pines and spruces that tower on the banks above, you are in another world, where time and distance are irrelevant. Writer Lane MacIntosh, who lives in Fredericton, only an hour from the Miramichi, speaks of the "powerful sensory experience." We can't find better words.

Canoeing

While the more developed (don't be alarmed at that word – development here means a log cabin overlooking a salmon pool or an occasional cluster of houses) part of the river runs close to Rte. 8, with several put-in points, the more pristine upper reaches are harder to get to. Happily, one stretch has a put-in and a take-out convenient to easily found roads, providing about 40 miles of river for a nice overnight trip. The Southwest Miramichi parallels the north side of Route 107 between Napadogan and Juniper, where the best put-in point is in a stand of tall pines, almost halfway between the two towns. The take-out is at Bloomfield Ridge, just off Route 625 near Boiestown.

> **TIP:** *Before putting your canoe in the water, get a copy of the* Southwest Miramichi Canoe Map, *a sturdy Tyvek document with river landmarks, location and classification of the rapids, and other information you'll need to explore the river. By custom and courtesy, fishermen have the right-of-way and you should paddle quietly behind them.*

Canoe Outfitters & Guided Tours

■ Rent canoes from **O'Donnell's Canoeing Adventures** (4439 Storeytown Road, Doaktown, NB E0C 1G0, ☎ 506/365-7924, fax 506/365-9080, e-mail cabin@nbnet.nb.ca). They operate from May through October, and offer day trips for $40 ($100 for a family of four) that put in at the Priceville Swinging Bridge and take out at their own log cabins (see *Where To Stay & Eat*, page 190) in Doaktown. Along this leisurely route you are likely to see bald eagles above you and salmon in the water below you as you

GUIDED TOURS OF THE MIRAMICHI: *If, after reading this section, you can't decide which to do first, and want someone else to sort out the details, provide the canoes, bikes and shuttle service, as well as food and lodging, call Roger Clowater at* ***Clearwater Hollow Expeditions****, McNamee, NB E0C 1P0, ☎ 506/365-7636 or 800/563-TRAIL (8724). Clowater is a Miramichi word meaning bundle of high energy wrapped in a sense of humor. Or if it isn't, it should be. All the Clowater clan – Roger, his sister Darla, and parents Perley and Phoebe – are involved in this third-generation business of helping visitors to see the Miramichi as they do, from the water in a canoe, from its hiking and bicycling trails, or across a table laden with Phoebe's legendary foods. You're bound to meet them if you are in the area for a while, and if you decide to let them put together a stress-free stay for you, you couldn't be in better hands. Prepare to laugh a lot and eat well.*

move along with the spirited current or paddle in the slow waters of the deep pools. A riverside picnic lunch is included, as is a stop to walk through New Brunswick's oldest covered bridge. If the area's unique history fascinates you, ask if you can have retired teacher Dan O'Donnell as your guide. (He also specializes in teaching beginners to fly-fish.)

Whether your guide is Dan or Gilbert Thiboudalt, you'll hear stories about the famed salmon pools you pass through on the way, including who owns them and who has caught what there. (Unlike many places, the best salmon pools here are owned by the adjacent landowners, and each fishing guide has access to certain pools where salmon are known to lurk.) Multi-day packages include a half-day tour and the use of canoes to explore different stretches of the river, with shuttle service from the cozy log cabins, where two nights' lodging is provided. They also offer fishing guides and can arrange for you to purchase a license.

■ **Clearwater Hollow Expeditions** (McNamee Road, McNamee, NB E0C 1P0, ☎ 506/365-7636 or 800/563-TRAIL), also operate from May through October and offer guided canoe trips. They provide shuttle service if you bring your own canoe. Rental rates are about $25 per day for a canoe; trailers are $25, and shuttle service runs from $50 to $75. Their most popular day trip is the "Canoe and

Barbecue," which includes canoes, instruction, guides, a shore lunch and a steak barbecue at their lodge on the river after the trip; it's a real value at $50 per person. Another day-long package includes a canoe, shuttle, and a picnic basket for two, filled with a way-above-average lunch. The "Put In Take Out" package provides two nights lodging, a canoe, equipment, and shuttle service, at $339 for a family of four. Owner Roger Clowater says the six-night Wilderness Canoe Expedition is "only for the hardy." Although it includes some class III and IV rapids and wilderness camps with very primitive facilities, anyone with enough paddling experience and a sense of adventure will enjoy it. After three days in the river from a put-in near Napadogan, you'll reach civilization and, along with it, more luxurious accommodations and dining for the rest of the trip. Along with the canoeing, expect to do a little land exploring to see waterfalls or venture into the cave where the infamous "Dungarvon Whooper" resides. If you dare, after Roger's campfire stories.

■ Debbie Norton at **Upper Oxbow Outdoor Adventures** in Sillikers, NB, ☎ 888/227-6100 or 506/622-8834, offers guided canoe excursions at $50 per person, including lunch, canoe, shuttle and instruction; or $30 per person without a guide.

■ **Cornish Corner Inn** in Stanley (☎ 506/367-2239, see *Where To Stay & Eat*, page 191) offers canoeing packages that include room, breakfast, a box lunch, canoe, a guide, and one of their justly famous dinners on your return, for $95 per person. Without a guide it's $65, about the best bargain you'll find.

AND THEY NAMED A TRAIN FOR HIS GHOST... *We don't need to worry about spoiling the campfire stories you'll hear in the Miramichi, since this one is never told the same way twice. The* ***Dungarvon Whooper's*** *long blood-curdling cry is heard by perfectly sane people (although everyone we know who has heard it has at least one trace to Miramichi ancestry). As the story goes, it is the ghostly wail of a young Irish lumberman who was found one morning without his wallet, and with his throat slit ear to ear. The fury of the blizzard that followed was so great that his bunkmates had trouble burying him properly, and his wail is heard to this day in the deep forests near the banks of the Dungarvon River, deep in the Miramichi.*

Tubing

Both Upper Oxbow Outdoor Adventures and Clearwater Hollow Expeditions offer tubing. Upper Oxbow's package is $15 per person with a life-jacket and transportation, or $20 with a lunch added.

Harbor & Bay Tours

If you don't want to get too up-close and personal with the river, **Staff's Charters Boat Tours** cruise in Miramichi Bay and along the harbor in Miramichi. Full-day (six-hour) tours leave from Burnt Cove near Neguac on the north shore of the bay, and go to uninhabited Portage Island's National Wildlife Area, where guests enjoy a driftwood beach fire and lunch, along with beachcombing, swimming, clam digging (they provide equipment and instruction), birding and island exploration. You can also jig for mackerel during the cruise. A trip to Portage Island costs between $15 and $20 per person, depending on how many passengers are on board, and you will need advance reservations. A shorter harbor tour is about $5, and leaves from Ritchie Wharf in Newcastle. Stafford Anderson, Jr., who runs the trips July-September, has a Coast Guard certified boat. Contact Staff's Charters at Box 3, RR2, Legacyville, Burnt Cove, NB E0C 1K0, ☎ 506/776-3217.

Fishing

The name Miramichi immediately conjures up pictures of fishing; it's almost a registered trade name among anglers, and all the greats have fished it. So can you, either on a week-long stay at one of the fishing lodges along the river, or on a *Day Adventure* for just one day. For current information on licensing, regulations and seasons, request a copy of *Fish New Brunswick* from the New Brunswick Wildlife Department, PO Box 20211, Fredericton, NB E3B 2A2, or pick up the *Aim and Angle Guide* at any provincial tourism office.

Most anglers book in at one of the fishing lodges in the area, which own some of the best fishing waters, but you can hire a guide and fish on a day basis. If you have never fished and would like to try the sport, you can learn with the best here. Most lodges offer expert instruction as part of your package.

For a day of fishing, with instruction, all equipment, guide and two meals, you can take advantage of a *Day Adventure* offered by **Miramichi Gray Rapids Lodge** on Route 118 in Blackville, ☎ 506/357-9784 or 800/261-2330, fax 506/357-9733. They have four private pools in a prime location.

FISHING OUTFITTERS & GUIDES

■ **Black Rapids Salmon Lodge**, PO Box 182, Blackville, NB E0C 1C0, ☎ 506/843-2346, fax 506/843-7755, offers comfortable accommodations, shared bath, three home-cooked meals, professional guides, and one mile of excellent private water on the Miramichi River, plus two miles of adjacent public water. Boats are used during the spring run-off, but bring waders to fish the pools in the summer. It's a lovely stretch of river, and the native lilies are exquisite. Rates are about $1,300 for four nights lodging and three days fishing, all inclusive.

■ **Pond's Resort**, 91 Porter Cove Road (PO Box 73), Ludlow, NB E0C 1N0, ☎ 506/369-2612, fax 506/369-2293, has a collection of pleasantly rustic cabins, hearty meals, licensed guides, and superb fishing. Bring your own tackle and gear, including waders. In addition to salmon, Pond's offers trout fishing, canoeing, and hiking. A three-day, three-night package is about $1,500.

■ To fish with a great Miramichi guide, contact the well-known fishing author **Wayne Curtis** at PO Box 225, Newcastle, NB E1V 3M3, ☎ 506/843-7890 in the summer, or write Box 294, Station A, Fredericton, NB E3B 4Y9, ☎ 506/452-9015 in the winter. Wayne grew up on the Miramichi, and knows the river intimately. He guides anglers expertly and can often be prevailed upon to share his memories of a childhood spent exploring this world-famous water with rod and creel. – *Sara Godwin and Charles James*

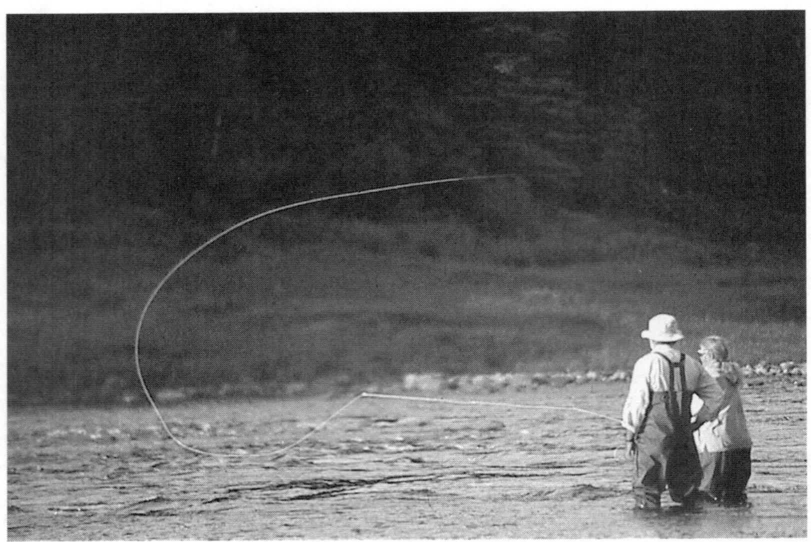

Fishing on the Miramichi.
(Photo by Charles James)

As elsewhere in the province (and other provinces as well) you can't just buy a fishing license and drop a fly in the water. The Miramichi is a scheduled river, which means it has salmon in it and is subject to several restrictions. First, if you are not a resident of New Brunswick, you must be accompanied by a licensed guide. The guide will know which pools are private and will have obtained permission, if needed, to fish wherever he takes you. Or, your guide will be employed by the lodge where you are staying, and you will be fishing in their pools.

> **TIP:** *If you fish the Miramichi, you'll want to stop at "Doak's."* ***W.W. Doak and Sons, Ltd.*** *(☎ 506/365-7828, fax 506/365-7762), on the main road in Doaktown, is a small shop with a huge reputation. It is known worldwide for its superb selection of fly rods, reels, lines, flies, and gear.*

On Snow

It's not at all unusual for the Miramichi area to be covered in white by early December, and the accumulation is enough to last into early April, so snow sports are a way of life for residents. In the city of Miramichi, the Recreation Department (☎ 506/623-2300) maintains **skating rinks**.

Skiing

The gentle, rolling riverside terrain is ideal for cross-country skiing, and you can be pretty sure of a good supply of snow. The **Miramichi Cross-Country Ski Club** maintains 15 miles of groomed trails of lengths from a quarter-mile to eight miles. On Mondays they have a Women's Ski Tour and on weekends frequently have moonlight skis. Their annual Loppet is part of the Provincial Loppet calendar. The daily trail fee is $3; $1 for children under 12.

Miramichi Gray Rapids Lodge, Route 118, Blackville, offers cross-country and snowshoe trails, as well as tobogganing and dogsledding. Mailing address is 326 MacDonald Avenue, Oromocto, NB E2V 1A7; ☎ 506/357-9784 or 800/261-2330, fax 506/357-9733.

Snowmobiling

Provincial Snowmobile Trail 42 runs from Fredericton to the Northumberland Strait, much of its distance along the Miramichi River. It follows the old rail line, the same trail used by walkers and cyclists in the summer. The distance from Fredericton to Miramichi is 133 miles via this trail.

Several snowmobile clubs groom and maintain the trails and hold events which visitors are welcome to join. These include **Miramichi Valley Snowmobile Club**, PO Box 622, Newcastle, NB E1V 3M3, ☎ 506/773-5607, fax 506/622-2119, and the **Nelson Snowmobile Club**, PO Box 295, Nelson-Miramichi, NB E0C 1T0, ☎ 506/778-8659. The **Rogersville Snowmobile Club** (☎ 506/775-6418, fax 506/775-1882) has races every Sunday at 1:30 pm, and salt-cod suppers every Friday evening.

The Miramichi Valley Club sponsors the **Annual Maritime Snowmobile Festival** in early February (☎ 800/459-3131 for information and dates).

You could hardly picture a more idyllic winter scene than **Schooner Point Log Cabins** with snow up to their eaves and

SNOWSHOE HIKING: *One of the most interesting winter experiences is to join a Micmac guide at the* ***Red Bank First Nation*** *for an hour's snowshoe hike followed by two hours of ice fishing. Along with snowshoes and fishing equipment, you will get a sample of traditional food and beverage, at $25 per person. reserve through the* Day Adventure *program or directly with Red Bank at ☎ 506/836-7146.*

walkways with snowbanks so high they seem like tunnels. They are the picture-perfect place for a winter getaway. Ten log cabins sit in an open spruce forest, each with cedar interior, fully equipped modern kitchen, electric heat and two bedrooms. Snowmobilers gather here, and the owners rent machines and equipment at $125 for the machine plus $20 insurance; add another $20 if you need extra gear. Helmet and trail pass are included in the basic fee. Beginners just trying out the sport can sign up for a day adventure which includes a snowmobile, all equipment, instruction, trail lunch and at least eight hours of guided touring, for $260 per snowmobile (two people can share a machine or each ride separately). If snowmobiles aren't your style, they can arrange for you to go smelt fishing through the ice. 192 Murdoch Road, Miramichi (Chatham) NB E1N 3A3, ☎ 506/778-2338, fax 506/773-9869.

Eastern Scenic Adventures (PO Box 398, Miramichi, NB E1V 3M5, ☎ 506/778-8573, fax 506/778-8222, e-mail skidoo@nbnet.nb.ca) also runs guided snowmobile trips, with machines and equipment (including suit and helmet) and lunch, at about $140 per person for half a day, $200 a full day. You can reserve through the *Day Adventures* program.

Ponds Resort (Porter Cove Road, Ludlow, NB E0C 1N0, ☎ 506/369-2612, fax 506/369-2293) offers snowmobile packages with trailside lodging beginning at about $45 per person per night, for those who bring their own machines. **Miramichi Gray Rapids Lodge** in Blackville (☎ 506/357-9733 or 800/261-2330; see *Skiing*, above) also has snowmobile packages.

Juniper Lodge (Juniper, NB E0J 1P0, ☎ 506/246-5223) offers a relaxed setting almost in the middle of nowhere. Juniper is on the North Branch of the Southwest Miramichi, on Rte. 107 about halfway between Stanley and Bristol. The lodge offers a relaxed atmosphere, home-cooked meals and access to trails, with lodging packages at about $85 a night per couple. You will need to bring your own machine or rent one elsewhere, although they do have fuel service at the lodge.

Betts Kelly Lodge (PO Box 177, Doaktown, NB E0C 1G0, ☎ 506/365-8008, fax 506/365-8007) has log cabins with full housekeeping facilities, close to snowmobile trails, in the same price range as Juniper.

Sledding & Sleigh Rides

Moonshadow Dogsledding Adventures, Giants Glen Road, Stanley, ☎ 506/367-2767, will teach you how to mush your own team of Eskimo dogs, for a day trip or a weekend of serious sledding. While the team rests, you can have lunch by an open fire.

Wine River Stables, PO Box 585, Chatham, Miramichi, NB E1N 3A8, ☎ 506/773-7648, offers hour-long sleigh-rides through the sparkling woods and fields of their ranch, followed by a home-cooked lunch in front of a roaring fire in their lodge. The cost is $12 per person.

Hoods Sleigh Rides, 410 Red Rock Road, Stanley, ☎ 506/367-2531, has sleighs and a log cabin where they serve meals and snacks after your sleigh ride.

Schooner Point Log Cabins (☎ 506/778-2338) can arrange for you to take a sleigh ride, which can include a lunch stop in a cabin with a warming fire waiting. These cost from $6 a person.

Sunny Side Inn, 65 Henderson Street, Miramichi, NB E1N 2R4, ☎ 506/773-4232 or 800/852-7711 (see *Where To Stay & Eat*), offers winter romance packages complete with a four-course candlelight dinner and an old fashioned sleigh ride, at $190 a couple.

■ On Horseback

Wine River Stables, PO Box 585, Miramichi, NB E1N 3A8, ☎ 506/773-7648, has trail rides year-round at their farm outside of Chatham.

Cornish Corner Inn in Stanley (☎ 506/367-2239; see *Where To Stay & Eat*) has wilderness horse trekking packages in the spring, summer and fall, which include lodging and meals at the inn.

Cultural & Eco-Travel Experiences

The long First Nation history of the area and the wide variety of immigrant populations makes the Miramichi a rich center for intermingling cultures. Each is represented in festivals and exhibits, and in the daily lives of the descendants. The area's concentration of Irish families makes it a natural venue for the largest **Irish Festival** in Canada each July.

Metepenagaig (Red Bank Reserve), 76 Shore Road, Red Bank, is a First Nation exhibit showing Micmac heritage and the people's relationship with the river and the land. It is open late June through August, daily from 10 am to 4:30 pm. In late June they hold the **Oxbow Pow Wow**. In mid-August is the **Burnt Church First Nation Powwow** at Diggle Point in Burnt Church. Both include drumming, dancing and traditional crafts. **Mi'kmaq Arts and Crafts** in Red Bank sells locally made handwork, including baskets. The Augustine Mound, an ancient burial site, is nearby, and the band office can give you directions. (For a unique winter experience learning ancient Micmac arts of ice fishing and snowshoeing, see the box on page 184.)

Music Festivals

The **Irish Festival** on the Miramichi (☎ 506/778-8810) brings Irish musicians from all over the world. Everything turns Irish, and the pubs do a lively business. Pipe and drum corps, a Festival Mass, dancing, Irish games and cultural events fill four days in mid-July.

The **Miramichi Fiddlers Weekend** (☎ 800/459-3131) brings French, Scottish, Irish and other traditional fiddlers together in early August, when you can join them for pancake breakfasts, a dance and a fiddlers' jamboree.

The following weekend brings the **Miramichi Folksong Festival** (☎ 506/623-2150), with well-known performers who come for the occasion, as well as (our favorites) the local artists singing traditional "Come All Ye" songs which are peculiar to the river. These are among the oldest known folksongs of the northeast, narrative ballads that nearly always begin "Come All Ye..." hence the name. This event has been going on for more than 40 years.

Farmers' Markets & Local Produce

Farmers' Markets provide not only fresh seasonal produce, but crafts, unique food gifts (honey, wild berry jams, and maple products), and a chance to mingle with local people you might not meet otherwise. The **Chatham Farmers' Market** is held on Fridays, 3 to 7 pm, throughout the growing season, on Water Street and the **Newcastle Farmers' Market** (☎ 506/622-0483) is in the Linden Recreation Center each Friday, 11 am to 3 pm.

Bay Breeze Farm, corner of Route 117 and River Road, Bay du Vin, NB E0C 1B0, ☎ 506/228-4437, grows plump, juicy strawberries that you can pick in the late spring in their fields overlooking Miramichi Bay. They are open daily, 9 am to 8 pm during strawberry season, and later in the summer for raspberries. Both are grown pesticide-free.

Sightseeing

The Woodsmen's Museum, Rte. 8, Boiestown, ☎ 506/369-7214, shows how timber made the Miramichi, long before it became one of North America's sportfishing meccas, portraying the heart and soul of that industry, and the days when it ruled the northland. It's an eye-catching museum, with two log-shaped buildings, a huge ax imbedded in one, a mammoth peavey in the other. One has alcoves furnished as a school, general store, cabin and a telephone office. But the real meat of the museum is, like the logging camp it portrays, outdoors. Here is reconstructed a typical loggers' camp, with bunkhouse, blacksmith and wheelwright shops, a pitsaw, sawmill, cookhouse, and machine sheds full of equipment. A narrow-gauge railroad runs through the woods and over a trestle; adults can ride it for $2, children $1. The museum is open May through September, daily from 9:30 am to 5:30 pm; admission is $5.

Miramichi Salmon Museum, Rte. 8, Doaktown, ☎ 506/365-7787, deals with the past, present and future of the Atlantic salmon, and with the sport of salmon fishing. An aquarium is stocked with live salmon, plus other species common

> ➔ **TIP:** *Although the principal attractions of the area are its natural setting and outdoor activities, several other places are well worth a stop. The don't-miss sights are the **Woodsmen's Museum** and the **swinging bridge**.*

to the river. Outside is an ice house, showing how ice was taken from the river and stored for use in warm weather. The museum is open June through September, daily from 9 am until 5 pm; admission is $4.

Doak Historic Site, Rte. 8, Doaktown, ☎ 506/453-2324, reflects the history of the town which was named for its builder, one of the town's earliest settlers. In it is the original furniture, and docents demonstrate early crafts and skills. Tour the barn and milkhouse of this early 19th-century farm, open late June to early September, Monday-Saturday, 9:30 am to 4:30 pm; Sunday, 1 to 4:30 pm. Admission is free, but donations are welcome.

MacDonald Farm Historic Site, Rte. 11, Bartibog, ☎ 800/561-0123, was built in the early 1800s by a Scottish veteran of the American Revolution. It is a good example of a self-contained farmstead, where everyday activities of the period – including cooking, gardening, caring for farm animals, and soapmaking – are carried on by costumed interpreters. It is open July-September, daily from 9:30 to 4:30; admission is $2.50.

Nelson Hollow Covered Bridge, the oldest in New Brunswick, is on a dead-end road just west of Doaktown. You can walk through it to inspect its construction.

The **Priceville Swinging Bridge** is not for those with acrophobia, especially after you've heard the story of how it and the people on it were swept away in a terrible spring flood. But thousands of people have crossed the new bridge in safety, and kids will love the long, scary walk above the water. It is on the McNamee Road, between Doaktown and Boiestown, crossing to the village of Priceville.

Miramichi Natural History Museum, 149 Wellington Street, Chatham, ☎ 506/773-7305, has an endearing collection that ranges from arachnids to Zulu spears, and includes the logs of the Cunard Steamship Line – not so unlikely when you know that the Cunard family is a local one. Look for fossils and for pre-European stone tools and implements of local native peoples. It is open daily in the summer, 10 am to 6 pm.

Ritchie Wharf in Newcastle is a newly constructed boardwalk, which has become a center for waterfront activities. The Tourist Office (☎ 800/459-3131) is there, in a lighthouse, as are cafés, shops a playground, and benches where you can sit and watch the river go by. Boat tours leave from here, and it's a good place to check in when you arrive, since any new activities and current events will be posted at the lighthouse. On Sunday afternoons there is frequently a live musical performance, which could be singers, fiddlers or a local band.

Beaubear Island, a Federal Historic Site where French families hid from the British troops during the Acadian expulsion, is a quiet, peaceful place with walking trails through the tall white pine forest. Local stories suggest that the masts for Lord Nelson's fleet at the Battle of Trafalgar came from this forest. One of the reasons it's so peaceful here is that there's no public boat access. You either have to paddle here yourself or find someone with a boat to bring you here. There's a picnic area on the eastern tip of the island.

Where To Stay & Eat

Chatham/Newcastle (City of Miramichi)

Sunny Side Inn is in a gracious big Victorian mansion high above the riverbank in Chatham. The restoration is excellent, incorporating modern comforts in an uncluttered 19th-century setting. *65 Henderson Street, Miramichi, NB E1N 2R4, ☎ 506/773-4232 or 800/852-7711.*

Schooner Point Cabins are built of cedar logs and stand near the East banks of Miramichi Bay. Guests can rent canoes there to explore the shore. Open year-round (see *On Snow*, page 183) prices run from $90-120 per night for four adults, or $535 a week. *192 Murdoch Road, Miramichi (Chatham) NB E1N 3A3, ☎ 506/778-2338, fax 506/773-9869.*

Country Inn & Suites is a modern motel-style accommodation in Newcastle, with nicely appointed rooms and a free continental breakfast. Expect to pay about $70. *333 King George Highway, Miramichi NB E1V 1L2, ☎ 506/627-1999, fax 506/627-1907.*

Beaubear Manor is a little grander than the average hostel, with antiques and a music room with a Steinway. They'll pick you up at the bus station free. *62 Riverside Dr., Miramichi (Nelson), NB E0C 1T0, ☎ 506/622-3036 ($).*

Cunard Restaurant is a local institution; a friend of ours remembers going there in her starched dresses for special occasions as a small child. They serve a combined menu of respectable Chinese dishes and standard Canadian fare, such as steaks and well-prepared seafood. *32 Cunard Street, Chatham, ☎ 506/773-7107.*

Saddlers Café also on the Chatham side of the river, serves pastas, seafood (including a Miramichi bouillabaisse) and vegetarian dishes overlooking the river in Lord Beaverbrook's former offices. It's open daily, 10 am to 9 pm. *331 Water Street, ☎ 506/773-4214.*

Boardwalk Café and Tea Room serves local dishes, including fiddlehead soup and quiche, shepherd's pie, and desserts of fresh berries. They open at 11 am, and lunch dishes are in the $6 range. It's an updated tearoom atmosphere with lace tablecloths and a nice view over the river. On Sundays, from 3 to 6 pm they serve a sumptuous tea. Of course, you can have tea and a dessert there any afternoon, but on Sunday they have scones and dainty tea sandwiches. *Ritchie Wharf, Newcastle, ☎ 506/622-6124.*

Portage Restaurant serves a standard menu of steaks and seafood, and is open from 6 am until 11 pm daily, with slightly shorter hours Sunday. *Rte. 11, Chatham, ☎ 506/773-6447.*

Along the Miramichi River

Victoria's Cottage Tea Room/Bed & Breakfast has comfortable rooms with a classy little restaurant downstairs serving lunch and tea, along with breakfast. Everything is made fresh (and from scratch) daily, and at lunch you might find giant hearty salads, salmon chowder, and sandwiches on homemade bread (all in the $3.50-$5 range), with dessert of lemon pie or fresh berries. In the morning toast will be homemade bread. Scones at afternoon tea are just out of the oven and the tea comes in a proper china pot. Rooms are $55 double, cot $10 extra. The log cabin on the same property is $50 for two, $10 each additional person. It has a small kitchen, with access to a barbecue area and riverside tables. *289 Main Street (Rte. 8), Doaktown, NB E0C 1G0, ☎ 506/365-7144 or 800/563-8724.*

O'Donnell's Cottages overlook the Miramichi River; it's quite common to share their sweeping lawns with a family of deer. The cabins are just rustic enough to make you feel like you're in a New Brunswick hunting camp, but have all the comforts, including fully equipped kitchens. Each has a front porch overlooking the riverbank. *4439 Storeytown Road, Doaktown, NB E0C 1G0, ☎ 506/365-7924, fax 506/365-9080, e-mail cabin@nbnet.Nb.ca ($$).*

Ponds Resort has riverside cabins and a large lodge where they serve meals to guests and others. It's a classic sporting camp, where you can depend on the conversation to center around fishing. They rent equipment and arrange for guides and licenses, too. Complete fishing packages with guide, equipment and three meals are $395 per person, per day. *Porter Cove Road, Ludlow, NB E0C 1N0, ☎ 506/369-2612, fax 506/369-2293 (rooms $-$$; cabins $$).*

Cornish Corner Inn has bright, comfortable rooms and a restaurant worth traveling for – pheasant, beef pie in a baked potato crust or scallops in premium sherry. Desserts are irresistible, as are breakfast scones. The hosts are energetic people with a fine-tuned sense of humor, who love the area and try to introduce guests to the best it can offer. They arrange a multitude of packages that include everything from horseback riding to mushroom hunting. The inn is open April until mid-December. *Main Street (PO Box 40), Stanley, NB E0H 1T0, ☎ 506/367-2239, fax 506/367-2230 ($).*

A large carved wooden moose calls your attention to **B&L Restaurant**, where you can get simple family-style meals at very reasonable prices. It's open 7 am to 9 pm, every day. *Rte. 8, Doaktown, ☎ 506/365-7907 ($).*

Darlene's Old Country Bakery and Tea House serves breakfast, lunch and tea, specializing in baked goods. On Saturday the special is baked beans and cornbread or biscuits. Seniors get a discount on Tuesdays. *Barnettville Road, Blackville, ☎ 506/843-9881 ($).*

■ Camping

Red Pines Park is at the Woodmen's Museum. Camping is a reasonable $7 a night, or $8.50 with hook-up. Firewood is available. *Boiestown, NB E0H 1A0, ☎ 506/369-7214, fax 506/369-7406.*

Enclosure Campground, a half-mile west of Newcastle, has a heated and supervised swimming pool and large kitchen shelters, as well as an activity center. Campsites are in a stand of tall pine trees. *Route 8, Miramichi, NB ☎ 800/363-1733 or 506/622-8638.*

The East Coast

Prince Edward Island protects this shore from the rougher tides of the Gulf of St. Lawrence, providing instead the calmer, warmer waters of the Northumberland Strait. Beaches and coastal marshland – prime migration stops for birds on the Atlantic Flyway – face these quieter waters. It is for these miles of white sand beaches, lapped by the warmest sea water north of Virginia, that the area from Miramichi Bay to Cape Tormentine (where the bridge links New Brunswick to Prince Edward Island) is best known. Kouchibouguac National Park protects a rare northern barrier island and miles of bog, marsh and forest joined by trails. Its low shore terrain is good for bicycling and the gentle seas for kayaking. Snowmobiling is the favored winter sport, but miles of cross-country trails bring skiers, too.

Geography & History

The region is defined on the north by the Miramichi River's mouth and the wide bay it forms. On the south it reaches to the east bank of the Petitcodiac River, a tidal estuary that brings the enormous force of the Fundy tides right into downtown Moncton. East of the Petitcodiac, the isthmus that connects Nova Scotia to New Brunswick narrowly prevents Nova Scotia from being an island. In 1997, a mammoth bridge was completed at Cape Tormentine, at last linking Prince Edward Island to mainland Canada via road instead of the ferry that previously connected it from the same point.

As a result of its unique position as the link to both these water-bound provinces, this part of New Brunswick has been a corridor through which travelers bent on other places passed, many hardly glancing around them on their way through. Moncton, the city through which all routes seem to pass (you can't cut straight up the coast from Fundy National Park to the Nova Scotia border, because the Petitcodiac River's vast tidal flats are in the way), is also generally ignored by tourists. It's been their loss, since the isthmus region has so many attractions of its own.

Historically, the area has also been a pivotal point. **Fort Beauséjour** was a French bastion until 1755, when the British gained control of it. In the same year the British solidified their position in Nova Scotia by deporting all those French farmers who refused to swear allegiance to the King after the British gained Nova Scotia, and many of them fled to this part of New Brunswick. In 1881, Acadians met in Memramcook, south of Sackville, and debated whether to join other French settlers and become part of Quebec. They decided against the union. The French influence is still strong along this shore.

Getting Around

To reach this region from the US border at St. Stephen or from Saint John, follow Rte. 1 to Sussex, where you join Trans-Canada-2. This takes you to Moncton and on to Sackville. In Dieppe, just east of Moncton, you can go north on Rte. 15, which follows the coast to Cape Tormentine, or you can follow Rte. 11 north from Shediac to explore the coast and Kouchibouguac National Park on your way to the Miramichi or Acadian Peninsula. The smaller, slower, but more direct route to Miramichi, Rte. 126, cuts off the coast through miles of largely unsettled woodland. It makes a good return route on which to avoid the coastal traffic.

Information Sources

- Tourist Information is available from the **Public Relations and Tourism Office** at City Hall, 774 Main St., Moncton, NB ☎ 506/853-3590, where you can get a free visitor guide and map of Moncton. From mid-May to Labor Day, a tourist information center at Magnetic Hill on TransCanada-2, at the intersection with Rte. 126, has information on the entire area.

- The **Sackville Information Centre** on East Main St. (Rte. 106) is staffed from June to October, ☎ 506/364-0431; from November through May, reach them at 506/364-0400.

■ In **Shediac** you can't miss the **Information Centre** on Main St., just as you enter town from Moncton, because of the giant 35-foot green lobster (quite a remarkable work of art) in front of it, ☎ 506/533-8800. The center is open from 9 am to 9 pm, June through September.

■ In **Aulac**, there's a large **Provincial Welcome Centre** on TransCanada-2 at the Nova Scotia border, ☎ 506/364-4090. For information on the shore **north of Shediac**, contact the **Tourist Information Centre** at 21 rue Main in Richibucto, ☎ 506/523-4547.

Adventures

One of Canada's least known natural wonders is **Kouchibouguac National Park**, pronounced "COO-she-boo-quack," a long stretch of low shore and coastal plain protected by bands of barrier sand bars. It is a center for nature and outdoor activities, as well as an excellent place to camp and swim. Stop at the park headquarters to get a copy of the free magazine The Osprey, which gives information about the park's many facilities and nature programs. Walkers and cyclists should also buy a copy of the park trail map. For information on the park, write Kouchibouguac, Kent County, NB E0A 2A0, ☎ 506/876-2443, fax 506/876-4802, e-mail kouch_info@pch.gc.ca. You must pay a fee of $3.50 per day, or $10.50 for a four-day pass, just to enter the park or use any of its facilities, including parking or its hiking trails. Children under six are free, ages six-16 pay $1.75, and seniors pay $2.75. A family day pass is $7 for one day, $21 for four days. A season pass is $17.50, $8.25 for youth and $13.75 for seniors.

■ On Foot

Kouchibouguac National Park is laced with walking and hiking trails. Some are as short and easy as the 10-minute walk on the boardwalk to Kelly's Beach, across tidal pools, inlets, and dunes to a true barrier island protecting the fragile wetland behind it. You can hike through a variety of ecosystems: beach, lagoon, barrier island, marsh, bog, and river banks. Because the terrain of the park is low shoreline, none of the hikes has any noticeable ascent. Ten nature trails, from a quarter-mile to more than eight miles in length, are shown on the park's trail map, which you should buy at the Visitors' Centre.

FAVORITE TRAILS IN KOUCHIBOUGUAC NATIONAL PARK

■ The level **Osprey Trail** follows the Black River for about three miles, a good vantage point for seeing the birdlife along its banks, including osprey diving in the lagoons for fish.

■ Also rich in opportunities for bird viewing is the **Beaver Trail**, less than a mile long, surrounding a beaver pond that is a favored bird habitat.

■ The **Bog Trail**, about a mile long, leads across the bog on a boardwalk to an observation deck and to a tower with a good overview of the bog area.

■ **Claire-Fontaine Trail**, about two miles long, follows the banks of Rankin Brook, steep at times, although the trail itself is level. It is mostly through forest, with nice views across the dunes of the delta.

■ The longest is the **Kouchibouguac River Trail**, which follows the river for about eight miles, passing the Sandstone Gardens, an interesting rock formation with a hanging red pine tree. A shorter route there is from La Source, which you can reach by car.

Escuminac Park on the southern shore of Miramichi Bay has an excellent beach for walking, with some unique natural attractions. Begin at the picnic area and walk east (to the right) along the beach, toward Point Escuminac. You will cross a creek which flows from the bog just inland. Soon the beach and bog meet, and you will walk underneath bluffs of peat moss, which get higher and higher, finally reaching more than 10 feet. Such oceanside bogs are quite rare (one of the few on the east coast of the United States is at Quoddy Head in Maine) and it is interesting to see the layers of peat and contemplate how long it took them to form. When you reach the lighthouse (not a picturesque old one), you have to return along the same route. The round-trip is about eight miles. If you are a dedicated beachcomber, you will like the coves along this beach, and will return with full pockets.

South of the national park, the **Bouctouche Sandbar** is a seven-mile strip of sand almost enclosing Bouctouche Bay. You can walk along the waterline (to avoid the strenuous work of slogging through the soft beach sand or the equally sandy road along the bar's center) to a lighthouse at the tip. The entrance to the bar is just south of Saint-Louis-de-Kent. The Irving Eco-Centre La Dune de Bouctouche protects an eco-system of rare plants, nesting terns and plover, fragile marsland and dunes.

The **South Richibucto Sandbar** is a little shorter (five miles) and without a lighthouse, but still a lovely beach walk. Follow Rte. 505 from Richibucto Village to Cap-Lumière, turning left along the shore until the road peters out. On this bar, the road is better walking and the views are best on the inland (left) side. When offered a choice, stick to the left where you can see over the marsh toward the neighboring island and mainland.

A trail leads into the **Sackville Waterfowl Park** from St. Paul's Anglican Church at the corner of King and East Main streets in the center of town. Another trail enters opposite the Information Centre on East Main St., where you can park your car. Trails and boardwalks cross the 55-acre marsh, a habitat reserved for birds and other wildlife (and the people who enjoy watching them). Nine species of duck breed there, and 150 other bird varieties may be seen. The park is open daily from 5 am until half an hour after sunset. Ask at the information center for a schedule of guided bird walks and for the brochure containing a map of trails and descriptions of flora and fauna in each of the park's habitats, which include open water, meadow, marsh and woods. At the far end of the park is a picnic area and the offices of the Canadian Wildlife Service, where there are interpretive displays on wetlands and the wildlife they support.

You can explore the **Tintamarre National Wildlife Refuge** from High Marsh Rd. in Upper Sackville. Look for a "crossroad" about six miles from the covered bridge; the smaller road to the left is the trail, which follows dikes and canals through the marsh, where you are bound to see abundant birds, especially the black ducks that nest here.

Guided Walking Tours

A *Day Adventure* program features a guided 2½-hour walking tour of the **Waterfowl Park** and the adjoining areas of the **Tantramar Marshes**, with historical and nature interpretation and a chance to use dipping nets to investigate the smaller creatures that inhabit the wetland ecosystem. Tours leave from the Sackville Information Centre daily, June-August, at 1 pm. The cost is $8, and includes coffee and donuts as well as a $5 certificate to use in local restaurants. ☎ 506/364-0431 for information.

On Wheels

Kouchibouguac National Park has more than 20 miles of level, nicely-surfaced bike trails through its interior and along the water. The longest extends from Rte. 117 near the bridge over the Kouchibouguac River all the way to Kelly's Beach and along the sea front, where it reconnects to Rte. 117. About half its length is along the river bank and shore. The primitive campground at Petit-large is only accessible by bicycle or on foot. Rent bicycles for about $5 an hour, $24 a day or $30 for two days at **Ryan's Rental Center** (☎ 506/876-3733) in the park, open weekends from late May to mid-June; daily until 9 pm through the first week of September.

You can also rent bicycles in the area at **Bouctouche Bay Chalet & Campground** (☎ 506/743-2848) in Saint-Edouard, about five miles from Bouctouche.

Sackville's portion of the former rail line has been converted to a cycling path along the border of the Waterfowl Park. This short section is reached from Dooly's on Bridge St. and the longer segments are accessed next to the Tantramar Regional High School.

Guided Bicycle Tours

- In Shediac, a four-mile bicycle path/walking trail leads from the center of town to Parlee Beach. **Unique Plus Adventures** leads bike tours in the area, ☎ 506/532-8898. Or you can take a guided bicycle tour with **Chediak Tours** (☎ 506/532-4585) to learn about the history, legends and culture of Shediac. This *Day Adventure* package includes a 2½-hour tour and light refreshments for $15 per person; it is offered between late June and late September.

- **Hub City Wheelers** in Moncton (☎ 506/386-1617 or 506/386-4481) sponsor Wednesday evening rides at 6:30 pm from May through October. They leave from Victoria Park and choose routes and distances to suit all cycling skills. Weekend day and overnight trips are scheduled throughout the season, some beginning in Moncton, others in Shediac, Kouchibouguac, Memramcook, Cocagne, and locations outside the immediate area, such as Grand Manan. Leaders and assistants are part of every group. Membership is $20 for an entire season. The highlight of the year is the annual Century Ride in August, with two routes; one is 100 miles, the other 100 km (60 miles). Both begin in Riverview, just outside Moncton, and travel west toward Petitcodiac.

■ On Water

Beaches

By far the best-known (and most used) beaches in the province, perhaps in all of Atlantic Canada, are those miles of golden sand that stretch east and north from Shediac. Warm and shallow water, fine clean sand in low flat bars, and tourist facilities geared to families with water-loving children make it the destination of nearly half a million tourists each season. Since the area is Francophonic, many of these visitors are from Quebec and other French-speaking areas of Canada.

Parlee Beach east of Shediac is the most crowded in the high season, but others north and east of the town are almost as warm and certainly less crowded. To find these smaller beaches, leave Rte. 15 or Rte. 11 and follow the roads along the waterfront, such as routes 134, 950, 955, 530, 475 or 505. One of these beaches, at the tip of Cap-Pelé east of Shediac, is being "improved" by the addition of park facilities, a canteen, a bar, a new road and a parking lot, so you can expect it to become quite crowded in the near future. Windsurfing equipment can be rented for $15 and hour or $60 a day at **Sandy Beach** in Cap-Pelé from Surf Ouest, ☎ 506/577-2218.

Beaches at **Kouchibouguac National Park**, unlike those only a little farther south on the Northumberland Strait, can be chilly – or downright cold – from the waters of the Labrador current, but by mid-July can be as warm as 70°. Inside the protected lagoons the water is bathtub warm on sunny summer days. Lifeguards are on duty at **Kelly's Beach**, which makes it more crowded than the unguarded ones where you'll find lots more room to spread your beach towel.

North of the national park at the outer edge of Miramichi Bay, **Escuminac Park** has excellent surf and dunes, with new boardwalks to protect the latter. South of the park is **Jardine Park**, with a good sandy beach, changing facilities, and campground.

Canoeing & Kayaking

Eight Class I (flatwater) rivers in Kouchibouguac National Park are easily toured by paddle-power. Canoe, kayak and boat rentals are available at **Ryan's Rental Center**, ☎ 506/876-2443. Ryan's is near the South campground, and open June through September from 8 am to 9 pm. Spring and fall hours are shorter. Expect to pay about $7 for an hour's canoe rental or $26 for a day. Single kayaks are about $5 an hour; doubles are $10, with no day-rate on either.

Campsites accessible by canoe are available from mid-May to mid-October in the park for a fee of $10 for two people, plus $2 for each additional person in a site. Firewood is included.

Marc's next to the Riverside Mall in Richibucto, ☎ 506/523-5921, rents canoes (including life jackets) for $8 per person per hour.

Unique Plus Adventures (☎ 506/532-8898) in Shediac rents canoes and kayaks and runs tours.

Canoe & Kayak Outfitters / Guided Tours

■ A 10-passenger canoe operated by **Voyageur Marine Adventure** gives those who would prefer to share the paddling a chance to see seals, common terns and piping plover at close range. Three-hour tours of the offshore sandbars leave daily, and cost $25 ($15 for under 12); reservations ☎ 506/876-2443.

■ **Kayakouch** in Saint-Louise-de-Kent, ☎ 506/876-1199, fax 506/876-1918, leads half-day kayak excursions with instruction in paddling, lunch, snacks, and all equipment. They welcome first-time kayakers as well as experienced paddlers. These trips explore the warm coastal waters of Kouchibouguac National Park, visiting lagoons, sandy beaches, barrier dunes, a colony of 300 grey seals, an island tern colony, piping plover and other fascinating birds of this rich shoreline. Evening paddles ($25) are cultural in focus and include a campfire by the river. The cost for a half-day guided trip is $50 per person; an eight-hour trip is $100. Their "Heart of Nature" trip is three days and two nights on the river, exploring the Black Lands Gully, a seal colony, shorebird habitats, the lagoon, estuary and dunes. The trip, including equipment and all meals, costs $300 per person. Kayakouch also rents kayaks for $25 a half-day and $40 for a full day.

Boat Tours

5 D Tours Ecotourism, Inc. runs boat tours from May through October from Shediac's waterfront; they leave from the wharf by the Tourist Information Centre. Tours inspect a fish processing

➔ **A MICMAC EXPERIENCE:** *Before the French or English arrived the land was home to Micmac people, many of whose descendants now live on reservations in the area. In Bouctouche you can join them on a pontoon boat to explore the river their ancestors have traveled for 10,000 years. "A Micmac Experience" includes a 1½-hour boat ride with historical and cultural narration from the Micmacs' perspective, plus samples of traditional foods. Along with the boat tour, which costs $20 and operates in July and August, the Micmacs offer several other tours and encounters with their ancient culture.* ☎ *506/743-9000 for information, or reserve through the* Day Adventures *program.*

and smoking plant in Cap-Pelé, a shipyard for fishing boats and wave-carved sandstone cliffs. Prices are about $25 adults, $15 children six-14. River cruises with on-board naturalists explore the St. Louis River and Kouchibouguac National Park, visiting habitats of seabirds and grey seals, and Tern Island, the second-largest tern colony in North America. The latter trips may be two hours ($29) or four hours ($45); longer ones include a guided walk in the dunes. They leave three times daily, mid-June through mid-September, from Saint-Louis-de-Kent, five minutes from the park. ☎ 506/576-1994, 800/716-TOUR, fax 506/576-6660 for reservations. Shorter sunset cruises include a traditional musician or storyteller, and sunrise trips include breakfast on board.

The 40-foot cabin cruiser ***Claire-Fontaine*** visits the tern colonies and seals, also with a naturalist on board, leaving from Ryan's Rentals in Kouchibouguac National Park. Two-hour narrated cruises cost $25 for adults, $15 for children, and run from mid-June to late September, ☎ 506/876-4212.

Seascape Divers, 705 East Main St., Shediac, ☎ 506/858-5663 or 800/858-3483, runs several tours along the coast from Shediac. One is a mussels and champagne evening tour and another cruises the coast to the Aboiteau Restaurant, a very good wharf-side seafood restaurant, where passengers disembark for dinner before returning to Shediac. Seascape also offers one-hour cruises along the shore and to Shediac Island.

On a cruise by **Classy Tours** of Cape Tormentine, ☎ 506/538-2981, you can take a boat under the giant spans of the new bridge to Prince Edward Island and hear about the construction of the longest bridge in the western hemisphere. Then try your hand at hauling lobster traps as you learn about these delicious crustaceans. The cost for a two-hour tour is $25 for adults and $15 for children; boats leave from the Marine Atlantic terminal and can be reserved through the *Day Adventure* program.

Down East Chartering at Cap-de-Cocagne, 10 miles north of Shediac, ☎ 506/533-6253, offers three-hour sailing cruises in the Northumberland Strait three times daily for $25 per person, or day-long cruises for $89. A live-aboard overnight sailing trip with hands-on instruction on sail handling costs $189 per person.

Learn to sail in a full-day, hands-on course aboard ***Tradewinds***, a 25-foot sailboat out of Shediac Bay Marina, ☎ 506/866-5441. *Tradewinds* and the 36-foot *Escapade* are also available for cruises of five hours to several days. Day or sunset sails leave at 10 am and 4 pm, and cost $25-50 per person. Longer trips with on-board accommodations are $300 per day.

For a tour of the Bouctouche River on a pontoon boat, see the box describing "A Micmac Experience" on the previous page.

Diving

Seascape Divers, 705 East Main St., Shediac, ☎ 506/858-5663 or 800/858-3483, offers scuba excursions and night dives at an old shipwreck. They also rent equipment.

Fishing

Lobster fishing trips are offered by **5 D Tours Ecotourism, Inc.**, Saint-Louis-de-Kent, ☎ 506/576-1994 or 800/716-TOUR, fax 506/576-6660, and by **Seascape Divers**, 705 East Main St., Shediac, ☎ 506/858-5663 or 800/858-3483. Seascape also runs mackerel fishing trips (the catch is best in August) and early morning shark fishing trips, which leave at 4 am and return about 10 am.

■ On Snow

Kouchibouguac National Park is the centerpiece of winter activity on the eastern coast, with cross-country skiing, snowshoeing, snowmobiling and winter walking trails, in addition to areas used for tobogganing. A three-mile trail in the park is set aside for winter walkers – those who prefer not to use either skis or snowshoes. The park does charge a trail fee for use in the winter, but we think the warming huts provided there make it well worth the cost.

Skiing

Cross-country skiing is very popular in this region of low coastal landscapes. **Club de Ski de Fond Boules de Niege,** the local ski club for the National Park area, sponsors a purely recreational loppet (cross-country meet) in early March, ☎ 506/876-2443. Many local parks have shorter trail systems that you can find through local clubs, many of which are responsible for maintaining the trails. Contact the **Beaver Cross-Country Ski Club** in Cocagne, ☎ 506/576-7927. In the Moncton area trails are maintained and events sponsored by the **Riverview Cross-Country Ski Club**, ☎ 506/386-4754.

SKI-AND-STAY PACKAGES

The **Kouchibouguac Motel and Restaurant** (☎ 506/876-2407, fax 506/876-4318) in St-Louise-de-Kent south of the park entrance on Rte. 134, has its own ski trail connecting to the 18 miles of groomed trails in the park, so you can literally ski right out your door. The motel rents skis and boots (with discounts to guests) and provides free ski trail maps. A package with two nights lodging, breakfasts, and a candlelit German dinner with wine is $178 per couple.

For $275 per couple, **Kayakouch** (☎ 506/876-1199, fax 506/876-1918), also in St-Louise, offers two nights lodging, a seafood or meat fondue dinner with wine, two Acadian brunches, a boxed lunch, a day's outdoor activity, and an Acadian soiree in the evening.

Habitant Motel (☎ 506/523-4421) in Richibucto near Kouchibouguac National Park has cross-country ski trails leading right from the door, connecting to the park's extensive trail network.

Chalets Nicholas (☎ 506/577-6420, fax 506/577-6422) in Robichaud east of Shediac packages a $65 night skiing experience through the *Day Adventures* program. Included is ski equipment, a night light kit, a guide and trail pass to a three-mile trail, followed by a meal at the clubhouse.

Little Shemogue Country Inn (☎ 506/538-2320, fax 506/538-7494) in Port Elgin adds a little romance to the package with a deluxe room, a five-course candlelight dinner in their highly acclaimed restaurant, a bottle of wine or champagne, snowshoes or a day of cross-country skiing or skating on the bay, all for about $200 a couple.

Kouchibouguac National Park's 18 miles of groomed trails are particularly attractive, not only for the stunning views from its mixture of wooded and open trails, but for the services along the way. Warming cabins with wood stoves and washrooms, as well as picnic tables, are spaced at closer than two-mile intervals, making this particularly attractive to families with small children or Sunday skiers who need to stop and rest often. The terrain is nearly level.

The cycling path on the former rail line in Sackville, bordering Waterfowl Park, is used for cross-country skiing in the winter. See *On Wheels* for access information. Beech Hill Park, also in Sackville, has two marked trails of one and two miles respectively.

Moncton's 450-acre **Centennial Park** has three ski trails, one of which is lighted at night. The nine miles of trails are particularly scenic, crossing several bridges over a brook.

Snowmobiling

The province-wide network of snowmobile trails is well represented along the coast, with a through trail extending from the Nova Scotia border to Miramichi and several inland trails connecting to create shorter circuit routes. Spur trails extend to Cape Tormentine and to Point Escuminac on Miramichi Bay.

The *Day Adventure* program offers several packages on the east coast for experienced or beginning snowmobilers. At **Seasonal Rentals** (☎ 506/523-4876) in Rexton you can get a night's lodging for two, a full day's use of a snowmobile, including accessories and insurance, plus direct access from your lodging to groomed trails, for $275 a couple. A half-day guided snowmobile tour with machine and insurance is $95 per person. Several other lodgings are located close to trails and offer special winter rates and packages that include such extras as meals or wine. At the **Habitant Restaurant and Motel** (☎ 506/523-4421) in Richibucto you can rent snowmobiles or take advantage of a winter package designed for beginners that includes a day of guided snowmobiling with dinner at the restaurant.

Chalets Nicholas (☎ 506/577-6420, fax 506/577-6422) in Robichaud (east of Shediac) offers a guided day excursion along the shore to the new Confederation Bridge, in a program designed especially for beginners. Snowmobiles and suit, insurance, instruction, guide, a hot lunch and a traditional Acadian dinner are included in the package for $270 a person or $300 for a couple sharing a snowmobile.

Snowmobile Clubs

■ The local snowmobile club in Shediac is **Safari 2000**, reached at ☎ 506/532-3074.

■ **Southeastern New Brunswick Snowmobile Association** is in Riverview near Moncton, ☎ 506/387-4131.

■ **Winter Wanderers** covers the Port Elgin area, ☎ 506/538-7877.

■ Near Kouchibouguac, contact the **Rexton Snowmobile Club** at ☎ 506/523-9252.

Dogsledding, Sleigh Rides & Skating

East Coast Dogsledding (☎ 506/743-8670) in Saint-Anne-de-Kent between Rexton and Bouctouche, combines dogsledding with winter fishing for speckled trout in their open pond in a *Day Adventure* package for $70. You get to keep a trout. Or you can opt for just the dogsledding.

Kouchibouguac National Park maintains tobogganing areas for which winter access fees are charged. You can arrange a sleigh ride at **Centennial Park** in Moncton by calling ☎ 506/853-3510, or take advantage of one of the winter packages offered by **Hotel Beauséjour**, which includes a sleigh outing at the park. Centennial Park also has a skating rink with a warming hut.

Chalets Nicholas in Robichaud (east of Shediac) has outdoor skating, with a clubhouse, ☎ 506/577-6420, fax 506/577-6422.

Kick Sleds

While kick sleds are quite common in Finland and elsewhere in Scandinavia, they are not often used in this hemisphere. Particularly good for families with small children, they combine sport for the driver with a sled-ride for a youngster. Picture an old-fashioned two-wheeled scooter with runners instead of wheels and a passenger seat under the handle bars; this will give you an idea of what they look like. **La Suite du Fond d'la Baie** (☎ 506/743-6265) in Bouctouche offers a half-day guided kick sled excursion along the town's remarkable dunes, followed by a fireside dinner of buffalo and a night's lodging, for $150 a couple. Children under 10 stay free. Or you can take a two-hour guided sled excursion followed by a hearty lunch, for $20 ($10 per child; free under age 10).

On Horseback

Outlaws Retreat Trail Rides in Sackville, ☎ 506/379-1014, offers riding between mid-September and June. In the summer they run a six-day riding camp for children; each child has their own horse and a family barbecue is held at the end of the week. The cost of this program is $225. In the winter they are equipped for sleigh rides.

Vallee de Memramcook Learning and Vacation Resort, a complete resort facility with cultural and ecological programs, has horseback riding on trails throughout its 520 acres of rolling hills. ☎ 800/268-2511 or 506/758-2511, fax 506/758-2149.

Cultural & Eco-Travel Experiences

At the crossroads of travel since the earliest days of settlement, this area has a rich blend of people from French, English, Irish and German origins. Most of the shore is Acadian country, where you will hear French spoken more than English. Moncton is 30% Francophone; here you'll find the French-language Université de Moncton and its free **Musée Acadien** in the Clement Cormier Building, ☎ 506/858-4088. The museum's collections visually document the daily life and culture of the Acadians who settled here after being driven out of Nova Scotia. Summer hours: Monday-Friday, 10 am to 5 pm; Saturday-Sunday, 1 to 5 pm. The rest of the year they are open Tuesday-Friday, 1 to 4:30 pm and Saturday and Sunday, 1 to 4 pm. The museum can be reached by heading north on Archibald Street.

One of Canada's best collections of Inuit art is on display at the **Bibliotheque Champlain**, weekdays 8:30 am to 11 pm, Saturday 10 am to 5 pm and Sunday 11 am to 5 pm, September through April. The Fine Collection of Inuit Art has 242 works by 150 artists.

Mount Allison University atop the hill in the center of Sackville had the first art museum in Eastern Canada, the **Owens Art Gallery**, established in 1894. The gallery is free and open year-round; weekdays, 10 am to 5 pm, and weekend afternoons in the summer; shorter hours the rest of the year. ☎ 506/364-2574 for information. Its collections emphasize works by European and North American artists, and it has made Sackville a center for artists. The university also has a museum of fossils housed in the **Avard Dixon Building**. The collection and other displays on the history of the earth are open to the public on weekdays, 9 am to 5 pm, and on weekend afternoons.

Struts Center art gallery on Lorne St. off West Main St., ☎ 506/536-1211, shows and sells works by numerous nationally known artists who live and work in the area.

An almost lost art is alive and well at the **Sackville Harness Shop**, the only manufacturer of handmade horse collars in North America. They are at 50 West Main St. at the top of the hill.

Le Pays de la Sagouine is an Acadian stage-set town, built to bring alive the characters and places in Antonine Maillet's fictional stories. Built on an island, this make-believe town is living theater, and you'll find yourself taking part even though you may not understand the language. Song, dance, fiddle music, Acadian food, traditional crafts, history and storytelling are all part of the theater; you can spend a day immersed in this Acadian atmosphere. It's on Rte. 11 in Bouctouche, ☎ 506/743-1400. Open daily, mid-June through August; admission is $7 adult, children $4.

Moncton has a **Farmers Market** at 132 Robinson St. on Saturday from 7 am to 1 pm, and on Wednesday from noon to 4 pm. Canadian and other ethnic foods make the market a good lunch stop; look for shish-kebab, farm sausage, homemade breads, pastries and fresh meats and produce. Crafts also have a prominent place here. The market is between Main Street and the river, ☎ 506/383-1749.

Pick your own fresh strawberries in July at **Poirier Farm** on Chemin Perry Rd. in Bouctouche, ☎ 506/743-2922.

■ Festivals

Acadian festivals celebrate this French heritage, especially on **Acadian Day**, August 15, in Saint-Louis and Richibucto, and at the Kent Museum in Bouctouche. During the week leading up to Acadian Day there is a pilgrimage to the Acadian shrine in

Rogersville. Other festivals recognize the main industries of the region, lumber and fishing, with a **Lumberjack Festival** in Bass River in early July (☎ 506/785-2227), a **Fishermen's Festival** in Collette in mid-July (☎ 506/775-2324), and a **Scallop Festival** in Richibucto in late July (☎ 506/523-9724). But the granddaddy of all seafood festivals is the **Lobster Festival** in Shediac (the town with the big lobster monument) early in July, ☎ 506/532-1122.

■ Natural Areas & Wildlife

The marshlands around Sackville and along the isthmus between there and the Nova Scotia border are world-class birding sites. Each summer the surrounding wetlands provide nesting sites for dozens of species of waterfowl and in August migrating shorebirds stop here – as many as half a million in a single flock. Sackville's **Waterfowl Park**, where 160 species have been recorded, begins right in the center of town (see *On Foot*, above) and **Tintamarre National Wildlife Area**, **Eddy Marsh**, **Fort Beauséjour** and **Cape Tormentine** all offer prime bird habitats. Dorchester Cape, at the end of the Bay of Fundy, has over 50,000 sandpipers daily during the birds' migration season in late July and early August. Bald eagles and peregrine falcons are sighted here, too. The Sackville Information Centre can give you a copy of the *Bird-Finding Guide* to help you locate the best places.

You can tour the **Tantramar Marshes** with the help of a self-guiding map and narratives, available free from the Information Centre in Sackville. The tour covers the largest man-made agricultural landmass in Canada, reclaimed from the sea by the use of dikes, canals and *aboiteaux* (drainage gates) by the Acadians in the 1700s. The tour includes short walks with driving.

Westcock Marsh, off Rte. 935 between West Sackville and Westcock, has a three-mile loop trail that follows one of these dikes along the sea. Along with good views, the dike provides a look at the marsh environment and its rich birdlife.

In late July and early August, the migration of a number of bird species, particularly sandpipers, reaches its height in the nutrient-rich mudflats at **Johnsons Mills**, south of Sackville. More than two million birds converge here, and one of the best ways to understand the phenomenon you are seeing is with a biologist as a guide.

The **Memramcook Learning and Vacation Resort** in St. Joseph has a program that combines a slide show at the center before following the guide (in your own vehicle) to Johnsons Mills for 1½ hours of bird observation and interpretation. High-quality binoculars and telescopes are provided (you may want to bring your own in case the group is very large). The cost is $10 per person, with a maximum of $20 per family. Tours are scheduled to coincide with the tides, so you will need to call for a schedule, but reservations are not necessary. ☎ 506/758-2511, fax 506/758-2149.

THE ACADIAN ABOITEAUX

The early Acadian settlers in New Brunswick and Nova Scotia found a way to grow crops in the rich sedimentary soil of the tidal valleys fed by the unusually high Bay of Fundy tides. Twice each day, tides of 20 or 30 feet wash in to fill long estuaries, covering acres and acres of mud flats. The Acadians devised a system of sea walls so strong that they would withstand the power of this wall of water. They began by planting several rows of strong trees at the points where the sea entered the marshes. Between these rows they laid cut trees in parallel stacks, filling the spaces between them with well-beaten clay to make them watertight. In the center of each of these dikes they made a trap-door – the aboiteau – to allow river water to flow out at low tide, but not let the sea flow in at high tide. While these held back normal tides, they purposely fell short of the extreme tides, allowing these to occasionally enrich the soil with their deposits.

Farther north, look for shorebirds and others – a total of 225 have been identified here – at **Kouchibouguac National Park**. Trails along the Black and Kouchibouguac Rivers provide the best variety, but the Bog Trail is also fruitful for birders. To learn what current sightings are, call either the **Moncton Naturalist Club**, ☎ 506/384-6397, or the **New Brunswick Bird Information Line**, ☎ 506/382-3825.

Magnetic Hill Zoo, off TransCanada-2 just outside of Moncton, has Canadian natives, such as the Arctic wolf, and rare exotics, including Siberian tigers and Dromedary camels. At 1 pm daily, join a staff member for "Meet the Keeper" and learn about particularly interesting animals. A special exhibit shows examples of the products that contribute to the depletion of rare animals, of particular interest to travelers who might not otherwise recognize objects made from endangered species. Open mid-May through mid-October, daily 9 am to dusk, ☎ 506/384-0303. Admission is $4.

Moncton is one of the best places to see the **tidal bore**, a wall of water that is pushed into the estuary's mud flats by the tremendous forces of the Fundy tides. A wide, deep gully of dark mud fills twice a day, as water is compressed into a very narrow space. Less dramatic than it was before the construction of a causeway, the sudden rise is still worth seeing. Go to Bore View Park, where a large sign gives the time of the tide's next sudden arrival.

Sightseeing

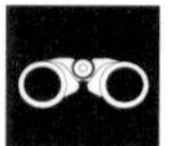

Fort Beauséjour National Historic Park, near Aulac at the Nova Scotia border, overlooks the Tantramar marshes and the inner edges of the Bay of Fundy. Built by the French, it was captured in 1755 by New England militia under British command and renamed Fort Cumberland. You can walk the earthworks and explore the underground passages as you learn about this tempestuous time in Canadian history, when this area played a pivotal role in the determination of which country would own Canada and New England, ☎ 506/536-0720. Admission is $2.25 for adults, less for seniors and children; the fort is open daily, 9 am to 5 pm, June through late October.

One of Eastern Canada's most visited attractions is **Magnetic Hill**, northwest of Moncton near TransCanada-2. As you near, signs tell you to drive down the slope, then cross to the left side of the roadway and stop your car by the white post. Put it in neutral, release the brake, and astonish your kids in the backseat by rolling back up the gentle slope to the top. It's an optical illusion, but for kids old enough to understand that it's not normal for things to roll uphill, it's worth the $2.

The free **Moncton Museum**, 20 Mountain Rd., ☎ 506/853-3003, hides in a new building behind the façade of the old City Hall. Permanent exhibits on Moncton history are upstairs; changing exhibits (often from Montreal's Museum of Fine Arts) are downstairs. Next door, and reached from the museum, is Moncton's oldest building, Free Meeting House, built in 1821. Over the years it has been used by a dozen different congregations in the city, including Protestant, Catholic and Jewish. Both are open daily in the summer, 10 am to 5 pm; in the winter, Tuesday-Friday and Sunday, 1 to 5 pm, Saturday, 10 am to 5 pm.

Also free is the **Thomas Williams Heritage House**, 103 Park St., Highfield, ☎ 506/857-0590. The 12-room Second Empire-style home has been restored to the elegance of its 1883 construction. Black marble fireplaces and fine wood paneling and carving are among its highlights. In the summer the Verandah Tea Room serves muffins, ice cream, tea, coffee and lemonade. Open May through mid-October: daily in mid-summer; in spring and fall, Monday, Wednesday and Friday from 10am to 3 pm.

Keillor House in Dorchester is a restored home depicting local life in the 19th century. Here also is the unusual **Maritime Penitentiary Museum**, whose exhibits range from the grim to the amusing – including examples of ways prisoners have tried to escape from the prison. Admission to both is $1 and they are open daily, 9 am to 5 pm, June through mid-September. ☎ 506/379-6633.

An unusual attraction in Sackville is the antennae farm of **Radio Canada International**. Here are the country's most powerful shortwave radio transmitters, broadcasting to Europe and South America. Free tours are offered between 10 am and 6 pm daily. You'll see the transmitters beside TransCanada-2, just east of town. ☎ 506/536-2690.

In Port Elgin, visit **Rosswog Farm Distillery** on Rte. 970 at Baie Verte. It was the first fruit farm distillery in Canada. ☎ 506/538-7405.

Where To Stay & Eat

Kouchibouguac/Bouctouche

Bouctouche's first rectory, built in 1880, has been transformed into **l'Auberge le Vieux Presbytere de Bouctouche 1880**. The original building has five suites with period furnishings; the two additions have modern rooms. Grounds and gardens border the sea and have a view of the lighthouse. Their excellent restaurant serves local seafood and other specialties such as pork medallions in a fig coulis. Don't miss the pâté of fresh and smoked salmon. *157 Chemin du Couvent, Bouctouche, NB E0A 1G0, ☎ 506/743-5568, fax 506/743-5566 ($$).*

The **Kouchibouguac Motel and Restaurant** is just south of the entrance to Kouchibouguac National Park. Its new owners are

> **➔ ACCOMMODATIONS ASSISTANCE:** *For a long list of cottage rentals in Shediac, and another brochure detailing lodging and restaurants, contact the **Town of Shediac**, PO Box 969, Shediac, NB E0A 3G0, ☎ 506/532-6156.*

from Germany, and have transformed the restaurant into a haven for those who love hearty knüdlen and delicate weiner schnitzels. Ask about their winter packages that include skiing in the park; you can ski right from your door. *Rte. 134, St.-Louise-de-Kent, NB E0A 2Z0, ☎ 506/876-2407, fax 506/876-4318 ($$).*

Habitant Motel and Restaurant is also near Kouchibouguac National Park, and connected to it by cross-country ski trails leading right from the door. Inside you'll find a heated swimming pool and sauna, in case the weather isn't right for swimming at the nearby beaches. It's a motel, but has the warm hospitality of an inn. You won't go wrong in the restaurant either. *PO Box 44, Richibucto, NB E0A 2M0, ☎ 506/523-4421 or 800/561-7666, fax 506/523-9155 ($$).*

Log cabins at **Richibucto River Resort** are each set on an acre of woodland overlooking the river. These cabins are especially attractive to riders since they have stables of Icelandic horses and riding trails. Launch your canoe from your own front yard. *Rte. 116, Upper Rexton, NB E0A 2L0, ☎ 506/523-4480, fax 506/523-4484 ($$).*

Les Chalets du Havre offers a newly built self-catering cottages on a secluded peninsula, but within a 10-minute walk from town. An attractive bonus is the summer shuttle boat directly to the shore at Kouchibouguac National Park. Canoes, kayaks, rowboats and bicycles are available for guests. *PO Box 555, Richibucto, NB E0A 2M0, ☎ 506/523-1570 or 800/277-9037, fax 506/523-9770; Web site www.new-brunswick.com/chalet.htm ($$-$$$).*

McPhail's Lobster Haven is a waterfront seafood restaurant and fish market. They also run boat tours. *Rte. 11 at Exit 27, ☎ 506/743-8432.*

South of Shediac

Hotel Beauséjour is a class-act downtown hotel. Although its rates are city level, look for bargains on weekends and in the summer. It's right where the action is, near restaurants, nightclubs, and the Capitol Theatre. The rooftop pool has a lifeguard and sun-

➲ **SEAFOOD LOVERS:** *One of the reasons people come to Shediac is to enjoy the abundance of fresh seafood, especially shellfish. Continental French and Acadian dishes are featured in local restaurants, and during the July Lobster Festival lobster dinners are less expensive than at other times. There's a lot of deep-fried seafood, but also mussels, scallops, shrimp and lobster prepared in classic and provincial French styles.*

deck, 24-hour room service, in-room movies, and non-smoking wings. See below for its two outstanding restaurants. *750 Main St., Moncton, NB E1C 1E6, ☎ 506/854-4344, 800/828-7447 in the US, 800/268-9411 in Canada, fax 506/854-4344 ($$$).*

Canadiana Inn is an 1880s mansion in a quiet neighborhood close to Main Street. Nice architectural details have been retained and the feeling is still that of a home, rather than a hotel. Public areas include Victorian parlors, verandas, and a dining room. Guest rooms are comfortable and homey and the hosts are warm and friendly. Breakfast is not included, but available at a reasonable cost. *46 Archibald St., Moncton, NB E1C 5H9, ☎ 506/382-1054 ($$).*

Victoria Bed & Breakfast is an elegant home transformed into lodgings. Antiques, lacy linens, duvets and soft robes pamper guests here; breakfasts are memorable. *71 Park St., Moncton, NB E1C 2B2, ☎/fax 506/389-8296.*

The **Université de Moncton** operates a hostel from May to August with lodging for about $25 a night. *North of the center of town via Archibald St., ☎ 506/858-4008.*

The elegant **Marshlands Inn** retains the molded ceilings, beveled glass windows, fine woodwork and an original William Morris frieze in the dining room that distinguish this Victorian building. Antique furnishings and original works by many local artists complete the decor. It's clear why Queen Elizabeth chose to stop for a respite here on her 1984 tour. The dining room ($$) has more than fine historic decor to offer, with a classic continental menu that adds some pleasant local surprises – fiddleheads as a side dish, blueberry sauce with breast of duck, smoked salmon layered with puff pastry. *59 Bridge St., PO Box 1440, Sackville, NB E0A 3C0, ☎ 506/536-0170, fax 506/536-0721 ($$).*

Savoy Arms Bed and Breakfast will appeal especially to fans of Gilbert and Sullivan's operettas. Room names and decor echo themes from their work, but in a playful way. Guests enjoy the genial hosts and the large, well-stocked library overlooking the backyard and terrace, where they may have breakfast in good weather. *55 Bridge St., PO Box 785, Sackville, NB E0A 3C0, ☎ 506/536-0790 ($-$$).*

Vallee de Memramcook Learning and Vacation Resort is a full-service resort with music and theater programs, a golf course, tennis, horseback riding and nature trails. Its 520 rolling acres are in a scenic valley between Moncton and Sackville. The restaurant, **Au Vieux College** ($$), serves seafood and other entrées in continental French style, with a selection of traditional Acadian dishes, including fricot, poutine rapée, meat pie and sugar pie. The menu has a good selection of heart-healthy dishes low in fat, which are marked by a symbol on the menu. The restaurant is open Wednesday-Sunday from 5 pm. *488 rue Central, PO Box 180, St.-Joseph, NB E0A 2Y0, ☎ 800/268-2511 or 506/758-2511, fax 506/758-2149 ($$).*

Chez Françoise is a comfortable inn in a late 19th-century house. Guest rooms are simply furnished, but the architectural detail of the public rooms is elegant, with leaded glass, fireplaces, and wood paneling. The croissants are the highlight of the complimentary continental breakfast. The inn is open May through December. Their dining room ($$-$$$) is open to the public, serving veal, salmon, and other dishes in a continental French style. Dinner is served from 5 to 10 pm, Sunday brunch from 11 am to 3 pm. *93 rue Main, PO Box 715, Shediac, NB E0A 3G0, ☎ 506/532-4233 ($-$$).*

The seven-room **Belcourt Inn** is right in the center of town. Handmade quilts cover brass beds in several of the rooms. The inn is open year-round, and has a loyal following of guests who return to its warm hospitality each year, so reserve well ahead. *112 rue Main, Shediac, NB E0A 3G0, ☎ 506/532-6098 ($$).*

Little Shemogue Country Inn is a four-star inn with a well-known dining room. It is furnished in Canadian and European antiques, and has only five guest rooms, so the atmosphere is more that of a fine country home. *RR 2, Hwy 955, Port Elgin, NB E0A 2K0, ☎ 506/538-2320, fax 506/538-7494 ($$).*

For a homey bed and breakfast at budget prices, reserve a room at **A.& A. Jacobs Bed & Breakfast**. It's a 70-year-old farmhouse only five minutes from the beautiful beaches of the Northumberland Strait. *Upper Cape Rd., RR 2 Port Elgin, Melrose, NB E0A 2K0,* ☎ *506/538-9980.*

The **Windjammer** is the premier eating place in Moncton, and looks like the captain's dining room aboard an elegant small ship. The changing menu may feature wild game, and will certainly offer finely prepared seafood. Their daily four-course prix fixe menu is reduced in price from 5:30 to 6:30 pm, the first hour of opening. They are busy every night of the week, so do make reservations ahead. *Hotel Beauséjour, 750 Main St, Moncton,* ☎ *506/854-4344 ($$-$$$).*

L'Auberge shares a chef with the Windjammer, but serves a slightly less ambitious and less expensive menu in a relaxed setting where families would feel as comfortable as couples dining tete-a-tete. We usually opt for the nightly specials, especially if they include the giant bowl of steamed mussels. For fine dining at affordable prices, you will never go wrong here. Open daily from 7 am to 10:30 pm. *Hotel Beauséjour, 750 Main St, Moncton,* ☎ *506/854-4344 ($$).*

Pastalli's Pasta House serves pasta and other entrées, most under $10, in an attractive atmosphere of carpeting and candlelight. Make your own garlic bread in unlimited quantities over an open grill, choosing from several herbed butters. Combinations are particularly good, such as pasta with fiddleheads, fennel or olives; the vegetable lasagna is excellent. We usually order the pasta sampler because we can't decide. Wines are very reasonably priced. Open Monday-Thursday, 11 am to 11 pm; Friday and Saturday, 11 am to midnight; Sunday, 4 pm to 11 pm. *Main St., Moncton,* ☎ *506/383-1050 ($-$$).*

Tivoli Bakery is open Tuesday-Saturday from 9 am to 10 pm and Sunday from 10 am to 7 pm, serving sandwiches, breads, pastries, sandwiches ($3-$5), soups and salads. Let them make picnic sandwiches for you or stop in the morning for a croissants ($1). *Main Street, Moncton,* ☎ *506/862-0011.*

Fisherman's Paradise is the place to sample it all, with their special of half a lobster, fried clams, scallops, stuffed shrimp, and a variety of fish, all for under $30. You'll find lobster prepared in a number of ways, and a good selection of non-fried seafood. Open daily, 11:30 am to 11 pm, from mid-April to mid-September. *Main St., Shediac,* ☎ *506/532-6811 ($-$$$), is at the east end of town, near Exit 37 on Rte. 15.*

> ➔ **DINING TIP:** *We know our friends in Saint John will be scandalized by this, but we think Moncton has the best collection of restaurants of any city in the province. Perhaps it's because it's a French city, and to the French, dining out is valued as an experience. Whatever the reason, you will be well-fed here, and find local people knowledgeable (as well as opinionated) when you ask for restaurant recommendations.*

Paturel Shore House serves forthright dishes of the freshest, finest quality seafood you'll find anywhere. The hearty lobster stew appetizer hardly leaves room for the entrée to come, and the seafood platter is gigantic. Open daily, 4 to 10 pm, from May through September. *Cape Bimet Rd., Rte. 133, Shediac,* ☎ *506/532-4774 ($-$$$).*

Fred's Restaurant is the place we go when we can't live another day without the world's best fried clams. Although we never order anything but clams here, we see happy people at neighboring tables wolfing down enormous lobster rolls and sandwiches on thick-cut bread. Fred's is open Sunday to Wednesday, 7:30 am to 9 pm; Thursday and Friday, 7:30 am to 10 pm; and Saturday, 7:30 am to 1 pm. *Rte. 15, Cap-Pelé,* ☎ *506/577-4269 ($-$$).*

Aboiteau Fisheries serves lobster-in-the-rough from a take-out a window in the back of the fisheries plant. Carry your clams, scallops, fish or chowder to tables in the enclosed picnic area. A tip on buying lobster: instead of getting a lobster dinner, go around the building to the fish market and choose live lobsters. Bring them back here and they'll cook them for you and provide plates, utensils and butter. It's not cheating – they suggested we do this to get the best market price. Only in New Brunswick.... *The Pier, Cap-Pelé, no phone ($-$$).*

The **Vienna Coffee House** is a casual restaurant serving hearty breakfasts – mega-omelets and eggs Benedict, lunches of creamy chowder or sandwiches on whole grain or white bread (baked here) and dinners. The evening menu is limited to a half-dozen choices, but good ones: chicken Kiev, Italian hot sausages with potato and sauerkraut, poached salmon and spareribs. This is a good choice for afternoon tea or a coffee break, accompanied by one of their luscious cakes or pastries: Fundy mud, chocolate velvet cheesecake or homey apple dumplings. *28 York St., Sackville, ☎ 506/563-0409 ($-$$).*

■ Camping

You'll travel far to find better-maintained campgrounds than those at **Kouchibouguac National Park**. Sites are large, mowed and well-spaced, the facilities spotless. This quality has not gone unnoticed, and the park is filled to the brim. You can reserve sites by calling ☎ 800/213-PARK, but half the spaces are held for those without reservations, so get there early in the day for the best chances and take a number for the next morning if you don't get a site. Fees range from $16 to $20. In addition to traditional campgrounds, two are not accessible by car. The Petit-Large area has primitive sites, with access by bicycle or on foot only. Sipu, on the riverbank, can also be reached by canoe. *Kouchibouguac, NB E0A 20A, ☎ 506/876-2443.*

Habitant Campground is close to the national park, and has a swimming pool and canteen. *PO Box 44, Richibucto, NB E0A 2M0, ☎ 506/523-4421, fax 506/523-9155.*

Jardine Municipal Park is a former provincial park now operated by the town of Richibucto. Serviced sites are $14, unserviced $12. *Richibucto, NB E0A 2M0, ☎ 506/523-4421.*

Escuminac Beach and Family Park is a former provincial park at Point Escuminac, on the southern shore of Miramichi Bay. It is now privately operated, with unserviced and partially-serviced sites at $10 and $16 a day, respectively. *PO Box 133, Baie Ste-Anne, NB E0C 1A0, ☎ 506/228-4532.*

Camping is available in a beachside setting at **Parlee Beach Provincial Park.** Rates are about $20 a day. *PO Box 1537, Shediac, NB E0A 3G0, ☎ 506/532-1500.*

Near the Confederation Bridge to Prince Edward Island, **Murray Beach Provincial Park** has campsites adjoining the white sand beach. *Cape Tormentine, NB E0A 10A, ☎ 506/538-2628.*

Nova Scotia

Introduction

Connected to the mainland by only a narrow isthmus, Nova Scotia seems like an island. Water surrounds it, and most of its towns and cities lie on the coast, which is ringed by roads designated as scenic routes. Each of these drives highlights an area, but each also points out the many contrasts that make Nova Scotia so interesting: past and present, sea and mountains, cosmopolitan and rural, all enriched by the three distinct cultures of Scottish, English and French.

IN THIS CHAPTER

- Chignecto
- The Evangeline Trail
- The Southern Shore
- Halifax & Environs
- Marine Drive & The East
- Cape Breton Highlands
- Cape Breton Lakes

Urbane **Halifax** is the commercial and political capital of the province, and the transportation hub of the entire region. Most flights into Atlantic Canada arrive here, and frequent flights connect it to cities in the other provinces. Its streets are lined with fine restaurants, many of them housed in historic buildings along the busy waterfront.

Nova Scotia's tri-cultural blend is a long-standing one. The **French** were the first Europeans to settle here, when Samuel de Champlain established a colony at Port Royal, now Annapolis Royal, in 1605. Over the next decades the French, who in this part of New France were called **Acadians**, spread along the west shore. **Scottish immigrants** came to the Pictou area in the mid-1700s, after France ceded Acadia to Britain. France had retained Cape Breton, which they continued to settle until the fall of their fortress at Louisbourg in 1758. Meanwhile the British populated new areas with immigrants from England and Scotland. A wave of Loyalists fleeing the American Revolution joined in the 1780s. Later, another influx of Scottish people settled in the Cape Breton Highlands.

You will see each of these cultures, alive and well today. French influence remains strong in the old Acadian areas and parts of

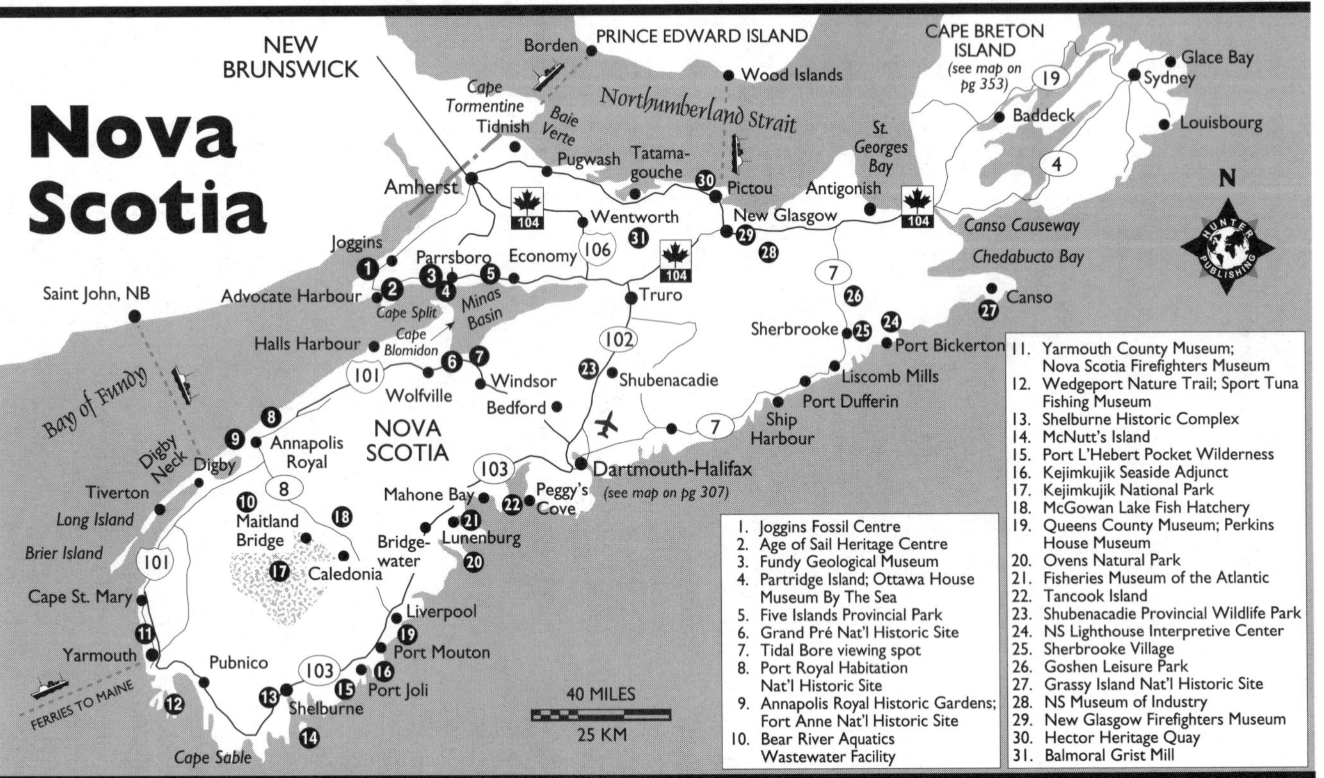

Nova Scotia
NEW BRUNSWICK
PRINCE EDWARD ISLAND
Borden
Wood Islands
Northumberland Strait
CAPE BRETON ISLAND (see map on pg 353)
Baddeck
Sydney
Glace Bay
Louisbourg
N
HUNTER PUBLISHING
Canso Causeway
Chedabucto Bay
Canso
Port Bickerton
St. Georges Bay
Antigonish
New Glasgow
Pictou
Tatamagouche
Pugwash
Baie Verte
Cape Tormentine
Tidnish
Amherst
Joggins
Advocate Harbour
Parrsboro
Cape Split
Cape Blomidon
Minas Basin
Economy
Wentworth
Truro
Shubenacadie
Sherbrooke
Liscomb Mills
Port Dufferin
Ship Harbour
Dartmouth-Halifax (see map on pg 307)
Bedford
Windsor
Wolfville
Halls Harbour
NOVA SCOTIA
Peggy's Cove
Mahone Bay
Lunenburg
Bridgewater
Liverpool
Port Mouton
Port Joli
Shelburne
Caledonia
Annapolis Royal
Maitland Bridge
Digby
Digby Neck
Saint John, NB
Bay of Fundy
Tiverton
Long Island
Brier Island
Cape St. Mary
Yarmouth
FERRIES TO MAINE
Pubnico
Cape Sable
40 MILES
25 KM
1. Joggins Fossil Centre
2. Age of Sail Heritage Centre
3. Fundy Geological Museum
4. Partridge Island; Ottawa House Museum By The Sea
5. Five Islands Provincial Park
6. Grand Pré Nat'l Historic Site
7. Tidal Bore viewing spot
8. Port Royal Habitation Nat'l Historic Site
9. Annapolis Royal Historic Gardens; Fort Anne Nat'l Historic Site
10. Bear River Aquatics Wastewater Facility
11. Yarmouth County Museum; Nova Scotia Firefighters Museum
12. Wedgeport Nature Trail; Sport Tuna Fishing Museum
13. Shelburne Historic Complex
14. McNutt's Island
15. Port L'Hebert Pocket Wilderness
16. Kejimkujik Seaside Adjunct
17. Kejimkujik National Park
18. McGowan Lake Fish Hatchery
19. Queens County Museum; Perkins House Museum
20. Ovens Natural Park
21. Fisheries Museum of the Atlantic
22. Tancook Island
23. Shubenacadie Provincial Wildlife Park
24. NS Lighthouse Interpretive Center
25. Sherbrooke Village
26. Goshen Leisure Park
27. Grassy Island Nat'l Historic Site
28. NS Museum of Industry
29. New Glasgow Firefighters Museum
30. Hector Heritage Quay
31. Balmoral Grist Mill

Cape Breton, and the Scottish have a definite imprint on the eastern shores and Cape Breton. In Halifax – and elsewhere – you will see more pictures of Queen Elizabeth II than of any Canadian public figure.

EVANGELINE

As you travel along the old French shore near Annapolis Royal, you will hear a lot about the expulsion of the Acadians, and about Evangeline, Longfellow's fictional Acadian lass who has become their symbol. It was the coming battle between Britain and France for control of North America that led, in 1755, to the expulsion of the Acadians. The British feared that these French farmers, although living in British territory, would be disloyal to the crown and provide support to the French in case of war (which everyone knew was coming). So, without warning, they threw them all out, and Acadians scattered to New Brunswick, Quebec, Louisiana and elsewhere. Many later returned to their farmland, where their descendants live today.

Getting to Nova Scotia

This is the easiest province to reach by air, since Halifax is the air hub of the Atlantic Provinces. **Air Nova**, the commuter partner of Air Canada, provides direct service from New York's Newark Airport and from Boston, as well as from most major Canadian cities; ☎ 800/776-3000 in the US, 800/565-3940 in Maritime Canada. From Halifax you can fly on to Sydney or Yarmouth. These three cities are also served by **Air Atlantic**, the commuter partner of Canadian Airlines International, ☎ 902/427-5500 or 800/426-7000 in the US; 800/665-1177 in Maritime Canada.

From New Brunswick you can follow TransCanada-1 over the isthmus to Amherst, or take a ferry from Saint John to Digby on Marine Atlantic's ***MV Princess of Acadia***, which crosses three times daily in the summer, less often the rest of the year. The crossing takes about two hours and 45 minutes, carrying both cars and foot passengers. One-way summer fares are $23 adult, $20.50 for seniors and $11.50 for children ages five to 12. These are reduced by $3-$5 off-season. To bring a car on the ferry it's $50 ($42.50 off-season), and you should make reservations. For infor-

➲ **TRAVEL TIP:** *Although Nova Scotia's tourist numbers are higher than those of its neighbors, very few places are crowded, and the easygoing pace remains even in the busiest summer months. And just because a lot of people come to Nova Scotia doesn't mean they all go to the same places; most never see the woodland and highland trails, or the rocky coast from the vantage of a kayak. You will have the woods and the waters almost to yourself.*

mation ☎ 506/636-4048 in Saint John, ☎ 902/245-2116 in Digby; elsewhere, ☎ 800/341-7981.

If you are driving from the eastern United States, you can cut 850 miles of driving by taking a water route. Prince of Fundy Cruises operates the ***MS Scotia Prince*** from Portland, Maine to Yarmouth, from May through October. It leaves Portland in the evening on alternate days, arriving in Yarmouth 11 hours later. The return cruise is a daytime crossing. You must have reservations from **Prince of Fundy Cruises**, International Terminal, Portland, ME 04101, ☎ 207/775-5616, 902/742-6460 in Yarmouth; 800/341-7540 or 800/482-0955 in Maine. One-way fares are about US$80 adult, $40 child, $100 auto, $35-100 for a cabin mid-June through mid-September, and US$60 adult, $30 child, $80 auto and $20-60 for a cabin May through mid-June and mid-September through October.

Marine Atlantic's ***MV Bluenose*** saves 600 driving miles on the six-hour, year-round route between Bar Harbor, Maine, and Yarmouth. From late June to mid-September, daily departures leave Bar Harbor in the morning, and Yarmouth in the late afternoon. Off-season, the service is not daily, but fares drop substantially. Summer fares are about US$45 adult, $25 ages five-12, $40 senior, $60 auto, late June through early September, and US$30 adult, $25 senior, $15 ages five-12, $50 auto, in June and early September through mid-October. For reservations, contact **Marine Atlantic Reservations Bureau**, PO Box 250, North Sydney, NS B2A 3M3, ☎ 800/341-7981 in the US.

You can also arrive in Nova Scotia by ferry from Prince Edward Island, leaving Wood Islands for a landing just north of Pictou. The new Confederation Bridge delivers you from Borden to New Brunswick, only a few miles from the isthmus leading to Nova Scotia.

However you arrive, once you are there getting around is very easy: TransCanada-104/105 runs the length of the province, and leads over the Canso Causeway to Cape Breton Island. The multilane Highway 102 leads south to Halifax. For much of the distance around the southwestern shores you can travel on arterial roads with somewhat limited access, which avoids driving through every little town if you are in a hurry. But since its little towns are part of the province's attraction, you will find yourself taking many of the little roads that hug the shoreline and lead across bridges to the tiny islands just offshore.

Nearly everywhere, the main roads go around the edges, with relatively few cutting across the interior to connect them. Villages are few in the inland area, where huge tracts of forested wild land are used for timber and water supplies, and little else.

Nova Scotia's Parks

Kejimkujik National Park lies in the province's wild western interior, on thickly forested, gently rolling hills, cut by lakes and streams. A small seaside section of the park preserves a rare wild and undeveloped coastline, with cliffs and beaches where piping plover nest.

Cape Breton Highlands National Park is one of Canada's signature parks, with mountains extending to the sea. Through the park, with views of the dramatic coastal cliffs, runs the Cabot Trail, circling the park's outer edges. Hiking trails criss-cross the highlands.

Blomidon Provincial Park is no slouch for scenery, either, encompassing the high bluffs of Cape Blomidon, which separates the Minas Channel from the Minas Basin. Miles of walking trails provide the best views of this scenic coast, and camping and day-use facilities are among the most used in the province.

Provincial parks with campgrounds are scattered through the province, all nicely maintained, many with beaches on either the ocean or lakes.

Fishing

Saltwater fishing does not require a license, and you might find cod, haddock, pollock, wolffish, flounder, mackerel, shad, rainbow smelt, striped bass, bluefish and dogfish. Bluefin tuna and blue shark are also taken along the coast but require special licensing. Size and take limits may vary from area to area, and all but mackerel, shad, smelt and squid have some limit. Cod and striped bass

➲ **FISHING REGULATIONS:** *A provincial fishing license is required for fishing in all fresh waters. In the two national parks you can buy a weekly license for about $10 a week or an annual license for $20. These are valid in any national park but not anywhere else.*

are more regulated than others. For all fishing details, contact the Department of Fisheries and Oceans, Yarmouth Division, ☎ 902/742-0871 or, in Halifax, PO Box 550, Halifax NS B3J 2S7, ☎ 902/564-7361. For information on tuna and shark, contact **Nova Scotia Saltwater Sport Fishing and Charter Boat Association**, ☎ 800/499-3474. The Department and the Association publish a *Saltwater Sportfishing Map*, available at most fishing supply shops and the major information centers.

TAKE CARE: *Waters along the Fundy shore, which includes the Minas Basin and Channel, Chignecto Bay, Cobequid Bay, and St. Mary's Bay, are subject to* ***Fundy tides****. More than 115 billion tons of water flow in and out every 12 hours, very suddenly, and not always exactly on schedule. If you are fishing in those areas, be sure you know the tide schedule, since the tides can be very dangerous.*

Information Sources

■ For information about all of Nova Scotia, call or write to **Nova Scotia Tourism**, PO Box 130, Halifax, NS, B3J 2M7, ☎ 800/565-0000 or 902/425-5781. Ask for the free, 300-plus-page *Doers and Dreamers Guide*, which has accommodations and campground listings, and descriptions of scenic routes, historic sites, festivals, and museums. Once there, any provincially operated information center will help you find a room through the Check-In system. On Cape Breton, ask for the *Cape Breton Bed & Breakfast List*.

■ ***Canoe Routes of Nova Scotia*** describes 70 canoeing areas with sketch maps and topo references, while ***Coastal Paddling Routes*** describes sea kayaking destinations. Both are available from the **Government Bookstore**, 1700 Granville St., Halifax, ☎ 902/424-7580, and you can get the latter from **Coastal Adventures** in Tangier, ☎ 902/772-2774.

■ *Passport to Diving* is a 48-page pamphlet of the **Nova Scotia Underwater Council**, Box 3010 South, Halifax, NS B3J 3G6, ☎ 902/425-5450.

■ ***Hiking Nova Scotia*** by Joan Light (Nimbus Publishing Ltd, 1995) and her ***Coastal Nova Scotia Outdoor Adventure Guide*** (Nimbus Publishing Ltd., 1993) are good hiking references. For hikes to waterfalls look at ***Waterfalls of Nova Scotia***, by Allan Billard (Sand Dollar Productions, 1997).

■ For hikes in Cape Breton, see ***Explore Cape Breton*** by Pat O'Neil (Nimbus Publishing Ltd, 1994). Two other guides to Cape Breton are ***Cape Breton's Cabot Trail*** by David Lawley (Nimbus Publishing Ltd, 1994) and ***A Traveler's Guide to Cape Breton*** by Pat O'Neil (Solus Publishing, 1996), which is a route-oriented directory.

Chignecto

Most travelers in Nova Scotia pass through one of its most interesting sections, sometimes twice in the same trip, without ever stopping. This triangular area is bounded by three bodies of water, two of them part of the fascinating Bay of Fundy tide system and the other the mild-mannered Northumberland Strait. Between them, in this quiet corner so often ignored, is a rolling, hilly land with sea bluffs, tidal estuaries and long, smooth warm-water beaches. Here too is the world's largest marshland and world-class fossil cliffs.

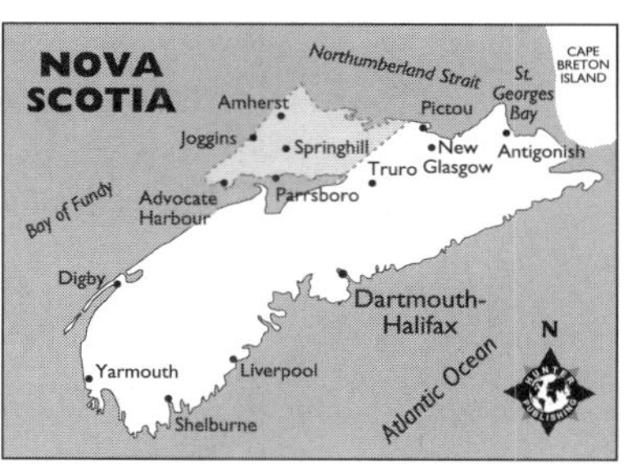

Geography & History

Geographically, Nova Scotia is very close to being an island. Between the New Brunswick towns of Port Elgin and Aulac, 15 miles apart at the end of the Cumberland Basin, and Amherst and the village of Tidnish facing them on the Nova Scotia side of the border, lies only the great Tantramar Marsh. It is the largest in the world, so vast that, except for the highway and a narrow road between Port Elgin and Tidnish Bridge, it forms an impenetrable barrier to the mainland. The marsh is an important waterfowl and bird sanctuary and breeding ground. The broad, gentle sweep of its grasses and the almost ethereal light that hovers over them has served as an inspiration to hundreds of Canadian poets and writers.

The land on the Nova Scotia side varies greatly, from the relatively flat and gentle shores of the north, to the low, but sharp and rugged mountains of inland Chignecto and its cliff-riven tidelands. From Truro to Advocate Harbour, its nearly 100 miles of southern shore are beaten and washed twice each day by the world's higest tides, for the Fundy's full force is concentrated here in the Minas Basin. Underlying the Chignecto plain is fossil-bearing sedimentary rock that surfaces at the shore near Parrsboro and Joggins.

The biggest town is Amherst, originally settled by Acadians and, after their expulsion, resettled by American Loyalists. Established as a town in 1764, the arrival of the railroad in the 1880s led to a splurge of growth as wool, steam boiler, railroad passenger car and shoe companies prospered. Along the coast from Truro to Advocate the twin industries of timber and shipbuilding prospered, sending off much of the lumber that built the cities of Eastern Canada.

Getting Around

From Halifax, Highway 102 leads to Truro at the eastern end of the Chignecto area. From Truro, Rte. 2 (Exit 14) or Rte. 4 (Exit 15) lead west along the shore. Rte. 2 continues as the **Glooscap Trail** before turning north through the inland and Springhill, to Amherst. Rte. 209 replaces it as the shore road (still the Glooscap Trail on maps), around the tip of the peninsula, following the shore to Amherst. A word of warning. The highway around the tip of the peninsula is very rough (especially in the winter and spring). If the temptation to turn around strikes, resist. The scenery is worth the jouncing, and from Advocate Harbour along the west side of the peninsula the road improves.

The roads along the north shore, Rtes. 366 and 6, are less of a challenge, as they wind through small harbor towns and past a low shoreline of beach and saltmarsh on their way to Pictou. Scenic side roads lead off to the shore, and you can follow them to windswept points and almost deserted beaches.

Through the center of the area, and the road most people stay on, is Highway 104, a branch of the now-split TransCanada Highway; its alter-ego is in Prince Edward Island, and they don't meet again until New Brunswick.

Adventures

■ On Foot

Hiking

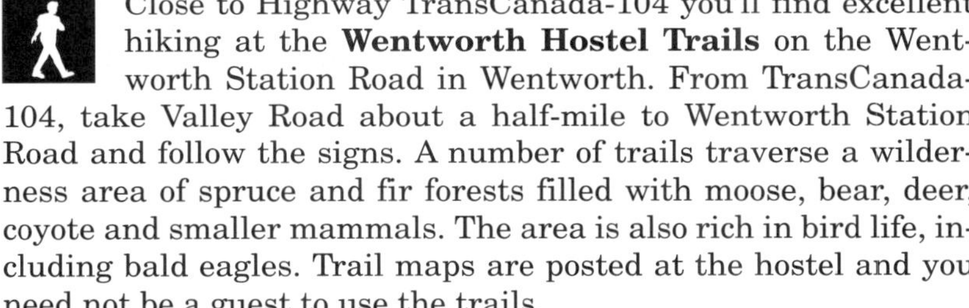

Close to Highway TransCanada-104 you'll find excellent hiking at the **Wentworth Hostel Trails** on the Wentworth Station Road in Wentworth. From TransCanada-104, take Valley Road about a half-mile to Wentworth Station Road and follow the signs. A number of trails traverse a wilderness area of spruce and fir forests filled with moose, bear, deer, coyote and smaller mammals. The area is also rich in bird life, including bald eagles. Trail maps are posted at the hostel and you need not be a guest to use the trails.

Traveling west on Rte. 2 at the village of Upper Economy, turn north onto River Phillips Road, continuing four miles to **Economy Falls Trail**. There are signs for the falls near the parking area where the trail enters the gorge. The trail is a fine hike, not only for the almost 100-foot waterfall, but for the wildflowers and ancient trees along the way. It's an in and out hike of about 2½ miles.

Along Rte. 2, about 20 miles east of Parrsboro and 35 miles west of Truro, **Five Islands Provincial Park** sits in a spectacular setting with a series of five islands receding into the Minas Basin, off a geological feature known as **The Old Wife**. The park itself sits on a peninsula that faces the Basin from atop a 300-foot cliff of fossil-bearing sandstone. Three trails in the park offer varied terrain and all of them can be hiked

> **WARNING:** *From The Old Wife, Moose Island, the largest and closest of the islands, seems reachable by foot at low tide.* ***Don't try it.*** *The currents between the mainland and the islands are dangerous and the tide rises so fast that you could be swept away. Remember, the tide rises about 50 feet here and to do so it has to move fast.*

within a day. The trails go through forests of mixed hard and soft woods, especially spruce, balsam fir, red maple and white birch. You'll see Schreber's and broom moss, star flower, wood sorrel, bunchberry, wood fern, and lily of the valley, and along the estuary route sea grasses and sea lavender, rare and beautiful when in bloom in August. You can dig clams on the mud flats, but keep a careful eye on the tide charts and the water, and ask at the entrance to be sure there is no red tide outbreak. For more information, contact Five Islands Provincial Park, District Office, Department of Lands and Forests, Box 428, Parrsboro, NS B0M 1C0, ☎ 902/254-3241, May-October 902/254-9911.

- The **Red Head Trail** starts near The Old Wife Point and, after going to the point for a view of the islands, runs east along the top of the high bluff through spruce forests to the lookoff point at Red Head, cutting inland before meeting up with the Economy Mountain Trail. Turn left if you want to go back to the campground or right if you want to continue on to the top of Economy Mountain.

- The **Economy Mountain Trail** begins heading south from a parking lot close to the entrance of the Park. After admiring the view from the top, continue on the trail and stay to the right to reach the campground or left at the intersection of trails to come out on the Red Head Trail along the cliffs.

- At the same parking lot, if you follow the trail on the north side of the road you will be on the **Estuary Trail**, following the shoreline of the East River. Shortly after starting on the trail go right and it will take you to the estuary and along its shore. When the trail again intersects, the trail to the left will return you to the parking lot. A right would take you to another parking lot near the Administration building and campground entrance. Red Head is three miles, Economy is three miles and Estuary is 2½ miles, but by linking all of them together, the total mileage is less than the sum of its parts.

If you do get a chance to walk the beaches at the foot of the cliffs between Red Head and the Old Wife look carefully at the exposed sandstone of the cliff. In it are embedded the fossils of some of the smallest dinosaurs (with skulls as small as two centimeters long), creatures that lived on this land during the Jurassic period, 200 million years ago. Look but don't touch unless you have a permit to take fossils, which you get from the Nova Scotia Museum in Halifax (see page 324 for information on the museum).

Wards Falls Trail is in Wharton, about 4½ miles west of Parrsboro on Rte. 209. A dirt road to the right, marked with a sign, leads to the parking area. The trail travels in to the falls and back on the same route, a total distance of about 4½ miles. Starting near the North Branch of the Diligent River, the trail crosses the river (in summer little more than a small stream), going through a plantation of white pine and then through a spruce forest, all the while following and criss-crossing the stream, as its ravine grows increasingly narrow and steep sided. At its end is a deep gorge caused by the Cobequid-Chedabucto fault, and the stream falls over it. We don't suggest hiking beyond this point, because it is steep, slippery and requires the use of ropes. The falls are at their best in the early spring when snow melt swells their waters, but the walk through the woods to the falls is nice even in the summer, when the falls are less dramatic.

For walks in the **Amherst Point Migratory Bird Sanctuary** through ponds, bogs and marshes filled with bird life, see *Cultural & Eco-Travel Experiences*.

Walking Tours

A Walking Tour of **Historical Downtown Amherst** highlights many of the elegant late 19th- and early 20th-century buildings from the heyday of its manufacturing past. At the Amherst Tourist Information Centre at 44 Lawrence Street, ask for the *Walking Tour* brochure and for the pamphlet *The Great Amherst Mystery*. The Centre is in a locally built Centennial Coach Car, built for high-ranking Canadian government officials and elegantly outfitted with oak paneling, brass tables and velvet curtains. From there, go to Victoria Street. At #50 you find the Victorian Gothic Old Customs House and at #54 the Courthouse, with carved arches over the first floor windows and curved pediments over the second floor windows. The two churches at #60 and #66 Victoria Street both date from 1846, but the one at #60, Christ Church, was built elsewhere 16 years earlier and moved here in 1846. Victoria Square lies between them. The Rhodes Steele Block at 65-69 Victoria Street is a turn-of-the-century Queen Anne Revival-style building in local red sandstone, while the Bank of Nova Scotia building at #79 was erected in 1887. At 98 Victoria the Dominion Public Building, from 1935, was originally the post office, a classic Greek temple-style built of greystone quarried in Wallace. Look for the hand-carved beavers and maple leaves that ornament the facade. Continue on Victoria Street to the corner of Acadia Street. At #129 is a department store that has been in business here since 1906.

Take Acadia Street to the right, and after passing Ratchford Street you come to the **Centennial Sun Dial** and beyond it the **Four Fathers Memorial Library**, which commemorates the four men from Amherst who participated in the creation of Canada. Retrace your steps to Ratchford Street and take it to **Trinity St. Stephen's United Church**, built in 1906. Take Havelock Street one block to the left, then cross to Princess Street. Local legend has it that at #6 (now a parking lot) a poltergeist wrought havoc in 1878 on young Esther Cox. Furniture was tossed, threats were written on the walls, knives were thrown and a neighbor's barn was burned after she had worked in it. At her place of work, chairs stacked themselves and dishes flew from the cabinets. Esther's ordeal ended when the spirit was exorcised by a Micmac medicine man.

While it might seem a bit strange to visit a barber shop, stop at **Bob's Barber Shop** at 6 Church Street, which hasn't changed in almost a century, with rows of shaving mugs and old-fashioned barber chairs. Head out Church Street and take Prince Arthur Street to the right, to Station Street, where you will find the 1908 **Intercolonial Railway Station** of red sandstone, still the railroad station for the town and serviced by VIA Rail on a regular basis. Continue down Station Street to Victoria Street, taking Lawrence Street on the left to return to the Centennial Car Coach.

Scenic Walks

On the Northumberland Strait, **Amherst Shore Provincial Park** is a good place to do a little walking and enjoy the north shore beaches and warm waters. In addition to a campground, there is a walk of about 1½ miles along Annebelle's Brook and along the shore, where there is a good swimming beach. From Amherst, take Rte. 366 north, and the park is a few miles east of Tidnish Dock. For more information, contact ☎ 902/661-6002 (in summer), or Department of Natural Resources, PO Box 130, Oxford NS B0M 1P0, ☎ 902/447-2115,

Ducks Unlimited is largely responsible for the creation of the wetlands at **Wallace Bay National Wildlife Area**, just off the shores of the Northumberland Strait between Pugwash and Wallace on Rte. 6, the Sunrise Trail. From Rte. 6 take the road to Wallace Bay, east of the Rte. 368 intersection. Look for the parking lot just before a bridge. The 2½-mile walk is over mostly level ground, on dikes built in the early 1970s; there are a number of observation areas and places to stop and identify birds along the way. Start the trail on a loop along a dike which protects the wetland from the salinity of the tidal river. At a fork, take the left branch between two wet areas to a wooded section. On the south side of the wetlands, the trail – now marked by blue jay figures on the trees – cuts along the side of the marsh and back to the parking lot. You can expect to see mergansers, wood ducks, several varieties of hawks, as well as more common waterfowl and song birds.

Wentworth Falls is off of TransCanada-104 on the Wentworth Valley Highway across from Ski Wentworth ski area. Gateposts mark the beginning of a short walk of about 200 yards to the falls of Higgins Brook. The falls are not a straight drop but rather a tight series of cascades over which the water drops more than 50 feet. It makes a good place for wading in the brook or for a picnic, but be sure to take your trash out with you, since this privately owned land could be closed if abused.

Guided Tours

- **Backroad Adventure Tours**, Box 37, Bass River NS, B0M 1B0, ☎ 800/353-4453, runs one- , three- , and five-day hiking tours along the Fundy coast and hinterlands where participants can watch the tides, dig fossils and see the wildlife of the area.

- **Scott Tours** (1707 Pryor Street, Halifax, NS B3H 4G7, ☎ 902/423-5000, fax 902/429-5535, e-mail rscott@fox.nstn.ca) also does occasional guided hiking tours into the Fundy area. In the north shore area contact **Wild Goose Eco Tours**, c/o Tatamagouche Centre, RR #3, Tatamagouche NS, B0K 1V0, ☎ 902/657-2231, fax 902/657-3445, for three- to five-day guided nature tours.

■ In The Air

For a different view of the world, **Pegasus Paragliding**, Diligent River, NS B0M 1H0, ☎ 902/254-2972, fax 902/254-2331, conducts paragliding lessons and flights from its hill in the Cobequid Mountains.

■ On Water

Water adventures come with a difference in this area where the shape of the land and the pull of the tides create the highest tides in the world – quite often more than 50 feet. Inland, this is an area of wilderness, with streams running into the waters on three sides.

On the Beach

The Northumberland Straits have some of the warmest waters on the northern east coast of the continent and there are several of them along Rte. 366 north of Amherst. The first one you come to from Amherst is on Rte. 366 at Tidnish, the **Tidnish Dock Provincial Park**. It was the site of a failed attempt to build a railway for carrying ships across the isthmus to the Bay of Fundy. Farther along, **Amherst Shore Provincial Park** has a fine beach; additonal choices a short distance beyond are **Northport Beach Provincial Park** at Northport, **Heather Beach Provincial Park** just west of Port Howe, and **Gulf Shore Provincial Park** on the peninsula north of Pugwash. On the end of the peninsula opposite Wallace, **Fox Harbour Beach** has unsupervised swimming and picnic facilities. All of the sites have changing rooms and picnic facilities, but only Heather Beach has supervised swimming. For information on any of these beaches write to Department of Natural Resources, 4917 Main St., PO Box 130, Oxford, NS B0M 1P0, ☎ 902/447-2155.

Canoeing & Kayaking

Parrsboro is center of water-based activities along the south shore. **Dinatours Adventures and Gifts**, Two Island Rd, Parrsboro, NS B0M 1S0, ☎ 902/254-3700, fax 902/254-3656, offers canoe trips on the wilderness streams from May through October. If the season is right you can fish along the way. If lucky you'll eat your catch and if not they'll feed you lunch. The tours are fully guided and equipped. Half-days are $45 for singles and $75 for couples; full days run $75 and $125; children under 16 are charged an additional $15 each. Dinatours also rents paddleboats, rowboats and fishing boats for $5 a half-hour or $8 an hour; they have special half- and full-day rates as well.

A New Brunswick company, **FreshAir Adventures**, offers kayak trips exploring this shore. Contact them at PO Box 146, Alma NB E0A 1B0, ☎ 800/545-0020 or 506/887-2249; fax May-

November 506/887-2262, December-April 902/895-2533; e-mail FreshAir@ fox.nstn.ca; Web site http://fox.nstn.ca:80/~freshair/.

Harbor & Bay Tours

Dinatours Adventures and Gifts, Two Island Rd, Parrsboro NS B0M 1S0, ☎ 902/254-3700, fax 902/254-3656, has both harbor and moonlight cruises in the Minas Basin and Channel areas near Parrsboro. With a minimum of five people, the harbour cruises run from May to October on Sundays at 1 pm and at other times on request. One of the exciting things about these cruises is their encounters with the huge Fundy tides of the basin. This is prime country for sightings of seals, seabirds and porpoises and a good chance to see the fossil-bearing coastal cliffs. Rates are $20 for adults ($35 per couple) and $10 for children under 16. The Moonlight Cruise operates from June to September from 8 to 12 pm each night during the full-moon weeks. Each cruise includes a beach cookout over a bonfire on an unsettled island. Adults are $15, children $10.

On the north coast, at Pugwash, the Pugwash River gathers its waters inland in a wide bay before emptying out into the Northumberland Strait. It is an area filled with seabirds and a good place to look for them. **Mystic Coast Adventure Tours**, c/o **Canadian Sterling & Goldsmiths**, PO Box 148, Pugwash Centre NS B0K 1L0, ☎/fax 902/902/243-2563, e-mail mysticco@auracom.com, has several different cruises on the river, using a stable 21-foot pontoon boat. The two-hour eagle nesting tour operates daily and costs $25 for adults, $15 for children under 16. There is a one-hour seal-watching tour offered at $15 for adults and $10 for children. During the summer and into early autumn they also run a 1½-hour harbor sunset cruise at 7 pm that goes out into the harbor and the Northumberland Strait as the sun sets ($15 adults; $10 children).

The *Meaghan & Derek* also sails out of Pugwash for a 2½-hour tour of the Northumberland Strait with **Water Tours & Charters**, ☎ 902/243-2382, cell 902/664-6305, fax 902/243-2382. Reservations are strongly suggested and there is a 20-person maximum for each trip. Water Tours operates from June to September and they do sea fishing tours on request. The captain tells the story of the town of Pictou, the town of Pugwash and of the industry that sustained them for many years.

Fishing

Sea fishing on the Fundy shore is limited but there is striped bass fishing at Bass River and off Portapique and rainbow smelt have been found at Upper Economy and Portapique. On the Northumberland Strait you will find mackerel everywhere along the coast. Rainbow smelt are at Cold Spring Head, Pugwash Point and in Tatamagouche Bay south of Sandville and at River John. Striped bass have been caught at Pugwash Point and at the inlet of Wallace Bay.

Guided Fishing Trips

■ **Dinatours Adventures and Gifts**, Two Island Road, Parrsboro, NS B0M 1S0, ☎ 902/254-3700, fax 902/254-3656, does fishing trips by reservation, providing all equipment and lunch. Fishing is for flounder, skate, northern shark and striped bass. The boat charges $165 for a half day and $265 for a full day. Trips run between July and October. They also do offer a guided fly-fishing trip for salmon along the Phillip River in mid- and late October; fees run $95 for half-day trips and $150 for a full day.

■ On Snow

Cross-Country Skiing

Five Islands Provincial Park permits the use of the Economy Mountain Trail and the park roads for cross-country skiing during the winter months, for a total of about 4½ miles of trails. Don't try Red Head; its proximity to the cliffs makes it too dangerous. Information about the park is available from the District Office Department of Lands and Forests, Box 428, Parrsboro, NS B0M 1C0, ☎ 902/254-3241.

Downhill Skiing

Ski Wentworth, Wentworth, NS B0M 1Z0, ☎ 902/548-2089, is located right off TransCanada-104 at Wentworth. It has a vertical drop of just over 800 feet, and the longest run is a bit over 1½ miles. There are 22 alpine trails, fairly evenly divided by skill level with nine beginner, eight intermediate and five expert. All slopes are open during the day and six are lighted for night skiing. The slopes are serviced by two quad chairs, two T-bars and two rope tows and operate from early December to mid-April, depending upon snow. There are also six miles of cross-country trails from novice to expert and special cross-country events through the season. The cross-country trails are groomed only for special events. Full outfit rentals are $18 per day (snowboards $22). Half-day tickets run from 8:30 am to 1:30 pm or 1:30 pm to 10 pm, and cost $25. Full day tickets, good from 8:30 am to 10 pm, cost $30.

Snowmobiling

Extensive snowmobile trails web all of the back lands in the area, cleared, built and maintained primarily by local snowmobile clubs and their members. Before using most of the trails, permits must be obtained from the Snowmobile Association of Nova Scotia.

> **CAUTION:** *Remember that although the region looks small on a map, these are large wilderness areas where help can be hard to come by. Always travel with a companion and go well-supplied with fuel and cold-weather necessities.*

The **Corridor Trail** through this section is Trail 104, starting on TransCanada-16 near Tidnish on the New Brunswick border. It threads its way southeast, crossing TransCanada-104 near Salt Springs and again near Folly Lake, in the territory of the Fundy Trail Snowmobile Club. It then cuts to the east and into another section of wilderness, around numerous small lakes and ponds to the facilities of the North Shore Snowmobile Club. It crosses Rte. 311 south of Earltown before heading south again to Mount Thom, west along TransCanada-104 to Kempertown then crossing the highway and heading off to the southeast.

In addition to the Corridor Trail, there are hundreds of miles of **club-maintained trails** with access to all parts of the area:

- From **Parrsboro**, for example, you can take **Trail 31** to **Trail 30**, then go west to end up in Advocate Harbour.

- Another option would be to take the trail at **Lower Economy**, then follow **Trail 3** to the Chisholm Trail Snowmobile Club facilities, and continue on to **Trail 5 east** and **Corridor Trail 104** (also labeled Trail 5C for a short section) east to the Cumberland Snowmobile Club facilities. From there take **Trail 1** south to **Trail 5B** north of Economy and follow it west to the trail you started on, returning to Lower Economy.

■ Likewise, east of TransCanada-104 from the Fundy Club facilities at the north end of Folly Lake, there are many trail choices through the wilderness between TransCanada-104 on the west and south and Rte. 246 on the north. **Trail 301** off Corridor Trail 104 will take you deep into the heart of this area.

Guided Snowmobile Tours

■ Guided snowmobile tours may be arranged through **Tidal River Ridge** (Moose River, ☎ 800/806-8860 or 902/254-3333), a lodge with two-bedroom cottages.

SNOWMOBILE TRAIL INFORMATION

■ If you plan to snowmobile, write or call the **Snowmobile Association of Nova Scotia**, Box 3010 South, Halifax, NS B3J 3G6, ☎ 902/425-5450, ext 324 for trail permits and maps.

■ You can also write directly to the several clubs in this area. For information west of the north-south part of TransCanada-104 at Wentworth, contact **Chisholm Trail Snowmobile Club**, c/o C. Soley, Five Islands, NS B0M 1K0, ☎ 902/254-3708. They maintain groomed trails. Or contact the **Cumberland Snowmobile Club**, c/o Keith Bowman, 230 Whitepine Road, Riverview NB, E1B 2X1, ☎ 902/597-3192. They are responsible for 300 miles of trails, including the Corridor Trail.

■ For the territory north and east of TransCanada-104 contact **Fundy Trail Snowmobile and Recreation Club**, c/o J. Cameron, Box 632, Truro NS, B2N 5E5, which has their clubhouse at Folly Lake and maintains 60 miles of trails. Also check with **Sutherland's Lake Snowmobile Association**, c/o Bruce Wylie, Box 69, Truro NS, B2N 5B6, and the **North Shore Snowmobile Club**, c/o Brian Sullivan, RR# 6, Truro, NS B2N 5B4, which has 65 miles of trails and a facility at West New Annan.

Cultural & Eco-Travel Experiences

In Portaupique east of the town of Bass River, there is a large **smelt run** in early May as the silvery fish return to the Portaupique River to spawn. Nearby, in the marshes, the remains of Acadian dikes can be seen along the river banks.

If you happen to be at the town of Economy on the second weekend of August, stop for the annual **Clam Festival** on Saturday. They have clams prepared every way possible, as well as lots of music and merriment.

Cobequid Interpretation Centre on Rte. 2 in Economy, ☎ 800/895-1177, is situated on the south side of the highway in the town of Economy. The centre is easily identifiable by the WWII era Observation Tower moved to this site to save it from tumbling over the cliff. The Interpretive Centre has staff members and exhibits to show the geological, natural and human story of the Cobequid basin and distributes information on the **Fundy Shore Eco-Tour**, a locally produced brochure guide to outdoor and other activities in the area. The tower provides wonderful views of Cobequid Bay and the Minas Basin.

A group of craftsmen started the **Glooscap Country Bazaar**, Economy NS, ☎ 902/647-2920, to promote quality local arts and crafts and their shop has prospered for more than 20 years. They sell handmade quilts and knit wear, ceramics, stained glass, woodenware and, for the hungry traveler, a bakery. They also sell locally grown produce. They're open on Saturdays and Sundays from 10 am to 6 pm in June, September, and October; from July through September they open daily from 10 am to 6 pm.

■ The Land: Geology & Fossils

Fundy Geological Museum, Two Islands Road, Parrsboro, NS B0M 1S0, ☎ 902/254-3814, fax 902/254-3666, e-mail fundy@ns.sympatico.ca. The museum explores, through its well-designed exhibits and audio-visual programs, the relationship between life and the land through the millennia. Exhibits include models of the landscapes of the Jurassic and Triassic periods, fossils from those periods millions of years ago and minerals exposed by the disintegration of the Fundy cliffs. It's open year-round and charges $3.50 adult ($6.50 family) during high season, free off-season.

➲ **A REAL GEM:** *The Fundy Geological Museum also sponsors the Nova Scotia Gem and Mineral Show (Web site www.nova-scotia.com/gemshow), held annually on the third weekend in August at the Lion's Recreation Center. Dealers from all over North America descend on Parrsboro to buy, sell and trade stones and minerals. There are also lectures on collecting minerals and fossils, stone cutting and polishing demonstrations, jewelry making and field trips to the mineral- and fossil-filled cliffs along Fundy's beaches.*

In addition to the Fundy Geological Museum there are a number of other interesting sites around Parrsboro. Coming into town on Rte. 2, follow the road to the left and across the arm of Parrsboro harbour toward the Geological Museum. Just beyond the museum is the road to **First Beach**, a great place to see the effects of the Fundy tides. At low tide the fishing boats are left high upon the beaches. If you continue on out the road toward Clarke Head there are wonderful views over the Minas Basin and you will eventually come to **Two Islands Interpretive Site** at famed **Wasson Bluff**, where fossilized imprints of the oldest-known dinosaur footprints were found. From the site a trail leads to the beach and the fossil-bearing cliffs. Collecting is strictly forbidden in this protected area.

Head south of Parrsboro past The Ship's Company Theatre and Ottawa House to **Partridge Island**, a peninsula sticking into the Minas Basin. The constant erosion of the seaside bluffs here continually showers the beach with semi-precious stones and minerals. Spring is the best time to come and walk the shore looking for treasures.

Dinatours Adventures and Gifts, Two Island Rd, Parrsboro NS B0M 1S0, ☎ 902/254-3700, fax 902/254-3656, has a series of mineral and fossil walks in the area. They search for agates, amethysts, and other minerals on a 2½-hour walk for $18, or $30 for a couple. Children under 16 are an additional $5. There is also a mineral tour of Cape Blomindon for $30 adults, $15 under 16 and a Five or Two Island Tour for $25 and $10 that lasts approximately four hours. The fossil tour goes to Wasson's Bluff, where the sea has exposed layers of the earth's history from the Carboniferous age. Rates are $18, $30 for a couple and children under 16 are $5. Walking tours are dependent upon the tides and they leave the beaches two hours before and after high tide. Call for reservations and times.

Parrsboro Rock and Mineral Shop and Museum, 39 Whitehall Road, Parrsboro, ☎ 902/254-2981, has, in their privately run museum, fossilized specimens of prehistoric amphibians, trees, plants and dinosaurs from the local area and around the world. The shop sells minerals, gemstones and fossils. They can also help you arrange for guided rock-collecting expeditions.

On the Chignecto Bay shore is **Joggins Fossil Centre**, Main St., Joggins, ☎ 902/251-2727, off-season 251-2618. The Centre features a large collection of fossils, including ferns, leaves, bark and roots of trees, as well as examples of prints left in the sedimentary soils by ancient creatures. They also have a large collection of geodes, quartz and amethyst crystals, amber, agates, orange and green gypsum, fluorite and many other minerals. There is a gift shop where you can buy examples. The Centre also has guided tours to the fossil cliffs daily from June through September. Check with them for times, which change according to the time of low tide each day. The Fossil Centre is open 9 am to 6:30 pm daily; admission is $3.50 for adults, with reduced rates for seniors and students. The guided Fossil Tours are $10 for adults.

Wildlife-Watching

In the northwest near Amherst is a chance to see the role wetlands play in the maintenance of healthy bird populations. The **Amherst Point Migratory Bird Sanctuary** has a series of trails through an area of ponds, bogs and marshes, some of which are natural; others are dikes and waterways built by Ducks Unlimited as part of their ongoing effort to foster waterfowl habitat. Sinkholes in the underlying gypsum deposits add another interesting aspect to the topography. Preserved as a sanctuary since 1947, this has become an important breeding ground for species such as the Virginia rail, gadwall, black tern and several other duck varieties. To get there take Exit 3 from Rte. 104 at Amherst and travel south. A Canadian Wildlife Service sign marks the entrance at the sanctuary.

Agriculture

The **Cumberland County Exhibition and Blueberry Harvest Fest**, PO Box 516, Oxford NS B0M 1P0, ☎ 888/395-0995 or 902/447-3285, fax 902/447-3100, starts on Tuesday of the last week of August and lasts through the following Saturday. Tuesday is 4-H day with the showing of young peoples' produce and livestock, Wednesday and Thursday bring horse competitions, Saturday has work horses and team competitions. The petting zoo, Thursday through Saturday from 10 am to 8 pm, is a popular family attraction. It's a real country event in a real agricultural area. Oxford is off Exit 6 of TransCanada-104 east of Amherst on Rte. 301.

The Dutchman's Cheese Farm on RR#1 in Upper Economy, ☎ 902/647-2751, is a cheese farm in the Netherlands style, with barn, cheese factory and farmhouse in one building. It also includes a cheese room, café-restaurant, gift shop and deck with views out over the Minas Basin. On the grounds are hiking trails, a series of interlinked ponds and a farmyard full of heritage animals. You can try the cheeses (mostly Goudas in plain or herbed varieties), walk the trails and see a type of architecture seldom seen on this side of the Atlantic. The café serves homemade soups, sandwiches and desserts and a special Sunday brunch and evening buffet supper, the latter by reservation only. The café is open daily from June to early October from 9 am to 7 pm. To see the farmyard, animals, playground and gardens, there is a fee of $5 for adults, $3 for kids, but this is credited toward meals or purchases anywhere on the farm. It's off Rte. 2 just past Brown Road.

You'll find the products of **Jost Vineyards** (Rte. 6, Malagash, NS, ☎ 800/565-4567 or 902/257-2636) on menus throughout all of the Atlantic provinces. Jost has 45 acres of vineyards and a shop that carries wine- and food-related goods and picnic supplies, including sausages and breads. They have picnic tables for you to use as well. Tours of the winery are given on a regular schedule, ending with a tasting.

Sightseeing

Ottawa House Museum By The Sea, ☎ 902/254-3814, sits below Partridge Island Road on the seaside, along a high bluff over the Minas Basin just outside of Parrsboro. Built in 1755, the house was purchased in 1871 by Sir Charles Tupper, a Premier of the province and Prime Minister of Canada, as a summer place. He was one of the Fathers of the Confederation, the group of men responsible for creating the Articles of Confederation that united Canada into one nation. The building has period rooms that show the life of Sir Charles and the shipbuilding and lumbering industries that were the life blood of this area for more than a century. Open daily from July to mid-September, noon to 8 pm. Nominal admission charge.

Age Of Sail Heritage Centre on Rte. 209 in Port Grenville, ☎ 902/348-2030, off-season 254-2932. Operated by the Grenville Bay Shipbuilding Museum Society, the award-winning museum seeks to brings to life the shipbuilding and lumbering that dominated this area for so much of its history. The main building is a restored church dating from 1857. Models, photographs and artifacts are used to document the lives and times of the people who settled and developed the lands along the Minas Basin. Open mid-May through Labor Day, 10 am to 6 pm, Tuesday through Sunday, and some weekends or by appointment in May, September and October. Admission $2 per person.

➔ **SHOPPING TIP:** *If you take the walking tour of Downtown Amherst (see* On Foot*) stop at* ***Victoria Court****, 7 Acadia Street, open Monday through Saturday from 9 am to 5 pm and on Friday until 8 pm. Inside there is a collection of small shops, including antiques, collectibles, and crafts. Thursday through Saturday from 10 am to 3 pm an* ***Artisan's Cooperative*** *sells a wide range of hand-crafted items, including furniture, stained glass, toys, art, hooked rugs and pottery. The Court is also home of* ***The Farmer's Market*** *of Amherst, open every Thursday from 10 am to 3 pm during the season, selling locally grown produce, meats, pottery, crafts, plants and much more.*

Cape d'Or Lighthouse, Cape d'Or, ☎ 902/664-2108. Just beyond Spencer's Island on Rte. 209, a road leads south to Cape d'Or Lighthouse, high on the cliff where the Bay of Fundy enters the Minas Channel. There is an interpretive center and restaurant in the old buildings of the light station, and on the surrounding grounds are hiking trails and good birdwatching.

In Parrsboro, follow the road south from the information center to find **The Ship's Company Theatre**, ☎ 800/565-SHOW (7469) or 902/254-2003 or 254-3000, one of the only theater companies operating aboard an historic ship. The M.V. Kipawo was built as a ferry in 1926 and was the last of the Minas Basin ferries. Sent to Newfoundland as part of the WWII war effort, she was brought back in 1982 and has become the home of a resident theater company. The theater focuses on innovative works by contemporary maritime writers. It's open July through September, Tuesday through Saturday at 8 pm and Sunday at 2 and 8 pm. Tickets are

$18 for adults, $16 for seniors and students, and $11 for children under 12. Dinner-and-show specials are $65, which includes dinner at one of three local restaurants and theater for two people.

Wallace Area Museum, 13440 Rte. 6 in Wallace, ☎ 902/257-2191 is one of those wonderful small local museums that captures the essence of the settlers and people of a town. In the modest home of mid-19th century shipbuilder James Davison, it tells his tale and that of many others from this community. It's generally open July to early September, daily from 9 am to 5 pm and off season from 1 to 4 pm.

In Tatamagouche, **Sunrise Trail Museum** on Main St. emphasizes the Micmac and Acadian experiences on the north shore as well as depicting the story of the area's agriculture and industry. They are open daily in the summer and weekends only in June and September.

The **Malagash Miners Museum** on RR#1, 19 North Shore Road in Malagash, ☎ 902/257-2407, is mining with a difference. From 1918 until 1959 salt was mined along the northerm shore of the Malagash peninsula. The museum has exhibits on the salt industry, including a video of a movie taken underground in the mines in the early 1940s. In addition to salt mining, the museum includes displays on the area's rich maritime and shipbuilding history. The museum is open mid-June through September daily, Monday through Saturday from 11 am to 6 pm, and opens at noon on Sunday. There is a modest entrance fee.

Balmoral Grist Mill, ☎ 902/657-3365, is just off Rte. 311 near the intersection with Rte. 256 south of Tatamagouche. Built in 1874, the mill is still operated by water power from an adjacent brook and millpond. Four specialized sets of millstones produced wheat, oat, barley and other flours as they have for over a century. Be sure to see the oat drying room with cast iron floor pieces to allow heat from a fire in the basement to dry the oats. The museum shop sells the flour produced at the mill and the world's best oatcakes, cookies made from the toasted oat flour. Expert interpreters will walk you through the entire milling process. Even for the non-historically inclined, this is a must. Even without the cookies, we think it's one of the most interesting historical sights in the province.

Nearby, the **Sutherland Steam Mill** on Rte. 326 in Denmark, ☎ 902/657-3365, represents another aspect of the history of the province. In 1891, a factory was erected for the manufacture of doors and windows and for the building and repair of carriages and sleighs. Owned by a father and son from 1894 until closure in

1958, the factory represents the entrepreneurial spirit of small businesses. The mill had its own sawmill, all operated by the second echelon of power, steam.

Historic Homes of Amherst

When the railroad ignited Amherst's manufacturing boom, the business owners built homes to befit their new prosperity. Their wealth produced a number of outstanding homes, many of which still stand, offering a unique chance to see a variety of Victorian building styles within a small distance. They are described in the brochure, *Amherst's Municipally Registered Homes*, which locates 17 of them. You can get it at the Amherst Tourist Centre or, if it is not open, drive or walk to Victoria Street West near Mill Street.

The **Lusby House** at 146 Victoria Street West dates from 1882 and is a three-bay Colonial Revival with characteristic large chimneys. At 27 Victoria Street West, the **Pugsley House** is a 1910 Queen Anne with fine wood texturing of the period. Continue on into town and Victoria will turn to the right and become Victoria Street East. At 163 is a home built for the general manager of the Robb Engineering Company, maker of rail passenger cars. The **Robb Engineering House** was built in 1870 in the Gothic Revival style and features a steep-pitched gable roof with matched dormers flanking a large central dormer. At #169 the **Munroe House**, also 1870, is another Gothic Revival with original gingerbread trim. The **Dickey House** at 169 was built later, in 1879, by which time the Second Empire style was in vogue, with a mansard roof and Italianate window bracketing. "**Victoria**," a 1907 late Victorian home, was built for a local barrister and businessman. Note the unusual use of stone turrets and bases for the porch and the conical tops of the towers. Further on at #183 is another 1870 Gothic Revival-style home, the **Townshend-Pipes-Rhodes House**, much changed from the original but still bearing many traces of the gingerbread and other details. Just beyond, #186 is the 1855 **Tupper House**, an early Victorian house of modified Gothic style and former home of Canadian Prime Minister Sir Charles Tupper, whose summer home in Parrsboro, Ottawa House, is open as a museum.

Where To Stay & Eat

Many of the lodgings and campgrounds in the province use the **Check Inns** centralized reservations service, ☎ 800/565-0000.

Wentworth Hostel is open all the time, with 20 dorm beds and family rooms. Reservations are recommended, and they do *not* take credit cards. There is a network of trails for hiking. From TransCanada-104 take Valley Road about a half-mile to Wentworth Station Road and follow the signs. *RR #1, Wentworth, NS B0M 1Z0, ☎ 902/548-2379 ($).*

Shady Maple B&B is on Rte. 2 just off Exit 12 of TransCanada-104, east of Glenholme. A small B&B, it's located on a working dairy farm where guests are welcomed to walk the grounds, swim in the pool or find out about dairy farming by visiting the barns. They serve a full four-course breakfast with their own fresh eggs, jelly and maple syrup. *Rte. 2, Masstown, NS, ☎ 902/662-3565 ($-$$).*

The Ro-Manse Inn B&B is a two-bedroom B&B with shared bath. It's just a quarter-mile off TransCanada-104 at Exit 11. They serve a full breakfast and are glad to offer advice on what to do in the area. *RR #1, Glenholme, Great Village, NS B0M 1L0, ☎ 902/662-3733 ($).*

Tidal River Ridge is at Moose River between Parrsboro and Five Islands. The four new cottages have two bedrooms, full bath and fully equipped kitchen. They are spaced well to ensure privacy. The extensive property lies along the shore of Moose River and the Bay of Fundy. There are hiking trails on the property, used for cross-country skiing and for snowmobiling. They are also adjacent to snowmobile trails. A week's stay is $500 for two, with extra persons at $7 per person per night. Rates are lower off-season. They also arrange guided hiking, cross-country skiing, fishing and skating. *RR1, Moose River, NS B0M 1N0, ☎ 800/806-8860 or 902/254-3333, Web site www.cottagelink.com ($$).*

Four Seasons Retreat has 10 fully equipped cottages with one-, two-, and three-bedroom cabins on Cobequid Bay. All have a fireplace and there is a hot tub and outdoor pool as well. Weekly rates are also available. *RR #1, Cove Road, Economy, NS B0M 1J0, ☎ 902/647-2628 ($$).*

The Sunshine Inn is a clean modern motel near Parrsboro on 68 acres near a 40-acre lake. Guests may swim in the lake and hike on the surrounding land. Open in May-October. *4487 Highway 2, Parrsborro, NS B0M 1S0, ☎ 902/254-3135 ($-$$).*

The Parrsboro Mansion is a European-style B&B with full breakfast, open from June 1 to the end of September and by reservation at other times. Three guest rooms all share a bath. It's in the heart of town and close to restaurants and the theater. They also arrange guided bicycle tours, as well as freshwater and saltwater fishing expeditions. *15 Eastern Avenue, Box 579, Parrsboro, NS B0M 1S0, ☎ 902/254-3339, fax 902/254-2585 ($$).*

The Maple Inn is near the center of Parrsboro and within walking distance of the town facilities. The owners have renovated and connected two 19th-century houses to provide five rooms with private baths and three that share two baths. There is also a two-bedroom suite with whirlpool bath. Rates include a full breakfast. *PO Box 457, 17 Western Avenue, Parrsboro, NS B0M 1S0, ☎ 902/254-3735 ($$).*

Cape d'Or Lightkeepers Guesthouse has a few rooms in the old lightkeeper's quarters of the Cape d'Or lighthouse. In addition to the guesthouse there is **The Lightkeepers Kitchen**, with a specialty of chili and chowders. *Advocate, NS, ☎ 902/664-2108 ($).*

Balmoral Motel is a modern motel on the outskirts of town. It offers clean, comfortable rooms, some with wonderful views over fields. The motel's dining room, **The Mill Room** ($) overlooks fields and the bay; last time we had lunch there we watched a family of deer ambling across the grass. The menu features well-prepared dishes, from seafood to German specialties; they serve hot oatcakes at breakfast. *Box 178, Tatamagouche, NS B0K 1V0, ☎ 902/657-2000 ($$).*

Amherst Shore Country Inn, on Rte. 366, offers formal dining along the north shore. Savor entrées such as chicken cordon bleu with brandy sauce. A full four-course meal is served at a single sitting, starting at 6:45 pm with cocktails. Dinner service begins at 7:30. The fixed menu changes daily; reservations are required. Rooms and suites are also available. *(Lornville, NS, ☎ 800/661-2724 or 902/661-4800 ($$$).*

Jubilee Cottage Country Inn is on Rte. 6; take Exit 1 or 3 from TransCanada-104. The small inn has three rooms, all with an ocean view. Room rates include a full breakfast and evening snack after wandering on the beach. The Inn also has a fine dining room that specializes in five-course candlelight dinners by reservation, featuring specialties such as baked salmon with ginger sauce, cheese-stuffed chicken breast and seafood. The fixed menu changes daily; the single seating begins at 7 pm. *Box 148, Wallace, NS B0K 1Y0, ☎ 800/481-9915 or 902/257-2432 ($$$).*

Windygates B&B, 129 North Shore Rd. In East Wallace, is a B&B with a difference. It's also a Highland cattle farm. Near the Jost Winery and the other attractions around Wallace, the B&B has its own nature trails and a view looking out over the bay. The private suite is only $60 for two people, including breakfast. *PO Box 266, Wallace, NS B0K 1Y0, Check-Ins, ☎ 902/257-2271 ($).*

Helm Restaurant & Lounge takes pride in its home cooking and features seafood and hot sandwiches. They are open Monday through Saturday from 7:30 am to 8:30 pm, and on Sunday from 11 am to 7 pm. *85 Victoria St., Amherst, NS, ☎ 902/667-8871 ($-$$).*

Country Rose Tea Room is open Monday through Saturday, serving soups, sandwiches, and quiche, all of which are homemade. *125 Victoria St., Amherst, NS, ☎ 902/667-0660 ($).*

Old Warehouse Café has a full menu, with chicken, beef, pasta, seafoods and soups. Open Monday through Friday, 8:30 am to 9 pm; open at 11 am on Saturday. *4 Havelock St., Amherst, NS, ☎ 902/667-1160 ($-$$).*

■ Camping

Hidden Hilltop Campground is a Good Sam Park campground off of TransCanada-104 south of Ski Wentworth and three miles north of Glenholme. They have fully serviced camper and RV sites as well as tenting areas, plus a large pool, track, playground, tennis courts, nature trail, horseshoes and a recreation building. Ask about their special weekend rates. *PO Box 166, Debert, NS B0M 1G0, ☎ 902/662-3391.*

Five Islands Provincial Park has 90 campsites with toilets, a dumping station, water and wood. They do not take reservations, but this is not a heavily traveled area. There is an unsupervised beach and clamming on the flats at low tide. Don't go onto the flats without knowing the tide schedule. *District Office Department of Lands and Forests, Box 428, Parrsboro, NS B0M 1C0, ☎ 902/254-3241; May-October, ☎ 902/254-9911.*

Fundy Tides Campground has 40 sites, of which half are serviced. The laundry, washroom and shower facilities are handicapped accessible. There is a full-scale ball park with regular league play, a playground, campfires and hayrides and they even have a craft shop. It's a good location from which to explore the tip of the peninsula. *Rte. 209, PO Box 38, Advocate Harbour, NS B0M 1A0, ☎ 902/393-2297.*

Loch Lomond Tenting and Trailer Court has tent sites in fields and in wooded sections as well as fully serviced trailer and RV sites. The site overlooks a mile-long stocked lake where they have a shallow swimming and wading beach. They also have a swimming pool, playground and amusement center. At the intersection of TransCanada-104 and Rte. 2 (Exit 4) take Rte. 2 south; it's just past the highway exit on the right. *Rte. 2, Amherst, NS, ☎ 902/667-3890.*

Amherst Shore Provincial Park has RV and tenting sites on a 45-acre site on the Northumberland Strait. The campground sits inland on Rte. 366 and another section of the grounds sits on the other side of the road with its own beach. The campground has facilities for wheelchairs. *In summer, ☎ 902/661-6002, or contact Department of Natural Resources, PO Box 130, Oxford, NS B0M 1P0, ☎ 902/447-2115.*

Nelson Memorial Park and Campground is on Rte. 6, 1½ miles from Tatamagouche. About half the 52 sites are serviced and have a choice of wooded or open. Recreational activities include walking trails, beach, pool, ball fields and a playground. *RR#3, Tatamagouche, NS B0K 1V0, ☎ 902/657-2730.*

The Evangeline Trail

The lush greens of the Annapolis Valley's farmlands roll gently to the sea along most of this coast, punctuated by the dramatic high headland of Cape Blomiden, which seems to challenge the

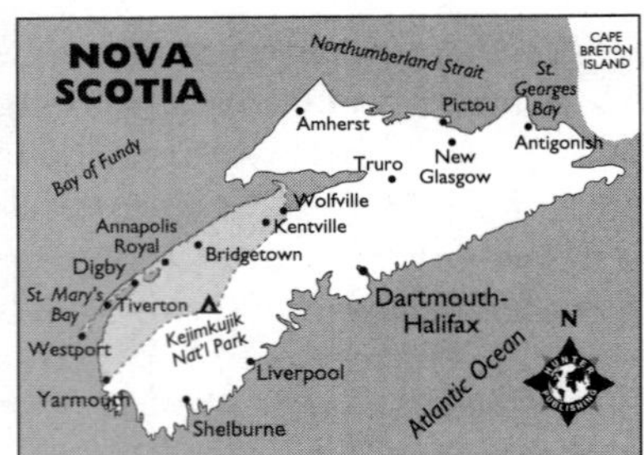

force of the Fundy tides by pointing a defiant crooked finger across the Minas Channel. This is Acadian country, still a rich blend of French and English cultures melded over more than two centuries of living together.

Geography & History

This southwest corner of Nova Scotia that separates the Bay of Fundy from the Atlantic is perhaps the best known and most heavily traveled part of the province. Ferries from three different ports bring passengers daily to this end of the island, and it is easy to reach in a leisurely side-trip from Halifax. The **Evangeline Trail** is the tourist office name for the route along the northern shore, which the Bay of Fundy separates from New Brunswick.

Evangeline, although a fictional character, has become the symbol of the Acadians, who still make much of their expulsion from these lands by the British in 1755. Once the French garrison at Fort Beausejour, near Amherst, had fallen, and the French had ceded Nova Scotia to the British, Britain allowed the farmers in this area (known as Acadia since Samuel Champlain began the first settlement in 1605 at Annapolis Royal) to remain. But when war with France seemed inevitable, they asked them to openly pledge allegiance to Britain. For those who didn't take the pledge the deportation order came in 1755, and they were forcibly expelled, many ending up in the French colony of Louisiana where their Acadian language and culture became what we now call "Cajun."

At about the same time British landlords decided to raise sheep on the small farms of Scotland and Ireland and the displaced victims of the "clearances" were enticed to replace the Acadians. The new province soon came to be known as Nova Scotia, the New Scotland.

New Englanders were the leaders and a substantial part of the British army that invaded and defeated the French at Louisbourg. After British domination was established in the late 1750s, many moved here to repopulate the lands left by the French. When the British were no longer at war with the French, they allowed the Acadians to return to their lands, which many of them did.

And so was born the cultural mix that remains today, as it does in the rest of the province, but with a stronger French accent along this Acadian coast. Agriculture, fishing and shipbuilding became predominant occupations and the region prospered. The Annapolis Valley is a rich agricultural area blessed with mild temperatures and good growing conditions. On the other side of North Mountain, the abundance of marine life enabled people there to prosper from the sea's harvest.

Getting Around

The Evangeline Trail, as it is shown on the provincial road map and on signs along the way, is **Rte. 101**, which leads from Halifax to Windsor, then travels close to the shore all the way to Yarmouth, and the beginning of the Lighthouse Route.

Few roads cut north-south across the wild interior, the main one being Rte. 8, which runs from Annapolis Royal to Liverpool, and provides access to Kejimkujic National Park in the center. Several side roads give access to a road along the very rim of the Minas Basin, a slow, but scenic way to get from Wolfville to Annapolis Royal. You can't follow the shore in a straight line and must wind your way on very rural, sometimes unsurfaced roads, but it is an interesting way to avoid the highway's sameness.

Information Sources

■ **Visitor Centre**, 21 Colonial Rd, Windsor, NS, ☎ 902/789-2690.

■ **Evangeline Trail Tourism Association and Welcome Centre**, 5518 Prospect Rd, New Minas, NS B4N 3K8, ☎ 800/565-ETTA or 902/681-1645, fax 902/681-2747.

■ The **Wolfville Visitor Centre**, Willow Park, Main Street (Rte. 1), Wolfville, NS B0P 1X0, ☎ 902/542-7000, is open daily 9 am to 7 pm July and August, 9 am to 5 pm, mid-May to October.

■ **Annapolis Royal and Area Information Centre**, Annapolis Tidal Power Project, Rte. 1, Annapolis Royal, NS, B0S 1A0, ☎ 902/532-5454, is open daily 9 am to 7 pm from mid-May to mid-October.

■ The **Evangeline Trail Visitor Information Office,** Digby, ☎ 902/245-5714, on the waterfront, opens daily from 9 am to 5 pm for the summer.

■ The **Nova Scotia Information Centre** is on the shore road to the ferry, opposite the Annapolis Basin. It's open daily from mid-May to mid-October.

■ Tours

Kan-Active Tours, RR #3, Waterville, NS B0P 1V0, ☎ 800/933-8687 or 902/538-8714, fax 902/538-8714, Web site www.valley-web.com/kanactive, has a number of tours of the Wolfville area that give a taste of the culture of the area. The "Mi'kmaq Legends/Acadian History/Mighty Tides" tour includes the Acadian influence at Grand Pré, the cliffs at Blomidon and the Look-Off (both with fine views of the Minas Basin), and artist studios. Other tours are available and they will also customize a tour for groups of four or more. Accommodations are in private cottages, inns or in resorts depending on the wishes of the traveler.

Tartan Tour Centre, 1595 Barrington Street, Halifax, NS B3J 1Z7, ☎ 902/422-9092 or 902/429-9787, can help you plan your trip, make lodging reservations and even arrange canoe, kayak or bicycle rentals for you. They can put together a schedule with all the things you are looking for. Rates for their services are $80 for a three-day trip, $100 for a five-day trip and $120 for a seven-day trip. They can also arrange day tours, including picnics. Open every day from 9 am to 7 pm.

Adventures

The northwest coast of Nova Scotia is a varied land, from the basalt cliffs of Brier and Long Islands to the fertile fields and orchards of the Annapolis Valley and the high wild forests and lakes of the inland. The shore is wed to the unusual tides of the Bay of Fundy. Those tides are magnified as they pass up the Minas Channel and Basin into the Avon River and Cobequid Bay. The tides drain most of the basin bringing nutrients and food for the sea creatures, making the area off Brier Island one of the richest habitats for whales, porpoise and dolphin. The wild high inland area is accessible to the adventuring traveler because of Kejimkujik National Park, PO Box 236, Maitland Bridge, NS B0T 1B0, whose facilities provide access while protecting the environment and the special nature of this place. Look there for hiking, canoeing, fishing, skating, cross-country skiing and coasting.

On Foot

Walking Tours

Across from the Blomidon Inn in Wolfville is a small and easy trail that leads to the water, a pleasant place for a short walk to see the birds and the tides. The town also has a "Self-Guided Walking Tour" with descriptive material on many of the historic buildings. Ask for it at the Visitor Centre. For a guided walking tour contact **Riven Woodworks**, 1341 Peck Meadow Road, RR #1, Wolfville, NS B0P 1X0, ☎ 902/542-3178. When Barry Brown is not making hand-fashioned walking sticks, canoe cups, wooden spoons and other wonders of wood he is happy to take you on a guided walking tour, which could be to the Acadian dikes.

Another popular hike is the **Acadian Dike Walk** that runs between the town of Wolfville and Grand Pré. Before the expulsion, the Acadians built a series of dikes along the tidal shore to take advantage of the rich soils of the tidal marshes and to protect them from erosion and the adverse effects of the saltwater. These hand-built barriers of clay and soil still stand, and today you can walk along the tops of them for two miles, admiring the handiwork of these long ago pioneers and watching the sea on the other side of the trail. To pick up the trail go to the Visitors Information Centre, ☎ 902/542-7000, on Rte. 1. It's a four-mile round trip over relatively flat and easy ground.

Hiking

The **Cape Split Trail** is an interesting hike. Just west of Wolfville on Rte. 1, take Rte. 358 north for access to Cape Blomidon and Cape Split. The Cape is a huge arm of land striking out into the Minas Basin and separating the Basin from the Bay of Fundy. Follow Rte. 358 to the end. Park in the parking lot and follow the trail to the right. It rises gently as it passes through mixed forests and out along the arm of land extending into the bay. As it advances, views open up to the west, revealing the raw Bay of Fundy, and to the east where the waters are relatively protected by the great barrier of Cape Split. The trail continues close to the edge of the rising bluff. These are eroding cliffs so avoid the edge, which could crumble and drop you hundreds of feet to the shore. Across the waters you will see the shores of the Glooscap Trail at Parrsboro and Diligent River. While there is an access to the beach level it is not recommended, as the cliff is erosive. If you do go to the shore know the tides; they rise fast and not strictly on schedule. If you are too far from the trail it could be deadly. This trail is about eight miles round-trip and takes from five to eight hours, depending upon how much time you take to savor it.

Take Rte. 1 out of Wolfville toward Kentville and keep an eye out for the signs for Kentville Agricultural Centre. At its entrance you will find the parking area for the **Kentville Ravine Trail**. This is only a half-mile trail each way into a ravine carved by the Elderkin River as it cuts through loose sandstone soils. The hemlock, red spruce and white pine forest is believed to be one of the oldest in the province, dating from the mid-1700s. The site is notable not only for the forest and the walk through the increasingly steep-sided ravine, but also for the 125 species of flowering plants that are found along its path and on its walls. At the end a long, narrow cascade puts the frosting to the cake.

RECOMMENDED READING: *A brochure entitled* **Annapolis County Parks and Trails** *is available from the Annapolis County Recreation Department, 354 George Street, PO Box 100, Annapolis Royal, NS, B0S 1A0, ☎ 902/532-2334, fax 902/532-2096. It lists 29 parks and walks of varying length throughout the county. Among the listings, for example, is the* ***Mickey Hill Pocket Wilderness*** *on Rte. 8, six miles south of Annapolis Royal. The Bowater Mersey Paper Co. has a number of these small and delightful "pocket" parks. This one has interpretive sites, marshland, boardwalk, suspension bridge, a treetop look-off and beach access, all on a walk of about a half-mile.*

To reach the **Delaps Cove Trails**, take the road from Annapolis Royal to Port Royal and watch for the dirt road to Delaps Cove on the right. Follow it to the trail head at the shore. There are two trials here, one two miles long and the other about a half-mile longer. **Bowhaker Trail** is a loop, and the easier of the two, starting on a rocky area, continuing through a forest and opening onto the shore. It then returns to a spruce and pine woods on the way back. Watch for the Christmas tree ferns in the forest sections, ferns almost four feet tall that make you believe in prehistoric fern forests. The longer **Charlie's Trail** is about a mile farther down the woods road. This is a very rough trail, requiring greater endurance because of the trail condition and rocky areas over which it passes. Looking at a map will tell you that this long northwest coast is a continuation of the Brier Island, Digby Neck area.

Kejimkujik National Park, Rte. 8, Maitland Bridge, is about a half-hour drive from Annapolis Royal. The centerpiece of the park is Lake Kejimkujik, with many of the facilities centered around it. The surrounding land is a mass of interconnected ponds and lakes. Many of the trails at Kejimkujik use the internal system of paved and unpaved roadways as part of their route. Stop at the Visitor Center on the way in for a map. After entering the park, keep to the left and park at the Merrymakedge beach parking area. Walk down the road over the outlet for Grafton Lake. On the right is the trail for **Peter Point** (under two miles) and **Snake Lake** (under two miles). Peter Point is good for bird-watching. Past those trails are **Gold Mines** (under two miles) and **McGinty Lake** (about three miles) trails on the left. Gold Mines is a self-interpretive trail detailing the mining that took place here, and McGinty Lake passes over glacial drumlins, one of which shows signs of a farm built there to take advantage of the rich soil.

A nice hike that gives a view of the whole area is the **Fire Tower Trail**, an 11-mile walk through soft and hardwood forests, ending at a fire tower. To get there, go past Merrymakedge Beach and follow the gravel road past the trails mentioned above. About four miles from the McGinty Lake Trail you will find the Fire Tower Trail on the right. On the north end of the park, the **Hemlocks and Hardwoods Trail** is a loop trail on the first leg of the **Channel Lake Trail**. Take the first trail to the right after the gravel road and when it intersects another trail (the Channel Lake Trail) go left. The Channel Lake Trail is a 15½-mile trip into the back woods; get specifics at the Visitor Center if you want to do this one. Be sure you pick up their excellent and inexpensive booklets entitled "The Mammals," "The Forests," "The Turtles," and "Dark Waters," which deals with the lakes, streams and fish.

Over on the coast is **Sandy Cove**. If you stand on the high point of the amazingly long, narrow strip of sand, rock and soil called Digby Neck and face south, you will be looking across St. Mary's Bay toward the Acadian shore. If you turn around there is a view across the Bay of Fundy toward New Brunswick. There are two beaches here, which make a nice beach walk; if you are a rock-

➲ **FOR BIRDERS:** *If you would like to see Brier Island with a guide who can show you the best birding sites, contact* ***Walk on the Wild Side****, Freeport Long Island, NS, ☎ 902/839-2962, on the Long Island side of the ferry to Westport.*

hound you can look along the cliff bottoms and perhaps find amethysts, agates and jasper.

The **Brier Island Coastal Walk** is a sensory triathlon for those with a wide variety of interests in the natural sciences. It combines birding, botany and geology, in one long, scenic hike. Many species of migratory birds use the island, it has rare wildflowers that grow in only one other place, and along the shore are rare minerals and curious hexagonal columns of basalt. To get there from Digby, travel out Digby Neck on Rte. 217, crossing on both ferries (easy to find, since the only road leads to the ferry landings). When you leave the second ferry, turn right toward, and past, Brier Island Lodge, to Northern Point and the Grand Passage Light and Alarm. The ride is up over heights and back down to the sea. The trail leads to the left along the shore. It passes Seal Cove and Pea Jack Cove, popular for mineral searches, and then leads to Cow Cove and the Brier Island Light and Alarm, originally built in 1809. This is also a popular rockhounding area and here you have two choices. You can continue along the shore of Mucklehaney Point, then return to the light on the same trail. Or you can take Lighthouse Road for a short distance, then follow Camp Road, to the right. It will go toward the sea and then around Po Gull Rock Road. You can follow it and come back into the town of Westport, where the ferry landed, and from which you can walk over the headland to your car. A shorter trail leads from the end of the shore road (go left as you leave the ferry) to **Green Head**, where the best examples of columnar basalt formations are found. For more on the natural attractions of Brier Island, see *Cultural & Eco-Travel Experiences*, page 267.

Another of the Bowater Mersey Paper Co. pocket wilderness areas is on Rte. 340 about nine miles south of Weymouth near the village of Corberrie. The **Wentworth Lake Pocket Wilderness** has nice walking trails here with interpretation stations.

On Wheels

Road Biking

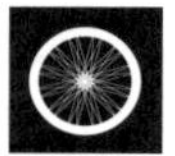

There is not a great deal of organized bicycling activity along the northwest shore on the Evangeline Trail, but it's a great area for cycling, particularly for families. While it has a rolling terrain, the hills are neither long nor steep.

In the area **north of Rte. 1**, between Wolfville and Kentville, is a whole warren of roads that wind between dairies and apple farms all the way to the Minas Channel and Minas Basin. Just west of Kentville, take Rte. 359 to Hall's Harbour, a small fishing village on the Bay of Fundy where, at low tide, the boats are sitting on the bottom with the docks far above. At high tide they are at wharf level, a dozen or more feet higher. From there double back a short way, take the road to Glenmont and continue east to Rte. 358. Take it to the left to The Look Off, which offers a view out over the Minas Basin, and then continue on to Cape Split or take a right to Cape Blomidon Provincial Park.

On the northeast side of Digby Harbour the estuary of the Annapolis River continues to separate a strip of land to Middleton and beyond. Down the center of that long narrow strip there is a ridge and on either side it slopes to water. All of the roads along that strip are country roads seldom traveled by tourists and great places to explore on a bicycle. Crossing the river at **Annapolis Royal**, for example, you can go southwest and take the road to Delaps Cove, then follow the shore route as far as you want. You could do this all the way to Cape Split on Cape Blomidon. At many points along the way are side roads that cut back across to Rte. 1.

> **BIKE TRAVEL TIP:** *Explore the area here while you wait for the ferry; with a bike you don't have to sit in line to hold a place. One word of caution, however: keep an eye on the ferry times. You will note that the closer you get to the ferry the more likely you are to encounter a clump of cars traveling fast to get to the ferry. Be aware of then and pull off to let them go by if you're uncomfortable. The rest of the time you just about have the road to yourself.*

While one unusually cranky innkeeper told us that no one bicycles on Digby Neck, driving down the road tells us a different story. The reason, the innkeeper told us, was the narrowness of the roads, but the roads are wide enough and so little traveled that riding here is a pleasure (with proper

Nova Scotia

precautions, of course). These roads are not any different than country roads in New England, so if you are comfortable there you should be here. Try the **Digby to Brier Island** route (Rte. 217) or parts of it. Along the way, take one of the side roads to the left and follow along the shore of **St. Mary's Bay**, or go uphill to the right to reach the shore along the Bay of Fundy.

Kejimkujik National Park, Rte. 8, Maitland Bridge, NS, has many miles of roads for bicycling, many of them gravel. Bikes are not allowed on the hiking trails. Bicycle rental is available at the park and costs about $3 per hour, $12.50 per day or $50 per week. Make arrangements at the Visitor Center. In addition to the park roads, there are some great roads out into the back country in the area south of the park entrance. From Kempt (we've looked in vain for the sister town of Unkempt), travel to Northfield or down to Harmony Mills and then to West Caledonia, Low Landing or Whiteburn Mines. Caledonia itself is a good destination with its museum and activities. Just south of the park, take a dirt road to the right to New Grafton, continuing to West Caledonia and from there into Caledonia before returning to the park via Rte. 8.

Bicycle Outfitters & Tours

- **Frame Break Bicycles**, 15 River Street, Kentville, ☎ 902/679-0611, is another choice in the area.

- **Freewheeling Adventures** has a six-day tour of the Evangeline route with an additional day of hiking and a half-day whale watch, a good well-rounded view of this area. Freewheeling has a full line of bikes, trailers and kayaks for rent. They also do kayak, bike and hike trips in the province. Contact Freewheeling Adventures at RR #1, The Lodge, Hubbards, NS B0J 1T0, ☎ 902/857-3600, fax 902/857-3612, e-mail bicycle @freewheeling.ca, Web site www.freewheeling.ca/ torlist.htm.

On Water

This region doesn't lack for water, and a fresh supply daily at that. A whopping 115 billion tons of water rush in and out twice a day, making timing crucial for most watersports. You need to know the daily tide schedule and be exceedingly careful to keep track of the whereabouts of the onrush. If you've never seen water arrive in a wall, it's hard to imagine how fast and powerful it can be.

TIDE CHARTS: *Tide information is published in the local papers, and all the information centers have pamphlets, tourist newspapers and brochures containing tide charts. You need to have this information.*

Canoeing & Kayaking

Fresh Air Adventures offers a great kayak trip around Cape Split, a rare and exciting experience. It starts in Hall's Harbour and travels up the coast, past waterfalls and rock formations to the jagged tooth end of Cape Split. The rate for the trip is $340 per person for three days and two nights. Contact them at PO Box 146, Alma, NB E0A 1B0, ☎ 800/545-0020, fax 506/887-2262 (May-November), 902/895-2533, 506/887-2249 (December-April), e-mail FreshAir@fox.nstn.ca, Web site http://fox.nstn.ca:80/freshair/.

South of Digby off the coast of St. Mary's Bay, **Hinterland Adventures & Gear** has a full range of canoeing and kayaking trips ranging from one day to three weeks. Options include inn-to-inn, day and wilderness trips, appropriate for all levels of paddlers. Guided tours and equipment rentals are available. Weymouth is at the end of an estuary off Rte. 101, Exit 27. Contact them at The Odyssey Centre, 54 Gates Lane, Weymouth, NS B0W 3T0, ☎ 800/378-8177 or 902/837-4092, fax 902/837-5156; e-mail odysseys@ns.sympatico.com; Web site www.valleyweb.com/odysseys.

RECOMMENDED READING: *A local group of canoe enthusiasts in the Annapolis area has put together a guide to the waters of the county. Contact* ***Canoe Annapolis County****, PO Box 100, Annapolis Royal, NS B0S 1A0, ☎ 902/532-2334, fax 902/532-2096; e-mail dryan.munnofan@clan.TartanNET.ns.ca. Their 157-page* **Canoe Guide** *has 22 canoe routes in the county and sells for $16. Each route has a skill rating from novice to intermediate and expert. There are route lists, day trips, overnight trips and river trips.*

Kejimkujik National Park, Rte. 8, Maitland Bridge, NS, has, without a doubt, the best freshwater canoeing in this area. When the Micmacs roamed this place the myriad ponds and interconnecting streams provided them a way to move from one side of the island to the other by water. Kejimkujik is a big lake filled with islands and lots of wildlife. The only settlement on it is the national park, leaving most of the lake a wilderness. The outlet of the lake is the Mersey River, a wide stream, perfect for viewing wildlife along its wilderness shores. A short portage at the end of the Lake at the Lower Mersey River Bridge will put you on Lake George where there is no sign of mankind other than your paddle stroke. On the north end of the lake is a 450-yard portage to Big Dam Lake, a long narrow body of water, half of which is clear enough to see fish on the bottom; the other half is the dark brown of iron-rich, boggy waters. Guided canoe tours conducted by national park interpreters are suitable even for those who have never canoed before. The wilderness canoeing opportunities for more experienced canoers are outstanding, but backcountry routes exist for beginners as well. The park has a concession at Jake's Landing where 14- to 17-foot fiberglass canoes can be rented for $3 an hour, $16 a day or $80 a week. They have roof-rack carriers and shuttle services. If your plans are for anything more than a half-day it's a good idea to reserve. Call **Pabek Recreation Limited**, PO Box 188, Caledonia, NS B0T 1B0, ☎ 902/682-2817.

A very short, but interesting paddle is at **Meteghan Falls**. From Rte. 1 north of Meteghan, take the road signposted Bangor. A bridge over the highway outside that town crosses the Meteghan River and you will see the falls several hundred feet upstream. Put in and paddle up to the falls. Only paddlers can get this close because the shore owners don't want their land used by the public.

Canoe Outfitters & Other Tour Operators

■ **Annapolis River Campground**, 56 Queen Street, Bridgetown, ☎ 902/665-2801.

■ **Back of Beyond Canoe Outfitters**, South Milford, ☎ 902/532-2497.

■ **Milford House**, Milford, ☎ 902/532-2671.

■ **Raven House**, Sandy Bottom Lake, ☎ 902/532-7320.

■ **Wade's Landing Marina**, Granville Centre, ☎ 902/532-7280.

■ **Loon Lake Outfitters**, Caledonia, ☎ 902/682-2220, rents equipment and is an outfitter as well, providing a full range of camping equipment rentals as well as canoe rentals.

■ Another outfitter operating in the park is **Wildcat River Outfitters**, RR #1, South Brookfield, NS B0T 1X0, ☎ 902/682-2822 or 902/682-2196 at Jake's Landing; fax 902/682-2114. They have canoes, boats, kayaks, paddle-boats and bicycles for rent.

■ Outside the park, several good outfitters can rent you a canoe and take you on short trips or an expedition. **Loon Lake Outfitters**, Maitland Bridge, RR #2, Caledonia, NS B0T 1B0, ☎ 902/242-2220 or 902/242-2290, is just north of the park entrance. Their canoe rental rates are comparable to those in the park. In addition, they rent a tent and full camping gear for as little as $35 a week for a two-person tent. A fully outfitted trip that includes all gear and food is $35 a day per adult, $23 per child. They can also provide maps of the water systems and guide services. As a sideline, owner Peter Rogers makes and sells handmade paddles and portage yokes.

■ **Kan-Active Tours** runs a broad range of tours in this area, including canoeing. Contact them at RR #3, Waterville, NS B0P 1V0, ☎ 800/933-8687 or 902/538-8714, fax 902/538-8714, Web site www.valleyweb. com/kanactive.

Boat Tours

Annapolis River Tours, Wade's Landing & Marina, Granville Centre, ☎ 902/532-7280. Lorry and Ardwith Wade take you on a two-hour narrated tour of the Annapolis River. This includes views of the Acadian dikes, the tidal power station and the wild-fowl areas along the river banks. Trips run from May through September; call for times, which vary with the tide schedules.

Whale-Watching

You will find almost all the whale watch excursion boats along the shore of Digby Neck and from the islands at its end. From Annapolis Royal it will take about two hours to get to Brier Island if heavy traffic doesn't lengthen the ferry wait. Always allow longer on Saturdays and Sundays. Nearly all the operators require reservations and you'll have to pay whether you show up or not. Allow plenty of travel time before departure time.

READ THE FINE PRINT: *Several boat operators guarantee whale sightings, which at least gives you an idea of how likely it is that you will see whales. But if you hit a bad whale day, do you get your money back? Probably not. Check those guarantees carefully: most give you a raincheck for another tour, which isn't much help if you're leaving the area soon. You can improve on your odds by booking a whale-watch very early in your stay so you'll have time to use a raincheck if you need to.*

It is important to know the ferry schedules. The ferry from East Ferry to Tiverton Long Island leaves hourly **on the half-hour**. At the other end of Long Island the ferry from Freeport to Westport, on Brier Island, leaves hourly **on the hour**. If you want to catch the next Brier Island ferry you have to go from Tiverton to the ferry without stopping along the way. If there is much traffic you may have to wait for the next departure an hour later. Not all boat trips require a ferry ride first; we've separated them into two groups.

Whale Watch Tours & Boat Tours

From the Mainland:

■ **Petite Passage Whale Watch** has a 34-foot boat with seating for 20; it's wheelchair accessible. The cruise is from three to four hours and they prefer reservations, but will take walk-on passengers if they have room. Cruises are at 8:35 am and 12:35 pm. Tickets can be purchased at the East Ferry General Store and are $33 for adults; half-fare for children under 12. It will take you 45 minutes to get to East Ferry from Digby. Contact Petite Passage at East Ferry General Store, East Ferry Digby Neck, NS B0V 1E0, ☎ 902/834-2226, evenings 902/245-6132, fax 902/245-4162.

■ **Bay to Bay Adventures** has an office in Little River on Digby Neck, about halfway between Digby and East Ferry. Passengers meet at the office and are taken to the boat at East Ferry. They use a real working lobster boat for the four-hour trips. They leave at 8:30 am, 12:30 and 4:30 pm daily during the summer. Bay to Bay Adventures is at Little River, NS B0V 1C0, ☎ 902/834-2618, fax 902/834-2939.

■ **Whale of a Time Sea Adventures** will accept walk-ins if there is room on the boat, but prefers reservations. The tours are 3½ hours or longer and leave at 8:45 am, 12:45 and 4:45 pm; each tour picks up passengers at Tiverton 15 minutes later. Deep-sea fishing and diving charters are also available; arrange in advance for these. Little River, NS B0V 1C0, ☎ 902/834-2867, e-mail whaletym@isisnet.com.

From the Islands:

■ **Pirate's Cove Whale and Seabird Cruises** uses the *M/V Todd*, a 34-foot lobster boat, for three-hour cruises. The cost is $33, but family rates are available. Sailings are at 8 am and 1 pm and they also offer a 5:30 sunset cruise if conditions are good. Reservations are required. Contact them at Tiverton, Long Island, NS B0V 1G0, ☎ 888/480-0004 or 902/839-2242, fax 902/839-2271; e-mail pcove@clan.TartanNET.ns.ca.

■ **Freeport Whale and Seabird Tours** sails from Freeport, the departure port for Brier Island, where the tidal rip is impressive. Cruises leave three times a day from mid-June to mid-October. Rates are $25 adult, $12 for ages three to 15. Contact Capt. Timothy Crocker, RR #1, Freeport, NS B0V 1B0; e-mail freeport @marina. istar.ca.

■ **Mariner Cruises** in Westport runs three cruises daily from June through October. A family business, their boat the *Chad and Sisters Two* is a 45-foot lobster boat-style with an enclosed cabin, a canteen and an open viewing deck. They have also teamed up with Walk on the Wild Side Nature Tours to present a morning-long nature walk of the island coupled with an afternoon sea tour of the whales, columnar basalt rock formations, seabirds and other mammalian sea life. Mariner Cruises, Brier Island, NS B0V 1H0, ☎ 800/239-2189 or 902/839-2346, fax 902/839-2070.

■ **Timberwind Cruises** sails the *Timberwind No.1*, a 35-foot sailboat. They leave from Westport at 9 am and 1 and 5 pm daily. The rate is $30 per person and they offer a fishing or sightseeing option to guests. Contact Timberwind at Westport, Brier Island, NS B0V 1H0, ☎ 902/839-2683.

■ **Slocum's Whale and Deep Sea Fishing Cruises** has trips at 8:30 am and 1:30 pm, with sunset cruises if conditions are right. Reservations are recommended but walk-in passengers are welcome on a space available basis. As the name states, they also have fishing cruises. Westport, Brier Island, NS B0V 1H0, ☎ 800/214-4655 or 902/839-2110.

■ **Brier Island Whale and Seabird Cruises, Ltd.** specializes in research and educational tours, using 52-foot and 45-foot vessels staffed by naturalists from their sister organization, BIOS (Brier Island Ocean Study). BIOS runs the "Adopt a Whale" research program. Contact them for tour information and schedules at Westport, Brier Island, NS B0V 1H0, ☎ 800/656-3666 or 902/839-2995, fax 902/839-2075, e-mail brierisl@TartanNET.ns. ca, Web site www.TartanNET.ns.ca/brierisl.html.

■ **Westport Whale Watch** is also part of the BIOS project. Their cruise emphasizes research and education and sails aboard the 45-foot *Captain Grumpy* with seats on the open viewing deck. On-board is Carl Haycock, who was a founder of BIOS and is an award-winning naturalist.

➲ **BIOS INFORMATION:** *If you are interested in more information on **BIOS**, contact them at **Brier Island Ocean Study**, PO Box 1262, Westport, NS B0V 1H0, ☎ 902/839-2960, 800/952-0225, 902/839-2467, Web site www.magi.com/~kk/BIOS, e-mail bioscarl@clan.Tartannet. ns.ca.*

Fishing

In the Avon River North of Windsor, off Hantsport, you can fish for rainbow smelt; off Wolfville you can also find rainbow smelt, as well as striped bass. In the Minas Channel, between Canady Creek and Chipman Brook, anglers will usually find ample ground fish. From the town of Digby, a protected harbor runs northeasterly into the estuary of the Annapolis River with the freshwater and saltwater transition occurring east of Annapolis Royal. In this section there is fishing for rainbow smelt and for striped bass. West of Annapolis Royal, off Smith's Cove and Deep Brook, are striped bass, while the whole of the basin is home to schools of mackerel. In the Bay of St. Mary, off New Edinburgh, are rainbow smelt and striped bass, with mackerel also showing up in the bay. Ground fish can be found along the south sides of Long and Brier Islands on St. Mary's Bay, off Cape St. Mary's and off Chegoggin, north of Yarmouth.

Kejimkujik National Park, Rte. 8, Maitland Bridge, NS is in a wilderness area with access via water to back country streams and lakes. A fishing license good for a week is $10, for a year $20, and is good for use in all national parks, but are **not** valid in provincial parks. Native fish and trout from the nearby McGowan Lake Fish Hatchery insure that the fishing is good. Canoes and boats are available for rent at Jake's Landing, inside the park, for $3 an hour or $13 a day.

Fishing Outfitters & Equipment Rentals

■ **North Mountain Outfitters** is an outfitter, as they say, for the serious sportsperson. Both Roger and Anna Ehrenfeld have been licensed guides since the 1970s and were founders of the Professional Hunting and Fishing Outfitters Association. They have a strong belief in the need to give clients value for their money. Lodging is in their clean, modern cottages and meals are home-cooked. From April 1 to the end of October they fish for striped bass in the Annapolis River; from June 10 through July 30 they fish the LaHave River for Atlantic salmon. From May 1 through June there is great fishing for rainbow and brook trout, and from mid-May to the end of June they will show you where the shad are on the Annapolis River. PO Box 187, Middleton, NS B0S 1P0, ☎ 902/825-4030.

■ Another outfitter is **River View Lodge Outfitters**, which guides anglers on the Medway River for salmon that weigh in at four to 24 pounds, the record for the river. Only fly-fishing is offered, with most of the fishing from boats, except for some wading as the waters recede. They have a main lodge with private rooms and a secluded wilderness camp. Greenfield, NS B0T 1E0, ☎ 902/685-2378 or 902/6685-2376 and 902/685-2433.

■ **Cape St. Mary's Charters and Tour Fishing** will do deep-sea fishing expeditions offshore. They have all of the necessary equipment and can even arrange to have your catch cooked for you. Call for rates and sailing times, which depend on the tides. Cape St. Mary's, ☎ 902/645-2519 or 902/649-2317.

On Snow

Some of the best of winter activities in this section are at Kejimkujik National Park, along Rte. 8 between Maitland Bridge and Caledonia. The hundreds of square miles of wilderness make it a perfect place for cross-country skiing, snowshoeing and skating on the lake. They also have winter camping available at no charge, with water and heated washrooms at the Visitors Center. The sites come with firewood. In Kings County, Eagle Outfitters conducts reasonably priced American bald eagle-watching tours from January to mid-March, when hundreds of eagles come to the area.

Skiing

Outside of Windsor, **Ski Martock** has a vertical rise of about 600 feet, with the longest run about a mile. Lifts are T-bars, rope tows and one quad chair. Night skiing is available. The main slopes are covered by snowmaking. The trails are from beginner to high intermediate and all trails are lighted for night skiing. They are open 9 am to 10 pm from December until (usually) April. RR #3, Windsor, NS B0N 2T0, ☎ 902-798-9501.

Cross-country skiing is best at **Kejimkujik National Park**, Rte. 8, Maitland Bridge, between Annapolis Royal and Liverpool. Kejimkujik has 30 miles of groomed trails, and over 40 miles of ungroomed trails. The **Big Dam Trail** on the north end of the entry road is groomed and follows the trails known in the summer as the Hemlocks and Hardwood Trail (a loop trail) and the Channel Lake Trail, a return distance of about five miles with some moderate hills. There are also groomed trails near the Merrymakedge Beach area with two warming huts at the beach. **Peskowesk Road**, the gravel road past the Grafton Lake outlet, and trails to **McGinty Lake** become groomed trails in winter. The first five miles of Peskowesk Road are groomed in winter but for experts, Peskowesk Road continues on for an additional 12 miles to Mason's cabin at Pebbleloggitch Lake. The cabin can be rented during the winter by prior arrangement. Shorter trails are off the groomed section of Peskowesk Road. There is ski equipment for rent near the park entrance and the park offers cross-country ski instruction and clinics.

At Wolfville, the **Old Orchard Inn Ski Touring Centre**, on Rte. 101, has 12 miles of trails consisting of five marked and groomed trails. They also have equipment rentals, lessons and of-

> **CAUTION FOR SNOWSHOERS:** *If you strike out cross-country, be sure to carry maps and a compass, tell the visitors center where you are going and when you plan to be back, and always use the buddy system.*

fer guided ski touring trips, including an overnight ski package. Ski, boot and pole rentals are $10 for half-day, $18 full day. Contact them c/o Old Orchard Inn, Box 1090, Wolfville, NS B0P 1X0, ☎ 800/561-8090 or 902/542-5751, fax 902/542-2276, Web site www. atcon.com/oldorchard.

Closer to Annapolis Royal, **Upper Clements Wildlife Park** uses their six miles of multi-purpose trails for cross-country skiing during the winter. They have beginner, intermediate and expert sections. Rte. 1, Upper Clements, ☎ 902/532-5924.

Ellenwood Provincial Park, Ellenwood Lake, NS, ☎ 902/761-2400. During the summer this provincial park, northeast of Yarmouth off Rte. 340, has a number of hiking trails. In winter these are put to use as cross-country and snowshoe trails.

Snowshoeing

Kejimkujik National Park is an excellent place for snowshoeing, with three designated snowshoe trails. There is a loop around Grafton Lake, a low man-made lake with lots of wildlife, that is about a mile long. Another, Farmlands Trail, is just over a half-mile and the third, Slapfoot Trail, is 2½ miles. In addition to the trails, those with experience and proper gear can snowshoe the backcountry.

Skating

Kejimkujik also offers skating. The Coves at **Jim Charles Point** and at **Merrymakedge Beach** are other good places to skate. Stay away from the areas where the streams enter the lake and from places where there is running water under the ice. Currents under the deeper sections of the lake may also cause the ice to be thin so stay toward the shore. There are warming huts at Merrymakedge Beach.

Snowmobiling

Complete information on trails is available from the **Snowmobile Association of Nova Scotia**, Box 3010 South, Halifax, NS B3J 3G6, ☎ 902/425-5450, ext 324. For local clubs and activities in this area, contact Hants Sno-Dusters, c/o Russell Burgess, RR #1,

Windsor, NS B0N 2T0, or the V.L.R.R. Snowmobile Club, c/o Randy Czapalay, Box 222, Wolfville, NS B0P 1X0, ☎ 902/542-3421.

■ On Horseback

Boulder Wood Stables is between Uniake and Windsor on Rte. 1 in the rolling landscape of apple country. They offer guided trail riding, instruction in English and Western saddle, an indoor arena and pony rides for kids. RR #1, Ellershouse, NS B0N 1L0, ☎ 902/757-1644 (cellular) or 902/499-9138 (evenings and weekends).

In the Annapolis Royal area, **Equus Centre** has a residential training center for children at Granville Centre, ☎ 902/532-2460. **Mandala Riding and Awareness Centre** provides instruction and riding; Arlington Road, Hampton, ☎ 902/665-2101.

Cultural & Eco-Travel Experiences

At **Grand Pré National Historic Site** a memorial park recalls the anguish of the original Acadian settlers who were deported from Nova Scotia in 1755. The memorial is built on the site of an original Acadian town of the 17th and early 18th centuries. A modern stone church set amongst gardens marks the religious devotion of the Acadians, whose plight is represented by a statue of Henry Wadsworth Longfellow's heroine, *Evangeline*. The chapel is open daily, mid-May to mid-October, from 9 am to 3 pm. Grand Pré, NS, ☎ 902/542-3631.

La Vieille Maison, Meteghan, NS, ☎ 902/645-2389. For followers of the Acadian saga, this museum continues the story of those who later returned, by documenting the Robichaud family, who lived in the house during the 19th century. Period furnishings, original documents and costumed interpreters bring their story to life daily, June through August from 9 am to 7 pm.

In the town of St. Bernard is a church that shows the devotion of two generations of Acadian catholics to their religion. **St. Bernard Church** was built between 1910 and 1942 of stone that was imported in its rough state to a local pier, then hauled by ox cart to the site to be hand-dressed by parishioners, who built one course per year. The church is open every day for visitors.

At Church Point, **St. Mary's Church** (☎ 902/769-2832) is said to be the largest and tallest wooden church in North America. The steeple, 185 feet tall, has 40 tons of ballast in the base to save it from the winds off the bay. During the summer there are bilingual tours of the church. Close by is the Université Ste Anne, where the church museum has a collection of vestments, furnishing and photos relating to the church and its parishioners.

Port Royal Habitation National Historic Site, Port Royal, ☎ 902/5232-2898. When Samuel de Champlain decided to settle the new world for France, in 1605 he and Sieur de Monts designed and built a stockaded set of buildings, centered around a courtyard, as a trading post. This was the first settlement of Europeans between Florida and Newfoundland. Burned by the British in 1613, it was rediscovered in the late 1930s and rebuilt. It has reconstructions of the chapel, governor's quarters, storage rooms, common rooms and bunkrooms of the traders who lived here, all based upon writings contemporary to the structure and archaeological excavations of the site. It's a unique chance to step back to the very beginning of our culture. The habitation is open mid-May to mid-October from 9 am to 6 pm. From Rte. 1 at Annapolis Royal go north to Granville Ferry, then turn left to Port Royal.

Port Royal Farm and Country Museum, Port Royal, NS, ☎ 902/532-5019. Rather than focusing on the great people, this one looks at the ones who made it work, the farmers. Collections depict country people and farming from the early days of settlement to the postwar era. It's close to the Habitation and open mid-May to mid-October, 9 am to 5 pm.

Acadian House and Potager, Annapolis Royal Gardens

Annapolis Royal Historic Gardens is one of the finest show gardens in North America, 10 acres of beautifully planned and expertly executed historical and horticultural beds. The Rose Garden has 2,000 bushes set among paths with green lawns, and the Governor's Garden is planted in the style and with the plants of the 1740s. The Victorian Garden celebrates the gardens that were popular during the town's commercial heyday, with plants that were new and exciting discoveries at that time. In a separate section are demonstration plots for current techniques and plants, and here you may well find dinner growing with the posies. There is even a winter garden where the plants are chosen for bark, stem shape or form that makes them attractive in the winter. On the back side of the garden the path looks out over the banks of the river and Acadian dikes built two centuries ago to allow use of the marshlands as food production fields. The gardens are a popular place for weddings, so you may have to sidestep around a happy couple and beaming parents. There is a modest admission fee. Open daily from May through October, 9 am to dusk. 441 St. George Street, Annapolis Royal, NS, ☎ 902/532-7018.

In Bear River near Digby, see the **Bear River Historical Society Museum**, a museum on the wharf featuring the history of the Micmac and the settlers. Open during the summer, Tuesday through Saturday, 10 am to 6 pm. River Road, ☎ 902/467-4172 or 902/467-3669.

At the Université Ste Anne, **Theatre Marc Lescarbot**, Church Point, NS, ☎ 902/769-2114, presents a musical adaptation of *Evangeline* in July and August on Tuesdays and Saturdays at 8 pm. Although the performance is in Acadian French, an English translation is available.

Mermaid Theatre of Nova Scotia has been providing top-notch theater for children for more than a quarter-century. Their works retell classic and contemporary children's tales using live actors and puppets. In their headquarters, open to visitors, is a collection of the puppets. It's open all year Mondays through Fridays 9 am to 4:30 pm. 132 Gerrish Street, Wolfville, NS B0P 1X0, ☎ 902/542-2202, ext 1373.

Atlantic Theatre Festival has become one of the major theater venues in eastern Canada. During the summer they mount three major productions, which may include contemporary playwrights, classic works or Shakespeare. The work of this company has been so acclaimed by critics that early reservations are advisable. Performances are held Tuesdays through Sundays from mid-June to early September. Tickets cost between $20 and $35 depending on the performance and seats. 356 Main Street, PO Box 1441, Wolfville, NS B0P 1X0, ☎ 800/337-6661 or 902/542-4242.

Wildlife-Watching & Geological Sights

The best whale-sighting waters on the east coast of North America are in the **Bay of Fundy**, between the Evangeline coast and New Brunswick. This is another fascinating result of the Fundy tides, which are rich in all levels of marine life, a candy shop for whales, each species of which follows its favorite bonbon into the bay in turn.

The first whales to arrive in spring are the finback and Minke whales and their close friends the porpoises. In June they are joined by the humpbacks and whitesided dolphins and after the beginning of July you might see a right whale. Pilot, beluga, sei and sperm whales have also been sighted from time to time. If you go on a whale watch here (and you should), you will probably see dolphins and porpoises cavorting in the sea alongside the boat.

Many of these trips originate on **Brier Island**, the second island at the end of Digby Neck. Along with whale-watching, the island is a center for birders, who come to see the migratory birds that stop here in the spring and fall. For a list of whale and bird-watching boats, see *Whale-Watch Tours & Boat Tours* on page 258.

The coast of **Brier Island** is marked by outcrops of large hexagonal columns of basalt crystals found in the rock formations. Looking like the ruins of some gothic structure, they are reminiscent of the Giant's Causeway in Ireland, or Fingel's Cave on the Isle of Staffa in Scotland. The best examples of these are at **Green Head**, where you can walk and climb on the rocky ledges around these columns. They are a short walk from the end of the shore road along the harborfront of Westport, to the left as you leave the ferry.

Getting to Brier Island is half the fun, as you skip from island to island on little shuttling ferries. You can't reserve space on any of them, and may have to wait for an hour, but rarely more, even in the busiest part of summer.

Much of Long Island is made up of columnar basalt rock formations which can be seen along the coast, where the sea has eroded and exposed them. On the south side of Rte. 217 you will see signs for **Balancing Rock**, a huge piece of columnar basalt at least 30 feet long, that has broken away from the cliff and is balanced vertically over the sea on the edge of another cliff. Records indicate that it has been on the precarious perch for over 200 years. A trail leads through fields to the rock.

Columnar rocks at Brier Island.

Winter travelers have the best view of the more than 400 **bald eagles** that come to Kings County between January and March. The best place for viewing is in Sheffield, between Canning and Centreville, north of Kentville. **Eagle Watching Tours** has winter eagle-watching tours. The minimum fee is $40 for up to two people and $15 per additional person. The eagles come to the area each winter because of a feeding station that began in the 1960s. Contact Eagle Watching Tours at RR #5, Canning, NS B0P 1H0, ☎ 902/582-7686, fax 902/582-7138, e-mail eagles@fox.nstn.ca, Web site www.valleyweb.com.eagletours.

Almost as unusual as the sight of so many eagles is the nightly spectacular staged by the resident flock of chimney swifts at Wolfville's **Robie Tufts Nature Centre** on Front Street, near the liquor store. A large factory chimney was about to be torn down when residents noticed that it housed a flock of chimney swifts. They kept the chimney and built a small nature center around it. Go about dusk to see their aerial display as the swoop in circles and return to their roost.

Belleisle Marsh. The marsh is a joint project of the province and Ducks Unlimited. It's off Rte. 1 north of Annapolis Royal and serves as a demonstration station for wildlife management and agricultural uses. There are walking trails through the marshes, which are breeding and resting grounds for many species of birds.

Shore Outdoor Adventure Nature Tours leads nature tours in the lower Evangeline Trail area. Contact them c/o Richard Hatch, West Chezzetcook, NS B0J 1N0, ☎ 902/827-3581.

Upper Clements Wildlife Park is about a mile beyond Upper Clements Park; a tunnel leads from it to the wildlife park. The animals are in enclosures along a trail through the woods, approximating their natural habitat. You'll see moose, Sable Island ponies, red deer and bald eagles, among others. The park is open from mid-May to mid-October, 9 am to 7 pm daily. Rte. 1, Upper Clements, ☎ 902/532-5924.

Oak Lawn Farm Zoo on RR #1 in Aylesford (☎ 902/847-9790) is a farm that grew into a zoo. It now has over a hundred species. Among the zoo's primary purposes is the breeding of animals on the Species Survival Plan list and on the CITES list. They have raised all of the primates, lions, tigers, leopards, cougars and jaguars here, as well as black and ruffed lemurs, tree kangaroos and north Chinese leopards. In addition to exotic species, they have examples of indigenous wildlife that were brought here for rehabilitation. Many of these are released back into the wild.

Of Tides & Water

Windsor is one of the best places to see the **tidal bore**, a wall of water that is forced up the estuary by the incoming tides. The Avon River is a bay-like body of water that extends up to the Minas Basin of Fundy, and where the Meander River flows into it is a good place to see the phenomenon. Check with the Visitor Centre at 21 Colonial Rd, ☎ 902/789-2690, for tide times and other locations.

Annapolis Tidal Power Project, 236 Prince Albert Road, Annapolis Royal, ☎ 902/532-5454. During the administration of Franklin Roosevelt it was proposed that the tremendous tides of the Bay of Fundy be harnessed for the production of electricity. While the project was never completed, there are periodic renewals of interest, and the Annapolis project has actually accomplished what was proposed earlier. At the plant there are interpretive displays that explain its operation and a tour allows you to see it first hand. Admission is free. Open daily from mid-May to mid-June, 9 am to 5:30 pm; mid-June through August, 9 am 8 pm; and September to mid-October, 9 am to 5:30 pm.

Off Rte. 8 near Kejimkujik National Park in Caledonia is **McGowan Lake Fish Hatchery**, ☎ 902-682-2576, where a half-million fry trout are hatched each year to be raised for release in the streams and ponds of the area. Most are speckled trout, a native species, and the fish here are bred from a combination of native fish and hatchery-reared brood stock. Fish bred here stay for a year and a half in the raceways until they are about nine inches long. Every aspect of their living conditions is carefully controlled. Look for the mixing chamber where brook water and deep lake water are mixed to make sure that the raceway temperature is optimal. Take the nature trail into the woods and along the lake before you go through the raceways, intake control house, hatchery and interpretive building and feed buildings.

At Exit 24 on Rte. 101 take the road to Bear River to see the **Bear River Aquatics Wastewater Facility**, which uses plants to remove contaminants and nutrients from the water. You can visit the greenhouse and see the process, look at the plants and watch the snails and other creatures. This could be the future. They are open daily all year, 1 to 5 pm, and offer tours from June through September. For more information, ☎ 902/467-3774, e-mail dryan.munofann@clan.TartanNET.ns.ca, Web site http://clan.tartanNET.ns.ca/munofann.

Sightseeing

The town of Windsor played a big role in the early days of Canadian hockey, so it's fitting that the **Windsor Hockey Heritage Centre** is located here. Along with original wooden pucks and hockey sticks hand-carved in one piece by the Micmac Indians, they also have photos, old equipment and other memorabilia associated with the early teams and players. The centre is at 128 Gerrish Street in Wolfville, ☎ 902/798-1800 or 902/542-2202, ext 1373.

Fort Edward National Historic Site in Windsor, ☎ 902/542-3631, is the oldest surviving blockhouse in Canada, a part of the fort built in 1750 when the British gained ascendancy in Nova Scotia. If you are following the Acadian saga you should stop here; it was one of the major assembly points for the deportation of Acadians in 1755. Open summers only.

Also in Windsor, **Shand House** on Avon Street, ☎ 902/798-8213, was the height of modernity when built in 1891, a trend-setter with electric lights, indoor plumbing and central heat. It's open June to mid-October, Monday through Saturday, 9:30 am to 5:30 pm; Sunday, 1 to 5:30 pm.

Historic items are on display at **Randall House**, 171 Main Street in Wolfville, ☎ 902/542-9775. After the 1755 expulsion of the Acadians Britain encouraged people from the southern colonies to settle here and after the American Revolution, Loyalists flocked here. Their possessions and those of their families are preserved at Randall House, open mid-June to mid-September, Monday through Saturday from 10 am to 5 pm; Sunday 2 to 5pm.

Upper Clements Park is in Clementsport, four miles from Annapolis Royal on Rte. 1. This is the theme park for the province, with all of the rollercoasters, convoy trucks and Evangeline Trains that you will want to see for a while. When the kids get tired of canoeing and bird-watching, bring them here for a break. The park is open daily from June to September, 11 am to 7 pm. For information, ☎ 888/248-4567 or 902/532-7557, fax 902/532-7681, Web site www.UpperClementsPark.com.

Fort Anne National Historic Site on St. George Street in Annapolis Royal, ☎ 902/532-2397, marks the spot where a fort has stood since the French built one in 1643. When the British took over in the 1750s they made this spot on the Annapolis River their stronghold. While the only remaining buildings are a 1700s gunpowder magazine and officers barracks, the impressive walls and ramparts are substantially intact. The siting of the fort, in the middle of town right on the river, makes this a nice place for a stroll. There is a small charge for admission to the barracks building where there are displays and exhibits, including a large 18-foot-long tapestry that tells the history of the area. The grounds are open all year, and the barracks is open mid-May to mid-October, 9 am to 6 pm.

The Historic Restoration Society of Annapolis County has been active in saving historic structures in town. Two of these are former Inns. The **Sinclair Inn** at 220 George Street, built in 1710, is one of the oldest buildings in Canada and has exhibits on construction techniques from the 18th to the 20th centuries. Open July and August; hours are variable. ☎ 902/532-7754.

The **O'Dell Inn Museum** is a restored Victorian stagecoach inn built in 1869. It has a large amount of exhibit space: 17 rooms, including a Victorian kitchen, a mourning room with fascinating Victorian memorials such as hair wreaths, and a section on shipbuilding with tools, ship models and half-models and other Maritime shipping memorabilia. It also has exhibits concentrating on the joys of childhood, showing the changes in games, toys and pastimes of children. 136 Lower St. George Street, Annapolis, ☎ 902/532-2041.

Sainte Famille Wines Ltd. in Falmouth is a Nova Scotia vintner that takes its name from the original Acadian name of the town. Tours of their operation are given from May to the end of October at 11 am and 2 pm. They are open Monday through Saturday, 9 am to 5 pm, and on Sundays at noon. Closed on Sundays from January through March. ☎ 800/565-0993 or 902/798-8311.

The area from Windsor through Wolfville and Kentville has long been a center for apple growing. In late May each year the apple trees bloom and Kentville has its **Annual Apple Blossom Festival** that includes orchard tours amid the wonderful scent of hundreds of acres of apple blossoms. They also have a big parade and other activities, but the blossoms are the experience. In fall, of course, this is an area for picking apples and drinking sweet cider. Call the Wolfville Visitor Center at ☎ 902/542-7000 for exact dates.

Where To Stay & Eat

Wolfville to Annapolis Royal

Blomidon Inn, a large inn in an elegant 1877 shipping magnate's home, sits on a sloping green lawn east of the center of town. The 26 rooms and five suites are nicely furnished and attractively decorated. The public rooms are elegant, with heavily molded and carved details in exotic woods. An afternoon tea and continental breakfast are included in the rates. *127 Main St., PO Box 839, Wolfville, NS B0P 1X0, ☎ 902/542-2291, fax 902/542-7461 ($$-$$$).*

Gingerbread House Inn is small and elegant, with two rooms and three suites. You would swear that this gingerbread-covered confection was built a century ago, but it wasn't; it is, in fact, quite new. Inside it's filled with the finest of contemporary furnishings and each room and suite has a private entrance. In a quiet residential section, it is a lush place to set down temporary roots. *Robie Tufts Drive, Box 819, Wolfville, NS B0P 1X0, ☎ 902/542-1458 ($$).*

Victoria's Historic Inn was built by an apple king in 1893, and all of the many exquisite details of this large Victorian mansion are lovingly preserved. Silk wall coverings and outstanding architectural detail meld with fine furnishings and decorative detail to make this a memorable place to stay. All rooms have private baths and many have whirlpool baths. There are six rooms and a two-bedroom suite in the main building and an additional six rooms in the renovated coachmen's quarters, including the ultra-quiet and private Hunt room. While breakfast isn't included, they do serve a nice full breakfast for under $4. The menu in the elegant dining room ($$-$$$) reflects the French ancestry of the original settlers of the region. Open daily during the summer and Tuesday through Sunday the rest of the year. *416 Main St., PO Box 308, Wolfville, NS B0P 1X0, ☎ 902/542-5744, 800/556-5744, fax 902/542-7794 ($$-$$$).*

Old Orchard Inn is a full-service, family-run inn with nice accommodations. Recreational activities include tennis, indoor golf, an indoor pool, and saunas. In the winter there are 12 miles of cross-country trails. Ski rentals are free for guests during the week and half-price on weekends. They also have a fine restaurant. *Box 1090, Wolfville, NS B0P 1X0, ☎ 800/561-8090 or 902/542-5751, fax 902/542-2276, Web site www.atcon.com/oldorchard ($$).*

Planters' Barracks Country Inn is a beautiful 1778 Georgian-style building that started life in the British army as Fort Hughes. A nearby building, also part of the inn and housing three of its rooms, served as the customs house. The public rooms retain the wide board floors and charm of the colonial period. All the rooms are large and have private baths, robes, hair dryers and comfortable wing chairs. Furnishings are largely antique. Open all year except from mid-December to mid-January. They will serve dinner for guests on 24-hour notice. The Acacia Croft Tearoom in the old customs house adjacent to the inn is open to the public. You can get a traditional ploughman's lunch here, sandwiches or tea with scones. To get here, take Rte. 358 toward Port Williams, west of Wolfville. *1468 Starr's Point Rd., R.R. 1, Port Williams, NS B0P 1T0, ☎ 902/542-7879, fax 902/542-4442, reservations 800/661-7879 ($$-$$$).*

Queen Anne Inn and **Hillsdale House**, within sight of each other, are two large, striking homes at the opposite extremes of Victorian style. Queen Anne is an example of Second Empire elegance, while Hillsdale is simpler, just showing the beginning of the New World's acknowledgment of its wealth. Both are fine lodgings, rooms furnished with the finest antiques, all carefully matched to the period of the house. While they are of museum quality, they retain a comfortable ease that makes them a joy to stay in. An excellent full breakfast is included in the rates. These

The Queen Anne Inn, Annapolis Royal.

inns are a treat and are within walking distance of downtown and the attractions. *4 Upper St. George St., PO Box 218, Annapolis Royal, NS B0S 1A0, ☎ 902/532-7850 ($$).*

Bread and Roses Country Inn is a late 19th-century Queen Anne-style brick mansion with tile fireplaces, woodwork and a grand central staircase providing access to the guest rooms. The guest and common rooms are furnished with period antiques, but the artwork is Inuit Indian and contemporary Canadian, a fresh combination. Stained glass in the inn is by the owner. They serve a full breakfast in the morning and tea and pastry in the evening, all included in the rates. *82 Victoria St. (off St. George St.), PO Box 177, Annapolis Royal, NS, B0S 1A0, ☎ 902/532-5727 ($$).*

Garrison House Inn has been behind its picket fence across from the Fort since 1854. The five rooms and one two-bedroom family suite are furnished in comfortable country style. They are open from June through October, but check for weekend openings the rest of the year. The dining room has a nice selection of entrées, including an Acadian jambalaya. They are open for all three meals, but breakfast is not included in the rates. *350 St. George St., PO Box 108, Annapolis Royal, NS B0S 1A0, ☎ 902/532-5750, fax 902/532-5501 ($$).*

Chez La Vigne is without a doubt the finest place to eat in town, and one of the best in the province. The menu is French and it is prepared and served to perfection. You'll seldom find a seafood dish as inviting as their ragu of seafood with scallops, shrimp, mussels and fish. They make everything here including their sorbets. It's very popular so reservations are suggested. They are open Tuesday through Sunday, all year, from 11 am to midnight during the summer and until 9 pm in winter. It's in the downtown section off Main Street. *17 Front St., Wolfville,* ☎ *902/542-5077 ($$).*

The Coffee Merchant is a handy place for breakfast or lunch, and it's well located right on the main street. They have muffins and bagels and sandwiches. On weekdays they are open 7 am to 11 pm and on weekends from 8 am. *334 Main Street, Wolfville,* ☎ *902/542-4315 ($).*

The Kitchen Door, a takeout place with a good reputation, is a popular place to get picnic lunches. They have tables outside, but you might want to stop here if you're going off hiking, canoeing or to the theater. *Front Street, Wolfville, no phone ($).*

Paddy's Pub Brewery is a pub in the traditional sense and they do their own brewing. The menu includes old-fashioned Irish stew, Tex-Mex specialties, pasta, steaks and fish. Brewery tours are given during the summer at 2 and 4 pm. They pour their own red-hued ale, a gold ale, a porter and a special seasonal ale. *42 Aberdeen Street, Kentville,* ☎ *902/678-3199.*

Leo's is a good, inexpensive and informal place for breakfast, lunch or a light dinner. Their signature dish is linguine with scallops, tomato and green onions in a saffron sauce; they also serve traditional fishcakes. The building, by the way, was built in 1712, making it the oldest in English-speaking Canada. There is a café on the first floor and the dining room and deck are on the second floor. *222 St. George St., Annapolis Royal,* ☎ *902/532-7424 ($).*

Newman's specializes in seafood, but the menu travels in many other directions. You might find braised black bear or locally raised mutton chops. They like to use local meats, seafoods and produce and the menu changes daily to take advantage of the changing harvests. They are open May through October for lunch and dinner. *218 St. George St., Annapolis Royal,* ☎ *902/532-5502 ($$).*

Near Digby & Brier Island

Bayshore B&B is a small but comfortable B&B with very reasonable rates that include a full breakfast. The two-room family suite overlooks the water and has a private bath; the other two rooms share a bath. It's open July and August by reservation or walk-in, but the rest of the year by reservation only. *Hwy. 1, PO Box 176, Saulnierville, NS B0W 2Z0, ☎ 902/769-3671 ($).*

Admiral Digby Inn is a modern motel-style facility three miles from Digby and a half-mile from the Marine Atlantic ferry dock. They have an indoor heated swimming pool and a dining room that's one of the better places in town to eat. *PO Box 608, Shore Road, Digby, NS, B0V 1A0, ☎ 902/245-2531 ($$).*

Brier Island Lodge and Restaurant could very well be the best place to eat on the island, with a menu of fresh seafood. The big dining room windows look out over the town of Westport and across Grand Passage to Freeport on Long Island. Turn right off the ferry and go up the hill to the lodge. The view is back across the rip tide to Long Island, and a short walk down the road will take you to Northern Point Light and Seal Cove. The rooms are modern, motel-style rooms with all the amenities. Rooms without an ocean view are $60 to $70; ocean-view rooms with queen beds and whirlpools are just over $100. *Westport, NS B0V 1H0, ☎ 800/662-8355 or 902/839-2300, fax 902/839-2006 ($$).*

Captain's Cabin has a home-style menu, featuring things that you won't have trouble getting the kids to eat. Pork, chicken, scallops (the town is famed for them), and fried clams as well as a good listing of sandwiches are all available. *2 Birch Street, Digby, ☎ 902/245-5133 ($).*

The Westport Inn is a small, family-run restaurant serving home-cooked food. You can get a quick lunch here from a range of sandwiches and soups. Go right from the ferry, then one street behind the main street. Park in the back. *Westport, ☎ 902/839-2675, fax 902/839-2245 ($).*

Cape View Restaurant is family-run, with fast food take-out as well. In addition to the usual burgers, fried clams and fried chicken they have Acadian dishes, including fishcakes. Open for breakfast, lunch and dinner from May through October, 7 am to 9:30 pm daily. They are on the road that leads to nearby Mavilette beach. *Mavilette, NS, ☎ 902/645-2250 ($).*

Red Raven Pub does serve poutine (French fries with brown gravy and cheese), an Acadian specialty. Thanks, just the same. They also have steaks, burgers, seafood, fried clams and a weekend brunch from 10 am to 2 pm. *100 Water St., Digby, ☎ 902/245-5533 ($).*

The Tiny Tattler is part of the B&B of the same name. They serve full dinners, including haddock and Digby scallops. *Central Grove, Long Island, ☎ 902/839-2528 ($-$$).*

Try the **Tiverton Seaside Lunch** at the ferry wharf, which offers take-out fast food, mainly seafood. *Tiverton, ☎ 902/839-2343 ($-$$).*

Near Kejimkujic National Park

The **Whitman Inn** is a large country farmhouse built in 1900. If camping is not your way but you want to enjoy all that Kejimkujik National Park has to offer, this 10-room inn is the place to be. All of the inn's rooms have private baths and are furnished with country antiques. The warm and welcoming hosts can suggest hiking trails, canoe routes or other activities. Set among nice lawns, the inn has an indoor pool, Jacuzzi and sauna. They arrange bike, canoe and kayak rentals during the summer and in winter can also set up ski, snowshoe or skate rentals. During each season they have special programs in photography, canoeing and nature painting. Their dining room is open Tuesdays through Saturday and they will take outside guests, but it is all by reservation. The ever changing menu takes advantage of the seasons but may include items such as haddock with chanterelles. This inn is a real find, especially for adventure travelers who want to come home to a bit of luxury. *RR #2, Caledonia, NS B0T 1B0, ☎ 902/682-2226, fax 902/682-3171 ($$).*

Milford House is right along Rte. 8 in South Milford. In the 19th century, when city people decided that they had to get back in touch with nature, they built rustic hotels like this one. The 27 cabins are scattered along the shore of a pristine lake where the presence of man is hardly noticed. All have a bath or shower and from one to five bedrooms. While comfortable, the rooms suffer from deferred maintenance and soft mattresses. At $139 to $151 a day we think they're a bit over-priced for their condition. The Milford's attraction, however, is as one of the very few remaining real old-time sporting hotels anywhere. That, and the proximity to nature, is what you are paying for. Put your canoe right into the water (rental canoes are available to guests) and paddle off into the myriad passages of the Mersey water system, or go up the road a short way to the national park. The dining room is the big old summer camp sort, where good, solid, family-style meals are served to guests daily. Open from mid-June to mid-September. During winter they have two heated cabins available for rent. *PO Box 521, Annapolis Royal, NS B0S 1A0, ☎ 902/532-2617 or 902/532-7360 off-season ($$$, including breakfast and dinner).*

■ Camping

Blomidon Provincial Park on Cape Blomidon close to Cape Split, has 70 RV and tenting sites with showers. Sites are both open and wooded. Facilities include a playground, beach access, a picnic facility and a nice set of hiking trails. It is also very close to the splendid trails at Cape Split. Many of the facilities are handicapped accessible. It is open mid-May through mid-October. *Blomidon, NS, ☎ 902/582-7319.*

Valleyview Provincial Park has 30 open and wooded sites on North Mountain. It has pit toilets and no showers but there is a dumping station. There is also a picnic facility. From Rte. 1 at Bridgeton take the road toward Hampton. *North Mountain, NS, ☎ 902/665-2559.*

On Long Island look for the **Moby Dick Campground** *(☎ 902/839-2290)*, which has 17 RV and tenting sites, or for **Fundy Sea Trail Camping Ground** *(☎ 902/839-2772)* with RV and tenting sites, a pool and a walking trail to the water. Both have signs on Rte. 217.

Kejimkujik National Park is a large park with so many campsites you can get lost looking for home. RV and tenting sites, most in the woods, spread out over a large area and sites are well spaced. The magic of this park is its location in the middle of the central wilderness of the island. In addition to campground sites, there are numerous wilderness sites scattered on the shores or on islands in the middle of the lakes. Activities at the park include fishing, swimming, hiking, and canoeing. The park requires an admission fee of $2.50 a day, six days for $6.75 per person, family rate $6 and $18 respectively. Camping rates are an additional $10.50 a day from mid-May to mid-October, $9 from May 1 to mid-

May and mid-October to mid-November. Back-country camping is $7.25 per day year-round, but winter camping in two designated areas of the main park is free and includes warm washrooms and showers at the Visitor Center. *PO Box 236, Maitland Bridge, NS B0T 1B0, 902/682-2772, fax 902/682-3367, e-mail nancy_spencer @pch.gc.ca, Web site http://parkscanada.pch.gc.ca.*

Ellenwood Provincial Park is an 86-site campground for RVs and tents. There is a full range of services, including showers, dumping station and picnicking. Recreational facilities include a playground, hiking trails and access to a freshwater beach. The campground is open mid-June to mid-October and most of the sites and facilities are handicapped accessible. *Ellenwood Lake, NS, ☎ 902/761-2400.*

The Southern Shore

The best known and most-visited part of the province, this southern shore is the Nova Scotia you are most likely to see in travel brochures, with its rock-bound harbor communities and lighthouses. So many of the latter line the shore that the tourist route along the south coast is called The Lighthouse Route. It may be the quintessential Nova Scotia, but to think of this area as just another row of postcard towns with tour buses would be selling it far short. There are a lot of reasons why all those other travelers choose the south coast.

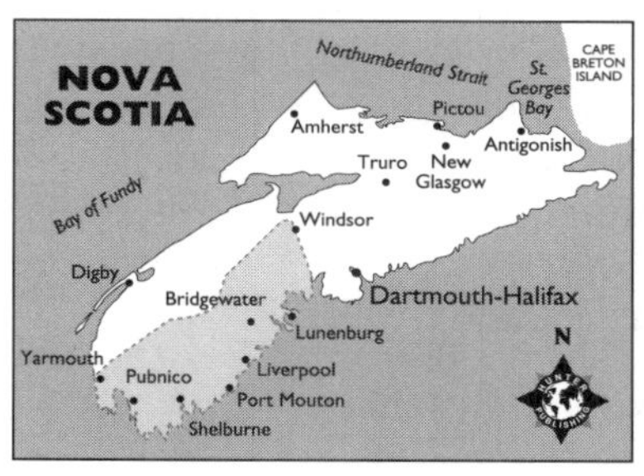

Geography & History

West of Halifax is a long, wide land, nearly half the mainland of the province, roughly shaped like the tail of a beaver. On the north, along the Evangeline Trail, it is washed by the Fundy tides, on the south by the Atlantic Ocean. The old seaport (and now ferry port) town of Yarmouth is at the far end, about 180 miles from Halifax.

This rocky southern coast is irregular and studded with islands, many of them drumlins formed of glacial debris. Much of the coast lies in low ridges, and between these are drowned river valleys. The coast is sinking (you don't have to hurry; it's been happening for a very long time) as a result of continental movement, which has flooded the beds of old rivers, creating the long bays and estuaries found along the shore. Two examples of this are Shelburne Harbour and the LaHave River, leading to Bridgewater. The underlying granite bedrock shows through in many places, particularly along the shore where the thin soils give way to rocky outcrops. Along the shore, small white sand beaches are formed from the eroded bedrock.

The human history of the area came late in the colonial period. It wasn't until the 1750s that significant settlement of the south coastal region began. The greatest spurt in growth came as a result of the American Revolution. As the tide of war turned against the British, Loyalist backers of the monarchy fled in the face of personal danger and having their property confiscated. Settling on the fine harbors of this coast, these former New England merchants, ship builders and seamen reestablished their former careers, building new towns and establishing new industries.

Shelburne is a fine example of these new towns that grew and prospered. Timber and fish harvested from the surrounding woods and seas were shipped to foreign markets and the money used to buy molasses, fabrics and furniture, which were in turn sold in the port on the return voyage, This trade reestablished many a fortune that had been lost to war.

During the war of 1812 they got back at their Yankee neighbors and many ship owners obtained authority from the crown to become privateers, preying on American shipping. Liverpool was a major privateer port. The lands behind the towns, however, remained wild and unsettled and the initial spurts of growth could not be sustained. Farming and fishing gradually supplanted shipping and shipbuilding. Tourism as an industry on the south shore began in the 1860s in Chester, when a few wealthy Canadian and American families built summer mansions along the shore and on the islands of the harbor. Yachts and small sailboats began to replace schooners and fishing boats and a new industry was born along the whole coast.

Getting Around

The most direct access into this section is from the Halifax area following Rte. 103, a limited access highway much of the way and continually being upgraded. Off the main route to the south are a number of small roads leading to points of land that jut into the sea. To the north is the great inland wilderness where settlements are few. Rte. 8 cuts all the way across to Annapolis Royal and west of Rte. 8 there is only one road that wanders into the central part of the peninsula.

Another way to get to this part of Nova Scotia is by ferry to Yarmouth from two ports in Maine. **Bay Ferries** sails the *Bluenose* on a regular schedule between Bar Harbor, Maine, and Yarmouth. Two offices: 121 Eden Street, Bar Harbor ME 04609, ☎ 888/249-SAIL (7245), ☎ 207/288-3395; and 58 Water Street, Yarmouth, NS B5A 1K9, ☎ 888/249-7245, 902/742-6800.

Prince of Fundy Cruises Limited, International Marine Terminal, 468 Commercial Street, Portland ME 04101, ☎ 800/341-7540 or 207/775-5616 operates between Portland, Maine, and Yarmouth Nova Scotia. The *Scotia Prince* leaves Portland at 9 pm on alternate days and arrives in Yarmouth at 9 am, departing Yarmouth on alternate days at 10 am and arriving in Portland at 8 pm. For fares and more information on both ferries, see the introductory chapter on Nova Scotia.

Information Sources

■ The large, modern **Provincial Visitor Information Center**, 342 Main Street, Yarmouth, is above the ferry docks, clearly visible as you get off the boat.

■ For information specific to the Yarmouth and Lighthouse or Evangeline Routes, check with the **Yarmouth County Tourist Association**, 355 Main Street, PO Box 477, Yarmouth, NS B5A 1G2, ☎ 902/742-5355, fax 902/742-6644.

■ At **Shelburne**, the **Tourist Information Centre** is at the foot of King Street on the waterfront, ☎ 902/875-4547. Open from 9 am to 9 pm mid-May to mid-October.

■ The **Lunenburg Tourist Bureau**, Blockhouse Hill Road, Lunenburg, ☎ 902/634-8100, is in a lighthouse.

They have a full supply of materials on the area, including maps of the town, a walking tour brochure and illustrated Heritage Society books on the houses of Lunenburg. It's open 9 am to 9 pm daily in summer.

■ **Mahone Bay Tourist Office**, PO Box 609, Mahone Bay, NS B0J 2E0, ☎ 902/624-6151, is on the east side of town on Rte. 3.

Adventures

■ On Foot

Yarmouth County Tourist Association, PO Box 477, Yarmouth, ☎ 902/742-5355, fax 902/742-6644, has an excellent walking tour of the city with a commentary on 26 buildings along its route and sketches of many of them. The brochure also has a short history and a description of the architectural styles that are seen along the way. They also have a walking tour of gardens and parks that was prepared by the Garden Club.

On Rte. 334, south of Yarmouth, is the **Wedgeport Nature Trail (Sentier de Nature de Wedgeport)**, Wedgeport, ☎ 800/566-TUNA (8862), starting at the Sport Tuna Fishing Museum. There are almost three miles of trails along the bay with 12 interpretive signs describing the natural and human history of the area. It's also a great place to see seabirds.

On the next peninsula down, take Exit 31 on Rte. 103 to the Pubnicos, one of the oldest Acadian areas in the province. **Pubnico Guided Tours**, Lower West Pubnico, NS B0W 2C0, ☎ 902/762-3029 are bilingual tour operators who conduct hiking and bird-watching tours in this area.

McNutt's Island Coastal Encounters, Dock Street, Shelburne, ☎ 902/875-4269 or 902/875-1180, fax 902/875-2294, has a number of walking and birding choices on guided trips to McNutt's Island, which sits like a stopper poised over the end of Shelburne Bay. Farmed in the past, the island is now returned to wilderness and is laced with roads and paths that provided pleasant walking from the beaches on the north end to the old lighthouse on the south end facing the open ocean. Operated by the lively and knowledgeable Eric and Donna Ensor, the company offers a Nature Walk and Seafood Chowder Lunch, Wednesdays through Fridays, for $35 adult, $25 under age 12. It includes a visit to the largest birch tree in the province, estimated to be 1,500 years old. On a Sunday Explorer trip from 1 to 7 pm, you can do your own exploration of the island and finish the day off with an "all you can eat" grilled salmon dinner on the island for $40 per person.

Port L'Hebert Pocket Wilderness, at Port L'Hebert, is another of those splendid wayside parks built and maintained by lumber companies. Take Exit 23 from Rte. 103 and travel down the east side of the harbor. The road will loop around to the other side of the peninsula, where there is a parking lot. The trail travels on a gravel path through a mixed forest to the shore and on boardwalks over bogs and to a salt marsh. The overall length of this loop trail is about two miles. The influence of the Gulf Stream tends to keep this area free of snow and ice for substantial parts of the winter and makes it good wintering grounds for a large number of water birds, including Canada geese, common eiders, black ducks and mergansers.

Kejimkujik Seaside Adjunct is a large chunk of land that encompasses almost all of the peninsula between Port Joli and Port Mouton. While large, it also is difficult to visit because the national authorities in charge of the park have not yet implemented a development plan for the park. Thus, while there are trails, they are rough and hard to get to. With that said, however, the positive side is that you will find here a a seaside wilderness essentially untouched by man. The peninsula serves as a wintering ground for several species of waterfowl, and there are nesting pairs of piping plover at St. Catherines Beach and Port Joli Beach.

The terrain here varies from muddy soil to bog to rocky outcrop with salt marshes and sand beaches interspersed. At this site you could expect to see common goldeneyes, oldsquaws, red breasted mergansers, common eiders, scaups, loons, black ducks and Canada geese, as well as the more common gulls and shore birds.

Two routes enter the area, and the two existing trails do not connect well. The shorter one, and the easiest to find, is off Port Joli Bay. From Rte. 103 take the Port Joli Road to the end where there is an area, albeit small, to leave a car. The trail starts here as an old two-rut road. It crosses the tip of the peninsula and comes out on the shore on the opposite side. For the other trail leave Rte. 103 at Exit 21, Port Mouton, and go to Southwest Port Mouton. The trail begins there as a gravel road. It's hard to find a place to put the car, as the neighbors obviously don't want visitors and have posted no parking signs as thick as leaves on a summer tree.

Liverpool to Summerville Trail is a part of the rails-to-trails system. This stretch, almost 15 miles long, parallels and crosses Rte. 3 and gives several options for stopping points. Like most rails trails, however, the drawback is that they do not loop and the return is along the same path. The walking is level and goes through a balsam fir and spruce forest with some maple and birch. It passes marshes and wetlands, providing an opportunity for wildlife and bird-watching along the way. You can pick it up at Paulis Road, outside Summerville, or at Hunt's Point, White Point, Five Rivers, McAlpine's Brook or at Liverpool on the west side of the bay.

The **Liverpool Historical Walking Tour**, c/o Queens County Museum, 109 Main Street, Liverpool, ☎ 902/354-4058, explores the history of this English town on a walk that takes about an hour. A brochure from the museum describes the houses and buildings along the way. **Fort Point Park** at the end of Main Street was the landing place of Champlain in 1604 and the site of a privateer fort that protected the town from American raiders during two wars with the United States.

Ovens Natural Park, Ovens Park Road. Take Rte. 332 south from LaHave, then Feltzen South Road and Ovens Park Road. Walking trails run along the top of high cliffs overlooking a beach below. The site of a gold rush in 1861, it's now a wild retreat with hiking and huge sea caverns to explore.

Off the coast of Chester, **Tancook Island**, seven miles out to sea and lying across the entrance to Mahone Bay, has a myriad of old roads and farm lanes. At one time heavily farmed, many of the fields are being reclaimed by nature. There is a regularly scheduled ferry that goes to the island from the wharf at Front Harbour on Water Street. Check the schedule to be sure that you don't miss the last one at night. The ferry does not take cars but a bike is okay. Close to the school on the island is a tourist information booth where you can get a map.

■ On Wheels

Bicycling along the south coast can give you intimate tours of small fishing harbors and tiny towns dating from the mid 1700s. Off of Rte. 103, three smaller roads wind their way down long fingers of land that jut into the sea forming harbors on either side. The main roads pass by the ends of these bays but some of the best riding is on the narrower and less busy roads, some unpaved, that circle the points. At the end of these you'll find attractive headlands, a few lighthouses and beautiful views over the sea to islands offshore. *The Nova Scotia Bicycle*

Book lists the entire 355 miles as a single route (route 12), not one to be done in a weekend. Along the way there are many towns with B&B accommodations.

The two Acadian areas near Yarmouth, settled by returning Acadians in the 1760s, on the Wedgeport and Pubnico peninsulas both make good trips, as does the Rte. 330 route around Cape Sable. At Shelburne a fine road runs along the harbour past Sandy Point to the end of the peninsula and back up the other side along Jordan Bay. The total loop mileage is about 25 miles.

At Bridgewater go down one side of the Bay to Riverport and Rose Bay and out to Kingsburg for a stroll of the beach, then return as far as the ferry on Rte. 332, cross the river and continue back to Bridgewater on Rte. 331, a distance of about 50 miles.

The rails to trails path between Summerville and Liverpool makes a nice, easy, 15-mile one-way trip. The **Summerville to Liverpool Trail** was one of the first of the system to be completed. It passes through an evergreen forest, marshes, swamps and bogs, providing a chance for wildlife and bird viewing.

Gabriel's Bicycle Tours on Main Street in Lunenburg, ☎ 902/543-4267 or 902/541-0909, runs cycling tours in and around Lunenburg on the coastal roads every day from 8:30 am to 3:30 pm during the summer. This is not an endurance test and there are stops at shops that show the work of local artists and craftsmen as well as breaks for snacks and lunch. Their relaxed pace is clear from their motto: "We take time to smell the roses."

The **Lunenburg Bicycle Barn**, RR #1, Garden Lots, Lunenburg, NS B0J 2C0, ☎ 902/634-3426, rents bicycles in the barn next to the Blue Rocks Road B&B. They also do bike repairs. The best possible way to see this beautiful road along the rocky shore is from a bicycle and these people are about as accommodating as you'll find anywhere. The rental rates are $8 half-day and $15 full day, or $90 for a week. They also have tandems and route maps and know the area well, so you can rely on their advice.

If you are in Chester, take your bikes on the ferry to **Tancook Island**, where miles of roads cover this sizeable island that lies across the mouth of Mahone Bay. Much of the farming on the island has been abandoned and the population is very small. The ferry leaves from a wharf at the end of Water Street. Take Duke Street or Valley Road into town from Rte. 3; they intersect at Water Street. Stop at the tourist information booth near the school for a map.

■ On Water

Canoeing & Kayaking

Pubnico Guided Tours, Lower West Pubnico, NS B0W 2C0, ☎ 902/762-3029, does canoe tours. The Pubnico peninsula is an Acadian settlement and one of the oldest in the province.

Rossignol Surf Shop at 216 Main Street in Liverpool has regular instruction and tour schedules from two locations in the area. Contact them at ☎ 902/354-3733, evenings and weekends 902/683-2530, fax 902/354-2560. At Summerville Beach Provincial Park the sessions are on Monday, Wednesday, Friday and Sunday at 10 am and 2 pm and from Port Joli Harbour they operate on Tuesday, Thursday and Saturday at 10 am and 2 pm. The two-hour sessions cost $35 and include basic instruction and a short tour. They can also arrange longer guided tours. Check with them for details.

Crescent Sea Kayak Tours at Crescent Beach, ☎ 902/688-2806, fax 902/688-2828, is on Rte. 331, east of Rte. 103 at Bridgewater. Off of Crescent Beach are several islands that provide protection from the sea and great waters to explore. The trips go to the LaHave Islands. Crescent accepts paddlers of any skill level, including beginners, and provides basic instruction. They have three trips daily, each three hours in duration, which leave at 9 am and 1 and 6:30 pm. Be there at least 15 minutes before departure time. Reservations are suggested. Rates are $30 for a single kayak and $50 for a double. They operate from June to September.

Mahone Bay Kayak Adventures has a number of guided kayaking options, including canoe and kayak rentals. Contact them at 618 Main Street, Box 360, Mahone Bay, NS B0J2E0, ☎ 902/624-6632, cellular 902/527-7101, e-mail seakayak@fox.nstn.ca, Web site http://fox.nstn.ca/~seakayak. The daily four-hour introductory ocean kayak clinics cost $45 and start at 10 am and 1 pm for single kayaks and at noon for doubles. The day-long introductory course is given on Thursdays and Sundays between 9 am and 5 pm and they supply not only the equipment but lunch as well. These usually include a guided trip to a set of islands so you can practice your newly acquired skills. These trips cost $85 per person. Off-season there are day-long guided river kayak tours that require wet suits and paddling jackets. They also require advanced skills such as an ability to do wet exits. Lunch and shuttle are provided and they start at 9 am, $85 per person. Mahone Bay

Kayak also has some great package trips, such as a two-day B&B Kayak and Cruising Tour where you paddle the water by day, meet up with a sailing vessel for transport to a country B&B for the evening and a good meal and then pick up with the kayaking again on the second day. They also have a two-day camping expedition and a midnight Island Paddle.

PROTECTING THE PLOVER... AND YOURSELF: *Be extremely careful in these areas to stay on paths and to avoid disturbing the plover or their nests. They are very rare and on the edge of extinction. A careless step or alarming noise could either destroy a nest or cause the parents to abandon it. On the other hand, wandering into nesting areas of gulls can be dangerous to you. If you see flying gulls looking nervous and starting to swoop low near you, back off. You're probably wandering into an area where their chicks are nested, and they will attack – ferociously.*

Mahone Bay Kayak is also very active in the industry, and the first weekend of July sponsors the Annual Nova Scotia Kayak Festival with special events, free lessons, free use of kayaks, a kayak swap-trade-sell and a guided starlight paddle. Admission is $40 per person or $60 per family. Single kayaks rent for $30 half-day, $45 full day and $30 per day after the first one. Doubles are $40, $65 and $40 for subsequent days. Canoes are $20, $35 and $20 for subsequebt days. All rentals include PFD, paddle, spray skirt, water jug, pump, compass and map.

Sailing

Oakland Centre for Outdoor Education, 189 Hirtle Cove Road in Mahone Bay, ☎ 902/624-8864, is dedicated to the promotion of sailing as a healthy outdoor activity. They have morning, afternoon and evening sailing lessons and they do half and full-day sailing cruises in Mahone Bay. The center also provides lessons for those who want to improve or polish their skills.

Sunnybrook Riding and Sailing, 340 Herman's Island Road in Mahone Bay, ☎ 902/634-3735, has a 37-foot Contessa sailing yacht and allows you to charter it and plan your own itinerary. Rates are $30 per hour, for a minimum of three hours; half-days $110 for five hours; full days $165 for nine hours. The rate is not per person, but for any size group.

Diving

Spectacle Marine Park and Area Underwater Dive Park, Port Mouton Harbour, contact Queens County Marine Park Association, c/o Janet Gatzke, RR#1, Port Mouton, NS B0T 1T0, ☎ 902/683-2188. The Association has identified 16 sites in Port Mouton Harbour that provide good diving opportunities for beginner and intermediate divers and two that are suitable for advanced divers at deeper levels. The harbor, which lies on the east shore of the Kejimkujik Seaside Adjunct, has reefs, shoals, underwater gardens and several wrecks.

Independent operators that can provide boats (but you must bring your own dive master) are: **Charolette & Aye**, ☎ 902/683-2752; **Polar Ice Charters**, ☎ 902/354-8078 and 683-2873; ***Nova Queen II*** (Donnie Winters), ☎ 902/354-4478; and **Neil Fisher**, c/o Brian Phiney, ☎ 902/354-4401. Tank refills are available at the fire station, 516 Main Street, Liverpool, ☎ 902/354-4530, by advance arrangement. There are no rental shops in the area so you will have to make those arrangements in Halifax.

Harbor & Bay Tours

Wedgeport Tusket Island Cruise is at the Sport Tuna Fishing Museum on Rte. 334 in Wedgeport, ☎ 800/566-TUNA (8862) or 902/663-4345, fax 902/663-4448, e-mail cyrille@istar.ca. Wedgeport, founded by returning Acadians in 1767, is the point of departure of these tours that sail around and visit some of the 365 islands that lie offshore. Long used by the Micmac Indians, the fishing continues with many fishermen's shacks on the rocky shores. June and July are the best times for viewing the thousands of migrating birds that pass through this area. If you are particularly interested in seeing birds, tell the Captain and he'll be happy to swing by islands where there are nesting bald eagles and another where there are nesting puffins, recent immigrants from the islands of Maine. The four-hour tour includes a stop at St. Martin's Island, named by the explorer Samuel De Champlain in 1604 and believed to have been a Micmac burying ground. The fare for the island tour is $30 adults, $15 between five and 12 years, and you can bring your own lunch and snacks or buy it at the wharf. But a better deal is to pay $40 ($25 for child between five and 12 years) and get a lobster and steamer dinner with the tour. In order to run they need to have at least 15 passengers. Fishing charters are also available, by reservation.

McNutt's Island Coastal Encounters, Dock Street, Shelburne, ☎ 902/875-4269 or 902/875-1180, fax 902/875-2294, has Wednesday and Friday lobster tours with supper on the beach at McNutt's Island. On Saturdays there is an all day Pelagic Birding cruise aboard the sailing vessel *Lady Madeline*. The 11-hour voyage includes a picnic lunch on the ship and a lobster supper on the beach of McNutt's. The fee for this cruise is $95 per person. On Sunday there is a birding expedition of about the same duration to the island looking for nesting terns, guillemots and other birds. Again, the fare includes lunch and a boiled lobster dinner on the shore.

Shelburne Harbour Adventure Tours, Shelburne Wharf, Dock Street, Shelburne, ☎ 902/875-1526, cellular 875-7767. Take a tour of the harbor of Shelburne and see the town from the water, as its seamen and fishermen have done for centuries. On the three-hour narrated tour you'll learn about salmon farming and the local fishing industry. All sailings are at 9 am, 1:30 pm and 5:30 pm. In June and September they sail Monday and Thursday through Sunday and in July and August they sail daily. Tickets are $20 adults and $15 for children under 12.

Creaser's Cove Boat Tours in Riverport, ☎ 902/766-4845, cellular 902/527-3257 and 902/527-6313, has two tours operating on different days from July through October. They will also do deep-sea fishing charters. The LaHave River is a long narrow estuary that runs far inland al the way to Bridgewater. The LaHave River tour is a round-trip cruise up the river, passing the shipyard where the *Bluenose* is sent for overhaul. These trips are Friday through Sunday at 9 am and 1 and 6 pm and last about three hours. Their LaHave Island and Marine Life Cruise goes outside the harbor and around the islands, where you may see seals, porpoise and possibly even eagles. The Island cruise is given on Tuesdays through Thursdays. Rates for each of the trips is $20 per person, under age five free. Call ahead, because it's a long trip to Riverport just to find out there is no room or that the trip was canceled. To get there take Rte. 332 along the north side of the LaHave River and turn right when you cross the bridge into Riverport. It's a bit over a half-mile on the right.

Star Charters, Ltd, c/o Keith Merrill, RR #1, LaHave, NS B0R 1C0, ☎ 902/634-3535 or 902/688-2351, does a 90-minute cultural and historical sailing tour of the harbor on the classic 48-foot wooden ketch *Eastern Star*. They sail at 10:30 am, and 12:30, 2:30 and 4:30 pm, and offer a sunset cruise during July and August.

Rates are $15.50 for adults; children under 18, $9.50. There is a special rate for families. The sunset cruise price is higher.

Look and Sea Glass Bottom Boat Tours, Fisheries Museum Wharf, Lunenburg, ☎ 902/527-6317, takes you on a tour of the harbor where you can see the town, a lighthouse and many other attractions of the area and also have a chance to watch the bottom of the sea glide by. Their 25-foot boat has a glass bottom with seats well placed to allow viewing of the sea bed along the way – the best way to see native fish in their own habitat. During the summer they operate daily from 9 am to 7 pm with departures every two hours. The tour takes 90 minutes. Adult fares are $20, children under 16 $10, family rate $50 for four family members.

When it's in port, the ***Bluenose II***, the pride of Nova Scotia, offers two-hour tours of the harbor under sail. This ship, a replica of the original prize-winning racing and fishing schooner, is one of the last of its type. Every year it sails to other ports in the province, in Canada and elsewhere in North America, serving as a symbol of the province. You never know where you'll find her, but home port is Lunenburg. The harbor cruise costs $20 for adults, $15 for seniors and $10 for children. For additional information write or call Bluenose II Preservation Trust, 121 Bluenose Drive, PO Box 1963, Lunenburg, NS B0J 2C0, ☎ 902/634-1963.

In Blue Rocks take Herring Rock Road and follow it to the end. It will pass several small fishing harbors eventually ending up at another harbor. **Lunenburg Whale Watching Tours** in Blue Rocks, ☎ 902/527-7175, searches out seals, puffins, seabirds and whales. They sail at 9 and 11 am and at 2 pm.

Captain Dave's Deep Sea Fishing Charters & Lobster Picnic Cruises, 5 Willowbend Ct, Bridgewater, NS B4V 3V9, ☎ 800/803-1321, 902/543-9317 or 902/543-3852, fax 902/543-6587, does a daily lobster picnic cruise to an abandoned island where a lobster dinner is served. The return is via colorful Blue Rocks, a real fishing village.

There are two Mahone Bays, one is a large body of water, the other a town of the same name. In the town, **Bright Sea Yacht Rentals**, Mader's Wharf, 643 Main Street, ☎ 902/624-1074, off-season 902/823-3352, has a variety of cruises in the bay, including two-hour cruises that leave at 9 am, noon and 3 and 6 pm. These sailing cruises explore the bay and its island and spot wildlife, including an occasional whale. The rate is $18.50 per person, but ask about family rates. They also have a full-day cruise in the bay and to the Chester basin on a sailing yacht for up to four persons,

The Bluenose II *in Lunenburg.*

priced at $152, with lunch at a seaside eatery. Bright Sea also has several yachts for bareboat rental.

You can see the many islands in Mahone Bay on daily boat tours that leave from **The Rope Loft** restaurant, Water Street, Chester, ☎ 902/275-3430. The boat sails through St. Margaret's Bay and out into Mahone Bay, passing many of the hundreds of large and small islands that dot the harbor. The boat sails from the wharf near the Tancook Ferry daily at 2 pm during the summer; the fare is $12 per person.

Fishing

Near Yarmouth and south along the island- and inlet-dotted coast, there is excellent fishing for rainbow smelt, all the varieties of ground fish, mackerel and, in season, for bluefish, particularly in the Tusket Islands to Pubnico Harbour area. In the big harbor between Green Point and Baccaro Point south of Rte. 103 at Cape Negro are good ground fish and on the other side of the peninsula, off Port Saxon and North Negro, are rainbow smelt and striped bass. Shelburne and Jordan Bays have good mackerel, smelt and ground fish, as do the shores off the east coast of western head south of Lockeport. Port Hebert Harbour is also a good place to seek ground fish and mackerel. Smelt and striped bass are found in the LaHave River and mackerel are found near its mouth. Another good place for ground fish is off the islands in Lunenburg harbour and the islands of Mahone Bay. Mackerel are generally easy to find in all of the small and large harbors along the coast.

Wedgeport Tusket Island Cruise at the Sport Tuna Fishing Museum on Rte. 334 in Wedgeport, ☎ 800/566-TUNA (8862) or 902/663-4345, although a cruise provider, also offers fishing charters on request in the fish-rich waters of the Tusket Islands.

Creaser's Cove Boat Tours in Riverport, ☎ 902/766-4845, cellular 902/527-3257 and 902/527-6313, provides harbour and river tours, but they will also run a fishing charter for you in the waters off the LaHave Islands or some of their other favorite haunts. You will find rainbow smelts in the river and at the outlet as well as mackerel, dogfish, blue shark, herring, pollock, haddock and cod.

Close by, **Captain Risser's Coastal Cruises** in Rose Bay, ☎ 902/766-4580, has three-hour cruises that operate daily from the Feltzen South Government Wharf. Theirs is a family fishing cruise and they supply all the gear and even clean and fillet the fish. They also do a sunset cruise. They operate between July 1 and August 31. Inquire at Ovens Park.

River View Lodge, Greenfield, NS B0T 1E0, ☎ 902/685-2378, 902/685-2376 or 902/685-2423, is an outfitter with comfortable lodgings in the interior of the peninsula, near Kejimkujik National Park, on the Medway River. The specialty here is guided fly fishing for Atlantic salmon, which run in the spring from mid-May into July. While most of the fishing is from a boat on the Medway, there is wading in some areas.

Elwood Lodge, East Dalhousie, ☎ 902/644-3009 or 617-729-5900, ext 214 in the US, is on Black Duck Lake and has guided fishing in the spring, with brown trout and smallmouth bass from mid-April to May and Atlantic salmon from mid-May until July 31. The lodge also has canoes for guest use on the lake and on Lake Torment and Saturday Lake.

Captain Dave's Deep Sea Fishing Charters & Lobster Picnic Cruises does daily fishing trips for shark, cod, pollock and haddock. Contact them at 5 Willowbend Ct., Bridgewater, ☎ 800/803-1321, 902/543-9317 or 902/543-3852, fax 902/543-6587. Reservations are suggested. The trips leave at 8 am and take a maximum of six people.

On Horseback

For trail and arena riding in the Mahone Bay area, contact **Ocean Trail Retreat and Horseback Riding**, c/o Chris Levy, RR #1, Mahone Bay, Rte. 3, NS B0J 2E0, ☎ 902/624-8824, fax 902/624-8899. In the same area, **Sunnybrook Riding and Sailing**, 340 Herman's Island Road, Mahone Bay, ☎ 902/634-3735, has a large outdoor horse riding arena and lessons available by the hour. They also give sailing lessons.

Cultural & Eco-Travel Experiences

Just south of Yarmouth off the peninsula jutting into an island-studded bay, the **Wedgeport Nature Trail**, ☎ 800/566-8862 (TUNA), runs along the shore of the harbor for three miles. Interpretive panels describe the bay and marshes and the waterfowl that inhabit the area. The trail begins at the Tuna Wharf on Tuna Wharf Road off Rte. 334. The islands are home to common, roseate and Arctic terns, black guillemots, storm petrels, blue herons, common puffins, herring and black back gulls, several varieties of ducks, geese and even eagles.

For **Ovens Natural Park**, on Ovens Park Road, take Rte. 332 south from LaHave, then Feltzen South Road and Ovens Park Road. A spectacular natural formation combined with the incursions of man, this area was the site of a gold rush in 1861. Sea caves line the beach and a stair goes down into a canyon where the booming of waves is heard as they smash into the chasm.

Hackmatack Farm Vintners, 813 Walburne Road, Mahone Bay, ☎ 902/644-2415, fax 902/644-3614, e-mail wine@fox.nstn.ca, is a family farm devoted to making the best product they can produce: grape, blueberry and other wines and products from the bounty of their farm near the north branch of the LaHave River. They also have their own honey, and a picnic area where you can watch their ducks and geese frolic.

Of Boats, Fish & The Sea

Mahone Bay Wooden Boat Festival, PO Box 609, Mahone Bay, NS B0J 2E0, ☎ 902/624-8443, is celebrated annually during the week that begins on the last weekend of July. The festival not only celebrates the town's long history of boat and shipbuilding, but the beauty of wooden boats themselves. Hundreds of active wooden boats of all descriptions fill the harbor, and there are tours of boat building yards, small crafts building and workshops on maritime skills, plus boat races, entertainment, parades, food and fireworks.

George James, Model Shipbuilding Sales, RR #3 Bridgewater, NS B4V 2W2, ☎ 902/543-8650, is a model shipbuilder who creates his models as the ships themselves were built, "plank on bulkhead construction." These exquisite ship models are made from rare woods and are based on the original plans.

Wildlife Wood Sculptor Ronald Redden, 788 Main St., PO Box 146, Mahone Bay, NS B0J 2E0, ☎ 902/624-9296 ($$). Uses a scale of 1:32 to create sinuous and wonderful carvings of whales. He captures the "stop motion" grace of these giants of the sea so perfectly that they bridge the line between art and science. One of his works captured a female humpback whale raising her newborn calf to the surface for air.

The **Sport Tuna Fishing Museum** in Wedgewood celebrates the glory days of sport tuna fishing off these shores, ☎ 800/566-TUNA (8862), fax 902/663-4448, e-mail cyrille@istar.ca. As late as the early 1960s there were as many as 30 boats a day going out to sport-fish the bluefin tuna. Many celebrities came to try their luck here: Amelia Earhart, Franklin Roosevelt, Kate Smith, Ernest Hemingway and others. In the late 1960s, the tuna migration pattern switched farther out to sea. Today they are hunted commercially to satisfy the Japanese market, but too far out for sport fishermen to follow.

Sightseeing

Yarmouth County Museum and Archives, Collins Street, Yarmouth, ☎ 902/742-5539, is off Main Street between the ferry and Frost Park. The museum has extensive exhibits on the work of the people who have lived here, displays related to the shipbuilding, fishing and shipping industries that played such an important role in the community. Their maritime collections include ship models and ship paintings. There are also a Victorian period parlor, bedroom, kitchen and nursery, a fully equipped blacksmith shop and costumes from their extensive collection. A nominal admission fee is charged. It is open Monday to Saturday, 9 am to 5 pm, and Sunday, 1 to 5 pm, from June to mid-October. From mid-October to May they are open Tuesday through Sunday from 2 to 5 pm.

Firefighters Museum of Nova Scotia, 451 Main Street, Yarmouth, ☎ 902/742-5525, has a large collection of equipment dating from 1819 to the present. Among the prized possessions are an 1880 Silsby Steamer, a 1926 American LaFrance hand-drawn pumper, a 1931 Model A ladder truck, and a 1933 Chevrolet Pumper. In July and August they are open Monday through Saturday, 9 am to 9 pm, and Sunday from 10 am to 5 pm. During June and September hours are Monday through Saturday, 9 am to 5 pm. From October to May, they are open Monday through Friday from 10 am to noon and 2 to 4 pm. There is a nominal admission fee.

Sheep raising and the processing of their wool into fabric was an important part of life in the early province. The **Barrington Woolen Mill**, Barrington, ☎ 902/637-2185, opened in 1884 and produced woolen fabric from local fleece for decades. It still has much of its original machinery, which still operates as part of the demonstration of spinning and weaving techniques. It continued to produce fabric until closed in 1962. It is open mid-June to the end of September, Monday through Saturday, 9:30 am to 5:30 pm; Sunday, 1 to 5:30 pm. There is a picnic area beside the river and close by are the 1765 Old Meeting House, the Western Nova Scotia Military Museum, a replica of Seal Island Light and the Cape Sable Historical Society Center.

The town of Shelburne, situated on a long bay with deep forests behind it, was a refuge for Loyalists who fled the United States after the American Revolution. Former New England ship owners, builders and merchants started these businesses again in their new home. A core of buildings from that time has survived along the waterfront and is the nucleus of the **Shelburne Historic Complex** on Dock Street, ☎ 902/875-3219. Most of the buildings and homes have been restored to their late 18th-century appearance and, while many of them remain private homes, they convey the sense of the town at its beginning.

One of them, the **Ross-Thomson House** on Charlotte Lane, is open for tours. This home was built and occupied by the family of George and Robert Ross who processed fish and local lumber and exported it, trading for consumer goods for the community. Their families lived here and operated the businesses until the 1880s. As was typical of the time, in the front of the house was a store with its long counters and barrels and shelves of goods. In the back, basement and second floor were the living spaces for the family.

Ross House is open daily from June to mid-October, 9:30 am to 5:30 pm.

Close by, on the sea side of Dock Street, the **John C. Williams Dory Shop** is the reincarnation of a dory building shop that operated here for decades. The dory was the smaller boat taken aboard big fishing schooners, such as the *Bluenose*, and used by fishermen out at sea to set and haul nets. They were designed for ease of handling, seaworthiness and for stacking so that they took up little room on the deck of the mother schooner. For wooden boat lovers this is an exciting place to see the fine old techniques of boat building applied. Although it is a museum, the boats they build are sold, on prior order, to people who intend to use them. They are built from the keel up using the old tools and the patterns used in this shop originally. The shop is open daily 9:30 am to 5:30 pm from mid-June to mid-September.

Near the dory shop on Dock Street is a working cooper shop, not a museum, but a real business actively engaged in the business of making wooden barrels and buckets. Its building looks as if it dates from the 1600s, but it is brand new, having served as the location for the market and interior shots in the movie "A" The Scarlet Letter, in 1994. The cooper's products are sold at the shop. Dock Street was also used in the 1992 movie *Mary Silliman's War*, in which it represented Fairfield, Connecticut during the revolution.

The **Shelburne County Museum**, also on Dock Street, ☎ 902/875-3219, is the exhibition venue for the museum complex for items related to the history of the town from the Micmac period and the 18th-century to the present. Associated with the museum is a geneological reference center with extensive information on Loyalists who came and settled or passed through the town. The museum is open mid-May through October, 9:30 am to 5:30 pm daily, and in winter from Tuesday through Saturday for the same hours. The museum shop of the complex, **Tottie's Crafts**, is at 10A Anne Street and specializes in fine hand-crafted items. Among the goods available are quilts, hooked items, placemats, pottery, glassware, and woodenware.

Queens County Museum, 109 Main Street, Liverpool, ☎ 902/354-4058, shows what a warehouse of a well-to-do merchant and privateer would look like. The house next door, the Perkins House, was the home of a privateer merchant, and the museum shows what his business was like. It also shows the lives of the Micmacs, shipbuilding and forestry. It is open all year. From June through mid-October, hours are Monday through Saturday, 9:30 am to 5:30 pm; Sunday from 1 to 5:30 pm. From mid-October to the end of May, they are open Monday through Saturday, 9 am to 5 pm.

The **Perkins House Museum**, Liverpool, ☎ 902/354-4058, next door to the Queens County Museum, tells a tale of mixed loyalties. In 1766 Simeon Perkins, aged 28 and a recent widower, took advantage of the offer of free land in Nova Scotia and resettled to Liverpool, building a home and store. He prospered and by the time of the revolution he was a ship owner. Although he still had relatives in the colonies, he was angered when his ships were damaged by American privateers and he obtained privateer papers himself to avenge his losses. His home, a low Cape, was twice extended as his new family grew. A careful diarist, he kept almost daily records of what went on around him. The home has been a museum since 1936 and is restored to the period of Simeon's occupancy. It opens June through October June through mid-October 9:30 am to 5:30 pm and Sunday 1 to 5:30 pm.

The **Hank Snow Country Music Centre**, Bristol Avenue, Liverpool, ☎ 902/354-4675, opened in 1996 in a former rail station, a short way from where Snow lived as a boy. The museum chronicles his life, awards and music and contains his 1946 Cadillac. If you're a country music fan, you'll enjoy this museum. If you like trains, visit the station master's office, which has local railroading materials.

Wile Carding Mill Museum, 242 Victoria Road, Bridgewater, ☎ 902/543-8233, tells the story of 19th-century sheep raising, important to local farmers both as a cash crop and for clothing their families. The carding of wool, brushing the fibers to properly align them, was a time-consuming process; mills like this one eliminated this step. The mill, with an overshot waterwheel, operated from the late 1800s until 1968. Restored, it gives an important insight into life in the 1800s. The Wile is open June to October, Monday through Saturday, 9:30 am to 5:30 pm, and Sunday, 1 to 5:30 pm.

The **DesBrisay Museum**, 130 Jubilee Road in Bridgewater, ☎ 902/543-4033, has other exhibits on the human and natural history of the town and area. It is open Monday through Saturday, 9 am to 5 pm, and Sunday, 1 to 5 pm, from mid-May to the end of September. From October to mid-May hours are Tuesday through Sunday, 1 to 5 pm.

Fisheries Museum of the Atlantic, on the waterfront in Lunenburg, ☎ 902/634-4794, chronicles the fishing industry, long a critical part of the economy of Nova Scotia, with Lunenburg at the heart of it. The story of the fisheries is told here not only in artifacts, but by two floating vessels and essential parts of two others. The salt-bank schooner *Theresa E. Connor* and the trawler *Cape Sable* are tied up at the wharf, ready for visitors to board and inspect. Nearby, at the end of the wharf, the wheelhouse and Captain's cabin of the side trawler *Cape North*, and the *Royal Wave*, a Digby scallop dragger, add to the picture of the fisherman's life at sea. There are three floors of exhibits on the sea, the fisheries and the people who made them, including the story of the *Bluenose*, Canada's legendary fishing schooner, which won all the races and has become a symbol of the grit of the people here. Admission is $4.50, family admission ticket available, rates likely to change. The museum is open daily from June to mid-October, 9:30 am to 5:30 pm, and on weekdays from mid-October to May, 8:30 am to 4:30 pm.

The **Settlers Museum,** 1 Main Street, Mahone Bay, ☎ 902/624-6263, is in a home that dates from 1850, and houses a fine collection of china, porcelain and enamelware. The museum also concentrates on items related to the first settlers of the town who came here in 1754. On the second floor, during July and August only, there is a display related to the town's history as a shipbuilding port when there were up to 11 firms actively building wooden boats.

Ross Farm Museum is on Rte. 12 in New Ross, ☎ 902/689-2210. A family farm and home to five generations of Rosses, the farm is now part of the Nova Scotia Museum and is caught in time, a real working farm and living museum. It's inland from Chester, about a 20-minute ride. Costumed docents perform the chores, and reverse-bred animals moo, bleet and cackle in the yard. On the farm is a working cooper, blacksmith and workshops, fully recreating the life of a farm of the 19th-century. Admission is $4.25 adults, 75¢ children ages five to 16 and families $9.75. They open daily June to mid-October, 9:30 am to 5:30 pm.

Chester Playhouse, 22 Pleasant Street, Chester, ☎ 800/363-7529, 902/275-3933, fax 902/275-5784, has a schedule of about 10 plays and musical theater productions from spring through December, with frequent performances in July and August. The box office is open Tuesdays to Saturdays from noon to 5 pm and 6 to 8 pm, and Sundays from 2 to 5 pm and 6 to 8 pm. Tickets are about $12 to $16, depending on the performance.

Where To Stay & Eat

Yarmouth to Shelburne

Murray Manor B&B is one of our favorites, just a few minutes walk up the hill from the ferry landing. If you come without a car they will pick you up. The three guest rooms in this wonderfully restored Gothic Revival cottage are on the second floor, each individually decorated. The fine taste of the warm and thoughtful hosts shows through in the details. They provide dressing gowns and even private bathmats for use in the shared bath. The privacy of the beautifully kept lawns and gardens is assured by a tall hedge around the property. The nearby streets with rows of Victorian homes make a great place for a stroll. Formal tea is served in the garden or parlor depending on the weather, from 3 to 4 pm, for only $5 per couple. *225 Main St., Yarmouth, NS, B5A 1C6, ☎ 902/742-9625 ($-$$).*

Victorian Vogue Bed and Breakfast is in an 1872 Queen Anne Revival building with a three-story turret, off Main Street, north of the ferry terminal. It has six rooms that share two baths. The owner serves an extensive breakfast of homemade goodies. *109 Brunswick St., Yarmouth, NS B5A 2H2, ☎ 902/742-6398 ($-$$).*

Best Western Mermaid Motel is a good, comfortable, well-maintained motel just a few minutes' drive from the ferry. In addition to guest rooms they also have five rooms with kitchenettes. Amenities include a heated pool and laundry facilities. *545 Main Street, Yarmouth, NS B5A 1S6, ☎ 800/528-1234, 902/742-7821, fax 902/742-2966 ($$).*

Rodd Grand Hotel Resort is a modern resort hotel, but in the grand old fashion. Turn left off the ferry terminal and it's just a few minutes away. What they don't have for recreation they can arrange, including hiking trips and kayaking. Owned by a prestigious Canadian chain, they have a pool and fitness center, as well as a dining room and dinner theater. Special packages are available. *PO Box 220, 417 Main Street, Yarmouth, NS B5A 4B2, ☎ 800/565-RODD, 902/742-2446, fax 902/742-4645, e-mail rodds@rodd~hotels.ca, Web site www.Rodd~Hotels.ca/.*

El Rancho Motel, R*te. 1, Yarmouth, B5A 1C6, ☎ 800/565-2408, 902/742-2408*, and **Coastal Inn Voyager**, *Rte. 1, Yarmouth, B5A*

1C6, ☎ 800/565-5026, 902/742-7157, are inexpensive motels close to the ferry landing on the main route into town.

Cooper's Inn combines history, hospitality and heavenly food. Part of the dining room of this 1785 house was brought here in a ship from Boston after its Loyalist owner decided to leave New England. The inn is a masterpiece of restoration, each of the seven rooms beautifully returned to the late 18th century and furnished with antiques, but each with its own modern bathroom. Recently the original roof dormers were restored and the top floor has been made into an outstanding two-bedroom suite with views over the harbor and town. Situated in the middle of the restored area, it is literally steps from all of the attractions of the museum complex and from the modern town one street behind it. Fresh fruits and homemade muffins for breakfast are complimentary. We travel miles out of our way to eat in the Coopers' restaurant ($$-$$$). The ingredients are impeccable and dishes are prepared with extraordinary finesse. Their huge sea scallops are tender, moist and delicately sauced, and the salmon, always on the menu but prepared differently every time, is never less than perfect. *36 Dock Street, PO Box 959, Shelburne B0T 1W0, ☎ 902/875-4656 ($$).*

Near Mahone Bay

Lane's Privateer Inn is an inn with full service, restaurant, lounge, patio and bookstore. The 27 rooms are all recently renovated. In summer there are bicycles and canoes available for rent. Part of the property was the home of a famed privateer and it's on the Mercey River. Next door they operate Lane's Privateer Bed & Breakfast, 33 Bristol Avenue, same telephone ($), which has three rooms with double beds that share a bath. Rates include a continental breakfast at the inn. *27 Bristol Avenue, PO Box 509, Liverpool, NS, B0T 1K0, ☎ 800/794-3332, 902/354-3456, fax 902/354-7220 ($$).*

River View Lodge is a destination lodge for fishing, canoeing and living near nature. It's inland and near the National Park. They have guest rooms in the main lodge with private bath and a large common living room. Three meals are served each day. They also have a wood-heated wilderness camp situated on a brook, with its own fishing pond. *Greenfield, NS B0T 1E0, ☎ 902/685-2378, 902/685-2376 or 902/685-2423 ($$).*

Elwood Lodge is another destination lodge on Black Duck Lake in East Dalhousie. Attractive modern quarters with common room and a whirlpool. Hiking is available in the area, as is fishing in a lake or for salmon in the Medway and LaHave Rivers. The rates include all meals: a six-night-five-day package with lodging, all meals and one guide for two people is $550. If you use the lodge as a vacation center, without a guide, the double rate for the same period is $125 per person, including lodging and meals. *East Dalhousie, ☎ 902/644-3009, or 617-729-5900, ext 214 in the US.*

Bluenose Lodge has lots of yard around it. The main building dates from 1863. Ashlea House, on the property, was built in 1889 on the last two lots of the town's common land. All of the nicely decorated rooms are different and have private baths. The Carriage House is especially suited for families. Rates include breakfast. *Falkland St., PO Box 399, Lunenburg, NS B0J 2C0, ☎ 800/565-8851 or 902/634-8851 ($$), e-mail bluenose@fox.nstn. ca, Web site www.grtplaces.com/ac/bluenose/.*

Compass Rose Inn has four rooms in a restored 1825 Georgian home, a block above the harbor. Rooms are furnished in period antiques and are comfortable; good beds with quilts create a country home feeling. It has an excellent restaurant ($$-$$$), serving some old-time favorites that you won't find elsewhere – finnan haddie, for example. *15 King Street, PO Box 1267, Lunenburg, NS B0J 2C0, ☎ 800/565-8509, 902/634-8509 ($$).*

Kaulbach House Historic Inn is a large Victorian with big bay windows. Six of the inn's eight rooms have private baths and all are comfortable and nicely decorated. The Tower room overlooks the harbor from its large sitting area. They serve a three-course breakfast. In the evening they serve dinner for guests only, for under $15. *75 Pelham Street, Box 1348, Lunenburg, NS B0J 2C0, ☎ 800/568-8818, 902/634-8818 ($-$$).*

The Lunenburg Inn is a very popular inn right on the edge of downtown. Seven rooms and two suites, all with private bath, are beautifully furnished. Built in 1893 and modernized, there are big porches on the first and second floors from which you can enjoy views of the water and the town. *26 Dufferin St., PO Box 1407, Lunenberg B0J 2C0, ☎ 800/565-3963, 902/634-3963 ($$).*

Topmast Motel has 16 rooms, all with balconies that overlook the harbor. They also have barbeques and picnic tables in case you want to have a picnic. *76 Masons Beach Rd., PO Box 958, Lunenburg, NS B0J 2C0, ☎ 902/634-4661, fax 902/634-8660 ($$).*

Blue Rocks Road B&B has three cozy rooms, all comfortable, with good beds and homemade quilts. They serve a full breakfast in the dining room. They are close to Blue Rocks and they rent bicycles, the best way to get around here. *RR #1, Garden Lots, Lunenburg, NS B0J 2C0, ☎ 902/634-3426 ($$).*

Sou'wester Inn is a small inn that overlooks the bay. Formerly a shipbuilder's home, each of its rooms has a private bath. Furnishings are a mix of antiques and good contemporary furniture; a full breakfast is included. The hosts are gregarious and full of information. *788 Main St., PO Box 146, Mahone Bay, NS B0J 2E0, ☎ 902/624-9296 ($$).*

Mecklenburgh Inn has four rooms that share two baths. It began its life as a rooming house in the 1890s and about 10 years ago was renovated into this attractive inn. The two front rooms on the second floor have access to the balcony that overlooks the street. Victorian antiques fit the period and spirit of the place. Breakfasts are hearty. Open June through October. *78 Queen St., PO Box 350, Chester, NS B0J 1J0, ☎ 902/275-4638 ($$).*

Captain's House Inn was built as a private home in 1822 and sits amid lawns shaded by trees. Each of the nine guest rooms has a private bath. The inn also has a first-class restaurant ($$$) where everything is made from the freshest ingredients and served with a flair. Lunch is served until 3 pm, dinner from 5:30 to 10 pm daily. *129 Central St., PO Box 538, Chester, NS B0J 1J0, ☎ 902/275-3501, fax 902/272-3502 ($$).*

Captain Kelley's Restaurant specializes is seafood. They prepare lobster anyway you like it and also serve nicely cooked clam, haddock and scallop dinners. The dining room is in an old, white sea captain's house and the decor is a mixture of modern and antiques. They open for dinner daily, but you can get lighter fare in Captain Kelley's Sports Pub in the same building from 11 am to 1 am daily. *577 Main Street, Yarmouth, ☎ 902/742-9191 ($-$$).*

Old School House Restaurant is a place for lighter fare, chicken dinners, lobster dinners and the like, as well as Reubens, fish and chips and corned beef sandwiches. *Barrington Passage, ☎ 902/637-3770 ($-$$).*

The Old Fish Factory, open for lunch and dinner, is on the floor above the Fisheries Museum. The specialty is seafood, always fresh and seldom deep-fried. They also have a good selection of steaks, chicken and pasta. The casual and comfortable atmosphere suits its dockside location. *68 Bluenose Drive, Lunenburg, ☎ 800/533-9336 or 902/634-3333 ($$).*

The Innlet Café looks across the bay to the houses facing the town's harbor. The menu, filled with specialties like the chef's signature dish of seafood skibbereen, an original casserole of scallops, shrimps and mussels with an Irish Cream sauce, also has a nice mixed grill. Open year-round daily for lunch, 11:30 am to 5 pm, and for dinner from 5 to 9 pm. *Edgewater Street, Mahone Bay, ☎ 902/624-6363 ($$).*

Mimi's Ocean Grill is an innovative place whose chef has imagination along with skill. Crabcakes are the most ordinary thing on the menu, but they're hardly ordinary. Reservations are recommended. *664 Main Street, Mahone Bay, ☎ 902/624-1349 ($$).*

Tingle Bridge Tea House, set on a small side hill beside the highway, is a place of gentility and British grace, serving hot tea (or coffee), fresh scones and jam, cheesecake and shortcake. You can also get a nice lunch of chowder or sandwiches. They are open May to November from noon to 6 pm, Wednesdays through Sundays. *RR#1, Mahone Bay, ☎ 902/624-9770 ($).*

Campbell House has wonderful country views from its wraparound windows. The menu features original dishes such as the chef's breast of chicken in a pumpkin-seed crust. Open Tuesday through Sunday, noon to 3 pm and 5 to 9 pm. *Lacey Mines Road, Chester Basin, ☎ 902/275-5655 ($$).*

To reach **Chester Golf Club**, follow Water Street past the ferry landing along the shore, then take Golf Club Road on the right. We're not talking stuffy country club here. This is a nice, casual place with friendly people who serve a good meal for a reasonable price. Fish and chips or a club sandwich with chips are about $5. All the local people eat here and the tourists don't know about it.

They also serve a good, cheap breakfast and dinner. Open from 8 am to 9 or 10 pm daily during the season, depending on the weather. *Golf Club Road, Chester, NS, ☎ 902/275-4543 ($).*

Julien's Pastry Shop Bakery & Tearoom is a wonderful bakery and pastry shop where breakfast is a delight and lunch or a picnic can be an adventure. Lots to chose from, and all of it is good. *43 Queen St., Chester, ☎ 902/275-2324 ($).*

■ Camping

Ellenwood Provincial Park has 86 sites for RVs and tents. There is a full range of services; recreational facilities include a playground, hiking trails and access to a freshwater beach. The facilities are also available for winter use. The campground is open mid-June to mid-October and most of the sites and facilities are handicapped accessible. *Ellenwood Lake, ☎ 902/761-2400.*

The Islands Provincial Park is off Rte. 3 a half-mile west of Shelburne. There are 64 sites on an island connected to the mainland by a causeway, accommodating RVs and tents in sites that are open or wooded. *Contact the Department of Natural Resources, PO Box 99, Tusket, NS B0W 3M0, in season ☎ 902/875-4304 or 902/648-3540.*

TH Raddall Provincial Park has 43 sites and eight primitive sites. It's on the shore and has six ocean beaches and one inner harbor beach. There are three miles of hiking trails and it's close to the Kejimkujik Seaside Adjunct. *East Port L'Hebert Road, Port Joli. Contact the Department of Natural Resources, Provincial Building, Bridgewater, NS B4V 1V8, or call the Queens Department of Tourism, ☎ 902/354-5741.*

Pine Hills Campground is a private campground close to Cape Sable and the Baccaro Peninsula. Some sites are open, others wooded. They have a pay shower to accommodate 10 serviced sites and five unserviced sites. Open April through October. *Rte. 103, Barrington, NS B0T 1V0, ☎ 902/656-3400.*

Risser's Beach Provincial Park is off of Rte. 331 east of Bridgewater, near Crescent Beach. It has 92 sites with all of the amenities for RVs and tenters. For recreation they have a playground, hiking trails, supervised swimming and beach access. There is also an interpretive display on one of the trails. *Contact the Department of Natural Resources, Provincial Building, Bridgewater, NS B4V 1V8, in season ☎ 902/688-2034 or 902/543-8167.*

Ovens Natural Park Family Campground is a private campground near the park. Take Exit 11 on Rte. 103 to Rte. 332, then head south to Feltzen South Road. The park can accommodate RVs and tenters in open or wooded sites. It has all of the facilities for 67 serviced sites and 80 unserviced sites. They also have a pool, an obstacle and orienteering course, and can arrange boat rides to the sea caves. It's open mid-May to the end of September. Camping fee is a minimum of $16. *Contact Drum Head Estates Ltd, Box 38, Riverport, NS B0J 2W0, ☎ 902/766-4621, fax 902/766-4344.*

Rayport Campground is a private campground between Lunenburg and Chester. Take Exits 9 or 10 from Rte. 103 to Rte. 3. There are 70 open and wooded sites for RVs and tents, with a laundromat. For recreation they have a solar heated pool, playground and game room. *Martin's River, NS B0J 2E0, ☎ 902/627-2678.*

Graves Island Provincial Park is close to Chester on Rte. 3 east of town. The 73 sites accommodate RVs and tents and have facilities for the disabled. Recreation includes a playground, hiking trails, unsupervised swimming, beach access and a boat launch. There is also an interpretive display. *Department of Natural Resources, Provincial Building, Bridgewater, NS B4V 1V8, in season ☎ 902/275-4425.*

Halifax & Environs

Halifax has everything going for it: a beautiful setting overlooking a bay, mild climate, an interesting history, a citadel, gardens and green space, lively arts and cultural life, and extraordinarily friendly people. And for the adventurous traveler, it has a harbor island to explore, paths to bicycle, a canal to canoe and interesting lively streets to walk in.

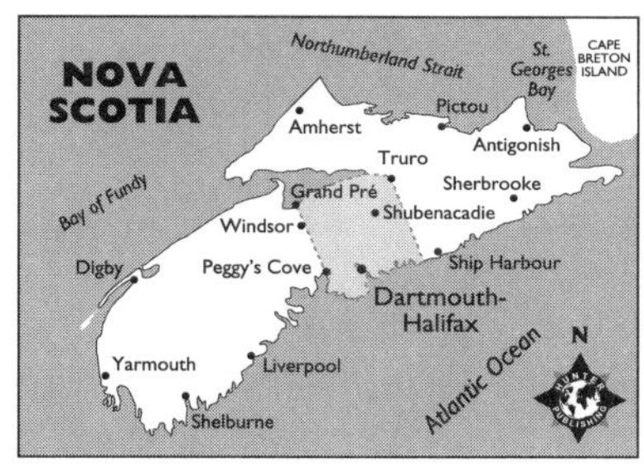

Geography & History

The historic clock tower in Halifax.

The facing cities of Halifax and Dartmouth, now part of the same municipality, share one of the finest harbors in the world. A long moderately narrow entrance with a large bay at the end, it was easy to defend and a natural stronghold when the British assumed control of the province. It is hard to believe that this large natural port wasn't settled until 1749, barely a quarter-century before the American Revolution. It was settled by the Earl of Halifax with the help of Bostonians and others from the New England colonies and some of the original buildings were assembled from parts pre-built in Boston. Within 50 years it was a sophisticated city with an impressive fort on the hilltop and an ornate clock tower erected by the punctilious Commander of the Halifax garrison, Prince Edward, the Duke of Kent, father of Queen Victoria.

Through both World Wars Halifax played a key role in support of the Allied forces as the major convoy assembly point. During World War I, a collision of ships loaded with munitions caused the largest non-nuclear man-made explosion in history, devastating both Halifax and Dartmouth.

Today it is a lively, sophisticated city of 115,000 people, with fine restaurants and hotels, an outstanding public garden, excellent museums and cultural events and a multitude of outdoor activities.

Getting Around

Halifax International Airport is the primary airport for the province. It is north of the city on Rte. 102, about 45 minutes from the

Dartmouth-Halifax

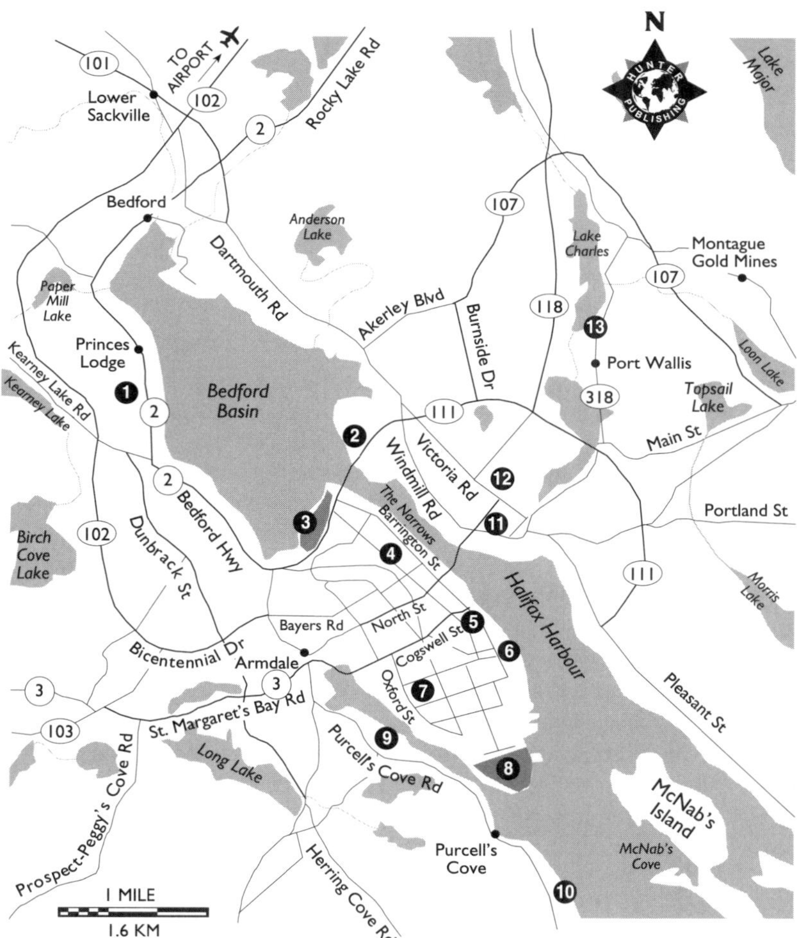

1. Hemlock Ravine Park
2. Bedford Institute of Oceanography
3. Seaview Park
4. Ft. Needham Park
5. Halifax Citadel Nat'l Historic Park
6. Maritime Museum
7. Victorian Public Gardens
8. Pt. Pleasant Park; Carleton Martello Tower
9. Fleming Park
10. York Redoubt Nat'l Historic Site
11. Dartmouth Park; Visitor Center
12. Micmac Mall & Tourist Bureau
13. Shubie Canal & Park

city center. **Aerocoach City Shuttle,** ☎ 902/468-1258, serves the airport from downtown hotels for $11 or $18 round-trip. There is also rail service to the city from Montreal via New Brunswick, daily except Wednesday. Contact **VIA Rail,** ☎ 800/561-3949; the station is at 1161 Hollis Street. Acadian Lines runs buses from Amherst, where they pick up passengers from New Brunswick bus lines. They also connect with lines to Cape Breton Island and Newfoundland ferries. Their depot is at 6040 Almon Street, ☎ 902/454-8279. **McKenzie Bus Lines,** ☎ 902/454-9321, has daily connecting bus passenger service to Yarmouth via the South Shore.

Information Sources

■ In the city of Halifax the **Nova Scotia Tourist Information Centre**, PO Box 130, Halifax B3J 2M7, ☎ 902/424-4247, is in Historic Properties on the waterfront. They are open daily, 8:30 am to 7 pm, from June through mid-September, and from September through June, Monday through Friday, 8:30 am to 4:30 pm. This is one of the best and most thoroughly stocked information centers anywhere and the staff knows the material and is eager to help. Their bookstore carries a good selection of travel material, including walking and nature guides. At the Halifax International Airport, ☎ 902/873-1223, there is another info center, also with a friendly and informed staff; a third is at the airport interchange of Hwy 102, ☎ 902/873-3608.

■ **Tourism Halifax**, PO 1749, Halifax B3J 3A5, ☎ 902/421-8736, fax 902/421-6897, is the information center specifically for the city. It's in the Old City Hall on Duke Street and they have a kiosk in the Public Gardens from June through August daily 9 am to 5 pm. In summer it opens daily, 8:30 am to 6 pm, and until 8 pm on Thursday and Friday. From September through May it opens 9 am to 4:30 pm, Monday through Friday. This center is the best place to pick up information on current performances and events; they have a bulletin board where events are constantly being posted. Ask here about attending the Mayor's afternoon tea.

■ Information is also available from the **Central Nova Scotia Tourist Association**, Box 1761, Truro B2N 5Z5, ☎ 902/893-8782, fax 897-6641.

Adventures

On Foot

Historic Walking Tours

The compact nature of Halifax makes walking the best way to see the sights. Start at the Tourist Center and walk along the waterfront through the old warehouses and wharves. The Ferry Terminal (with ferries to Dartmouth) is close by, and just beyond are the *HMCS Sackville*, a corvette that saw duty on World War II convoys, and the *CSS Acadia*, an historic hydrographic ship that charted the Arctic, at their berths behind the Maritime Museum. The Atlantic Marine Pavillion (open June through mid-September daily 10 am to 7 pm) at Sackville Landing Park has interpretive materials on sea life, including live fish. Take a right and go up Sackville Street to Hollis Street. Continue on and when you cross Prince Street on the left you will pass Province House, the oldest legislative building in Canada, and on the right the ornate building of the Art Gallery of Nova Scotia (open year-round, Tuesday through Friday, from 10 am to 5 pm, weekends noon to 5 pm).

Turn left and go up George Street through the **Grand Parade**, Halifax's original military parade grounds. On the left is **St. Paul's Church**. It is the oldest building in the city and was prebuilt in Boston and shipped here when the city was founded in 1749. It survived the Great Explosion of 1917 but has two fascinating mementos of that day. It is the oldest Anglican church in Canada. On the other end of the Parade is **City Hall**, a granite classic of Victorian monumental municipal architecture. Continue on George Street. The **Town Clock** straight ahead was built by order of the Duke of Kent, Commander of the Garrison, in 1794. His daughter Victoria, born after his time here, became Queen.

Next to the clock, stairs lead to the **Citadel**, ☎ 902/426-5080, which is open 9 am to 6 pm daily, June through August, and 10 am to 5 pm from September through May. Guided tours are available or you can explore on your own. The **78th Highlanders**, dressed in kilts and with pipes skirling, parade here in the summer. At the southwest corner of the citadel grounds, on the opposite side of Sackville Street, are the **Public Gardens**, one of the best gardens in North America, with acres of carefully tended grounds. You can take Sackville Street back downhill, passing along Barrington Street to shop on the way.

A different **walking tour** touching upon a different group of historic buildings is published by the Alexander Keith Brewing Company. The brochure, entitled *Alexander Keith's Magical History Tour*, is available at the information center. **DTours**, ☎ 902/429-6415, does a 90-minute walking tour of the historic area for $3. **Murphy's on the Water**, Cable Wharf, 1751 Lower Water Street, ☎ 902/420-1015, does a 1½-hour walking tour of the downtown and historic district and another to McNab's Island. **Scuttlebutt N Bones**, ☎ 902/829-2592 or 902/429-9255, has lightweight wireless communication systems for their walking tours so you don't have to snuggle up to the guide to hear what is said. They tell you not only about the buildings, but interesting details, stories and old gossip as well.

Parks & Nature Walks

Hemlock Ravine has a 350-year-old stand of hemlocks and almost five miles of hard-surface walking trails. It's on Kent Avenue off the Bedford Highway, close to the city. When John Wentworth, last Royal Governor of New Hampshire, hurriedly left that state and came here, he built a rustic cottage. When Prince Edward, Duke of Kent, came here as Commander in Chief of Royal Forces in 1794, John loaned him his place and Edward created an estate for himself and his mistress, Julie St. Laurent. Though most of the buildings are gone, the park, with its paths and flowing brooks, remains. The hemlock and birch groves in the ravine are original growth dating to before the settlement of the city and are 80- to 100-feet tall. The area is also home to a number of woodland birds.

Shubie Park in Dartmouth (take Waverly Road and then either Jaybee Drive or Locks Road) has loop trails that run alongside the old Shubenacadie Canal for about 1½ miles. Along the way there are interconnections with other multi-use trails that lead through Sullivan Pond Park and on to trails along Lake Bannok and Lake Micmac.

Point Pleasant Park is on the tip of the peninsula south of town, and originally was a vital part of the city defenses. It is now a peaceful park with water on three sides and 25 miles of walking paths wending their way through lawns and trees. It's a popular getaway where Haligonians go bird-watching, walking, jogging, bicycling and cross-country skiing. Roads literally honeycomb the park, creating lots of options, but the best is along the shore route of Cable, Arm and Shore Roads, passing many of the old artillery batteries, and with views out over the harbor on three sides. While bicycles are allowed on weekdays, they are banned on weekends and people on foot have the place to themselves. No motor vehicles of any type are allowed on the interior or circumferential roads. From downtown follow Barrington Street south to Inglis Street. Take it to Young Street or Tower Road on the left; either leads to the Park.

Sir Sanford Fleming Park, off Purcell's Cove Road, Rte. 253, is on the west side of the North West Arm, a narrow bay that cuts off part of Halifax. Sir Sanford was an immigrant Scotsman who was instrumental in the building of the Canadian Pacific Railway and he built a summer estate named "The Dingle" here. In 1908, to celebrate the 150th anniversary of representative government be gave 95 acres to the city as a park. There are five walks on the grounds of the park. If you enter the park from Dingle Road, to the parking lot on the left, and walk back up the road, you will find **Cottage Trail** next to the driveway for the Fleming Cottage. It will take you into the woods and circle back to the parking lot or, if you take the left branch in the woods it will bring you to the Loop Road Walk, which is a large circular path in the woods with a central trail to a look-off. You can then take the trail back to Dingle Road. Opposite the beginning of the Cottage Trail, another, the **Crossland Ice Trail**, leads to the **Frog Pond Trail** and to the Recreation Center. There is another parking lot for this trail on Purcell's Cove Road.

The 1,200-acre **McNab's Island**, at the end of Halifax Harbour, was originally part of the harbor defenses, with several gun emplacements scattered around. The long narrow island has many beaches and trails for walking or exploring. The island is now uninhabited and is a nature reserve and natural recreation area. For boat access to McNab's Island, see *Harbor & Bay Tours*, page 315.

MacLeod Bird and Nature Tours, Site 14A, RR #4, Armdale, NS B3L 4J4, ☎ 902/852-5209, have more than 20 years experience and are members of the Nova Scotia Bird Society. They conduct guided half-day and full-day bird and nature tours in the areas surrounding Rte. 333 and the Peggy's Cove peninsula, to Brier Island at the end of Digby Neck on the north Shore and other popular birding and nature spots in the province.

Victoria Park, in Truro, has over a thousand acres inside the city. A deep gorge cuts through the park, a dramatic focal point, reached by a pleasant walk along gravel paths up through the valley. Most of the way the trail is wheelchair accessible. The trail rises gradually as it enters more deeply into the cleft until it reaches Howe Falls, a high waterfall that tumbles from a fault in the rocks into a pool below. Wooden stairs lead up to the head of the falls, from which other trails lead throughout the park.

■ On Wheels

Shubie Park in Dartmouth has hard-surface trails through the park that interconnect with other multi-use trails through Sullivan Pond Park, as well as trails that run along the shores of Lakes Bannock and Micmac.

Point Pleasant Park, on the tip of the Halifax peninsula, is an outstanding place for a family bike trip. Relatively level, there are 26 miles of roads that wind in and around the point of land between the end of the harbor and North West Arm. Throughout the park there are old artillery batteries and remains of the many forts that were part of the harbor defenses. If you take Cambridge Drive from the parking lot, keep to the right onto Cable Drive. You will pass the Old Chain Battery, continue on as the road name changes to Arm Road and then take the loop to the right around Point Pleasant. As you come back out onto the main road, turn right and follow what is now called Shore Road. On the right you will pass Point Pleasant Battery at the very end of the point. Farther along there is a picnic area along the road with barbeque facilities. Opposite the breakwater and the container pier take Fort Road to Fort Ogilvie, built in 1793 and reinforced in 1862. Return to Shore Road and follow it, turning onto Birch Road, which you follow back to the park office, turning left back to the parking lot.

> **POINT PLEASANT PARK BIKING RULE:** *For some unknown reason, the park bans bikes on Saturdays, Sundays and holidays. They also require that both hands be on your handlebars.*

The big peninsula that extends south and west of Halifax is within easy reach of the city and provides two loop rides, one longer than the other, that will give you a good look at the small fishing villages that have made Nova Scotia famous. The loop through **Portuguese Cove** starts at the Armdale Rotary, a crazy place with several layers of traffic trying to get across each other, and goes out Herring Cove Road (Rte. 349) a short distance. As a side trip, take the first left after you get on Rte. 349 and follow it to the Mont Blanc anchor. In the explosion of 1917, the anchor from the French munitions ship flew through the air all the way from the opposite corner of the city to this spot. You can follow the curving road up to Purcell's Cove Road or return to Rte. 349. Take Rte. 349 to the left a short way then follow Rte. 253, Purcell's Cove Road. This will take you inland along the North West Arm past Sir Sanford Fleming Park, a good place to stop for a rest or a picnic.

The road then follows the coast along some very attractive roads to Herring Cove, a small fishing village. From there take Rte. 349 south to Ketch Harbor and then on to Sambro, where, when the fog isn't too thick, you'll see Sambro Light, an old red-and-white-striped lighthouse. Just past Sambro, continue on out toward Pennant. You will see signs for **Crystal Crescent Beach**, two beautiful big curving sandy beaches, another good rest stop. Return to Sambro and take a left onto Rte. 306, following it inland through wilderness country through Harrietsfield, until, just past the end of Long Lake, you again meet Rte. 349, Herring Cove Road, which you take left back to Armdale Circle. This route is about 30 miles and is a bit hilly but the traffic is less than on the Peggy's Cove route.

The **Peggy's Cove** route also starts at the Armdale Circle but you take Margaret's Bay Road halfway around the circle and follow it to Rte. 333, which you take to the left toward Prospect and Peggy's Cove. Follow it inland through Hatchet Lake and on to White Lake and Shad Bay. At each of these are optional side trips to Terrence Bay and Prospect, each out a road to the end of its own peninsula. Prospect is a timeless little fishing village with nice walking trails along the wild seashore and a cozy B&B. Prospect would be a good headquarters from which to see this area or to split the trip into a two-day jaunt. From Shad Bay continue to McGrath Cove (with a possible side trip to the East Dover peninsula) and on through West Dover to Peggy's Cove, one of the most photographed and heavily touristed villages in the province. Be careful on the rocks here, rogue waves can sweep people out to sea.

From Peggy's Cove, Rte. 333 heads north along the east shore of St. Margaret's Bay through a series of attractive fishing villages. At Upper Tantallon take Rte. 3 east, back to Armdale Circle. This trip is about 55 to 60 miles, without side trips; its down side is that traffic can be heavy, particularly in summer when all of the tour buses from Halifax head out to Peggy's Cove.

Bicycle Outfitters & Guided Tours

■ **Velo Halifax Bicycle Club**, PO Box 125, Dartmouth B2Y 3Y2, ☎ 902/423-4345, is centered in the Halifax metropolitan area. They offer cycling trips throughout the province, as well as in the metro area. Trips are graded by degree of difficulty, with A being the toughest and D being the easiest. C and D trips all have sweep riders to assist anyone with problems.

■ **Atlantic Canada Cycling**, Box 1555, Station M, Halifax B3J 2Y3, ☎ 902/423-2453, fax 423-2452, is a tour planner and information center that can give you free advice on places to bike or help you plan a more extensive trip. They also have guidebooks and a referral service, and host an annual cycling festival.

■ **Murphy's on the Water**, Cable Wharf, 1751 Lower Water Street, ☎ 902/420-1015, has mountain bike rentals from their Cable Wharf location on the waterfront, April through November, Mondays through Fridays.

■ On Water

Canoeing

The **Shubenacadie Canal**, Dartmouth, ☎ 902/462-1826, was built in the 19th century to connect Halifax Harbor with the Bay of Fundy. Long disused, it has been restored and makes a great place for canoeing. The canal connects a series of ponds and streams across the province.

Canoe & Kayak Outfitters and Guided Tours

■ In Dartmouth you can rent canoes at **Mayak Ventures**, 59 Glenwood Avenue, Dartmouth, ☎ 902/463-9639. They also have scheduled guided tours or can customize one for you.

■ **DKS Wilderness Experiences**, 38 Sussex Street, Halifax, ☎ 902/477-4488, rents canoes and camping equipment and outfits guided trips of from one to seven days, including all equipment and transportation.

■ **Sea Sun Kayaking**, Box 1749, Fairfield Road, Halifax, ☎ 902/452-2978, conducts guided half- and full-day and overnight tours from Halifax for beginner and more advanced paddlers. They provide instruction, kayaking courses and will also rent equipment.

■ South of the city, **Halifax Canoe & Kayak Rentals, Limited**, West Dover Seaside Cottages, 6029 Peggy's Cove Road, Halifax, ☎ 902/499-8264, does daily and weekly canoe and kayak rentals that include all equipment and roof racks. They prefer advance notice. If you are flying in, they will pick you up in Halifax and bring you back.

Harbor & Bay Tours

When the *Bluenose II* is in town you can get a sailing tour of the harbor on board this famous schooner. Visits, particularly in summer, are rare, so don't miss the chance if you have it. It docks behind the Maritime Museum of the Atlantic near the *CSS Acadia*. For information, ☎ 902/422-2678 or 902/424-5000.

Murphy's on the Water, Cable Wharf, 1751 Lower Water Street, ☎ 902/420-1015, operates several water cruises daily from the historic waterfront. Check directly with them or at either information center. Among them are cruises to McNab's Island, harbor cruises aboard a stern-wheel vessel and narrated cruises of the harbor and North West Arm. *Harbour Queen* is a stern-wheel paddler that offers dinner cruises from 6 to 8 pm, Thursday through Sunday ($30 per person), a two-hour Sunday brunch cruise at 11:30 am ($20), a country dance cruise Wednesday nights at 7 pm ($16), and a Sunday night party cruise at 9 pm ($16). A two-hour historical cruise leaves at 10 am and noon ($16 adult, $10.50 children ages five-16) on the *Haligonian III*.

Murphy's also has **fishing charters** on board the *Stormey Weather*. Fishing trips are five hours and leave at 9 am and 2:30 pm every day; equipment is included. They also have a 75-foot sailing vessel, the *Mar II*, that does a lunch cruise every day from noon to 1:30 pm for $17. There is also a cocktail cruise at 6:30 and a midnight cruise Friday and Saturday at 11:30 pm, each at $17 per cruise. Reservations required.

The **McNab's Island ferry** leaves from Cable Wharf next to the Ferry Terminal at 9 am and returns at 2 pm; another trip leaves at 2:30 pm and returns at 7:30 pm. Round-trip fares are $10 adults, $6 children; they will also accept bicycles.

Four Winds Charters, c/o Ken Merlin, 180 Hillside Drive, St. Margarets Bay, ☎ 902/492-0022, sails from Unit 4 on Cable Wharf in Halifax. While they are outfitted for fishing, they will also do whale-watching and harbour tours on request and ferry to George's and NcNab Islands. The McNab's fare is $8.50, a 1½-hour harbor tour is $10 adult, $5 for children six-12, and the deep-sea fishing 12 miles offshore costs $36 per person. Whale-watching trips in July and August cost $20 adult, $10 child.

Tax Sea on the Harbour, 1535 Shore Road, Eastern Passage, ☎ 902/471-3181 or 902/458-7128, also operates a harbour taxi service from Cable Wharf on the Halifax waterfront and will help personalize a harbour tour.

On the Dartmouth side of the harbor, **McNab's Island Ferry and Nature Tour**, Fisherman's Cove, Eastern Passage, ☎ 800/326-4563 or 902/465-4563, leaves from the Government Wharf all year for trips to McNab's Island. Take Rte. 322 south from Dartmouth.

Peggy's Cove Water Tours, Peggy's Cove, ☎ 902/823-1060 or 902/456-3411. The boat is the *So Much to Sea*; it leaves from the Government Wharf at Peggy's Cove. Tickets for the cruise are sold there but it's best to reserve ahead. Two cruises are offered, a half-hour photo-taking tour and a three-hour whale-and-puffin-watch tour that goes out to Pearl Island, where puffins breed. The much-photographed fishing village of Peggy's Cove is at the end of St. Margaret's Bay, on a wave-splashed rocky point carved thousands of years ago by a glacier.

Shubenacadie River Adventure Tours Ltd., Rte. 215, South Maitland, ☎ 902/471-6595 or 902/443-9735 is north of Halifax and runs a narrated scenic tour of the Shubenacadie and Stewiake Rivers. Bald eagles, herons and various species of ducks are often sighted along the route. The tour fee is $20 per person. From Halifax take Rte. 102 to Exit 10 and follow Rte. 215; they'll be on the right at South Maitland.

Hunting the Tidal Bore

At the head of Cobequid Bay the Shubenacadie River is about the only place for the flood of the Fundy Basin to go. At high tide the heavier saltwater pushes up the river, forcing the freshwater backward, forming reverse rapids in the river and a wall of water that can be as high as 10 feet. Unlike most river rafting, which is over rocks and boulders, this rafting is over smooth shallows and sand bars with rising water. All of the following providers use Zodiac-type boats that are fast and maximize the experience. They also provide rain suits and flotation devices. It is a good idea to wear old clothes and bring a spare set and a towel in case you get wet from the spray; they have showers at their landings. They all run between mid-May and mid-October and reservations are recommended. Call for tide times. Most want you there an hour early for orientation and to make sure you get the earliest start. It's fun and exciting, but not terribly dangerous.

Shubenacadie River Adventure Tours Ltd., Rte. 215, South Maitland, ☎ 902/471-6595 or 902/443-9735, has a variety of tours, including a two-hour and a three-hour tidal bore adventure. The trip covers more than 26 miles of the river, as you follow the bore up-river, crossing up and over and literally playing in the tidal bore. The size of rapids chosen can be determined by the riders. Fares for the 3½-hour tour are $50 for adults and $40 for children under 13. The two-hour tour is $10 less. From Halifax, take Rte. 102 to Exit 10 and follow Rte. 215; they'll be on the right at South Maitland.

Shubenacadie River Runners, 8681 Rte. 215, Maitland, ☎ 800/856-5061 or 902/261-2770, is another provider of tidal bore rafting. Their tour is four hours long and follows the bore up the Shubenacadie River. The rafting fee, which includes lunch and beverage, is $65 per person for adults and $58 for children under 12.

Tidal Bore and Upriver Rafting is run by Hilbert and Eppie Kohl from their private park along the Shubenacadie. Contact them at Shubenacadie Tidal Bore Park, RR4 Shubenacadie, ☎ 800/565-7238 (RAFT) or 902/758-4032, e-mail raftcamp@fox.nstn.ca. They, too, use Zodiac craft to run the rapids on their four-hour trip starting 12 miles downriver. From their welcome center high above the river you walk down wooden stairs to a deck to challenge the waves or to watch others doing so. The two-hour trip is $45 for adults and $35 for children under 12; the four-hour trip is $60 adults, $50 children.

Tidal Bore Rafting, Ltd, ☎ 902/752-0899 or 902/755-5560, operates tours out of Maitland and chase the tidal bore 18 miles up the Shubenacadie River to a takeout at Rines Creek. A ham, beef or salmon sandwich and a soft drink are included in the price, which is $65 for adults and $55 for children 12 and under. Water time is three hours and overall trip time about five hours.

Fishing

A number of party boat and charter fishing expeditions are available in the greater Halifax area. In addition to Murphy's on the Water (see page 315), **Capt. Eli's East Coast Charters** has fully equipped boats and offers packages from mid-June to mid-November. Scheduled departures are at 8 am, 1 or 2 pm, and 7 pm. The fishing package, which even includes rain gear and fish filleting, is $37 adults, $32 seniors, $25 children. Contact Capt. Eli Richards, 1745 Lower Water Street, Boat Tour Center, Halifax, ☎ 800/665-3608 or 902/422-3608.

New Dawn Charters, 553 Purcell's Cove Road, Halifax, ☎ 902/479-2900, has a 40-foot Cape Island boat that they use for fishing off the ledges of Chebucto Head, about 15 miles offshore. They also do whale-watching, diving trips and individualized harbor tours, as does **A&M Sea Charters**, Box 376, 87 Government Wharf Road, Eastern Passage, ☎ 902/465-6617.

■ On Snow

Cross-Country Skiing

Skiing is not a big activity here because the warming influence of the ocean melts the snow or turns it to freezing rain. However, there are some good cross-country skiing spots in the area, with the summer walking trails used for skiing in the winter. Try the paths along the Shubenacadie Canal in Dartmouth at **Shubie Park**. **Point Pleasant Park** at the southern end of the Halifax peninsula has 26 miles of roadways that are barred to all motorized vehicles (including snowmobiles) and it's a good place to go after a fresh snow. Across the North West Arm, **Sir Sanford Fleming Park** has trails that are good for cross-country skiing. North of the city, the Bedford Recreation Department has created five miles of trails called the **Jack Lake Trails**.

■ On Horseback

Two farms northwest of Halifax have horses. **Hatfield Farm Cowboy Adventure**, 1821 Hammonds Plains Road in Hammonds Plains, ☎ 902/835-5676, is open all year and has a good range of horse-related activities. In addition to trail riding they offer hayrides; in winter they have sleigh rides. Private riding is also available and they have overnight excursions with camping. The 1½-hour, 2½-mile trail rides are held eight times a day in summer, beginning at 8:40 am and ending at 7:10 pm; the last winter ride starts at 2:40 pm. From June through September you do not need a reservation, but during the rest of the year you must reserve ahead. Cost is $21.50 for adults; $16 for children ages nine to 14. They will train beginners. There are also pony rides for $4.50. Take Rte. 102 out of Halifax, then Rte. 213 west at Exit 3.

Wyndgate Farm, 156 Windsor Junction Crossroad, Windsor Junction, ☎ 902/861-2279, has a lighted indoor arena. They also have trail rides, hay rides and sleigh rides and are open all year. Take Rte. 102 from Halifax to Exit 4 (Rte. 101), then take Rte. 354 north.

Southwest of the city and a little bit closer, **Isner's Riding Stable**, 1060 Old Sambro Road, Harrietsfield, ☎ 902/477-5043, is a close six miles from the Armdale Rotary. They will be glad to give lessons or take you on guided horseback rides by reservation. The Isner's also can provide hay rides and sleigh rides if the conditions are right. From the Armdale Rotary, take Herring Cove Road (Rte. 349 to Rte. 306 and follow the latter to Harrietsfield).

Cultural & Eco-Travel Experiences

The province celebrates its immigrant heritage at **Pier 21**, PO Box 611, ☎ 902/425-7770. The equivalent of America's Ellis Island, over 1½-million people started new lives here. During World War II, 368,000 Canadian troops set sail for the battlefields and over 100,000 refugees sought asylum through the port. When completed (it's in the beginning stages now), it will have exhibits on the immigrants, a resource center, theater and performance hall.

The **Black Cultural Centre for Nova Scotia**, 1149 Main Street, Dartmouth, ☎ 800/465-0767 or 902/434-6223, preserves the story of black migration into, and out of, the province since the first black person arrived in 1606. Black Loyalists came to Nova Scotia in great numbers beginning in 1783 and black communities were formed in over 48 areas around the province. The tales of these people and of their lives are preserved in the exhibits and materials collected here.

Black Heritage Tours offers tours of Halifax and Dartmouth ($18), Peggy's Cove ($20), and a Halifax City and Country Tour ($25) that shows not only the highlights of the city but delves into the black experience here as well, telling the tale of the Africville section of Halifax that was taken down in the 1960's. Tour prices are based on a minimum of seven persons but the tours can be taken with fewer for a higher fee. Contact Carolyn and Matthew Thomas, 2032 #7 Highway, East Preston, NS B2Z 1G1, ☎ 902/462-2011, e-mail cgrt@atcon.com.

Bordered by Sackville Street, Spring Garden Road, Summer Street and South Park Street, the **Public Gardens** are among the finest Victorian gardens on the continent. Acres of beautifully laid out gardens are shaded by tall stately trees. These include rose gardens and formal flower beds that bloom throughout the summer. Plantings are integrated with the fountains, ponds and walkways to create a variety of garden textures. In classic Victorian style, there is a bandstand where free public concerts are given on Sunday afternoons. The Friends of the Public Gardens give tours by appointment. Call them at ☎ 902/422-9407. The gardens are open daily from 8 am to sunset.

Cole Harbour Heritage Farm Museum, 471 Polar Drive, Cole Harbour, ☎ 902/434-0222 or 902/462-0154. As the city of Halifax grew, it put pressure on adjacent lands that had been market gardens and dairy farms. Cole Harbour has preserved a bit of that heritage in a collection of seven buildings that keep a family farm alive. Giles House, the oldest in town, is the only building moved here; all of the others have been part of this working farm for over a century. The farm has a blacksmith shop, a main barn, a market barn once used as a weekly farmer's market, a crib barn, carriage shed and a main house with a tea shop on the veranda. Gardens demonstrate techniques used by farmers to get produce to market before their competition. A path through a former pasture leads to a marsh and a pond with a boardwalk and other trails lead into wooded parkland.

The Farm at Naturally Nova Scotia, 2769 Lawrencetown Road, Dartmouth, ☎ 902/4234-7206, is a working farm growing products for the Naturally Nova Scotia Health Products and Design company. It's on a restored 19th-century farm and has walking paths, display beds, a forest walk and a bevy of animals. They grow extensive beds of herbs.

Discovery Centre, 1593 Barrington Street, ☎ 800/565-7487 or 902/492-4422, is filled with hands-on exhibits on such things as momentum, waves and illusions. They also have math games and workshops. Open Monday through Saturday, 10 am to 5 pm, and Sunday, 1 to 5 pm. Admission is $4 for adults; there are special rates for seniors and children.

Shubenacadie River Adventure Tours Ltd., Rte. 215, South Maitland, ☎ 902/471-6595 or 902/443-9735, has a 250-acre tract of land along the Shubenacadie River. In addition to their tidal bore rafting tours they also have a one-hour forestry tour, during which they explore an Acadian Forest and a managed plantation. Part of the tour is a demonstration of Christmas tree shearing. The cost of the tour is $5 per person.

You don't have to ride on top of the **tidal bore** to enjoy it. This rushing current pushed on by the Fundy tides develops into a wall of water from one to several feet high – highest during full moons in August or in autumn. **Tidal Bore Park**, on the grounds of the Palliser Restaurant in Truro is one of the best places to see this twice-daily phenomenon. Be there at least 10 minutes before the expected time of the bore. Tide tables are generally available in town or call Dial-a-Tide, ☎ 902/426-5494. The park, on the banks of the Salmon River, is floodlit at night for easier viewing.

Shubenacadie Provincial Wildlife Park, Shubenacadie, ☎ 902/758-2040, fax 902/758-7011, is on Rte. 2, north of town, reached by Exit 10 off Rte. 102. The park has reindeer, moose, cougars, and Sable Island horses in the collection and a host of native birds, including several varieties of ducks and swans. The animals are in large enclosures with room to roam and many of the birds are not penned. At the entrance to the park, the **Creighton Forest Environment Centre** is dedicated to the study and teaching of and about the forest and their inhabitants, and the relationship of humans and their forestry practices to the health of both. The park is open mid-May to mid-October, 9 am to 7 pm.

■ Music & Theater in Halifax

Nova Scotia International Tattoo, PO Box 3233 South, Halifax, NS B3J 3H5, ☎ 800/563-1114 or 902/420-1114 or 902/451-1221, fax 902/423-6629, Web site www.nstattoo.ca. There is no better word to describe this show than extravaganza. Presented the first week of July every year for almost 20 years, the show combines pageantry, music, dance and acrobatics. It is held in the enormous Halifax Metro Centre and more than 2,000 international military and civilian performers participate. Past groups have included pipe bands from Britain, the Quantico Band of the US Marine Corps (yearly since 1980), the Copenhagen Police Band, the Gymnastics Display Team of the Paris Police Department, the Royal Netherlands Air Force Band and the US Army Drill Team. Even though the Metro Centre holds thousands, it's better to reserve tickets early. The Tattoo is so popular that the *QE II* once delayed sailing so passengers could attend. Performances are at 7:30 pm; ticket prices range from $12 to $24.

Theater and music are very much alive in Halifax; you can choose from stage or dinner theater, the symphony, or Celtic, jazz or rock music. Two popular venues for music and performances are the **Metro Centre,** 5284 Duke Street, ☎ 902/451-1221 (tickets), 451-1202 (schedule), and the **Dalhousie Arts Centre** at Dalhousie University, 6101 University Avenue, ☎ 800/874-1669 or 902/494-3820, open noon to 6 pm, Monday through Saturday. Also in summer there are free noontime concerts, usually Wednesday-Friday, on the Grand Parade.

The **Neptune Theatre,** 1903 Barrington Street, Unit B24, Halifax B3J 3L7, ☎ 800/565-7345 or 902/429-7300, fax 429-1211, is a professional repertory company that has been active here for more than 30 years.

The Eastern Front Theatre is a new company producing works written and performed by Atlantic Canadians. Members (you can be one for $10) get to sit in on playwright readings and working rehearsals. Performances are at the Dalhousie Arts Centre and other locations in the city. Contact the theatre at PO Box 11, Dartmouth Main Postal Station, Dartmouth B2Y 3Y2, ☎ 902/466-2769, fax 424-5327, Web site www.chebucto.ns.ca/culture/EF/EF-home.htm.

Grafton St. Dinner Theatre, 1741 Grafton Street, ☎ 902/425-1961 ($$$), operates Tuesday through Sunday evenings with a program of musical comedies. Entrée options include prime rib, salmon, or chicken. The **Historic Feast Co,** Historic Properties, Upper Water Street, PO Box 3004S, ☎ 902/420-1840, fax 902/429-8487 ($$$), has three different shows through the year, some based on the past, some spoofs of other shows. Ticket price includes soup or salad, an entrée of your choice, dessert and beverage.

Symphony Nova Scotia, ☎ 902/421-1300, presents concerts throughout the year at various places in the city. The repertoire of the orchestra is broad and includes classical, maritime, Celtic, blues and jazz. Some of their performances are at the Metro Centre. Call for program, dates and locations.

The **Saint Cecilia Concert Series** is performed at St. Andrew's United Church, 6036 Coburg Road. Tickets and information are available from the box office of the Dalhousie Arts Centre, ☎ 800/874-1669 or 902/494-3820.

Sightseeing

■ In Halifax

If you have time for only one museum in Halifax, make it the **Maritime Museum of the Atlantic**, 1675 Lower Water Street, ☎ 902/424-7490. Its exciting exhibits and displays bring the maritime history of the province and the North Atlantic to life, and show the role the sea has played in all facets of local life. When the *Titanic* sank, the rescue operations were centered here, survivors landed here and the recovered dead were buried here. The exhibits include items found on the sea and others later recovered and tell the tale of the ship and the people on board. Excellent multimedia exhibits chronicle the 1917 collision of two ships in the harbor that caused the Halifax explosion, through photographs and the tales of survivors. Also part of the museum is Queen Victoria's Royal Barge, given to the museum by Queen Elizabeth II. Over 200 model ships from old sailing craft to ocean liners, freighters and naval ships are in the collections. Another part of the museum is in an old ship chandlery, where items were bought to outfit ships for sea.

At berths close to the museum is the ***HMCS Sackville***, a corvette class known for bouncing around like a cork in heavy seas, that saw duty during the Battle of the Atlantic in the convoys that kept Britain alive. The last of its type, the ship can be toured daily. The ***CSS Acadia*** is also open for touring, after long years of service charting the bottom of the Arctic and North Atlantic. An adjacent wharf also serves as the berth for the *Bluenose II* and visiting tall ships. The museum is open from June to mid-October, Monday through Saturday, 9 am to 5:30 pm; Sunday, 1 to 5:30 pm; and Tuesday, until 8 pm. From mid-October to the end of May it opens Tuesday through Saturday, 9:30 am to 5 pm; Sunday, 1 to 5 pm; and Tuesday until 8 pm. The *Sackville* (☎ 902/429-5600) is free and open the same hours as the Museum in summer, but from October through May is open Monday through Saturday, 10 am to 5 pm, and Sundays from noon to 5 pm.

Air buffs have their day at a pair of aviation-related museums. **Atlantic Canada Aviation Museum**, ☎ 902/873-3773, at Exit 6 of Rte. 102, is at the main entry of the Halifax International Airport, with a collection of aircraft and related memorabilia ranging from Alexander Graham Bell's *Sliver Dart* to modern jet aircraft;

they even have a V-1 buzz bomb of the type that terrorized London. Open late May to early September, daily 9 am to 7 pm.

South of Dartmouth is the **Shearwater Aviation Museum**, 13 Bonaventure Avenue, ☎ 902/460-1083, at the Shearwater Airport. The airfield itself was opened by the US Navy Flying Corp under Lt. R.E. Byrd, the polar explorer, in 1918. Long a naval airbase, the museum has an extensive collection of naval aircraft, photos and related materials that tell the story of naval combat, submarine patrol and search and rescue missions. It is open July and August, Tuesday, Wednesday and Friday, 10 am to 5 pm, Thursday until 8 pm, and Saturday and Sunday, noon to 4 pm. September through October and April through June, it's open Tuesday through Thursday, 10 am to 5 pm, Saturday noon to 4 pm.

The Citadel, ☎ 902/426-5080, is hard to miss atop its hill in the center of Halifax. Take nearly any street uphill from the waterfront and you'll get there. From the Citadel you'll have a wide view over the city and harbor. Started in 1749 with the founding of the city, the fort took its present shape in 1856. Never subjected to attack, its battlements remain in excellent condition for exploring. At noon daily there is a ceremonial firing of the noon gun. The **Army Museum**, with a collection of military material and memorabilia, is on the grounds of the Citadel. The grounds of the Citadel are open all year but the displays open mid-May to mid-October from 9 am to 5 pm.

Old Town Clock, Brunswick Street on the Citadel Grounds, was put there to encourage punctuality. Prince Edward, the Duke of Kent, had it erected in 1803 to teach his subjects the habit of timeliness. It has dominated the town since and become one of its symbols.

St. Paul's Cathedral and **The Parade**. The parade was the original town square of the city, used by British troops for parading and as a gathering place for inhabitants. It still serves that function and around it you will find not only the 1888 City Hall but several restaurants and pubs that keep going late into the night. At the south end is St. Paul's Cathedral, the original church in the town, the wooden frame of which was made in Boston and shipped. The church became the first Anglican Cathedral outside of Britain in 1787. Look over the doors in the entry for a wooden sill embedded there during the explosion. The front pew on the left is reserved for the Queen (or King as the case may be).

The **Nova Scotia Museum of Natural History**, 1747 Summer Street, ☎ 902/424-7353, is behind the Citadel on Summer Street. Here the mystery and history of the natural world of the province is explored. The fossil remains found in the province are exhibited and explained here, along with a real whale skeleton. In addition to the world of plants, sea life and animals, exhibits feature the Micmacs, with examples of items made and decorated with dyed porcupine quills. The museum is open all year. From June through mid-October hours are Monday through Saturday, 9 am to 5:30 pm; Sunday, 1 to 5:30 pm; and Wednesday until 8 pm. From mid-October through May they are open Tuesday through Saturday, 9:30 to 5 pm; Sunday, 1 to 7 pm; and Wednesday until 8 pm. Admission is $3; $6.50 for a family. It's free Wednesday nights from 5:30 to 8 pm.

Point Pleasant Park is on the tip of the peninsula south of downtown. Originally part of the defenses of the city, it has one of the few Martello towers in North America. The park is open all year and the tower can be toured daily during July and August from 10 am to 6 pm. There is an admission charge.

Where To Stay & Eat

In Halifax

Hotel Halifax is a modern full-service hotel right in the midst of all of the major downtown activities. The city and provincial information offices are a just a few blocks away, as is the historic waterfront restoration and museums. The hotel is connected to a major indoor shopping mall. All of the rooms have been recently refurbished and are large and well furnished. They get high marks from us for the friendly and knowledgeable front desk staff who are always ready to help (it's another place we arrived dripping like drowned rats – we seem to make a habit of it). They have a large heated indoor pool, a big whirlpool, and an exercise room with saunas. *1990 Barrington St, Halifax, NS B3J 1P2, ☎ 800/441-1414 or 902/425-6700, fax 902/425-6214 ($$-$$$).*

Lord Nelson Hotel was probably the finest hotel in town when built. It has a stunning lobby, but the ornate dining room and other common rooms are now gone. The rooms are plain but comfortable and, for the city, are reasonably priced. *South Park St, PO Box 700, Halifax, NS B3J 2T3, ☎ 800/565-2020 or 902/423-6331 ($$).*

Halliburton House Inn is an upscale option with the quiet feeling of a private home. Placed in a series of three historic row houses, the inn has a sitting room for guests and a first-class restaurant. The rooms are individually decorated with antiques and fine reproductions. There is ample free parking for guests. It's also handy to the restaurants of Spring Garden Street. *5184 Morris St, Halifax, NS B3J 1B3, ☎ 902/420-0658, fax 902/423-2324 ($$-$$$).*

The **Waverly Inn** is a large Victorian mansion where Oscar Wilde once stayed. It has a lot of excesses of the Victorian age and the furniture is generally true to the period. They have free parking for guests. *1266 Barrington St, Halifax, NS B3J 1Y5, ☎ 800/565-9346 in the Maritimes, 902/423-9346, fax 902/425-0167 ($$).*

The Garden Inn is a guest house near the University with pleasant comfortable rooms and free parking. Breakfast does not come with the room but can be found close by. *1263 South Park St, Halifax, NS B3J 2K8, ☎ 800/565-0000 or 902/492-8577 ($-$$).*

Queen Street Inn Tourist Home is in a small Victorian home with an engaging host. It has one of the most astounding collections of Canadian art outside of a museum. The cozy, comfortable rooms are nicely furnished with antiques. *1266 Queen St, Halifax, NS B3J 2H4, ☎ 902/422-9828 ($$).*

Across the harbor, a 10-minute walk from the Halifax ferry, is **Stearns Mansion**, with five beautiful rooms furnished in Victorian antiques. Two rooms (at a higher rate) have large Jacuzzis. Rates include a four-course breakfast. *17 Tulip St, Dartmouth, NS B3A 2S5, ☎ 902/465-7414, fax 902/466-8832 ($$).*

Inexpensive city lodging is at **Heritage House Hostel**, where there are group, private and family rooms that have undergone a renewal in recent years. Shared baths. *1253 Barrington St, Halifax, NS B3J 1Y2, ☎/fax 902/422-3863.*

Historic Properties has converted an old warehouse originally built to hold goods taken from American ships by privateers during the war of 1812. It now features three restaurants, the elegance and price rising with the floor. **Upper Deck Restaurant**, ☎ 902/422-1501 ($$), on the top floor, serves a menu with an emphasis on seafood dishes but offers a good selection of other items. The large room is nicely divided into smaller dining areas. Dishes are well prepared and beautifully served by a knowledgeable staff. On the second floor, the **Middle Deck Pasta Works**, ☎ 902/425-

1500 ($-$$), specializes in pasta dishes and is a good choice for family dining at lower prices. They also have steaks and seafood. On the first floor, the **Lower Deck Good Time Pub**, ☎ 902/422-1289 ($), serves pub food like burgers, sandwiches or fish & chips. It's also the place for maritime music, and on weekends it can be crowded and noisy. There is a $3 cover charge for the music on Wednesday through Sunday nights. *Upper Water Street, on the waterfront.*

Sweet Basil Bistro is a trattoria serving nouvelle Italian cuisine. Pasta dishes are varied, with a lot of local seafood influences. The service is good, and the atmosphere is casual and romantic. *1866 Upper Water Street, ☎ 902/425-2133 ($-$$).*

Salty's on the Waterfront has dining rooms on the first and second floors, with views over the harbor. Casual and light meals are served on the first floor, which has an outdoor deck. The second floor offers more formal dining. They specialize in seafood. *1869 Lower Water Street, ☎ 902/423-6818 ($$-$$$).*

McKelvie's offers many seafood dishes, with quite a few prepared other ways than fried. There is a good selection of alternatives for non-seafood lovers, too. The menu has a welcome international touch. *1680 Lower Water Street, ☎ 902/421-6161.*

Haliburton House, at the inn of the same name, is one of Halifax's most popular fine-dining restaurants. The small, intimate dining room has a nice offering of well-prepared entrées, and is especially noted for its game dishes. The menu changes frequently and always has one or more hard-to-find specialties. *5184 Morris Street, ☎ 902/420-0658 ($$-$$$).*

Il Mercato is a pasta and pizza restaurant with a contemporary country Italian atmosphere. They have many interesting pasta offerings, and the focaccia and pizzas are out of the ordinary. *5475 Spring Garden Road, ☎ 902/422-2866 ($-$$).*

Paloma, off Spring Garden, serves tapas, paella Valenciana, shrimp dishes, braised rabbit, Basque beef stew, Mediterranean bouillabaisse and other dishes, all well prepared and perfectly seasoned. The small, intimate dining room features live Spanish guitar music on weekends. *1463 Brenton Street, ☎ 902/429-2425 ($-$$).*

Granite Brewery brews three ales of their own and serves British ales as well. The menu is pub fare, with sandwiches, burgers and steaks predominating. They also have a smoked salmon club, beef and beer stew, jambalaya, peppercorn chicken and a number of other entrées. *1222 Barrington Street, ☎ 902/423-5660 ($).*

La Perla is on the second floor and is one of the favorites in the city. They serve a nice selection of northern Italian dishes in a townhouse atmosphere. There is parking in a lot around the corner on a side street, but it's easier and more fun to take the short ferry ride across the harbor. Just make sure that you don't miss the last ferry back. *Wyse Road, Dartmouth, opposite the Ferry Terminal, ☎ 902/469-4231 ($$-$$$).*

MacAskill's Restaurant makes a nice outing from the city. Eat on the patio in summer or in the dining room; from either you get great views back across the harbor to Halifax glittering in the night sky and reflected in the water. Seafood is nicely prepared, as are steaks and pasta. Take the ferry and leave the driving to them. *88 Alderney Drive, Dartmouth Ferry Terminal Building, Dartmouth, ☎ 902/466-3100 ($$).*

Outside Halifax

The Inn On The Lake is more like a small resort on Lake Thomas, with big comfortable rooms that are quiet even on very busy weekends. It's just minutes from the airport and they will pick you up or take you to the airport so you can turn in your car early. The staff couldn't be more helpful or genuinely interested in your welfare. In addition to their standard rooms, they have suites, some with kitchenettes, fireplaces or whirlpool baths. facilities include tennis, shuffleboard, swimming and boating. They also have a good restaurant (where they are very nice about serving people arriving late from the airport). Don't miss the cedar-planked salmon. *PO Box 29, Waverley, NS, B0N 2S0, ☎ 800/463-6465 or 902/861-3480, fax 902/861-4883 ($$).*

Prospect Bed & Breakfast was once a convent, but what the good sisters left behind is now a comfortable, beautifully decorated B&B. The shingled and turreted inn is right on a bay, perfect for canoeing or kayaking, and is close to walking trails along the deserted seacoast. All rooms have private bath. Rates are on the low side of moderate for attractive, bright rooms with the best beds. A home-baked continental breakfast is included. Ask if room 5, in the turret, is available. They can set you up with boat tours, water-skiing or deep-sea fishing, or provide a picnic lunch to be enjoyed on a private island. Guests can also arrange for an evening meal here; the specialty is grilled salmon. *Box 68, Prospect Village, NS B0J 2V0, ☎ 800/SALTSEA or 902/852-4492 ($$).*

Havenside Bed & Breakfast is in a new building close to the water's edge. Guests have complimentary use of a canoe and can indulge in a big breakfast after a morning paddle. All rooms have bath en suite and there is a game room with a pool table, a sitting room with fireplace and a deck for enjoying the water. Havenside is off Rte. 333, six miles north of Peggy's Cove. *225 Boutilier's Cove Road, Hackett's Cove, NS B0J 3J0, ☎ 800/641-8272 or 902/823-9322; e-mail webbk@atcon.com ($$).*

Sprucehaven Bed & Breakfast has two guest rooms, each with private bath, and serves a hearty continental breakfast and an evening tea and snack. They also have a library, which guests may use. *5397 Rte. 289, RR #2 Upper Shubenacadie, NS B0N 2P0, ☎ 902/671-2462 ($).*

The Palliser Hotel is right along the Salmon River and the Tidal Bore. The motel-style accommodation has clean and comfortable rooms. On the grounds is a tidal bore interpretation center, and the river is floodlit at night for viewing. Room rates include a buffet breakfast. The dining room serves chicken, lamb, steak and seafood dishes as well as sandwiches. Guests receive a 15% discount on meals. *Tidal Bore Road, PO Box 821, Truro, NS B2N 5G6, ☎ 902/893-8951 ($).*

The Silver Firs Bed & Breakfast is a gracious inn in an 80-year-old home. There are four air-conditioned rooms, all with private bath. Guests have the use of a paneled library. A full breakfast is served in the dining room or on the veranda overlooking the rose garden. At Exit 14 on Rte. 102 (Rte. 236) take Robie Street and watch for Prince Street on the right after the cemetery. Just after Longworth Street the B&B will be on the left. *397 Prince Street, Truro, NS B2N 1E6, ☎ 902/897-1900 or 902/893-0570 ($$-$$$).*

White Sails Bakery is in Tantallon, north of Peggy's Cove, along the west shore of St. Margaret's Bay. It's a good place for a pastry stop or to break for lunch. They have a nice array of fresh-baked pastries and breads and a selection of sandwiches to eat there or take out for a picnic. Closed Monday and Tuesday. *12930 Peggy's Cove Road (Rte. 333), Tantallon, ☎ 902/826-1966.*

Golda's Café & Tea Room, along the road to Peggy's Cove, is a bright, upbeat little tea room that's a nice stop for breakfast, lunch or dinner. The affable hostess, probably Golda's daughter, will whip you up a bowl of chowder, a lobster roll or a sandwich. The decor is a quirky mixed retro; the food is top notch. *816 Prospect Road (Rte. 333), Goodwood, ☎ 902/876-1264.*

■ Camping

Shubie Park, run by the City of Dartmouth, has a campground near a lake. It's on Jaybee Dr, off Rte. 318, and has pay showers, washrooms, laundromat and a canteen, plus supervised swimming. The park season is mid-May to September. *Box 817, Dartmouth, NS B2Y 3Z3, ☎ 902/435-8328. Off-season, call ☎ 902/464-2121.*

Juniper Park, near Exit 4 on Highway 103, has wooded and open campsites on a lake. They have washrooms and pay showers. Swimming is available in the lake. Open June through mid-September. *Box 6, Site 15, RR 3, Armdale, NS B3L 4J3, ☎ 902/876-2814.*

Woodhaven Park has about 200 wooded and open sites for RVs and tents, most serviced. Its location makes it a good jumping off place for forays into the city, Peggy's Cove area or along the south coast. It has pay showers, washrooms and a laundromat. Amenities include a pool and a recreation hall. Open May through October. *Hammond Plains Road, Rte. 213, Hammonds Plains. Mail to 70 Lorne Avenue Dartmouth, NS B2Y 3E7, ☎ 902/835-2271, fax 835-0019.*

Marine Drive & The East

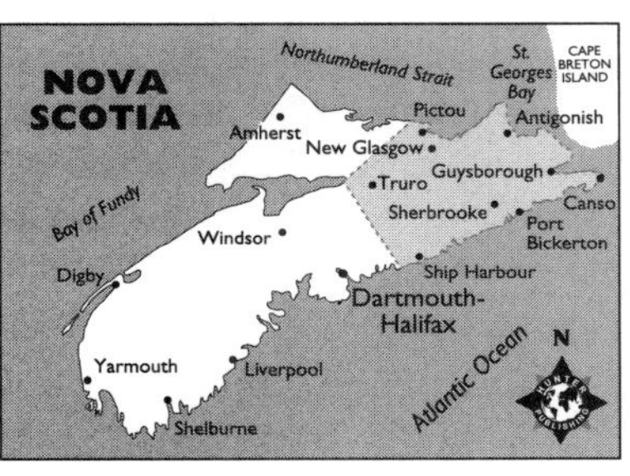

Although the north shore is well known as the Scottish heart of Nova Scotia, with its famous Highland festivals, the southern shore, called The Marine Drive, is nearly always bypassed by travelers returning from Cape Breton Island, in favor of the faster TransCanada 104 directly to Truro. They miss a great deal: a rocky coastline with some very fine – and uncrowded – white beaches, good kayaking waters, and a fascinating restored village from the last century, a museum in which people actually live.

Geography & History

The southern shore east of Halifax is called, for tourism purposes, The Marine Drive, and it wanders along a shoreline so irregular and cut with estuaries that one of them must be crossed on a ferry and another requires a long inland swing to bypass it. At the far end of the region is the long Cape Canso, not to be confused with the canso Causeway, to its northwest, leading to Cape Breton Island.

There are three major population centers along the eastern north coast, Pictou, New Glasgow and Antigonish, all of which have a decided Scottish flavor. When Britain acquired the land from the French, it granted thousands of acres to companies in the colonies that later became the United States, in order to establish English dominance rapidly. One of the earliest towns, Pictou, was first settled by six immigrant families from Philadelphia in 1767, but quickly took on a highland flavor when they were joined in 1773 by 200 Scots, who arrived on the *Hector*, a replica of which is being built in the museum on the harbor. Pictou became the entry port for Scots who fanned out into other communities inch. The incentive to emigrate for the Scottish farmers was free passage, a farm of their own and provisions for a year.

Along the coastal area of this section you will find many small villages whose residents are engaged in fishing. Small inland towns are farming and lumbering communities, often widely separated in the heavily wooded and unsettled interior.

Getting Around

From New Brunswick, **TransCanada-104** will take you through the northern part of this area, all the way to the Canso Causeway. The northeast end of Marine Drive begins on Rte. 344 at the causeway. From Halifax take Rte. 102 to Truro for the northern part and to get to the Marine Drive from Halifax take the MacDonald Bridge to Dartmouth and at Victoria Street follow the signs for Marine Drive.

Information Sources

- Information on the area is available from the **Nova Scotia Tourist Office,** junction of Rte. 6 and Rte. 106 in Pictou, just off the rotary, open daily 8 am to 8 pm from mid-May to mid-Oct. On TransCanada-104, **Pictou County Tourist Association**, 980 East Rivere Rd, New Glasgow B2H 3S5, ☎ 902/755-5180, fax 902/775-2848, has an information cabin 18 miles south of town, open 8 am to 8 pm daily in summer.

- In Antigonish, the **Nova Scotia Tourist Office** is open July and August from 8 am to 8 pm in summer, and 8 am to 5 pm in June and September. They are at 56 West St., Antigonish, ☎ 800/565-0000 or 902/863-4921, Exit 32 off Rte. 104.

- The **Antigonish/Eastern Shore Tourist Association** has information on the eastern north shore and Marine Drive. Contact them at Musquodoboit Harbour, NS B0J 2L0, ☎ 902/889-2362, fax 902/889-2101.

- Additional information on the Marine Drive area can be obtained from the **Tourist Bureau**, Whitman House, 1297 Union St., Canso, NS B0H 1H0, ☎ 902/366-2170. It's open daily from late May to September, 9 am to 6 pm. The

Guysborough County Tourism office, PO Box 49, Guysborough, NS B0H 1N0, ☎ 902/533-3731 also provides information on this area.

■ On the west end of the Marine Drive, the **Musquodoboit Railway Museum and Tourist Information Center**, Rte. 7, PO Box 303, Musquodoboit Harbour, NS B0J 2L0, ☎ (902) 889-2689, has full tourist information services and is open daily, 9 am to 5 pm, during July and August; in June and September hours are 9 am to 4 pm.

Adventures

■ On Foot

Hiking

West of Antigonish a rough back country road leads to the trail for **Cutie's Hollow Falls**, on the James River. This attractive site is a series of three wide falls that drop like a veil from one level to the other, a distance of over 50 feet. The hike is difficult, through a number of wet areas and with one ford of the James River, but the hike is a nice one with a real reward at the end of the trail. The trail is about 1½ miles, the last part beginning shortly after the ford and up a steep slope, along the top of a high embankment and then down a marked trail to the river bed and the falls. The trail is used by all-terrain vehicles and is therefore easy to follow. From TransCanada-104 near the Pictou-Antigonish county line at Marshy Hope, follow a rough, marked road north just under four miles to a collection of woods camps. Follow the trail on the right side of the road.

Just over a mile south of Guysborough on Rte. 16, take Rte. 401 and immediately on the right after the road to Roachvale will be a parking lot for the **Guysborough Nature Trail**, a 2¼-mile hiking and nature trail along the gravel bed of a former railroad line. This will be part of the TransCanada Trail and is a project of the Guysborough County Trails Association. It wends its way through spruce and fir woods and across varied terrain. There are two look-off points with views over Cooks Cove. At its south end the trail again intersects Rte. 401 and you have the option of retracing your steps or following Rte. 401 back to the parking lot.

At Canso, off of Rte. 16, the **Chapel Gully Trail** is a wonderful mix of natural and historic points. It passes through woodland, over tidal flats and rocks, across a bog and even includes places to swim and picnic. The length of the trail is about 6¼ miles over forest trails, rocks, raised boardwalks and across a wooden footbridge over Chapel Gully, a long narrow sea inlet. The area abounds with wildlife that includes moose, deer and mink, which might be seen or heard playing around the water's edge. An excellent pamphlet with a map and detailed trail and wildlife descriptions is available from the Eastern Tip Trails Association, Attn. Harry Dollard, PO Box 235, Canso B0H 1H0, ☎ 902/366-2311.

Also in the Canso area is **Black Duck Cove Day Use Park**, with a trail system of just over two miles. Take Rte. 16 toward Canso but take the right hand turn to Little Dover, a small fishing village, and follow the signs through the town to the park on the far side. A combination of gravel paths and boardwalks circle the peninsula between Black Duck Cove and Dover Harbour. Start by taking the boardwalk past the beach along the **Coastal Trail** around the point, where you will find great sheets of flat rocks sliding out into the water. The trail then follows along the harbor, eventually ending back at the parking area. **Bluff Point Trail** is a cut-back trail that allows you to avoid the point and the **Keefe Point Trail** is a shortcut back to the parking lot. There is also a nice sandy beach with changing facilities, and a canteen with a craft shop. The trails are open for use during the off-season.

On Rte. 7 at Liscomb Mills, watch for the bridge over the Liscomb River. There is a nice small waterfall there, really more a series of cascades at the point where the river becomes tidal. On the east side of the river, look for a sign for the **Liscomb Hiking Trails**. The peninsula was once a busy place, with a sawmill, shops and homes, none of which remain, all reclaimed by the forest. There are several trails with varying terrain covering the Mayflower Peninsula but they are all moderately difficult because of the steep and uneven land. Wear hiking boots, especially if you take the trail to the right along the banks of the Liscomb River.

A long peninsula on Mushaboom Harbor leads to Taylor Head at the village of Spry Bay, where you'll find **Taylor Head Provincial Park**, on Rte. 7 between Mushaboom and Spry Harbour. This is an area of opposing syncline and anticline geological pressures that formed and continue to form the area. Interpretive signs describe these features and the interactive effects of the sea and the land upon the plant and animal life of the intertidal zone of the park. The park has four hiking trails along the beaches and salt marshes. From the parking lot the **Spry Bay Trail** (about 2½ miles) is a loop that circles the central part of the peninsula and the shore of Spry Bay. Part of this loop, the **Headland Trail** (about five miles) circles the peninsula along the shore to Taylor Head, returning along the shore of Spry Bay to rejoin the Spry Bay Trail. The **Bob Bluff Trail** (about two miles) is an out-and-back wooded trail along the shore of Pyches Cove, with occasional views of Mushaboom Harbour to a bluff. Beyond the bluff the trail continues as **Bull Beach Trail,** past Ranger Bluff and along Mushaboom Harbour. The **Beach Walk Trail** (about 1¼ miles), a walk along a barrier beach, starts at Pyches Cove and heads in the opposite direction. A white sand beach, picnic facilities and a full-service canteen on the dunes make this a nice place for an afternoon outing.

Between Ship Harbour and Jeddore Oyster Ponds is a loop road that goes around the Clam Harbour peninsula. Just west of Clam Harbour take the short road to **Clam Harbour Beach**. The trail, an easy 2½-mile return trip, is a pleasant walk along small beaches and over coastal rocks in an area that is a refuge and wintering place for Canada geese and golden eye and black ducks. The wild roses bloom profusely in the spring and wild iris are here all summer. The background is a white spruce and balsam forest with a few hardwoods.

At Musquodoboit Harbour is a long road along the peninsula to **Martinique Beach Provincial Park**, a beautiful beach on the seldom traveled shore east of Halifax. There are good swimming and picnic facilities and a bird sanctuary. For freshwater swimming stay on Rte. 7 to **Porter's Lake Provincial Park**, West Porter's Lake Rd, Porter's Lake, ☎ 902/827-2250, where there is also a picnic area.

Hiking Outfitters & Guided Tours

■ **Camtech** operates Riverview Nature Tours along the beautiful St. Mary's River. They are located at the Sherbrooke Tourist Center, Sherbrooke, B0J 3C0, ☎ 902/522-2192, fax 902/522-2435.

■ **Turnstone Nature Tours** is an outfitter that runs hiking trips in the north shore, Marine Drive and Cape Breton (PO Box 974, Antigonish, NS B2G 2S3, ☎ 902/863-8341 or 902/386-2884, e-mail tnt@grassroots.ns.ca, Web site www.grassroots.ns.ca/~tnt). Their five-day land and sea tour starts at Halifax airport, visits Taylor Head Provincial Park, Sherbrooke and the St. Mary's River before heading across the wilderness of the interior to Antigonish. After exploring St. George's Bay and Pomquet village, the tour moves on to Cape Breton Island. Turnstone also has one- or two-day guided tours to the rock-bound headlands of Cape St. George, where fossils are found and where there is a nice beach. Half-day trips examine a pond with an active beaver lodge, visit a white gypsum cliff to examine a cormorant colony, and a barrier beach (called a *barachois*) to see herons, gannets, terns and perhaps even a bald eagle. Special tours can also be arranged. The company is owned by trained naturalists who have extensive knowledge of the flora, fauna and geology of the province. Their rates start at $15 adult, $10 child and they also have family rates.

■ On Wheels

The area surrounding Pictou is good for bicycling, and tours are operated by the **Pictou County Cycling Club**, PO Box 254, Pictou, NS B0K 1S0, ☎ 902/755-2704 or 752-8904. Visitors are invited to join them. The club season is from May to October and they have a number of tours, including overnight jaunts, on a regularly scheduled basis throughout the season. Their tours always have designated lead and sweep riders.

Velo Halifax Bicycle Club, PO Box 125, Dartmouth B2Y 3Y2, ☎ 902/423-4345, also does periodic trips in this area.

The St. Mary's River area around Sherbrooke is fairly level and provides some enjoyable touring. **Camtech**, ☎ 902/522-2192, fax 902/522-2435, on the main street of town just outside the secondary entrance to the museum village, has bike rentals for $5 an hour or $25 per day and they have kid's bikes, bike trailers, helmets and water bottles. They can supply you with maps and advise.

■ On Water

On The Beach

On the North Shore, **Caribou Provincial Park**, which also has a campground, has a large beach. From here you can watch the Prince Edward Island ferry come and go. It's off Rte. 6 northwest of Pictou. North of New Glasgow on Rte. 348 there is swimming at Powells Point Provincial Park, and a bit further on is the large and very popular Melmerby Beach Provincial Park, which has full facilities including canteen and supervised swimming. Pomquet and Bayfield Provincial Parks, north of TransCanada-104 at exits 35 and 36 respectively, both have supervised swimming on St. George's Bay.

There are several good beaches along the Marine Drive, the first at **Port Shoreham Provincial Park**, off Rte. 344 east of Guysborough. Just beyond the village of St. Francis Harbour, the park has a nice swimming beach and picnic tables, with a view across the bay toward Guysborough and the Canso peninsula. On the Canso Peninsula, **Black Duck Day Use Provincial Park** has an attractive beach, as does **Tor Bay Provincial Park** on Rte. 316. There are other beaches at **Marie Joseph**, and at **Spry Bay** and **Taylor Head**, both mentioned in the *On Foot* section. **Clam Harbour**, also mentioned there, and **Martinique Beach** on Musquodoboit Harbour have nice sandy beaches.

For freshwater swimming go to **Porter Lake Provincial Park** or the nearby **Lawrencetown** and **Rainbow Haven** beaches. Swimming at all of these sites is unsupervised, but all have changing rooms and most also have a canteen. The waters along this shore are warm in the summer because of the proximity of the Gulf Stream and the water tends to be warmer than beaches along the northeast United States.

Canoeing & Kayaking

One doesn't usually think of a canoe as a way to get to a waterfall, but **Carding Mill Brook Falls** may be reached only by water. Country Harbour is a long narrow inlet of the sea between Port Bickerton and Isaac's Harbour North on Rte. 211. A ferry carries the Rte. 211 traffic across the harbor. Park on the west side of the ferry. You'll be able to put in at the ferry landing. Paddle north along the west side of the harbor past the mussel farm (that's what those blue barrels are) for about a half-hour and you'll come to the outlet of brook just past a small peninsula that juts out into the water. Look for a path along the shore of the brook and beach your canoe, following the path upstream to the falls. The falls, actually a fast cascade, is fed by the overflow from a boggy area above. The whole of Country Harbour is over nine miles long and is a beautiful protected area for canoeing or kayaking. Rte. 316 parallels it on the east side and on the west there is nothing from its mouth at the ocean on the south to the end of the harbor in the north. When parking, pull well off the road and make sure that you don't block or impede the places needed for the ferry.

The eastern shore has a number of inlets and harbours that are great places for sea kayaking. The long harbor at **Guysborough** off of Chedabucto Bay offers protected paddling. On the Canso peninsula **Dover Harbour** and the harbor off Rte. 316 at **Whitehead** are also nice. Farther west along the coast, Country Harbour, mentioned above, and the St. Mary's River are nice long estuary trips. Off of **Liscomb** and **Marie Joseph** are nice harbors with islands. The section between **Spry Bay and Lawrencetown** is a warren of long inlets and off-shore islands that includes **Spry Bay, Tangier, Ship Harbour, Clam Harbour, Jeddore Bay, Musquodoboit Harbour** and **Chezzetcook Harbour**. As with all kayaking, these should only be done with the proper equipment and always with at least one companion. You should also be careful to watch the weather, because it can change rapidly along this open Atlantic coast. With these cautions in mind, there are miles of wild shoreline and unsettled islands there to explore.

Canoe & Kayak Outfitters

■ **Turnstone Nature Tours**, an outfitter from Antigonish, deals primarily with hiking and nature tours but will arrange guided canoe trips on request. Although they are in Antigonish, they can set up trips in any of several areas along the north shore, on the Marine Drive or on the inland lakes. Contact them at PO Box 974, Antigonish, NS B2G 2S3, ☎ 902/863-8341 or 902/386-2884, e-mail tnt@grassroots.ns.ca, Web site www.grassroots.ns.ca/~tnt.

■ **Coastal Adventures**, PO Box 77, Mason's Point Road, Tangier, NS B0J 3H0, ☎/fax 902/772-2774, is the outfitting company of Scott Cunningham, recognized in Europe and throughout North America as a leading expert and proponent of kayaking. Scott's books on kayaking define the sport in the province. Guided half- and full-day trips, as well as longer multi-day expeditions are available and novices are welcome. They offer trips among the neighboring islands and longer expeditions to locations in Cape Breton and other places in Atlantic Canada. They also offer introductory and advanced sea kayaking lessons, including eskimo rolling and kayak handling techniques. The introductory lessons are given each Saturday, Sunday and holiday from mid-April through October, 9:30 am to 5 pm, for under $80 per person. Canoe rentals are $25 for four hours, $35 a day, $50 per weekend, or $175 per week.

Single kayak rentals are the same as canoes for half- and full-day, and $60 and $195 for weekend and weekly rentals. Doubles are also available for slightly higher rates. On the next to last weekend in June they host the annual Atlantic Canada Sea Kayakers Meeting.

■ Along the Marine Drive one of the prettiest places to canoe or kayak is the St. Mary's River near Sherbrooke. From the sea to Sherbrooke are more than 12 miles of waterway along the shores of the wide tidal river. Canoe and kayak rentals are available from **Camtech**, ☎ 902/522-2192, fax 902/522-2435, on the main street of town just outside secondary museum entrance. Rates for canoes and kayaks are $6 an hour or $35 per day.

Harbor Cruises

Carefree Cruises, c/o Gregg MacDonald, RR #1, Pictou, NS B0K 1H0, ☎ 902/485-6205, operates daily cruises of the Northumberland Strait, Pictou Harbour and Pictou Island during July and August. They also do a Scottish historic tour and by charter will do fishing trips and evening cruises. Check with them if you want to go out in June or September; they do offer cruises then but the schedule varies. The boat leaves from the Caribou Ferry wharf, five miles from Pictou; follow the signs for the PEI Ferry.

Jiggs & Reels Boat Tours, RR #1, Merigomish, NS B0K 1G0, ☎ 902/396-8855, runs a tour of Pictou Harbour and of the Northumberland Strait from the New Glasgow waterfront daily, July through late September, on a certified 32-foot boat. The Captain's name is Angus MacDonald – how much more Scottish can you get? There is a guided tour of the area, colorful commentary, sightseeing and Scottish music, which is occasionally live. The three-hour tours are from 9 am to noon, 1 to 4 pm and 5 to 8 pm, with a maximum of 18 people per tour. Make sure to reserve your space.

Fishing

If you have your own boat the coast along the North Shore and Marine Drive is full of fishing opportunities. The predominant fish along these shores and bays is mackerel but you will find others as well. On the north shore, **Merigomish Harbour** is a large protected bay where you are likely to find mackerel and rainbow smelt. St. George's Bay offers some of the best fishing territory and the broadest range of fish. The great trophy fish, the bluefin tuna, is caught here in record sizes. Mackerel, of course, are found in most places and dogfish are also found all along the shore. In Antigonish Harbour rainbow smelt are found near the outlet of the South River and they can also be found in the Canso Strait at Auld's Cove and Medford. Rainbow smelt can be found at St. Francis Harbour on the outlet of the Goose Harbour River, Guysbrough Harbour, the St. Mary's River, Jeddore Harbour, Musquodoboit Harbour, Chezzetcook Bay and Lawrencetown Bay. For ground fish try the areas off Cape Canso, the inlet of St. Mary's River, the waters of Clam Harbour and Little Harbour areas and Jeddore and Chezzetcook Inlets. Striped Bas can be found at Antigonish Harbour, off Bayfield and at Chezzetcook Inlet.

Cultural & Eco-Travel Experiences

Festivals

Things Scottish are one of the reasons for being in this part of the province, and there is nothing more Scottish than the **Highland Games at Antigonish**, held every summer since 1863. Clan gatherings, Celtic workshops, ceilidhs (informal gatherings for Celtic music and dance), concerts, youth competitions, and many other events are held at Columbus Field in town. Competitions include the classic hammer throw, broad-jumping, caber tossing, foot races and the more recreational highland dancing, while pipe bands march and skirl between events. For a finale, pipe bands with hundreds of pipers mass for one last joyful celebration of Scottish heritage. For details call or write the Antigonish Highland Society, 274 Main St., Antigonish, NS B2G 2C4, ☎ 902/863-4275.

During the months of July and August **Festival Antigonish**, ☎ 902/867-3954 or 800/563-7529, presents professional theater, drama, musicals, revues and children's theater at the Bauer Theatre on the campus of St. Francis Xavier University. Call for the schedule of this long-running summer arts festival.

Local Culture

The centerpiece of Pictou is the **Hector Heritage Quay**, 29-33 Caladh Ave., ☎ 902/485-8028. The quay marks the beginning of Pictou as a major port and of Scottish influence in the province. A 2,000-square-foot interpretation center tells the story of the migration of Scots, beginning on the battlefield of Culloden Moor, that carries them through their arduous 10-week voyage to arrival in Pictou. The scenes, exhibits and dioramas engage all the senses. Outside, a fully-equipped 18th-century shipyard is busily engaged in constructing a faithful replica of the *Hector*. You can visit the woodworking and blacksmith shops, talk to the craftsmen and watch the making of history. In mid-August the Hector Festival provides a joyous five-day celebration of Scottish heritage.

Micmac Country Craft Shop, Greenhill, ☎ 902/396-3844, is right off TransCanada 104, five miles west of New Glasgow. This shop is a chance to encounter the Micmacs (also spelled Mi'kmaq, and several other ways) and their handmade crafts. In addition to the expected moccasins, miniature birch bark canoes and T-shirts, you'll also find handsome woven split wood baskets and fine example of quill work, a traditional craft made from dyed porcupine quills.

J. Willy Krauch & Sons Smokehouse, off Rte. 7 in Tangier (look for the signs), smokes salmon, eel and mackerel the old-fashioned way, with a recipe and technique brought from Denmark. The fish are delicately flavored, yet when finished are not fully cooked. They supply the British Royal Family. If they're not too busy, they are happy to show guests through the brining and smoking process. ☎ 800/758-4412 or 902/772-2188, fax 902/299-9414.

Mulgrave Road Theatre, 68 Main Street, Guysborough, ☎ 902/533-2092, features a professional touring company of long standing in the area. It performs here on a varying schedule and also appears elsewhere in the province. Call for current productions and performance schedules.

The Fisherman's Life Museum, Jeddore Oyster Ponds, ☎ 902/889-2053, is just off Rte. 7. Onshore fishing was an important part of life along this coast for more than a century, and thousands of families were engaged in the trade. The simple lives of these hardy, proud people are captured at this museum, which preserves the home and workplace of one such family. You first see the fishing shack and dock with the dories tied alongside, the inside full of tools, nets, tubs and gadgets used by the fisherman. On a knoll across the street is the simple cottage where the family lived, in this case the same family for the entire time of its occupancy. Furnished as it was decades ago, it is a fitting tribute to their determination and hard work. The museum is open June to mid-October Mondays through Saturdays, 9:30 am to 5:30 pm, and from 1:30 pm on Sundays.

Wildlife & Natural Areas

North of Sherbrooke off of Rte. 7, the small town of Goshen has taken over an abandoned private hunting preserve and established the **Goshen Leisure Park**, ☎ 902/783-2571, Web site www.grassroots.ns.ca/guys/guyswel.htm. It is actually a wildlife park full of wild and unusual animals and birds. Large naturalized cages hold skunks, porcupines, an entire fox family, and birds, including a bald eagle. Many of the animals have been brought here for rehabilitation. The eagle, for example, has a wing injury that will prevent his return to the wild. Part of the park is a petting zoo where children can see and touch animals and birds close up. This is a great walk in the country and a fine way to see some of the mammalian inhabitants that you probably wouldn't see otherwise. From Rte. 7, take Rte. 276 to Goshen, then follow Rte. 316 a short way to the park on the left side of the road.

WHAT'S UNDERFOOT

The geology of the northern and eastern part of the province is different from the southern region. By studying the rocks, geologists have learned that the northern section developed from a shallow and storm-tossed sea in the Ordovician period about 430 million years ago. Fossil remains, particularly in the Arisaig area and the Cobequid mountains, show that they were formed under a shallow sea, with enough sunlight and food to support a number of animal species in the seas. Examining the Ordovician rock in the southern sections, however, they find a sedimentary rock with few fossils, indicating a deep sea with little light or nutrients.

Continental plate movements have lifted and shifted rock of various periods, forming valleys that are actually faults between different ages of rock. The last ice age advanced and retreated several times before it melted, wearing away the softer tops of inland hills, which were made of newer sedimentary rock, leaving them flat on top, with the volcanic precambrian bedrock exposed or lying just beneath thin layers of glacial till.

The Old Hall Wilderness Heritage Centre, 4694 Rte. 7, Porter's Lake B0J 2S0, ☎ 902/827-2364. In an old community hall area residents have created an environmental study place, with exhibits on natural history, animals and the impact that man and his activities has on the natural world. A 60-square-foot relief model shows the unusual nature of the land, and other exhibits show the role of the lake as a shipping route and of the lumbering industry that once predominated here. A video program shows lumbering as it was once practiced.

Arisaig Provincial Park, Rte. 245, north of New Glasgow and Antigonish, has a one-mile interpretive trail describing the development of this part of the province. The rocks here were formed from silts laid down in a shallow sea 430 million years ago, when the land masses of the world were all close together. Rich in very early fossils, the area has been studied by scientists for over a century. Fossils found include brachiopods, clams, snails, trilobites, graphtolites, nautiloids and bryozoans. There is an excellent brochure on the park that discusses its geologic history and describes the fossils found there. There is also an access point to the beach.

Sightseeing

McCulloch House & Hector National Exhibit Centre and Archive on Old Halliburton Road in Pictou, ☎ 902/485-4563, is an archive and library for materials on the history and genealogy of the area. The historic 1806 McCulloch House has been restored, with original furniture and artifacts from the town's history. There is also an ornithology collection that Audubon cited as one of the best of its day.

Grohmann Knife Factory, 116 Water St., Pictou, ☎ 902/485-6775, is a German knife maker that started here in 1956 and now sells knives around the world. They make a complete line of kitchen knives for the homemaker and for the professional chef. There are also sport and pocket knives for hunting, fishing and general outdoor uses. Grohman has tours of their factory and an outlet store.

The **Carmichael-Stewart House Museum**, 86 Temperance Street, New Glasgow, ☎ 902/752-5583, was built by the town's founder, James Carmichael, as a wedding present for his son. In 1810 he opened a general store and later began a shipbuilding business. The house is an imposing Victorian with cut shingle work on its tower and a matching band between the first and second floor. Inside, the home contains fine examples of period stained glass and some of the original family furnishings. It also serves as the home of the Pictou County Historical Society, whose collections focus on the shipbuilding and coal mining industries that prospered here. During the summer the museum hosts Victorian teas with costumed docents in the mansion's gardens. From June through August it's open Monday through Friday, 9 am to 4:30 pm, and Saturday, 1 to 4:30 pm.

Nearby, and accessible by a path through Peace Park across from Carmichael House, is the **New Glasgow Firefighters Museum**, opened in 1993 and containing equipment and vehicles from the town's first horse-drawn steam pumper (1877) to a 1917 chain-driven American LaFrance pumper. The museum is in a glassed-in building behind the library, off Archimedes Street. Take Exit 25 north from TransCanada 104. You will be on Rte. 348, East River Road, which becomes Archimedes Street. The museum is about two miles from the highway.

The Crombie House, Abercrombie St., New Glasgow, ☎ 902/755-4440, is an art gallery that features works mainly by Canadian artists. It houses the Sobey Art Foundation collections, including works of the Group of Seven and those of many contemporaries of the Group. Unfortunately the museum is open only on Wednesdays during July and August, 9 am to noon and 1 to 4 pm.

The Nova Scotia Museum of Industry, Foord Street, Stellarton, ☎ 902/755-5425, fax 902/755-7075, is off Exit 24 of Trans-Canada 104. On the site of the former Foord coal mines, this is the largest museum in the province and it tells the story of the impact of industrialization on the people of Nova Scotia. In the museum are the *Samson* and the *Albion*, the two oldest locomotives in Canada and among the oldest in the world. This is a place for adults and kids to get a feel for the burst of creative energy that followed the harnessing of water and steam power and the invention of modern manufacturing techniques. The Museum is open all year.

Grassy Island National Historic Site, Visitor Centre, Whitman House Museum, 1297 Union St., Canso, ☎ 902/366-2170. Situated on an island offshore, Grassy Island was the site of one of the earliest settlements, a fishing station, now returned to nature. It is accessible by boat, and you can obtain schedules and make arrangements at the Visitor Centre. While there, watch the video program about the village, see the diorama and examine artifacts found during excavations. An interpretive trail runs around the island itself. The site is open daily, 9 am to 6 pm, from June to September. No admission charge.

Nova Scotia Lighthouse Interpretive Centre, 640 Lighthouse Road, Port Bickerton, ☎ 902/364-2000, is less than five miles south of the Country Harbour cable ferry on Rte. 211. The old keeper's house of the Port Bickerton Light has been made into an interpretive center for all of the lighthouses in the province and tells of the roles they played and the lives the keepers led on these lonely outposts. The centre is at Lighthouse Beach Park and is open daily from the end of June to mid-October, 10 am to 8 pm. Admission is $2, or $5 for a family pass.

In the 1960s the province undertook the preservation of an entire way of life at **Sherbrooke Village**, Sherbrooke, ☎ 902/522-2400. Originally settled in the 1700s as a farming community, the town boomed in the 1860s when gold was discovered in the area. More gold was extracted here, in fact, than in the Klondike strike in Alaska. Within 50 years the mines closed and a long decline set in. Much of the architectural heritage of the boom period remained unchanged, and the museum was established in the 1960s to save it from destruction.

Almost all the old town was incorporated into the museum, an unusual combination of a living town mixed with buildings restored for museum purposes. Twenty of the buildings have been restored to their original purposes as homes, stores and tradesmen shops, and are open to the public, with the original trades demonstrated inside. The blacksmith is busy at his anvil and in the boat builder's shop a replica of an original river barge is being built the old way. In the old Sherbrooke Hotel, a restaurant now serves lunch and afternoon tea, featuring traditional Nova Scotia dishes as well as soups, sandwiches and salads.

A short distance away from the main town, and well worth seeing, is the MacDonald Brothers water-powered up and down sawmill and, across the street from it, a period lumbermen's camp on the shore of a pond. To get to the camp you will walk along the sawmill's hand-dug mill race, which was a prodigious task.

The mill at Sherbrooke.

The museum is open daily, June through mid-October, 9 am to 5:30 pm. Admission is $4 adults, $2 children, with a family maximum of $12. Admission is free at the MacDonald sawmill.

The information office at the museum's entrance is staffed with well-informed guides who can answer questions about the museum. They also have information on lodging, dining, attractions and activities in the area.

Musquodoboit Railway Museum and Tourist Information Center is an appropriate after-life for a Victorian station house. It is still serving travelers, but now as a visitor information center. The museum portion has a large collection of railroad memorabilia displayed in the restored waiting room, station master's offices and freight rooms. Outside you'll see passenger and freight cars. The museum is open daily, 9 am to 5 pm, during July and August; 9 am to 4 pm in June and September. Admission is free. They are on Rte. 7; contact them at PO Box 303, Musquodoboit Harbour, NS B0J 2L0, ☎ 902/889-2689.

Where To Stay & Eat

If you are traveling in the northern part of this area in the spring or during August, reserve lodging well in advance. The available rooms fill up during university graduation and the Highland Festival.

On the North Shore

The **Braeside Inn** is a stately older hotel, with comfortable, newly carpeted guest rooms. A family business operated by engaging and hospitable hosts, there is an ongoing program of renovation and upgrading here. Common rooms are attractive and inviting and display the hosts' personal collection of antiques. There is an excellent dining room, casual, but in an elegant setting, with rose-colored linens on tables that overlook the harbor through big bright windows. The menu is continental with many Nova Scotia specialties, including filet mignon, salmon, lamb and lobster. *126 Front St., Pictou, NS B0K 1H0, ☎ 902/485-5046 or 800/565-0000, fax 902/485-1701 ($$).*

The **Consulate Inn** was the US consulate at the end of the Civil War. Today there are rooms and housekeeping units in the charming old stone building and in an adjoining cottage. Attractive and comfortable, antique and classic furnishings are blended in an atmosphere that puts guests at ease. Rates include continental breakfast. *115 Water St., Pictou, NS B0K 1H0, ☎ 902/485-4554 ($-$$).*

Pictou Lodge Resort was built in the 1920s as a log cabin resort getaway for Canadian Pacific Railway executives. The rustic cabins, on a secluded section of seashore 2½ miles from the PEI Ferry landing, are homelike and comfortable, good for uncomplicated relaxation. The resort has a wide range of sport facilities and activities and there is excellent golfing nearby. The dining room in the main lodge ($-$$) serves a choice of well-prepared dishes with an emphasis on Nova Scotia specialties. The setting is in a large log baronial hunting lodge. *PO Box 1539, Pictou, NS B0K 1H0, ☎ 800/495-6343 or 902/485-4322, fax 902/485-4945 ($$).*

Walker Inn, on the upper floors of an 1865 townhouse, couldn't be more centrally located. It's only a few minutes' walk to the Hector reconstruction. All the rooms have been completely renovated and are beautifully furnished and quiet. The engaging young Swiss owners also serve a three-course dinner by reservation. *34 Coleraine St., Pictou, NS B0K 1H0, ☎ 902/485-1433 ($$).*

Old Manse Inn, close enough to downtown to walk, is in an 1874 mansion on the hillside overlooking town. Take Exit 32 on Rte. 104 to the William Henry Government Building, turn left on Hawthorne Street and take the second left onto Tigo Park. Rates include a full breakfast. *5 Tigo Park, Antigonish, NS B2G 1M7, ☎ 902/863-5696 or 902/863-5259 off-season ($-$$).*

Sunshine Café is owned by Chef Mark Gabrieau, trained in the classic French style and now applying it to create an exciting menu. The focus is on locally farmed mussels and scallops, seafood from local fishermen, and fresh vegetables, grains, fruits, cheeses and meats from local farmers. The lighthearted, casual atmosphere in the dining room is a counterpoint to the serious finesse of this kitchen and its health-conscious menu. *332 Main St., Antigonish, ☎ 902/863-5851 ($-$$).*

Stone House Café serves a mixture of German specialties, seafood, sandwiches, and pizza in a casual downtown second-floor dining room. In the summer they have outdoor patio seating. *13 Water St., Pictou, ☎ 902/485-6885 ($).*

The Press Room in a former newspaper plant, is another casual and inexpensive option for burgers, fish & chips, sandwiches and similar fare in a pub setting. Saturday brunch includes steak and eggs. *50 Water St., Pictou, ☎ 902/485-4041 ($).*

On Marine Drive

Sea Wind Landing Country Inn is newly built and sits out on a peninsula by itself, overlooking beautiful Charlos Cove, south of Cole Harbour. Rooms in the old inn building are cozy, while those in the new separate building are more expansive. All are comfortable and attractive. The emphasis here is on nature, with plenty of shore to walk. The inn's *Sugar Island Life Excursion* is done on their 30-foot cruiser, which travels to nearby islands to see seals and birdlife. They also have trail directions, so you can explore neighboring lands and beaches. *RR2 Charlos Cove, NS B0H 1T0, ☎ 800/563-INNS, 902/525-2108 ($$).*

St. Mary's River Lodge is a comfortable five-room guest house by the river in Sherbrooke. They also have two separate summer houses, one in Liscomb and the other at Port Hilford, which they will rent for a few days or by the week. The lodge has a dining room open for breakfast, lunch and dinner, and features Swiss specialties. It's close to the historic village. *PO Box 39, Sherbrooke, NS B0J 3C0, ☎ 902/522-2177, fax 902/522-2515 ($$).*

Kelley's Housekeeping Cottages has cottages along the St. Mary's River, as well as walking trails. *Box 127, Main Street, Sherbrooke BS B0J 3C0, ☎ 902/522-2314 ($).*

Liscomb Lodge is one of the resorts operated by the provincial government. Located on the Liscomb River and the ocean, it offers a multitude of recreational opportunities, including hikes along the shore or through a vast wilderness inland. The river and bays surrounding the offshore islands make interesting canoe and kayak destinations. The resort has its own private marina. The dining room, which overlooks the river, specializes in planked salmon. *Rte. 7, Liscomb Mills, NS B0J 2A0, ☎ 800/665-6343, 902/779-2307 ($$-$$$).*

Marquis of Dufferin Seaside Motel is under new, enthusiastic ownership and is being steadily renovated and upgraded. Comfortable rooms (all with new mattresses) overlook the harbor. The Marquis also has its own dock and offers canoes and bicycles for use by guests. The dining room's continental menu is lively and creative, and it has quickly become one of the best-regarded restaurants on the south shore. They use local produce, meats and seafood. In summer meals are served on a deck overlooking the harbor. *RR1, Rte. 7, Port Dufferin, NS B0J 2R0, ☎ 902/654-2696, fax 902/654-2970 ($-$$).*

Black Duck Seaside Inn looks like an old Victorian mansion, but it's really all new. Bright attractive rooms and a nice sitting area on the second floor landing make this a very pleasant place to stay. If you bring your canoe or kayak you can use their floating dock. The dining room menu is as attractive as the room itself, with many traditional dishes and a few that are the specialty of the owner. We liked the unique fisherman's lasagna. Breakfast is included in the rates *25245 Rte. 7, Port Dufferin, NS B0J 2R0, ☎/fax 902/885-2813 ($$).*

Salmon Lake Lodge is set on the shores of a beautiful lake and the cottages, some with kitchenettes, are nicely spaced; some are on a wooded island connected by a causeway to their other grounds. They also have a campground and offer boat and canoe rentals. There is a good restaurant in a wonderful knotty pine lodge with a big fireplace and large windows overlooking the lake. The menu includes salmon, scallops au gratin, steaks, chops, even liver and onions, and there is a kids menu. West of Port Dufferin take Rte. 374 north, then take a left to the lodge after about 4¾ miles. *RR #1, Sheet Harbour, NS B0J 3B0, ☎ 902/885-2534, reservations 902/885-2058 ($$).*

Camelot Inn is close to the intersection of Rte. 7 and the high-speed provincial artery of Rte. 107. Sitting on five acres of land, the inn is in an attractive Victorian cottage overlooking the rapids of the river that flows past. *Musquodoboit Harbour, NS B0J 2L0, ☎ 902/889-2198 ($$).*

Bright House Restaurant serves lunch and dinner daily from June to October in a large old colonial-style house close to the back entrance of the museum. They offer traditional Nova Scotia fare and seafood; one specialty is scallops in Pernod. Behind the restaurant is a bakery that makes all of the breads and pastries for the dining room; it also sells to the public. *Main Street, Sherbrooke, ☎ 902/522-2691 ($-$$).*

English Garden Tearoom, on Rte. 7 past Ecum Secum and Necum Teuch (two of the area's many interesting local town names), serves breakfast, lunch and dinner. They have fish & chips, hot and cold sandwiches and, in the evening, a fixed dinner menu. From June through August they are open Monday and Wednesday through Saturday, 8 am to 9 pm and on Sunday, 10 am to 9 pm. From September through May they open Wednesday through Monday, 10 am to 9 pm. *Moser River, ☎ 902/347-2870 ($).*

Family Fries is a locally owned and operated fast food place offering fish & chips, fried clams, and lobster salad. The staff is friendly and outgoing and the food well prepared. It's popular with local people. *Rte. 7, Ship Harbour, no phone ($).*

■ Camping

Caribou Provincial Park has 82 RV and tent sites on a sand spit in the Northumberland Strait. From here you can watch the Prince Island Ferry go back and forth. Off Rte. 6 northwest of Pictou. *PO Box 457, New Glasgow, NS B2H 5E5, ☎ 902/752-3181, seasonal phone 902/485-6134.*

Salt Springs Provincial Park is an inland camping facility with 60 RV and tent sites, both open and wooded. There is also access to freshwater fishing on West River and Sixmile Brook, the two streams that bound the park. Picnic grounds, available to day visitors, are well separated from campers. It's right off TransCanada 104 west of New Glasgow. *PO Box 457, New Glasgow, NS B2H 5E5, ☎ 902/752-3181, seasonal 902/925-2752.*

Boylston Provincial Park, a small area, has 35 RV and tent sites with flush toilets but no showers. There are picnic grounds and a dumping station. There is also frontage on the ocean with unsupervised swimming. The park is open mid-June to September. *☎ 902/533-3326, across the bay from Guysborough.*

Salsman Provincial Park is on the Marine Drive near Issacs Harbour North. It's close to the intersection of Rte. 316 and Rte. 277, which crosses Country Harbour by ferry between Issacs Harbour North and Stormont. Salsman has 40 RV and tenting sites and a dumping station. *Mailing address 190 Beech Road, RR #7, Antigonish, NS B2G 1R6, ☎ 902/863-4513, seasonal phone 902/328-2999.*

East River Lodge Campground and Trailer Park is a private facility close to Sheet Garbor, Mushaboom and Taylor Head Provincial Park. Reservations are accepted for their 38 sites, 28 of which have water, sewer and electric service. There are free hot showers and a laundry. You can cool off in the river while the kids play in the playground or use the recreation hall. It's open mid-May to mid-October. *West East River Road, Sheet Harbour, NS B0J 3B0, ☎ 902/885-2057 or 885-2864.*

Farther down Rte. 7 at Jeddore, **E.F Webber Lakeside Park and Campground** has 53 sites, 10 of which are unserviced. They have free hot showers, flush toilets, and a laundry and there is swimming, a playground and a recreation room. It's open mid-May to mid-October. From Rte. 7, just east of Jeddore Oyster Pond, take the road north to Upper Lakeville for 2½ miles. *RR #2, Oyster Pond, Jeddore, NS B0J 1W0, ☎ 902/845-2340.*

Porter's Lake Provincial Park has 165 RV and tent sites, showers and facilities for disabled persons. It is on a lake formed in an earth fault. The lake is 15 miles long and makes a good place for canoeing and boating. There is unsupervised swimming. Fewer than five miles away, Lawrencetown Coastal Heritage Park has Lawrencetown and Rainbow Haven Beaches that both offer ocean swimming, with changing rooms and a canteen. Conrad's Island Provincial Park is also close by and offers a varied coastal ecosystem with tidal marshes that are an important bird breeding site. *West Porter's Lake Rd, Porter's Lake, NS B0J 2S0, ☎ 902/827-2250.*

Cape Breton Highlands

The drive through the highlands on the Cabot Trail is often listed among the most scenic drives on the continent, and we wouldn't argue. The landscape is open, but not barren, with low green moorland and upland bogs at its elevations and green forests in its valleys. Although much of the area is strongly Scottish, on the west coast you will find French communities, such as Cheticamp.

Geography & History

Between 1763 and 1775 about 20,000 Scots abandoned the highlands of their homeland and moved across the seas to Cape Breton, a place that looked close enough to their bonnie braes to make them feel wanted. A few years later, when the British government began the "Clearances" of small farmers and herdsmen from the estates of Scotland in order to allow English landlords to raise sheep, more Scotsmen joined them. The Irish, too, came as a result of the clearances in that land and as a result of the potato famine in the 19th century. These immigrants and their descendants give Cape Breton, especially the northern section, its distinctly Celtic flavor.

The primary man-made feature in the northern part of Cape Breton is the **Cabot Trail**, a sinuous two-lane highway that winds in three dimensions through the highland mountains and along the high-bluffed shores of the sea. When it opened in the fall of 1932, the 181-mile-long road was the first highway to link most of the towns through which it passes.

Getting Around

Access to Cape Breton is over the Canso Causeway, the deepest causeway in the world, completed in the 1950s. Don't confuse the Canso Causeway with the town of Canso. The town is many long miles east, on Cape Canso, while the causeway crossing is on Rtes. 4 and 104 just east of Auld's Cove.

Almost all the road-accessible parts of the Highlands are along the coast. From the causeway, **Rte. 19**, called the Ceilidh (pronounced KAY-lee) Trail, is the primary route north. It generally follows the coast, cutting inland near Port Hood, passing through Mabou at the end of its beautiful bay and coming out to the sea again at Inverness. At Dunvegan it cuts inland through the various Margaree villages and returns to the sea again at Margaree Harbour. If you want to follow the sea take Rte. 219 at Dunvegan. At Margaree Harbour, Rte. 19 ends and you will have to take the Cabot Trail, the only road around the north end of the island and without a route number.

If you want see a little of the west coast, then cut back to the lakes area or Louisbourg, take the Cabot Trail **south** at Margaree Forks to Rte. 105 south of Baddeck, about 24 miles (40 km).

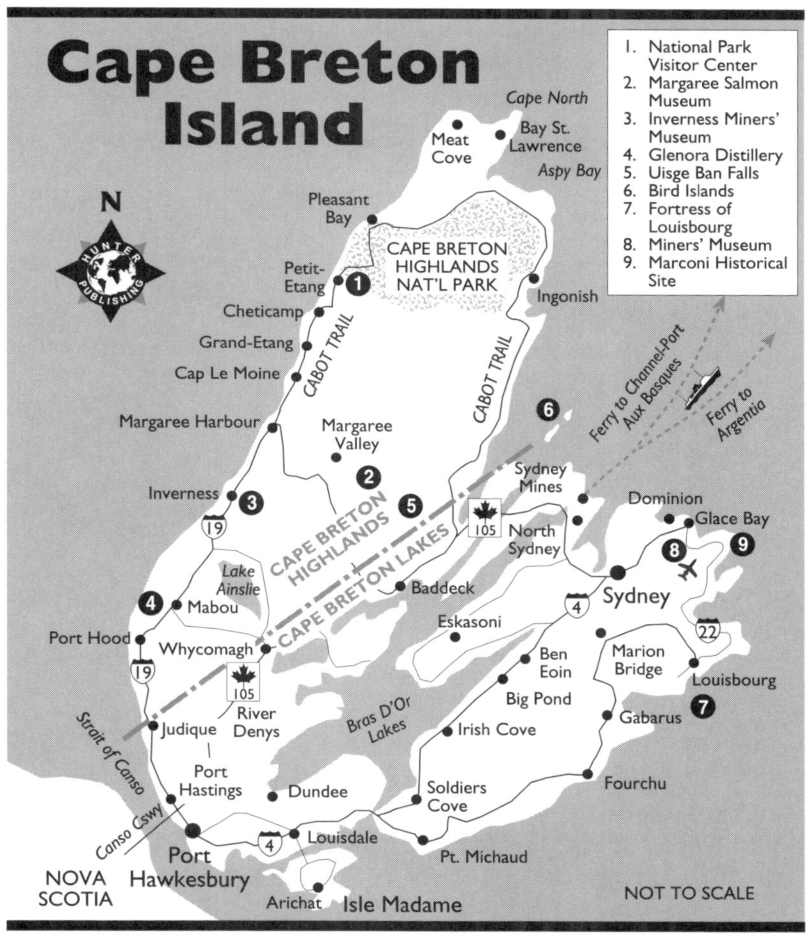

The **Cabot Trail** is a magnificent drive, rising and falling from low coastal coves and beaches to the highlands and mountainsides, which often end abruptly in sea cliffs. Inland from the highway there is only a wilderness of mountains and lush northern forests, often giving way to views of the sea. The road turns inland along the north border of the Cape Breton Highlands National Park to Dingwall, on Aspy Bay. From Cape North an interesting side trip leads through North Harbour to Meat Cove. The unpaved road travels through pure wilderness and along cliffsides to a spectacular view at the end.

Another option from Port Hastings, which brings you directly to the eastern side of the Cabot Trail, is to take **Rte. 105** north through Whycocomagh and Baddeck. At the head of St. Ann's Bay, a left turn puts you on the Cabot Trail.

Information Sources

■ **Tourism Cape Breton Inc.**, PO Box 627, Sydney, NS B1P 6H7, ☎ 902/565-9464, can provide information on Cape Breton, including places to stay.

■ For information on the western area, contact the **Inverness County Recreation/Tourism Department**, PO Box 179, Port Hood, NS B0E 2W0, ☎ 902/567-2400.

■ Eastern area information may be obtained from the **Victoria County Recreation Dept.**, PO Box 370, Baddeck, NS B0E 1B0, ☎ 902/295-3231, fax 902/295-3444, Web site http://org.atcon.com/ceilidh/victoria.htm, e-mail verdt@atcon.com.

■ **Cape Breton Highlands National Park**, Ingonish Beach, NS B0C 1L0, ☎ 902/285-2691 or 224-3403, fax 285-2866, TDD 285-2691, is the general contact for all things in the National Park.

Adventures

Throughout much of this region, steep hills rise as you look inland, and along the shore the mountains sometimes end suddenly, falling in sheer cliffs to the sea. The trails along the coastal sections run through forests and an occasional field before coming out onto highpoints above the sea, with views over the ocean and back along the coastal cliffs. Inland trails provide occasional views over the mountains around you. The forests tend to be thick, but the trails are usually well maintained and marked. But whether you are hiking, skiing or snowmobiling, remember that you are near wilderness areas, particularly as you move farther inland, and you should carry maps and proper equipment including a good compass.

The Inverness County Tourism Department (contact informaton above) and several hiking and skiing groups have jointly produced an excellent map, called *Trails of Inverness County*, that shows most of the area's hiking, skiing, horseback riding, biking and snowmobiling trails. Most of these trails are built and maintained by volunteers from surrounding villages.

On Foot

Hiking

The **Cape Mabou Trail Club**, Box 528, Inverness, NS B0E 1H0, is also good source for information on hiking the western side. The club has created a series of trails over Cape Mabou, some of which traverse the inland highlands and one that climbs through spruce forests from McDonald Glen over the seaward shoulder of the cape. The MacDonald Glen trail end has a side trail leading to a scenic overlook with views south along the west coast. To reach the trail from the Mabou end, take Rte. 19 and turn left after crossing the bridge. Follow that road until you see the trailhead sign on your left, with a wide place where you can park. To get to the Sight Point end, take Rte. 19 north. Just before Inverness, a small paved road leads to Banks of Broad Cove. From that take the unpaved Broad Cove Road to the right along the coast to Sight Point. The trail, from one end to the other, is approximately 6.3 miles over moderately rugged terrain.

The **South Highlands** and **Bear Trap trails** also leave from Sight Point. The South Highlands Trail starts from an elevation just under 1,500 feet and climbs to more than 3,000 feet. Just past its highpoint, the trail intersects the Bear Trap Trail, which runs south along MacIssacs Glen Brook, and a gravel road that leads back to MacDonald Glen. The combined length of both trails is 8.8 miles over rugged uphill terrain.

Also accessed from Broad Cove Road is **Black Brook Trail**, which takes off on the east side of the road at a sharp turn. It climbs from near sea level to an altitude of over 3,000 feet. At the top it connects with an unpaved road that leads to the also unpaved Cape Mabou Road. A short way beyond, about halfway to Sight Point and just before crossing Stewart's Brook, the **Rosner Farm Trail** wends its way to meet with Black Brook Trail at the high point. They are each about two miles long. Both trails have steep sections; they can be combined to make a circuit.

> **TRAIL MAPS & INFORMATION:** *Hiking maps and information are available from the National Park information centers at Cheticamp and Ingonish.*

On the east side of Rte. 19 near Strathlorne, about three-quarters of

Nova Scotia

PARK PASS REQUIRED: *Remember, before using any of the facilities at Cape Breton Highlands National Park you must buy a pass* ***when you enter the park*** *at the Cheticamp or Ingonish visitors center. They can not be purchased within the park or at the north end.*

the way from Mabou to Inverness, take the Foot Cape Road to the right to the **Strathlorne Nursery Trail**. This is a moderately easy two-mile trail through a clear-cut area of well-spaced trees and a thicker forest of many mixed species.

In the Margaree area take the Cabot Trail highway south at Margaree Forts to Northeast Margaree (which, for some reason is south of Margaree Center) and turn north toward Margaree Center. Follow the signs to Brown's B&B. The **Eagle Nest Trail** leaves from there, an easy one-mile trail into the inland areas.

In **Cape Breton Highlands National Park**, several good hiking trails begin from the Cabot Highway. Near the Information Center on Rte. 19 north of Cheticamp are two trails used for hiking in the summer. **Le Chemin du Buttereau Trail**, near the campground entrance, is a fairly flat three-mile trail that has a small loop on the far end and a return via the original path. There are old foundations of early Acadian settlements along the trail. **L'Acadien Trail** also has remnants of Acadian settlement and is on the east side of the road a short distance from the Buttereau trail, leaving from an information center. This six-mile loop trail rises to about 1,200 feet but is a fairly easy hike with good open views from the top. Close by, behind the information center at the Robert Brook group campground, the **Trous de Saumons Trail** is another fairly level trail of about eight miles, following the Cheticamp River. There is an observation pool along the way where you can see salmon swimming in the river. This trail is also used by mountain bikers.

A bit farther up the road, **Corney Brook Trail** is an out-and-back five-mile hike that follows Corney Brook through its gorge and into the hills to Corney Brook Falls. The trailhead is in the parking lot just north of Corney Brook. A short way north of Corney Brook, just after the road turns inland, a gravel road on the left leads to **Skyline Trail**. This is mostly a loop trail with short double-backs at each end, traveling over the highlands that the highway circles. At the top are great views over the ocean.

Fishing Cove Trail is a short distance away on the west side of the road, accessed by a gravel road. The trail follows Fishing Cove River down its steep-sided valley to the sea, where there is a wilderness campground.

Benjie's Lake Trail is a change of pace from climbing in the hills. Most of its two miles is over wet marshes and through coniferous forests, some parts crossing over boardwalks. Moose are plentiful here and sightings are common, but don't approach them or make sudden movements. They weigh more than half a ton and can be quite dangerous.

Louisbourg, Cape Breton Island.

On the right side of the Cabot Trail, past Pleasant Bay, the **McIntosh Brook Trail** is a short hike along McIntosh Brook to its falls; you can return on an alternate path through the forest. Just before the Benjies Lake Trail is the **Bog Trail**, less than a half- mile walk into a living bog, on a boardwalk from which you can see insect-eating pitcher plants and other bog flora.

Near Ingonish, the **Cape Smokey Trail** travels more than 600 feet above the sea for much of its length, with beautiful views.

Cape Smokey is one of the highest mountains in the highlands and juts out into the sea. The trail leaves from Cape Smokey Provincial Park and is just under five miles long. There are a number of look-offs and good wildlife-watching especially for bald eagles. Be very careful when walking along the cliff sides.

Also in the Ingonish area, take the road out to Keltic Lodge to reach the **Middle Head Trail**, which leads over the sea along the narrow peninsula.

North River Provincial Park's North River Trail rises over a thousand feet, but the reward at the end is a hundred-foot waterfall. The trail follows the North River and its East Branch, crossing and recrossing it. The river is noted for salmon and several side trails give access to salmon pools where, during the season, you can see them swimming. From the Cabot Trail at North

River Bridge north of St. Anns, take Oregon Road, just north of the bridge. It's about three miles to the park. It's nearly a 10-mile hike to the waterfall and steep in parts. A short, steep trail leads to an old road that dwindles to a trail; be sure to note the point where the connector trail meets the old road, since it can be hard to find on the way back. It's a long hike so leave enough sunlight to get back.

Rock Climbing

To get in touch with active rock climbing enthusiasts, contact **Climb Nova Scotia** through Sport Nova Scotia at ☎ 902/425-5450, Frank Gallant at ☎ 902/422-6687, or the Trail Shop at 6210 Quinpool Road, Halifax, ☎ 902/423-8736.

Hiking Outfitters & Guided Tours

Several providers offer walking and hiking tours in the Highlands, with different packages and destinations.

■ **Cabot Trail Outdoor Adventures**, Jersey Cove RR 1, Englishtown, NS B0C 1H0, ☎ 902/929-2546, offers a hiking and sea kayaking weekend.

■ **North River Kayak Tours**, 40 Beaumont Avenue, Sydney River, NS B1S 1J5, ☎ 902/567-2322, Web site www.chatsubo.com/nrktours/home.html, leads a kayaking and hiking trip that climbs to a waterfall.

■ Near Ingonish, **Ocean Vistas Walking Tours**, c/o Wendy Gibbs, Box 23, Ingonish Beach, NS B0C 1L0, ☎ 902/285-2489, offers short walks in that area and will do personalized hiking tours along the Cabot Trail.

■ **Regal International Tours, Inc.**, Box 44208, Bedford, NS, B4A 3Z8, ☎/800/565-8183 or 902/861-1066, and **Scott Tours**, 1707 Pryor Street, Halifax, NS B3H 4G7, ☎ 800/262-8644 or 902/423-5000, both provide packages that include all accommodations, meals and ground transportation.

■ The **Green Highlander Lodge** is an outfitter that guides hiking trips to North River Falls. For the especially fit, they offer a special canoe adventure upstream to Indian Brook Falls that includes paddles through quiet pools as well as rough portages over the boulder-strewn stream bed through a high-walled gorge. Contact the lodge at PO Box 128, Baddeck, NS B0E 1B0, ☎ 902/295-2303, Web site www.capebretonnet.com/baddeck/greenhighlander.

On Wheels

Only the hardy will want to try it, but Rte. 19 and the Cabot Trail itself are very popular with experienced bicyclers. The terrain varies greatly, but is very hilly, with particularly long mountain climbs in the northern highlands. While this is a major paved two-lane highway, it is wide and has good sight lines. Between the towns of St. Joseph du Moine and Great Etang, the Pembroke Trail is a challenging mountain bike trail past Pembroke Lake and on along Forest Glen Brook. Trous de Saumons Trail, behind the information center north of Cheticamp, is an eight-mile trail shared by mountain bikers and hikers.

Bicycle Outfitters & Guided Tours

■ At the north end of the national park, **Sea Spray Cycle Center**, RR#2, Dingwall, Smelt Brook, NS B0C 1G0, ☎ 902/383-2732, rents mountain bikes and offers maps and guidance on trips in the northern highlands, of varying distances and for all skill levels. They also have guided backcountry off-road trips. Both east and west of Digwall, roads offer pleasant cycling through small villages and settlements overlooking small harbors and the sea.

■ If you are an intermediate to advanced cyclist, **Freewheeling Adventures**, RR#1, Hubbards, NS B0J 1T0, ☎ 902/857-3600, fax 902/857-3612; e-mail Bicycle@ freewheeling.ca, Web site www. freewheeling.ca, offers a five day cycling tour of the Cabot Trail, including some secondary roads. Rates are about $1,175 and include four nights at inns, most meals and van support. Trips begin in late June and are offered through October. They also have a five-day Cape Breton on- and off-road trip for intermediate to advanced mountain bicyclists; cost is about $1,200 and it is offered from June through October.

■ **Island Eco-Adventures**, Box 34, Baddeck, NS B0E 1B0, ☎ 902/707-5512, 902/295-3303, rents touring and off-road bikes, camping equipment and can provide advice and self-guided tours.

■ **Strait Mountain Bike Association**, PO Box 166, Port Hastings, NS B0E 2T0, is also a good source of information for bicycling on Cape Breton.

■ On Water

Canoeing & Kayaking

Cape Breton's large harbors and rivers offer good canoeing and sea kayaking. Of particular interest are Mabou Harbour, Cheticamp, North and South Ingonish Bay and Ingonish Harbour and St. Ann's Harbour and Bay. Cape North sticks out into the middle of Aspy Bay and on either side of it smaller bays are protected by sand barriers. Called North Harbour and South Harbour, these abound with wildlife and are wonderful places for canoeing and kayaking.

REFLECTIONS ON THE WATER

A sea kayak gives you a different perspective on the land, and as I move slowly round the rocky points and under the tree-lined banks of North River, and out into St. Ann's Bay, I have a lot of time to look at it. Bald eagles soar overhead, then land and perch in the trees to kayak-watch. Cormorants dry their big, unwieldy-looking wings on a row of pilings at the old dock, and I drift quietly near, hoping my bright orange vest will be mistaken for a harmless bit of flotsam. But I'm discovered and the bird flies to another piling.

Angelo, the guide, paddles alongside to tell us about the broken-down wharf and the large ruin on shore. This was the site of a lumber mill; quite an operation, judging from the size of the remaining walls. Angelo is full of local history, and we can picture the North River filled with logs. He tells us of one particularly big log-jam that broke. The logs got away and some of them drifted as far as Newfoundland (where they probably became houses in some grateful town).

Out on the point, we find a narrow pebble beach and stop to stretch our legs (actually, after a morning in a kayak, my knees need to bend, not stretch), while Angelo whips together a little something: hot tea on a tiny stove, thick slices of his mother's homemade bread slathered with wild berry jam. Here we learn about the Normanites, a fanatical religious group that drifted off course in a storm and landed here a century ago. This wild and now unsettled shore is alive with stories, and with ghosts of the people whose homes were once where the eagles now perch.

Canoe & Kayak Outfitters

■ One of our favorite places to kayak is where St. Ann's Bay cuts deeply inland, forming a spectacular seascape. Here Angelo Spinazzola, a singer and songwriter (when he finds time) runs **North River Kayak Tours**, 40 Beaumont Avenue, Sydney River, NS B1S 1J5, ☎ 902/567-2322, Web site www.chatsubo.com/nrktours/home.html. He will take you around the scenic and historic shores of St. Ann's Bay on a three-hour ($55), full-day ($85) or moonlight ($55) paddle. The three-hour trip includes a picnic lunch and the full-day trip has a lunch of steamed mussels. There are discounts for groups of three or more and he will also do customized tours. Special packages are also available, such as a two-day kayaking and hiking trip with a night at a beautiful riverside B&B. A kayaking fundamentals program is also offered.

North River Kayak also rents both kayaks and canoes. Fees are $25 for a single kayak for three hours ($35 for a double); canoes are $20 for the same period. Seven-hour rates range from $35 to $55. From the Cabot Trail at North River take Murray Road, opposite the Presbyterian church, for about 1¾ miles. Call ahead to find out what time trips are leaving, or to reserve a kayak.

■ **Eagle North Canoe and Kayak Rentals**, 299 Shore Road, Cape North, ☎ 902/383-2552, has rentals for paddling around the waters of South Harbour at $15 an hour or $30 a half-day. The rental includes life vests and you can also rent binoculars for wildlife-watching. Shore Road is off the Cabot Highway near the Hide Away Campground.

■ For extended kayaking tours in the Cape Breton highlands, contact **Island Seafari** at 20 Paddy's Lane, Louisbourg, NS B0A 1M0, ☎ 902/733-2309, e-mail seafari@atcon.com, Web site http://business.auracom.com/seafari.

■ **Island Eco-Adventures**, Box 34, Baddeck, NS B0E 1B0, ☎ 800/707-5512 or 902/295-3303, also rents canoes, life vests and cartop racks and can give advice on the best local places to go.

■ **Green Highlander Lodge**, POB 128, Baddeck, NS B0E 1B0, ☎ 902/295-2303, has canoe and kayak rentals. On the south shore of Bras d'Or Lakes, **Kayak Cape Breton and Cottages**, West Bay, Roberta, NS B0E 2K0, ☎/fax 902/535-3060, is another source for rentals. They also do kayaking on the Margaree River, conduct a three-day kayak tour of Port Hood and Henry Island, and a five-day Cape Breton Highlands tour along the coast from Cheticamp to Meat Cove.

Boat Tours Near Cheticamp

At Little Judique Harbour just south of Port Hood, **Port Hood Island Tours, Ltd.** has a three-hour tour of Henry and Port Hood Islands and the adjacent west shore of Cape Breton. Tours depart at 9:30 am, and 1 and 4:30 pm. A guide provides information on folklore, shipwrecks, the shore and its geological development, and the avian and marine life around you. They even have fishing gear so you can catch supper. Contact them at RR#2, Shore Road, Box 123, Port Hood, NS B0E 2W0, ☎ 902/567-2400,

Tour the harbor or even charter a trip to Margaree Island with **Margaree Harbour Boat Tours**, ☎ 902/235-2848. During the tour there are sightings of whales, seals and birds, including an occasional eagle. Trips are at 9 am and 1, 2 and 6 pm.

Near the southwest entrance to the **Cape Breton Highlands National Park**, Cheticamp has five whale- and seabird-watching tour operators, all leaving from the wharf in the center of town. This is Acadian country and you'll usually get a good dose of Acadian culture and folklore thrown into the bargain. Rates are $20-$25; children six-12, $10-$12. All operate from May to October.

L'Escaouette Whale Cruise, PO Box 249, Cheticamp, NS B0E 1H0, ☎ 902/224-1959, cruises around Cheticamp Island and north along the coast. They are on the boardwalk and have two cruises in the morning, another at 4 pm, and moonlight cruises in the evening.

Whale Cruisers Ltd, PO Box 183, Cheticamp, NS B0E 1H0, ☎ 800/813-3376 or 902/224-3376, fax 224-1166, was the first whale-watch operation in Nova Scotia. In May and June they run tours at 9 am and 6 pm; in July and August they add a 1 pm sailing. From August until mid-September the last sailing is at 5 pm. After that date there are trips at 10 am and 4 pm.

Laurie's Motor Inn has their own whale watch cruise, **Seaside Whale and Nature Cruises**, ☎ 902/959-4253, leaving at 9 am, 1 and 5 pm daily from the boardwalk downtown.

Cap Rouge Ltée, PO Box 221, Cheticamp, NS B0E 1H0, ☎ 902/813-3376 or 902/224-3606, has tours and cruises on the *Danny & Lynn* at the government wharf in July and August, 8 am, 1 and 5 pm daily.

Acadien Whale Cruise, c/o L.A. Muise, PO Box 97, Cheticamp, NS B0E 1H0, ☎ 902/224-1088, was the second whale watch in town. They operate from La Chaloupe wharf in Cheticamp. From June to August 15 they leave at 9:15 am, 1:15 and 6:15 pm daily; from August 15 to mid-September the last cruise departs at 5:15 pm.

Pleasant Bay lies at the point on the Cabot Trail where the highway turns inland along the park's northern boundary on its way to Dingwall. It is totally surrounded by wilderness and there are no settlements along the coast from here to the northern tip. **Highland Coastal Tours and Charters**, Pleasant Bay, NS B0E 2P0, ☎/fax 902/224-1825, has three-hour cruises along this wild coast from mid-June through mid-September, three times a day. Before August 15 they leave at 9:30 am, 1:30 and 5:30 pm; after that date departures are at 10 am, 1:30 and 5 pm. Along the way there is whale- and bird-watching. Fares for the 48-foot *Sonya Maria I* are about $20, less for children; they also have a family rate.

Boat Tours - North Cape & East Coast

To do your bird- and whale-watching under sail, book aboard the schooner ***Tom Saylor***, ☎ 800/872-6084 or 902/383-2246. The boat is a 52-foot, two-masted schooner; she leaves from near the Markland Resort three times daily on sightseeing, whale- and bird-watching trips around Aspy Bay. The captain has done whale research voyages in the Arctic and Antarctic.

The area around the northern tip of the island offers more water-based adventures. Rates for all of the following providers are about $25 for adults, half-price for children; most offer special family rates. ***Fan-A-Sea VI***, Bay St. Lawrence, ☎ 902/383-2680, has coastal tours and 2½-hour whale- and seal-watching excursions on a 27-foot fiberglass boat. Tours depart from the Bay St. Lawrence wharf at 10 am, 1 and 4 pm daily.

The ***Wayne & Freda***, ☎ 902/383-2268, leaves the government wharf in Bay St. Lawrence for coastal tours and whale- and bird-watching at 10 am, 1 and 5 pm daily. Your whale sighting is guaranteed by Captain Burton.

Island Whale Watch and Nature Tours run by Capt. Kenneth McClellan of Meat Cove, ☎ 902/383-2379, goes out of Bay St. Lawrence harbor on whale watches. This boat is equipped with an underwater microphone so that you not only see whales, but hear them as well. The owner/captain also has a campground on the windswept head of Meat Cove, where the entertainment is watching whales cavort offshore. Tours leave at 10:30 am, 1:30 and 4:30 pm in July and August (and, weather permitting, in June and September).

Leaving the same wharf in Bay St. Lawrence is **Captain Cox's Whale Watch**, Capstick, ☎ 902/383-2981 (summer) and 902/492-0325 (winter). The 2½-hour whale and sea animal trip includes eagle and seabird sightings as well. He uses a traditional 32-foot Cape Island boat and is a trained marine biologist.

Highlander Whale Watch and Scenic Tour, ☎ 902/383-2287, has departures at 9 and 11:15 am, 3:45 and 6 pm daily from Bay St. Lawrence and will adjust times for groups. Their rate is slightly lower than the others in Bay St. Lawrence.

On the east end of South Harbour, turn off the Cabot Trail to Smelt Brook and White Point. In addition to a nice drive along the north coast, you will come to **White Point Whale Cruise and Nature Tour**, White Point, ☎ 902/383-2817. Whale trips are on a 32-foot boat; they look for humpback, pilot and minke whales. Along the coast you will see sea caves and a multitude of seabirds – and maybe even an eagle. From there you can continue back to the Cabot Trail at Neil Harbour.

Sea Swell Ventures at Neil Harbour, ☎ 902/563-6455, fax 902/336-2204, does whale, bird and fall foliage coastal tours leaving from Neil Harbour, where the Cabot Trail meets the east side of the island.

At the southeast corner of the national park, **Sea Visions Sailing Tours**, Ingonish, ☎ 902/285-2058, operates the 57-foot sailing schooner *William Moir*. Offered are whale- , porpoise- , seal- and bird-watching trips; you may even see puffins. Trips are at 10 am, 1:30 and 4:30 daily from the Ingonish ferry wharf and cost $25, half-fare for children.

Diving

Nova Scotia Scuba Association, Box 22136, 7071 Bayers Road RPO, Halifax, NS B3L 4T7, ☎ 902/457-7451, is the best source for diving information. They have buddy lists, outfitters, equipment providers, sites and tour provider information.

Cape Breton Tours has dive tour packages that include dives on a tanker and a 200-year-old 74-gun wreck, plus others. Contact them at 24 Kings Road Sydney, NS B1S 1A1, ☎ 902/564-6200, fax 567-0988, e-mail homespun@atcon.com.

Divers World has sales and rental facilities as well as instruction and information. They are at Unit 11, 2 Lakeside Park Drive, Halifax, NS B3T 1L7, ☎ 902/876-0555, fax 902/876-7079; e-mail divrwrld@fox.nstn.ca.

Fishing

Salmon fishermen should try the North River at **North River Provincial Park**. Noted for its salmon, the river can be reached from the North River Trail (see *On Foot*). At North River Bridge take Oregon Road to the park.

Many of the boats used for harbor tours also provide fishing opportunities. Rather than repeat information in the *Boat Tours Near Cheticamp* section above, we'll just list the ones that do fishing trips by name, and you can refer back for contact information. For deep-sea fishing in the Judique-Port Hood area, see Port Hood Island Tours on page 362.

Cap Rouge Ltée in Cheticamp does trips for cod and mackerel with occasional catches of hake, flounder, pollock and herring.

Highland Coastal Tours and Charters in Pleasant Bay does fishing trips mainly as charters, but might take you if they are going out. The coast off Pleasant Bay is totally unsettled so there's little competition for the fish.

In Bay St. Lawrence contact **Fan-A-Sea VI** for deep-sea and shark fishing. They also do diving trips on request. The ***Wayne & Freda*** in Bay St. Lawrence specializes in shark fishing and their motto is "no fish – no fee." See also *Boat Tours – North Cape & East Coast*, on the preceding two pages.

On the east side of North Cape, at Neil's Harbour, **Sea Swell Ventures** specializes in shark and mackerel fishing with rod and reel, and in cod jigging. They supply the bait and gear or you can take your own. Rates are slightly lower than at Bay Lawrence.

FISHING THE MARGAREE & THE DEEP BLUE SEA

Since Nova Scotia does not require guides, if you're an experienced angler or already know Cape Breton well, buy a copy of *The Handbook for the Margaree, 3rd Edition*, by James T. Grey, Jr. It may be the most detailed description of a river, pool by pool, lie by lie, ever written. It, and a good map, will get you to good fishing on the Margaree. The book is available at the local fishing museum, most bookstores, and at the Normaway Inn. If you'd like to hire a great guide for fishing the Margaree River, contact Ed McCarthy, R.R. 1, Little Narrows, Cape Breton, NS B0E 1T0, ☎ 902/756-2442. An expatriate American, Ed fell in love with the Margaree River years ago and knows every pool, run, and lie from top to bottom. His casting is superb, and his tips on flycasting alone are invaluable: any fish are a bonus. Ed's rates are $140 per day.

Margaree Harbour Boat Tours offers deep-sea sportfishing that's great fun for children and adults alike. Captain Leo Burns supplies everything you need, and the fishing is often fast and furious. The catch can include cod, mackerel, halibut, and rockfish that are ugly beyond belief. You get to take the fish, fresh-caught and cleaned, home for dinner. As a prelude to the fishing, Captain Burns takes you out to Margaree Island Wildlife Preserve to see whales, seals, and all sorts of birds, including bald eagles, great blue herons, black-backed gulls, northern gannets, and guillemots. Bring binoculars, a warm jacket or windbreaker and wear rubber-soled shoes. *– Sara Godwin and Charles James*

On Snow

Cross-Country Skiing

While you won't find world-class Alpine skiing along this route, there are some enjoyable downhill slopes at Cape Smokey, along with a good offering of cross-country trails. The snow is better on Cape Breton than it is farther south in the main part of Nova Scotia. Ski Margaree, The Secretary, Margaree Valley, NS B0E 1H0 is a good source of information on the many cross-country ski options in the Margaree area.

During the winter, the **Strathlorne Nursery Trail** between Mabou and Inverness (see *On Foot*) becomes a cross-country ski trail, but the beginning point moves to the north end of the nursery, on Rte. 19 at Strathlorne. The trail goes through a forest of mixed tree species, has loops in the mixed forest and in a clear-cut area, then returns over the same track.

The major cross-country ski area, however, is around Margaree Center. The **Center-Valley Trail** circles Margaree Center, running along the side of the Margaree River for a good part of the way. On the north end, at the east side of the Ingraham Bridge, is a shorter **Meadow Trail**.

Another series called the **Badlands Trails** leaves from Hatchery Road and Big Intervale Road at Portree. On the south side of Big Intervale Road is another major network of cross-country trails with an access off of Fielding Road. At the end of the unpaved road to Big Intervale is another network known as the **MacKenzie Bowl Trails**. Access these from the East Big Intervale Road in Big Intervale. Near Margaree, the **Normaway Inn**, ☎ 800/565-9463, 902/248-2987, has two- and three-mile trails for use by guests and visitors.

On the north end of the island are two excellent private cross-country ski areas, both charging the national park rate of $5 individual, $10 family per day. They are open from Christmas to the end of April, snow conditions permitting. **North Highlands Nordic Ski Trails**, ☎ 902/383-2732, is in Cape North at the Northern Victoria Community Centre. These trails are run by a ski club and they groom daily if needed. They use the green, blue and black symbols of downhill to mark the difficulty of trails, which run from half a mile to nearly five miles long. The waxing room and rentals at the Community Centre are available to the public when the center is open. They can arrange for lessons if you call in advance.

South Ridge Trails, South Ridge Rd, RR#1, Dingwall B0C 1G0, ☎ 902/383-2874, is a little over three miles off the Cabot Trail and has two trails, neither of which is groomed. The easy trail is three miles long, through forest along the Aspy River valley. The other trail, moderate, is a loop of just over four miles through the pines, along the ridge between the Middle and South Aspy Rivers. There are views of the mountain ranges. South Ridge has a ski shop for equipment sales, rental and waxing. They also have a lighted area for evening ski lessons. Rental and lessons should be arranged in advance.

Cape Breton Highlands National Park has 60 miles of cross-country trails. For groomed ski trail conditions call ☎ 902/285-2549; for information and cabin rental call the Ingonish Park Warden at ☎ 902/285-2542. Check at the Park information center for maps and conditions. Trails in the National Park are groomed from Wednesday to Sunday and a Park Ski Pass is required for groomed trails. Ungroomed trails are free and the Park Use Fee required in the summer does not apply in winter. Ski pass rates are $5 daily or $35 for the season, $10 and $55 for family passes. Winter camping is available at the Black Brook Ski Trails, with privy, waxing and a warmup building. The warmup building can be rented for overnight use; they provide a wood stove and wood but there are no beds. At Mary Ann Falls the cabin can be rented with wood stove and wood. Wooden benches serve as bedroll bases. Tent rates at Black Brook are $10 per night ($30 for four nights), the warm-up building is $30 per night ($90 for four nights) and the Mary Ann Falls cabin is $15 per night.

North of Cheticamp, two hiking trails near the information center double as cross-country trails in the winter (see *On Foot*). Ungroomed **Le Chemin du Buttereau** begins off the east side of the road just before the information center. Behind the information center the **Trous de Saumons Trail** is almost three times longer. Both are moderately level terrain. Beyond Corney Brook, the trail at **Benjie's Lake** is also used in winter as a cross-country trail, but it's not groomed. This level pathway through wet and marshy areas is popular with moose.

The following trails are all groomed and accessible from the National Park entrance north of Ingonish on the east side of the park. The **Black Brook Trails** are about 15 minutes ride north of Ingonish and offer three options. The first is the **Black Brook Trail**, which has easy and moderately difficult sections. It's a three-mile trek through a boreal forest with views of the Black Brook River. **Warren Lake Trail** travels just under two miles on its way to and from Warren Lake, the largest lake in the park. The **Mary Ann Falls Trail** is the longest (about 15 miles return). Over its course the trail rises 1,500 feet. The payoff is the view over the coastline and of the high inland plateau. On the return leg the trail passes Warren Lake. There is a warming hut at Mary Ann Falls. Anyone using the Mary Ann Falls Trail should be equipped to deal with sudden and dramatic weather changes. In this same area is the **Gold Mine Trail**, so named for the gold mines that were worked in this valley from the late 1800s until World War II. Follow the paved road at the park entrance to the Grafton Lake fish hatchery. It is an easy run through forest along the Clyburn River valley, with views of Franey Mountain.

➲ SKI INFORMATION LINE: *For general ski information in the Cape Breton area during the winter months, call* ***Cape Breton Tourism****, ☎902/565-9464, ext SKI.*

Also on the east side, the **Gaelic College** at St. Ann's, PO Box 9, Baddeck, NS B0E 1B0, ☎ 902/295-3441, fax 295-2912, has 4½ miles of trails. Check with them for the details on the trails. The College is on a hilltop just north of the TransCanada-105 intersection.

Island Eco-Adventures, Box 34, Baddeck, NS B0E 1B0, ☎ 800/707-5512 or 902/295-3303, rents cross-country equipment and can provide guided and self-guided tours.

Downhill Skiing

For downhill skiing try Ski Cape Smokey, Box 123, Ingonish Beach, NS B0C 1L0, ☎ 800/564-2040 or 902/285-2778, Sydney area 902/539-ISKI, fax 902/285-2615, e-mail larry@nscn.ns.ca. It has the highest vertical drop (1,000 feet) in the province and spectacular views. The longest run is about 1½ miles with several others of reasonable length. A full range of trails from novice to expert are serviced by a quad chair and snowmaking equipment. The lodge has a canteen, lunch service and a full-service lounge. In mid-February they hold the Cape Smokey Snowboard Race and Valentine Dance. Ski packages are available from Keltic Lodge-White Birch Inn (see *Where To Stay & Eat*) and they have a listing of area accommodations that are open in winter. Full-day adult weekend rates are $28 (weekdays $22); complete ski rental is $21 per day. Ski Cape Smokey is open from mid- to late December until

April, depending on the snow. Hours are 9 am to 4 pm; closed Tuesdays and Wednesdays.

Snowmobiling

As is true of most of the Atlantic provinces, snowmobile trails on this route are operated and maintained by clubs in key areas. It is important to remember here that settlement is only along the coast; inland there is nothing but wilderness. Cape Breton offers some fine and exciting snowmobiling, but it takes planning.

Snowmobile Rentals & Trail Information

- The **Alpine Snowmobile Club**, c/o Blaise Moran, RR2, Port Hood, NS B0E 2W0, ☎ 902/787-3085, operates 36 miles (60 km) of trails.

- Farther north are the **Inverness Capers Snowmobile Club**, c/o Jerome MacEachern, RR1, Inverness, NS B0E 1N0, (no phone), and the **Highland Snowmobile Club**, c/o Patrick Larade, Box 367, Cheticamp, NS B0E 1H0, ☎ 902/224-2690.

- At Margaree contact **The Margaree Highlanders Snowmobile Club**, c/o Basil MacLean, Box 5, Margaree Harbour, NS B0E 2B0.

- Trail information is available through the **Snowmobile Association of Nova Scotia**, Box 3010 South, Halifax, NS B3J 3G6, ☎ 902/425-5450, ext. 324.

- **Island Eco-Adventures**, Box 34, Baddeck, NS B0E 1B0, ☎ 800/707-5512 or 902/295-3303, has snowmobile and clothing rentals, and will provide advice and maps of the best local trails.

■ On Horseback

Just before reaching Inverness on Rte. 19, follow Broad Cove Banks Road to the right a short way to **Cameron Farm Horseback Riding**, ☎ 902/258-2386, where you can take trail rides. Children are welcome, too. Their riding trail runs along the side of MacIssac Pond. In addition to trail rides, **Normaway Inn**, on Egypt Rd. in Margaree Valley, ☎ 902/248-2987, offers wagon rides if arrangements are made in advance.

➲ **FOR EXPERIENCED RIDERS:** *For a different riding experience, try* ***Cheticamp Island Icelandic Riding Tours****, c/o Kevin Scherzinger, Cheticamp Island, NS B0E 1H0, ☎ 902/224-2319. Between mid-June and mid-September they conduct guided tours of the island on Icelandic horses, descended from the horses brought by the Vikings. These tours are for experienced riders and are by reservation only. Along the way you'll see beaches, moorlands and views of the sea and mainland. In the autumn they conduct a foliage trail ride.*

Little Pond Stables, ☎ 902/224-3858, are a quarter-mile off the Cabot Highway on Petit Etang Road, about 2½ miles north of Cheticamp. In addition to trail rides they give riding lessons.

On the east side of the Cabot Trail at North River Bridge **Boots and Saddles Trail Rides**, Robert MacRury, Box 22, RR #4, Baddeck, NS B0E 1B0, ☎ 902/929-2365, has a stable of Newfoundland Ponies, a Celtic breed, that he uses for his trail rides. He is open daily from May to November but reservations are required.

Nova Scotia

Cultural & Eco-Travel Experiences

■ Festivals

Celtic Colours International Festival, 197 Charlotte Street, Sydney, NS B1P 1C4, ☎ 800/565-9464 (information), 888/553-8885 or 902/562-6700 (reservations), fax 902/539-9388, e-mail colours@chatsubo.com, Web site www.chatsubo.com/colours/. Celtic and Gaelic music and art have become synonymous with Cape Breton and many of its musicians are recognized around the world for the quality of their work. While the festival is new, it has already become one of the major musical events of the province and of the world of Celtic music. Scheduled for the fall when the foliage is at its height, the festival promotes Celtic culture via the media of music, art and craft. During a nine-day period in early October some of the world's top-ranked Celtic musicians come to Cape Breton for performances all over the island, with as many as three or four in different places every night. Most of the venues are 12 to 30 miles apart, a few are farther away.

➲ **FESTIVAL & EVENT INFORMATION:** ***Inverness County Recreation/Tourism Department****, PO Box 179, Port Hood, NS B0E 2W0, ☎ 902/567-2400, publishes an extensive list of events and festivals throughout the county. There are Ceilidhs, dances, stepdances, Tall Ship events, horse racing, heritage festivals, suppers, outdoor events, concerts and theater. The listing is by date and all necessary information is provided. Write to them for a copy or pick one up at the major information centers on the island.*

Added to the mix are the finest up-and-coming artists and groups from around the province. Recent performers have included the internationally known Chieftains, Natalie MacMaster, Capercaille, Sharon Shannon, Ashley MacIsacc and Rita MacNeil. Also performing during the festival are a massed Gaelic choir comprised of six Gaelic choirs from around the province, the Cape Breton Fiddlers Association and the Danhsa Breacan Dancers. A *Feis an Eilan* (Festival of the Island) is presented and the Gaelic College participates in the festival, leading a song workshop and milling frolic. Workshops, a Gaelic trade show, a *Feis Mhabu* Gaelic festival at Mabou and stepdance workshops are held during the day. There's piping, fiddling, singing, guitars, and just about every other type of traditional music. Performance dates and locations change every year so contact them for a schedule well in advance.

Cape Breton is Celtic to the core, so ceilidhs and square dancing are a normal part of life and take place on a regular weekly basis. Some regular year-round ones are: **Family Square Dances** at **Glencoe Mill** on Thursday nights (it's well known but off the main track, so ask for directions at Mabou); also on Thursday night, **ceilidh** at the Legion Hall, **Inverness**; **ceilidh** Wednesday nights at **Mabou** and **Family Square Dances** on Saturday nights at **West Mabou**. At **Cheticamp** there is **Music on the Boardwalk** every Tuesday and Friday night from 6:30 to 8:30 pm.

At the outdoor theater of **Cheticamp** campground at Highlands National Park, **Les Amis du Plein Air** sponsor concerts of Scottish and Acadian music and dance every Sunday night during July and August. These concerts include folk singers, Highland dancers, bagpipers and fiddlers. Shows run from 8:30 to 10 pm. Admission is under $5 and children under 12 are admitted free.

The **Gaelic College of Celtic Folk Arts,** PO Box 9, Baddeck, NS B0E 1B0, ☎ 902/295-3441, fax 295-2912, at St. Anns, is the place to steep yourself in Scottish culture. They offer summer courses in Gaelic language, music, bagpiping, drumming, Scottish dancing, Cape Breton stepdancing, weaving and kilt making. The shop has over 200 Tartans in stock.

The College also operates **The Hall of Clans**, open daily in July and August from 8 am to 10 pm, until 7 pm in May and June as well as September through December. In addition to the exhibits on Scottish history, an exhibit details the life of Angus MacAskell, an eight-foot-tall native who was known as "The Cape Breton Giant." A full selection of kilts and tartans are available by the yard, as well as book and music sections.

A Scottish festival, the **Gaelic Mod**, is held at the college the last weekend of August with dance competitions and music. On the second weekend of August the College hosts the St. Ann's Highland Festival and on the third weekend is the Festival of Scottish Fiddling.

A look into French Acadian culture can be found in St. Joseph du Moine at **Le Theatre des Moineaux**, Rte. 19, St. Joseph du Moine, ☎ 902/235-2855, for reservations and information. They present a dinner theater with music, mime and dance. A full multi-course meal is served, with a choice of entrée, and there is a cash bar. It's held in the Parish Hall of St. Joseph du Moine, Monday through Friday at 7 pm; the show starts at 7:30.

■ Craft & Art Studios

Cape Breton Island, especially in the highlands, is noted for the quality and variety of its art and craft studios. Cheticamp is especially noted as a center for Acadian rug hooking, which you can watch in progress at several places, and even try your own hand at it in the museum at the Artisans Cooperative, on your left as you enter the center of town. All along the Cabot Trail you can watch potters and other craftsmen at work, and buy their art in dozens of galleries, many of them co-operatives. We mention only a few of our own favorites; you will find more.

Mabou Village Gallery, Rte. 19 in Mabou, ☎ 902/945-2060, open spring through autumn, is a gallery featuring the art of Suzanne MacDonald and unique pieces of pottery, glass, weaving, wood and wool. The art exhibited is in oils, watercolor, acrylic and photography.

Cape Breton Clay, Margaree Valley, ☎ 902/248-2860, fax 248-2307, is the studio and showroom of Bell Fraser, a young 1990 graduate of the Nova Scotia College of Art and Design, whose outstanding pottery and clay designs set her apart from others. Her works feature animals from the sea: fish, lobsters, and other shellfish.

Flora's Cape Breton Crafts, Point Cross (Cheticamp), ☎ 902/224-3139, fax 224-1213, is one of the largest of the outlets for crafts on the island. Just south of Cheticamp, they carry sweaters, tartans, wall hangings, placemats, pottery and a multitude of other well made objects, but their forte is Cheticamp hooked rugs. They have one of the largest selections with over a hundred local women supplying rugs of all sizes. Cheticamp hooked rugs are noted for their unique designs and soft pastel colors.

The culture of the Acadians is preserved and explored at **Les Trois Pignons**, Cheticamp, ☎ 902/224-2612 or 2642. It is a community center, museum, genealogical center and the home of the Elizabeth Lefort Gallery of tapestry and rug hooking. Rug hooking is a fine art in this part of the province and some of the best are found here.

At Dingwall, overlooking South Harbour, **Tartans and Treasures**, South Harbour, Dingwall, ☎ 902/383-2005, has a wide selection of tartans including kilts. The Treasures part of the name refers to the other handmade crafts in the shop including carvings, models, lambskin rugs and slippers and Native Canadian crafts such as soapstone carvings and dolls. **The Trade Shop**, nearby at Cape North, right on the Cabot Trail, also offers a selection of fine locally crafted items.

Lynn's Craft Shop and Art Gallery, 36084 Cabot Trail, Ingonish, ☎ 902/285-2735, combines a collection of outstanding local crafts with the gallery of artist Christopher Gorey. Working in oils, tempera and most recently in watercolor, his works document the richness of the Nova Scotia and Cape Breton countrysides and the lives of the people.

The St. Anne's Bay area has a number of artisans and craftsmen's shops. An unusual shop with a traditional but unusual craft, **Knotstalgia**, Indian Brook, ☎ 902/929-2113, exhibits the work of Greg Mason, who fashions useful and ornamental items from rope, following the traditions of the sailors of the past. Among the objects available are Celtic cross placemats, napkin rings, fisherman's whisks, picture frames and knotted walking sticks.

In the same area, **Leather Works**, Indian Brook, ☎ 902/929-2414, features handmade leather products, from reproduction leather fire buckets to belts and other accessories. It's open daily from May to October and by appointment the rest of the year.

Iron Art and Photographs, ☎ 902/9292821 or 929-2318, is at Tarbot on the Cabot Trail north of St. Anns. It features metal sculpture and photography by artists Carol and Gordon Kennedy.

Wild Things, between Tarbot and North River Bridge, ☎ 902/929-2021, is the shop and studio of three exceptionally talented artists who fashion works of art from wood, using the grain and character of the wood to dictate the final form of the work. The shop is open mid-June to mid-October daily.

At the intersection of the Cabot Trail with Oregon Road at North River Bridge, the **School on The Hill**, ☎ 902/929-2024, is open daily from 8:30 am to 6 pm (until 7 pm in the summer). It has a broad collection of fine crafts, both useful and decorative, each crafted by an island craftsman.

Wildlife-Watching

Whales and seabirds are plentiful, especially off the west coast and in Aspy Bay, at the North Cape. You will find concentrations of whale, bird and nature trips at Margaree, Cheticamp, Pleasant Harbour, Bay St. Lawrence, Dingwall and Ingonish. Because nearly all the sightseeing tours from Cheticamp and other ports are also whale- and bird-watching trips, we have listed these under *Boat Tours*, page 362. If wildlife is more than a casual interest for you, choose a trip with a marine biologist or other scientist on board.

The captain of the schooner ***Tom Saylor***, ☎ 902/872-6084 or 902/383-2246, which leaves from near the Markland Resort three times daily for whale- and bird-watching trips around Aspy Bay, is also captain of whale research voyages in the Arctic and Antarctic.

The captain of **Captain Cox's Whale Watch** on Aspy Bay is a trained marine biologist. Capstick, ☎ 902/383-2981 (summer) or 902/492-0325 (winter).

Margaree Island Wildlife Preserve, off the western shore near St. Rose, is a bird sanctuary, home to nesting seabirds. A boat trip there is a multifaceted wildlife viewing experience, and you will likely to see whales, seals and all sorts of birds, including bald eagles, great blue herons, black-backed gulls, northern gannets, and guillemots. **Margaree Harbour Boat Tours**, ☎ 902/235-2848, runs trips at 9 am and 1, 2 and 6 pm daily in the summer and fall.

A WHALE AND BIRD TRIP FROM CHETICAMP

The emphasis with Whale Cruisers is primarily on whale-watching, for fin, pilot, and minke, but Captain Cal Poirier also makes a serious effort to include good sightings for bird watchers. Possible species include cormorants, guillemots, gannets, and bald eagles. As you should on any trip on the seas around Cape Breton, bring binoculars, a warm jacket or windbreaker, and wear rubber-soled shoes. Rates are $25 for adults, $10 for children. You'll find Whale Cruisers at Government Wharf, Cheticamp Harbour, opposite the big stone church, ☎ 902/224-3376 or 800/813-3376, fax 902/224-1166, Web site www. whale-cruises.com. – *Sara Godwin and Charles James*

Sightseeing

South of Mabou on Rte. 19 take a left onto Rankinville Road to **The Old Pioneer Cemetery**. It contains the graves of the earliest settlers, including that of Benjamin Worth, a Loyalist from New Jersey who was the town's first settler. The Mother of Sorrows Pioneer Shrine was built in the 1920s as a memorial to the pioneers buried at the cemetery. It's a beautiful small version of the typical Cape Breton church, but the interior is remarkable, the walls and ceiling of natural tongue-and-groove Douglas fir. Take a right from Rte. 19 just before the Mabou bridge. It's a short distance on the left.

If you like the Scottish *Uisge Beatha*, water of life, stop at the **Glenora Distillery** on Rte. 19 in Mabou, ☎ 800/839-0491 or 902/258-2662, fax 902/258-3572. They make a single malt Scotch that is still aging in their warehouse, but you can take a tour of the distillery from 9 am to 5 pm, for a fee. While waiting for the Scotch to age (it should become available in a few years), you can try their dark, white and amber rums. There's a bagpiper at the door to welcome you and they usually have live Celtic music inside from 6 to 8 pm, Monday-Saturday, and on Sunday from 3 to 7 pm.

The **Margaree Bicentennial Society Museum**, ☎ 902/235-2426, was a bicentennial project of the town of Margaree. The museum of local history and life is open from the last week of June through Labor Day weekend, exhibiting antiques and historical memorabilia.

The North Highlands Community Museum in Cape North (no phone) is in a split log building in the same style as the home built by the earliest settlers, about 1812. Originally a settlement of Scots dispossessed from the highlands of Scotland in the mid-1700s, it was an isolated fishing and farming community with no road connection until 1932. The museum is a fascinating collection of the household, fishing, farming and logging tools used by the pioneers and there is a display of artifacts on the 1761 wreck of the *Auguste*, found in Aspy Bay in 1977. The museum, at the intersection of the Cabot Highway and the road to Aspy Bay, is open 10 am to 6 pm.

Cape Smokey Provincial Park, off the Cabot Trail south of Ingonish Ferry. There are splendid views from this park on the top of Cape Smokey. **Cape Smokey Lodge**, Ingonish Ferry, NS B0C 1L0, ☎ 902/285-2778, fax 285-2615, is a ski area in the winter and has a lift to the top of Cape Smokey. From the top you can see Glace Bay, Spanish Bay, Point Aconi and the Bird Islands.

Guided Tours

While a private car is the most convenient way to see the Highlands, and almost essential to most outdoor activity, several locally owned bus and van tour companies can take you around the Cabot Trail.

- **Glengael Holidays**, PO Box 1632, Sydney, NS B1P 6T7, ☎ 902/439-8777, ☎/fax 902/539-5664, e-mail glengael @magi.ns.ca., gives area tours.

- **Tartan Tours**, Visitors Centre, 1595 Barrington St., Halifax, NS B3J 1Z8, ☎ 902/422-9092, offers "Coastal Claw" and "Explorers Route" itineraries. They also have multi-day passes and can arrange inexpensive lodging along the route. The Explorers Route pass allows seven days of travel within 30 days for $290; Coastal Claw allows 10 days within 30 for $365.

- **Wind Dancer Discovery Tours**, Box 743 Port Hawkesbury, NS B0E 2V0, ☎ 902/625-1412; e-mail windance@ atcon.com, has a number of hiking and auto tour options. The Cabot Trail Tour is a 12-hour automobile excursion for $60 per person. A North River Falls hike is also $60. The 10-hour Mabou Highlands hike (for experienced hikers) and Margaree Valley Tour are $50 per person. They also have a walking tour of the beaches of the Ceilidh and Fleur-de-lis trails for $5 an hour per person and Family Square Dance Tours in the Margaree Valley area at the same rates.

■ **Cape Breton Tours**, 24 Kings Road Sydney, NS B1S 1A1, ☎ 902/564-6200, fax 567-0988, e-mail homespun@atcon.com, has a daily tour of the Cabot Trail from Sydney, North Sydney and Baddeck for $55 per person. They have a wide range of other options, including wreck diving, sailing and whale and bird-watching.

■ On Mondays, Wednesdays and Fridays the vans of the **Fortress Louisbourg Shuttle Service** run an eight-hour Cabot Trail tour leaving Baddeck at 9 am; cost is $52 for adults, $29 for ages 16 and under. Contact Bannockburn Discovery Tour, Box 38, Baddeck, NS B0E 1B0, ☎ 902/295-3310.

■ Eileen Kotlar of Baddeck operates **Island Highlights Tours**, Box 584, Baddeck, NS B0E 1B0, ☎/fax 902/295-2510. She gives mini-van tours of the Cabot Trail and Highlands. Tours are tailored to each group; rates vary but are competitive. There is a minimum of four persons.

■ **Rhodora Research and Design**, Box 116, Grand Etang, NS B0E 1L0, ☎ 902/224-2849, is operated by David Lawley, an experienced naturalist who provides guide services. His rates are $200 per day or $150 per half-day. He will work with you to create the trip you want, whether by foot or car, on the main road or into the wilderness.

■ **Airmac Flight Centre**, at Port Hawkesbury Airport, ☎ 902/625-5053, will arrange personalized air tours of the island, or charter service anywhere in the Maritime Provinces.

Where To Stay & Eat

Because of the linear nature of the Cabot Trail and the distances involved, lodging and dining options are listed below in geographical order.

➲ **ACCOMMODATIONS SERVICE:** ***Check-In Nova Scotia***, *Nova Scotia Information and Reservations, PO Box 130, Halifax, NS B3J 2M7,* ☎ *902/425-5781 or 800/565-0000, fax 902/453-8401, can help you with reservations throughout the island. The* ***Cape Breton Bed & Breakfast*** *brochure is available from Tourism Services, C.P. 1448, Sydney, NS B1P 6R7,* ☎ *902/565-9464, or from any visitor center. It lists B&B accommodations all over the island. You can reserve directly or use Check-In Nova Scotia. Rates range from $40 to $60 and may be in modest homes or restored historic properties. The provincial information office at Port Hastings, just over the causeway on the right, will also help you find lodging.*

Near the Canso Causeway

Auberge Wandlyn has modern rooms, TV, an indoor pool, exercise room, and laundry. The dining room serves breakfast and dinner. *Rte. 4, PO Box 558, Port Hawkesbury, NS B0E 2V0,* ☎ *902/625-0621, fax 902/625-1525 ($$).*

Maritime Inn Port Hawkesbury is part of a well-regarded chain. Three miles from the causeway, it's a modern hotel with large rooms and outdoor and indoor pools. *689 Reeves St., PO Box 759, Port Hawkesbury, NS B0E 2V0,* ☎ *902/625-0320 or 888/662-7484, fax 902/625-3876 ($$).*

On the West Coast

Clayton Farm Bed & Breakfast is a farmhouse in a scenic setting; the large guest rooms share a bath. The house is set on a point and has water views over the harbor. *Rte. 19, PO Box 33, Mabou, NS B0E 1X0,* ☎ *902/945-2719, fax 902/945-2719 ($-$$).*

Duncreigan Country Inn is elegant, almost luxurious, all the more surprising for the moderate rates. Rooms are large and modern, but furnished in the best of traditional taste. The view from some rooms is across the harbor to the lighted spire of the village church. They also have one of the finest dining rooms in the province, serving the best local produce, lamb and seafood. It's a favorite oasis for others besides us, so dinner reservations are suggested. *Rte. 19, PO Box 59, Mabou, NS B0E 1X0,* ☎ *902/945-2207 ($$).*

The modern **Glenora Inn** is at the Glenora Distillery, just north of Mabou. The attractive motel-style rooms are in a courtyard formed by the distillery and its restaurant. A clear mountain brook runs through the grounds. The dining room ($$-$$$) serves a varied menu, such as rack of lamb, chicken parmesan or salmon, as well as some Scottish dishes. Dinner is often accompanied by Gaelic or bagpipe music. *Rte. 19, PO Box 181, Mabou, NS B0E 1X0, ☎ 902/258-2662 or 800/341-6096, 800/565-0000 in Canada, fax 902/258-3133 ($$).*

Inverness Lodge By The Sea has 10 hotel and 15 motel units near the sea. It's close to the beaches, hiking and other attractions of the area. Rooms are modern and comfortable and they have a dining room that serves three meals a day. *Rte. 19, PO Box 69, 15787 Central Ave, Inverness, NS B0E 1N0, ☎ 902/258-2193, fax 258-2177 ($$).*

West Lake Ainslie Cottages offers nine fully equipped housekeeping cottages overlooking the west end of Lake Ainslie, the largest lake in the province. They have both one- and two-bedroom units. In addition to the modern well-kept cabins, the owners can provide fishing and hunting guides and even picnic or catered meals by prior arrangement. At Strathlorne on Rte. 19, take the Lake Ainslie Road for seven miles. *RR 3, Inverness, NS B0E 1N0, ☎ 902/258-2654, evenings only ($$).*

Duck Cove Inn is a motel with units overlooking the Margaree River as it meets the sea. Most of the rooms have water views and some have balconies. They also have a restaurant. The inn is open May to November. *Margaree Harbour, B0E 2B0, ☎ 902/235-2658 or 800/565-9993, fax 902/235-2592 ($$).*

Mill Valley Farm is a small B&B in a fully restored century-old farmhouse. There are 147 acres, filled with forest and apple orchards, to roam on foot or by cross-country skis before enjoying the whirlpool bath. Take the first right north of the Margaree River Bridge. *Off Rte. 19, PO Box 15, Margaree Harbour, NS B0E 2B0, ☎ 902/235-2834 ($).*

Normaway Inn has guestrooms in the main lodge and one- or two-room cabins. The inn building dates from 1927, situated on 250 acres of land set among hills. They have their own dining room and dinner is usually accompanied by live music. It's open May to November. *Egypt Rd, Box 100, Margaree Valley, NS B0E 2C0, ☎ 902/248-2987, 800/565-9463, fax 902/248-2600 ($).*

Heart of Harts has four housekeeping cottages and five rooms in the restored 19th-century home. Walking, cross-country skiing and snowmobiling are available. A full Scottish breakfast is served in the morning; gourmet meals are served in the evening if reservations are made by mid-afternoon. We haven't stayed here, but several friends recommend it highly. *Box 21, North East Margaree, NS B0E 2H0, ☎ 902/248-2765, fax 248-2606 ($ cabins, $$ rooms).*

The Mull Café and Deli, operated by the energetic Mullendore family, is a great place to stop for lunch, dinner or supplies for a picnic in the Highlands. They offer not only salads, soups and sandwiches, but big fat deli sandwiches and entrées as well. Lunch prices are in the high-budget range. Dinner entrées might include lemon chicken supreme and scallops in wine. *Rte. 19, PO Box 59, Mabou, ☎ 902/945-2244, fax 945-2154 ($-$$).*

Frizzleton Market is an interesting combination of restaurant, craft store, antique store and cultural experience. They serve sandwiches on their own homemade multigrain and potato breads. It's open from 10 am to 6 pm. *Cabot Trail, Northeast Margaree, ☎ 902/248-2227.*

L'Auberge Doucet Inn, just south of Cheticamp, has eight rooms in a contemporary home. They also have a deck with views of Cheticamp Island and the Cape Breton Highlands. Rates include a continental breakfast. *PO Box 776, Cheticamp, NS B0E 1H0, ☎ 902/646-8668 or 902/224-3438 ($$).*

Laurie's Motor Inn is a modern motel with attractive and comfortable rooms in various sizes and styles. Some of the rooms have balconies and the motel is located on the main street close to the activity of the seafront and downtown. Their dining room ($$) serves seafood and Acadian specialties; local musicians occasionally perform in the lounge. *Rte. 19, PO Box 1, Cheticamp, NS B0E 1H0, ☎ 902/224-2400 or 800/959-4253, fax 902/224-2069 ($$-$$$).*

The Laurence Guest House, a B&B, overlooks the coast with splendid views of the colorful sunsets. Rooms are good sized and furnished with antiques. Evening tea is served in the parlor. Open May through October. *Rte. 19, PO Box 820, Cheticamp, NS B0E 1H0, ☎ 902/224-2184 ($).*

Les Cabines Du Portage, Cheticamp Sporting Camps, have six housekeeping cabins with two double beds and furnished kitchenettes and three two-bedroom cottages that will sleep six, with fully furnished kitchens. Views are over the mouth of Cheticamp harbor. *412A Main Street, Cheticamp, NS B0E 1H0, ☎ 902/224-2822 ($$).*

Chez Renée Café is just south of Cheticamp. Acadian and French cuisine dominate the menu, but they even have some Chinese dishes, burgers, sandwiches and salads. It's one of the most popular places in the west coast area. *Rte. 19, Grand Etang, ☎ 902/244-1446 ($).*

Restaurant Acadien has friendly wait-staff dressed in Acadian costume. The most popular thing on their Acadian menu is the chicken fricot, but you'll find many more local favorites that are hard to find elsewhere. Visit the craft coop before leaving. Open June-October. *774 Main St, Cheticamp, ☎ 902/224-3207 ($).*

The entrance to **Le Gabriel Restaurant** looks like a lighthouse, which is appropriate. Its specialty is seafood, but they also serve steaks and other traditional fare. You'll find a few Acadian dishes as well. On Tuesdays they have square dancing; from Wednesday through Saturday popular music is played; and on Saturday afternoons the sounds of fiddling fill the air. *Rte. 19, Cheticamp, ☎ 902/224-3685, fax 224-1213 ($-$$).*

The dining room at **Harbour Restaurant** in downtown Cheticamp overlooks the harbor. As you might expect, the specialty is seafood. *Le Quai Mathieu, Rte. 19, Cheticamp, ☎ 902/224-2042 ($$).*

The Rusty Anchor sits at the point where the Cabot Highway turns inland. Seafood is the specialty here, but they also have a nice salad bar. *Rte. 19, Pleasant Bay, ☎ 902/224-1313 ($$).*

The oyster and mussel bar and plentiful locally caught seafood have been drawing customers to **The Black Whale** restaurant for more than 20 years, and the cooks are kin to the fishermen who catch it. *Rte. 19, Pleasant Bay, ☎ 902/224-2185 ($-$$).*

North Cape & The East

Oakwood Manor Bed & Breakfast was built in the 1930s by the father of the present owner. It's snuggled into 150 acres of hillside. Walls, ceilings and floors are of oak with inlays of maple. They serve a full breakfast at the kitchen table. Rooms are comfortable and have in-room sinks, but share baths. *North Side Road, Cape North, NS B0C 1G0, ☎/fax 902/383-2317 ($).*

Highlands By the Sea was built a hundred years ago as a church rectory. It's a pleasant and inexpensive bed-and-breakfast with shared baths, in a fishing village setting just south of Bay St. Lawrence. *St. Margaret's Village, NS B0C 1R0, ☎ 902/383-2537 ($).*

Burton's Sunset Oasis sits on a hillside over the harbor. This small housekeeping hotel is close to the whale-watch boats and to activities at the tip of the island. *Bay St. Lawrence B0E 1G0, ☎ 902/383-2666, fax 902/383-2669 ($).*

Morrison's Pioneer Restaurant, next to the museum, occupies a building that was the center of local activity when it housed the general store. It is still a local gathering place because of this family-style restaurant. *Rte. 19 at Bay St. Lawrence Rd, Cape North, ☎ 902/383-2051 ($$).*

The Markland is a first-class country resort in a first-class location. It has both rooms and separate pine-paneled cabins with fully equipped kitchens. The dining room ($$$-$$$$) is one of the island's best, with innovative cuisine such as *mille-feuille* of lobster with sweet corn-butter sauce. Canoes and bicycles are available to guests. They also book whale-watching cruises on a two-masted schooner berthed nearby, the *Tom Saylor. Box 62, Dingwall, NS B0C 1G0, ☎ 902/383-2246 or 800/872-6084, fax 902/383-2092 ($$$-$$$$).*

Keltic Lodge has 72 rooms and 26 cottages in buildings that range from the baronial main lodge to the modern White Birch Inn and rustic two- and four-room cabins. All are impeccably cared for and tastefully furnished. Special packages are worth looking into. In winter they offer a ski package for $54 a person that includes lodging, continental breakfast, buffet dinner and ski ticket discounts for both downhill and cross-country skiing. This is a full-service resort with an outdoor pool, freshwater lake, three tennis courts, an 18-hole golf course and lots of beach. The location is striking, on its own forested rocky point of land jutting into the ocean, atop rocky cliffs that fall into the sea. **The Purple Thistle** dining room ($$$) is their top-of-the-line restaurant and serves outstanding entrées. The other eating place, the **Atlantic Restaurant**, is more casual and a bit less pricey. *Middle Head Peninsula, Ingonish Beach, B0C 1L0, ☎ 902/285-2880, 800/565-0444, fax 902/285-2859 ($$$$, including dinner and breakfast).*

Smokey View Cottages, just over a mile from the park entrance, has four new two-bedroom cottages with full kitchens and barbecues. They also have a playground. *Box 238, Ingonish Ferry, NS B0C 1L0, ☎ 902/285-2662 ($$-$$$).*

The Stephens' B&B is one of the nicest B&Bs we've seen on the island. This fine old country home is lovingly cared for, tastefully furnished and just right for relaxing. Set high on the bank over the Murray River, you can look out over the river and neighboring hillsides. North River Kayaking is just down the street. To get here, from North River Bridge take Murray Road opposite the church. *North River, RR #4, Baddeck, NS B0E 1B0, ☎/fax 902/929-2860.*

Lobster Galley is a big, friendly restaurant at the intersection of the Cabot Trail and TransCanada-105. It's best known for seafood, particularly lobster (which you pick from a tank), but they have a good general menu as well. *St. Ann's, ☎ 902/295-3100 ($$).*

■ Camping

Cape Breton Highlands National Park has several campgrounds; see descriptions below. Reservations are not accepted at any of them and availability is first-come, first-served. The park admission fee must be paid in addition to the daily camper fee. Rates run from $14-16 per night, with the fourth night free. Campgrounds are open from late May to early October. *Ingonish Beach, NS B0C 1L0, ☎ 902/224-2306 or 285-2691 for all areas; special numbers listed separately below.*

- **Cheticamp** (☎ 902/224-2310): Near entrance to the park. 20 unserviced wooded sites for tents and RVs. Showers, theater, kitchen shelters with wood stoves.
- **Corner Brook:** Open sites on the ocean. Kitchen shelters with wood stoves, playground, beach (unsupervised), self registration.
- **MacIntosh Brook:** Pleasant Bay area. 10 unserviced sites. Open in wooded valley. Kitchen shelters with wood stoves, self registration.

■ **Big Intervale:** Cape North area. Open sites on the river. Kitchen shelters with wood stoves, self registration.

■ **Broad Cove** (902/224-2524): Ingonish area. 193 unserviced sites, 83 RV sites. Open and wooded sites near the ocean. Showers, kitchen shelters with wood stoves, swimming, playgrounds, theater.

■ **Ingonish:** 90 unserviced sites, both open and wooded. Showers, kitchen shelters with wood stoves, swimming in July and August.

MacLeod's Beach Campsite is a west-facing campground with a quarter-mile of beach on warm sea, bracketed by highland bluffs. They offer fully serviced wooded and open sites, with shower and washrooms as well as a laundry. *Dunvegan, RR #1, Inverness, NS B0E 1N0, ☎ 902/258-2433, fax 258-2653.*

Plage St. Pierre Beach and Campground has fully serviced RV and tent sites. Amenities include a laundry, canteen, beaches, boardwalk and nature trails, tennis courts, volleyball, miniature golf and more. *PO Box 430, Cheticamp, NS B0E 1H0, ☎ 800/565-0000 (in Canada), 800/341-6096 (US), 902/224-2112 or 2642, fax 903/224-1579.*

Meat Cove Camping is at the end of a long road that is gravel for the last part; the drive alone is a reason to come here. There are 20 campsites perched (we don't use this term lightly) on a highland bluff with spectacular views into the Gulf of St. Lawrence. The campground has toilets and showers and sells firewood. These are rustic campsites with primitive facilities. Sit on the hillside and watch whales cavort below or join the owner for one of his whale watch cruises in Bay St. Lawrence. *c/o Kenneth McLellan, Meat Cove, NS B0C 1E0, ☎ 902/383-2379.*

Hideaway Campground and Oyster Market has 25 unserviced sites and five with electricity. There is a playground, plus canoeing, fishing and swimming in the Aspy River. They also have canoe and kayak rentals, and Aspy Bay oysters on the halfshell for sale. *RR #2, Dingwall, NS B0C 1G0, ☎ 902/383-2116.*

Dino's Camping Trailer Park has 25 open serviced sites (18 with sewage hookups) for $13.50. They offer showers and a place to buy groceries. Open June through October. *Box 64, Victoria County, Ingonish, NS B0C 1K0, ☎ 902/285-2614.*

Cape Breton Lakes

No wonder the Scots felt so at home in Cape Breton: not only did it have the moor-covered highlands, but its lowlands are filled with long narrow lakes, reminiscent of Scottish lochs. More heavily French than the north, this region has a rich ethnic blend of Gaelic, Gallic, and English traditions.

Geography & History

The eastern side of Cape Breton is characterized by low hills, the huge expanse and several arms of Bras d'Or Lakes and the low marshy areas of the lands south of Sydney. From St. Anns Harbour east is essentially a series of islands connected by bridges and ferries, making east-west travel difficult. Bras d'Or Lakes fill the center of the area, with openings to the sea through the St. Andrew's Channel in the north and an historic canal at St. Peter's Bay in the south.

Except around Sydney, North Sydney, Sydney Mines and Glace Bay, settlement is mostly along the primary routes or a few hundred feet from them. Away from the highways, the land is mostly wilderness. This proximity of wilderness to civilization is one of the exciting things about Cape Breton.

Where the Highlands of Cape Breton were settled primarily by Scots, the areas to the east have a broader blend. The French settled early and the Fortress of Louisbourg, southeast of Sydney, became the stronghold of the French Empire in North America. So many francs were spent on its construction that Louis XIV is reported to have said that he expected any day to see its spires rising on the horizon. The scourge of British-held New England, it was attacked and finally destroyed in 1758 by New Englanders under British command.

The English may have taken control, but the French heritage is still obvious throughout the area, particularly in the place names. Isle Madame, in the south at the Strait of Canso, is another center of French culture and settlement. The Sydney area also has a black heritage, a result of the British transportation of slaves freed during the British invasion of the Chesapeake Bay in 1813.

With the British dominant after the fall of Louisbourg, the English influence and settlements spread. It's interesting to note that although 32,000 Loyalists emigrated to Canada during the American Revolution, only 140 of those families settled in Cape Breton.

Getting Around

Despite the sprawling form of the lake, you have more options for routes in the south than in the highlands. If you are primarily interested in getting to the Ferry in North Sydney, or to the restoration at Fortress Louisbourg, take Rte. 104 from Port Hastings to Port Hawkesbury. From here the fastest route is to continue on Rte. 4 through St. Peter's and on to Sydney. You'll see more of the countryside, however, if you opt for the only slightly slower pace of Rte. 4 to St. Peter's. Along the way you can detour onto Rte. 320 for a trip around Isle Madame.

From St. Peter's, Rte. 4 follows the southeast shore of Bras d'Or Lakes, through small settlements and with views out over the wide lake. To get to the Newfoundland ferry, take Rte. 125 north to North Sydney. For Louisbourg, take Rte. 125 east a short distance to Rte. 327, which you follow to Louisbourg.

Rte. 105, the TransCanada Highway, follows the northern shore of Bras d'Or Lake, and the un-numbered Bras d'Or Scenic Drive follows the shoreline from St. Peter's through Dundee to Rte. 105 just south of Whycocomagh. The Bras d'Or Scenic Drive continues most of the way around the lake.

An optional route to the Sydney-Louisbourg area is to take Rte. 105 from Port Hastings through Whycocomagh and to follow the Bras d'Or Scenic Drive at the ferry over the St. Patrick Channel to Little Narrows. At Little Narrows you can turn left or right; either way you will end up at the bridge in Iona. Take the bridge over the Barra Strait to Great Narrows, where you again have two options. If the Newfoundland ferry is your primary goal, take Rte. 223 along the east shore of the St. Andrews Channel to the town of Bras d'Or. If Louisbourg is the objective, follow the Bras d'Or Scenic Drive along the southern and eastern sides of the peninsula to Rte. 4, following it north toward Sydney.

Information Sources

■ For information on all of Cape Breton Island, contact **Tourism Cape Breton Inc.**, PO Box 627, Sydney, NS B1P 6H7, ☎ 800/565-9464.

■ **Victoria County Recreation Dept.** can send you information on the area west of Baddeck to the north tip of the island. Contact them at PO Box 370, Baddeck, NS B0E 1B0, ☎ 902/295-3231, fax 295-3331, Web site http://org.atcon.com/ceilidh/victoria.htm, e-mail verdt@atcon.com.

■ **Richmond Tourism**, PO Box 658, Louisdale, NS B0E 1V0, ☎ 902/345-2700, covers the south end of Bras d'Or Lake, including the St. Peter's area and Isle Madame.

■ **Northside Visitor Information Centre**, Purves St., North Sydney B2A 1B9, ☎ 902/794-7719, is next to the Marine Atlantic Terminal (follow the signs for the Newfoundland Ferry). It's open 9 am to 8 pm daily.

■ **Fortress of Louisbourg**, St. Peter's Canal, PO Box 160, Louisbourg, NS B0A 1M0, ☎ 902/733-2280, fax 733-2362, TDD 733-3607, can send you information on happenings there.

Adventures

■ On Foot

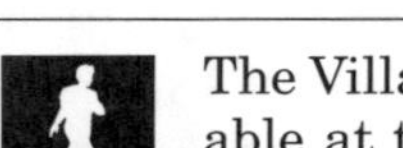

The Village of St. Peter's has a handy walking map, available at the Information Center just west of the canal or from Richmond Tourism, Box 658, Louisdale, NS B0E 1V0, ☎ 902/345-2700. A pleasant walking trail follows the coast of St. Peter's Bay along the abandoned rail line and to ruins of 17th- and 18th-century British forts in Battery Provincial Park. Picnic facilities are available at the park. Seven miles east of St. Peter's on the Fleur de Lis Trail is Point Michaud Beach, with two miles of sand beaches for swimming, walking and beachcombing.

Highland Hill Trail is on the island in Bras d'Or Lakes that lies between Iona and Grand Narrows. If you follow it to the lookouts on Cains Mountain, you can see all of the four counties of Cape Breton, and if you read the trail's interpretive panels, you'll learn about modern forest management and silviculture. To reach the trailhead at MacKinnons Harbour from Rte. 105, take Rte. 223 (and the ferry), turning south at the ferry landing. Signs lead you from McKinnons Harbour, along Barra Glen Road to Highland Hill Road. Stay to the right after the MacNeil sawmill and the parking lot will be on the left. The trail is wide and well maintained but there are steep sections on the mountain. It is like a series of stacked loops with each loop larger than the previous. As a result there are several options, the shortest being 1½ miles and the longest (the entire outside loop) just under five miles. From the parking lot take the left-hand trail. As you progress, you will pass two additional trails on the right. Either of these cuts across to the return trail (turn right at the far end), but if you follow them you will miss the views from the mountain.

Uisge Ban Falls drops 50 feet into the pristine highlands and was believed by the Indians to be a place of special spiritual value. The trail is about 4½ miles, with a shorter option. It passes through an old clear-cut regrown to young forest and then into old growth forests with red and sugar maples, hemlock and white pine that may be as old as 200 years. Naturalists will want to watch for rare wildflowers, plants, mosses and lichens along the route. At the fork in the trail, close to the trailhead, a left will take you on the most direct route, but we suggest the northbound trail along the river to the right. It crosses Falls Brook and then follows the North Branch of the Baddeck River before curling back inland to the south. Go right when you come to the intersection with the more direct trail, continuing along the brook to the falls. Return on the shorter trail. To get there take Exit 9 at Baddeck and go to Baddeck Bridge, then take MacPhees Road to Baddeck Forks. A left at the intersection leads to the parking lot.

A bit farther south at **Whycocomagh Provincial Park**, on Rte. 105, a 1½-mile return-trip trail goes to the top of Salt Mountain, 750 feet above the lake. From the top are views of the mountains and over the lake. The mountain gets its name from saline springs on its slopes.

Sydney Harbour is a long, broad inlet that forks into the Northwest Arm and the South Arm. Across the South Arm from the city is **Petersfield Provincial Park**, Department of Natural Resources, RR#6, Sydney, NS B1P 6T2, ☎ 902/563-3370. The property was first settled in 1787 by David Mathews, a Revolutionary War-era mayor of New York City, who escaped after being accused of plotting to assassinate George Washington. He became a high official on Cape Breton, and at his death the property passed through the hands of other wealthy owners, who established fine gardens there. While each of the four mansions that once stood there are gone, a number of pleasant and easy walking trails lead through the former gardens and to Point Amelia. Among the gardens of the estate was an extensive wildflower garden that included many species not native to this area. Many of these have acclimatized themselves, making the grounds unusually interesting. Picnic sites and many of the trails are wheelchair accessible. The park is officially open from mid-May to mid-October but is available to the public year round. Take Exit 5 from Rte. 125 west of Sydney and travel north to Westmont Road (Rte. 239). The entrance is about a half-mile on the left.

The trail at **Cape Breton** gives you the chance to walk to the easternmost point in Nova Scotia (aside from a few offshore islands), see the remnants of the last ice age and appreciate the power of the sea. This trail is about 9½ miles long and follows the coastline closely, partly over beaches, cobble and gravel. It is moderately difficult, both for its length and for the terrain. Part of it is right on the beach and other parts are on the cliffs above the rough Main-à-Dieu Passage. Take Rte. 22 east from Sydney to Louisbourg and then follow the Marconi Trail north through Little Lorraine, a bit over two miles to a dirt road on the right, near the top of a hill. The dirt road ends near a beach, which you can walk along to Baleine Head. You can see the Fortress at Louisbourg on clear days. Follow the shore line to Hummocky Point and then along the beach of Kelpy Cove to Cape Breton, the eastern point of the main island. Continuing along the coast the trail follows the shore of Anse aux Cannes (Bay of Dogs). On the north end of the Bay, Convict Point juts into the sea and the trail continues along the top of the cliffs above the Main-à-Dieu Passage to the town of Main-à-Dieu. Along this leg look off to sea for Scatarie Island, a home for fishing families until the 1940s and now a wildlife sanctuary for Arctic hare and rock ptarmigan. In Main-à-Dieu, the trail ends at a road, which you can follow to the main highway and walk along it to the Baleine dirt road and your car.

North of Main-à-Dieu, the **Main-à-Dieu Trail** leads over a low gravel and sand-covered area of glacial moraine. These glacial droppings have created a cobble beach. Follow the directions to the Cape Breton Trail, but pass by the Baleine Road and continue on through the village of Main-à-Dieu to a parking lot on top of the hill on the other side of town. The trail is about three miles and is best walked at low tide. Parts of the trail along cliffs can be eroded, so be careful. Take the trail downhill to the beach and across a shallow channel at the mouth of Hall Pond. On the far side of the channel follow the trail through the trees to the top of Moque Head. Scatarie Island lighthouse, directly ahead, marks the other side of the Main-à-Dieu Passage. From Moque Head the trail continues along the shoreline of Mira Bay before deteriorating at a cut-over. Return along the same route.

The **Gull Cove Trail** at Gabarus, along the southern shore of Gabarus Bay, is a good place to see how glacial till and the tides combine to form barrier beaches that enclose freshwater ponds. At the end of the trail there is a chance to explore the remains of an abandoned fishing village. From Sydney take Rte. 327 south from Exit 7 of Rte. 125 through Marion Bridge to Gabarus. A gravel road leads from the breakwater on the far side of town to the cemetery, where you can park. The trail is about eight miles long and, while moderately level, is usually wet, so you'll want waterproof shoes. The trail goes around Harris Lake, behind a barrier beach. It then follows the shore, past remnants of two stone walls, and around Lowell Point. You will see the small Hardy's Point jutting into the sea and then the small Gull Cove, and the shore sweeping out to Cape Gabarus. The cliffs on the far end of the cove are unique for this part of the coast. Gull Cove is the site of a former fishing village and it's fun to find the foundations and try to picture what it was like as a living village. Backpackers can camp here. While the trail continues from here around Cape Gabarus and down the coast for an additional 15 miles, only the most experienced and well equipped hikers should follow it, because of the severe weather conditions that occur unexpectedly along this section. The extended trail runs out along the barrier beaches of Cape Gabarus, Winging Point and Fourchu Bay, an area that offers little protection and where the waves can crash over the fragile protective barriers taking everything in their path.

Guided Hiking Trips

■ An interesting walking tour on the east shore of Bras d'Or Lakes is with John Willie MacInnis, a naturalist who grew up in this area and who delights in telling others of its natural history. His company is **Big Pond Eagle Tours**, Big Pond, NS B0A 1H0, ☎ 902/828-3052, and the rates are $15 age 12 and over, $5 under age 12. The tour takes you down an old country road and through fields, accompanied by tales of the natural world around you and the people who have inhabited it. Big Pond is about halfway between St. Peter's and Sydney.

■ The **Green Highlander Lodge** outfits guided hiking trips to North River Falls and Uisge Ban Falls, both north of Baddeck. They also guide hiking trips in western Cape Breton. Contact them at PO Box 128, Baddeck, NS B0E 1B0, ☎ 902/295-2303, Web site www.capebretonnet.com/baddeck/greenhighlander.

■ On Wheels

Bicycling Equipment Rentals

■ **Kayak Cape Breton and Cottages**, West Bay, Roberta, NS B0E 2K0, ☎/fax 902/535-3060, on the south shore of Bras d'Or Lakes between St. Peter's and Dundee, rents mountain and touring bikes. Rates are $10 per day, $45 per week.

■ **Island Eco-Adventures**, 16 Chebucto Street in downtown Baddeck, ☎ 800/707-5512 or 902/295-3303, rents touring and off-road bikes and does repairs. They offer hourly, half- and full-day rates. Cycling and camping equipment is also available for rent, and they can advise you on the best and most interesting routes, as well as make suggestions on guided tours and cycle camping. Write c/o Brian Doncaster, PO Box 34, Baddeck, NS B0E 1B0.

■ **The Outdoor Store**, Chebucto St., Baddeck, ☎ 902/295-2576, e-mail outdoor@atcon.com, has bicycle rentals, a full repair shop and conduct cycling tours. They also carry a full line of camping equipment and outdoor clothing.

■ **Wheels and Reels**, 7535 Main St., Louisbourg, ☎ 902/733-2933, offers a full range of bicycle rental from youth to adult. Rentals include helmet, lock and a map of local bike routes. Rates are two hours for $8, half-day $14, full day $20 and weekly $80. They also have car racks and children's bicycle seats for rent. They're open 9 am to 7 pm and also rent fishing equipment.

On Water

Canoeing & Kayaking

Experienced kayakers will want to explore some of the island's best ocean routes, off the east coast. While enjoyable to explore, these are on the open Atlantic Ocean and should only be taken by strong, experienced kayakers or with experienced guides. Mira Bay and the broad meandering Mira River have tall cliffs and seacaves, and the wide Gabarus Bay at Kennington Cove, south of Louisbourg, or at Gabarus off of Rte. 327, has cliffs, seabirds and seals. At Scatarie Island, across the Main-à-Dieu Passage northeast of Louisbourg, you'll find shipwrecks and warm water swimming. Or try Cow Bay and Louisbourg Bay, once one of the busiest harbors in the new world.

The broad and expansive Bras d'Or Lake is too large to see in only one trip. In the northern part of the lake you might try the long reaches of Great Bras d'Or, the St. Andrew's Channel or the Indian Islands area of East Bay. On the west and south shores look at Denys and North Basin, St. Patrick's Channel or West Bay and St. Peter's Inlet. If you bring your own canoe or kayak most of the outfitters have special prices that allow you to join their groups or to hire a guide for your own explorations.

Harvey Boat Renters, Public Dock, Baddeck, ☎ 902/295-3318, doesn't do tours, but they do rent kayaks and sailing craft. Kayak rates are $10 per hour and $40 a day. A 16-foot Hobie catamaran is $22 per hour or $88 a day. They also have motorboats: a 12-foot fiberglass boat with a 15-hp motor is $30 per hour or $120 per day. Sailboats are also available; a 12-foot Widgeon is $15 an hour or $60 a day, a 28-foot Aloha is $185 a day, and a 32-foot Ontario is $235 a day. They have a number of boats of each type available.

At Roberta on the Bras d'Or Scenic Drive between St. Peter's and Dundee **Kayak Cape Breton and Cottages**, West Bay, Roberta, NS B0E 2K0, ☎/fax 902/535-3060, rents canoes and kayaks for use on the lake. Canoes and single kayaks are $20 for a half-day, $35 for a full day, or $120 per week. Double kayaks are $30-$50 or $165 per week. Kayak Cape Breton also has several guided kayak and canoe tours on the lake, a lake and ocean combo, a trip along the shores and islets of Point Michaud and Grand River and trips to Port Hood, the Margaree and Cheticamp. Two-day trips are $175, three-day $280, and the five-day Cape Breton trip is $490. One-day guided river kayaking trips are $80 per person and include introductory kayak lessons. More extensive lessons, including a whole day of perfecting the Eskimo roll and rescue, are available. A morning lesson is only $25; for another $10 they'll throw in a short guided tour after the lesson. Minimum of two people. Check with them for dates of special trips.

South of Sydney, **Paradise Kayak Tours**, 220 Byrnes Lane, Marion Bridge, NS B0A 1P0, ☎ 902/733-3244, offers three-hour ($45) and full-day ($120) kayaking adventures. Tours include instructions and lessons on shallow waters; beginners are welcome. They also will help more experienced kayakers brush up on their technique. Equipment rental is available only to tour customers.

The Baddeck River and the Bras d'Or Lakes provide pleasant canoeing and kayaking waters. The **Green Highlander Lodge** does guided 3½-hour trips on the Baddeck River that are suitable for all levels of experience, for $45 including lunch. The 2½-hour evening paddles are topped off with a barbecue on the shore for only $30 per person. Canoe rentals are $10 an hour, $25 a half-day and $50 a full day. Kayaks are $30 an hour, $50 for a half-hour and $85 a full day. Close to Baddeck you will be able to see bald eagles, wood ducks, ospreys and several varieties of small mammals. Contact them at PO Box 128, Baddeck, NS B0E 1B0, ☎ 902/295-2303, Web site www.capebretonnet.com/baddeck/greenhighlander.

Island Eco-Adventures, Box 34, Baddeck, NS B0E 1B0, ☎ 800/707-5512 or 902/295-3303, also rents canoes, life vests and cartop racks and can give advice on the best local places to go.

On the east coast of Cape Breton, **Island Seafari Sea Kayaking**, 20 Paddy's Lane, Louisbourg, NS B0A 1M0, ☎ 902/733-2309 or 902/567-4878 (cellular), offers a wide variety of tours including three hours, day, two-day and extended. They also have kayaking courses for $30 per person. The rates include guide, kayak, equipment, PFD's and snorkeling and fishing equipment and run from $38 for the three-hour tour to $170 for the two-day tour. Rental rates for kayaks are (singles) $25 a half-day, $45 a full day, and (doubles) $35 a half-day, $65 a full day. Packages including lodging at local inns cost between $182.50 (one-day and overnight tour) and $250 per person (two days kayaking, one night lodging).

Harbor & Bay Tours

St. Ann's Harbour Boat Tours, Box 33, Englishtown, NS B0C 1H0, ☎ 902/929-2563, gives a different vantage point to see the harbor and surrounding mountains. Narrated cruises leave from their dock on Rte. 312 close to the ferry landing at Englishtown.

When Nova Scotia planned its exhibit at the 1967 World's Fair in Montreal, they built a 47-foot replica of a fishing schooner like those that had been the glory of the Maritimes at the turn of the century. The schooner *Atlantica*, a two-masted kissing cousin of the *Bluenose*, was the ship, and it now cruises the Bras d'Or Lakes and as far away as Prince Edward Island. **Tor Bay Charters Ltd.** is operated by Gordon and Mary Pellerin, teachers who spend their summers on board the schooner. The ship can accommodate up to four passengers, and they are willing to adjust the itinerary if bookings allow. They will arrange transportation from Halifax International Airport. Contact PO Box 12, Larry's River, NS B0H 1T0, ☎ 902/525-2516, fax 533-3554, e-mail torbay@auracom.co, Web site http://business.atcon.com/torbay/.

➲ **BIRDERS TAKE NOTE:** *For birding cruises to the Bird Islands off St. Ann's Bay, and eagle-watching cruises on Bras d'Or Lakes, see* Wildlife-Watching, *below.*

Loch Breagh Boat Tours, Government Wharf, Baddeck, ☎ 902/295-2016 or 295-1565, provides tours of Bras d'Or Lakes at 10 am, 1:30 and 4 pm daily. They have a special golf package that allows golfers to cruise down the lake to the Dundee Resort course, play a game and cruise back. They also have an occasional evening cruise on the lake.

Perhaps the queen of the Bras d'Or cruising fleet is the two-masted schooner ***Amoeba***, Government Wharf, Baddeck, ☎ 902/295-2481 or 295-1426, e-mail amoeba@auracom.com. Built in 1977, she sailed the Virgin Islands before coming to Bras d'Or. There are regular 1½-hour tours of Bras d'Or Lakes with plenty of seating on deck, leaving at 11 am, 2, 4:30, and 6:30 pm daily, from June through September. The fare is $16 for adults, $14 for seniors and $8 for children ages eight-15.

In 1917 Alexander Graham Bell launched the 54-foot yawl ***Elsie*** as a gift to his daughter and her husband. Now fully restored, this historic vessel, based in her old home port of Baddeck, is available for charter sailing on Bras d'Or Lakes. *Elsie*, c/o Odessey Cape Breton, PO Box 737, Baddeck, NS B0E 1B0, ☎ 800/565-5660 or 902/295-3500, fax 902/295-3527.

At Big Pond, on the east shore of Bras d'Or Lakes and about halfway between Sydney and St. Peter's, there are two options for sailing the lake and enjoying its birdlife. **Cape Breton Lake Charters**, RR#1, Big Pond, NS B0A 1H0, ☎ 902/828-2476, has a two-hour guided boat tour along the shore in an 18-foot runabout operated by Calum MacPhee. For one or two people the fee is $50; for up to four, $75. The other option is to take a day sail with Pat Nelder on his 30-foot sailboat to the MacPhee Islands in East Bay. The rate is $350 for a maximum of four people. Both operators can arrange customized tours on request.

On the south end of the Lake, **Super Natural Sailing Tours**, RR#1, St. Peter's, NS B0E 3B0, ☎ 800/903-3371 or 902/535-3371, fax 902/535-2209, offers cruises aboard a 50-foot catamaran from the Johnstown Market in Johnstown, on Rte. 4, about 20 minutes from St. Peter's. A mesh net on the back of the boat collects plankton that you can see with the on-board microscope. It's part of the naturalist's maritime program. Two marine biologists operate the cruises, and can tell you about the creatures that live in the waters as well as the eagles and other birds overhead. The 2½-hour tours depart at 10 am and 1:30 pm from mid-May to the end of October. Adults are $28; children ages six-12, $14. Refreshments are available on board and there is seating in the cabin or on deck. Sailing is smooth on a cat, and it is wheelchair accessible.

Cruising

While this book does not cover cruising (a number of books cover that subject in great detail), the popularity of the Isle Madame area and Bras d'Or Lakes prompts us to include marinas in this area.

- On Isle Madame, **Isle Madame Yacht Club**, Box 186, Arichat, NS B0E 1A0, ☎ 902/226-1020 or 226-1674, fax 226-9312, or **Lennox Passage Yacht Club**, D'Escousse, NS B0E 1K0, ☎ 902/226-2187 or 625-2400, VHF Channel 68.

- At St. Peter's, **St. Peter's Lions Club Marina**, Strachan Cove, St. Peter's, NS B0E 3B0, ☎ 902/535-2309.

- On Bras d'Or, **Lake Dundee Resort Marina**, RR#2 West Bay, NS B0E 3K0, ☎ 902/345-0430, fax 345-2697, VHF Channel 68.

Diving

Safari Divers, Port Hawkesbury, NS B0E 2V0, ☎ 902/625-3751, is a full service outfitter that sells and services equipment and has guided wreck tours, scallop dives and even spear fishing for trout in their own pond. They also fill tanks and are open seven days a week.

On Isle Madame there is good diving in Chedabucto Bay, and **Vollmer's Island Paradise Inc.**, PO Box 53, West Arichat, NS B0E 3J0, ☎ 902/226-1507, fax 226-9853, has an extensive program of diving from July through September. They dive on the 1971 wreck of the tanker *Arrow*, now resting in two pieces at a depth of 27 feet, and on several other wrecks. They feature underwater photography and video. A dive master, lessons and diving center are available for all levels of experience.

Fishing

Wheels and Reels, 7535 Main St., Louisbourg, ☎ 902/733-2933, is one of those rare places that rents fishing equipment. They can also tell you where the best local places are. Rates are $4 for two hours, $5 half-day, $6 full day and $5 a day for multiday rentals. They also have bait and lures. If you know you're going to need equipment, call and reserve.

■ On Snow

Skiing

Downhill skiing is available in the lakes area at **Ski Ben Eoin** (pronounced *Ben Yon*), PO Box 3, East Bay, NS B0A 1H0, ☎ 902/828-2804, fax 902/828-2550, recorded ski conditions 902/828-2222. The 30-year-old area has 11 trails from beginner to expert. All of them are covered by snowmaking, essential here, where the Gulf Stream tempers air temperatures. Beginner and instruction slopes are set apart from the general ski area, a boon to both beginners and advanced skiers. Although the vertical drop is only 500 feet, the longest run is a comfortable 3,500 feet. The main trails are served by a triple chairlift and others by a platter and a rope tow on the beginner slope. A rental shop has snowboard and ski rentals, including parabolics. Lifts run, weather permitting, from mid-December to April, Sunday through Friday, 9 am to 10 pm, and on Saturday from 9 am to 6 pm. Lift prices vary with time (from two hours to six+ hours) and lifts. A ticket for six or more hours for the chairlift is $24, $33 with ski rental; a three-hour

> **➲ CROSS-COUNTRY SKIING:** *While many of the hiking trails in the lakes area would make good cross-country trails, snow in this area is fairly unreliable. The best cross-country skiing is in the highlands around Ingonish and in the North Cape area near Dingwall.*

Nova Scotia

ticket is $20 ($30 with rental). Ski Ben Eoin has a busy schedule of events throughout the season including races, teen ski socials, Carnival Weekend and a New Year's Eve Family Affair with skiing, fireworks and bonfires.

Island Eco-Adventures, 16 Chebucto St., Baddeck, ☎ 800/707-5512 or 902/295-3303, rents lightweight snowshoes in the winter. Write c/o Brian Doncaster, PO Box 34, Baddeck, NS B0E 1B0.

Cultural & Eco-Travel Experiences

La Picasse, Petit de Gras, Isle Madame, ☎ 888/811-0118 or 902/226-0002, serves as a cultural center for the French residents of Isle Madame, with classrooms and programs to preserve Acadian culture in the area. Exhibitions of crafts and art and handmade items are for sale and a small cafeteria-style restaurant serves good Acadian food. Production Picasse, PO Box 362, Petit de Grat, Isle Madame, NS B0E 2L0, operates an earthenware pottery at La Picasse, producing hand-painted vases and items bearing maritime scenes. Tours are available all year, Monday through Friday 9 am to 4 pm.

On the Port Hawkesbury waterfront, **The Creamery** houses the new Artisans Co-op. It sells works of art and other products handmade in Cape Breton. During July there is a quilt market at The Creamery.

■ Ceilidhs & Festivals

Sunday evenings at 7 pm in July and August there are **concerts** on the Granville Green, at the bandshell just off the main street of Port Hawkesbury overlooking the Strait of Canso. These concerts feature Cape Breton singers and musicians and have included such performers as the Rankin Family. It's a celebration of the Acadian and Gaelic heritage of the island and of the music they have produced.

Baddeck is the home base of **Centre Bras d'Or Festival of the Arts**, Rave Entertainment, 197 Charlotte St. Suite 2, Sydney, NS B1P 1C4, box office ☎ 800/708-1811 or 902/295-2787, offices 902/539-8800. The festival is a celebration of music and the visual arts that continues from June to October. During July and August there are musical productions from the classics to Cape Breton folk music almost every night. The Mainstage for musical productions is at Baddeck Academy; the Masonic Hall in the center of town is the venue for all Soundscapes and theater productions. More than 50 performances are presented during the season.

During August the Gaelic College of Celtic Arts and Crafts holds the **A Ceilidh Series**, at the Englishtown Community Hall on Rte. 312. This summer-long ceilidh series features major Cape Breton performers in programs that begin at 9 pm on each performance date. Admission is $7. Contact the college for specific dates at PO Box 9, Baddeck, NS B0E 1B0, ☎ 902/295-3411, fax 295-2912, e-mail gaelcoll@atcon.com, Web site www.taisbean.com/gaeliccollege.

During July and August ***Feis An Eilein*** (Festival of the Island), PO Box 17, Christmas Island, NS B0A 1C0, ☎ 902/622-2627, holds its festival at the town of Christmas Island, on Rte. 223 just over the Barra Strait at Iona. Feis is a community group dedicated to the preservation and teaching of the Gaelic language and culture. Programs include Gaelic language and song and a stepdance program held once a week for four weeks, Gaelic learning and activity camps for young people, fiddling lessons and information sessions, song workshops and ceilidhs. Programs change from year to year.

Along Rte. 4 on the east shore of Bras d'Or, the **Annual Ben Eoin Fiddle and Folk Music Festival** features top names in country and folk music, including many of the leaders in Cape Breton music, at the Ben Eoin ski area. The concert is held on the middle weekend of August from 1 to 6 pm.

On the last weekend of June the Northside Highland Dancers Association begins its **Annual Dockside Ceilidhs** at the outdoor theater on the North Sydney Waterfront next to the Atlantic Marine Ferry Terminal. Ceilidhs continue daily at the outdoor theater, July through September, with performance times keyed to the departure time of the Newfoundland Ferry. On Tuesdays and Thursdays performances are at 1:30 pm, Wednesday and Friday at 11:30 am and Saturday and Sunday at 8 pm. Weekday performances are about an hour in duration and weekends run 1½ to two hours. For a schedule, ☎ 902/794-3772, fax 794-4787, or stop at the Visitors Information Centre (see *Information*, page 388).

On the last Saturday of November the **Annual Scottish Concert** is presented at St. John's Anglican Church Hall on Pierce St., North Sydney, featuring dancers, pipers, fiddlers and singers.

July 1 is celebrated throughout Canada as **Canada Day**, the anniversary of Canadian confederation. In Sydney Mines, the celebrations are in Miners Memorial Park at 38 Pitt Street and in North Sydney at Smelt Brook Park on Pierce Street. Starting on Monday of the second week of August the **Annual Cape Breton County Exhibition** is held at the Exhibition Grounds on Regent Street, North Sydney. This county fair lasts for a week and includes agricultural, forestry and marine exhibits, a midway, shows and performances and horse shows.

The heritage of Cape Breton's Scottish immigrants is celebrated at the **Nova Scotia Highland Village Museum**, 4119 Rte. 223, Iona, ☎ 902/725-2272. On the first Saturday in August the village holds **Highland Village Day**, with ceilidhs, dances and other special Scottish activities; throughout the summer they hold other special events. Authentic buildings that have been brought to the site from around the island include houses, a general store, carding mill, blacksmith shop and school. There is also a replica of a Hebrides Island "black house." The museum is open from June to September, Monday through Saturday, 9 am to 5 pm; Sundays, 10 am to 6 pm. Admission is $4 adults, $8 family. On the first Sunday of July and the end of August the Village has a traditional Cod Fish Supper, and during July and August, on Saturday nights, they have round and square dancing under the stars. On the first Sunday of August is the annual Highland Village Day.

Beaton Institute of Cape Breton Studies, University College of Cape Breton, Glace Bay Highway, Sydney, ☎ 902/539-5300 ext 327, is the college's archive of Cape Breton history and culture. The documents and materials extend from the colonial period to the present and cover the social, industrial and cultural history of the island and its varied ethnic groups. Items include recordings of ethnic music and current Cape Breton music makers. From June to September, it's open free, Monday through Friday from 8:30 am to 4 pm; from September through May, hours are 8:30 am to 4:30 pm.

Cape Breton Centre for Heritage and Science, 225 George St., Sydney, ☎ 902/539-1572. The Centre concentrates on the social and natural history of the island and presents it in a series of in-house and traveling exhibits. It is free and open all year. From June to September, daily hours are 10 am to 4 pm; the rest of the year, Tuesday through Friday, 10 am to 4 pm and Saturday 1 to 4 pm.

The Louisbourg Playhouse, 11 Aberdeen St., Louisbourg, NS B0A 1M0, ☎ 888/733-2787, 902/733-2996, Web site www.

gdlewis.ednet.ns.ca/lsbrg/playhs.html. The playhouse is a unique setting, originally built for the Disney movie *Squanto: A Warrior's Tale*. It opens in mid-June and runs every evening at 8 pm until into the fall, presenting Fortress Follies (a family comedy and music show), the Soundscapes Concert Series with Cape musicians on Wednesday and Friday evenings, and a variety of other productions. On Sunday afternoons at 3 pm, matinee performances are given by local entertainers.

Wildlife-Watching

Hertford and Ciboux Islands lie off the east coast about 1½ miles north of the entrance of St. Ann's Bay. Called the Bird Islands, their steep cliffs provide nesting grounds for a variety of seabirds. **Puffin Boat Tours**, Box 33, Englishtown, NS B0C 1H0, ☎ 902/929-2563, has narrated tours to them. Their dock is on Rte. 312 near the ferry landing at Englishtown. The fare is $25 per person and reservations are suggested.

PUFFINS GUARANTEED

Captain Joe Van Schaick has been taking tours out to the Bird Islands to see seabirds and seals for the last 25 years. From May to August, you'll see Atlantic puffins, razorbills, and black-legged kittiwakes; from May to September, you'll find black guillemots, great cormorants, double-crested cormorants, herring gulls, and great black-backed gulls. Puffins are guaranteed between May 15th and the end of August. Bald eagles can be sighted from June to September. Nearly 200 gray seals (a species once thought to be extinct) can be seen between June and September. To reserve, which is a good idea, contact Bird Island Boat Tours, RR#1, Big Bras d'Or, NS B0C 1B0, ☎ 800/661-6680 or 902/674-2384. They leave from the Mountain View By The Sea Cabins and Campground. The 2½-hour cruise, which costs $27 for adults and $12.50 for children, has a cruising time to the islands of about 40 minutes. The settlement of Big Bras d'Or is north of Rte. 105 between Great Bras d'Or and the St. Andrews Channel. They also offer a package of two nights B&B and two boat tickets for $110 for two people. – *Sara Godwin and Charles James*

Bras d'Or Lakes are home to over 200 pairs of nesting bald eagles, the largest concentration in eastern North America. You can often see them as you drive or hike near the lake, but you are almost certain to spot them from a boat, especially if the skipper knows where the nesting sites are. **Super Natural Sailing Tours** in St. Peter's, ☎ 800/903-3371 or 902/535-3371, fax 902/535-2209, offers naturalist-conducted cruises; see page 396.

On the banks of the Mira River in the Sydney/Louisbourg area, **Two Rivers Wildlife Park** is operated by the NS Department of Natural Resources, exhibiting a large number of the birds and animals native to the province. You can usually see deer, black bears, cougars, bald eagles, coyotes and Sable Island horses. Animals in the park are enclosed in large naturalized areas. To get there take Exit 7 from Rte. 125 (the Sydney circumferential) and follow Rte. 327 south to Marion Bridge, then take Sandfield Road west along the Mira River for six miles.

Sightseeing

Marble Mountain Museum and Library, Bras d'Or Scenic Drive, Marble Mountain. Marble quarrying and limestone mining were once a big industry here, and the museum tells the tale of the quarries and of the families that drew their livelihood from them. It's a fascinating collection of artifacts, photographs, documents and books that brings their story to life. In an old schoolhouse on a hillside, the view from the museum is over Lake Bras d'Or and over the fields where the houses of the workmen once stood. Open summers Monday to Saturday, 10 am to 6 pm and from 1 pm on Sunday. It's free, but donations are heartily welcomed.

Miners' Museum, 42 Birkley St., Glace Bay, ☎ 902/849-4522 or 849-8022, reminds visitors that coal mining was a major Cape Breton industry, with the largest part of it centered in this area. It includes guided trips through the Ocean Deeps Colliery, a miners' village with a period house and a company store, and a simulated mine ride. Retired miners serve as guides (which gives the museum much more immediacy than most) and the museum has its own coal mine. In 1967 a group of miners and retired miners formed a singing group called the Men of the Deeps, now internationally known for their songs of miners and working men. They give live performances in the museum auditorium on most Tuesday nights during the summer. The Museum is open all year, from

10 am to 6 pm (7 pm Tuesdays), daily from June to September and Monday through Friday, 9 am to 4 pm the rest of the year. Entry fees are $6 for adults, $3 for children. The mine can be damp and cool, so dress accordingly.

Port Hastings Historical Museum and Archives, Church St., Port Hastings, ☎ 902/625-2951. With displays on the town's history, this museum is particularly fascinating for its exhibits on the construction of the Canso causeway and the disruptive effect that it had on the families of ferrymen and on the local economy. Free, it is open April to September, but hours vary.

The canal at St. Peter's helped to make the town the commercial center of this part of the island. The **St. Peter's Canal** was first completed over 140 years ago, opening Bras d'Or Lakes to the ocean on its south end. Originally motivated by a desire to avoid the long sail out around Cape Breton on the east side of the island, it now allows sailing and pleasure craft easy access to the lake. You'll find it on the east side of town, where **Battery Park** extends along its east side.

The **Nicholas Deny Museum**, St. Peter's, sits along the canal in a building believed to be similar to the trading post that the early explorer and fur trader established here in 1650. It houses a collection of artifacts from the town's history. The museum is open June through the end of September daily from 9 am to 5 pm and charges a nominal admission.

Also in St. Peter's, the **Wallace MacAskill Museum**, Rte. 4, St. Peter's, ☎ 902/535-2531, honors the marine photographer with a display of his work and items from his life in his childhood home. The museum has occasional craft demonstrations. Open daily July and August, 10 am to 6 pm, and weekends in September, 10 am to 6 pm.

On the waterfront in Arichat the **Le Noir Forge Museum**, Arichat, ☎ 902/226-9364, is a traditional blacksmith shop that began making ironwork for the shipbuilding industry in the 1700s. The museum also houses artifacts from the town's history. It's open daily, 10 am to 6 pm, from May to September. There is usually a blacksmith on duty operating the equipment and narrating the history of the shop. **The Island Forge**, Larry Keating, RR#1, Port Royal, NS B0E 3J0, ☎ 902/226-9364, operates the smithy and has handmade ironware for sale, including fireplace tools, ornate utensil sets, shelf brackets, coat hangers, lamps and custom wrought iron railings.

Railroad enthusiasts will want to see the two railroad museums on Cape Breton, one at Orangedale and the other at Louis-

➲ **FAMILY FUN:** *Close to Louisbourg on the Marconi Trail,* ***Fish'n Critters U-Fish & Mini Zoo*** *in Little Lorraine has two fishing ponds where you can catch trout for a fee. You can use your own rod or one of theirs. Kids really like this place.* ☎ *902/733-3417.*

bourg. The **Orangedale Railway Station Museum**, Bras d'Or Scenic Highway, Orangedale, ☎ 902/756-3384, is a 19th-century station that operated until 1990. It houses artifacts, a model railroad and original furnishings. It is south of Rte. 5 (Exit 4) at Iron Mines on the Bras d'Or Scenic Drive. There are several rail cars on the grounds. It's open mid-June to mid-October, Monday through Saturday, 10 am to 6 pm; Sunday, 1 pm to 6 pm. Admission is free. **Sydney and Louisbourg Railway Museum**, Main St., Louisbourg, is in the 1895 stationhouse, the roundhouse and freight shed. The shed houses a working model of the line and the roundhouse is a display center where concerts and dances are held from time to time. They have two passenger cars, a box car, tanker and caboose. It's open daily from the beginning of June to the end of September, 9 am to 7 pm. Free.

The **Alexander Graham Bell National Historic Site**, Chebucto St., Baddeck, ☎ 902/295-2069. The museum has extensive displays on the life and work of the famed inventor, including his work on a proposed hydrofoil and on the *Silver Dart*, an early airplane. Bell and his family spent much of their lives in Baddeck and they had deep affection for the town and the island. A play and slide shows illustrate his, and the family's lives. The museum is in a large and bright modern building, but the family home is unfortunately not a part of the museum, which is open in July and August daily from 9 am to 8 pm, in June and September, 9 am to 7 pm, and 9 am to 5 pm in October and May. Admission is $3.75 adults, $2 youth from mid-May to mid-October only. On the first Thursday afternoon of June, July, August and September a Garden Tea is held at the museum.

Sydney has a pair of restored homes that both date from about 1787. The **Cossit House Museum**, 75 Charlotte St., ☎ 902/539-7973, was the home of the city's first Anglican minister and several of the rooms have been furnished in accordance with the contents listed on his 1815 estate inventory. Open daily from June to mid-October, 9:30 am to 5:30 pm, free. The **Jost House**, 54 Charlotte St., Sydney, ☎ 902/539-0366, was the home of a well-to-do town merchant. It has a number of special collections, including an unusual marine display. The house provides fine examples of the changes in the building over the course of its existence. Open all year; in July and August, Monday through Saturday, 10 am to 4 pm; from September through June, Tuesday through Friday, 10 am to 4 pm and Saturday, 1 pm to 4 pm.

St. Patrick's Church Museum, 89 Esplanade, Sydney, ☎ 902/562-8237, a classic small stone church, is the oldest Catholic church on the island (1838) and now serves as a community museum. Walking tours of the town originate at the church.

North of Sydney on Rte. 28 (the Colliery Route), **Fort Petrie** at New Victoria is being restored as an educational center. It will focus on the role of Sydney and its harbor fortifications during World War II, when Sydney served as a major gathering place for allied Atlantic convoys. Built in 1939, the fort guarded the entrance to Sydney Harbour from submarine attack until it was decommissioned in 1956. Open summers only, there is a picnic area and beach.

A short distance further on, past New Victoria and the lighthouse, **Colliery Lands Park** is on the outskirts of New Waterford. The park is on the site of two coal mines and contains memorials to the more than 300 local men who died in mining disasters. There is a display area with a mine slope, cars, and coal boxes near the original mine entrance. The entire area from Sydney to Glace Bay and Port Morien contained large deposits of coal and was the site of many mines, one of which still operates. Mine shafts generally sloped out under the ocean, as at New Waterford where the working face of the only remaining colliery is almost 3½ miles offshore. Monuments and sites at New Waterford, Reserve Mines, Dominion, Glace Bay and Port Morien recount this history and the struggle of miners with their employers.

Marconi National Historic Site, Timmerman St., Glace Bay. In 1902 Guglielmo Marconi perfected his idea for wireless transmission of message across the Atlantic and conducted the first radio operation from Glace Bay. A model replica of his radio station and an exhibit of his work is on display. Open June to mid-September daily from 10 am to 6 pm; free.

Don't miss **Fortress of Louisbourg National Historic Site** on Rte. 22 in Louisbourg, ☎ 902/733-2280 or 902/733-2280. This attraction alone is a sufficient reason to come to Cape Breton. It is a massive rebuilding (the largest reconstruction in North America) of the fortress town built early in the 1700s as the centerpiece and bastion of France's North American empire. A threat to British interests in New England, it was attacked several times before it was finally taken; it was blown up by New Englanders in 1758.

➡ TIPS FOR SEEING THE FORTRESS: *While it is possible to rush through the fortress in a few hours, you really should plan on a day to savor this astounding place. It is an adventure into the past, giving an entirely different perspective into the Colonial period of the entire eastern North American coast. Pick up goodies to eat at the town bakery or have a meal at any of the three restaurants located in the restoration (dining on authentic period foods). Buy reproductions of antique handicrafts or talk to a costumed guard about the British threat.*

Beginning in the 1960s with meticulous archaeological research, a substantial part of the fortress city has been rebuilt and populated with authentically costumed docents who recreate the lives of the French citizens of the time. The huge stone walls have been restored and official residences, private homes of the high born and lowly, stores, bakery and trade shops have been rebuilt on their original sites, faithfully following historic drawings and accounts of the original town. The documentation and the story of how its restorers learned about its construction and appearance is told in exhibits almost as interesting as the fortress itself.

A bus from the visitors center, where you must park, takes you to the outskirts of the fortress town. Be sure to wear comfortable walking shoes, since there's a lot of territory to cover, and bring a jacket or sweater. It is usually cool on this windswept peninsula. Open daily in July and August, 9 am to 7 pm, and from 9:30 am to 5 pm in May, June, September and October. Facilities are limited in May and October. Admission $11 adult, $5.50 over age five, $27.50 family.

Where To Stay & Eat

In the South

Auberge Wandlyn has modern rooms, TV, an indoor pool, exercise room, and laundry. The dining room serves breakfast and dinner. *Rte. 4, PO Box 558, Port Hawkesbury, NS B0E 2V0, ☎ 902/625-0621, fax 902/625-1525 ($$).*

Maritime Inn Port Hawkesbury is part of a well-regarded chain. Three miles from the causeway, it's a modern hotel with large rooms and outdoor and indoor pools. *689 Reeves St., PO Box 759, Port Hawkesbury, NS B0E 2V0, ☎ 902/625-0320 or 888/662-7484, fax 902/625-3876 ($$).*

Kayak Cape Breton and Cottages has newly built two-bedroom log housekeeping cottages on the southern shore of Bras d'Or Lakes. Nicely maintained, they have access to the water and, as the name indicates, they also rent kayaks, canoes and bikes. There is a minimum two-night stay; in July and August the minimum is three nights. *West Bay, Roberta, NS B0E 2K0, ☎/fax 902/535-3060 ($$).*

Carter's Lakeside Cedar Log Cottages has four one-bedroom cottages that sleep four and one two-bedroom cottage right on the southern shore of Bras d'Or Lake, all new fully equipped housekeeping units. Across the street are hiking trails and places for wilderness camping; they have rowboats and fishing. It's open all year and in winter cross-country skiing, skating and ice fishing all begin here. *RR#2, St. Peter's, NS B0E 3B0, ☎ 902/535-2453 ($-$$).*

Indian Point Lodge is on a large peninsula that juts into bay-like Grand River, protected by a barrier beach. The lodge is a group of log cottages set amongst fir trees along the shore. Each is fully equipped with ranges, refrigerators and TV. Grand Rivers is on the Fleur de Lis Trail in the seldom-visited area south of Louisbourg and near Michaud Point. *Grand River, NS B0E 1M0, ☎ 902/587-2410.*

Bras d'Or Lakes Inn is a big log lodge close to the St. Peter's Canal, offering attractive wood paneled rooms and furnished with custom-built wooden furniture. The family-style dining room serves good wholesome fare. *General Delivery, St. Peter's, NS B0E 3B0, ☎ 902/535-2200 or 800/818-5885, fax 902/535-2784 ($$).*

Dundee Resort is a full-service resort in the southwest corner of Bras d'Or Lakes on Bras d'Or Scenic Drive. Its 60 hotel rooms and 39 housekeeping cottages are large, modern and attractively furnished. Its big draw is the award-winning 18-hole public golf course, so popular that there's a cruise from Baddeck to allow golfers to play there. The resort has its own marina, indoor and outdoor pools, canoes, kayaks and motorboats, and a beach on the world's largest saltwater lake. Their excellent dining room is open to the public. The resort is open from May to the end of October.
RR#2, West Bay, NS B0E 3K0, ☎ 800/565-1774 or 902/345-2697 ($$$$).

D'Escousse Bed & Breakfast is a cozy little B&B in a 19th-century home with wonderful gingerbread embellishment. If this were Prince Edward Island you'd look for Anne of Green Gables. *PO Box 510, D'Escousse, Isle Madame, NS B0E 1K0, ☎ 902/226-2936 ($).*

L'Auberge Acadienne on Isle Madame is a handsome new 17-room inn with large guest rooms, centrally located for enjoying this French island. The dining room serves Acadian specialties. Biking and kayaking packages are available. From May to October they run "Hiking Isle Madame" on the island for $137 per person. *PO Box 59, Arichat, Isle Madame, NS B0E 1A0, ☎ 902/226-2200, fax 902/226-1424 ($$).*

Vollmer's Island Paradise Inc. is way out on the western end of Isle Madame on Janvrin Island peninsula. These seven housekeeping cottages are newly built, private and nicely maintained. Walking, canoeing and fishing are nearby and the Vollmers operate a diving service from July through September, including lessons and equipment. Their restaurant serves family-style meals, by reservation only. *PO Box 53, West Arichat, NS B0E 3J0, ☎ 902/226-1507, fax 902/226-9853, Web site www.taisbean.com/vollmers/ ($$).*

Claire's Café is really run by Claire, with the occasional help of her sister. Both food and company are good, and if you're interested she'll tell you all about the town and island. It's open 9 am to 9 pm. *D'Ecousse, Isle Madame, ☎ 902/226-1432 ($).*

Au Bord de la Mer is open Monday through Friday from 11 am until 8:30 pm, Sunday 11 am to 8:30 pm. Their lunch and dinner menu often features Acadian dishes. Petit de Grat is way out on the east end of the island. It's in the Acadien Cultural Centre, La Picasse, on the way into town. *Petit de Grat, Isle Madame, ☎ 902/226-0011 ($$).*

Cookie's Chowder House, where homemade seafood and corn chowders are the specialty, also has a daily home-style entrée, salad special, and sandwich special, as well as pizza. On Rte. 4 along the east shore of the lake. *Johnstown Market, Johnstown, ☎ 902/535-2442 ($).*

A HOUSE WITH A STORY

Maison Emile-Mouchet B & B was a fairy tale come true for Jean-Guy Duguay and Maurice Leblanc. Through a series of magical coincidences, they saw the three-story house (built in 1863) and fell in love with it, only to learn it was not for sale. Not long afterward, a colleague mentioned that he had to go to West Arichat to sell his mother's home. As they chatted, they realized it was the house they'd fallen so in love with. They bought it on the spot, furnishings and all. Staying at Maison Emile-Mouchet is like staying with Acadian friends. The conversation, whether in French or English, is delightful, the breakfasts are generous and delicious, and the house – well, you'll want to move in. It's the perfect base for biking around Isle Madame, hiking to Cap Rouge, or exploring islands that can only be reached at low tide. *1448 Highway 206, West Arichat, Isle Madame, NS B0E 3J0,* ☎ 902/226-9740, fax 902/226-1911, e-mail nmw@web.apc.org, Web site www.web.apc.org/~nmw ($-$$). – *Sara Godwin and Charles James*

Near Baddeck

Green Highlander Lodge has three suite-style rooms that will sleep up to six persons. It's in the old lodge on the main street of town over the Yellow Cello restaurant. *PO Box 128, Baddeck, NS B0E 1B0,* ☎ *902/295-2303, Web site www.capebretonnet.com/baddeck/greenhighlander ($$-$$$).*

When you see **Castle Moffett** on the hillside above the highway, you'll blink and look again. It's a castle, complete with crenelations, sitting on 185 acres of wooded grounds high over Bras d'Or Lake. Inside, the antique- and art-filled public rooms and bedroom suites are as elegant as you would expect in a new-world castle, but very comfortable. Reservations are required. West of Baddeck and overlooking the upper end of the St. Patrick's Channel, Castle Moffett is a unique experience and close to some of the best activities on the island. A number of special multi-night packages are offered that include admission to local museums and attractions, canoeing and kayaking, fishing, golf and sailing. *Box 678, Baddeck, NS B0E 1B0,* ☎ *902/756-9070, fax 902/756-3399, ($$$-$$$$).*

Auberge Gisele has rooms in the original inn and in an adjacent modern building. Amenities include a whirlpool, sauna, and solarium. They have a dining room serving stylish continental dishes and where the menu changes often. *387 Shore Rd, PO Box 132, Baddeck, NS B0E 1B0, ☎ 902/295-2849, fax 902/295-2033 (high $$).*

Duffus House includes a pair of 19th-century houses close to the center of activity, but with shared gardens for relaxed evenings. Rooms are furnished with antiques and each has its own character. *2878 Water St., Box 427, Baddeck, NS B0E 1B0, ☎ 902/295-2172, off-season 902/928-2878, fax 902/752-7737 ($$).*

Telegraph House is noted for its charm and the warmth of its hospitality. Centrally located, there are rooms in the newer motel annex or in the original house. The dining room serves family-style fare. *Chebucto St., PO Box 8, Baddeck, NS B0E 1B0, ☎ 902/295-9988 ($$).*

Highland Heights Inn is a bright and attractive motel adjacent to the Highland Village Museum. Every room has a view over the Barra Strait. Their dining room serves family fare three meals a day with an emphasis on seafood and local specialties; all of their breads and pastries are homemade. *Rte. 223, PO Box 19, Iona, NS B0A 1L0, ☎ 800/660-8122 or 902/725-2360, fax 902/725-2800 ($$).*

Annfield Manor Country Inn is an eye-catching, column-fronted 29-room mansion in a garden. Room rates include a full breakfast. Their dining room serves lunch and dinner by reservation. Turn right at Exit 18 of Rte. 105 in Bras d'Or. *Church Rd, Bras d'Or, NS B0C 1B0, ☎ 902/736-8770 (low $$).*

Herring Choker Deli, Café and Bakery, west of Baddeck on Nyanza Bay, is a good place to pick up assorted things for a picnic or to get supplies for a hike. *Nyanza, ☎ 902/295-2275 ($).*

Bell Buoy Restaurant is right on the main street of town and serves a big seafood dinner menu, with good choices for those who want something else. The lunch menu has a nice selection of sandwiches under $7 and entrées under $8. The view over the lake is great, and the staff couldn't be friendlier. It opens at 11:30 am daily. *Chebucto St., Baddeck, ☎ 902/295-2581, winter 902/564-6752 ($$).*

Lobster suppers are a tradition throughout the Atlantic provinces and Cape Breton is no exception. **Baddeck Lobster Suppers** is one of the best known and it is open daily for lunch, 11:30 am to 1:30 pm, and dinner, 4 to 9 pm, from June to October. The lobster comes with unlimited seafood chowder and steamed mussels, salad, bread and desserts. *PO Box 669, Ross St., Baddeck, ☎ 902/295-3307 ($$).*

The Baddeck Fish Company Restaurant is, at last, a seafood place where they don't fry everything; in fact, they don't fry anything. The cooking method of choice here is high-pressure steam and the result is delicious. Try the St. Ann's Bay mussels, the steamed lobster with potato salad, or the seafood chowder dinner with haddock, scallops and crab (we can't stop at one bowl of this, although they are quite large). Roast chicken and salmon are also on the menu, along with sandwiches and salads. Casual dining. *Chebucto St., Baddeck, 902/295-1238 ($-$$).*

Near Sydney

Rockinghorse Inn, an 1891 High Victorian mansion, is being lovingly restored to show its stained glass, bronze statuary and decorative oak detail. They serve high tea in the afternoon and elegant dinners, both by reservations made a week in advance. The library contains a collection of Cape Breton histories relating to the steel and mining industries. *259 King's Road, Sydney, NS B1S 1A7, ☎ 902/539-2696 ($$-$$$).*

Park Place B&B, in the downtown area close to restaurants, is in a turn-of-the-century two-story home. *169 Park St., Sydney, NS B1P 4W7, ☎ 902/562-3518 ($).*

Dove House B&B offers the comfort and convenience of lodging in a Victorian home overlooking the harbor, only minutes from the Newfoundland ferry. *108 Queen St., North Sydney, NS B2A 1A6, ☎ 902/794-1055 ($$).*

Gowrie House Country Inn is a large, Georgian-style mansion retaining much of its decorative detail and set among outstanding gardens. No modernization has been undertaken here, and several rooms share a Victorian bath. It is notable for its antiques, old club style, and elegant and pricey dining room. Modern rooms are in a separate building, nicely set in the gardens. *139 Shore Rd, Sydney Mines, NS B1V 1A6, ☎ 902/544-1050 ($$$).*

Louisbourg Harbour Inn is in the eight-room home of a sea captain, later occupied by a series of mariners' families. Beautifully restored rooms are furnished in antiques and antique reproductions. Most of the bedrooms have whirlpool baths. *PO Box 110, 9 Warren St., Louisbourg, NS B0A 1M0, ☎ 888/888-8INN or 902/733-3222 ($$).*

Cranberry Cove Inn is a large Victorian mansion, newly refurbished, but keeping its period charm and warmth. Rooms are bright and cheerful, furnished with antiques and reproductions; some have whirlpools. The dining room has a menu of innovative and nicely prepared dishes, especially seafood, and they always have at least one vegetarian option. *17 Wolfe St., Louisbourg, NS B0A 1M0, ☎ 902/733-2171 ($$).*

Point of View Suites certainly has points of view; it's on a private peninsula in Louisbourg harbor. Eight housekeeping suites have full kitchen facilities and private balconies or patios. Guests have the chance to enjoy a nightly lobster boil at the private beach house along with views of the bay and Fortress. *5 Lower Commercial St., Louisbourg, NS B0A 1M0, ☎ 888/374-8439 (VIEW) or 902/733-2080 ($$).*

Westminster Abbey is unique. It's probably the island's only restaurant serving English-style fish & chips, fried clams and hot dogs from a double-decker London bus. *On the Boardwalk, Sydney. No phone ($).*

The Grubstake Dining Room's Wild West façade might distract, but the menu includes items such as poached scallops with sautéed mushrooms, milk-poached salmon with garlic butter, steak au poivre flambé and country-style pork steak. Their motto says it all: "An oasis in a deep-fried desert." Open June through September from noon to 9 pm. *1274 Main Streeet, Louisbourg, ☎ 902/733-2308 ($$).*

Tigger's Treasures and Tea Room, near the upper Mira River and Two River Wildlife Park, is a stopping place for tea or lunch. They also have a gift shop with a nice selection of craft items. *3850 Rte. 327, Marion Bridge, ☎ 902/727-2653.*

Singer and songwriter Rita MacNeil has now turned her home, a former schoolhouse, into **Rita's Tea Room**. She lived here with her family when she was not on the road. Stop in for tea (or coffee), sandwiches or baked goods, browse the gift shop and look at the memorabilia. Open daily 9 am to 7 pm from June through mid-October. *Rte. 4, Big Pond, ☎ 902/828-2667.*

■ Camping

Whycocomagh Provincial Park has 75 campsites with wood grills and firewood, RV dumping station. Boat launch into Lake Bras d'Or and hiking trail. *PO Box 130, Whycocomagh, NS B0E 3M0, ☎ 902/756-2339; May-October, ☎ 902/756-2448.*

➔ **PROVINCIAL PARKS:** *For information on Provincial Parks, contact Parks and Recreation Div., Department of Lands and Forests, RR#1, Belmont, NS B0M 1C0, ☎ 902/662-3030.*

Mountain View by the Sea Cabins and Campground has three housekeeping cottages and 16 campsites (eight serviced), with a laundromat, canteen, showers, a dock and beach swimming. *Big Bras d'Or Road, Big Bras d'Or, NS B0C1B0, ☎ 800/661-6680 or 902/674-2384, fax 674-2742 ($$).*

Glenview Campground is on Rte. 252, just off Exit 5 of Rte. 105 at Whycocomagh. It has 79 tent and trailer sites with water and electricity, of which 48 have sewer hookups, modern washrooms with showers as well as a laundry. Activities include a pool, horseshoes, hiking and a playground. *PO Box 12, Whycocomagh, NS B0E 3M0, ☎ 902/756-3198.*

Seal Island Campground is on the shore of the Great Bras d'Or Channel near the Seal Island Bridge. Seal Island is a family camping area with tent and RV sites, some of which are serviced. Showers, a laundromat, groceries and LP gas are at the campground, which has hiking, boating, swimming, a recreation hall, horseshoes and a game room. *RR#1, Bras d'Or, NS B0C 1B0, reservations ☎ 800/565-000, info 902/674-2145.*

Englishtown Ridge Campground, close to the Rte. 312 ferry from the Cabot Trail across St. Ann's Harbour, has open and wooded tent sites, RV sites with full hookups, showers, a laundromat, and a canteen with a family room and fully licensed café and bar. Rates are $15-$20, depending upon services. It's open from mid-May to October, and off-season rates are available. *Rte. 312, Englishtown, NS B0C 1H0, ☎ 800/565-0000 or 902/929-2598, off-season 902/674-2373.*

Driftwood Tent & Trailer Park, with frontage on Bras d'Or Lake, has serviced and unserviced open and wooded sites, showers, laundromat and trailer rentals. Activities include canoe and sailboard rentals, swimming, fishing, boating, horseshoes and a playground. From Exit 18 off Rte. 105, take George's River Highway 1½ miles. From Rte. 125 take Exit 2 north on Johnston Rd. *c/o Raymond Howatson, PO Box 222, North Sydney, NS B2A 3M3, ☎ 902/794-4519.*

River Ryan Campground has both fully serviced RV sites, a tenting area and on-site trailer rentals. The campground is on Lingan Bay and offers canoe and boat rental, swimming in the bay, fishing, volley ball, horseshoes, playground and a rec building. There is also a nature trail. From Rte. 4 east of Sydney take Gardiner Rd to Rte. 28 and then left on Rte. 28. *Rte. 28, River Ryan, NS B1H 4K2, ☎ 902/862-8367.*

Louisbourg Motorhome Park is right at the docks in the center of town. If convenient location is important, stop here. The downside is that it's much like a parking lot with no trees or cover and sardine-like sites, but they are clean and tidy and the people very nice. Tent sites are $8; RVs are $10 unserviced and $15 serviced. Washrooms (including a wheelchair-accessible one) and free hot showers are available. It's open June to October and the office is open 9 am to 9 pm daily. *Box 10, Louisbourg, NS B0A 1M0, ☎ 902/733-3631.*

St. Peter's Campground is an RV campground with 30 fully serviced sites, including cable TV. The facility is newly built and has children's and adult pools as well as washrooms, laundry, showers, rec hall and arcade. *Rte. 4, PO Box 226, St. Peter's, NS B0E 3B0, ☎ 902/535-3333, fax 535-2202.*

Battery Provincial Park has camping for RVs and tents in a park setting along the St. Peter's Canal. *St. Peter's, NS B0E 3B0, ☎ 902/535-2032.*

Prince Edward Island

Introduction

The long red beaches and warm gentle waters of Prince Edward Island represent, to us, the accumulated memories of idyllic summers. These happy Julys and Augusts meld in retrospect into one long beach, punctuated by pots of fresh-dug clams steaming over a campfire, with a backdrop of miles of green, gold and terracotta fields covering a rolling landscape, like a lumpy featherbed. Please don't expect us to be objective here.

You will notice that we have strayed (as we are likely to do in PEI) from our pattern of breaking a province into small regions. We did this because PEI is small, and because so many activities, outfitters and adventures involve the whole island. Many people, for example, cycle the entire length of the island on the Confederation Trail in a single trip. Or rent a kayak in Charlottetown to paddle in bays from St. Peters to Malpeque. But don't let the island's size mislead you: it packs a lot of activity in a tidy little sea-wrapped package.

Geography

Geographically, the island is a great red sandstone mass cast adrift in the Northumberland Strait. It is separated from New Brunswick by nine miles of sea between Cape Tormentine and Borden and from Nova Scotia by 14 miles of sea between Caribou and Wood Islands. Much of the shoreline is red sand beach backed by eroded red sandstone cliffs 15 to 30 feet high, in places forming natural arches – and off the North Cape, a giant elephant.

The rolling hillsides are covered with rich fields of farmland. In spring, summer and fall there is a kaleidoscope of color – brick red soil contrasted with golden fields of wheat and green masses of potato plants. Behind them are dense forests of evergreens which, along the coastal regions, are stunted by the strong prevailing winds. Deep river estuaries cut into the land, almost dividing it into three segments. On the north coast, barrier beaches from Alberton in the west to Tracadie Bay in the east protect harbours that provide not only a bounty of fish and shellfish but exciting canoeing, kayaking and fishing.

History

The first European settlement on the island was late by North American standards. In 1720 the French settled at Port la Joye, at the entrance to what is now Charlottetown Harbour. Other French settlements began at about the same time, notably on the west end where the French flavor of its original Acadian settlers is still strong. After only 38 years, Port la Joye was captured by the British and a new fortification was added, Fort Amherst.

Charlottetown was settled soon thereafter and in the next several decades Scottish and Irish settlers began to arrive. To this mix were added a few settlers and refugees from the American colonies before and after the Revolution. Originally farmers, the settlers soon took on fishing and then shipbuilding, succeeding in all. They also became merchants and traders and to this day have a broad-based economy in which fishing, fish farming, farming and commerce play equally important parts.

We should note two more historical events that you will meet in PEI. Charlottetown was the scene of the conference where the Articles of Confederation were drawn up, creating Canada as we know it (but without Newfoundland). These sites have the same hallowed significance to Canadians that Independence Hall and the Liberty Bell have to Americans, as do the men who met here, who are called the Fathers of Confederation, sometimes simply The Fathers. Charlottetown has some very nicely done historical programs centering around this exciting time in its history.

The second is a more recent phenomenon, based on an endearing series of children's fiction by Lucy Maud Montgomery that center around the adventures of "Anne of Green Gables." Anne has so captured the hearts of the world – most recently the Japanese – that the entire north-central part of the island is known by the tourist designation of "Anne's Land." Much is made of Anne, some of it quite charming, but some of the attractions are... how do we say it nicely? A quarter of a million people visit the sites annually. When it all becomes too suffocating, just think of the local people, who can't even run to the corner for a gallon of milk without fend-

Shore at Prince Edward Island National Park.

ing off tour buses and Japanese wedding parties. Fortunately, it's only a short way through Cavendish to the island's loveliest beaches and miles of woodland walks.

Getting Around

The primary route to Prince Edward Island is **Rte. 16** in New Brunswick from Aulac to Cape Tormentine. This once meant a 45-minute ferry ride, and often a wait. The 24-hour ferry service was part of a commitment to permanent communication made to the island when it joined the confederation. That commitment took another step in the summer of 1997 with the opening of the **Confederation Bridge**, a nine-mile span over the Northumberland Strait from Cape Tormentine to Borden.

The other highway access to the island is still by ferry. At Caribou, Nova Scotia, **Northumberland Ferries Ltd.** operates a car ferry to Wood Islands on PEI. This 14-mile ferry takes 75 minutes and operates 24 hours a day. From Rte. 104 west of New Glasgow, Nova Scotia, take Rte. 106 to Caribou.

From Borden or Wood Islands, take TransCanada-1 to get to the provincial capital, **Charlottetown**. Three designated touring routes, one for each county, lead travelers around the island. The

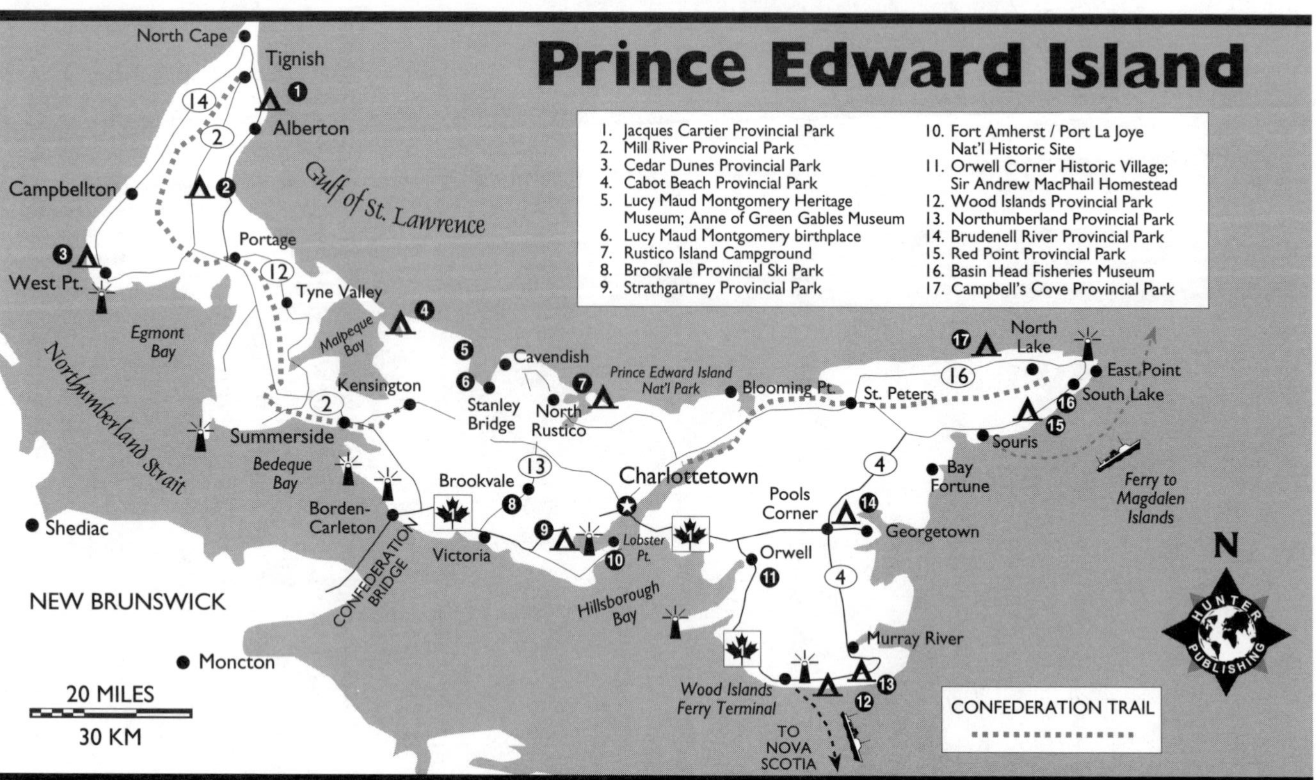

Prince Edward Island
1. Jacques Cartier Provincial Park
2. Mill River Provincial Park
3. Cedar Dunes Provincial Park
4. Cabot Beach Provincial Park
5. Lucy Maud Montgomery Heritage Museum; Anne of Green Gables Museum
6. Lucy Maud Montgomery birthplace
7. Rustico Island Campground
8. Brookvale Provincial Ski Park
9. Strathgartney Provincial Park
10. Fort Amherst / Port La Joye Nat'l Historic Site
11. Orwell Corner Historic Village; Sir Andrew MacPhail Homestead
12. Wood Islands Provincial Park
13. Northumberland Provincial Park
14. Brudenell River Provincial Park
15. Red Point Provincial Park
16. Basin Head Fisheries Museum
17. Campbell's Cove Provincial Park
North Cape
Tignish
Alberton
Campbellton
West Pt.
Egmont Bay
Portage
Tyne Valley
Malpeque Bay
Gulf of St. Lawrence
Kensington
Summerside
Bedeque Bay
Borden-Carleton
Confederation Bridge
Northumberland Strait
Shediac
Moncton
New Brunswick
20 Miles
30 KM
Cavendish
Stanley Bridge
North Rustico
Brookvale
Victoria
Prince Edward Island Nat'l Park
Charlottetown
Lobster Pt.
Hillsborough Bay
Blooming Pt.
Pools Corner
Orwell
Wood Islands Ferry Terminal
To Nova Scotia
St. Peters
Georgetown
Murray River
Bay Fortune
Souris
North Lake
East Point
South Lake
Ferry to Magdalen Islands
Confederation Trail
N
Hunter Publishing

western, more sparsely settled part of the island is explored from the **Lady Slipper Drive**, which circles the shoreline of Prince County, about 180 miles. Follow the signs with the pink lady slipper; the route numbers change often but the signs don't. The faster route is Rte. 2, which runs pretty much up the center.

The eastern region, King's County, has **King's Byway Drive**, which also circles the shoreline, a distance of about 234 miles. Follow the signs with the purple crown, and here too, expect the route numbers to change frequently. From Charlottetown, Rte. 2 will take you north along the Hillsborough River and then across the peninsula to the port town of Souris, the starting place for the ferry trip to the Magdalen Islands. TransCanada-1 serves the southern part of the county, as far as Wood Islands, and Rte. 3 is the fastest route to the Brudenell area, with Rte. 4 leading to the southern shores of St. Mary's Bay.

The third county is Queen's County, in the central third of the island, circled by **Blue Heron Drive**, along its outer edges and close to the ocean, about 120 miles. Route 2 runs almost straight across the center from Charlottetown to Kensington but, as a look at the map will tell you, there is no fast straight road from the entry point at Borden to the north shore area. TransCanada-1A from Borden will take you quickly to Summerside and Rte. 2.

Information Sources

■ Information on the province is available from **Tourism PEI**, PO Box 940, Charlottetown, PEI C1A 7M5, ☎ 888/PEI-PLAY (888/734-7529), 902/629-2400, fax 902/629-2428, Web site www.peiplay.com, e-mail tourpei@gov.pe.ca.

■ On the island end of the Confederation Bridge, stop at **Borden-Carleton Gateway Village**, which has a large selection of materials and is open daily, 8 am to 10 pm, in early summer; 9 am to 9 pm from mid-August to early September; and from 9 am to 5 pm the rest of the year.

■ **Charlottetown Visitor Information**, City Hall, 199 Queen Street, Charlottetown, PEI C1A 4B7, ☎ 902/629-4116, is open daily in July and August, 8 am to 5 pm, and 9:30 to 5 pm the rest of the year.

■ **PEI Tourist Information Centre**, Water Street, Charlottetown, PEI C1A 7M5, ☎ 902/368-4444, is open 8 am to

10 pm daily in July and August, and from 9:30 to 5 pm the balance of the year.

■ In addition to the information centers in Charlottetown, there are others at: **PEI Tourist Information Centre**, Rte. 13, Cavendish, PEI C0A 1N0, ☎ 902/963-7380; **New London Tourist Association**, Rte. 6, New London, PEI C0B 1M0, ☎ 902/886-2315; and **Kensington Area Tourist Association**, Broadway, Kensington C0B 1M0, ☎ 902/836-3031.

■ In the eastern part of the island, stop at the **PEI Tourist Information Centre**, Wood Islands, PEI C0A 1B0, ☎ 902/962-2015; **PEI Tourist Information Centre**, junction of Rtes. 3 and 4, Pooles Corner, PEI C0A 1G0, ☎ 902/838-0670; and **PEI Tourist Information Centre**, Rte. 2, Souris, PEI C0A 2B0, ☎ 902/687-7030.

■ In the west, visit **PEI Tourist Information Centre**, Rte. 2, Portage, PEI C0B 1V0, ☎ 902/859-8796; **Spinnaker's Landing Tourist Information Centre**, Harbour Drive, Summerside, PEI C1N 5R1, ☎ 902/436-6692; **West Prince Tourism Association**, Gard Rd. (in West Prince Industry Centre), RR 1, Alberton, PEI C0B 1B0, ☎ 800/565-2299.

Adventures

The differences between the adventures here and in other Atlantic provinces are a matter of degree. Yes, there are some cliffs, but they are friendly drop-offs where the sea has eroded the sandstone shore. The bays are low and gentle, most of them quite protected from the full fury of the sea. There are abundant routes for bicycling, but no athlete-challenging mountains to climb, just rolling hills through colorful countryside. In short, this is a laid-back and casual place for relaxed enjoyment. This doesn't mean that you can't be challenged, only that you don't have to be.

Many of the activities in the center of the island are located inside **Prince Edward Island National Park**, Parks Canada, 2 Palmers Lane, Charlottetown, PEI C1A 5V6, ☎ 800/213-PARK or 902/672-6350. The National Park includes most of the north shore of Queens County from Tracadie Bay on the east to New London Bay on the west. It protects the delicate shoreline from excessive use while keeping it available to the public. Within its borders are sand dunes, beaches, red sandstone cliffs, salt marshes, clam flats, freshwater ponds and woodlands. The park presents opportunities for hiking and walking on the beaches and designated hiking trails, swimming in the warm waters of the Gulf of St. Lawrence, sailboarding, kayaking and canoeing in its protected bays and rivers, cycling on its roads and around the periphery, tennis and bird-watching. While the park season is from June through September (when park fees are collected), the facilities are open the rest of the year without services and without fee.

On Foot

The Confederation Trail

Canada's great new TransCanada Trail, known in PEI as the **Confederation Trail**, is built here upon the bed of the former Canadian National Railway. In 1989 the rail line was shut down; since then many miles of the railbed have been converted to rolled stonedust surface. Along its way the trail passes through small towns and villages presenting many choices of lodging and dining. The problem with a rail-trail, of course, is that they don't loop, so if you want to end up in the same place you started you have to double back.

If you intend to backpack across the province this is the best way to do it. The only traffic you will encounter on the trail, except at highway crossings, is bicycles. The runs between towns are short enough to give you a great deal of flexibility in planning your stops. Many of the outfitters and trip planners listed in the *On Wheels* section below can help make arrangements for you along the trail; some can arrange luggage transfers, so you don't even have to carry a full pack. See particularly those listed in the Central area; most of them operate throughout the whole province.

CONFEDERATION TRAIL MAP: *A map is published and updated annually by the association that is overseeing the building of the Confederation Trail, changing as new sections are added. You can get a copy at the major information centers, particularly those along the trail route.*

The trail is also good for those touring by automobile, who just want to get out of the car periodically and wander into the countryside. Get the map and stop for a short walk on the trail whenever your highway crosses it. A look at the map will show you what is interesting along the trail nearest you –

good view points and even beaver dams are shown on the trail map.

On the eastern tip, the trail starts at Elmira, fittingly at the old railroad station, now a museum. At last notice the trail was completed all the way to Mount Stewart, south of Savage Harbor, and another section was under construction from there to Scotchfort. Segments along the trail generally run about five miles between towns; most segments have special attractions. For example, between Elmira and Baltic is an attractive pond and between Bear River and Selkirk is the Larkin's Pond Bridge Lookout. The total distance from Elmira to Mount Stewart is about 44 miles.

On the west side of the island the starting point for the trail is the zero mileage marker at Tignish, on the northern tip. From there the trail drops down to St. Louis, just over 6½ miles, and then to Alberton, on Cascumpec Bay, an additional six miles. Currently the end point of the trail is at Kensington, on the east side of Malpeque Bay, about 75 miles from Tignish. Work continues on the intervening 75 miles and should be completed soon.

Other Hiking & Walking Areas

The Confederation Trail is not the only rail-to-trail project on the island. At Montague on the island's eastern shore, along the north bank of the Montague River, a spur line has been made into a walking/cycling trail. It follows the river for awhile, then cuts inland through the town of Brudenell, crossing the head of the Brudenell River and skirting the edge of Brudenell River Provincial Park. At the intersection of a side route to Cardigan, turn right and follow the trail to Georgetown on the end of Cardigan Point. This route is about 12 miles each way.

The Harvey Moore Wildlife Management Area, Rte. 4, Murray River, ☎ 902/838-4834, is due to the dedication of Harvey Moore, a leading Canadian conservationist, to the protection and preservation of birds and particularly waterfowl. An extensive trail system runs through the area, where young birds can be seen early in the season. The sanctuary was a personal project of Mr. Moore, and his family still owns and manages it. You can fish for trout in one of their small ponds in July and in another in August for a small fee.

Sir Andrew MacPhail Homestead, Rte. 209, off Highway 1, Orwell, ☎ 902/651-2789. At the home of this noted 19th-century Canadian there are several interpretive trails through the fields and forests surrounding the historic homestead. The shortest of these will take about 20 minutes and the longest about 45. There is also a museum and dining room on the property.

The **Walking Tour of Summerside** is entitled "Of Merchant, Fox and Sail," a theme that succinctly captures the town's history. Starting with a Loyalist farming settlement in 1785, it became a merchant center, a shipbuilding port, a rail center and, for decades, was the world center of the silver fox industry. You can pick up the well-done brochure at the Eptek Centre on Green Shores Common at Harbour Drive. The walk takes you through the historic central part of the city, pointing out over 20 of the city's more prominent buildings. A longer version of the walk extends into a different area, adding more buildings from the late 19th and early 20th centuries. This was the period of Summerside's greatest wealth and success, when fashion made the silver fox popular, and gave birth to the industry that dominated Summerside for years. Many of the mansions seen along this route were built for the leaders of that trade.

Hiking Outfitters & Guided Tours

■ **Outside Expeditions**, c/o Bryon Howard, Box 2336, Charlottetown C1A 8C1, ☎ 800/207-3899 or 902/892-5425, is run by a husband and wife team who conduct tours all over the Atlantic provinces. In PEI they have a variety of walking tours to suit your ability and time. The guided tours start at $39 and they use local guides who know the territory. On Wednesday or Friday nights you can walk to a lobster bake on the beach. They also have kayaking and bicycling. Visit their shop at the end of the North Rustico Road.

■ **Scott Walking Tours**, 1707 Pryor Street, Halifax, NS B3H 4G7, ☎ 800/262-8644 or 902/423-5000, e-mail rscott@fox.nstn.ca, operates a number of walking trips on the island, including a six-day trip. Their trips walk from inn to inn.

On Wheels

Bicycling on PEI is a joy, with pleasant country roads and little traffic, if you stay away from the route between Charlottetown and Cavendish. Your first look at a map will tell you that the terrain is not severe. The roads tend to run as straight as a die and, while there are hills, they are gentle and rolling, enough to add interest but not enough to be a serious obstacle. You will pass farmland and more farmland. This is a potato raising land and they send hundreds of tons to the other provinces and to the United States. They raise mostly red potatoes (which for many years we believed to be red because of the color of PEI's soil).

The choice of where to go is almost infinite, as long as you stay off the main routes like Rte. 2. Use the **Confederation Trail** to avoid the main roads. The Confederation Trail (see *On Foot* above) is part of a massive Canadian project that will someday result in a trail over 5,000 miles long, starting in Newfoundland and ending in Vancouver, British Columbia. On this island it runs, or will run, from Tignish in the west arm to Elmira on the tip of the east arm, a total of about 165 miles. While the trail is useful to walkers, it is even more useful to a bicyclist. Use the trail for part of the trip and then create a loop by using the smaller back roads. Many of the outfitters and trip planners listed here can help you make arrangements and some can arrange luggage transfers as well. See particularly those listed in the central area, since most of them operate throughout the whole province.

The Confederation Trail ends at Elmira, at the island's easternmost tip, a good place to start. You can rent bicycles at the railroad museum here, where the trail begins. You could also start at Souris and take the branch line of the trail to Harmony Junction, where you have a choice of going east to Elmira or west toward Mount Stewart. From Souris to Elmira is about 14 miles. Another option is to take Rte. 305 to Hermanville, following Rte. 16 along the north coast past the tuna fishing port of North Lake Harbour and then on to Elmira. From there take the trail back to Harmony Junction and then to Souris. South of Souris in the Brudenell area another converted rail line at Montague makes a nice bike path all the way to Georgetown at the end of Cardigan Point (See *On Foot*).

Bicycling Outfitters & Guided Tours

■ Bicycle rentals can be found at **A Place To Stay Inn**, which is open all year and rents mountain bicycles. Their rates are $20 a day, $80 weekly. 9 Longworth Street, Box 607, Souris, PEI C0A 2B0, ☎ 800/655-STAY or 902/687-4626.

■ Carol Carter operates **Cycle East** from the Elmira Railway Museum at Elmira. Rates include helmets, racks, and other equipment. Rte. 16A (Box 91), Souris, PEI C0A 2B0, ☎ 902/687-4087.

■ Closer to the Savage Harbour area, **Trailside Café and Adventures** is on the Confederation Trail and will not only rent you a bike with all the trimmings, but can provide route maps, advice and can even fix you up with a picnic, shuttle service, customized tour packages and accommodations. They are open every day from May through October, 9 am to 5 pm, and in July and August until 9 pm. 61 Main Street, Mount Stewart, PEI C0A 1T0, ☎ 888/704-6595, 902/676-3130 or 902/892-7498; in winter 902/368-1202.

■ **Venture Out Vacations** is open from May through October and will arrange tours on PEI and on the Magdalen Islands. Souris is the only departure point for the Magdalen ferry. He also has bike rentals. c/o Allan Arsenault, RR #1, Souris, PEI C0A 2B0, ☎ 902/687-1234.

■ One of the most popular places to rent bikes is **MacQueen's Bike Shop**. It's one of the biggest bike shops in the province, with a good selection of rental bikes and equipment. Bikes come with all of the gear and they also offer emergency road repair service for $25. They suggest reservations, especially during the busiest periods. They know their stuff and can provide you with trail and route maps and suggestions. They also operate **MacQueen's Island Tours** (same phone numbers) for those who want to do independent bike touring but need help with the details. They can set up accommodations, dining, rentals, road repairs, luggage transfer and other pain-in-the-neck details. Both are open all year. 430 Queen Street, Charlottetown, ☎ 800/969-2822, 902/368-2453 or 902/894-4547.

■ **Fun On Wheels** has bikes for rent by the hour, day and week and they provide helmets, etc. They are open mid-May through September from 8 am to dusk. 19 Great George Street, Box 2952, Charlottetown, PEI, ☎ 902/368-7161, winter 902/672-2870.

■ On the north shore in the Anne's Land area, **Northshore Rentals**, Brackley Beach, ☎ 902/672-2022, is open all year and can outfit the whole family with a bike and equipment, as can **Smooth Cycle** in Cavendish, ☎ 800/310-6550 or 902/566-5530, and **Sunset Campground Bike Rentals**, on Rte. 6 beside the Cavendish Boardwalk in Cavendish, ☎ 800/715-2440 or 902/963-2440. They have beach bikes and bikes for all members of the family in the $12 to $17 per day price range. They are open mid-June to September, 8 am to 10 pm.

■ South of Kensington are rentals at **Wheels Bicycle Rentals**, in Kelvin Grove, open all year. Half-day rentals are $10.95, daily $14.95, and weekly $69.95. They will deliver free in the Summerside-Kensington area. ☎ 800/255-5160 or 902/836-5189.

■ **Bike By The Sea** is a bicycle tour outfitter that has tours through out the province. Tours operate between July and the end of August and cover most parts of the province. Some trips combine other experiences, such as biking and golfing or biking and kayaking. They also have trips geared to the needs and desires of people over 50. 45 Woodgarden Crescent, Scarborough, ON M1E 3K3, ☎ 888/BIKE-PEI or 416/284-8516.

■ Another outfitter that has bike trips throughout the province is **Freewheeling Adventures**. They have five- and six-day tours that travel from inn to inn and eat at the best local restaurants. They also provide equipment and will help you select the trip that fits your skill level and interests. They offer trips from June through September. Contact them c/o Cathy Guest, RR #1, Hubbards NS B0J 1T0, ☎ 902/857-3600 or 902/857-3612.

■ Another well-regarded outfitter is **Outside Expeditions**, which has a shop at the end of the road in North Rustico. They provide guided trips across the island or help you to design your own and give you a hand with logistical support. Trips range from half-day jaunts to six-day expeditions, and they know the best trails. The day fee rate is $39. c/o Bryon Howard, Box 2336, Charlottetown, PEI C1A 8C1, ☎ 800/207-3899 or 902/892-5425.

■ **Smooth Cycle** provides guided bicycle tours of the city every Tuesday from mid-June to mid-September for $28, which includes the bike, helmet, personal guide and a snack. Their staff are all cyclists and are eager to share their knowledge of trails and routes with customers. They also provide full bike rental packages. 172 Prince Street, Charlottetown, PEI C1A 4R6, ☎ 800/310-6550 or 902/566-5530.

■ **Atlantic Canada Cycling** can supply you with free advice, tour planning services, guidebooks and supplies from May through October. Contact them c/o Gary Conrod, Box 1555 Station Central, Halifax NS B2Y 2Y3, ☎ 902/423-2453, fax 902/423-2452, e-mail cycling@ fox.nstn.ca, Web site www.fox.nstn.ca/~cycling.

■ On Water

Beaches

There's no escaping them, and even confirmed "we aren't going to fritter away our vacation lying on the sand" travelers succumb to PEI's beaches. Hardy New England kids who think of all saltwater as something that turns their ankles blue in five minutes can't believe these warm waters, where they can happily splash about all day without a shiver.

On the East Cape, **Campbells Cove Provincial Park**, off Rte. 16 just west of North Lake Harbour, has unsupervised swimming, as does **Red Point Provincial Park** off Rte. 16 north of Souris. **Panmure Island Provincial Park**, at Panmure Island, off the east side of the island near Brunnell River, has beautiful white sandy beaches with supervised ocean swimming. It's off Rte. 17, the King's Byway, at Gaspereaux where you follow Rte. 347 a short distance. There is also a campground in the park. **Northumberland Provincial Park**, Wood Islands, Parks Division East, Box 370, Montague, PEI C0A 1R0, ☎ 902/962-2163, offers unsupervised ocean swimming on the southern part of the same coast.

The north shore of the central part of the island has some of the best beaches of all. Most are red sand, eroded from the sandstone cliffs that back them. Others are white sand and backed by dunes. **Prince Edward Island National Park** covers all of these beaches, at Dalvay, Brackley Beach, Rustico Island, North Rustico, Cavendish and New London. There are so many miles of beach that you are sure to find a quiet spot, and just about all of these beaches are supervised.

Cedar Dunes Provincial Park, at the southwest corner of the province, is right on Lady Slipper Drive, on Rte. 14. It has lots of beautiful sandy beach for wandering and it's in a part of the island that is practically unsettled, so they are blissfully uncrowded. Swimming here is supervised. There is a big black and white striped lighthouse and you can climb up to the lantern deck to see the island spread below. The park also has a camping area.

You'll find unsupervised swimming at Campbellton, Skinner's Pond or supervised swimming at **Jacques Cartier Provincial Park,** south of Kildare. **Green Park Provincial Park**, near Port Hill, also has unsupervised swimming, as does **Linkletter Provincial Park** on Sandy Cove, just west of Summerside.

Canoeing & Kayaking

Leaving right from Charlottetown, there are enough canoeing and kayaking opportunities to use up several vacations. The **Hillsborough River** starts there and runs north for almost 50 miles into the countryside, passing shorefront that is essentially unsettled. On the south side of the city, **Charlottetown Harbour** runs west into the North River for several miles and opposite the city and across the harbor, the **West River** extends well inland, all the way to (and beyond) Strathgartney Provincial Park at Strathgartney, more than half the way to Victoria.

All along the east coast, south of Souris, are a myriad of bays and estuaries that are ripe for canoeing. The **Souris River** runs well inland and **Rollo Bay**, just south of it, connects to **Fortune Bay** and the **Fortune River**, a wild coastline. At Bridgeton is the head of the **Boughton River**, a drowned river estuary. **Cardigan River** on the north side of Cardigan Point also runs well inland, past Cardigan along shores that have still not seen a bulldozer.

On the Georgetown side of the Cardigan peninsula is an immense watershed that would take weeks to explore. The first is the **Brudenell River**, accessible from the Provincial Park, and across a tapered peninsula is its neighbor, the **Montague River**. Both of these lead into **Georgetown Bay** and then into the huge **St. Mary's Bay**, protected from the Atlantic by Panmure Island. The long **Murray River** starts west of the town, passes it and then continues on for miles, widening out to embrace several sizeable islands and passing by a number of small inlets before arriving at the sand barrier across its mouth at Murray Harbour. On the south coast, **Orwell Bay** runs well inland via the Vernon River and a number of coves cut deeply inland.

In the western part of PEI, the entire north shore of the western arm, from the Kildare River north of Alberton all the way across almost to Kensington, is one gigantic kayaking and canoeing opportunity. It's a vast area, one where the first challenge is to know and appreciate your own skill level, endurance and planning capabilities. The whole shore along this section is protected by a barrier beach and within the barrier are **Cascumpec Bay** and its associated **Mill River Bay** and **Foxley Bay**, the **Conway Narrows** and the enormous **Malpeque Bay**, famed for oysters and filled with bays and inlets to explore. On the south shore consider the **Percival River** or **Summerside Harbour**, **Dunk River** and **Bedeque Bay**.

Canoe & Kayak Outfitters - Guided Tours

■ **Outside Expeditions** has a shop at the end of the road in North Rustico and they paddle in the waters of the National Park. On windy days they do their instruction and paddling on a nearby river. They offer half-day excursions at 9 am and 2 and 6 pm daily and a kayaking course the first Saturday of each month. The half-day trip is $45 and for $49 you can kayak to a lobster bake on the beach on Wednesday or Friday nights. They also conduct a seal-watching trip on the eastern part of the island every Sunday for $85 and a 24-hour Discovery Kayak Adventure starting at $159. Kayak rentals are available from their North Rustico site for $25. c/o Bryon Howard, Box 2336, Charlottetown, PEI C1A 8C1, ☎ 800/207-3899 or 902/892-5425.

■ **Trailside Café and Adventures** is a bicycle outfitter, but also does watersport rentals. Mount Stewart is close to the head of the Hillsborough River, a south-flowing stream that comes within two miles of Savage Harbor on the north shore and nearly cuts the island in two parts. 61 Main Street, Mount Stewart, PEI C0A 1T0, ☎ 888/704-6595, 902/676-3130 or 902/892/7498, winter 902/368-1202.

■ **Paddle PEI** operates a full-service kayak shop from the National Park. They offer half- , full- and two-day trips and rent equipment as well. The canoeing and kayaking available in the Brudenell River and Georgetown Bay are outstanding. They are able to handle all skill levels from beginner up. They open June through September, 9 am to 8 pm. 41 Allen Street, Charlottetown, PEI C1A 2V6, has a location at Brudenell River Provincial Park, ☎ 902/652-2434.

■ **Watersport PEI** has canoes, boats, sailboats and windsurfers for rent. They open mid-June to September daily from 10 am to dusk. Rte. 6, Stanley Bridge, ☎ 902/886-2323 or 902/886-3313.

■ **Fun On Wheels** has kayaks and canoes for rent and can provide PDF's and other needed equipment. Hourly, daily and weekly rates are available, 8 am to dusk, from mid-May to the end of September. 19 Great George Street in Charlottetown, ☎ 902/368-7161, winter 902/894-4837.

■ South of Charlottetown on one of the arms of the West River, **St. Catherine's Cove Canoe Rental, Inc.**, St. Catherine's, ☎ 902 675-2035, provides canoes for a paddle along the Elliot River, an arm of the tidal West River that starts opposite Charlottetown Harbour. Here the river is rural and bucolic with views of the hills along the shore. The rentals are from a small farm with lots of barnyard animals for kids to enjoy. They operate from dawn to dusk but are dependant on the tides, so it's best to call ahead for a reservation and the best times. Open May 1 to late October from dawn to dusk. Rates are $7.25 per hour or $24 per day.

Harbor & Bay Tours

On the eastern end of the island **Captain Garry's Seal and Bird Watching Cruises**, Murray River, ☎ 800/496-2494, 902/962-2494 or 902/962-3846, operates two boats to almost certain seal-spotting grounds, where you may see seal pups if you go quite early in the season. They also do sunset cruises. Trips run from mid-June to the end of September.

Cruise Manada Seal Watching Boat Tours, c/o Capt. Dan Bears, Box 641, Montague C0A 1R0, ☎ 800/986-3444 or 902/838-3444, operates an award-winning cruise on the Montague and Brudenell Rivers, two of the biggest in the province. Their three boats are equipped with roll-down sides that allow a full view but protect from spray. The narrated cruise visits seals in the harbor, bird sites, and mussel farms, all while you take in the sights of and enjoy the complimentary refreshments. They run from mid-May to the end of September.

Cardigan Sailing Charters, Box 7, Cardigan C0A 1G0, ☎ 902/583-2020, take guests on a 30-foot mahogany sailboat in beautiful Cardigan Bay, off the entrance to Georgetown Harbour, from late June to late September. Departures are at 10 am and return in late afternoon. It costs $50 per person for an unforgettable ride.

From Charlottetown, **Imperial Harbour Cruises**, ☎ 902/628-5263 (LAND) or 902/368-2628(BOAT), depart from the Prince

Street Wharf for a cruise of the harbor with a description of the history and the passing sights. Daytime and sunset cruises run daily from June through September. Prices vary with the cruise and range from $8 to $20.

There is a unique chance in Charlottetown to do your own harbor tour. **Island Houseboat Holidays, Inc.** has 8x35-foot houseboats that sleep six for rent at berths in Charlottetown. Take your home-away-from-home and travel up the Hillsborough River, which runs north of the capital and almost cuts the island in half. Or sail into the West River or up into the North River. Reservations are required. Available between mid-April and mid-October. c/o Sanderson/Miller, 65 Douglas Street, Charlottetown, PEI C1A 2J4, ☎ 800/840-5322, winter 902/566-1104.

To sail through Charlottetown's harbor on a typical salt banker, look for the ***Mercy Coles***, ☎ 902/892-9065, at Peake's Wharf, behind The Prince Edward Hotel. They sail daily at 10 am, 2 pm and 6 pm in the summer. These two-masted schooners were used for fishing throughout the 19th century.

On the western side of the island, **Avery's Fish Market and Crafts**, Alberton, ☎ 902/853-3474 (FISH), operates the *Andrew's Mist*. It does deep-sea fishing by day, but at night Captain Craig Avery offers an evening cruise in beautiful Alberton Harbour. The best part is that they serve complimentary mussels on the cruise and the price is only $15 per person.

Fishing

PEI was once famed for its bluefin tuna fishing, and we're happy to report that after a several-year absence, the tuna are back. North Lake, the main port for tuna fishing, is in the northeast corner of the island on Rte. 16. The season is between July 1 and November 1. **Bruce's Tuna and Deep Sea Fishing By Rod and Reel,** ☎ 902/357-2638, operates two boats from North Lake for sport fishing. **Coffin's Tuna & Deep Sea Fishing** (☎ 902/687-3531, winter 902/357-2030); **MacNeill's Tuna and Deep Sea Fishing** (☎ 902/357-2454), and **Prince Edward Island Sport Fishing Association Inc.** (☎ 902/838-3723); all also sail from North Lake in search of the bluefin. **North Lake Tuna Charters Inc.** (☎ 902/357-2894) sails between July 1 and the end of August. They all supply the equipment.

Wild Winds Deep Sea Fishing and Tuna Charters at Savage Harbour, ☎ 902/676-2024, operates 3½-hour trips from July to

➔ **FRESHWATER FISHING:** *Prince Edward Island does not require a guide to fish in its streams, but you'll probably need one unless you're very familiar with the island or know someone who is. Many of the streams have only local names, quite a few don't show up on tourist maps, and access to the fishing holes is often through privately-owned fields and pastures. Most of the freshwater sportfishing here is for trout. Like much else on the island, fishing here feels very much like a 19th-century pastoral idyll, complete with small boys carrying wicker creels and migratory songbirds singing their hearts out. A good fishing guide for the island is* ***Scott Mitchell****, Bonshaw Post Office, Bonshaw, PEI C0A 1C0, ☎ 902/675-2318. His rates are $50, including taxes, for half-day trips; full-day excursions are $100.* – Sara Godwin and Charles James

mid-September. They supply all equipment and take care of your catch.

The north shore of the central part of the island is headquarters for a fleet of deep-sea fishing boats, and you can catch a variety of saltwater fish, with mackerel predominating.

Our kids learned to fish with family-operated **Gauthier's Deep Sea Fishing** in Rusticoville, ☎ 902/963-2295 or 902/963-2191. They are one of the oldest fishing trip services and, we think, one of the best. It's a class act and they pay extra attention to children. They have rods, reels, tackle, and rain gear and will clean your catch at the end of the trip. We've fished with them for 30 years. In late August they will also take you to tuna territory. Open July to early September.

Aiden Doiron's Deep Sea Fishing in North Rustico, ☎ 902/963-2442 or 902/963-2039, runs daily fishing trips aboard the *Dougie D* and *Island Prince* between July 1 and mid-September. They supply the rods and bait. They will also do charter and shore line cruising trips by prior arrangement. Early risers get free coffee aboard and they have a market and canteen at the wharf where you can get fresh or cooked lobster or fresh seafood to cook at your campsite.

Also operating out of North Rustico are **Barry Doucette's Deep Sea Fishing**, ☎ 902/963-2465 or 963-2611, and **Bob's Deep Sea Fishing**, ☎ 902/963-2666 or 902/963-2086. Both supply all equipment and will clean and bag your catch on their 3½-hour trips. **Bearded Skipper's Deep Sea Fishing**, North Rustico Wharf, ☎ 902/963-2334 or 902/963-2525, also provides the same services. Barry and the Bearded Skipper are open July 1 to early September and Bob stays open a week or so later.

Salty Seas Deep Sea Fishing at nearby Covehead Harbour, ☎ 902/672-2346 or 902/672-2681, operates from July to the end of September. Their guarantee: "No fish, no charge." **Richard's Deep Sea Fishing**, ☎ 902/672-2376, also operates from Covehead Harbour during the same months.

In Alberton, facing the Gulf of St. Lawrence on the western side of PEI and handy to the provincial park, **Avery's Fish Market and Crafts**, Alberton, ☎ 902/853-3474 (FISH), operates the *Andrew's Mist* on daily fishing trips, but you should call ahead for times and reservations. They supply all necessary equipment and will clean and bag your catch for you. Deep-sea fishing is $20 adults, $18 under age 12.

Freshwater fishing in a private pond is available at **Ben's Lake**, Rte. 24, Bellevue, ☎ 902/838-2706. Ben's is a good place to practice catch and release with trout. Or, for a fee, you can take the fish home for dinner. It's open all year. Fishing licenses are not required.

At Rollo Bay off of Rte. 2 just southeast of Souris, **Rollo Bay U-Fish**, ☎ 902/687-2382, has fishing on their own pond, where licenses are not required. The fees depend on whether you choose catch and release or catch and keep.

■ On Snow

Skiing

While there is some skiing here, it is limited by the nature of the terrain and the weather conditions. The relatively flat, rolling ground doesn't lend itself to downhill skiing. But that doesn't mean it's missing altogether. **Brookvale Provincial Ski Park** in Crapaud, ☎ 902/658-2925, is a small area with chairlifts and night skiing. Although you probably wouldn't plan to spend your Alpine skiing vacation there, it gives a little variety to a winter trip. You couldn't ask for a less threatening place to learn downhill skiing than at the PEI Alpine Ski School, Brookville, ☎ 902/658-2142.

The relatively mild temperatures caused by the moderating effect of the Gulf of St. Lawrence, and the Gulf Stream off the Atlantic side, makes snow cover uncertain along the coasts, but when there is snow, several places have groomed trails. The gentle terrain makes skiing a pleasure (for those of us who think cross-country need not be an ordeal to be fun). **Brudenell River Provincial Park**, Roseneath, Parks Division East, Box 370, Montague, PEI C0A 1R0, ☎ 902/652-8966, winter 902/652-2356, has well-groomed trails that travel through the woods in a lovely shore-side setting. The park is off Rte. 3, between Georgetown and Roseneath, and has a resort and dining room adjacent.

At **Mill River Provincial Park**, Parks Division West, RR #3, O'Leary, PEI C0B 1V0, ☎ 902/859-8786, winter 902/859-8790, you'll find that trails are also well groomed, and suitable for beginning skiers. This park is right off Rte. 2, which runs up the center of the west part of the island. It's a big park overlooking a long arm of Cascumpec Bay.

Prince Edward Island National Park, Parks Canada, 2 Palmers Lane, Charlottetown, PEI C1A 5V6, ☎ 800/213-PARK or 902/672-6350, stretches along the north coast from Tracadie Bay on the east to New London Bay on the west. It has groomed trails, all quite level, and nice sea views.

Southwest of Charlottetown, **Brookvale Nordic Touring Centre** in Crapaud, ☎ 902/658-2925, has miles of beautifully tended trails, which are used for major cross-country ski competitions. They also have lighted trails for night skiing.

Snowmobiling

Some of the best snowmobiling in the province is along the **Confederation Trail**. See the *On Foot* and *On Wheels* sections above for general descriptions of the trails. The relatively level nature of these trails makes them a good corridor, connecting local trails across the island. You'll find clear signage and clubhouses along the trail, along with towns where you can find food and lodging. Rent snowmobiles at the Mill River Resort, ☎ 902/859-3555, on Rte. 2, south of Alberton, in Mill River Provincial Park, and at Dennis Motors, ☎ 902/831-2229, in Ellerslie, in the Tyne Valley, also in the western part of the province.

■ On Horseback

Close to the Provincial Park, **Brudenell Trail Rides** in Roseneath, ☎ 902/652-2396 or 902/838-3713 in winter, has guided hour-long rides along the beach of the Brudenell River estuary, every day from June to the end of September. These rides are $15 and they also have a half-hour ride for $10 and sunset rides for $18.

Also on the east side of the island, **Lakeside Trail Rides**, West St. Peters, ☎ 902/961-2076, leads hour-long rides by the beach from mid-June to mid-September for $9. Their hours are 7 am to 9 pm. It's near the entrance to the Crowbush Golf Club.

Close to the center of Anne's Land, **Cavendish Trail Rides**, ☎ 902/963-2824, is located in Cavendish and provides a chance for a quiet ride on a country trail, much the same as Lucy Maud Montgomery might have enjoyed. They also have pony rides in the barnyard for younger children. They are open late June to September, daily 9:30 am to 8 pm at $8 per ride.

Just a three-mile trot south of Cavendish, **Grant's Trail Rides**, (no telephone), operates their rides from Mayfield on Rte. 13. They have over 2½ miles of private trail with a separate pony trail for kids. Open mid-June to September, $8 per ride. They also have small farm animals for children to pet.

Jeannie's Trail Rides, Ltd, Hunter River, ☎ 902/964-3384 operates from June to September and has a 2½-mile trail through woods and fields. A separate trail for children on ponies and the farmyard animals make this fun for the whole family. Open daily, June through September from 9:30 am to 8 pm. Rides are $7.

Millstream Trail Rides, Brackley Beach, ☎ 902/672-2210, on Rte. 15 at Britain Shore Road, also has rides. They're open mid-June to mid-September from 10 am to dusk daily. Rates are $9 for trail rides and $3 for a child's ride in the paddock.

South of Stanley Bridge on Rte. 254, **Ride Brimstone Hollow**, ☎ 902/886-2225, is across from the Devil's Punch Bowl (which might give you some idea of where the name came from). They promise a trail ride like no other and operate from mid-June to September daily, "sunup to sundown."

North Bedeque is on Rte. 1A, west of Borden, and there you will find **Meadowside Stables**, ☎ 902/888-2568. For $10 you can enjoy an hour-long ride along quiet back roads and river banks in this almost unknown part of the province. They are open Monday through Saturday all year. You should make reservations.

G&J Trail Rides, Coleman PO, ☎ 902/859-2393, has trail riding in the western section every day from 10 am to 6 pm. The fee is $7 per ride; they are open from late June to early September.

Nail Pond Bed & Breakfast & Trail Rides, in Nail Pond (near Tignish), ☎ 902/882-2103, is on the far northern tip of the western peninsula. They arrange trail rides for their B&B guests and for others.

Cultural & Eco-Travel Experiences

Two museums, less than 12 miles apart, tell the story of the island Acadians, early French settlers. **Acadian Museum of PEI**, Rte. 2, Miscouche, ☎ 902/436-6237, is a new museum where visitors learn about Acadian culture from 1720 to the present through audio-visual presentations and exhibits. They also have extensive genealogical resources. Miscouche is on Rte. 2 west of Summerside, and the museum is open year round, Monday to Friday, 9:30 am to 5 pm, and in summer daily during the same hours.

The **Acadian Pioneer Village** at Le Village Resort, ☎ 800/567-3228 or 902/854-2227, is a reproduction of a small Acadian village of log buildings. The church, family homes and school bring back the lives of the early Francophone settlers. Five murals at the village tell the tale of the settlers and their lives. They are open mid-June to mid-September, 9:30 am to 7 pm.

College of Piping, 619 Water Street East, Summerside C1N 4H8, ☎ 902/436-5377, is dedicated to the preservation of the Scottish heritage of the island. From late June to early September they present performances of bagpipes, Highland dance, fiddling, and stepdancing on Thursday nights. Check with them for other performances and on lesson in Highland piping, Scottish snare drumming, Highland and stepdancing, piano, fiddle and tin whistle. An historical exhibit details the story of Scottish immigrants to the island.

Indian Art and Craft of North America, Box 176, Lennox Island, PEI C0B 1P0, ☎ 902/831-2653, on the Lennox Island reservation, has a fine collection of Indian-made crafts and artwork, including Micmac items. They have a large selection of Micmac-made split ash baskets. They also have Iroquois, Ojibway and Navajo items. In addition to a variety of basket styles they have porcupine quill baskets, masks, dream catchers, stone and wood carvings, decoys, pottery, leather items and jewelry in stone, shell, bone, feather and beads. Lennox Island is north of Tyne Valley; to get there, continue north on Rte. 12 to Rte. 163.

Culture Crafts Co-operative Association, Ltd, PO Box 8, Richmond, PEI C0B 1Y0, ☎ 902/831-2484 or 902/854-3063, also makes hand-split ash baskets, reviving a craft of the island's potato industry. For almost two centuries potato pickers here used these baskets to hold their produce. You can watch as the tree is split with a wooden maul and strips of wood are prepared by pounding and shaving. In addition to baskets they sell wood carvings, quilts, hand woven rugs, pottery and willow and driftwood furniture. They're on Rte. 2, 15 miles west of Summerside.

Island Farmhouse Gouda, Inc, RR #9, Winslow North, PEI C1E 1Z3, ☎ 902/368-1506, is another agricultural enterprise. The Cheese Lady makes wonderful Gouda-style cheese, and you can buy it at the farm, where you can see the operation. They are open Monday through Saturday, from 10 am to 6 pm. Take Rte. 2 west a short way from Charlottetown, then take Rte. 223 north, on the way to the north shore.

Irish Moss Interpretive Center on Rte. 14 in Miminegash, ☎ 902/882-4313, explains yet another harvest. This small tufted seaweed has many commercial uses – you've probably used it on your shoes, taken it to feel better and eaten it in one of your favorite desserts. Here you can learn how it grows, how it is harvested and what it is used for.

Island Nature Trust Tours, c/o Kate MacQuarrie, Box 265, Charlottetown C1A 7K4, ☎ 902/566-9150, fax 902/628-6331 operates between mid-May and the end of October. Their tours concentrate on nature history and the birds, fish, animals and earth of the island. On the tours they visit dunes, woods, beaches, cliffs and wetlands for a broad look at the ecology of the island. Rates depend on the tour but whole day rates start at $125, and they will customize your tour if there is something in particular you want to see.

■ Wildlife-Watching

Prince Edward Island National Park protects a shoreline rich in wildlife habitats: sand dunes, beaches, cliffs, salt marshes, clam flats, freshwater ponds and woodlands. To explore the park from June through September, you must pay a fee, but the facilities are open the rest of the year without a fee. For information, contact Prince Edward Island National Park, Parks Canada, 2 Palmers Lane, Charlottetown, PEI C1A 5V6, ☎ 800/213-PARK or 902/672-6350.

BIRDING ON PRINCE EDWARD ISLAND

The great birding sport on Prince Edward Island is spotting rarities. A bird may be rare because the species is endangered, or because it's outside its normal range. Rarities are found here every year, birds blown off course by storms or high winds. Or, during the spring and fall migration, birds sometimes fly far afield. Take copious notes, get a photo if you can, and report your sighting at the **Bird's Eye Nature Store** in Charlottetown (41 University Avenue, ☎ 902/566-3825) or to the **PEI Natural History Society**, PO Box 2346, Charlottetown, PEI C1A 8C1.

More than 250 species have been recorded at PEI National Park, but the star is the rare and endangered piping plover that nests in the sand dunes. Nesting areas are carefully protected, but you can see piping plovers on uncrowded portions of the beach. Covehead, Brackley, and Rustico all have large sheltered bays, where you can see shorebirds from mid-July through autumn. The best birding is at the ponds inside the dunes early in the morning.

Right smack in the middle of town, Charlottetown Harbour offers excellent birding. Common terns nest on the old bridge pilings spring and summer; double-crested cormorants use the same pilings in late summer as they gather for their migration south. A variety of gulls, ducks, and shorebirds are also here. Look closely and you may spot harbour porpoise and harbour seals as well.

One of the richest birding spots is Malpeque Bay, dotted with islands, almost all of which contain nesting colonies of great blue herons, common terns, greater black-backed gulls (the largest of all the gulls), herring gulls, and double-crested cormorants. Osprey also nest around the bay. During migration Canada geese, black ducks, common mergansers, red-breasted mergansers, common goldeneye, and both scaups are seen in substantial numbers. Thousands of double-crested cormorants stage here in September and October preparing to heading south for the winter, creating what a knowledgeable local birder calls "one of the greatest wildlife spectacles in the Maritimes." Good vantage points are along the shore at Gillis Point, Belmont Provincial Park, and Hamilton. In September, ask about boat tours to Hog Island for spectacular viewing. – *Sara Godwin and Charles James*

Nature programs and walks are scheduled regularly during the summer, and the park visitors center has ample material on the wildlife you can see there. Get a copy of *Birdlife of the Prince Edward Island National Park*.

RECOMMENDED READING: *Handy books are* Familiar Birds of Prince Edward Island *and* 25 of the Best, Easy to Reach Birding Spots on Prince Edward Island, *both by Geoff Hogan. Get a good, detailed map to go with the latter; its maps are inscrutable, except, perhaps, to locals.*

Harbor seals summer in the broad estuaries, especially those of Brudenell and Murray Rivers, on the eastern shore. Seal watch trips go out of Murray River and Montague. **Captain Garry's Seal and Bird Watching Cruises**, ☎ 902/962-2494 or 902/962-3846, operates two boats out of Murray River to some of the surest seal-watching territory around. Early in the season you may see seal pups. Garry's boats also go to Bird Island where cormorants, blue herons and terns are common.

Cruise Manada Seal Watching Boat Tours in Montague, ☎ 800/986-3444 or 902/838-3444, cruises on the Montague and Brudenell Rivers.

Seals winter on the ice floes off the **Magdalen Islands**, where they pup in late February. It's one of the coldest venues for wildlife-watching, but the experience of seeing baby harp seals born is one you'll never forget. Tours, which can be arranged by **Atlantic Marine Adventure Tours**, ☎ 506/459-7325, are not cheap. Before reserving, check other options. Consider a package tour with an international nature vacation company such as **Natural Habitat**, ☎ 800/543-8917, which offers five-day trips that include hotel accommodations, transportation from Halifax, and other extras, for $1,700.

HERON HAUNTS: *The largest great blue heron colonies in North America are found in eastern Prince Edward Island. Anywhere along the Souris Causeway will offer good viewing, but the restaurant at the east end lets you do your birding in a civilized manner, over a proper cup of tea or pot of hot coffee. Great blue herons in goodly numbers are on the mud flats and in the salt marsh; the best time is in August. Flocks of Canada geese and brant also congregate here, and osprey are common.* – Sara Godwin and Charles James

Prince Edward Island Marine Aquarium, Rte. 6, Stanley Bridge, ☎ 902/892-2203, gives you a close-up look at seals playing. Elsewhere the tanks of fish show who lives under all that water around you. The aquarium is open mid-June to mid-September, daily 9 am to dusk, admission $5 adults, children six-14, $2.50.

You wouldn't expect to find them here on an island in Canada, but at **Buffaloland** there is a herd of American Bison. The park has a 100-acre fenced area with a boardwalk to a platform where you can watch the buffalo and whitetailed deer browse. There is no admission fee and they are open all year. In Montague, north of Murray River on Rte. 4, ☎ 902/652-2356.

Sightseeing

In the Eastern Region

Orwell Corner Historic Village is an actual little town that gradually died away about a century ago and has been restored to its 1895 appearance. The streets were never paved, the store front never modernized, and the result is a Brigadoon feeling of having been dropped into a different time. The tiny general store with an old-time Post Office, a dressmaker's shop, a farmhouse, the old village church, and the old school, cluster at the crossroads of two rutted paths that were once the main road. In the kitchen of the farmhouse there's a flip-top baking table that makes us wonder if we really do have all the modern conveniences today. People in the barns and workshops will discuss the old farming techniques and you can learn about village social life at a real ceilidh every Wednesday evening during the summer. Cookies and scones are served in the Community House in the morning and sandwiches are served from 11 am to 4 pm. Or you can order a picnic in a wicker basket to eat on the grounds. They are open from mid-May to late June and September to late October, Tuesday through Friday, 10 am to 3 pm, and late June through August, Tuesday through Sunday, 9 am to 5 pm. Admission is $3. Rte. 1, Orwell, Vernon Bridge RR 2, Orwell Corner, PEI C0A 2E0, ☎ 902/651-2013 in summer, 902/892-9127 in winter.

Sir Andrew MacPhail Homestead in Orwell has many items related to Sir Andrew's fascinating life, including letters exchanged with some of the leading figures of his time. Sir Andrew was one of those bigger-than-life men of the 19th century: medical doctor, magazine editor, professor and writer on public policy.

> **➔ AND FOR BIRDERS...** *Take the meandering nature trail from the handsome old Sir Andrew Macphail Homestead into the forest, where woodland birds and songbirds fill the trees. Brown creepers, the secretive boreal chickadee, hermit thrush, evening grosbeak, and a half-dozen species of warblers, including the mourning warbler, are all possible sightings. Five different woodpeckers, including the black-backed woodpecker, are also here. Ruffed grouse drum on hollow logs, and hawks soar, including the northern goshawk and sharp-shinned hawk. Some 40 species are commonly seen here, which makes for a pleasant and productive bit of birding.* – Sara Godwin and Charles James

Among his avocations was scientific investigation of agriculture to improve farm production. Rte. 209, off Highway 1, Orwell, PEI ☎ 902/651-2789.

Basin Head Fisheries Museum, Rte. 16, Basin Head, ☎ 902/357-2966, is just east of Souris. Inshore fishing long played an important role in the economy of the island, and here you can learn about the lives of those who engaged in it. Small buildings exhibit gear, boats, photographs and other artifacts Dioramas illustrate the methods they used and the ecology of the sea they fished. There is a boardwalk to a white sand beach, and they have programs on coastal ecology. Open daily in July and August, 10 am to 7 pm; in the spring and fall, hours are Monday through Friday, 10 am to 3 pm.

In Central PEI

Province House (☎ 902/566-7626), at the corner of Richmond and Great George Streets in Charlottetown, is an active legislative building and still houses the Provincial Legislature. It was here that Canadian leaders gathered in 1864 to discuss a possible union of the provinces, making this the "Birthplace of Confederation." Several rooms have been restored to their appearance at the time of the historic meeting and are open for viewing when not in use. It's open daily in June and September through mid-October 9 am to 5 pm, July and August 9 am to 6 pm, and mid-October through May weekdays 9 am to 5 pm.

Ardgowan National Historic Site, Corner of Mount Edward Road and Palmers Lane, Charlottetown, ☎ 902/566-7050. This historic Victorian home of William Henry Pope, one of the prime movers in the Confederation movement, was the site of a grand party for participants in the Confederation conference. It is now the headquarters of the Department of Canadian Heritage. Its gardens are open to the public and are a fine example of a private Victorian garden, with a croquet lawn and ornate hedges. During July and August guided walks of the gardens are given weekly.

Beaconsfield Historic House, 2 Kent Street, Charlottetown, ☎ 902/368-6600, was built in 1877 by James Peake, Jr, a shipbuilder. His home reflected his wealth, with imported chandeliers, marble fireplaces, central heat and gas lighting. The exterior shows the influence of the Victorian Second Empire, with its mansard roof and ornate wraparound veranda, but adds Georgian detail with bonnet-roofed dormers on the third floor. It's on the waterfront and open all year, September to June, Tuesday through Friday and Sunday from 1 to 5 pm; in July and August, 10 am to 5 pm daily. Admission is $2.50 for adults, children under 12 free.

Fort Amherst, Port La Joye National Historic Site, Rocky Point, ☎ 902/675-2220, is the place where European influence on the island began. While about all of the French settlement and fort are gone, the foundations of the British 1758 fort are still there. Open from May through November, it is staffed mid-June to September daily from 10 am to 6 pm. Take TransCanada-1 south from Charlottetown and then follow Rte. 19 (Blue Heron Trail) north to Rocky Point and the Park.

Lucy Maud Montgomery Birthplace, New London.

The popularity of Lucy Maud Montgomery's semi-autobiographical island girl, Anne, has created a culture of its own in the central part of the island. Of the several Anne museums and souvenir shops with Anne everythings, we've culled these: **Anne of Green Gables Museum** at Silver Bush, Rte. 20 in Park Corner, ☎ 902/436-7329, is one of the primary places associated with the life of Lucy Maud Montgomery. It was the home of her aunt and uncle, the Campbells, and it was in this house that Lucy was married in 1911. It contains many items associated with her life and the characters of her novels. Thousands of Japanese flock here each year, many to be married at this home. **Lucy Maud Montgomery Birthplace**, corner of Rtes. 6 and 20, New London, ☎ 902/886-2099 or 902/436-7329, is a modest little house, where you can see a fairly typical island home of the late 1800s, and Lucy's wedding dress. **Lucy Maud Montgomery Heritage**

Museum on Rte. 20 in Park Corner, ☎ 902/886-2807 or 902/886-2752, was the home of her grandfather, a place she visited often and which played a big part in her books. **Site of Lucy Maud Montgomery Home**, Rte. 6, Cavendish, ☎ 902/9963-2231, is a pleasant stop, even though the home is gone. The fields, trees and pathways that she loved and wrote about are still here. The site and the bookstore/museum here are run by her great-grandson, John MacNeill, and his wife, Jennie.

Woodleigh Replicas and Gardens has over 30 scale models of English (and Scottish) buildings, from castles that you can walk through to the tiny Shakespeare's home. All of this is set in 40 acres of beautiful gardens and lawns. They are open daily from early June to mid-October. In June, September and October, hours are from 9 am to 5 pm; in July and August they stay open until 7 pm. Admission is $6.50 adults, $6 senior and youth, $3.50 children. Family rates are available. In Burlington, ☎ 902/836-3401, fax 902/836-3620, e-mail woodleigh@pei.sympatico.ca.

St. Paul's replica at Woodleigh.

The Victoria Playhouse is a professional repertory theater that has been presenting drama and musical productions in the town's historic theater for more than 16 years. Theater/dinner packages are available. Off Rte. 1, Victoria, in the Maritimes, ☎ 800/925-2025 or 902/658-2025.

Harbourfront Jubilee Theatre operates a professional-level theater through the summer, with a pair of shows that alternate night. Works of contemporary playwrights and musicals are the fare. Tickets run about $17. For information contact The Wyatt Centre, 124 Harbourside Drive, Summerside, PEI C1N 5Y8, ☎ 800/708-6505 or 902/888-2500, fax 902/888-4468, e-mail hjtpei@auracom.com, Web site http://pei.auracom.com/jubilee.

In The West

The **Keir Memorial Museum**, Rte. 20, Malpeque, ☎ 902/836-3054, has exhibits on the inhabitants of the area from Micmacs through the Acadians to the Scots and Brits, and on the oyster industry that has made Malpeque famous throughout the eating world. It is open July 1 through August, weekdays, 9 am to 5 pm, and weekends 1 to 5 pm, for a nominal admission.

International Fox Museum and Hall of Fame, 286 Fitzroy Street, Summerside, ☎ 902/436-2400. From the late 19th and well into the 20th century the raising of fox fur for the international markets was a major industry in the Summerside area. One of the leading families in the trade were the Holmans and their home has become the museum. The key to the success of the trade here, and what made Summerside the center of international trade was the development of a breed of silver fox. The museum documents the growth and decline of the industry.

Eptek National Exhibition Centre, 130 Harbour Drive, Summerside, ☎ 902/888-8373, on the waterfront, is a large multi-use exhibition center with gallery space, where there are changing exhibits, usually art- or history-related traveling shows from across Canada. Open all year. In July and August hours are 10 am to 4 pm daily; from September through June, Tuesday through Friday, 10 am to 4 pm, and Saturday and Sunday, 1 to 4:30 pm. Admission is $2.

Spinnakers' Landing, on the waterfront in Summerside, is just an enjoyable place to hang out, with specialty shops in a reproduction village setting on an attractive boardwalk extending along the shore. There are daily boat rides, a wooden boat builder demonstrates his craft while building an actual boat and local artists perform along the boardwalk. An interpretive display with video tells of the island fishing industry. It's open daily from mid-June to mid-September, 9:30 am to 9:30 pm.

Green Park Shipbuilding Museum and Historic Yeo House, Rte. 12, Port Hill, ☎ 902/368-6608, examines the province's shipbuilding industry in the 19th century and you can wander through the home of one of the town's leading builders. The museum deals with the history of ships here and how they were built, while the steep gabled Queen Anne house, with an interesting cupola, shows the lifestyle of a prosperous family. Open June to September, $2.50 adults, under 12 free.

Prince Edward Island Potato Museum, 22 Parkview Drive, O'Leary, ☎ 902/859-2039, shows how important the potato is to the local economy and culture. The museum deals not only with the history of the potato's journey from Peru, but also with growing the lowly spud and the changes that have taken place over the years. It's also the community museum, with an old schoolhouse, chapel and log barn. They have a snack bar that sells, of course, potato snacks.

Alberton Museum, Church Street, Alberton, ☎ 902/853-4048, is in the former courthouse. Built in 1878, it now houses items related to the history of the town as far back as the Micmac, the fishing and farming industries and the lives of the people who settled and lived here. It's open from June 1 through August.

Where To Stay & Eat

In the East

Forest and Stream Cottages are some of the most attractive cottages we've been in, and at very reasonably prices. Fully insulated and all-electric, they have kitchenettes and a grill and picnic table outside. There are hiking trails on the property and the lake side is a good place for bird viewing. They are open May through October. *Murray Harbour, PEI C0A 1V0, ☎ 902/962-3537 ($-$$).*

The Inn at Bay Fortune is a class act, the kind of place you want to settle into for a while. All of the rooms have natural wood floors, fine furniture and nice details, including cassette players, hair dryers and full tiled baths. The rooms sit around a courtyard, except for two that are in a tower. At the top of the tower is a guest common room with a broad view out over the countryside and water. Built by the playwright Elmer Harris (who wrote Johnny Belinda), it was once the home of actress Colleen Dewhurst and has become one of the leading small inns in Canada. The restaurant keeps pace, with a sophisticated menu firmly based in local ingredients. We are not alone in rating it as one of the best in the

Maritimes, with its constantly changing menu and a bright, elegant dining room. *Rte. 310, R.R. 4, Souris, PEI C0A 2B0, on Route 310 near Highway 2, ☎ 902/687-3745 summer, fax 902/687-3540, off-season 860/296-1348, e-mail innayft@peinet.ca ($$$).*

The Matthew House Inn is within an easy walk of the Magdalen Islands Ferry, even if you are carrying luggage. The historic house has been meticulously restored and converted into a charming inn without sacrificing any of its elegance or grandeur. Rooms all have private bath and the common rooms are stunning. It is consistently rated one of the best in the province, and rightly. Thoroughly hospitable and friendly hosts have lots of material and maps on where to fish, bicycle, canoe and hike. *Box 151, Souris, PEI C0A 2B0, ☎ 902/687-3461 ($$$).*

Sir Andrew MacPhail Homestead is a wonderful old home, and their dining room is a nice place to meet a few Scottish dishes if you don't already know them. They have haggis, bannocks, fish, and beans made with an heirloom bean grown on the farm. They also have a roast of some variety, a poultry dish and a vegetarian entrée each day. The dining room is set with nice china on linen tablecloths and is lit at night by oil lamps. Dining here is a great experience. They serve June through September, Tuesday through Sunday, 11:30 am to 2:30 pm, and Wednesday through Sunday, 5 to 8 pm. *Rte. 209, off Highway 1, Orwell, PEI ☎ 902/651-2789 ($$).*

Central PEI

Prince Edward Hotel is a large hotel close to the center of downtown activity. It's a Canadian Pacific Hotel; do we need to say more? Rooms are large, nicely furnished, very comfortable and have all the amenities. Services and facilities include in-room movies, same day cleaning and laundry, large indoor pool, fitness center, a masseuse, sauna and whirlpool bath. It's stylish, but very hospitable. *18 Queen Street, Charlottetown, PEI C1A 8B9. ☎ 800/828-7447, in the US, 800/268-9411 or 902/566-2222, fax 904/566-1745 ($$$).*

MacLauchlan's Motor Inn is an in-town motel, associated with the Best Western group. In addition to standard rooms and suites they also have housekeeping units available. Rooms are attractive and comfortable and there is an indoor pool and a sauna. They have a restaurant and are handicapped accessible. *238 Grafton Street, Charlottetown, PEI C1A 1L5, ☎ 800/528-1234 (US) or 800/463-2378 (Canada), 902/892-2461, fax 902/566-2979 (low $$$).*

Dundee Arms Inn gives you the option of a room or suite in the original 1903 town mansion or a more modern room in the 10-unit motel. All are nicely furnished, but the inn rooms have period furnishings and the tone of the original structure. Rates include a continental breakfast. *200 Pownal Street, Charlottetown, PEI C1A 3W8, ☎ 902/892-2496, fax 902/368-8532 (low $$$).*

Fitzroy Hall is close to the downtown area, but in a residential area. This 1872 home has been recently brought back to life as an attractive B&B. Nicely decorated, it is furnished with antiques and all six rooms have private baths. Rates include a full breakfast. *45 Fitzroy Street, Charlottetown, PEI C1A 1R4, ☎ 902/368-2077 ($$-$$$).*

Heritage Harbour House Inn is a four-room B&B close to the center. Two of the rooms have private baths. A garage is available for bicycles. *9 Grafton Street, Charlottetown, PEI C1A 1K3, ☎ 800/405-0066 or 902/892-6633 ($$).*

Altavista B&B is an attractive B&B overlooking the water. It has two rooms with private baths. Canoeing is available. *2 Altavista Crescent, Charlottetown, PEI C1E 1M9, ☎ 902/894-4248 ($$).*

Orient Hotel has been a presence in town for many decades. Newly renovated and beautifully decorated, it continues to offer attractive and comfortable accommodations to travelers. Guests may unwind in the hotel's tea shop with a welcoming cup. *Main Street, Victoria, PEI C0A 2G0, reservations Box 162, Charlottetown, PEI C1A 7K4, ☎ 800/565-ORIENT or 902/658-2503, fax 902/658-2078, e-mail orient@pei.sympatico.ca ($$).*

Dalvay By The Sea Inn & Restaurant is one of the finest restaurants on the island and probably among the top-ranked in the country. Chef Richard Kemp has an international reputation; his menu here features dishes with a contemporary flair, all prepared from the freshest local ingredients. Presentation approaches fine art. All the fuss over the restaurant should not overshadow the very fine lodgings of this resort hotel. *Off Rte. 6, Grand Tracadie, ☎ 902/672-2048 ($$-$$$).*

Dundee Arms Inn has two eating places. The **Hearth and Cricket Pub** ($) is casual and cozy, the local roost of the upwardly mobile. The menu tends to the pub side of dining; it's open Monday through Fridays, noon to 1 am, and Saturday, 11:30 am to 1 am. The more formal **Griffon Room** ($$-$$$) emphasizes seafood but has a good selection of alternatives. *200 Pownal Street, Charlottetown, ☎ 902/892-2496.*

The Lord Selkirk is more than simply an elegant and reliable place to dine. The chef has been here for years and has earned his reputation for innovative and delectable cuisine. In the evening you can dine to piano music. Reservations are suggested. *Prince Edward Hotel, 18 Queen Street, Charlottetown, ☎ 902/566-2222 ($$-$$$).*

Sirenella Ristorante is a small gem with a quiet, comfortable feeling. The menu is northern Italian and features a nice selection of seafoods, often paired with pasta. It's right in the downtown area near the Confederation. Make reservations, because it is popular and small. *83 Water Street, Charlottetown, ☎ 902/628-2271 ($-$$).*

Brothers Two offers pub and restaurant dining with a full line of well-prepared entrées in the dining room. The difference here, however, is that they have a dinner theater, presented by **Feast Dinner Theatres**, that has been running in the summers since 1979. The theater is upbeat and enjoyable, featuring contemporary stuff poking fun at just about everything. The atmosphere is casual and easygoing. *Kent and Pownal Streets, Charlottetown, ☎ 902/629-2321 ($$, including theater presentation).*

Cedar's Eatery has a definite Lebanese twist, but there are plenty of other choices. At lunchtime there are soup-and-sandwich specials and a full array of sandwiches. At dinner you'll find kibbe, grape leaves, shish taouk or one of their not so exotic offerings. Reservations aren't necessary. *81 University (between Fitzroy and Kent Streets), Charlottetown, ☎ 902/892-7377 ($-$$).*

Outside Expeditions is an imaginative activities outfitter that does lobster bakes on the beaches of the north shore. There is nothing quite like a clambake and this is one PEI version. Complete dinners on the beach are $55 and offered from June through October on Wednesday and Friday nights. Reservations recommended. See them at their shop at the end of North Rustico Road. *c/o Bryon Howard, Box 2336, Charlottetown C1A 8C1, ☎ 800/207-3899 or 902/892-5425.*

One of the real traditions in PEI is the **church lobster supper**, fitting for a place surrounded by the sea. Expect to pay $21 to $30 for a lobster dinner with steamed mussels and chowder. Non-lobster meals are $12-$16, and kids meals are $3.50-$10. **St. Ann's Church Lobster Suppers**, St. Ann's, ☎ 902/964-2385, is on Route 224 east of Stanley Bridge. It started these lobster suppers and theirs is very popular. They also serve steak, scallops, sole, or pork chops. No longer the homey little weekly event of our childhood, it's become big business, with a license for beer and wine and live entertainment. They serve from 11:30 am to 2 pm and 4 to 9 pm, the last Monday in May to the first Saturday in October, except Sunday. Another good choice is **New Glasgow Lobster Suppers**, ☎ 902/964-2870, in the New Glasgow recreation center on Route 224. They serve from 4 to 8:30 pm, early June to mid-October, but July and August are the busiest times.

In the West

Silver Fox Inn was built in 1892 for a local lawyer and in 1925 became the home of a successful fox breeder. Note the decorative bargeboard and the effect created by the sun passing through the holes drilled in it. All the fine woodwork has been preserved and rooms are furnished with period antiques. A continental breakfast is served. *61 Granville Street, Summerside C1N 2Z3, ☎ 800/565-4033 or 902/463-4033 (low $$).*

West Point Lighthouse is an inn as well as a functioning lighthouse. Two of the nine rooms are in the tower; one, the Tower Room, is positively regal. All have private baths and two have whirlpools. Guests share a common room and there is a museum on the property. Cedar Dunes Provincial Park is adjacent. The licensed restaurant's specialty is West Point Lobster Stew. *West Point, c/o Carol Livingstone, RR #2, O'Leary, PEI C0B 1V0, ☎ 902/859-3605, 800/764-6854 or 902/859-3117 off-season, fax 902/859-3117, Web site www.maine. com/lights/others.htm ($$).*

Tignish Heritage Inn hides behind the St. Simon and St. Jude Church off Maple Street, located there because it was a convent before being converted into a beautiful inn. All 17 rooms have private bath and include a continental breakfast. Tignish is close to all of the sights and activities of the North Cape. *Box 398, Tignish, PEI C0B 2B0, ☎ 902/882-2491 ($$).*

Meme Jane's Restaurant is a family-style restaurant with a good selection of Acadian fare, including rapure (a delicious baked combination of pork and grated potatoes), pâté, and an unusual dish we've found only here: *Père Michele*, which means Father Michael. It's a pork pie with apples and Sultana raisins, a traditional dish served when the circuit-riding priest came to dinner. The restaurant also serves homemade soups, sandwiches, burgers and other fare, including a hefty-size seafood platter (the only thing on the menu over $10) heaped with shrimp, scallops, mussels and several varieties of fish. *6 Lady Slipper Drive, Miscouche, ☎ 902/436-9600 ($).*

Seasons in Thyme is the creation of Chef Stefan Czapalay, in a small town 60 miles from Charlottetown. Open spring through fall, he chooses only the best and freshest of local produce, meats, game, fish and seafoods, coaxing them into a contemporary regional cuisine within the European tradition. Neither casual nor formal, the dining room is attractive and comfortable, with a touch of elegance added by the linen combination of dark green and off-white. His use of herbs and spices is deft, his presentation artful. In spring and fall he opens Tuesday through Sunday, 4 to 10 pm and from mid-June through mid-October the same days from 10 am to 10 pm. This restaurant is one of the top three places to dine on the island. *Tyne Valley, ☎ 902/831-2124, fax 902/831-3357 ($$).*

Fox Tea Room is located in the Holman Homestead/Fox Museum. One of the best places to eat in town, the restaurant is in the comfortable rooms of an old Summerside mansion. Full dinners come with appetizer such as smoked salmon or sausage croustades and a choice of entrées from poultry to beef. Meals are accompanied by breads made on the premises and their desserts are excellent. In summer there is an outdoor patio; at any time it is a good idea to reserve. *286 Fitzroy Street, Summerside, ☎ 902/436-6707 (lunch $, table d'hôte $25).*

Brothers Two charges about $25 for theater and dinner. A friendly, casual pub and restaurant with a long-running summer dinner theater presented by **Feast Dinner Theatres**. The menu emphasizes lobster, salmon, shrimp and mussels, but there are lots of other choices. The cheerful staff adds to the experience. *Water Street East, Summerside, ☎ 902/436-7674 .*

Camping

Campbell's Cove Provincial Park, a 23-acre campground on the northeast point of the island, is off Rte. 16 on the Northumberland Strait. They have kitchen shelters, fireplaces and a dumping station. The park is on an unsupervised beach. *Campbell's Cove, Parks Division East, Box 370, Montague, PEI C0A 1R0, ☎ 902/357-2067, winter 902/652-2356.*

Red Point Provincial Park is a small but attractive campground on the Atlantic side of the northeast peninsula, a few miles north of Souris. They are able to handle both large RV's and tents and have kitchen shelters, fireplaces, and a dumping station. They also have a supervised beach and playground. *Red Point, Parks Division East, Box 370, Montague, PEI C0A 1R0, ☎ 902/357-2463, winter 902/652-2356.*

Brudenell River Provincial Park in Roseneath is a large campground with lots of facilities and services. They can accommodate both RV's and tents. The park sits along the beautiful Brudenell River, and recreational opportunities are outstanding. There is a championship 18-hole golf course here as well as horseshoes, tennis, lawn bowling, canoeing, kayaking, and horseback riding. They also have a hotel with a fully licensed dining room. *Parks Division East, Box 370, Montague, PEI C0A 1R0, ☎ 902/652-8966, winter 902/652-2356, off Rte. 3 between Georgetown and Roseneath.*

Stanhope Campground is an attractive seaside park on the north shore. The park has a lot of services, including a laundromat. For recreation there is supervised swimming, a playground, programs, and sports equipment loans, and there are hiking trails close by. Wood fires are allowed in the kitchen shelters only. Open mid-June to early September. To get here take Rte. 25 off of Rte. 6. *Stanhope, Parks Canada, 2 Palmers Lane, Charlottetown, PEI C1A 5V6, ☎ 800/213-PARK or 902/672-6350.*

Northumberland Provincial Park is close enough to the Wood Islands ferry to allow you to scoot over to Nova Scotia for the day. The park has a nice ocean beach and a place to dig clams. RVs and tents are accommodated and there are kitchen shelters, laundromat and a dumping station. In addition to a series of park recreation programs, there is also a trail through a seaside forest showing the effects of the ocean and the wind on forest growth. There is a camper's store in the park. *Wood Islands, Parks Division East, Box 370, Montague, PEI C0A 1R0, ☎ 902/962-2163, winter 902/652-2356.*

Rustico Island Campground is on the long barrier beach that forms and protects Rustico Harbour. One of the most popular camping areas on the entire island, this is a hard one to get into, but one of our favorites. On the ocean side are miles of beaches for walking, swimming (supervised) or sunning. On the other side there is a red sand beach where generations of campers (including us) have dug clams for their supper. These are not serviced sites and the use of wood fires is limited to kitchen shelters and designated fire pits. This is a rare chance to camp among the dunes. Recreation here is walking, jogging on the beach and windsurfing. *Rustico Island, Cavendish, Parks Canada, 2 Palmers Lane, Charlottetown, PEI C1A 5V6, ☎ 800/213-PARK or 902/672-6350.*

Cavendish Campground is a fully serviced park run by the federal government; it concentrates on not only preserving the natural environment, but on enjoying it, too. Natural history programs are offered by the park both here and at other locations. There is supervised ocean swimming on a big sandy beach and hiking on trails close by. Campfires are limited to kitchen shelter stoves only. It is open early June to late September. *Cavendish, Parks Canada, 2 Palmers Lane, Charlottetown, PEI C1A 5V6, ☎ 800/213-PARK or 902/672-6350.*

New Glasgow Highlands Camp Cabins and Camping is on Rte. 224 in New Glasgow, a quiet country area near a fishing pond. They have cabins, where you bring everything but the tent, and campsites where you bring that too. It's close to the Hunter River, which feeds into a long arm of Rustico Bay. They have a heated pool and a playground and the north shore beaches are close by. They have a long season from May 1 through October. *N, c/o Les Andrews, RR #3, Hunter River, PEI C0A 1N0, ☎ 902/964-3232.*

Strathgartney Provincial Park is a small park 12 miles south of Charlottetown and right on TransCanada-1 for easy access. The park is also on one of the long arms of the West River, also known as the Elliot River. They have a kitchen shelter, laundromat and dumping station. There is a nature trail and swimming within five miles at Argyle Shore Provincial Park. *Churchill, Parks Division West, RR #3, O'Leary, PEI C0B 1V0, ☎ 902/675-7476, winter 902/859-8790.*

Cabot Beach Provincial Park is on the big beautiful bay famed for its oysters. It's right on Rte. 20 and they take RV's and tents. They have supervised ocean swimming and recreation and nature interpretive programs for campers. *Malpeque, Parks Division West, RR #3, O'Leary, PEI C0B 1V0, ☎ 902/836-8945, winter 902/859-8790.*

Cedar Dunes Provincial Park is at the southwest corner of the island on Rte. 14. Campsites are suited to both RVs and tents. For recreation there is a supervised swimming beach on the ocean, an interpretive nature trail, sports equipment for loan, and interpretive nature programs. It's open from late June to early September. *Parks Division West, RR #3, O'Leary, PEI C0B 1V0, ☎ 902/859-8785, winter 902/859-8790.*

Mill River Provincial Park is right off Rte. 2, which runs up the center of the west part of the island. It sits on a long arm of Cascumpec Bay, making it a perfect place for canoeing or kayaking. It will accommodate tenters and RV's and has kitchen shelters, dumping station and laundromat. Supervised swimming, canoeing, sailboarding, golf (18 holes, par 72), tennis, racquetball, sports equipment loan and a playground are available. There is also a motel and a full-service licensed dining room. It's open from late June to early September. *Parks Division West, RR #3, O'Leary, PEI C0B 1V0, ☎ 902/859-8786, winter 902/859-8790.*

Jacques Cartier Provincial Park has serviced and unserviced sites for RVs and tents on 22 acres facing the Gulf of St. Lawrence. They have a kitchen shelter, a laundromat, a canteen and supervised ocean swimming. It's north of Alberton on Rte. 12 and is open from late June to early September. *Parks Division West, RR #3, O'Leary, PEI C0B 1V0, ☎ 902/853-8632, winter 902/859-8790.*

Newfoundland Introduction

It's difficult to separate Newfoundland from the sea that batters it on every side, grinding its stone to the sand and cobble that fill the crevices between its headlands, and carving the island into its multi-armed shape. Its stony core is exposed on every side, so visible that its natives call their land simply "The Rock." They are caught between a rock and a wet place, and although this has shaped their way of life, more significantly it has chosen the people who would live there.

IN THIS CHAPTER

- The Avalon Peninsula
- Bonavista & Terra Nova
- The Burin Peninsula
- Gander & The Kittiwake Coast
- Exploits Valley & Baie Verte
- Bay d'Espoir & Fortune Bay
- The Great Northern Peninsula
- Southwest Newfoundland

As a homeland, it's never been a place for sissies. It was fish – principally the cod – that attracted and kept the first settlers here, and that has formed the core of the Newfoundland economy, ethic and culture, just as surely as the rock forms its physical core. Only the hardy came, survived and stayed on, breeding generations of people who could take the hard knocks with good humor, or at least a wry good grace. However stunningly beautiful its scenery – and we think it among the finest our continent can offer – it is the people who will linger in your heart after you've left their rock.

The cod that brought people here in the first place seemed inexhaustible, and was, until the small boats that put out from the jagged rock into an often angry sea were suddenly competing with Russian and Japanese fish processing plants housed in huge ships that vacuumed the sea's bottom clean and made fishermen an endangered species.

The challenging and rigorous climate Newfoundlanders endure is balanced by the most extraordinary scenery in eastern North America. Wherever land meets sea, around the entire island of Newfoundland, it does so dramatically. The Appalachian Mountains end abruptly at the Gulf of St. Lawrence, and where

➲ SAYING IT RIGHT: *Newfoundland is correctly pronounced with the accent on the "land", rhyming with "understand." While this may seem strange when you first hear it said locally, it does make sense. The name originated when it was the new-found-land. The natural emphasis, when you say those three words together, is on the noun: land. As time went by, the name became an official one, and as the three words ran together, the original pronunciation stayed.*

they end the rock has been worn by glaciers and rivers into deep fjords that reach between the mountains like great long fingers.

A Separate History

Newfoundland was one of the earliest places explored by Europeans, possibly the first landfall in the New World. Vikings settled briefly about 1000 AD and the Italian explorer John Cabot, on behalf of England, stopped in 1497, carving what was perhaps the first graffiti in the new world on a rock there. The English settled soon after, and fought off French and Dutch incursions to establish it as a fishing base. Remote from both Europe and the emerging colonies farther south, Newfoundland grew in its own independent way, largely ignored, and liking it that way.

It was the last province to join Canada, after World War II, during which it was still a British Colonial outpost. Even then, the vote was a very close one, and it has maintained closer ties with England than its neighbors have. The city of St. John's, its largest and its capital, still has something of the air of an outpost of the British Empire.

North America's closest point to Europe, Newfoundland was important to early communications and flight. In 1901 Marconi received the first transatlantic wireless message at the stone tower that still stands on Signal Hill. The same tower was Lindbergh's last sight as he left on his historic transatlantic flight. Trepassey and Harbour Grace, both in the Avalon region, are important places in the annals of early flight, and Gander, in the center of the island, was the major refueling point for transatlantic flights until fairly recently. It was a major refueling stop and supply base in World War II.

Newfoundland & Labrador

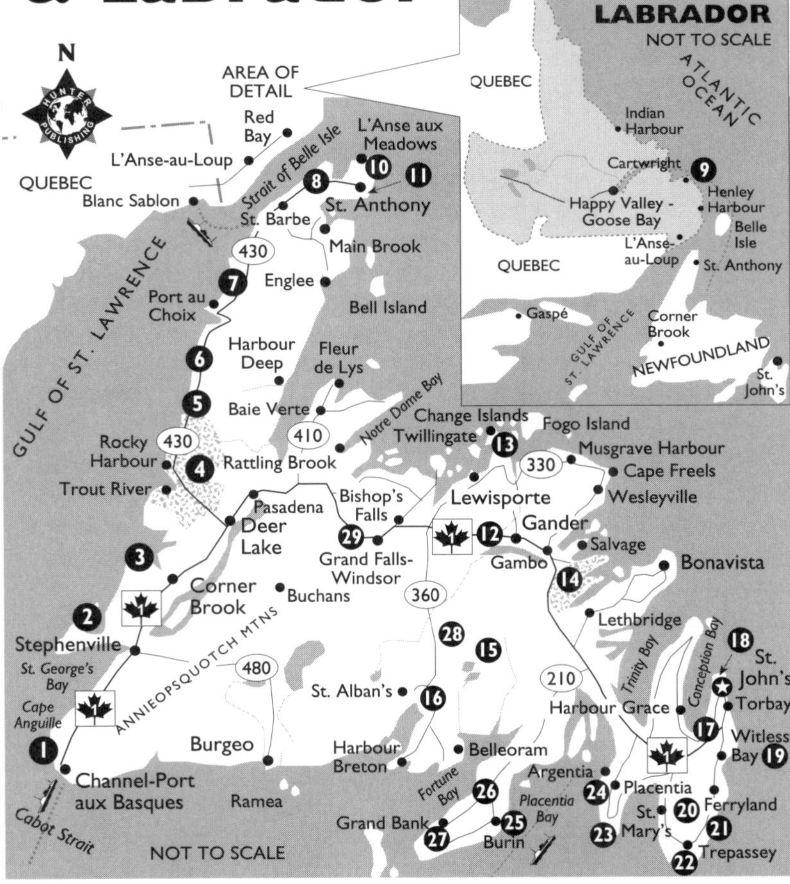

1. J.T. Cheeseman Provincial Park
2. Piccadilly Head Provincial Park
3. Blow Me Down Provincial Park
4. Gros Morne Nat'l Park
5. The Arches
6. Table Point Ecological Reserve
7. Port au Choix Nat'l Historic Site
8. Watt's Point Ecological Reserve
9. Gannet Islands Ecological Reserve
10. L'Anse aux Meadows Nat'l Historic Site
11. Grenfell Mission Headquarters
12. Notre Dame Provincial Park
13. Dildo Run Provincial Park
14. Terra Nova Nat'l Park
15. Bay du Nord Wilderness Reserve
16. Jipujikuen Kuespem Provincial Park
17. Butter Pot Provincial Park
18. Signal Hill National Historic Site; Cape Speare Nat'l Historic Site
19. Witless Bay Ecological Reserve
20. Avalon Wilderness Reserve
21. Chance Cove Provincial Park
22. Mistaken Point Ecological Reserve
23. Cape St. Mary's Ecological Reserve
24. Castle Hill Nat'l Historic Site
25. Burin Heritage House
26. Frenchmans Cove Provincial Park
27. Southern Newfoundland Seamen's Museum; Fortune Head Ecological Reserve
28. Middle Ridge Ecological Reserve
29. Wildlife Interpretive Centre

OUTPORTS AND RESETTLEMENT

Wherever you go along the coast of Newfoundland, you will hear references to outports and to the resettlement. Here's the story: Long before Newfoundland had a road system, fishermen, sometimes accompanied by their families, built homes in coves and bays closest to their favorite fishing grounds. They and their families came and went by boat. Many of these settlements grew into good-sized towns, but many remained tiny villages of a dozen or so families. Some were served by ferries, others bought their bulk supplies during the twice-yearly visit of a schooner filled with barrels of flour, sugar, grains and other staples. These isolated towns without road access were called outports. Gradually, many of them were connected to nearby towns by roads, but others remained completely isolated or were connected only by cart trails over rough headlands. Often children attended school in neighboring towns, walking several miles a day over these trails. Remember, we told you Newfoundland wasn't settled by sissies.

Shortly after Newfoundland became a province of Canada, from 1950 to 1977, the provincial government undertook a massive resettlement program, urging, cajoling and in some cases forcing residents of these towns to move elsewhere. One way they did this was to take away the town's school teacher and access to medical care. Some communities held their ground and refused to be resettled. Fogo Island is one of these. All along the coast, you will find old paths leading to the remains of these towns. Year by year the few remaining buildings fall closer to the ground and are more overgrown, but you can still see standing houses in some, along with fishing stages and other remains. We've mentioned trails to several, but you can ask local people nearly anywhere about abandoned outports in their area and get directions to more.

Getting Around

With the building of the Confederation bridge that links Prince Edward Island to the mainland, Newfoundland is now the only province you can't drive to. You can drive as far as the ferry landing in North Sydney, on Cape Breton Island in Nova Scotia, where you have a choice of two routes, both operated by **Marine Atlantic**, ☎ 800/341-7981; in North Sydney, 902/794-5814; in Port aux Basques, 709/695-2124.

Both routes leave from North Sydney, on Cape Breton Island, Nova Scotia. The shorter (five hours) sails to Port aux Basques, on the southwest coast; the longer (14 hours) arrives in Argentia, in the Avalon, but still some distance from St. John's.

The Port aux Basques ferry sails every day all year round, several times a day in the summer. The fare is about $60 for automobiles, $20 for adults, $9.50 for children. Dormitory sleepers are $7-$13, depending on which boat you travel on. Cabins add $50 to $100 to your fare. You should make advance reservations for your car, and must arrive one hour before departure to claim it. **DLR Coachlines**, ☎ 709/737-5912, travels to St. John's from Port aux Basques, with stops at cities and various points on the Trans-Canada Highway.

The ferries to Argentia operate only three times a week from mid-June through September. Passenger fare for the overnight trip is about $55 adult, $27 ages five-12; cars cost about $120; cabins cost $125; a reclining chair, $15. Cabin and car spaces on the North Sydney-Argentia ferries are always heavily booked, and well in advance. You must arrive one hour early to claim your reservation. **Newhook's Transportation**, ☎ 709/726-4876, connects the Argentia ferries to St. John's.

If you are not visiting other Atlantic provinces, it is probably easier to fly to The Rock on one of the frequent Air Nova or Air Atlantic flights from Halifax. **Air Nova** is the commuter partner of Air Canada, ☎ 800/776-3000. **Air Atlantic** is the commuter affiliate of Canadian Airlines, ☎ 800/426-7000 in the US, ☎ 800/665-1177 in Canada. You will probably have to change planes in Halifax before continuing to Newfoundland. The biggest disadvantage to flying there is having to rent a car to explore the island, an expensive proposition whoever you rent from.

Distances are great, and travel is further complicated by the fact that most settlements are around the edges, often separated by miles and miles of cliff, and connected only by long roads that

> **CAUTION:** *Moose and fog are the two major road hazards. Most accidents with animals happen at night, closely followed by early evening, when moose are most active. If there's fog, drive with your low beams on, instead of high beams; you'll see the road much better.*

lead from the central artery of TransCanada-1, which runs east-west across the northern half. A map of Newfoundland shows the difficulty of getting between points; a straight line may be the shortest distance, but there's no way to travel in one.

These great distances make it hard to see some of the most spectacular of the island's scenery; it takes a long trip to combine the Avalon (including all its various arms), Burin and Northern peninsulas with the magnificent headlands of the southern coast. When you consider that nearly every point of land you see on a map of the province ends in soaring cliffs, with tiny fishing villages clinging to the coves beneath them, you can see how frustrating it is to plan an itinerary there. But consider this and be consoled: most Newfies have never been to all these either.

Renting A Car

Buses connect the major points, but you'll need a car to travel into the countryside, unless you plan your whole trip with an outfitter who will provide your transportation. Car rental agencies are in St. John's, Corner Brook, Deer Lake and at the airport in St. Anthony. Reserve your car in advance (and after checking prices carefully) from **Avis**, ☎ 800/879-2847; **Budget**, ☎ 800/268-8900; Hertz, ☎ 800/263-0600; **Thrifty**, ☎ 800/367-2277; or **Tilden**, ☎ 800/387-4747.

> **CAR RENTAL RATES:** *With insurance, taxes, and other charges, a week's car rental in Newfoundland might cost $700. The unusual cost is due to the almost unanimous policy of charging a per-kilometer rate. As we write, only one, Tilden, offers unlimited mileage and, although their rate is higher, if you plan to cover a lot of miles it's worth the higher rate to avoid an outrageous surcharge for distance.*

Traveling Backcountry & Woods Roads

Some of the most fascinating adventures you can have in Newfoundland involve traveling on woods roads, the network of unpaved roads and tracks carved through the wilderness by timber companies and others. These are the only routes to many places, and the shortest, most interesting routes to others.

BACKCOUNTRY DRIVING TIPS

A few tips will make travels safer and, hopefully, give you a little more confidence.

- Begin any long trip early in the day.

- Always begin with a full gas tank, food, water, blankets or plenty of warm clothing and insect repellent.

- Carry a topographical map and, if possible, a map drawn for you by a local person, as well as your notes made as he draws it. The latter are vital, because sometimes this running commentary provides the only descriptive detail that distinguishes one track through the woods from another.

- Once on the road, if there's a large puddle in front of you, don't drive through it with both wheels. Keep one side of the car on the shoulder. If you can't, send your passenger out to wade through it or take soundings with a stick. If you don't know how to drive in mud or at least in deep slushy snow (which is much the same), don't try to drive through any puddles on a deeply rutted road.

- Don't straddle rocks in the road; keep one side of the car as close to their summit as possible and take them on an angle.

- Don't let your natural stubbornness ("I'm going to do this because I never give up") lead you into continuing when common sense says the road is impassible or dangerous. Most vehicles are equipped with reverse gear, and you can back out of a bad place easier than you can get someone to haul you out when you've gone too far. Assuming you could find someone.

Finding someone to draw you a map is not as hard as it might seem, but you may need a little persistence. Local information offices are accustomed to helping tourists, not adventurers. If they think a road is not open, ask them who will know for sure. Hosts in the information offices sometimes hesitate to tell you about anything not in the provincial tour guide. They are afraid you'll fall

➲ **MILES VS. KILOMETERS:** *Most people in Newfoundland will give you the distance in miles, even younger people who've learned metric in school, because that's how they think of distances. Be sure to ask which if you're not sure. Canadian rental car odometers will give readings in metric; so will road signs and the provincial highway map. Written directions on brochures here may use miles. You need to be really fast in conversions, at least in approximations. The quickest translation is two kilometers to a mile, plus a little. To translate longer distances, ignore the last digit and multiply the rest by six. For example, change 100km to 10; 10x6=60 miles. You'll figure out your own system; if you're the sort who irons dishtowels, you'll carry a pocket calculator. We don't do either.*

over the edge of the waterfall or be blown off a trail and they'll feel responsible for sending you there. Understand this and you have the first clue. If they can't (or won't) tell you, ask who can – that gets them off the hook. If you ask someone else's advice, they aren't to blame. Sympathize with them – jobs are scarce up here. And hope they know someone who works in the woods – a timber scout for Abitibi is golden.

OF TIME & THE WEATHER

Newfoundland is on "Newfoundland Time," which is half an hour ahead of Atlantic time. When it is noon in Boston and New York, it is 1:30 pm in St. John's.

The Gulf Stream currents keep coastal temperatures moderate year-round, but the price of this warm air is fog, created when it meets the cold Arctic Stream. Daytime temperatures are often quite warm in the summer, but evenings are always cool, and at sea – even in a protected bay – you should always carry a sweater and a waterproof jacket. The rule is that the minute you've decided what the day's weather will be, it changes. Winter temperatures are not bitter on the coast, but the wind can be brutal. Inland is very cold in the winter. The best year-round advice on clothing is to layer. We've begun hikes in the morning with five layers, been too warm in one by noon, and had to add them all back when the fog rolled in at 2 pm. For **weather information**, call ☎ 709/772-5534.

Newfoundland's Parks

■ **Terra Nova** is on the eastern coast, a low shoreline deeply indented by a fjord. Its thick evergreen forests are crossed by hiking trails that also lead to lakes and wilderness campsites. Abandoned fishing settlements, called outports, are connected by trails and by a boat shuttle.

■ **Gros Morne** is Eastern Canada's (many would argue ALL of Canada's) most spectacular park, meeting the sea with dramatic deep fjords, its deep inland lakes contained by 2,000-foot cliffs. Hiking and climbing are the main adventures, but fishing is close behind.

■ **Provincial parks** are in a state of flux. Like several other provinces, Newfoundland is in the process of privatizing many of its provincial parks, retaining only the major ones and those which encompass some outstanding natural feature in need of protection.

Many of the parks offer beaches, all have camping. Since printed material here lags behind reality, and because the status can change abruptly, you may find parks referred to as provincial when they are, in fact, privately operated. For the most part, the new management has retained the features that made the provincial parks a favorite with serious campers: well-spaced sites, good maintenance, hiking trails, and an absence of amusement park gimcracks. Several have retained the interpretive nature programs that enrich the provincial park experience.

PROVINCIAL PARK & WILDLIFE RESERVE RESTRICTIONS: *Snowmobiles, while a common form of winter transportation all over the province, are prohibited in provincial parks, as are ATVs. This is also true in wildlife and wilderness reserves, such as the Avalon Wilderness Reserve. You can't even use them on roads in these. To enter a wildlife reserve at any time of year, you must have an entry permit, which you can obtain from the Department of Environment and Lands, Park Division, PO Box 8700, St. John's, NL A1B 4J6, ☎ 709/729-2431.*

Hiking

Some of the best and most scenic trails in the province lead very close to its precipitous ocean cliffs. Sometimes you must choose between the very edge of a cliff and the dense tuckamore, not really a choice at all, since the intertwined, wind-stunted limbs of the small trees and shrubs of tuckamore form a mat that you could only get through with a chainsaw. Never take these coastal trails in the rain or in a high wind.

Even the lower ledge rocks can be dangerous in high seas, when waves can suddenly sweep people from rocks that were perfectly dry seconds earlier. Once in the Atlantic at this latitude, there is little chance of getting out or of being rescued. In developed areas like Cape Speare, signs warn walkers of undercut cliffs and especially dangerous areas, and it is important to pay attention to the warnings. But on more remote trails, there will be no signs, not even trail markers.

It's a good idea to remember that Newfoundlanders are a hardy, self-reliant lot. They are not wimps and they do not think that people need to be protected from their own stupidity or carelessness. They are sensible and they give the rest of the world credit (however mistakenly) for taking sensible precautions. Therefore, you will not find danger signs in obviously dangerous places, as you would in the United States. Unless you know for a fact what is under the cliff edge, don't stand on it. It could be crumbling shale, its surface held together by matted grass.

Flora & Fauna

A happy surprise for those traveling in the short summer, will be to find all the flowers blooming at once. Farther south, they bloom in succession, but here evolution has favored those which bloom early enough to form seed before the summer's end. The result is that species bloom all at once. July is the peak season, when lilac, lupine and iris are all in bloom. Iris seem to grow everywhere; a low bright purple variety blooms on the windswept moorlands along the sea, while taller ones grow in roadside puddles formed of blowing salt spray.

Moose are not native to the island of Newfoundland, but were first introduced near Howley, in 1878, when two Nova Scotia moose were released into the wild. In 1904, four more – these from New Brunswick – were released in the Gander Bay area. These six animals grew into the herd of 125,000 that now covers all parts of the province. Major herds of caribou are found in the wilderness areas, with herds of 15,000-16,000 each in the Avalon and Middle Range (south of Gander and Grand Falls).

MOOSE WARNING, AGAIN

While you may be anxious to spot a moose during your trip, you don't want to spot it just as it jumps in front of your car. Accidents involving moose are serious, because of the tremendous weight of the animal and its height. When struck by a car, the moose's body is at windshield height and often crushes the roof or hits passengers at head level. Fatalities are fairly common in these accidents.

Moose are the undisputed kings of the wild, and with no predators they have no fear. A car is just another small animal to a moose, who expects the car to flee as other animals would. So the moose will either stand his ground or actually charge the car, with a rack of antlers that smashes right through windshields.

■ Keep a watch for moose appearing from the roadsides whenever you are traveling through wilderness areas, but particularly around dawn and dusk, or at night. If you must travel in remote areas (and this includes TransCanada-1) at night, both driver and passengers should constantly scan the roadsides ahead for dark shapes or any sign of movement in the underbrush that might signal a moose about to cross the road.

■ If you see a moose in the road, stop and pull off to the side. At night, turn off your headlights so the moose will not be blinded by them and wait for the moose to leave the road. Under no circumstances should you get out of your car when a moose is near.

■ If you see moose near the roadside in daylight and want to photograph them, try to do it from the car. If you cannot, or if the moose are some distance away, get out of the car very slowly, and don't move too far from the car. Leave the engine running so you can get away quickly if the moose should suddenly head toward the road. Usually the moose will continue eating and ignore you, but if you have accidentally come between the parent and a young moose – which might be hidden in the brush on the opposite side of the road – the moose could charge with amazing speed. It is hard to believe how fast such a seemingly cumbersome and ungainly creature can run.

Very few other places in the world can approach Newfoundland's concentration of seabird nesting sites, with more than a dozen show-stopping sites and over 5½ million breeding pairs. One of the world's major gannetries is at Cape St. Mary's; Baccalieu Island alone is home to three million nesting pairs of Leach's storm petrels and one of only three breeding sites for northern fulmar. It also has a significant colony of puffins, but the continent's largest concentration of these is on an island in Witless Bay, near St. John's.

Fishing

As a tourist destination, Newfoundland is most widely known by anglers. All the great names have fished its waters, which the legendary fly-fisherman, Lee Wulff, brought to world attention. Seven-pound brook trout are almost common; lake trout grow to 40 pounds. More than 200 salmon rivers flow throughout the province, with reports of salmon weighing as much as 40 pounds. Newfoundland has more than 75 fishing outfitters listed in the ***Newfoundland & Labrador Hunting and Fishing Guide***, available free from the Tourism Branch of the Department of Development, PO Box 8700, St. John's, NF A1C 5R8, ☎ 709/576-2830.

Only two non-residents may fish with one guide. With three, you need two guides. If you book a fishing trip through an outfitter, guides come as part of the package. The only difference is whether the ratio of guides is one-on-one or one for every two people fishing.

FISHING REGULATIONS: *Rules are strictly enforced, and prohibit non-residents from fishing in any scheduled salmon river without a guide. The only exception to that is if you are fishing with a direct relative (not your third cousin's brother-in-law) who is a Newfoundland resident. Unscheduled waters, which include ponds, lakes and trout streams within 800 meters (a bit over 800 yards) of a provincial highway, are open to licensed non-residents. Beyond that you must have a guide or a resident relative. The definition of a provincial highway is whether it has a route number, which you can determine by looking at a highway map.*

Information Sources

■ The agency responsible for tourist information is the **Department of Tourism, Culture and Recreation**, PO Box 8730, St. John's, NF, A1B 4K2, ☎ 709/729-2830 or 800/563-6353.

■ Information on Labrador is available through **Destination Labrador**, 118 Humphrey Rd., Bruno Plaza, Labrador City, NF A2V 2J8, ☎ 709/944-7788 or 800/563-6353.

■ On the Web, find cultural and tourist information at **www.wordplay.com**. Local and regional information centers are listed under *Information Sources* in the beginning of each chapter. When you ask for information, be sure to mention any specific interests, such as fishing, birding, canoeing or sea kayaking, since some of these have special publications.

■ *Hiking Guide to National Parks and Historic Sites of Newfoundland*, by Barbara Maryniak, Goose Lane Editions, $12.95, is invaluable for hiking in Gros Morne National Park – and elsewhere, too – but you really need it there.

■ Although it focuses on the geological sights in Gros Morne National Park, the geology of all Newfoundland is explained in text and diagrams in *Rocks Adrift: The Geology of Gros Morne National Park*, which you can buy at the Gros Morne visitors center. The complicated forces and movements of the earth's crust are clearly presented and the color photographs show what the landscape actually looks like.

■ For a very personal look at The Rock and some good travel tips, look for *Come Near at Your Peril* by Patrick O'Flaherty, published by Breakwater, 100 Water St., St. John's, NF A1C 6E6.

■ Look for additional information on canoeing from **Newfoundland Canoeing Association**, PO Box 5961, St. John's, NF A1C 5X4.

■ A very thorough guide to kayaking areas is *Canyons, Coves, and Coastal Waters*, from Eastern Edge Outfitters,

Box 17, Site 14, RR2, Paradise, NF A1L 1C2. It costs $21.95, plus $6 shipping to the US, $2.50 in Canada.

■ Serious birders will want the free *Field Checklist of the Birds of Insular Newfoundland and its Continental Shelf Waters*, from the Natural History Society of Newfoundland and Labrador, Box 1013, St. John's, NF A1C 5M3.

■ Topographical maps are available from the **Department of Environment and Lands,** Crown Land Division, Howley Bldg., Higgins Line, PO Box 8700, St. John's, NF A1B 4J6.

The Avalon Peninsula

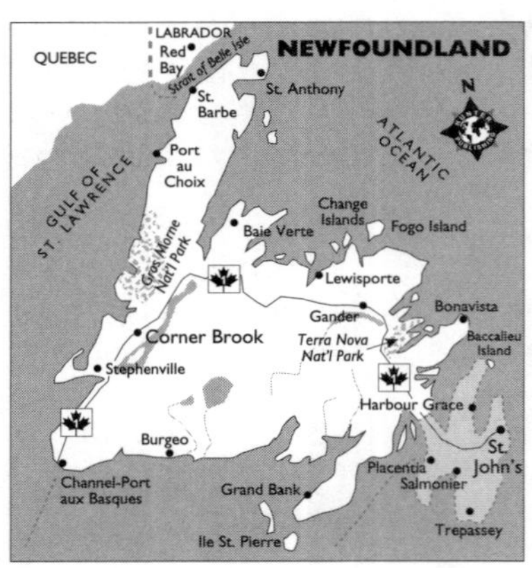

Although you could hardly describe as compact this lopsided H made up of four long peninsulas hanging off the map of Newfoundland by a narrow, fogbound isthmus, it *is* more compact than the rest of the province. And, in a way, it is a mini-version of what you'll find elsewhere. Although it doesn't have the fjords of the Northern Peninsula, it certainly doesn't lack for dramatic cliff-lined coasts. For the traveler, it has the advantage of being close to the capital and the major airport, as well as to one of the ferry terminals that connect the island to the mainland. For that reason, it is the most often visited part of the province.

But don't expect crowds, even in St. John's. And don't expect St. John's to be a glitzy, sophisticated city. It has more of an air of provincial capital about it, but a lively, rollicking one. You'll find more pubs than boutiques, more hearty, lusty Maritime music than symphonic works. It is a real city, its narrow harbor filled with ships from all over the world, its streets lined with Victorian wooden homes and brick mercantile buildings. You can't help liking it, even when the wind is blowing hard enough to pin you to the side of one of them.

Geography & History

Like Maine and New Hampshire, the Avalon is a newcomer to North America; each was once part of the African plate, which bumped into North America briefly (in geological terms), and left bits of itself behind, about 200 billion years ago. But although its origins are different from the rest of the island, the geological differences are not apparent; it looks just as much like a rock adrift in the sea as the rest of the province does.

It is the easternmost part of the province, with St. John's at its northeast corner. Marine Drive, north of the city, leads around high headlands and deep coves to the lighthouse at Cape St. Francis. This is the smallest arm of the H.

South of the capital is the widest of the four peninsulas, ending in two capes: Cape Race (the scourge of navigators since the arrival of the first ships) and Cape Pine, the two separated by Trepassey Bay. The long arm of St. Mary's Bay divides this region from Cape St. Mary's, a long, wide and sparsely settled area that forms the southwesternmost part of the Avalon.

The most northerly part extends between the waters of Trinity Bay and Conception Bay. The roads connecting its coasts, routes 70 and 80, are collectively known as the Baccalieu Trail, and the area is sometimes called the Baccalieu Peninsula, taking its name from the Portuguese word for cod.

The Portuguese and the Basques were the first settlers in the area, with seasonal camps along the shore where they dried and salted cod to be carried back to Europe. One of these, in Renew on the southern Avalon, provisioned the *Mayflower*, which stopped on its way to Plymouth in 1620. It was to the Avalon that the early explorers and settlers (except for the Vikings) came, so you'll bump into these tidbits of history as you travel. St. John's was the first permanent European settlement in the New World, begun only 31 years after John Cabot sailed into its long, protected harbor in 1497. From a remote summer fishing station, the settlement at St. John's grew to a thriving seaport, the hub of shipping across the Atlantic.

Getting Around

If you arrive by air, it will be through St. John's Airport, a new, small, and very personal terminal where you can see everything you need as you enter from the runway: the lone baggage carousel (usually with your luggage already waiting for you – it seems to have the fastest retrieval of any airport on earth), the tourist information desk and the car rental representatives. Downtown is six miles away, and if you don't pick up a rental car immediately, a Bugden's taxi will take you there.

DLR Coachlines carries passengers between St. John's and the ferry landing at Port aux Basques, ☎ 709/737-5912, and **Newhook's Transportation**, ☎ 709/726-4876, connects with the Argentia ferries. There is no train service.

The *St. John's Visitor Guide* has a map of the central part of the city, which is quite easy to find your way in. The only thing the map can't tell you is which of the streets go almost straight up the hill; as a rule of thumb, if a street runs perpendicular to the harbor, it's steep. **Metrobus**, ☎ 709/722-9400 ($1.50 adults, $1 children), connects major hotels with the harbor area and the malls on the outskirts, on the way passing many of the city's attractions.

You really do need a car to do any serious exploring outside St. John's. Much of the area is sparsely populated and buses run infrequently, or not at all to some areas.

You can take a quick look at any one of the peninsulas on a day trip, but not with time to stop and see much. And certainly not with time to enjoy any of the adventures they offer. We mention it only to suggest how long it takes to get to the farthest points. Handily, roads run along the outer edges, usually within sight of the shore, connecting the little ports, so you can see nearly each peninsula on a circular loop, repeating very little. This makes planning your routes fairly easy, since choices are few.

Information Sources

- For information, contact the St. John's Economic Development and Tourism Division, in City Hall on Gower Street (PO Box 908), St. John's, NF A1C 5M2, ☎ 709/576-8106, fax 709/576-8246, open weekdays from 9 am until 4:30 pm. Or stop at their desk at the airport or visit their railway car on Harbor Drive, open daily June through September.

■ The best source of information on the Baccalieu Trail is at the **Tourist Information Office**, Rte. 70, Harbour Grace, NF A0A 2M0, ☎ 709/596-5561, open daily, 9 am to 6 pm, May through October. It's easy to spot, next to the restored DC-3, *Spirit of Harbour Grace*, a memorial to the aviation pioneers who used the little airstrip on the hillside above.

Adventures

The Avalon has a good sampling of the kinds of adventures that await you elsewhere in the province, with year-round activities and a healthy share of wildlife to discover. In fact, it has better opportunities for viewing a wider variety of wildlife than any other area of its size in the province (or anywhere else in the Atlantic provinces).

■ On Foot

Walking Tours

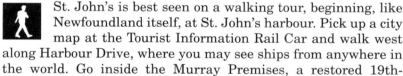

St. John's is best seen on a walking tour, beginning, like Newfoundland itself, at St. John's harbour. Pick up a city map at the Tourist Information Rail Car and walk west along Harbour Drive, where you may see ships from anywhere in the world. Go inside the Murray Premises, a restored 19th-century mercantile building, the city's oldest.

Leave by the door on the opposite end, through the courtyard and onto **Water Street,** once a pathway for early explorers and settlers, known as the earliest main street in the Americas. Walk right along Water St., between the façades of Victorian commercial buildings to the granite **Courthouse**. Behind the Courthouse, the steep hill continues, and you should climb it via Church Hill, to see the rows of restored wooden Victorian row houses in their original bright colors. The city's major churches are along this route, and they present a catalog of ecclesiastical architecture, beginning with the neo-Gothic Anglican **Cathedral of St. John the Baptist**, with its fine stained glass windows. Crossing the strange sloping intersection, continue climbing to the Roman Catholic **Ba-**

silica of St. John the Baptist, whose towers you can see ahead of you.

> **RECOMMENDED READING:** *Begin your exploration of this region with a copy of* **Trails of the Avalon**, *by Peter Gard and Bridget Neame, which has maps and descriptions of some of the area's best walks.*

You are now at the topmost point of the tour; now it's all downhill. Military Road leads past the Basilica to the **Colonial Building**, where you should stop to see the painted decorations in the legislative chambers, open on weekdays. As Military Road reaches King's Bridge Rd., you will pass the 1836 **St. Thomas Church,** Newfoundland's second-oldest church. Here you reach Cavendish Sq., where you turn a sharp right onto Gower Street, past another group of Victorian houses. Go downhill (left) on King's Rd., to the **War Memorial,** on the spot where, in 1583, representatives of the British Crown proclaimed Newfoundland a territory. Below is **Harbourside Park**, stretching along the harbor to the Rail Car where you began.

You can take a more thorough tour, learning about the five centuries since its first European contact, with **St. John's Historic Walking Tours**, ☎ 709/738-3781. **Terry's Tours**, for which you do not need a reservation, leave five times daily from the Tourist Rail Car on the harbor. Hour-long walks, with tales of intrigue, treachery, enemy attack, and the origins of some of St. John's colorful place names, cost $5.

Northwest of the city center, **Pippy Park** has walking trails, as does **Bowring Park,** off Waterford Bridge Road, a few miles from the center. There paths go alongside ponds, through well-kept gardens and through light woodlands between two streams as they meet to flow into the harbor. Guided hikes in the park are $3 in the spring and summer, ☎ 709/576-6134.

Abutting Pippy Park is the Memorial University **Botanical Garden**, on Mt. Scio Rd., ☎ 709/737-8590. Its trails and walkways lead through extensive native plant collections, as well as display beds of annuals, perennials and herbs. Naturalist-led walks are available Saturday mornings at 11:30 from May to November, and at other times (call to find out when). Admission to the garden is $2 adults, $1 for seniors and children. It's free the first Thursday of each month.

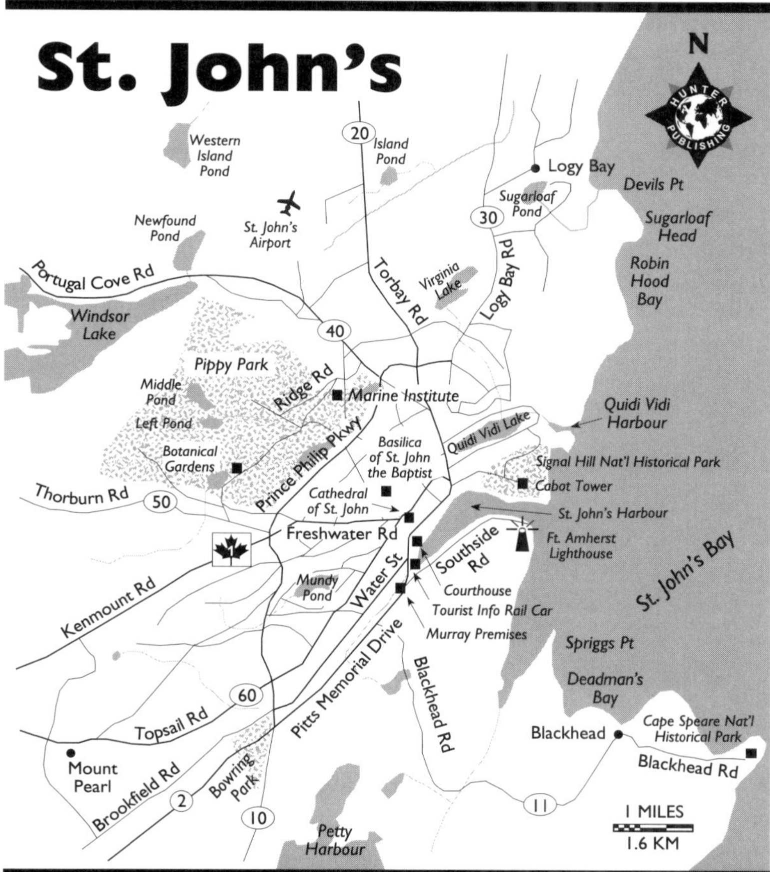

Hiking

On the way to **Signal Hill**, at the intersection of Duckworth Street and Signal Hill Road you'll find the beginning of a hiking path that skirts the tops of the sea cliffs. The path has some steep, rugged stretches, but also has fine views of the icebergs that fill local waters in the spring and summer. If you continue along the shore on this trail you can hike all the way to the historic battery at Quidi Vidi.

From Quidi Vidi, a section of town that was once a tiny fishing port, **Rennie's River Walk** follows the river connecting the Quidi Vidi Lake to Long Pond, in Pippy Park. Follow Signal Hill Road to Quidi Vidi Road, then turn right onto Forest Road. A left at the fork will take you downhill to the lake, and the beginning of the trail. It's a little under four miles one-way.

The East Coast Trail is among the most spectacular hikes in Canada (or anywhere, for that matter), following the shore from Topsail, which is southwest of St. John's, around the tip of Cape St. Francis (about 30 miles), then south along the coast to Cape Race, at the far southern end, another 150 miles. Although the entire trail is not finished, large sections are completed, and local groups work year-round to complete more and maintain what is open. The trail will be suitable for wilderness camping and have access to B&B accommodations along the way.

When complete, the East Coast Trail will incorporate a series of feeder trails that make shorter loop hikes possible for day hikers. For the latest information on what segments are open, you can call ☎ 709/570-7509 or check the East Coast Trail Association's Web site at www.paragon.nf.ca/ eastcost/ect.htm. One of the earliest completed sections also made it possible to reach the natural sea geyser, **The Spout**, on a trail leading from Bay Bulls north to Shoal Bay.

North of the city you can hike a section of the old pre-automobile lane along the shore from Torbay to Flat Rock, entering from the beach in Torbay, off Rte. 10, at the end of Lower St. Follow the dirt road north along the shore until it turns inland, then follow the old grass-covered lane along the shore. You can go all the way to Flat Rock Point, or you can cut back to the road at any of several places. For a scenic shorter walk along the ledges to Flat Rock Point, begin at the gravel bank just before Flat Rock, where you can park and take a dirt road leading toward the shore. When it forks, go left (north) up the hill (to a fine view over the bay), then along a high ledge that gradually slopes down to the point. You can return along the other side of the point, walking on the flat ledges, to the village (stopping for tea at the Tides Inn) and walk back along the road to the gravel bank where you parked.

South of town at **Cape Speare**, where an 1836 lighthouse perches on a cliff at the most easterly point in North America, hiking trails lead to sweeping sea views and to a World War II gun battery, with underground passages to explore. In the late summer you can pick blueberries beside this and the other trails that lead along this headland.

A challenging all-day trip for hikers in good condition begins at **Cape Speare** and follows the shore line to **Ft. Amherst**, across the harbor from St. John's. It's about seven miles of up and down, but a rewarding route, with a waterfall hidden in Deadman's Bay, a needle-shaped rock pillar and an abandoned outport. A shorter section of the same trail includes many of its attractions, but can be made into a loop by returning to the road via the trail that once led to the outport settlement of Freshwater.

Hiking south from **Cape Speare to Petty Harbour,** a distance of about seven miles, begins with a high, rugged coastline, but after crossing a bog (where you can find cloudberries in the late summer and fall) it drops to lower ledges and passes a prime whale-watching site at North Head. From Cape Speare to North Head is about a two-hour hike, and quite easy.

> **TUCKAMORE:** *The biggest problem for hikers is the dense mat of tangled trees that grows along many of the shores here. It's called tuckamore, and it is impenetrable. In other environments, when a trail is blocked by a wash-out or fallen tree, you can simply go around it, but in tuckamore you can only do so where sheep have made a tunnel through it. It helps, at these times, if you are no taller than a sheep.*

In **La Manche Park**, farther south on the road to Ferryland (Rte. 10), hiking trails leading to an abandoned fishing village and to a waterfall. The **La Manche Falls Trail** begins at the picnic area and follows the stream to the falls, about an hour's round trip. Although the bog and boreal forest you'll pass are not uncommon habitats in Newfoundland, the marsh is quite unusual here.

The **La Manche Village Trail** is less than a mile long, and also takes about an hour. It begins from the fire exit road, close to the park's boundary, and leads to an outport (a fishing village without year-round road access) that was destroyed by a storm in 1966. You will see the deep harbor, known as one of the best in the Avalon, and the cellar holes of the houses, stores and other buildings.

At **Chance Cove Provincial Park** a trail goes along the shore (part of the East Coast Trail) as far as Frenchmans Point, about three miles round-trip. It goes through some moss-covered forest and along the cliff edge to an open meadow at the point, from which you can see the coast to Point Race. For variety, if the sea is calm, return along the shore, where you're sure to see seals.

Along TransCanada-1 west of St. John's is the entrance to **Butter Pot Provincial Park,** one of the province's most-used parks. Hiking trails there lead through the low forests of spruce and balsam, and over rocky barrens to the strange rounded outcrops that gave the park its name. These provide some elevated lookout points, where you'll get views over the bay. The hike to Butter Pot Hill is about four miles round-trip. Not far from the beginning of the trail, take the short side-trail to the right to see some glacial erratics in the forest. You'll see more when you get to Butter Pot Hill. Check the bulletin boards at the park for the interpretive program schedule, which includes guided hikes.

At the northern tip of the Baccalieu Trail (Rte. 70) is the precipitous village of **Grates Cove**. Until the mid-1960s there was a carving in the rock here, left by **John Cabot** verifying his landing. It was chiseled off the ledge by thieves, but historians had already authenticated it. A monument now marks the spot, but the little town's other historic attraction is still there: **Grates Cove Rock Wall National Historic Site**, ☎ 709/587-2326. These unusual stone-walled gardens and enclosures are scattered about the hillsides, connected by a network of **walking trails**. They lead along the brows of the points that enclose the harbor, high above the sea, and in winding routes to the shore – to the Cabot rock site, the head, Wiggy's Beach, Shaw's Marsh, Dancin' Place Pond and other destinations where the scenery is uniformly superb. There's no map of them, but you don't need one, since at this elevation and across open moors, you can always see where you are.

Ask at the museum in Harbour Grace, also on the Baccalieu Trail, for the free guide and map to a **walking tour** of historic buildings.

Farther south along Rte. 70 in Bay Roberts, the **Bay Roberts East Walking Trail** (☎ 709/786-3482) wanders along the coast, past the ruined walls and cellarholes of the town's early settlements at Juggler's Cove and French's Cove.

Several trails lead from the little community of Cupids, close to Brigus. A two-mile trail begins on the opposite side of the harbor from the village, near the unmistakable hulk of the old fish plant. **Rip Raps** is an abandoned community, reached by the trail with blue markers. **Spectacle Head** is an elevation from which you can see, on a clear day, all the way from Baccalieu Island, off the far end of that peninsula, to Cape St. Francis, north of St. John's. That trail is marked with white blazes.

Another trail to the abandoned settlements of **Noder Cove**, **Deep Gulch** and **Greenland** leaves from the cemetery behind the Anglican Church at Burnt Head. To reach Burnt Head, drive east from Cupids on Sea Forest Drive, turning right onto Burnt Head loop, and following it to the church. The trails are signposted from the rear of the cemetery. Green markers lead, appropriately, to Greenland, red to Nodor Cove, and yellow to the community of Deep Gulch. It's about two miles of fine scenery, with old foundations and stone walls.

Guided Hiking Tours

■ You can explore these trails, those of the wilderness reserve of the Avalon interior and more coastal trails accompanied by an experienced guide from **Southern Shore Eco Adventures**, PO Box 125, Ferryland, NF A0A 2H0, ☎ 709/432-2659. They specialize in nature explorations throughout Avalon, so you can expect to find the caribou herds and the prime birding and seal-watching sites with them.

■ On Wheels

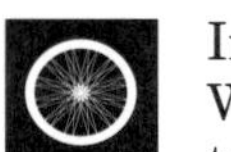

In St. John's, the woodland paths of **Bowring Park**, off Waterford Bridge Road a few miles from the center of town, are popular for cycling. You can join a tour or rent bicycles from **Avalon Bicycle Tours** in St. John's, ☎ 709/576-1951.

■ On Water

Water is what the Avalon has plenty of; even in its most inland reaches, the center of the Avalon Reserve, you're never far from a lake. Long arms of water reach between the cliffs to form tiny sheltered beaches where locals and New Englanders find pleasant swimming. The rest of the world finds the water too cold and heads for the shallow waters of inland ponds and lakes. The loveliest beach in the entire area is, we think, the one at the former **Northern Bay Provincial Park**, ☎ 709/584-3465, at the upper end of the Baccalieu Trail, north of Carbonear. It sits under cliffs, with caves at one end and a waterfall at the other.

Canoeing & Kayaking

The **Avalon Wilderness Reserve** can be crossed by canoe, in a three- to five-day trip. The put-in is at Cape Pond, reached by taking Rte. 10 to Cape Pond Rd., south of Burnt Cove. The pond is about six miles from Rte. 10. The canoe route goes northwest through a succession of ponds, with portages over barrens and a take-out at Peak Pond, off Rte. 90, just south of TransCanada-1. There are no river runs and no challenging rapids, but a wilderness of ponds, peatlands and barrens, where you are likely to see caribou, geese, moose, beaver, and several varieties of duck. The ponds that make up the route are shown in darker blue on the map in the *User's Guide to the Avalon Wilderness Reserve*. In order to use the area, you must obtain a free permit, which you can get, along with a map of the Reserve, from the Parks Division, PO Box 8700, St. John's, NFA1B 4J6, ☎ 709/729-2431.

The **Rocky River**, which runs roughly parallel to Rte. 81 between TransCanada-1 (south of the western end of the Baccalieu Trail) and St. Mary's Bay, is the largest river system in the Avalon, and you can canoe it from Markland to its mouth in Colinet. In high water during the spring runoff, you can canoe it in a day. At low water, the rocks which gave the river its name become obstacles, and you'll spend more time carrying the canoe than it spends carrying you. If you love portages, go late in the season. In periods of extraordinary flooding, the river can be quite dangerous.

Apart from a couple of places where you can see Rte. 81 in the distance, the route is pure wilderness, with moose, and even otters a likely sight. The take-out is just before the falls, a mile from Colinet, where you will see the bridge as Rte. 91 crosses the river. Access roads are near the bridge. Expect a few scrapes on your canoe, since you will certainly have close encounters with the rocks, boulders and ledges in the riverbed.

You can begin a longer trip, with wilderness camping, in Whitbourne, making your way along the string of lakes between there and Markland.

Some of the most rewarding kayaking anywhere, in terms of the variety and quality of what you'll see from the water, is in **Witless Bay**, south of St. John's. Launch sites are plentiful, with roads leading to gentle beaches in several places, and small villages on the shore. The wildlife is spectacular (the bay is a wildlife reserve) with North America's largest puffin and kittiwake colonies, and thousands upon thousands of nesting seabirds. Wear a hat. Fortunately whales don't fly, but they almost seem to as they breach in the waters of the bay, and you don't want to be there when they do. Seals are a common sight. Since this is a reserve, you can't get closer than 50 yards from Green Island, or closer than 50 feet from the others. The islands are out a bit, facing open sea, so expect rough conditions and watch for sudden fog or other weather changes in the outer areas of the bay.

Canoe & Kayak Outfitters - Guided Tours

■ **Southern Shore Eco Adventures**, PO Box 125, Ferryland, NF A0A 2H0, ☎ 709/432-2659, has guided sea kayaking tours of Witless Bay and other areas of the Avalon coast.

■ About an hour south of St. John's in Cape Broyle, off Rte. 10 between Witless Bay and Ferryland, you can take an all-day guided sea kayak tour with **Wilderness Newfoundland Adventures**, ☎ 709/747-NFLD (6353). The trip is through the waters of the wildlife sanctuary, where you are likely to see whales, dolphins, puffins and eagles, and in the early summer, icebergs. Always there are the sea caves and seastacks, waterfalls and arches that mark the shore of the Avalon and its islands. The trip includes a picnic lunch, which you will eat on an island. With kayak, guide, and lunch included, a day's excursion is $100 per person. Longer trips are possible, too.

■ Full-day guided kayak trips around Cape Broyle, exploring sea caves and waterfalls that drop into the ocean from the cliffs, are offered by **Eastern Edge Outfitters,** in Paradise, ☎ 709/782-1465. Instruction is included, as is all equipment, so the trips are suitable for beginners as well as experienced paddlers. Another day-long trip explores the waters of Great Island Bird Sanctuary, sea caves and the abandoned town of La Manche. A third goes into the sea caves along the Marine Drive shore, north of St. John's. The cost of any of these is $100.

■ Combine canoeing and trout fishing with **Island Outdoor Adventures,** ☎ 709/364-4411. You'll set out with canoe, rod and frypan and cook your catch for lunch. A licensed guide is part of the package, which is offered from early June until mid-August.

Boat Tours

In this area where whales follow the capelin and other small fish in their annual migrations, you are likely to see whales quite near the shore and in the bays, so any boat tour becomes a whale watch. For trips especially designed to find whales, see *Cultural & Eco-Travel Experiences*, pages 488-490.

Scan the harbor in St. John, along Pier 7, for sailing tours, which leave from there throughout the summer. **Adventure**

Tours of Newfoundland, in St. John's, ☎ 709/726-5000 or 800/77-WHALE, takes passengers aboard the schooner *Scademia* for two-hour sails along the harbor, through the Narrows and to Cape Speare. The cost for a two-hour sail is $20. **J&B Schooner Tours**, ☎ 709/753-SAIL, offers five cruises daily, with shorter evening and sunset cruises. On Monday seniors pay half-price.

Chance Cove Ventures, PO Box 53, Renews, NF A0A 3NO, ☎ 709/363-2257, operates a 10-passenger boat for daily tours of the Cape Race area. Tours leave from Chance Cove Provincial Park, and explore the unforgiving coast which has been the scene of more than 350 recorded shipwrecks. They also explore abandoned fishing communities; the season is May through October.

Tour the waters and coastline of Conception Bay by boat with **Dawson Boat Tours**, Conception Bay South, ☎ 709/834-7130 or 5874, fax 709/834-7130. The trip circles Bell Island (scene of the only German attack on a North American land target during World War II) and Kellys Island.

Scenic Shag Rock and other landmarks on the coast of Trinity Bay, on the opposite side of the peninsula, are among the sights you'll see from the *MV Reality*, with **Shagrock Boat Tours**, ☎ 709/588-2759. Tours leave from Whiteway, about 20 miles north of TransCanada-1 on Rte. 80, along the west side of the Baccalieu Trail.

In nearby Dildo, on the same coast, you can explore Dildo Island in a stopover during a tour with **Dildo Island Boat Tours**, ☎ 709/582-2687. The island was the site of a cod hatchery a century ago, and has evidence of several aboriginal cultures. You can visit the excavations of a Dorset Eskimo site on the island.

To view the gannet-covered sea stack and cliffs of Cape St. Mary's Ecological Reserve from the sea, reserve a space on board the *Catherine Alesha*, from St. Brides, ☎ 709/337-2660 or 709/337-2614. Along with the birds, you'll see the coastal cliffs from a new perspective, and sail through the waters off St. Vincent where humpback, fin and minke whales feed on the fish in July and August.

Although it's close to one of the Avalon's prime whale-viewing spots, you won't see whales while you're cruising aboard **Fleming's Little Ocean Discovery Boat Tours** in St. Vincent's, ☎ 709/525-2943. Their stable pontoon boats explore the magnificent **Holyrood Pond**, a long arm of the sea that reaches 15 miles inland between high banks, looking very much like a Scottish highland loch (even to the brooding sky that seems common here). A long bar of sandy beach and cobble nearly blocks the end of the pond, which is further barred by a bridge, where Rte. 90 meets Rte. 10 at the southwest corner of the peninsula south of St. John's.

Diving

Off the southeast coast of the Avalon, guarded grimly by Cape Race lighthouse, is the famed **Graveyard of the Atlantic**, where the sea floor is strewn with shipwrecks. Cape Race lies at the main transatlantic navigation point, where ships headed for ports in North America changed direction, and it overlooks the scene of some of history's most famous sea disasters. This is where the *City of Philadelphia* and the *Anglo Saxon* were lost, and not far away is where the *Titanic* sank. Many of the dozens of ships lost here lie in water about 20 fathoms (120 feet) deep, two to five miles offshore, and are easily accessible to divers.

Vessels sunk by a German U-Boat in World War II provide a diving site close to St. John's in Conception Bay, off Belle Isle.

Diving Outfitters

- **Chance Cove Ventures**, PO Box 53, Renews, NF A0A 3NO, ☎ 709/363-2257, will take you on a three-hour dive for $30. It is wise to contact them in advance to reserve a date. You can also sign up for their diving trips at the Downs Inn in Ferryland or through Southern Shore Eco Adventures, PO Box 125, Ferryland, NF A0A 2H0, ☎ 709/432-2659.

- On the coast of Trinity Bay at the western side of the Baccalieu Trail, **Shagrock Boat Tours**, ☎ 709/588-2759, has a dive platform and provides diver pick-up with an inflatable craft. Dive tours leave from Whiteway, about 20 miles north of TransCanada-1 on Rte. 80.

- **Oceanus Adventures**, ☎ 709/738-0007, packages dive vacations, with staff and equipment prepared to guide physically impaired divers.

Windsurfing

Some of Canada's best windsurfing is in Newfoundland, with several prime sites in the Avalon; St. John's has the highest average windspeed (12 knots) of any city in Canada, and the Avalon shores are known for the consistency of their winds. Try Quidi Vidi Lake (except in June, July, and early August, when it's reserved for row-

> **FISHING EXPEDITIONS:** *A unique trip combining salmon and brown trout fishing is operated by Sea Run Outfishing Adventures, PO Box 30054, St. John's, NF A1G 1T3, ☎ 709/368-6880. Sailing on a Grand Banks schooner, groups can travel by sea between rivers, around the coast of the Avalon. Accommodations can be in B&Bs or camping along the shore – or a combination of both.*

ing) and Long Pond on the University campus, where you can rent boards and take lessons. Nearby Paradise has Octagon Pond, a paradise for windsurfers and site of several championship competitions.

On Conception Bay, about 20 minutes from the city on Rte. 60, **Foxtrap, Chamberlain** and **Topsail** beaches are all accessed by roads, but icy ocean waters require wetsuits. In Dildo Bay, not far from TransCanada-1 on the western loop of the Baccalieu Trail, has steady winds and cold water. At the southern end of Cape St. Mary's, the protected saltwater **Holyrood Pond** has good wind, warmer water and a launch from the former provincial park or outside the park at Path End.

Fishing

In the 1880s, brown trout – German browns and Lochlevens – were introduced into the Avalon, where they have thrived and flourished. They inhabit nearly every river system, including the scheduled salmon rivers. Locals call them sea trout, because they migrate to the sea each year, as salmon do. In fact, they develop scales and are sometimes confused with salmon because of their silvery appearance. The Canadian record for a sea run brown trout is a 28.5 pounder taken at Lower Pond, in Witless Bay. This estuary, not far south of St. John's is a regular source of trophy trout. The season for browns is longer than for other species, opening during ice fishing season in February and continuing through September, so you can fish for them when all other fishing seasons are closed.

■ On Snow

This far north, you can expect snow to be a normal part of winter life, so nobody makes a big deal of it. Cross-country skiing isn't confined to groomed trails, and you may find snowshoe tracks as commonly as those of the snowshoe hare. Renting snowshoes may be difficult, but if you ask the host in your B&B, there's a good chance they'll have a couple of pair in the shed. Or their neighbors will.

Skiing

Northwest of the city center, **Pippy Park** has cross-country ski trails (as well as ponds which become skating rinks), and you can also ski on the trails of **Bowring Park** (see *On Foot*, above).

Butter Pot Provincial Park has a network of four miles of cross-country ski trails beginning at the park office, where you will find a trail map posted. Most of the trails follow the park roads, but some of them use the summer hiking trails and one longer trail circles Big Otter Pond. Most are suitable for intermediate to advanced skiers. There is a warmup station just off the main access road, near the administration building. For information and conditions, ☎ 709/759-2584.

For a day's downhill skiing from St. John's, you can go to **White Hills** in Clarenville without a car via **Ski Express**, ☎ 709/682-1644. They leave the city at 7:30 am to arrive at the slopes at 9:30 am, returning at 5 pm, for a 7:30 arrival back at St. John's. The rate for transportation only is $25; for transportation and a full-day pass, $50; with ski rentals, $70.

On the western side of the Baccalieu Trail, **Dildo Run Provincial Park** grooms four miles of cross-country trails, mostly novice to intermediate. The views across the inlet are an added attraction, ☎ 709/629-3350.

■ On Horseback

Earle's Riding Horses, Rte. 74, Carbonear, ☎ 709/596-7854, has trail rides, pony rides for kids and night riding. They also have a petting farm for children and other amusements at the ranch. Carbonear is on the Baccalieu Trail, on the east shore of the peninsula.

In Brigus you can join guided rides through the woods and meadows with **Wheelwright Trail Rides**, ☎ 709/528-1020.

Cultural & Eco-Travel Experiences

Cape St. Mary's is dear to the hearts of Newfoundlanders, partly because of a well-loved song, *Let Me Fish Off Cape St. Mary's*, which you'll hear wherever Maritime music is played. It's a haunting song of the sea and of homeland, and it sums up the feelings of the Irish settlers and their descendants, who still populate the southwest corner of the Avalon. The region even looks like Ireland, with its green, fog-swept moorland. Here you will notice an even heavier layer of Gaelic in the speech. But you'll hear the Celtic influence in all the music in Newfoundland, especially in the maritime-influenced pubs of St. John's. Nearly every pub has live music, usually a maritime group, at least some evenings, and when the weather is good, you can stand on George St. and hear the rich plaintive chords and rousing choruses of several at once, with a French or Scottish fiddle tune wavering on the evening breeze as well. You can be sure of Irish music at **Erin's Pub**, 184 Water St., ☎ 709/722-1916, and Celtic bands several nights a week at **O'Reilly's Irish Pub** on George St., where you can also get Irish food.

Cape St. Mary's.

Pigeon Cove Productions, ☎ 709/754-7324, has weekly events at various pubs and local halls, featuring traditional Newfoundland music and dance, including instruction in local folk dancing.

In early August, the **George Street Festival** brings five nights of top Newfoundland bands, ☎ 709/576-8455, and the **Newfoundland and Labrador Folk Festival** in Bannerman Park, ☎ 709/526-8508, brings story telling, dancing and traditional music.

Also in the summer, the **Signal Hill Tattoo** recreates the sounds – and sights – of military drills from the 1800s. It's a grand show, performed on the parade grounds of Signal Hill at 3 and 7 pm on Wednesday, Thursday, Saturday, and Sunday from mid-July to mid-August. Other local celebrations often call for tattoos at other times, so it's a good idea to call and verify times.

For the most up-to-date information on what's happening where, read the free newspaper, *Signal*, listing all the pubs and their music schedule each week.

Archaeology

To learn more about the colony that Lord Baltimore founded in 1621, follow Rte. 10 south from St. John's to the **Colony of Avalon Archaeology Project** in Ferryland, ☎ 709/432-2767 summer, 709/432-2820 year-round. The lord and his family didn't like the Newfoundland winters and quickly moved on to Maryland and his better-known place in history, but the colony continued and the remains of its buildings are being unearthed right beside the harbor. To date, they have discovered a staggering half-million artifacts, in what many believe to be the best preserved colonial settlement in British North America.

You can watch the excavations close-up, and visit the excellent museum, which displays some of the artifacts and recreates their archaeological and historical context very nicely. You can also visit the laboratory upstairs to see the latest finds sorted, cleaned and reconstructed. Down at the dig, be sure to note the privy at the tide line – it may well be the continent's first flush toilet. You can look into the excavations at the dig anytime, but the museum is open daily 9 am to 7 pm, mid-June through mid-October; admission is $2, or $5 for a family. The shop at the museum is well worth touring, too, exhibiting and selling some fine Newfoundland art and craft work.

Unlike most archaeological digs, you can actually get your hands dirty in this one. Week-long programs, with lodgings at the nearby Downs Inn, allow you to join a research team. You'll be trained and assigned to real working jobs in the field. For details, contact Aiden Costello at the Downs Inn or **Southern Shore Adventures**, ☎ 709/432-2659.

To visit the excavations of a Dorset Eskimo site on an island in Trinity Bay, take a tour with **Dildo Island Boat Tours**, ☎ 709/582-2687. The boat makes a stop at the island during its regular tours.

Geology

The scenery, which is the combined work of geology, weather and the sea, is an adventure in itself. Wherever you find coast here you will find sea cliffs, or rocky ledges. Beaches are very rare, except the small ones caught in the deepest coves and in well-protected bays. It's hard to suggest where the scenery is at its best, since it's spectacular nearly everywhere. Grates Point, at the far tip of the Baccalieu Trail, Cape Speare, Cape St. Mary's, Race Point, and Cape Pine are perhaps the most dramatic, but that leaves out the stunningly beautiful little harbors enclosed by rock outcrops. Quidi Vidi in St. John's is one of these. South of the city, off Rte. 10, Brigus South is one of the most rockbound harbors in a province where rockbound harbors are almost commonplace, with tiny fishing shacks and boats, and a cemetery of white crosses on a steep green slope, all surrounded by cliffs. Its namesake, Brigus, on the southern end of the Baccalieu Trail, is another, with a harbor almost completely encircled by steep, rounded rock outcrops. Brigus is often compared to Norwegian fishing villages for its dramatic setting (although its houses are more reminiscent of New England).

All the dramatic scenery isn't along the shore: near St. Catherine, at the head of St. Mary's Bay, **The Cataracts** is a deep gorge with a waterfall. A very steep set of wooden stairs leads down into it, with bridges crossing the stream below the falls. These make viewing the falls from several angles safe, without ruining the wild beauty of the place. To get there, follow Rte. 91 from Colinet, then follow signs onto an unpaved road, about two miles to the falls.

Those interested in **fossils** should go to **Mistaken Point Ecological Reserve**, which has the oldest multi-celled marine life fossils found in North America. They are also the world's only deepwater fossils of their age, which is over 620 million years, and this is the only site that contains such a variety – over 20 different deepwater creatures. A trail leads from the road to Cape Race, but it is not easy to follow across the moors, and once you get to the right place, you still may not see the object of your trek. If you are passionately interested in fossils, we suggest getting a guide through **Southern Shore Eco Adventures**, PO Box 125, Ferryland, NF A0A 2H0, ☎ 709/432-2659. No fossil collecting is allowed in the reserve.

A second, lesser-known fossil site of major importance is at **Manuels River Linear Park**, Rte. 60, Manuels, ☎ 709/834-2099.

FOR BERRY LOVERS

If you travel in late August or early September, you will be tempted to stop often to pick the wild blueberries that grow along the trails and roadsides. Newfoundland harvests well over two million pounds of these tasty little berries each year commercially, which doesn't count the jars and jars of blueberry jam put by and the rows of blueberry pies baked in homes all over the province.

■ Brigus celebrates this harvest in mid-August with the **Brigus Blueberry Festival.** The program includes everything from a regatta to a theatrical walking tour of town led by local players, but you can be assured of leaving with blue teeth after you've sampled the pies, muffins, pancakes, even if you choose not to enter the blueberry pie-eating contest. You can learn all about blueberries from exhibits by the Department of Agriculture.

■ Newfoundland's abundant wild berries are also the focus of attention at **Rodrigues Markland Cottage Winery** in Markland, ☎ 709/759-3003. Markland is south of Whitbourne on Rte. 81, a few miles south of TransCanada-1. Blueberries and partridgeberries are made into wine here; both of those, along with bakeapples (the local name for the rare northern cloudberries) are made into liqueurs. Tours are conducted and wines sold Monday-Saturday, 9 am to 5 pm.

■ Wild berries are also the business of **Kit n' Kabootle**, 3 Prospect St., St. John's, ☎ 709/726-3838. They create jams, chutneys and other preserves from partridgeberries and blueberries, including a wild partridgeberry honey mustard, wild blueberry chutney, and partridgeberry apple almond chutney. You can visit them and sample the latest creations or pick up recipes at their Fine Food factory, just off King's Rd, uphill from Duckworth St., on Saturday afternoons between 1 and 5 pm.

Pick up a copy of the excellent trail guide at the tourist chalet, where the trails begin, to follow either of two trails along the river. Fossil evidence here is, like that of Mistaken Point, more than 600 million years old, and you can find fossilized trilobites in the loose shale. You may collect these, but you cannot chip any loose from the rock. Guided hikes are on Sunday afternoons and Tuesday evenings. A **Family Campfire** program each Thursday evening in July and August brings locals and visitors together to learn about the unique and undeveloped Manuels River system, and to have a good time singing around the campfire.

■ Wildlife-Watching

In St. John's, Pippy Park at the edge of Long Pond has the only public **Fluvarium** in North America, ☎ 709/754-FISH. What, we asked, is a Fluvarium? It's an underwater viewing station that gives a close-up, year-round view of the insects, plants and fish that live underneath the water. Summer hours are from 9 am to 5 pm daily, with hourly guided tours. Winter hours are shorter, but the Fluvarium is especially interesting then because you get to see what's happening under the ice.

Creatures that live in saltwater are the specialty of the **Ocean Studies Centre** in Logy Bay, on the Marine Drive north of St. John's, ☎ 709/737-3706. Tours of this working research station, and its discovery room, let you see an aquarium full of fish and reach into the touch tank to feel the creatures. Films, exhibits and the explanations of the guide tell about the natural history of the area and the work of the center. Tours take about an hour, and begin each hour, by advance reservation only in the winter and on a first-come basis in July and August. Tours are $2.50 for adults, $1.50 for under age 18 and seniors.

Near The Cataracts, on Rte. 91 in Colinet, there is a **salmon ladder** and holding pool at **Rocky River Falls**, ☎ 709/521-2719. It's open daily 9 am to 5 pm, July through mid-November, and it's free. The best time to see salmon active there is in the early part of the season. Each year the Salmon Enhancement Project holds 70 adult salmon, which produce about 150,000 eggs, of which 120,000 are expected to hatch.

From almost anywhere along the Avalon it's hard *not* to watch whales if you're traveling in June or July, when as many as 20 species breach and spout wherever the water is deep enough for them, often right along the shore. Between the whales and icebergs in the water, it's difficult to remember to watch the road. Good places to look for them from the shore are at the village of **Flat Rock**, on the Marine Drive north of St. John's, and from the natural breakwater at **St. Vincent's**, at the outlet of Holyrood Pond. Stop here, especially in the spring and early summer, to watch humpback whales cavorting in the waters just offshore.

WITLESS BAY ECOLOGICAL RESERVE

Witless Bay Ecological Reserve is made up of four islands off the east coast of the Southern Avalon Peninsula. It has the continent's largest colony of Atlantic puffins (over 90,000 pairs), and the world's second largest colony of the nocturnal Leach's storm-petrel. Nearly 95% of the Atlantic puffins in North America breed in Newfoundland. More than two million seabirds come to nest, breed, and feed their chicks on the capelin – small, silvery herring-like fish which run from mid-June to mid-July. In addition to Atlantic puffins and Leach's storm-petrels, birders are likely to see black-legged kittiwakes, common murres, thick-billed murres, black guillemots, razorbills, herring gulls, and the great black-backed gull, the largest of all gulls. The rare northern fulmar has been spotted breeding on Great Island in the reserve.

The seabirds return every year from the open sea to breed on the islands in Witless Bay. On the boat ride out to see them, you're likely to see both whales and dolphins. The world's largest concentration of humpback whales is found in these waters, as well as fin and minke whales. If you're lucky, you'll get to watch whales spyhop, blow, and breach, and you may even spot a whale calf or two. – *Sara Godwin and Charles James*

Several boats take passengers into Witless Bay, most leaving from Bay Bulls, some from Bauline East and the town of Witless Bay. These latter are close to the reserve, so trips are shorter – less time is spent getting there – and less expensive. Prices from Bay Bulls run about $30-$35, from closer ports $15-$20. Some operators have a shuttle bus from major hotels in St. John's. Bring binoculars, a camera, and a bird identification guide. Dress warmly, even in the summer, bringing a windbreaker and a hat that covers your ears.

Witless Bay Boat Tours

The following boats tour Witless Bay; all are Coast Guard approved:

■ **O'Brien's Whale and Bird Tours,** Bay Bulls, ☎ 709/753-4850 or 709/334-2355, fax 709/753-3140, e-mail obriens@netfx-nc.com. O'Brien's runs five trips a day in heated, wheelchair accessible, tour boats. The rate varies depending on the time of the tour: both early and late are less than the mid-day tours.

- **Gatherall's Puffin & Whale Watch**, Bay Bulls, ☎ 709/334-2887 or 800/41-WHALE. Six trips a day, from 10 am, May through October, in a heated boat with special viewing area for children.

- **Capt. Murphy's Bird Island and Whale Tours,** Witless Bay, ☎ 709/334-2002 or toll-free 888/783-3467. Six trips daily, from 10:30 am to 7 pm, late June through early September. The sanctuary is two miles from their dock, making their travel time shorter, but they spend longer in the sanctuary than the one-hour tours below. The cost is about $20.

- **Seabird Boat Tours**, Bauline East, ☎ 709/334-2098. Ten minutes from the reserve, their two boats do one-hour tours, leaving every hour, 8 am to 8 pm.

- **Great Island Boat Tours**, Bauline East, ☎ 709/334-2621. One-hour tours daily, 8:30 am to 8:30 pm every hour-and-a-half.

- **Ocean Adventure Boat Tours**, Bauline East, ☎ 709/334-2636. One-hour tours, daily 8 am to 8 pm.

- **Wildland Tours**, 124 Water Street, St. John's, ☎ 709/722-3335, takes full-day trips beginning with a boat tour of Witless Bay and continuing to the lower Avalon to see the caribou herds or to Cape St. Mary's to see gannets.

At almost any time of year you are likely to see gray harbor seals from the beach at **Chance Cove Park**, off Rte. 10 about halfway between Ferryland and Trepassey. Bird- and seal-watching boat trips leave from the campground, but you need to reserve a space with **Southern** Shore Eco Adventures in Ferryland, ☎ 709/432-2659.

The **Avalon Wilderness Reserve** spreads across much of the center of southern Avalon and is home to 13,000 caribou, the most southerly herd of its size found anywhere. Just because the reserve is their home doesn't mean they actually live there. In the winter, spring and early summer, the best place to see them is along Route 10 between Trepassey and Pete's River. They graze along the roadside, wander across it, and – if you don't get too close – pose for photos. Although you'll probably see them along Rte. 10, searching for them is a good excuse to explore the southernmost point of the Avalon Peninsula and the lonely village of St. Shotts, whose waters are so exposed that fishing boats had to be pulled onto the shore at night for safety. On the way there, you'll pass the road to nearby Cape Pine Lighthouse, through another area where caribou are usually plentiful.

Later in the summer the caribou migrate north into the Avalon Reserve, where finding them takes a little more effort. Ask in Trepassey, or at the new **Caribou Interpretation Centre** to find out where they've been seen recently. The Province is building the caribou center near the intersection of Rte. 10 and the road to St. Shott's, but the exact construction schedule is still not definite as we write. If you see a building at the intersection, you'll know that's it.

If the caribou are not accessible outside the vast reserve, the best way to see them is to take a caribou tour with **Southern Shore Eco Adventures**, PO Box 125, Ferryland, NF A0A 2H0, ☎ 709/432-2659.

GAZING AT THE GANNETS

Cape St. Mary's Ecological Reserve, ☎ 709/729-2431, is one of the world's premier birding experiences. Northern gannets are large, handsome, graceful seabirds, with greeting, courtship, and breeding rituals as elegant and formal as a minuet. They dive from as high as 100 feet in the air, plunging spectacularly into the sea to fish for capelin, herring, and mackerel.

Cape St. Mary's is one of those rare sites where it is possible to observe thousands of nesting birds at close range without disturbing them. More than 26,000 pairs of northern gannets breed on a sea stack only a few feet from seaside cliffs where the birds, nests, and chicks can easily be watched. The northern gannets arrive in March and depart for the open sea in late September.

Cape St. Mary's also has 10,000 pairs of black-legged kittiwakes, 10,000 pairs of common murres, and the world's southernmost colony of thick-billed murres. In addition to the 60,000 seabirds, there are bald eagles, peregrine falcons, ravens, water pipits, horned larks, and many species of migrating shorebirds (lesser golden plover, black-bellied plover, and whimbrel among them).

Gannet greeting display at Cape St. Mary's.
(Photo by Charles James)

A clearly marked half-mile trail (a 20-30 minute walk) follows the cliffs from behind the interpretive center. The center itself is jam-packed with informative displays that provide a clear understanding of fascinating gannet behaviors – skypointing, bowing, fencing, and begging. The weather is often cold, damp, windy, and foggy. Dress warmly, wear sturdy, water-resistant hiking boots, and bring binoculars or a spotting scope.

Bird Rock at Cape St. Mary's is free; there is a nominal charge to visit the interpretive center. The 35-page pamphlet *Cape St. Mary's: Guide to the Ecological Reserve* by Alexander Burnett is outstanding, and available here. Also useful is *Seabirds and Major Seabird Colonies of Newfoundland and Labrador* by David Snow, a free guide published by the Department of Tourism. – *Sara Godwin and Charles James*

The Reserve is at the southwestern tip of the Avalon Peninsula, off Rte. 100. The turnoff is three miles east of St. Bride's. Although the closest views are from the shore, you can get another perspective on the sea stack, as well as the surrounding coastal cliffs, on board the ***Catherine Alesha*** from St. Brides, ☎ 709/337-2660 or 709/337-2614. On the way there, you'll sail through the waters off St. Vincent where humpback, fin and minke whales feed on the fish in July and August.

WILDLIFE PHOTOGRAPHY TOURS: *Photographers keen on getting the best shots of the Avalon's abundant wildlife, both bird and mammal, should look into* ***Wilson Photography Tours****, PO Box 648, Eastern Passage, NS B3G 1M9, ☎ 902/465-2750. Led by professional photographer Dale Wilson, whose work has appeared in National Geographic and Natural History magazines, and who also teaches photography, the tours concentrate on those places with the best opportunities for serious photography: Witless Bay and Cape St. Mary's, and the Avalon caribou herd.*

At the far northern point of the Avalon, off the Baccalieu Trail, is the **Baccalieu Island Ecological Reserve**, the world's largest colony of Leach's storm petrels, with six million petrels and thousands of puffins, kittiwakes, murres, and other seabirds. They can fly to the island but, as we write, you can't get there. Until recently, a boat took birders out to the island on a regular schedule, but the boat was destroyed in a storm, and it is uncertain whether the service will be resumed. Be sure any information you get on this is current, since several local tourist brochures have not been reprinted since the boat service stopped. For the latest word, contact the Tourist Information Office, Rte. 70, Harbour Grace, NF A0A 2M0, ☎ 709/596-5561, open daily, 9 am to 6 pm, May through October.

To see caribou, and other indigenous animals in enclosures specially designed to maintain the natural habitat of each species, stop at the **Salmonier Nature Park,** on Rte. 90, not far south of TransCanada-1, ☎ 709/729-6974. A two-mile nature walk follows a boardwalk across a bog and woodland trail through the forest, where you'll see and learn about flora and fauna you might not see in the wild, including moose, snowy owls, beavers, red foxes, bald eagles, peregrine falcon, spruce grouse, otters and hare. It's open Thursday-Monday, noon to 7 pm, June through mid-October; admission is free.

CARIBOU

Caribou thrive in open, barren landscapes and in coniferous forests. In the summer they eat green plants and mushrooms, and in the winter lichens and small evergreens. Lichens are their principal food, and they may eat a dozen pounds a day. The great expanses of windswept barrens on the Avalon provide plenty of food for the herd, which is healthier than most in the province.

One measure of their health is the amount of energy expended on antler production: big antlers are a sign of a healthy animal. Some of the world's record antlers are found on males in the Avalon herd. Unlike most other animals, female caribou also have antlers, but a lower than average percentage of females in the Avalon herd are antlered. In the spring, females move to their calving grounds, near Little Harbour and Murphy's River.

Sightseeing

To see what life was like for colonial officers in the early days of empire, visit **Commissariat House** on King's Bridge Rd. in St. John's, ☎ 709/729-6730. The beautiful Georgian building, restored to its 1830 appearance, is furnished in Brussels carpets, English china, silver, lace, and fine paintings appropriate to the lifestyle of an Assistant Commissary General who supplied non-military goods and services for troops at the local garrisons. Admission is free and the building is open daily, June to mid-October, 10 am to 5:30 pm.

Exhibits on native peoples of Newfoundland and on 19th-century daily life of European settlers fill the **Newfoundland Museum**, 285 Duckworth St, ☎ 709/729-2329. Furnishings and toys, a schoolroom, cooperage, fishing stage, and grocery store fill in the picture of life in the last century. Open daily 9 am to 4:30 pm in July and August, shorter hours the rest of the year, the museum is free.

The Newfoundland Transport Museum, 212 Mount Scio Rd., ☎ 709/722-7224, features a different transportation theme each year. Permanent outdoor exhibits, open daily, daylight hours, include a collection of railway passenger cars and a locomotive. Open daily, 10 am to 6 pm, in July and August. Admission is by donation.

Cathedral of St. John the Baptist, 68 Queen's Rd., ☎ 709/726-5677, has a Gothic-style nave, of Scottish sandstone and rough-hewn Newfoundland stone. It is particularly known for its carved pews and the 36 stained-glass windows, which, combined with its architecture, make it an important example of Gothic revival. Free tours are given late May to mid-October, 10:30 am to 4:30 pm.

Several attractions crown **Signal Hill**, overlooking the entrance to the harbor, ☎ 709/772-5367. The view alone is worth the trip up the hill. Midway, the park's Visitor Centre shows the history and importance of Signal Hill and the harbor it guarded. Next come the ruins of **Queen's Battery,** established by the British in the 1700s and enlarged during the War of 1812. Replicas of 32-pounder guns represent the 1860s period. Atop the hill, **Cabot Tower** was begun in 1897 as a lookout and signal tower. Here Guglielmo Marconi received the first transatlantic wireless broadcast from England in 1901, and the tower maintains communications with the world through an amateur radio station, open during the summer. Admission is free, except for special events, and the Visitor Centre is open mid-June to Labor Day, 8:30 am to 9 pm daily; the rest of the year 8:30 am to 4:30 pm daily. The grounds are open year-round.

Also commanding an elevation overlooking the sea is **Cape Speare National Historic Site**, ☎ 709/772-5367. The 1836 lighthouse, perched on a rocky cliff, is at the most easterly point in North America, about seven miles southeast of St. John's. A World War II gun battery has underground passages connecting gun emplacements with magazines. A Visitor Centre interprets the history of Cape Speare and guides explain the lighthouse, from mid-June to early September.

On the Baccalieu Trail about halfway up the peninsula is the charming **Victoria Lifestyles Museum**, next to the Hydro station in Victoria, ☎ 709/596-1004. This assemblage of small buildings includes an historical museum, an active cooper shop, blacksmith, sawmill and other relics of local life in the last century.

On the western shore along Rte. 80 is the **Sparkes Heritage House Lifestyle Museum** in Sibley's Cove, ☎ 709/586-2337 or 2241. Costumed interpreters show what life was like for a fisherman's family of the 1930s. It's open daily, 10 am to 6 pm, late June through early September, and admission is $1.

Continuing south along Trinity Bay you'll come to the **Heart's Content Cable Station**, Rte. 80, ☎ 709/729-2460 or 583-2160. This free museum preserves the site – with all its operating equipment – where the first transatlantic telegraph cable came ashore after it was laid along the ocean floor by the ship *Great Eastern* in 1866. It served as the major communications connection between Europe and North America for an entire century. Exhibits show the difficulty of laying 2,000 miles of underwater cable and guides in the Operations Room demonstrate how the messages, all in Morse Code, were relayed to their destinations all over the continent. You can see the end of the cable inside the building, and across the road, disappearing into the sea. The museum is open 9 am to 5:30 pm daily in the summer.

Just south of Heart's Content (you'll love some of the town names up here), in the village of Dildo, about seven miles north of the junction of Rte. 80 and TransCanada-1, is the **Dildo Interpretive Center**, ☎ 709/582-3339. Aquariums display the fish in the Bay, and exhibits based on nearby archaeological excavations show the Maritime Archaic, Dorset and Beothuk native cultures. Another set of exhibits concern the local fishing industry and the experimental cod hatchery operated here a century ago.

You don't have to be an early flight enthusiast to be impressed by the **Harbour Grace Airstrip**. About four miles north of the DC-3 and tourist information kiosk, take Bannerman Lake Road west, following the sign uphill. At the end of the pavement, go right, then stay on the major road until you cross the lower end of the field. The road then turns and follows the field to the top, where a simple stone monument lists the early aviators who began their transatlantic flights at this primitive field. Amelia Earhart started her solo transatlantic flight here on May 20, 1932, and the view you see is very close to what she saw as she raced down the hill and into history.

The departure log with their signatures, flight plans, and photographs of the planes and pioneer aviators who used this field are in the **Conception Bay Museum**, Water St., Harbour Grace, ☎ 709/596-1309. You may recognize the names of some of these planes: *The Pride of Detroit, Winnie Mae* and *Southern Cross*. If you don't, the free booklet *Dirt Strip to Glory*, available here, will tell you more. A room is devoted to the notorious pirate, Peter Easton, whose fort stood where the museum now stands.

Hibbs Cove, which sits precariously perched at the end of a long narrow strip of highland (reached by a long narrow strip of road), south of Harbour Grace, has the **Hibbs Cove Fishing Museum**,

☎ 709/786-3912 or 709/786-3900. This assemblage of historic home, fishing museum, schoolhouse, fish shed and flake where fish is dried sits in the hollow and on rocky hummocks with ledges behind, begging you to get out your camera. World War II buffs will want to see the anchor from SSPLM 27, torpedoed at Bell Island by German subs during the war. The museum is open Monday-Saturday, noon to 5 pm; Sunday, 1 to 6 pm. Admission to all buildings is $2.

> **SIGHTSEEING TIP:** *While you're in the area visiting the Hibbs Cove Museum, stop at the* ***Copper Kettle Tea Room*** *and the crafts shops in Port de Grave along the way. All combined, this makes a nice excursion.*

Farther south, about 20 miles from the TransCanada-1, is **Brigus**, a destination in itself because of its beautiful rock-bounded harbor (see *Cultural & Eco-Travel Experiences*, above). Brigus was the home town of Captain Robert A. Bartlett, captain of the ships for Peary's 1898, 1905 and 1908 polar expeditions. You can visit his home, **Hawthorne Cottage**, on Main St, ☎ 709/528-4004. Along with illustrating the lifestyle of a prosperous Victorian family, the house contains memorabilia of his Arctic adventures. It's open daily, 10 am to 6 pm, June through August. Admission is $2.50.

Almost opposite, in a restored stone barn, is the **Brigus Museum**, 4 Magistrate's Hill, ☎ 709/528-3298, with more material on Bartlett and on the town's seafaring history. It's open Monday-Friday, 10 am to 6 pm; Saturday-Sunday, 10 am to 8 pm, from mid-June through August; admission $1.

Don't leave without visiting the harbor and **The Walk**, a large stone outcrop, which was pierced by a tunnel in 1860 so people could get from the town to the harbour.

At **Cupids**, close to Brigus, is the site of the first English settlement in North America, which began here in 1610. There is an archaeological excavation of the original plantation. You can visit the dig in the summer and see the artifacts they've recovered in the free **Cupids Museum**, ☎ 709/528-3477 or 709/596-1906, open Monday-Friday, 11:30 to 4:30; Saturday-Sunday, noon to 5 pm; from mid-June through mid-September.

At the southern end of the Avalon is **Trepassey** and the charming little **Trepassey Museum** on Main St., ☎ 709/438-2044. Trepassey was an important early base for the flying boats, and you'll see photos of Amelia Earhart, who left here as a passenger to become the first woman to cross the Atlantic by air. Local religious and household items are interesting displays as well. The museum is open in July and August, Monday-Saturday, 10 am to 5 pm, and Sunday, 1 to 5 pm. Admission is $1.

Placentia, on the west coast of the Avalon near Argentia, where the ferry from Nova Scotia lands, was once the French capital of the province, founded in 1662. You can see why the site made a good stronghold when you look down on the town and its protected harbor from **Castle Hill National Historic Site**, off Rte. 100, ☎ 709/227-2401. The remains of the fort are open daily, 8:30 am to 8 pm, mid-June through August; and 8:30 am to 4:30 pm, September through mid-June.

Where To Stay & Eat

The St. John's Area

By any measure the best and most conveniently located of St. John's hotels is the modern **Hotel Newfoundland**. Most of the rooms, which are very well-decorated, have harbor views. A swimming pool, sauna, whirlpool, squash courts and other fitness facilities round out the services you'd expect at a CN property. For dining, the menu at the hotel's Cabot Club ($$-$$$) is stylish, and the chef turns a fine hand to the classic dishes. You can sample some of the more humble, but legendary Newfie specialties, like fish and brewis (pronounced FISH'n-brews) from the informal buffet at The Outport. *Cavendish Sq., St. John's, NF A1C 5W8, ☎ 709/726-4980 or 800/268-9411 in Canada, 800/828-7447 in the US, fax 709/726-2025 ($$$).*

About a mile from downtown, also with a pool, is **The Battery Hotel and Suites**. *100 Signal Rd., St. John's, NF A1A 1B3, ☎ 709/576-0040 or 800/563-8181, fax 709/576-6943 ($$).*

Among the city's several more elegant bed and breakfast homes is the downtown **Kincora Hospitality Home**. The Victorian home is furnished in fine antiques (the beds are astonishing), and its engaging host serves a full hot breakfast on fine china. *36 King's Bridge Rd. (at Empire Ave), St. John's, NF A1C 3K6, ☎ 709/576-7415 ($$).*

Just as classy, in a turreted Queen Anne mansion at the opposite end of town (but on a bus line), is **Waterford Manor**. Antiques furnish large rooms, and you can have breakfast served at your own window table or in the stately dining room. Either way, it's a full show. *185 Waterford Bridge Rd., St. John's, NF A1E 1C7, ☎ 709/754-4139, fax 709/754-4155 ($$).*

Compton House is in a fully modernized 1919 mansion a bit out of the center, but on a bus line. Bright, spacious rooms and suites may have whirlpool baths and/or working fireplaces. *26 Waterford Bridge Rd., St. John's NF, A1E 1C6, ☎ 709/739-5789 ($$).*

Monkstown Manor has big bright rooms in the easygoing homey surroundings of an in-town row house. Shared baths have double whirlpool tubs. *51 Monkstown Rd., St. John's, NF A1C 3T4, ☎ 709/754-7324, fax 709/722-8557 ($$).*

Overlooking a bay on the Marine Drive, where you can often see whales, is **The Tides Inn**. The sunporch in front, with a sea view, is a tearoom. Although it's out of the city, it's only 15 minutes from the airport. *407 Windgap Rd., Flatrock, NF A1K 1C4, ☎ 709/437-1456 ($-$$).*

Eight miles south of St. John's is the attractive cove-set village of Petty Harbour and **Orca Inn**. Petty Harbour is a good base for hikers exploring the Cape Speare/North Head area on the Coastal Trail. *PO Box 197, Petty Harbour, NF A0A 3H0, ☎ 709/747-9676, fax 709/747-9676 ($).*

The most interesting menu in town is at **Stone House**. Wild game and fresh local seafood predominate, prepared in unexpected and stylish ways. Wild boar chops, moose steak with partridgeberries, pheasant (prepared with pecans and red currants when we last tried it) and a wine-rich stew of wild meats highlight the menu. Their own gravlax is our starter of choice (and the pâté of wild game with chanterelles a close second). *8 Kennas Hill, ☎ 709/753-2380 ($$-$$$).*

You'll find innovative, appealing fusion cuisine at **The Cellar**. Intimate surroundings are, as the name suggests, in an old stone cellar. *Baird's Cove (off Water St), ☎ 709/579-8900 ($$-$$$).*

Vegetarians will rejoice (Newfoundland is not known for its way with vegetables) at **Stella's Natural Foods Restaurant**. So will anyone who loves desserts. We like Stella's black bean burritos. *106 Water St., ☎ 709/753-9625 ($$).*

Cavendish Café, *73 Duckworth St,* ☎ *709/579-8024 ($)*, serves soups and sandwiches, and **Classic Café**, *364 Duckworth St.,* ☎ *709/579-4444 ($)*, offers budget seafood and local beers around the clock.

Mary Jane's has fresh-baked breads and pastries, sandwiches and salads. It's a good source of lunches to carry off and eat by the sea. A good choice for picnics. *377 Duckworth St,* ☎ *709/753-8466 ($).*

For a breakfast of local favorites – baked beans with bologna, fish and brewis, fish cakes, salmon and eggs, or toutons (fried dough, served with molasses or syrup), go to **Zachary's** on Cavendish Square. Later in the day you can get home-style comfort foods, fried fish, and pasta. *71 Duckworth St.,* ☎ *709/579-8050 ($-$$).*

For a relaxed pub with sturdy meat pies at lunch, set sail for **The Ship Inn**. *265 Duckworth St.,* ☎ *709/753-3870 ($).*

Southwest of the city, in Conception Bay South, look for **Soirée**. The dishes are home-style and well prepared, and they specialize in using the rare berry, called "bakeapples" locally, cloudberries elsewhere. Open every day in the summer from Tuesday-Sunday, January-May. *Rte. 60 in the settlement of Killigrews,* ☎ *709/834-4282.*

Along the Baccalieu Trail

On a street of fine old homes is **Keneally Manor**. It was built in 1839 by two schooner captains and is a fine home for a bed and breakfast, furnished with period antiques. *8 Patrick St., Carbonear, NF A0A 1T0,* ☎ *709/596-1221 ($$).*

Overlooking period gardens opposite the museum are the elegant restored 19th-century rooms at **Garrison House**. Full breakfasts are included, and fine dinners of local seafood are served by reservation only. They're worth reserving. *Water St., Harbour Grace, NF A0A 2M0,* ☎ *709/596-3658 ($$).*

Rothesay House is a 1919 Queen Anne-style home furnished in antiques. Each bedroom has a sitting are and some have fireplaces. *Water St., Harbour Grace, NF A0A 2M0,* ☎ *709/596-2268 ($$).*

Brittoner offers bed and breakfast in a restored Victorian home on the harbor. *12 Water St. (PO Box 163), Brigus, NF A0A 1K0,* ☎ *709/528-3412 ($-$$).*

Skipper Ben's B&B is in a big, comfortable home overlooking the harbour. Breakfast is bountiful. *Box 76, Cupids, NF A0A 2B0,* ☎ *709/528-4436 ($-$$).*

North Street Café serves lunches of soups, meat pies and sandwiches, and tea with scones, jam and fresh cream. *North St. in Brigus,* ☎ *709/528-1393 ($).*

For dining out in Carbonear, locals choose **Fong's Restaurant**. Like many Chinese restaurants here, Fong's also has a complete menu of western favorites, from seafood to steaks. *143 Columbus Dr.,* ☎ *709/596-5114 ($$).*

We've eaten fish and brewis from Tickle Cove to Mistaken Point and never have we had such a fine plateful, tasty and succulent, as we had one recent afternoon on the outdoor deck at **Land's End Restaurant** in Grates Cove, at the northern tip of the Baccalieu Trail. It's well-named, since the restaurant is at the end of the road at the end of the town at the end of the peninsula. The view is as good as the food, which includes local fish, and homemade pies. It was worth driving to the end of the earth for the best craft shop, as well. *No phone ($).*

The Southern Avalon

We like **The Downs Inn** in Ferryland. We liked it when Aiden Costello's mother was the innkeeper and we like it now that Aiden is the host. Its comfortable rooms overlooking the harbour are warm and inviting, while retaining the building's history as the village convent. We think the nuns would approve, and we bet they'd have liked the hefty sandwiches and good desserts in the tearoom Aiden has opened in their parlor, too. You can walk to the archaeological dig and museum, and take your morning constitutional around the downs, an almost-island beside the harbor. Aiden is a gold-mine of information on adventures – from kayaking to finding the caribou – in this part of the Avalon. *Route 10 (PO Box 15), Ferryland, NF A0A 2H0,* ☎ *709/432-2808 or 709/432-2163 ($).*

The **Trepassey Motel and Restaurant** has comfortable, modern rooms and the best dining room ($) in many miles. The salmon is nicely prepared, and they offer alternatives to the usual fried fish. *PO Box 22, Trepassey, NF A0A 4B0, ☎ 709/438-2934 ($-$$).*

Northwest Bed & Breakfast offers two pleasant rooms with a private guests' entrance and shared bath. Breakfast in the kitchen includes conversation with the engaging hosts. *Rte. 10 (Box 5, Site 14), Trepassey, NF A0A 4B0, ☎ 709/438-2888 ($).*

The **Harold Motel** is convenient to the ferry in Argentia. Ask for their excellent brochure on the area's attractions. *PO Box 142, Placentia, NF A0B 2Y0, ☎ 709/227-2107 ($).*

Bird Island Resort has rooms, efficiencies and suites close to the ecological reserve at Cape St. Mary's. A kitchen is available for guests, as are laundry facilities, playground, barbecue pit, and fitness room. *Route 100, St. Bride's, NF A0B 2Z0, ☎ 709/337-2450 ($-$$).*

Whalen's Hospitality Home is 30 minutes from the ecological reserve at Cape St. Mary's. "Hospitality home" is Newfoundland for B&B; the breakfast here is continental. Full breakfast and other meals are available by reservation. *Rte. 100, Branch, St. Mary's Bay, NF A0B 1E0, ☎ 709/338-2506 ($).*

Atlantica Inn and Restaurant has five plain motel rooms, spotless and comfortable. The restaurant ($) is open 7 am to 8 pm, serving no-nonsense homey foods (liver and onions, $6), fried seafood, and sandwiches. *Route 100, St. Bride's, NF A0B 2Z0, ☎ 709/337-2860 or 2861 ($).*

■ Camping

Butter Pot Provincial Park is open mid-May through August, with 140 campsites, available with and without hookups. Swimming, boating, hiking, a miniature golf course, trout ponds and other facilities make it a popular weekend getaway for people in St. John's. *TransCanada-1, Holyrood, ☎ 709/570-7573 or 800/866-CAMP.*

La Manche Provincial Park has a campground with 69 well-spaced sites in the woods by a pond; it is open June through Labor Day. It's a favorite with birders, since over 50 species have been identified here. *Rte. 10, Bauline East, NF, ☎ 800/563-NFLD.*

Chance Cove Provincial Park has an unsupervised free camping area with 25 open campsites near the sea. The biggest crowd you'll see here is of gray and harbor seals, or of birds, since it's a stop, in the spring and fall, on the Atlantic flyway. Bird- and seal-watching boat trips begin at the campground. *Rte. 10, between Portugal Cove and Cappahayden.*

One of the happy transitions of the provincial park scuttle has been at **Northern Bay Provincial Park**. Now privately operated by its former ranger, the park is being improved to add some conveniences without losing its spacious campsites and air of tranquil seclusion. The beach is set below cliffs, next to a tumbling waterfall. Sites are mowed weekly, and an overflow field provides for late arrivals. Thumbs up for this one; camping is $9, day use of the beach $3, and they accept reservations. If you can't carry all your gear on the airplane, they can rent you a tent and cookstove, and will meet you at the airport. *On the Baccalieu Trail north of Carbonear, ☎ 709/584-3465.*

On the northern edge of St. John's, **Pippy Park Trailer Park** has a campground with 158 sites for tents and trailers, open May through September. *Nagles Pl., St. John's NF A1B 3T2, ☎ 709/737-3669, fax 709/737-3303.*

Bonavista & Terra Nova

In the peninsula and island-studded mainland coast that surround Bonavista Bay are clustered two of Newfoundland's best-known places: the historic old seaport of Trinity and one of the province's two national parks. Water surrounds all. Long arms of the bay reach into the land, including the deep fjord of Clode Sound, which separates the two sections of this region. As the kittiwake flies, it's less than

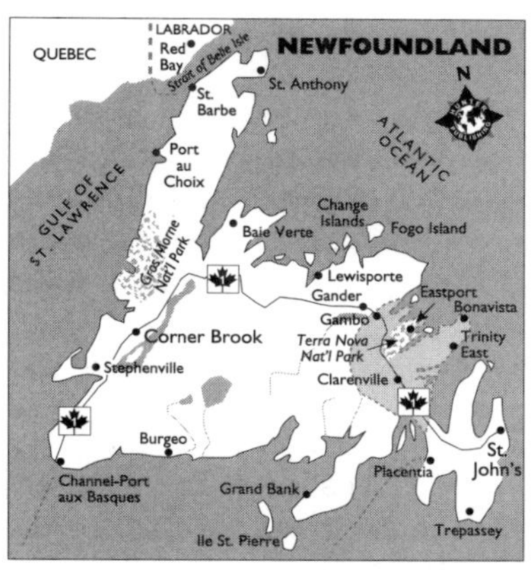

25 miles from Bonavista to Salvage. To drive it is three times that distance.

Geography & History

West and north of the Avalon, the Bonavista Peninsula divides Trinity Bay from Bonavista Bay. Trinity Bay is the long, relatively wide body of water that nearly separates the Avalon from the rest of Newfoundland, ending at the mountainous isthmus.

Like the Avalon, of which it is geologically a part, the Bonavista coast is irregular, rocky and abrupt, rising to high headlands that drop suddenly into the sea. These cliffs make the protection of its deep harbors all the more inviting (and important to its history).

John Cabot stopped at Bonavista in 1497, and Queen Elizabeth II came 500 years later to celebrate the anniversary. In typical Newfoundland style, the welcome was warm and rousing, but the weather was foul for Her Majesty's visit.

Trinity, a bit south of Bonavista on the peninsula's east coast, seems to have a monopoly on historic firsts, however. In 1615 the first English court of justice held outside of England convened in Trinity to settle fishermen's claims. In 1796, the smallpox vaccine was first used in North America. Trinity Roman Catholic Church is the oldest church building in Newfoundland, built in 1833. Trinity flourished as a trade and commercial port until the railroad made its shipping obsolete in the early 1900s. Today, it thrives on visitors, who come to enjoy its beautiful setting overlooking the bay, its museums and restored buildings, most of which are still lived in. The more adventurous of its visitors come here for its kayaking waters and for the walking trails that lead to a string of abandoned fishing settlements.

Terra Nova National Park occupies a large share of the mainland opposite the Bonavista Peninsula, along Clode and Newman sounds. Although its shore is scenic, it can't match the drama of Gros Morne National Park, and its emphasis is recreational, with golf, a resort hotel, supervised beaches, and playgrounds, as well as its more adventuresome attractions of interpretive programs, boat tours, hiking and bicycling paths.

Reached from the northern end of Terra Nova, on Rte. 310, the Eastport Peninsula is ringed by fine coastal scenery, secluded beaches, and recently reclaimed hiking trails to abandoned outport towns. Fishing villages, such as Salvage, try to stay alive in the face of a declining fishery.

Getting Around

TransCanada-1 runs along the spine of the isthmus connecting the Avalon to the rest of the island, and continues its northerly route through the center of Terra Nova National Park. It completely bypasses the Bonavista Peninsula, which is reached by Rte. 230, with the connecting Rte. 233 shortening the approach from the north. Rte. 230 goes all the way to the tip, ending in the town of Bonavista, with other side roads branching off it like the veins of a leaf, leading to other smaller towns along the shore and in the deep coves at the end of smaller bays. Rte. 236 runs along its northern shore, making a good loop route.

Information Sources

- Information on this region can be found in the very useful annual *Newfoundland and Labrador Travel Guide*, free from the **Department of Tourism, Culture and Recreation**, PO Box 8730, St. John's, NF A1B 4K2, ☎ 800/563-6353 or 709/729-2830.

- Additional material is available from the **Bonavista Area Regional Development Association**, PO Box 87, Bonavista, Bonavista Bay, NF A0C 1B0, ☎ 709/468-2200.

- Information on the Bonavista Peninsula is also available from the **Interpretation Center**, Rte. 239, Trinity, NF A0C 2H0, ☎ 709/464-2042, open daily, 9 am to 6 pm, mid-June through mid-October.

- **Terra Nova National Park** information is available from the provincial tourism department, or at the park headquarters, ☎ 709/533-2801. The headquarters is open daily, 10 am to 8 pm, mid-May through mid-October.

Adventures

Many of the outdoor activities in this region are in Terra Nova National Park, but you must pay an admission fee of $3.25 for one day, $9.25 for four days. Family rates are $6.50 for one day and and $19.50 for four days. You must pay this fee in order to leave

TransCanada-1 anywhere in the park, even to stop for lunch at the lodge or to visit the Marine Interpretive Centre.

■ On Foot

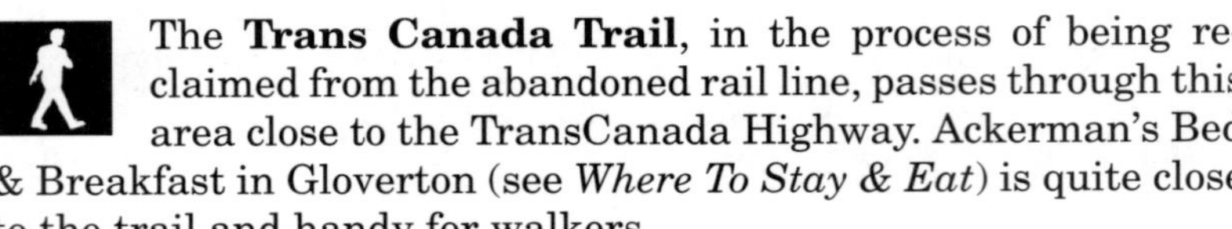

The **Trans Canada Trail**, in the process of being reclaimed from the abandoned rail line, passes through this area close to the TransCanada Highway. Ackerman's Bed & Breakfast in Gloverton (see *Where To Stay & Eat*) is quite close to the trail and handy for walkers.

Walking Tours

A road once connected the town of Winter Brook, on the northern shore of the Bonavista Peninsula, to the village of Sweet Bay, crossing a point of land that extends into the long reach of Sweet Bay. Replaced by the newer, but longer, Rte. 230, the road is now a walking path, with beautiful views across Sweet Bay.

In King's Cove, take Rte. 235 along the north shore of the Bonavista Peninsula and follow streets uphill until you come to **St. Peter's Church**, a big white building with an interesting history told on its sign. Park at the church and follow the old road along the ridge behind it. In August we counted over 30 varieties of wildflowers in bloom along this track in a 20-minute (one-way) walk to the lighthouse at its end. Along the path are also signs telling the history of Pat Murphy's Meadow (immortalized in a song by the McNultys) and of the home that once stood at the lighthouse.

From the tall, windswept cliff where the lighthouse stands you can see whales, icebergs and open sea, as well as the steep, irregular coast across Blackhead Bay, where collapsed sea caves have left great gouges in the cliffs.

Trails along the shore around Trinity are described in the little booklet *Welcome to Trinity Bight*, which you can get free at the information center in Trinity. Several lead from Trinity East, perhaps the best of them to a waterfall called **The Trussle**. Also from Trinity East you can climb for the view from the top of **Brown's Lookout**, or take the **Farm Pond Trail** past the pond to see the seabirds and view at **Sam White's Cove.**

From Port Rexton, you can walk around the harbor to **Bailey's Head**, then to Devil's Cove and Skiff Cove. The walk to Skerwink Point is longer, about an hour, past a changing series of sea views punctuated by whales.

We think a perfect walking trail should combine interesting terrain, good scenery, wildlife, history and a rewarding destination at the end, with an element of discovery. And when we get there, we don't want to find a crowd that came by car or a chairlift. It's a lot to ask of a single walk, and most trails fulfill only a few of these ideals. But in New Bonaventure, at the end of Rte. 239, close to Trinity, we found, on the advice of Lloyd Miller at the Riverside Lodge in Trouty, a trail that measures up on all counts. When we're far away and dream of Newfoundland, as we often do, **Kerley's Cove** is in the dream.

Park at the Anglican Church at the top of the hill, and take the trail leading downhill from the end of the parking lot. When it crosses the end of a freshwater lake, look back for views of the church. As you climb the ledged hill, think of the children who used this path every day, summer and winter, back and forth to school in Bonaventure. Just before a soggy area where you'll have to walk along the slanting ledge to keep your feet dry, look for the "devil's tracks" in the ledge. Only the older boys dared walk slowly here, and their stories scared the little kids into a dead run past it. Climb another hill and descend into the deep green vale and rock-bound harbor that was once the thriving outport of Kerley's Cove. The first foundation you'll see, with a rusting bedstead leaning against it, was the home of Lloyd Miller, now owner of the Riverside Lodge. There's no sign now of the Millers' fishing stage, but around the hill, deeper in the cove, are the remains of two or three others. Continue around, carefully, crossing the brook where moose often come to drink, to explore (very carefully) the high-rent district where the town's three "mansions" stood. You can see the last of them, its turret fallen over, but its decorative moldings and corner braces make it clear that it was the grandest home in town. You may meet, here or on the trail, a group of friendly horses who pasture on the grassy slopes.

Your enjoyment of this trail will be greatest if you've been a guest at the Riverside Lodge, and been lucky enough to find Lloyd Miller at home. Take your notebook, and he might draw you a map of the houses and flakes, and tell stories of the two separate Miller families that lived in many of the 25-30 homes that made up Kerley's Cove. His was one of the families resettled when the town was abandoned, but he grew up there and has a wealth of memories to share – how the bulk supplies came in the spring by schooner out of Catalina, and why nobody painted their house red.

Hiking Trails

An exciting project is underway on the Eastport Peninsula, where you can walk along the shore and over the headlands to reach a series of these abandoned fishing towns which were closed down by the Canadian government between 1950 and 1970. Local groups in the Eastport area have done a monumental job of reclaiming the old trails, disused for many years, and often overgrown. Begin walking the six-mile Heritage Trail at Crooked Tree Park in Sandy Cove or at the Salvage Fisherman's Museum at the other end. The trail council plans to have rides available for a reasonable fee to return you to your lodgings or to your car at the other end. When the entire project is completed, there will be an interpretation center at the Sandy Pond end of the trail.

The first segment is the **Ridge Trail**, running from Sandy Pond, overlooking a pond and Clay Cove, on the north side of the bay. At the end of this section is a stream with a waterfall. **The Ponds** continues up to a headland, passing another waterfall and some nice long views. **The Junipers** heads down through backcountry, over a rock face and past a beaver lodge in a pond. Each section of trail in turn brings different views and new terrain, as they cross a barren (once part of the ocean floor) and drop down into abandoned settlements. On the last leg, close to Salvage, the trail descends into a bog filled with pitcher plants. As the trail develops, it will have more interpretive signs telling about the history of the old settlements and the unusual geology of the headland. Hikers will learn what a droke is (a wooded area reserved for fishermen to select timbers for building and repairing their boats) and have a set of cards to help them identify the flora and fauna. It's an ambitious project, with a lot of energetic people involved in it; if you enjoy the trail and want to help, we know they'd appreciate your becoming a member, for a $10 donation. Lynn Stephan, at Laurel Cottage Bed & Breakfast, is active in the project, so if you are staying there, ask her for the latest developments.

Terra Nova National Park has more than 50 miles of hiking trails, described in a trail map book you can buy for $5.50 at the Park Visitors Centre. You can hike to some deserted fishing villages on the **Outport Trail** from the Newman Sound Campground, the park's longest trail at about 11 miles. You can hike portions of the trail by taking advantage of the regularly scheduled boat service that brings campers to the backcountry sites along the shore. The whole trail takes about six hours, allowing for stops to investigate the shore and enjoy the scenery. Along the trail are the mudflats of Newman Sound, boreal forests, the summit of Mt. Stamford, and the former outports of Minichins Pond and South Broad Cove. Mt. Stamford is on a mile-long side trail, but worth it for the views, which may include icebergs and/or whales.

Blue Hill Trail, under three miles long, begins at the Blue Hill Lookout Tower, and goes to a pond with a sandy beach. Glacial erratics and a graminoid fen (a type of bog with barely moving water) are interesting sights. To learn how the glacial erratics got to the park, take **Ochre Hill Trail**, a three-mile walk beginning at the Ochre Hill Lookout, where there are interpretive signs that explain the local geology and the work of the glaciers in forming the landscape.

■ On Wheels

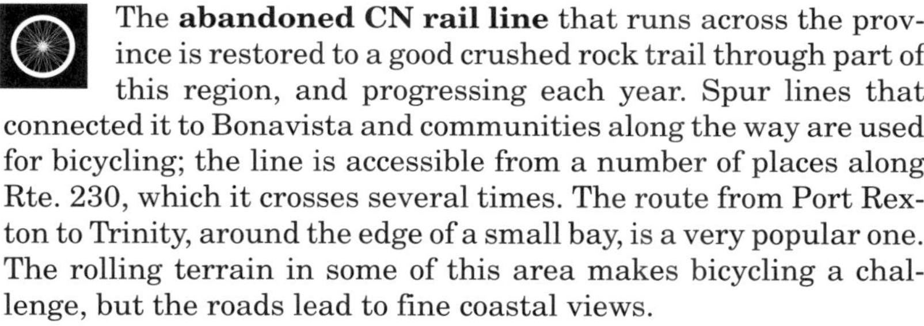

The **abandoned CN rail line** that runs across the province is restored to a good crushed rock trail through part of this region, and progressing each year. Spur lines that connected it to Bonavista and communities along the way are used for bicycling; the line is accessible from a number of places along Rte. 230, which it crosses several times. The route from Port Rexton to Trinity, around the edge of a small bay, is a very popular one. The rolling terrain in some of this area makes bicycling a challenge, but the roads lead to fine coastal views.

Bicycle Outfitters & Guided Tours

- Guests at **Campbell House** in Trinity, ☎ 709/464-3377, can rent mountain bikes to explore the area. You can also rent bikes from North East Treks, in Clarenville, ☎ 709/466-2036 or 709/466-3350.

- **Freewheeling Adventures** based in Hubbards, Nova Scotia, ☎ 902/857-3600, fax 902/857-3612, cycles the Trinity area on tours with a fixed base at Campbell House, whose owner is herself an avid cyclist. Each day's trip explores a different route on the Bonavista Peninsula. The trip costs $1,280 (including tax) per person, with $100 additional if you need to rent a bicycle. This trip is scheduled so you can combine it with their cycling tours of either the Burin Peninsula or the Viking Trail.

■ On Water

For your choice of secluded beaches, or a quiet lakeshore park, go to **Sandy Cove** on the Eastport Peninsula. Two beaches, one saltwater and one freshwater, share a parking area at Crooked Tree Park. If you follow the road back along the shore a bit, you'll find a walking trail along a ravine that leads to the other end of the Sandy Cove beach. Or you can walk there along the shore, choosing a spot of sand on the way. At the freshwater pond are changing facilities and picnic tables.

Lockston Path Provincial Park, on Rte. 236 in Port Rexton, has 56 campsites for both tents and RVs, with an unsupervised beach, boat launch and one-mile walking trail.

Canoeing & Kayaking

The deep arm where Trinity Bay lies seem made especially for kayaking, with protected waters and an irregular, interesting shoreline studded with points and abandoned outports, plus a few small islands. Sea caves are interesting to explore, but it's not wise to go inside these low-ceilinged ones, since a sudden swell could crash your head into the rocky ceiling without warning.

Terra Nova National Park has eight backcountry campsites accessible only by canoe. Four are on the wooded shore of Beachy Pond, four on Dunphy's Island. Five more sites on the shore of Dunphy's Pond can be reached by canoe or a three-mile trail. The four-mile length of Southwest Arm is calm, and takes between two and three hours to paddle; Sandy Pond and Dunphy's Pond are about a six-mile trip, and take about five hours, with a short (a quarter-mile) portage. You need a (free) permit to do this so park rangers will know you are out there.

Experienced paddlers can put in at Terra Nova Lake and follow the Terra Nova River to its mouth in Alexanders Bay (or take out at the river crossing of TransCanada-1). This course does not go through the National Park; Terra Nova Lake is in the town of Terra Nova, reached by the unpaved Rte. 301, which leaves TransCanada-1 about halfway through the park. With a portage of just under a mile, you can also make this trip from the ponds in the park, with a permit. Any of these are challenging trips and only for those with a lot of paddling experience. Rangers at the park headquarters can give you advice and information on water levels.

The waters inside the deep fjords of the park are calm and rarely even ruffled, making them good for beginners, but the shores are varied enough to keep anyone interested.

Canoe & Kayak Outfitters - Guided Tours

■ Random Island, which is bounded by North West Arm and Smith Sound at the southern end of the Bonavista Peninsula, is the destination for a two-day guided kayak adventure by **Eastern Edge Outfitters** in Paradise, ☎ 709/782-1465. Instruction is included, as is all equipment, so the trip is suitable for beginners as well as experienced paddlers. Random Island is carved with bays and sheltered inlets, so the waters are fairly calm under the towering cliffs where eagles are a common sight. All along this coast are abandoned outports that were thriving communities until the resettlement program moved their residents elsewhere. The campsite is near one of these, so you'll have a chance to explore its cellar holes and overgrown cemeteries. The third day of the trip moves to the Avalon coast to paddle in the bird sanctuary and visit another outport nearby. The cost of this trip, including transportation, equipment, meals and one night's lodging in a B&B, is $500.

■ You can explore the shoreline of Trinity Bay for a day or at leisure with **North East Treks** in Clarenville, ☎ 709/466-2036 or 709/466-3350. Rent a sea kayak for an hour or a day, or join a guided trip (the best idea if you don't know the waters) for a full day for $125, including equipment and lunch. Instruction is included, so the trips are suitable for beginners. Longer trips, from one to five days, include camping and all meals. In May and June, icebergs are the focus of trips into some of the best iceberg waters anywhere. In July, August and September, interpreters/guides take you where the sea life is, to watch three varieties of whales and two of dolphins, as well as the seabirds that also follow the return of the fish. Also in the summer, you can sign on for a five-day exploration of Smith Sound, and the islands that dot it. The first and last days are spent traveling to the sound on board a yacht, the three middle days are spent in kayaks, exploring the coastline from an island base-camp. The rate is $485 per person. **North East Treks** also rents canoes, and has designed three-day canoe adventures to introduce you to three different Newfoundland environments. On day trips, based at their own B&B in Clarenville, guides take you canoeing along the coast, through the boreal forests and in the barrens. If you prefer, you can camp out one of the nights. The rate is about $100 a day, and the trip is offered only twice each season.

■ You can rent canoes and kayaks at the concession at Sandy Pond in **Terra Nova National Park** or launch your own canoe there, ☎ 709/677-2221.

Boat Tours

Sailing from Bonavista around the cape and into Trinity Bay, you get stunning views of the lighthouse and the dramatic headlands with **Landfall Boat Tours**, ☎ 709/468-2744, fax 709/468-1278. Two-hour trips leave three times a day.

Visitors get a greater feel for life in the days of sail, when Trinity was an important commercial center, by exploring its waters under sail with **Atlantic Adventures** at Trinity Wharf, ☎ 709/464-3738. The owners of the nearby Peace Cove Inn run nature and history cruises aboard a 46-foot sailboat, which often sails right alongside whales. Other adventures on his sailboat/motor cruiser include exploring deserted outports, looking for fossils, and watching for seals, eagles and other birds.

The cruiser ***Willing Mind*** strikes a nice blend between the two things Trinity and its waters have the most of: history and wildlife. Whales, eagles, kittiwakes and guillemots are everyday sights in Trinity Bay, and passengers can enjoy seeing them as they learn the rich lore of the area with photo-CD technology to show them pictures and maps of the area as it once was. Tours of outports left to time's ravages mean more with a look at what they looked like a few decades ago as thriving fishing settlements. Several tour are scheduled each day. Contact **Historical Harbour Boat Tours**, Trinity, ☎ 709/464-3355.

From Southport, at the point where Random Sound meets Trinity Bay, you can tour abandoned outports, see the hundreds of rock carvings left by a ship's crew in the 1700s, visit a lighthouse and watch the puffins at Duck Island with **Southport Adventure Boat Tours**, ☎ 709/548-2248, fax 709/548-2580. This little-explored region is filled with surprises, including the wrecks of fishing vessels at the former community of Loreburn. On either tour you'll see bald eagles that nest on the cliffs of Southwest Arm.

Three tours leave each day, May through September, weather willing, and cost $25 and $30, depending on which route you choose. The two routes are so different that you may choose to take both and make a day of it. You can add a night in their village B&B for $35.

On Smith Sound, which separates Random Island from the Bonavista Peninsula, you can explore the abandoned outports and look for eagles, ospreys and whales with **Random Island Charter Boats** in Peltey, ☎ 709/547-2369, fax 709/547-2348.

In Terra Nova National Park, **Ocean Watch Tours,** Saltons Wharf, ☎ 709/533-6024, runs several tours daily, from mid-May through October, at $19-$26. They combine sightseeing, whale-watching, fishing and watching for bald eagles. On any of these cruises you're likely to see icebergs in the spring and early summer. Trips along the coastal fjords are 2½ hours, ocean watch expeditions run three hours, and sunset cruises to visit an outport last two hours. Their boat, the *MV Northern Fulmar*, takes passengers to the isolated campsites and provides a hiker/camper ferry service. They will drop you off at a back-country site after your tour if you are camped there or want to hike back.

A ferry connects Burnside, on the Eastport Peninsula, to **St. Brendan's Island**, one of the few ferry-connected islands left after the resettlement of the outport communities. The island is well worth visiting; fare is $13.50 for car and driver ($7 if the driver is a senior), plus $4.50 for each adult and $2.50 for children and students. The crossing is 45 minutes and the ferry makes five daily round-trips in the summer, three in the winter. The island is a mini-Ireland, with accents redolent of the Auld Sod. It's hilly, barren and covered with boggy ponds and scrubby trees, and has about 350 residents. Ask anyone in town for directions to the home of **Mr. Beresford**, who builds scale models of sailing schooners and who loves visitors. He can't hear what you say, but you will enjoy listening to him.

Windsurfing

Near Clarenville, you can launch from the public wharf at **Shoal Harbour**, and on the Eastport peninsula there is excellent windsurfing at **Sandy Cove** and **Eastport Beach**.

Fishing

A one-day trout fishing fee in **Terra Nova National Park** is $4.50, $6.50 for a seven-day permit and $14.25 annually. Salmon fishing fees vary, as does the season, if it is open at all; Northwest River is the only scheduled salmon river in the park. All other waters are closed to salmon fishing. Fishing with artificial flies, bait and spinners is allowed in most ponds in the park; lead sinkers, jigs and weights are strictly prohibited.

■ On Snow

Terra Nova National Park is open in the winter for camping, with some enclosed, winterized kitchen shelters at Newman Sound Campground, Sandy Pond and Southwest Arm, where fires are permitted. One section of Newman Sound Campground is kept open and has heated washrooms and hot water. After mid-October there are no campground fees. The Administration Building in the center of the park is open year-round on weekdays, 8 am to 4:30 pm. Ice fishing is allowed on Big Pond and Dunphy's Pond, with a park fishing permit.

Skiing

Terra Nova National Park has groomed ski trails, and there's a ski shop in winter at Terra Nova Park Lodge. The lodge is open year-round and offers winter packages for skiers, ☎ 709/543-2535 (for reservations) or ☎ 709/543-2525 (for information). For trail conditions, ☎ 709/533-2801.

The park's side roads, which are not plowed in the winter, make very good ski trails, especially those to Ochre Hill Blue Hill, Sandy Pond and Salton's Beach. Dunphy's Pond Trail is a particularly good one, and leads directly from the main highway, not far from its southern boundary. Close to Terra Nova Lodge, the golf courses offer good skiing and open landscapes overlooking the water (or ice). At low-snow times, this route may be closed, so check at the lodge or headquarters before using it.

The **Clarenville Ski Club**, ☎ 709/466-1412, maintains 30 miles of cross-country trails, 15 of which are groomed. They can also provide beginners with lessons in cross-country skiing. A small downhill ski area in Clarenville has a vertical drop of 600 feet, with 16 runs.

Snowmobiling

The abandoned CN rail line that runs across the province is in the process of being reclaimed as part of the TransCanada Trail, and in this area it is already in use as a snowmobile trail. On

TransCanada-1 in Port Blanford near the intersection of Rte. 233, **Terra Nova Hospitality Home and Cabins**, ☎ 709/543-2260, fax 709/543-2241, has trails connecting to the old rail line. The whole area is webbed with snowmobile trails, and the owners of the lodge can give you good advice and directions for scenic rides. You can rent snowmobiles at **Wiseman's Sports** in Clarenville, which is connected to Port Blanford by the old rail line around Thornburn Lake.

On the peninsula, the spur line leading to Bonavista is a popular route for snowmobilers; you can go from Trinity right into Clarenville, where it connects to the TransCanada Trail.

The **Heritage Trail** system from Sandy Cove to Salvage is designed for use by snowmobilers; look for trail markers with a cluster of red berries in the winter (the summer hiking trails are marked with a white flower).

On Horseback

Ride Away Trails offers overnight trail rides with a guide, barbecue, campfire and camping. Rides leave from the Splash-N-Putt Resort (we didn't name it) on TransCanada-1 at Eastport Jct., ☎ 709/533-2541. They also offer trail rides as short as one hour, daytrips and multi-day trips. Trail rides are $13 for one hour, $60 for a day (with lunch), overnight $100, weekends $200. Tents are provided, but you will need to bring your own sleeping bag on overnight trips.

You can arrange to tour the village of Eastport and the area by horse and buggy at **Pingent Bed and Breakfast**, 17 Church St. in Eastport, ☎ 709/677-3021.

Cultural & Eco-Travel Experiences

Although dramatic sea caves and arches are not unusual along the coast, most of them are inaccessible or very difficult to see, under the cliffs of points and headlands too dangerous to approach even by boat. A happy exception is the **sea arch** at Tickle Cove, a tiny settlement at the end of a road off Rte. 235 in Plate Cove East, on the northern shore of the Bonavista Peninsula. The whole point is not only very beautiful, but a geologist's playground. On the way to Tickle Cove you pass through Red

Cliff, a fishing settlement set entirely on ledges of a deep burgundy red. Honest.

At Tickle Cove the rocks change colors from one cliff to the next, and are broken and worn into shapes. Just before a little bridge, turn left (there may be a little hand-painted sign to "The Arch") and continue between houses until you reach an impasse in someone's backyard. There's room to park. Walk toward the headland to your left, following the trail and climbing over the rocky spine (another sign may encourage you here). Watch the rock colors, as a stripe of green rock cuts through the red. The arch is in the headwall in front of you; just as interesting is the little cove to your right, where the sea has worn the ledges under your feet into fantastic convoluted shapes and patterns. True beachcombers will return with their pockets sagging with beautifully colored water-smoothed rocks from this cobble cove.

The best-known coastal formation on the peninsula is **The Dungeon**, close to Cape Bonavista Lighthouse in Bonavista. This enormous sinkhole with two giant arches, was formed when the sea undercut a layer of soft rock while pillars of hard rock remained. A sturdy wooden platform makes viewing safe and signs explain how the hole was formed, with interesting drawings showing how it looked at each stage and how it will look as the sea continues to wear away the stone. The views of the headlands from this high ridge are splendid.

Terra Nova National Park has a daily **Junior Naturalist Program** which gives children hands-on experiences and lively lessons on the environment. These programs are free, and may include puppet shows, or a chance to inspect insects at close range. Evening programs for the entire family are also free, and may focus on a particular native animal, forest fires, sea creatures or the human history of the park lands. Guided walks with a naturalist are $2 for adults, $1 for ages 6-16, $5 for a family.

On the Eastport Peninsula, the **Burnside Project** is an archaeological dig excavating an early Paleoeskimo site, rare in Newfoundland. They have already uncovered over 2,000 artifacts at the stone quarry and learned that the Beothuk settlement there was built on top of an earlier Paleoeskimo one. The arrowheads and stone tools recovered, dating back 5,000 years, have provided the best evidence yet discovered on the advance of technology among the stone-age peoples in Newfoundland. You can take a 20-minute boat ride to the sites at 1 pm on summer weekdays, when the dig is in progress. Be prepared for a steep climb from the landing to the quarry. Artifacts from the site are displayed at the small museum and interpretive center at Burnside, where exhibits and guides explain the site, the finds, and the human and natural history of the area, ☎ 709/677-2474. The museum is open Monday-Friday, 10 am to 8 pm, Saturday-Sunday, noon to 6 pm, June through August. It's free, but like all research programs, they welcome your donation. The museum is six miles north of Burnside.

Wildlife-Watching

For up-close-and-personal whale encounters, sail with **Atlantic Adventures**, Trinity Wharf, ☎ 709/464-3738. On their nature and history cruises aboard a sailboat, you are likely to see a wide variety of birds, too, including bald eagles. See *Boat Tours*, above; any travel by water is likely to be a whale-watching or birding experience.

The park transport boat, *MV Northern Fulmar*, takes passengers on cruises to view the coastal scenery and discover marine life in the sea. Their **Ocean Watch Expedition** (☎ 709/533-6024) is more than sightseeing, with a chance to take part in whatever research project is underway. Whales and icebergs are often part of the experience. Sunset cruises travel along the coast to outports, stopping to see bald eagles on the way.

One of the best vehicles for watching sea life is the almost silent kayak, and the waters of Trinity Bay are filled with interesting creatures you can learn more about on a guided kayak tour with **North East Treks** in Clarenville, ☎ 709/466-2036 or 709/466-3350. From July through September you can expect to see humpback, minke and fin whales, and white nosed and white sided dolphins. Puffins fly within feet of your kayak, then dive and swim for awhile before taking flight again; you are certain to see guillemots and most likely eagles, too.

On Rte. 230 in Lethbridge, the Wildlife Division maintains an interesting **Wildlife Interpretive Centre**, ☎ 709/467-5800. Its displays address environmental issues and have mounted specimens (all victims of accidents) and good bird models by a local conservation officer, Len Penney. Although the models at the center are not for sale, Len lives in nearby Summerville, and you can arrange to see and buy others, ☎ 709/462-3416. The center is a good source of information on wildlife in the area.

In Terra Nova National Park, the **Marine Interpretation Centre** at Saltons Day Use Area is open daily, 9 am to 9 pm, June through August; shorter hours in September and October. Admission is $1.25. Interactive displays explain the dynamics of the sea and its creatures.

Sightseeing

Hiscock House in Trinity, ☎ 709/464-2042, has been restored to its original 1910 appearance. Displays show the everyday family life of a hardworking woman who raised six children after her 39-year-old husband drowned in 1893. It is free, and open daily, 10 am to 5:30 pm, June through mid-October.

The 200-year-old **Green Family Forge**, ☎ 709/464-3720, is open daily, 10 am to 5:30 pm, mid-June through mid-September, with an admission fee of $2.

Perhaps the most remarkable building is the newly reconstructed **Lester-Garland House and Premises,** ☎ 709/464-2042. Only a few years ago it was a ruin, consisting of a low stone foundation and a portion of a tumbled brick chimney. Today it is an elegant mansion, with fine wood floors, and only the kitchen, where the remnants of the chimney once stood, shows its long road to recovery. There you can see the archaeology of the house in cutaway segments. The house has many pieces of the family's original furniture, which was tracked down in England, including a mahogany table made from a log found floating in the sea by a local ship, off the coast of Portugal. The house is open daily, 10 am to 6 pm, mid-June through mid-October, and is free.

Next door is the reconstructed **Ryan Building,** which was, from the late 16th century to 1952, an accounting office, warehouse and general store. The store shows the merchandise available in a commercial port the size of Trinity. It is free, and open daily, 10 am to 5:30 pm, June through mid-October.

In the early 19th-century **Tibbs House**, you'll find the Trinity Interpretation Center, with excellent displays combining early documents, photographs and artifacts to explain the town's history. If you plan to hike to the outport towns, notice the large display showing their locations. Ask for a copy of the booklet *Welcome to Trinity Bight*, with history, things to see, and suggestions for walks.

An unusual drama with a cast of actors portraying moments in village history is the **Trinity Pageant**, Interpretation Center, ☎ 709/464-3232. It's held Wednesday, Saturday, and Sunday at 2 pm in July and August, donation $5. The audience walks around town with the characters, and local places provide the stage sets.

Beyond Trinity on the Bonavista Peninsula, roads to Little Catalina and Maberley, a short detour off Rte. 230, take you to **Arch Rock** and other dramatic cliffs.

In Bonavista, go all the way to **Cape Bonavista Lighthouse,** ☎ 709/468-7444. One of Canada's oldest, It was built in 1843, and has historic displays. Like most lighthouses it's on a point overlooking the sea, so the views are splendid. Admission is free and it's open daily, 10 am to 5:30 pm, mid-June through mid-October.

On the waterfront, look for **Ryan Premises National Historic Site** on Old Catalina Rd, ☎ 709/772-5364, open 10 am to 6 pm daily, mid-June through mid-October; free. The premises includes a restored 19th-century residence, shop, fish shed, store and carriage shed. Daily programs explore the history of the fisheries and the lives of the families associated with it, using live theater, interpreters, and demonstrations of early crafts.

In the fishing village of **Salvage** on the Eastport peninsula, visit the **Fisherman's Museum,** ☎ 709/677-2609. It's on a hill overlooking the harbor, and has old fishing equipment, household utensils and photographs of the outports that lie beyond Salvage. It also has one of the unique step-back wood stoves once common here. It's open daily, 9:30 am to 7:30 pm, mid-June through August. Admission is $1.

The village of Salvage is well worth seeing even if the museum isn't open, since it clings to the sides of steep hills and rocks that surround a harbor. No matter where you stand, there's a view of the harbor, wharves, boats, red fishing sheds and square white houses. It still has an active fishing fleet.

For a different kind of wheeled travel, **Trinity Loop Fun Park and Railway Village** in Trinity East is a nicely done amusement park with a miniature train ride around the historic train loop, used by early trains to descend the steep hillside from the hills to the shore village. We don't normally suggest amusement parks, but this one does preserve a fascinating bit of local railroad history. The park is open daily from 10 am to 7 pm, the railway museum from noon to 7pm, ☎ 709/464-2171. Admission to the park is $2.50 adults, $2 for seniors and children under 12.

Where To Stay & Eat

On the Bonavista Peninsula

Although they are both very small (two and three rooms respectively), two B&Bs are conveniently located in the town of Bonavista, about a mile from the Ryan Premises, on the way to the lighthouse, which is less than two miles. Walkers could easily explore the town and the scenic point from either of them: **Abbott's Cape Shore B&B**, *PO Box 689, Bonavista, NF A0C 1B0,* ☎ *709/468-7103 ($)*, and **White's Bed and Breakfast**, *21 Windlass Dr. (Box 323), Bonavista, NF A0C 1B0,* ☎ *709/468-7018 ($-$$)*. White's rents bicycles.

The owners of Southport Adventure Boat Tours also welcome travelers to their homey **By the Pond Bed and Breakfast**. There are two comfortable rooms and a patio, in a small fishing village. What could be more relaxing? *Southport, Trinity Bay, NF A0E 2A0,* ☎ *709/548-2248, fax 709/548-2580 ($).*

Campbell House is in the village and within an easy walk to everything. This beautifully restored 1840 home is set in an authentically restored outport garden. Coffee and tea are always available, and you can rent mountain bikes. The owner can give you good advice on cycling routes and walking trails. A tidy two-bedroom cottage on the shore has a kitchen and a porch overlooking the fishing wharves. Open late May through mid-October. *Trinity, NF A0C 2H0,* ☎ *709/464-3377, off-season 24 Circular Rd, St. John's, NF A1C 2Z1,* ☎ *709/753-8945 ($$).*

Peace Cove Inn is also open late May through mid-October. It's located in a small settlement in a turn-of-the-century home, and has a warm, homey atmosphere. They serve family-style meals at moderate prices. A small apartment is good for families. *Trinity East, NF, A0C 2H0,* ☎ *709/454-3738 or 709/464-3419, off-season 709/781-2255 ($$).*

If you seek blessed sleep, try the bed in which Newfoundland's first Anglican bishop slept, at **Bishop White Manor** in Trinity. The home is a fine example of the architecture of Trinity at its peak, when it was the capital of the fisheries and of trade and commerce. It's a rare chance to stay in a fine home from the early 1800s. *Trinity,* ☎ *709/464-3299 ($$).*

Riverside Lodge is open April through October and overlooks the long, narrow harbour of a tiny fishing village only four miles from Trinity. You should eat here at least once, since Annette Miller's homecooked meals of fresh-caught cod or salmon are legendary, not to mention generous. Meals are served daily at 7 pm. Rooms are homey and comfortable. Lloyd Miller can tell you a lot about the abandoned outport towns; he grew up in one. *Box 9, Trouty, NFA0C 2S0, ☎ 709/464-3780 ($).*

For a nice blend of modern menu and old favorites of local kitchens, go to **Old Trinity Cookery**. Local dishes include pea soup, cod prepared in a variety of ways, and baked apples filled with wild blueberries. They serve three meals a day in the summer and you can bring your own wine. *Trinity, ☎ 709/464-3615 ($$).*

Dock Marina Restaurant charbroils steak and serves chicken and ribs along with traditional Newfie favorites, and the dock setting provides good scenery to go with your meal. *Trinity Wharf, ☎ 709/464-2133 ($$).*

Coopers, near the Trinity turn-off, is a plain, friendly restaurant, and the place to try a local favorite, fried cod tongues ($7.95). They stay open until 11 pm, which is good to know if you arrive in town late. *Rte. 230, ☎ 902/875-4656 ($).*

For a pick-me-up, breakfast or lunch, go to **Trinity Bake Shop**. The chili is filled with meat, the sandwiches are on fresh-baked bread and the cookies are delicious (we know, we've sampled every kind). *In Trouty, ☎ 709/464-3777.*

In the Terra Nova Area

Near the intersection of Rte. 233 is **Terra Nova Hospitality Home and Cabins**. The newly-built lodge and its tidy row of housekeeping cabins are nicely furnished. Home-cooked meals are available ($15 for a full salmon dinner), with advance notice, in a bright common area with a cathedral ceiling. A full breakfast is included in the room rate, even for those with housekeeping cabins. The cabins have whirlpool baths, and there's a sauna in the main lodge. *TransCanada-1, Port Blanford, NF A0C 2G0, ☎ 709/543-2260, fax 709/543-2241 ($$).*

The Trans Canada Trail, in the process of being reclaimed from the abandoned rail line, passes through this area close to the Trans-

Canada Highway. **Ackerman's Bed & Breakfast** is quite close to the trail and handy for walkers. *In Gloverton, ☎ 709/533-2810.*

Inside the park, you'll find modern hotel rooms and well-equipped efficiencies at **Terra Nova Park Lodge**. A full-service resort overlooking the golf course, the lodge is a lively place, well designed for families. All rooms have extra beds, and there is a heated outdoor pool. **Mulligan's Pub** ($-$$) serves light meals and the **Clode Sound Dining Room** ($-$$) overlooking the golf-course serves lunch and dinner, with a menu of wild game and seafood. *Port Blanford, NF A0C 2G0, ☎ 709/543-2535 (for reservations) or 709/543-2525 (for information) ($$).*

A B&B doesn't have to be in a century-old home to be warm, inviting and a pleasure to come home to, as proven by the lovely **Laurel Cottage**. Rooms are thoughtfully furnished and decorated with hand-painted walls. Bathrooms are positively luxurious. A full breakfast with homebaked breads and jams of local wild berries is served on fine china, in a dining room that overlooks gardens. But for all its decorator magazine look, it's just like popping into a friend's house. *41 Bank Rd, Eastport NF A0G 1Z0, ☎ 709/677-3138 ($-$$).*

Pingent Bed and Breakfast has attractive, comfortable rooms in the village. The owner's art studio is next door. *17 Church St, Eastport, NF A0G 1Z0, ☎ 709/677-3021 ($).*

Little Dernier Restaurant has a good selection of nicely prepared dishes, served in a brand new glass-enclosed dining room. Their partridgeberry tarts are a treat. *Eastport, NF, ☎ 709/677-3663 ($).*

■ Camping

In Terra Nova National Park, **Newman Sound Campground** has 417 tent and RV sites, showers, laundry facilities, and a store. The more rustic **Malady Head Campground** has 153 sites for tents only. Particularly attractive to adventure travelers are the park's backcountry campsites. Without road access, they can be reached by hiking trails, or by a scheduled ferry service. Two are in abandoned outports, once-thriving villages reached only by sea or on foot. More backcountry sites are set around **Beachy** and **Dunphy's Ponds** and on **Dun-**

phy's Island, and are accessible only by canoe or hiking trail (Dunphy's Pond only). All campers must pay the daily park entrance fee in addition to the campground fee, which is $14-$16 a night for Newman Sound and $12 for Malady Head. Weekly rates save the cost of one day out of seven. Primitive backcountry sites are $8, for a maximum of four persons in a site. *Reservations are accepted for campsites, ☎ 709/533-2801.*

Lockston Path Provincial Park has 55 campsites with an unsupervised swimming beach. Open mid-May through mid-October). *Rte. 236, Port Rexton, ☎ 800/866-CAMP.*

Putt-N-Paddle is the new name of the old and well-loved Jack's Pond Provincial Park, at the very top of the isthmus leading to the Avalon. Campsites are well kept, some open, some under trees, some on the lake, all $10 a night. The beach is free for day use (unlike most parks, which charge admission for the beach), and has boats for rent. They do not accept reservations. The park adjoins a three-mile stretch of the old Cabot Highway, which is now used as a walking and cycling trail. *At Arnold's Cove; no phone.*

The Burin Peninsula

Travelers tend to ignore the Burin or treat it only as a route to the "exotic" French islands (where, we have to admit, the wine is good). They should spend more time here, stopping to look at its tiny villages along the sea and explore its moor-covered headlands. It *is* a long way down to the foot of the peninsula, where the action is. But the road never seems monotonous, with a good chance of seeing caribou wandering among the stone outcrops and glacial debris that dot its slopes. The drive is especially beautiful in the fall, when the bogs turn a deep red.

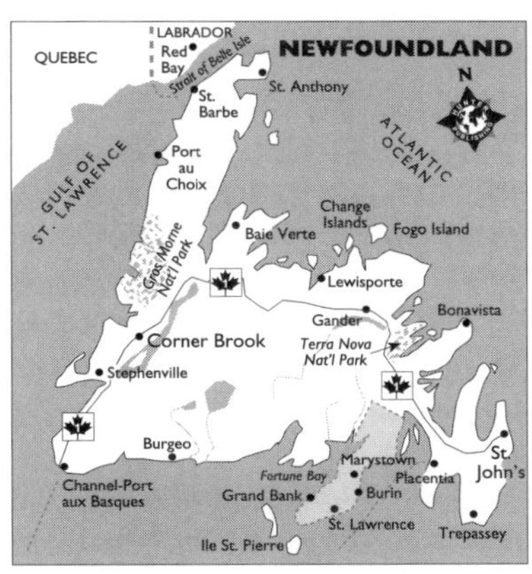

Geography & History

On a map, the Burin always reminds us of the hind foot of a snowshoe hare. Its main (and only, most of the way) road runs along a high plateau, through wilderness barrens of high bogs and stunted trees. A few side roads lead to tiny fishing villages, two of which have ferries to outports.

If architecture in Grand Banks, one of the Burin's two main commercial centers, looks a bit more like New England than Newfoundland, it's because the captains and fishing families here had more contact with Boston than with St. John's, beginning in the 1500s, when fishing started here, until this century. The first record of year-round settlement in Grand Bank is from the 1600s when the French controlled the Burin. They lost it in 1713, and 50 years later lost it permanently in a treaty that left them only the tiny base at St. Pierre and Miquelon, within sight off the west coast. The area's economic heights began in the 1880s, and until 1940 it was the undisputed capital of the Newfoundland banks fishery.

Getting Around

Rte. 210 travels almost due southwest from TransCanada-1, which it leaves about seven miles north of Sunnyside, until it reaches Marystown, nearly 100 miles away. Below Marystown the roads divide, with Rte. 220 circling the end of the peninsula, a trip we heartily recommend for its scenery. Rte. 210 continues on to Grand Bank. Although it is less centrally located, we prefer Grand Bank, with its main business streets along the busy harbor, as a headquarters on the peninsula.

To give you some idea of the distances, it would take about 2½ hours to drive around the base of the Burin from Grand Bank to Marystown if you didn't stop at all, which you certainly will (or you wouldn't have chosen this guidebook).

From the village of **Fortune**, almost in the backyard of Grand Bank, you can make a 70-minute crossing to St-Pierre, a department of France, which you can see from the end of the peninsula. You need reservations on the ferry, which you may be able to get only if you make lodging reservations on the island at the same time (both are handled by the same travel agency and they like to sell packages). You cannot take a car to St-Pierre, but you can rent bicycles on the island or tour in a bus or taxi.

Ferries can take you from St-Pierre to the larger island of Miquelon and the other smaller islands. To reserve on the passenger ferry, contact **St-Pierre Tours** in Fortune, ☎ 709/832-0429, or in St. John's at ☎ 709/722-3892. The ferry leaves daily at 9 am and returns at 4:30 in July and August, less often the rest of the year. The fare is $47 for adults, $27 children.

Fishing flakes, Burin Peninsula.

Information Sources

- Information on the Burin is included in the "Eastern Region" section of the annual *Newfoundland and Labrador Travel Guide*, free from the **Department of Tourism, Culture and Recreation**, PO Box 8730, St. John's, NF A1B 4K2, ☎ 800/563-6353 or 709/729-2830.

- You can get more specific information on the Burin from **Marystown Visitor Information Center**, PO Box 757, Marystown NF A0E 2M0, ☎ 709/279-1211. It's easy to spot, in a little lighthouse-shaped building on Rte. 210, north of Marystown, open daily from 9 am to 6 pm, mid-June through August. The staff there couldn't possibly be nicer, and we have found them particularly helpful in tracking down obscure waterfalls and places the average tourist doesn't ask about.

- For information on the French islands, contact **Agence Regionale du Tourisme**, Place du General de Gaulle, BP 4274-97500 St-Pierre, ☎ 508/41 22 22 or 800/565-5118, fax 508/41 33 55. It's open daily, 9 am to 6 pm, June through

August, and Monday-Friday, 9 am to noon and 2 to 6 pm, September through May.

Adventures

■ On Foot

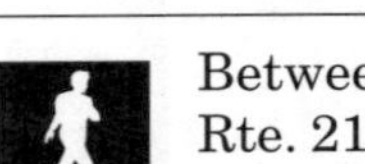

Between Marystown and Grand Bank Rte. 213 loops off Rte. 210, leading to the town of Garnish, where you'll find several walking trails. About two miles from the turn-off, near the elementary school, look for a sign for the **Long Ridge Hiking Trail**, which gives some nice views over the beaches and the open, unsettled moors. If you follow the road along the shore to the right, to the end of the town, you will find the lane leading to the old Point Rosie lighthouse. It's passable only to four-wheel-drive vehicles, but it makes a nice walking trail. Other trails lead to Deep Water Point and Mount Serat. Ask at the Community Centre on the waterfront for trail information; there's talk of preparing a map of these paths.

In the handy *Grand Bank Visitors Guide* and in the also-free *Heritage Walk* brochure, you'll find a one-mile tour of the town, with descriptions of the several good examples of Queen Anne architecture that line its streets. You will also see examples of the commercial buildings, or "premises" common to seafaring towns in Newfoundland.

A three-mile trail across **Grand Bank Head** leaves Grand Bank from Christian Road, at the far west end of town, or you can begin at the recreation complex next to the high school off Main St. The trail crosses the barachois at the end of Admiral's Cove Pond, then climbs the headland. Follow the trail to L'Anse aux Paul Rd., at the end of the beach, then follow the highway back to town – or return on the same path for a different set of views over Fortune Bay.

In St. Lawrence, leave the main road to find **Herring Cove**, tucked under the hillside north of town (Water St. East leads along the left side of the harbor from the center of town). This tiny cove has two fishing stages above a red sand beach, and the unusual **Umbrella Tree**, with picnic tables on a mowed hillside. A trail leads over a little bridge and climbs to **Calapouse Head**, for excellent views over the two narrow coves that surround the head.

Serious hikers with a head for heights might want to take the trail from **Rushoon to Red Harbour**, a mere six miles as the crow flies. On a long point, reached only by ferry from Petit Forte, you can hike across the tip from South East Bight to Great or Little Paradise, both outports that are still very much alive.

➔ **HIKING TRAILS IN BURIN:** *In the town of Burin, trails to several outports are often steep as they climb over the precipitous headlands, but the scenery is outstanding. There are, as yet, no trail maps, and the paths aren't marked, but if you ask at the* ***Burin Heritage House****, ☎ 709/891-2217, someone can draw you maps or give you directions.*

■ On Wheels

The lower end of the Burin is circled by the gently rolling Rte. 220. Never long out of sight of the sea, it runs along a low coast of moorland that rises in places, especially along the eastern end, to more dramatic headlands with offshore islands. Small side roads lead to little harbors and beaches, through expanses of green bog, dotted with the bright red blossoms of the pitcher plant. In the fall the foliage of many of these bog plants turns red. Because the landscape is moorland with few trees, vistas are broad, and for much of the way you can see the island of St. Pierre, so close you can distinguish individual houses. It's fun to go home and tell your friends that you were bicycling within sight of France. Or you can take your bike over on the ferry and tell them you went cycling on the French islands.

Among the features of this area that make it so pleasant to bicycle through are the everyday touches of local life that you might not notice from a car, such as the fishnets hanging to dry along the guard rails.

Guided Bicycle Tours

■ **Freewheeling Adventures** based in Hubbards, Nova Scotia, ☎ 902/857-3600, fax 902/857-3612, offers a five-day tour, with three days cycling the Burin from Goobies on TransCanada-1 to Fortune, and a day spent cycling on Miquelon. This all-inclusive van-supported trip costs $1,265 (including tax) per person, with $100 additional for bike rental if you don't bring your own.

■ On Water

Canoeing & Kayaking

The Narrows and the Creston Inlet in Marystown are good canoeing waters. You can rent canoes from **Stage Head Tours and Rentals** in Marystown, ☎ 709/279-2214. They are located on the north side of the Canning Bridge.

Boat Tours & Ferries

Ferries run from Petit Forte to South East Bight on the east side of the peninsula, and from Terrenceville to Rencontre East, on the west. This ferry is the first in a series that link the outports along the south coast to road links in the Burin, Harbour Breton, Burgeo and Port-aux-Basques. For many towns this ferry is the only access. Unfortunately, it does not carry cars, so it is not helpful to travelers who must explore each of the four roads to the south coast separately on a go-and-return route.

Woody Island lies just off the coast, tucked into the corner where the Burin leaves the mainland. You can take a relaxing two-day trip there with **Island Rendezvous**, 14 Westminster Dr., Woody Island, NF A1N 4N1, ☎ 709/364-3701 or 800/504-1066, fax 709/364-3701. The boat that takes you from the mainland also takes you on a tour around the island the next day. Woody Island was resettled, its residents moved elsewhere, its communities left to the weather and the sea. You can explore the old burial grounds, cellar holes and harbors, picnic on the beaches, and enjoy the scenic trails at leisure, staying in a B&B with all meals included. The experience here is a good one for several couples or families to share, since it includes a shore-side campfire with Newfoundland music and other sociable activities.

Two-hour (or longer) tours on a boat with open or enclosed deck, are offered in Marystown by **Stage Head Tours and Rentals**, ☎ 709/279-2214. Tours of the long harbor and inlet (with a good look at the resident seal family) are in the morning. Afternoon bay tours visit communities along the shore. Environmental tours are especially planned with children in mind, with a chance to haul a lobster trap, catch creatures from the sea bottom and look at the sea floor with a "bottom looker." An evening tour includes a barbecue on board. Stage Head will also drop you and your gear off at a secluded beach where you can spend the day or camp overnight. Their dock is on the north side of the Canning Bridge.

Windsurfing

The fresh waters of Golden Sands Park, a private recreation park in Marystown, about a 30-minute drive from Grand Bank, are some of the province's best for windsurfing. South of Grand Bank, overlooking the islands of St. Pierre and Miquelon, Point May has a pebble beach, from which you can sail in the swells of the open strait between Fortune Bay and the Atlantic. For information on windsurfing events, including the annual Golden Sands Weekend when the Breakers Club in St. John's travels to the Burin, call **George Hodder** at ☎ 709/891-1524.

Diving

Stage Head Tours and Rentals at the Canning Bridge in Marystown, is equipped to bring scuba divers to several good dive sites with excellent visibility, ☎ 709/279-5050.

Fishing

A scheduled salmon river runs through **Grand Bank**, and the Garnish and Salmonier Rivers in the same area are also salmon fishing areas. On the east coast, **Red Harbour** is known for salmon fishing.

Cultural & Eco-Travel Experiences

The Burin Peninsula **Festival of Folk Song and Dance** is held each year in early July in Burin, and other traditional song and dance programs are held throughout the summer at the outdoor stage at Heritage Square in Burin. Garish's Bakeapple Festival is in mid-August and, as you may have learned by now, has nothing to do with apples. This is the local name for the hard-to-pick orange berry of the northern bogs, called cloudberry elsewhere. Look at local calendars for church and community-sponsored events, such as "Jiggs Dinners" (corned beef and cabbage), pea soup suppers, local "Come Home Year" events and Canada Day (July 1) celebrations. And, if you can get a space on the boat, go to St. Pierre for the Bastille Day fêtes on July 14.

LOCAL PRODUCTS: *Peat and kelp are products of the area around Lamaline, on the south shore. Peat taken from the bogs here is still used as fuel, and sold throughout Newfoundland. If you are interested in either peat or the harvesting of kelp, stop at the GLADA building on the east side of town to see the displays.*

Grand Bank has a **Producers Market** on Saturdays, 10 am to 3 pm, in the school ground on Main St. in good weather, or at 7 Water St. in less than good weather. You'll find fresh berries, homemade preserves and breads, vegetables, seafood and crafts.

While we usually don't suggest escorted driving tours, we can't talk about the southern Burin without mentioning **Burin Historical Tours**, ☎ 709/832-0301. Jodi Bartlett leads intelligent, interesting trips that get inside the culture and the folklore, as well as into the spirit of the area and its history. Half-day tours, one for each side of the Burin, are $30 each; a full day is $50. You'll see all the nooks and crannies, including a beach known as the "whale graveyard."

Fortune Head Ecological Reserve, between Fortune and Grand Bank, is another of Newfoundland's several important geological sites. The jagged cliffs on the headland expose a bit of the earth from 500-600 million years ago, showing the boundary between the Cambrian and Precambrian periods. While such junctions are visible in a few other places, the times of their formation vary due to other influences, so the scientific world needed to find *the* exposure that was the most representative and therefore would define the boundary. In 1992, the Global Stratotype was declared to be here at Fortune Head. This particular site was chosen because the fossil remains of the first multi-cellular organisms were more recognizable here than elsewhere. You can follow a dirt road up to the marker, and walk about 250 yards to the site, but don't expect to see the fossils easily. These are not gastropods the size of your fist lying about on the ground. They are trace fossils left by burrowing organisms as they crawled about in layers of sand, then on the ocean floor. They are on the sea face of the cliffs, not easily accessible and not easy to identify once you're there. And, of course, it is absolutely forbidden to pick up so much as a flake from the cliff.

Wildlife-Watching

The Manx Shearwater rarely visits North America; most colonies are found in the British Isles. The only known breeding colony of this bird is on **Middle Lawn Island**, about a mile off the south coast of the Burin near Lord's Cove. To visit the island, contact **Gus Walsh** in Lord's Cove, ☎ 709/857-2619. Other birds you can expect to see on the island are black guillemots, Leach's storm petrels and several gull varieties.

MIDDLE LAWN ISLAND MYSTERY: *Local people began to notice the Manx shearwater here in the mid-1970s. By 1981, the population was about 350 birds. Ornithologists still have no idea why the birds came here or chose to nest so far from their native breeding grounds. Nor do they know why the colony chose, and has limited its nesting to this island, when other surrounding islands have identical habitats of grasses on a peat base above cliffs, with a maximum elevation of about 200 feet above the sea.*

Creston Inlet, in Marystown, is home to a sizable family of harbor seals. **Red Harbour Head** and **Grand Bank Head** are favorite lookout spots for whale-watchers. Along Rte. 211, from Terrenceville to Grand Le Pierre, you may see caribou in May and June. (If you're really serious about seeing them, however, you're better off in the Avalon.)

Sightseeing

To understand the rich history of the Grand Banks fishing schooners and the fisheries they made possible, visit the **Southern Newfoundland Seamen's Museum**, Marine Drive, Grand Bank, ☎ 709/832-1484. It has ship models, historic photographs, and artifacts of the schooner days. It's free and open Monday-Friday, 9 am to noon and 1 to 5 pm; Saturday and Sunday, noon to 5 pm.

George Harris House Museum of Local History, 16 Water St, Grand Bank, ☎ 709/832-1574, is only one of the many Queen Anne-style buildings dating from the early 1900s in Grand Bank. George Harris's father was the "father" of Newfoundland's fisheries off the Grand Banks, taking his schooner to the Banks in 1881.

➲ **STRANGE HISTORY:** *In Taylor Bay there's a cluster of houses you could easily miss. Look for the house on the inland side of the road that's not set square to the road. This bit of independence was not the work of a landscape designer, but of the peculiar tidal wave that hit the coast in 1929. It moved the entire house to the position you see today, and they left it there. Other homes, even those some height above the shore, were not so fortunate, and were swept out to sea, along with the families in them. You can learn more about this bizarre disaster at the GLADA building in Lamaline.*

His success there launched the industry that was to sustain Newfoundland for nearly a century. He built this home as a wedding present for his son. The house, a fine example of the Queen Anne style popular early in the 20th century, has been restored and shows the community life of Grand Bank at its most prosperous. It is free and open daily, 10 am to 4 pm, July through August.

On a hill above the harborside village of Lawn is the **Lawn Heritage Museum**, a small house filled with local history, including old photographs. Be sure to see the hand-knit long-johns in the kitchen. It's open from 10 am to 6 pm daily, May through September. They request (gently) a $2 donation, and offer the use of their picnic table in the yard overlooking the harbor and the hills that rise behind it.

In St. Lawrence, the **Miner's Museum** on Rte. 220, ☎ 709/873-2222, shows early and modern mining methods used here in Canada's only fluorspar mine. It also chronicles the life of the miners. It is open daily, 10 am to 6 pm, July through August.

Burin's setting, clinging to the steep rocky outcrops above Ship Cove, makes it a destination. But the **Burin Heritage House**, ☎ 709/891-2217, is one of Newfoundland's finest museums. Quality exhibits are nicely displayed and interpreted, both by useful signs and by spirited guides. You can wander through on your own, but the free guides will tell you stories that make the whole peninsula come alive. Outports, shipwrecks, Beothuks, and domestic details – they're all there in this fine old home on the hill. It's free, and open May through October, Monday-Friday, 9 am to 5 pm; Saturday-Sunday, 1 to 8:30 pm.

➲ **INTERESTING HISTORY:** *In the Burin Heritage House, you will learn how, in the tiny school room, Newfoundland children once had to write their exams in shorthand. This was to cut the cost of shipping paper to England, where they were all corrected. (Evidently English education officials didn't trust local teachers to assess their students' progress.)*

Where To Stay & Eat

At the start of the Burin route only 15 miles from TransCanada-1 are the modern log cabins of **Kilmory Resort**. Two-bedroom cabins have kitchenettes and decks, and the resort offers canoe and boat rentals, boat tours and winter sports. *PO Box 130, Swift Current, NF A0E 2W0, ☎ 709/549-2410, fax 709/549-2204 ($$).*

To stay in one of the vintage captain's houses, reserve a spot at **The Thorndyke**. Rooms are late '40s, but the location is great. *33 Water St, Grand Bank, NF A0E 1WO, ☎ 709/832-0820 ($).*

Recently refurbished rooms are comfortable at **Granny's Motor Inn**. The popular restaurant ($-$$) serves standard dishes; no surprises here, just reliable good food. *Hwy. Bypass, Grand Bank, NF A0E 1OW, ☎ 709/832-2180, fax 709/832-0009 ($-$$).*

Opposite the museum in a beautiful village setting overlooking the harbor is **Heritage Square B&B**. Breakfasts are always good, positively grand on weekends. *37 Seaview Dr, Burin, NF A0E 1E0, ☎ 709/891-1353 ($-$$).*

Harbourview Restaurant does indeed have a view of the busy harbor, as well as typical local seafood dishes. They also offer boat excursions and guided tours. *Water St., St. Lawrence, ☎ 709/891-1353 ($).*

■ Camping

Between Marystown and Grand Bank is **Frenchman's Cove Provincial Park**. Its 76 tent sites are set in low woodlands along a beach. As we write, it is still a provincial park, but its future is uncertain. It's such a nice facility that if the province does scuttle it, hopefully the town will take it over. *Rte. 213, Frenchman's Cove, ☎ 709/826-2753.*

Gander & The Kittiwake Coast

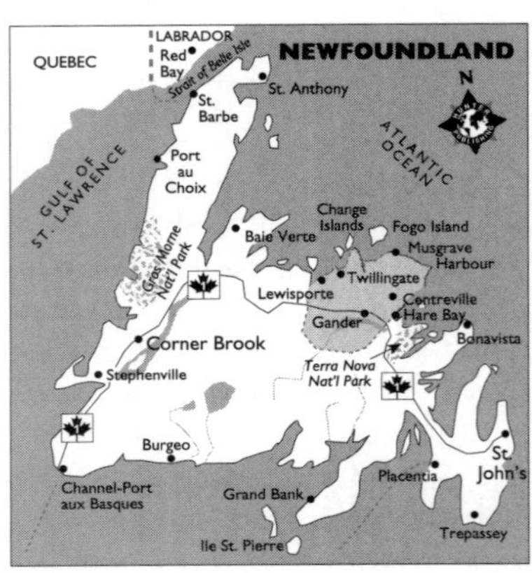

Icebergs and aviation are two prominent themes in this area of north central Newfoundland. As North America's closest fog-free point to Europe, Gander was a refueling and supply point for transatlantic flights until the 1960s, when refueling was no longer necessary. North of Gander, the coast is lower than in many other parts of the island, and an almost constant parade of icebergs drift by in spring and early summer, usually accompanied by whales and seabirds.

Geography & History

The coast of Hamilton Bay is more level and less dramatic than other edges of The Rock, with beaches, dunes, long low rocky points, and fishing harbours set astride clusters of flat round rock outcrops which Newfoundlanders call "sunkers." North of this coast are clusters of islands, one group connected to the mainland by causeways, the other by ferries. Among the latter is Fogo Island, designated by the Flat Earth Society as one of the four corners of the earth. To its west is the sprawling group that includes New World Island and the two Twillingate Islands. Here the shore is more ragged, with irregular rock headlands and deeply cut coves and channels.

This area was the summer fishing grounds of the **Beothuk** people (pronounced Bee-AW-thuk), who still inhabited this and much of Newfoundland's interior in the 1600s. Caribou hunters in the winter, they migrated to the coast in the spring, where they lived on seals and salmon. When Europeans arrived, the Beothuk were friendly, but the new settlements along the shore began to interfere with their fishing places. The resulting conflicts, however, were not as deadly to the Beothuks as the tuberculosis these newcomers had brought with them. The Beothuk were reduced to scattered bands and, by 1829, were extinct.

Until the 1930s Gander was marked on maps as the remote rail milepost 213. Then, with acute foresight, the British Air Ministry (Newfoundland was not yet part of Canada) chose the fog-free slopes above Gander Lake as the location for an air base. That decision turned out to be very important to the defense of allied Europe during World War II, when it became the supply link and refueling point for nearly all military aircraft headed to Europe. The town that grew alongside the main runway was little more than a military base, but its name became synonymous with transatlantic flight, even after the war, when it continued the same function for commercial air traffic.

Finally, the Boeing 707 made the refueling stop, and Gander itself, unnecessary. But Gander had by that time grown to a town, and its residents decided to move it away from the airstrip, locating it several miles west. They named their new streets after famous aviators and flight pioneers – look for Rickenbacker Rd., Markham Place and Yaeger St. – and decorated them with vintage aircraft. Today it is a thriving town, and one of very few in Newfoundland that did not grow from a fisheries port. A port it was, but not for boats.

Getting Around

At Gambo, you can either whiz directly to Gander on Trans-Canada-1, or take Rte. 320 north to Rte. 330 to explore the shore of Hamilton Sound. You can return to Gander on this road, making what Gander residents call "The Loop," or continue along the coast on Rte. 331, making a side-trip to Twillingate via Rte. 340, then continuing on Rte. 340 south via Lewisporte to TransCanada-1. Lewisporte, in a protected bay filled with tiny islands, is a favorite yachting center and the southern port for ferries to Labrador.

Gander International Airport provides direct air access to the area, and major car rental agencies are represented there. **Rent a Wreck** has an office in Lewisporte, ☎ 709/535-2355. Coastal ferries to Labrador leave Lewisporte every four days, mid-June through early September, operated by **Marine Atlantic**, ☎ 800/341-7981.

Twillingate and Lewisporte are towns with enough activity that you can explore them, and the waters around them, without a car, arriving by bus from Gander or St. John's. **North Eastern Bus Line**, ☎ 709/747-0492 or 709/884-2570, fax 709/368-8830, travels to Twillingate three times a week, returning on alternate days.

Information Sources

- Information on the area is in the Central Region section of the free annual *Newfoundland and Labrador Travel Guide*, which can be obtained from the **Department of Tourism, Culture and Recreation**, PO Box 8730, St. John's, NF A1B 4K2, ☎ 800/563-6353 or 709/729-2830.

- For more detailed local material, contact **Tourist Information: Visitors Center**, 109 TransCanada Hwy., Gander, NF A1V 1P6, ☎ 709/256-7110, or **Kittiwake Coast Tourism Association**, 109 TransCanada Hwy, Gander, NF A1V 1P6, ☎ 709/256-5070.

- For the Lewisporte area, contact **Lewisport Tourism Department**, 252 Main St. (PO Box 219, Lewisporte, NF A0G 3A0, ☎ 709/535-2525, fax 709/535-2695.

Adventures

■ On Foot

A hike along the barren rocks of **Brimstone Head** on Fogo Island could convince you that it really *is* one of four corners where the earth ends. From Tilting, you can take Turpin's Trail to Wild Cove; other trails lead along headlands to the abandoned settlements at Lock's Cove, Lion's Den and Eastern Tickle, providing a good day's worth of walking on the island.

Twillingate Island has some very scenic hikes across its rocky heads and through boggy cove-side meadows, with icebergs usually in sight. A short walk from Little Harbour leads to a giant sea arch (one you can actually get to and walk through – very unusual). From the harbor follow the sign to "Jobe's Cove." It's about a half-hour round-trip. A longer hike leaves from the road to French Beach, on the Durrel side of the harbor, and leads over the interior to Codjack's Cove.

Twillingate Island Guided Hikes, ☎ 709/884-5683, give you the opportunity to see the island with someone who can tell you not only about the plants and geology of this interesting landscape, but of its people, folklore and history. Two- or three-hour hikes are only $20 for a group of four, $5 for each extra person.

Sea arch near Twillingate.

For haunting echoes of Gander's past, wander through the ghost town of the **original Gander**. From the airport access road take Garret and Circular Roads to wander around its checkerboard of streets with military-base street names now bordered by low woods instead of quarters. Signs identify points of interest in some places. You can almost hear the ceaseless aircraft sounds of the early 1940s.

Thomas Howe Demonstration Forest, two miles east of Gander on TransCanada-1, ☎ 709/256-6878, has newly developed walking trails in the area surrounding Gander International Airport. The visitors center and self-guided interpretive trails show the processes of forest management at work. Trails take from 20 minutes to an hour respectively. There is a picnic area at the site.

A short (half-mile) but very pleasant trail links the visitor center with the Beothuk archaeological site at **Boyd's Cove** (see *Archaeology*, below).

A woods road from Jumpers Brook, on Rte. 351 just east of Bishop's Falls, leads to the base of **Mount Peyton**, the highest elevation in central Newfoundland, at 1,600 feet. The climb is only moderately difficult, and the view stretches for miles. If you'd like to do this, or other wilderness hikes, with a guide, check the trips offered by **Caribou Adventure Tours**, PO Box 284, Lewisporte, NF A0G 3A0, ☎ 709/535-8379. They offer backpacking trips into wilderness areas or short hikes in the Lewisporte area, guided by a local biologist. It's an excellent opportunity to see local wildlife: they report 100% success in caribou sighting, but also look for the smaller creatures and plant life along the trail.

A beautiful place to walk along the beach, where the sand is smooth and flat, is **Cape Freels**, on Rte. 330 as it swings south above Bonavista Bay. Instead of turning to go into the village of Cape Freels, continue straight on the unsurfaced road and go out to the cape itself. The road is pretty churned up, so you'll want to park and walk, which you can do for quite a distance, with only birds for company.

■ On Wheels

Rte. 330, the route along the low, flat Kittiwake Coast, is hardly ever out of sight of the sea. When you tire of the road, follow little lanes into the villages.

The **Change Islands** are also good for bicycling. You can take your bike over on the ferry or borrow from your hosts if you stay at **Seven Oakes Island Inn and Cottages**, ☎ 709/621-3256.

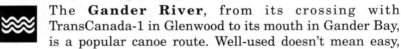

Guided Bicycle Tours

■ Mountain bike with **Caribou Adventure Tours**, PO Box 284, Lewisporte, NF A0G 3A0, ☎ 709/535-8379, who lead day trips and overnight bike/camping trips to Mount Peyton, near Bishop's Falls. Old forest roads lead deep into the wilderness that lies just south of the TransCanada Highway through this region.

■ On Water

Canoeing & Kayaking

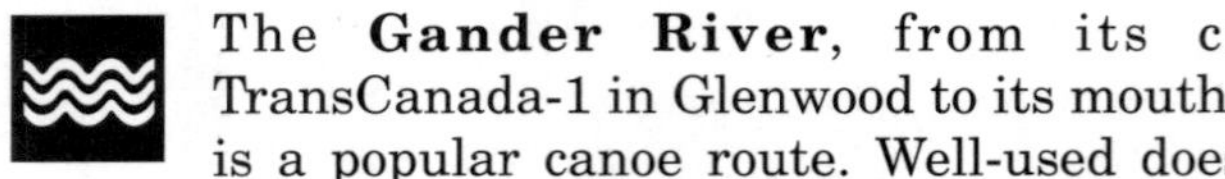

The **Gander River**, from its crossing with TransCanada-1 in Glenwood to its mouth in Gander Bay, is a popular canoe route. Well-used doesn't mean easy, since there are two chutes that can be very dangerous. Portages around Big Chute and Little Chute are well-worn by the feet of sensible less-experienced canoeists. Splinters of the canoes of others are floating around with the icebergs in Hamilton Sound. The rest of the trip is Class I all the way, but technical waters around boulders and the often strong winds on the more open ponds closer to Gander Bay can slow you down. The 35-mile trip will take experienced paddlers all day, without winds; it's safer to plan on two and begin looking for a campsite early, since marshy shores make finding them difficult. We're not personally as fond of this stretch

➲ **A DIFFERENT BOATING EXPERIENCE:** *To try your hand with a craft unique to the area, rent a traditional red Newfoundland dory from* ***Twillingate Adventure Tours*** *on Main St. overlooking the harbor,* ☎ *709/884-5999 or toll-free 888/447-TOUR. We admit to a prejudice for the lines of a dory, but these have to be among the most graceful ever designed, and you'll see them lined up at harbors in these islands. The waters of Twillingate Harbour are like glass, and you can navigate around them safely even if you've never rowed a boat before.*

of river, which has a lot of developed areas; we like more wilderness, but it is easy to get to and has some good areas for seeing ospreys, bald eagles and other birds.

The **Northwest Gander River**, which rises in the wilderness west of Rte. 360, is one of the province's best canoe rivers, a Class I river with some stretches of Class II rapids. It is not considered dangerous, but its riffles and rapids are challenging; lining is required on some rapids, except for expert paddlers.

Outfitters & Guided Canoe Trips

- **Gander River Guiding Services**, ☎ 709/676-2628, or **Glen Eagles Enterprises** next to the Irving Station in Appleton, ☎ 709/679-2232, can provide river guides for the Gander River and make shuttle arrangements to get you and your car reunited after you reach Gander Bay. They can also arrange trips to explore the upper river.

- Canoe trips on the Gander River, either one-day excursions or multi-day canoe/camping trips, are the specialty of **Caribou Adventure Tours**, PO Box 284, Lewisporte, NF A0G 3A0, ☎ 709/535-8379. Your guide will be a biologist well versed in the fauna and flora, as you watch for ospreys and other birds, as well as moose frequently seen along the river.

- **N.W. Gander Lodge** on the Northwest Gander River south of Glenwood, ☎ 709/754-5500 or 709/579-8055, does two- and three-day canoe trips on the Northwest Gander River, which can be combined with canoeing the lower Gander River all the way to the ocean.

- You can rent canoes from **Para Sport** in Little Harbour (five minutes west of Gander on TransCanada-1), ☎ 709/651-2126.

Boat Tours & Ferries

Rte. 335 leads to **Farewell**, an appropriate name for the ferry port to the Change Islands and Fogo Island. Separate ferries depart year-round, with six sailings to the Change islands in the summer and four to Fogo. The Change Island fare is $5.25 for car and driver ($2.75 senior driver), $1.75 for additional passengers ($1 seniors and children). The fares to Fogo are about $1.50 more ($.75 more for senior driver).

Explore the shores of the Change Islands on a small fishing boat with **Change Island Adventure Tours**, Main Rd. (North End), Change Islands, ☎ 709/621-3106. The two-hour tour will often be joined by a local fisherman, who will tell about fishing in these waters; you'll hear also about island life as you pass tiny settlements clustered around their distinctive red fishing stores and stages. Three tours leave daily, at $15 for adults, $12 for seniors and $10 for children under 12.

Flat Earth Boat Tours, from Fogo Island, ☎ 709/266-2745, use a small boat to tour the domain of puffins, whales and icebergs, and see the smaller islands around Fogo. You can stop to hike or beachcomb on the islands, or bring a picnic.

High Seas Sailing Charters at the Yacht Club docks in Lewisporte, will take you on a three-hour, half-day, or full-day tour under sail on the 41-foot *Windborne III*. You can also learn to sail a keelboat with certified instructors, in a variety of courses from an introductory lesson to a full course. Contact them at 6 Young St., ☎ 709/535-2214 or 535-3222, fax 709/535-3225, e-mail highseas@cancom.net, www.cancom.net/~media/highseas.

Twillingate is the center for whale and iceberg-watching, with three tours leaving daily on **Twillingate Island Boat Tours** at The Iceberg Shop, ☎ 709/884-2242 or 800/611-BERG. Expect to learn a lot about icebergs from these experts. **Twillingate Adventure Tours,** also on Main St., ☎ 888/447-TOUR or 709/884-5999, leaves three times daily on a 40-passenger tour boat, with wheelchair access. Both operate May through September.

Beothuk Indian Adventure Tours, Boyd's Cove, ☎ 709/656-3333, does tours through the waters between New World Islands and the mainland peninsula, past the Boyd's Cove Beothuk archaeological site. They use a stable pontoon boat, for a very smooth ride that even non-boat-fanciers will enjoy. Reservations are not essential if you arrive 30 minutes before the scheduled departures at 10 am, 4 and 7 pm, but it is better to call first in case they have booked a group that fills the boat.

In Lewisporte, you can explore the bay islands, some with abandoned outports, and feast on lobster or mussels in front of a beach campfire at an island cabin, with **Island View Tours**, 106 Main St., ☎ 709/535-2258. In season, you can invite an iceberg to lunch – or at least choose a spot next to one. The owner of this boat will also take you to a former Beothuk campsite on an island.

The only saltwater cruise we know of where you have a good chance of seeing whales, icebergs and moose on the same trip is with **Kittiwake Boat Tours** in Lumsden, about halfway around "The Loop" of Rte. 330, on Hamilton Sound, ☎ 709/530-2401 or 530-2360. Whales and icebergs you expect here, but the moose – about 15 of them – live on an island about five minutes offshore. In the course of the cruise you can haul a lobster trap, visit capelin fishermen, jig for cod, or land to do a little beachcombing on an island where two-centuries-old coins have been found. Three tours a day cost $20 for adults, $10 for children six-15. They also make day-long trips to the Wadham Islands to see puffins and other seabirds, including razor bills (see *Wildlife-Watching*, page 547).

Glen Eagles Enterprises in Appleton, ☎ 709/679-2232, can take you on a boat tour to remember, on a traditional Gander River Boat. Designed especially for the stretch of the river from Glenwood, where it crosses TransCanada-1, to its mouth at Gander Bay, these boats have evolved over the years from a twin-stemmed boat that was poled, to a square-sterned craft with a 20-25 hp motor. Glen Eagles guides will take you on a ride in one of these, through the chutes and the Long Rattle, an exciting way to see the river.

Diving

Devon House, an inn on Exploits Island near Lewisporte, ☎ 709/535-2509, fax 709/535-0805, can arrange for you to spend a day diving in the crystal-clear waters of Exploits Bay; bring your own scuba gear.

Windsurfing

Bring a wet suit to **Sandy Cove** on Fogo Island so you can say you've surfed off the end of the earth. The water is cold – which won't surprise you when you see the icebergs drifting past – but the winds are constant and the beach sandy, as the name suggests.

Fishing

The **Indian Bay** area has some of the province's best trout fishing in the Indian Bay Watershed, where one-pound trout are not uncommon. Indian Bay Brook is a scheduled salmon river as well. The whole area is accessible by high-wheeled vehicles. **Indian Bay Connections** on Rte. 330 in Indian Bay, ☎ 709/678-6337, fax 709/678-2284, offers professional guides, cottages and RV sites for anglers.

The **Gander River** is big and fast, best fished from boats. Some pools can be waded, but for the most part, shore fishing is not practical.

Fishing Outfitters & Guided Trips

■ To learn fly-fishing from experts or to arrange a fishing trip in the Gander River area, inquire at **Caribou Adventure Tours**, 19 Premier Drive (PO Box 284), Lewisporte, NF A0G 3A0, ☎ 709/535-8379. They offer guided trips in search of both salmon (the Gander is a real success story in salmon repopulation) and brook trout.

■ Fishing guides are also available through **Gander River Guiding Services**, ☎ 709/676-2628, or **Glen Eagles Enterprises** in Appleton, ☎ 709/679-2232. Glen Eagles can furnish you with everything you need to fish the Gander River – gear, rainwear, flotation vest, waders, even your fishing license, for fishing trips as short as half a day. A full-day Glen Eagles fishing package includes a guided trip in a traditional Gander River Boat (see *Boat Tours*, above), waterproof clothing, life vest, fishing equipment, and lunch.

GANDER RIVER WILDERNESS LODGE EXPERIENCE

Beaver Lodge is deep in the wilderness, on a small island with quiet woods and lovely wildflowers, including wild orchids. The Lodge provides comfortable private rooms, three hearty meals a day, professional guides (at ratio of 1.5 guides per client), and boats. You supply your own tackle and gear: rods, reels, lines, flies, fishing vest. Smart anglers in this unpredictable Newfoundland weather layer their clothing (T-shirt, turtleneck, wool shirt, sweater, and a warm jacket), then peel down to whatever the weather dictates. Raingear and waterproof boots are essential. When you plan to spend time in a remote lodge, pack binoculars, bird books, wildflower identification guides, a couple of good books, and any personal items you need, especially prescription medications, since you are a long way from the nearest mall. Beaver Lodge, c/o Wayne Thomas, PO Box 455, Grand Falls-Windsor, NF A2A 2J8, ☎ 709/489-9673 or 709/489-5054, fax 709/489-3181. Rates are $220 per person per day for the complete package. – *Sara Godwin and Charles James*

■ On Snow

Skiing

Notre Dame Provincial Park on TransCanada-1 south of Lewisporte, ☎ 709/535-2379, has six miles of cross-country trails with a ski chalet. **Dildo Run Provincial Park**, on New World Island, has a warm-up cabin built by the local community, and about four miles of trails connected so you can make a two-mile, three-mile, or four-mile loop. The warm-up shelter is in the central portion of the loop.

Several local ski clubs maintain trail systems, some of them quite extensive. The **Island View Club** in Twillingate (☎ 709/884-2862) has four miles of groomed trails, with a cabin. They give lessons.

A new winter sports facility in Gander called **The Runway** (☎ 709/651-HILL), has a combination of outdoor activities for snow-lovers. Cross-country trails cover nine miles at the **Howe Demonstration Forest**, connected to the Runway facility by a two-mile trail. The Howe Forest has both challenging and gentle terrain, with several choices of loop trails. Five downhill trails at the Runway, serviced by a T-bar lift, have a good vertical drop for their length, which is not very long, but the half-pipe for snowboarders is the longest so far in Atlantic Canada, at 1,100 feet. Rentals are available. The whole facility (except Howe Forest) is right on TransCanada-1, within walking distance of the cluster of hotels and restaurants near the tourist chalet.

Snowmobiling

Woods roads honeycomb the **Indian Bay Watershed**, kept clear by the steady flow of anglers who flock there during fishing season. These roads are used by snowmobilers in the winter to enjoy this relatively level and unspoiled environment. You can rent snowmobiles at **Indian Bay Connections** on the main highway in Indian Bay, ☎ 709/678-6337, fax 709/678-2284. They also have professional guides.

N.W. Gander Lodge on the Northwest Gander River south of Glenwood, ☎ 709/754-5500 or 709/579-8055, is well-located for snowmobile trips, providing a comfortable base lodge and all equipment. The terrain includes the central barrens and woodlands, using woods roads and the vast trackless wilderness areas, as well as the rivers themselves when ice conditions permit. The lodge is between the grounds of two caribou herds, so sightings are frequent.

Farther north along the Kittiwake Coast, **Barbour's Bed and Breakfast** in Lumsden, NF A0G 3E0, ☎ 709/530-2107, can arrange snowmobile trips along the low, scenic northern shore.

Cultural & Eco-Travel Experiences

Icebergs are the big talk around Hamilton Sound, and in a normal year you can see them drifting by in the distance or caught in the harbors and bays to sit until they melt or wander off on a changing current. Even locals come to see the really big ones that drift close to shore; in fact, iceberg-watching is as popular a sport with natives as it is for those who visit here from warmer waters. The best season is May through mid-July.

Icebergs create a wildlife ecosystem, attracting seabirds, fish and whales feeding on plankton that thrives in water around icebergs. You will often see those intrepid travelers, the kittiwakes, hitching a ride on top of one.

To learn more about icebergs, stop at the distinctive blue **Iceberg Shop** on the waterfront in Twillingate, ☎ 709/884-2242. This free interpretive center has informative displays about sea ice, as well as sweatshirts with icebergs on them, a nice change from the palm-tree T-shirts your neighbors bring back from the Virgin Islands. The whale and iceberg photography is excellent.

ABOUT ICEBERGS

Icebergs are not static things: they drift and change shape as they melt, sometimes developing towers and arches. When their weight becomes unbalanced, they flip over with a huge splash – you don't want to kayak too close to one for this reason. When an arch forms, the increased surface melts more quickly, and the iceberg eventually breaks in two.

The icebergs you see drifting past are borne by the Labrador Current, and they may have taken several years to reach Newfoundland since calving from the glaciers of Greenland and Baffin Island. As many as 400 may reach Newfoundland waters each year. The makeup of ice that forms each winter in bays and coves has a lower salt content than the ocean icebergs and freezes more easily. You can tell these random pieces of ice, as well as "slob ice" from the Labrador Sea, because iceberg ice has a blue-green color and the others don't. And you thought ice was ice.

➲ **ICEBERG TIPS:** *The small pieces (about the size of a modest house) you see are known as "bergy-bits."*

Icebergs in Newfoundland.

Archaeology

A major discovery at **Boyd's Cove** north of Gander provided important new insights on the Beothuk, who inhabited the coast seasonally before the coming of Europeans. At the Boyd's Cove **Beothuk Interpretation Center** off Rte. 340, ☎ 709/656-3114, 11 house pits, stone foundations of mamateeks (the Beothuk's circular dwellings) dating from 1650 to 1720 were excavated, yielding artifacts and information on the group's everyday lives. The excavation, for the present, is completed, and the encampment has been covered and returned to grass, surrounded with a raised walkway to permit a clear view. The half-mile trail from the Visitors Centre to the site interprets the forest, beaches, stream and meadows where the Beothuk spent their summers. Inside the modern Visitor Centre, a film, displays and well-informed guides, explain what is known about the Beothuk people. The exhibits are very well done. It is a shame that most of the actual artifacts recovered have been moved elsewhere, instead of being displayed at the site where they were found. We hope that they are being used for research and will be returned. The center is open daily, 10 am to 5:30, June through September, and is free.

Geology

> **LOCAL COLOR:** *We love the Dover town motto: "With a fault to be proud of."*

Through Dover, not far north of Gambo on Rte. 330, runs the northern end of the **Dover-Hermitage Fault Line**, visible evidence of the two different plates that collided and separated over 400 million years ago. To the east is a portion of the African plate that stuck when the rest of it went to Africa. To the west is the North American plate. (It was the force of this collision that caused the upthrust of the Appalachians, of which Gros Morne National Park is the northernmost end.) Climb to the top of the lookout, where there are interpretive signs, and look out over the notch between the higher elevations; the other end of the fault is at Fortune Bay on the lower reaches of the Bay du Nord River.

■ Wildlife-Watching

Twillingate is one of the prime whale-watching areas on the Newfoundland coast. You can often see humpback, fin, minke and pilot whales, as well as dolphins. Harp seals may be seen around Twillingate in May, June and sometimes into early July.

The **Wadham Islands,** which include **Penguin and Cabot Islands**, are a bird sanctuary where you can see puffins, razorbills and other members of the auk family. You can also see eider ducks and gannets, the only booby found in cold northern waters. The islands lie off the east end of Hamilton Sound, southeast of Fogo Island, and can be reached on a full-day trip with **Kittiwake Boat Tours**, in Lumsden, ☎ 709/530-2401 or 709/530-2360. These islands are reputed by local tradition to have been a breeding ground for the now-extinct great auk, and the flat surface of Penguin Islands would lend credence to that. Early European seamen called the black and white flightless auks penguins, so the name Penguin Island on old maps suggests that they saw them there.

Cape Freels beaches are populated with hundreds of small seabirds, on a strip of oceanic barrens.

Sightseeing

Gander's new **North Atlantic Aviation Museum** on TransCanada-1 just west of the Visitors Center, ☎ 709/256-2923, is devoted to the history of flight, especially to the role Gander played in World War II. The museum is open daily, 9 am to 9 pm, mid-May through early September, 8:30 am to 4:30 pm, September through mid-May, admission $3 adults, youths and seniors $2. You can climb into the cockpit of a DC-3. In the first week of August is the annual Festival of Flight, with aviation-related activities and even more vintage aircraft.

Somber and moving is the **Silent Witness Memorial**, near TransCanada-1 and the airport. This monument is dedicated to the 258 members of the 101st Airborne Division, the "Screaming Eagles," killed in the 1985 crash as they returned from a peacekeeping mission in the Sinai.

Bonavista North Regional Museum, off Rte. 330, Wesleyville, ☎ 709/536-2077, is big, and chock full of interesting artifacts, antiques and exhibits that really give a sense of what life has been

➔ MORE LOCAL COLOR: *At the Barbour Heritage Site you'll hear the story of one of the owners whose boat was driven off course while returning from St. John's in 1929 and ended up in Tobermory, Scotland. We told you the winds blew in Newfoundland.*

like in these small coastal towns. We admit to a fondness for these community attics, but this one's especially good. Admission is $2. and it's open daily, 1 to 6 pm, longer on Tuesday and Wednesday in July and August.

Newtown has a beautiful setting, perched on a cluster of low, rocky outcrops connected by bridges, and one of these is the **Barbour Heritage Site**, ☎ 709/536-2441. It centers around two fine old homes, one a Queen Anne, and both filled with the everyday furnishings and treasures of several generations of families. Open late June through early September, 10 am to 8 pm daily, admission $5, students $3.

WHAT'S IN A NAME?

Farewell may be an appropriate name for the jumping-off point to the islands, but no name could be less appropriate than Change Island, where nothing seems to have changed in the last century, except for the addition of a few cars. Red fishing stores sit over the docks, and little boats bob in the water or putt around through the *tickles* (a charming Newfoundland word for a narrow channel). At Puncheon Cove there is a largely abandoned settlement.

Fogo Island is only a bit more changed from its early ways, and flatly refused to be resettled when the government tried to move its residents to the mainland in the 1960s (bully for Fogo, we say). You'll find a beach at Sandy Cove, although few people – even adventurous ones – are likely to swim long in waters shared with icebergs. Visit the town of Seldom, with a sheltered fishing harbor, lighthouse and abandoned community nearby.

Bleak House Museum in Fogo on Fogo Island, ☎ 709/266-2237, is a restored 1816 merchant home, with many of the original family pieces. It's free and open July and August.

Twillingate is a busy, attractive town and a center for tourist services. Its long history is well-shown in the **Twillingate**

Museum on North Island, ☎ 709/884-2825. In the spacious Anglican rectory on the hill, it records both great events and simple homey details, such as a nursery complete with baby clothes, cradle and other baby furnishings, with the loving care of a community that values its past. The museum, and the excellent craft shop (look for the delicate miniature snowshoes and the embroidered Grenfell parkas) on its first floor, are open daily, 10 am to 9 pm, June through early September. Admission is $1.

A church on the Kittiwake Coast.

The Prime Berth at the causeway on Twillingate Island, ☎ 709/884-5925, shows the history of inshore fishing through its aquarium, equipment and artifacts, a quirky assemblage of fascinating things. On the shore is a fishing stage and premises you can visit. It's open daily, 10:30 am to 8:30 pm, mid-June through September, costs $2, and has a craft shop.

Over the Top Museum on Rte. 340 in Birchy Bay, ☎ 709/659-3221, is a 1900-era home containing a museum of local history, with a fine model of a locally built schooner, implements of daily living, and exhibits on local history. Outside is a reconstruction of a winters tilt, the tiny structure and wharf built by fishermen for winter use in remote places. A short trail leads to the top of Jumper's Head, for a view of the surrounding shore. It's open in July and August; admission is $1.50.

Spinning Wheel Crafts and Bye the Bay Museum, Main St., Lewisporte, ☎ 709/535-2844, is a craft cooperative with an especially good selection of hand-knit sweaters and mittens. You will also find homemade jellies from wild local berries, including cloudberries. Admission to the museum, a good collection that includes a penny organ, a kerosene-heated iron, and a very nice hand-hooked tapestry, is 50¢. Both are open daily, 9 am to 9 pm, in July and August; Tuesday-Saturday, 9 am to 5 pm, June and September through December.

Where To Stay & Eat

Near TransCanada-1

Accommodations and dining in Gander are more abundant than in other places in central Newfoundland, with several hotels lining the highway and more in the town.

Hotel Gander has modern rooms, free meals for kids under 12, and 20% discounts for seniors. Several extras make it a good value. *100 TransCanada Hwy, Gander, NF A1V 1P5, ☎ 709/256-3931, fax 709/651-2641 ($$).*

Sinbad's Motel is attractive, with modern rooms and a surprisingly sophisticated dining room menu ($$). This restaurant is our hands-down choice in town, open for three meals daily. Roomy efficiencies have dining and sitting areas and modern kitchens. Children under 18 stay free, under 12 eat free. *Bennet Drive (PO Box 450), Gander, NF A1V 1W8, ☎ 709/651-2678 or 800/563-4900 ($$).*

We'll always remember the hospitality at **Cape Cod Bed and Breakfast**. We rang the doorbell soaked to the skin and muddy after hiking in the rain at Boyd's Cove, and they treated us as though we'd arrived dressed for the Queen's tea party. They even did our laundry while we went out to dinner. Full breakfast on fine china and nice decorator touches in the rooms, too. *66 Bennett Drive, Gander, NF A1V 1M9, ☎ 709/651-2269 ($-$$).*

Northgate Bed and Breakfast has warm, well-decorated rooms in a home where you feel comfortable reading in the parlor after dinner. A hearty full breakfast is sociable, with engaging hosts introducing guests to each other. Plan to have a lobster cookout and boat ride with them during your stay. *106 Main St, Lewisporte, NF A0G 3A0, ☎ 709/535-2258 ($).*

The boat ride to the island and three meals are included in your stay at **Devon House**. The last remaining home on an island that once had 100 residents, Devon House is a beautifully restored mid-19th-century residence, with a licensed dining room serving traditional Newfoundland dishes. The price, all inclusive, is $100 per person. *Exploits Island (PO Box 430) Lewisporte, NF A0G 3A0, ☎ 709/535-2509, fax 709/535-0805.*

Brittany Inns is a motor inn with modern rooms and a pleasant dining room ($$) serving alternatives to fried fish. *Rte. 341 (PO Box 730), Lewisporte, NF A0G 3A0, ☎ 709/535-2533 ($$).*

Gateway Restaurant serves a standard menu, heavy on seafood (why do we keep restating the obvious in sea-bound Newfoundland?). It's right down the street from the Northgate Bed and Breakfast. *126 Main St., Lewisporte, ☎ 709/535-8510 ($-$$).*

For a mid-day pick-me-up, stop at **Shirley's Home Baking** on Premier Drive. *Lewisporte, ☎ 709/535-3030.*

The Islands

Crewe's Heritage Bed and Breakfast overlooks the harbor in the center of town, within sight of the dock where you can take whale-watch trips. Open June through September. *33 Main St, Twillingate, NF A0G 4M0, ☎ 709/884-2723 ($).*

Anchor Inn has modern guest rooms (some with wheelchair access) and a dining room overlooking the harbor. The menu is longer and has more variety than you usually find in Newfoundland; the fisherman's brewis served here as an appetizer is very good. *PO Box 550, Twillingate, NF A0G 4M0, ☎ 709/884-2777 ($$).*

Harbour Lights Inn sits above Twillingate's harbor in a well-restored historic home. Dinner is served by reservation; their surprising menu includes dishes from South Africa. *189 Main St., Twillingate, NF A0G 4M0, ☎ 709/884-2763, fax 709/884-2701 ($$).*

Beach Rock Bed and Breakfast has cozy rooms in a casual, homey atmosphere, serving breakfasts and dinners in the kitchen, and generous amounts of good humor. Seafood feasts are available for houseguests and others by advance reservation. It's in a tiny harbor village close to Twillingate. *RR 1 (PO Box 350), Little Harbour, NF A0G 4M0, ☎ 709/884-2292 ($).*

Seven Oakes Island Inn and Cottages overlooks the ocean from an island setting. The large heritage home once belonged to a prosperous island merchant; meals are available to guests, as are rowboats and bicycles. *PO Box 57, Change Islands, Notre Dame Bay, NF A0G 1R0, ☎ 709/621-3256 ($-$$).*

Along the Kittiwake Coast, where Rte. 330 reaches the shore of Bonavista Bay, you'll find **Barbour's Bed and Breakfast**. It's in a small, new home, and its two guest rooms have private baths. If you are traveling with children, you may be happy to hear that childcare is available. *Lumsden, NF A0G 3E0, ☎ 709/530-2107 ($).*

Near Wesleyville, **The Yellow Teapot Inn** is a B&B with a restaurant (☎ 709/536-3307, $) in an adjoining building. They are at the far eastern end of the town, near the hospital. *54 Main St., Badger's Quay, Bonavista Bay, NF A0G 1B0, ☎ 709/536-5858 ($).*

■ Camping

Notre Dame Provincial Park has 100 campsites; amenities include a convenience store, unsupervised beach and nature activities. *TransCanada-1 (PO Box 489), Lewisporte, NF A0G 3A0, ☎ 709/535-2379.*

Dildo Run Provincial Park has 55 campsites, some with hookups. *New World Island, ☎ 800/866-CAMP.*

Formerly a Provincial park but now operated by the town, **Smallwood Park** has well-maintained campsites and a rushing waterfall on Middle Brook, with a salmon ladder. *Gambo.*

The former **Windmill Bight Provincial Park** is now operated by the town. Its campsites, all without hookups, are a mix of open and shaded and cost $7 a night. Neither of its two beaches – one fresh, one salt – is supervised; a $3 day-use fee allows access to both. *Near Cape Freels, where Rte. 30 turns south on its way back to TransCanada-1.*

The Exploits Valley & Baie Verte

Travelers driving across Newfoundland in a hurry find the stretch from Grand Falls to Deer Lake the most tedious, with mile after mile of wilderness broken only by a few small settlements. The TransCanada Highway swings abruptly north here, leading to the doorstep of the beautiful Baie Verte region, whose irregular coastline engendered place names like Wild Cove and Confusion Bay.

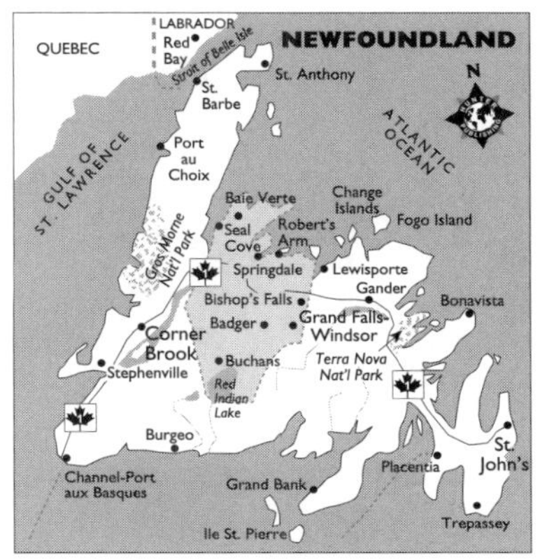

Geography & History

The long Bay of Exploits reaches south, forming a natural boundary between the western and southern shores of Notre Dame Bay and the group of islands that includes Twillingate. The Exploits River, which begins in the long Red Indian Lake, gives the southern part of this area its name: the Exploits Valley. Grand Falls-Windsor, at a falls in the Exploits, is its largest commercial center, on the TransCanada Highway.

North and west of the Exploits Valley is the Baie Verte Peninsula, bounded on the east by Notre Dame Bay. To the west, White Bay separates it from the Great Northern Peninsula.

Lumber, mines, and mileposts on the route of CN's Newfie Flyer sums up much of the inland history, while fishing brought the first European settlers to the protected harbors of Notre Dame Bay. Before that, the Paleeoskimo Dorset peoples hunted seals here. The town of Botwood may seem quiet now, but in World War II it was the Royal Air Force's bombing and reconnaissance anti-submarine seaplane base, visited by everyone from President and Mrs. Roosevelt to Winston Churchill to Bob Hope. Its aviation history is even older: it was the departure point for the first scheduled transatlantic flight in 1937, and a stopping point for the Lindberghs on their 1933 non-stop transatlantic flight.

Getting Around

TransCanada-1 links the two parts of this region in a long S-curve. From it only two routes lead south: Rte. 360 dropping almost straight to Fortune Bay on the south coast, and Rte. 370, which heads toward Red Indian Lake. If you are headed to Port-aux-Basques or Burgeo, on the southwest coast, you can travel a remote unpaved woods road along the lake, a dubious shortcut described (with full disclaimers) in the *On Wheels* section, below. Heading north from Grand Falls, Rte. 350 offers the choice of two roads that end at Notre Dame Bay, leading to the towns of Fortune Harbour and Leading Tickles.

Farther west, Rte. 380 leads to another group of coastal towns, as does Rte. 390, which takes you to the 400-foot Rattling Brook Falls. Rte 410 leads the length of the Baie Verte Peninsula, with offshoots to a number of scenic fishing settlements. As elsewhere on the Newfoundland cast, you can follow any road to a harbor-side village, most with incomparable settings. Fleur de Lys and Seal Cove are especially scenic.

Information Sources

- At the intersection of TransCanada-1 and Rte. 390 is the very helpful **Green Bay Information Centre**, which is open year-round. There is another on TransCanada-1 at Grand Falls-Windsor.
- Write or call ahead for information from the **Exploits Valley Tourism Association**, Grand Falls-Windsor, NF A2A 2J7, ☎ 709/489-7251.

Adventures

■ On Foot

Hiking

The **Alexander Murray Hiking Trail** in King's Point on Rte. 391 is a four-mile trail to the top of the 1,006-foot summit of Hay Pook. From here you can see the length of Southwest Arm and out to open sea (with icebergs) to the north and the Topsail mountains 50 miles to the south. On the way up you'll pass three waterfalls and a deep gorge with a 700-foot sheer cliff, which is about a one-hour hike if you don't want to climb to the top. Plan at least four to five hours for the round-trip and wear boots, since the trail is rough and rocky. Don't try it in wet weather. The trail leaves Rte. 391 close to its intersection with the road to the village of Rattling Brook.

The town of **Little Bay Islands** is on an island reached by a 45-minute ferry ride. From there, trails lead all over the island, many to abandoned communities, and one to the top of **Pole Hill.** From here you can look down on the village, its almost enclosed harbor, and the group of surrounding islands that give the town its name.

North of Point Leamington, on Rte. 350 north of Bishop's Falls, a trail leads to East Tickles, about a 45-minute hike one way. Here you will find a group of **Newfoundland ponies**, one of three in this area. Another group is on the north side of **Cull's Island**, where the road past Leading Tickles ends. Follow the trail to **Sprunes Garden**, about a 15-minute walk. The third group of ponies lives on an island (see *Boat Tours*, below).

Guided Hiking Trips

■ **Aspen Brook Adventures** in Aspen Brook on TransCanada-1 west of Grand Falls (☎ 709/489-7675), leads hiking tours to explore the area around Hodge's Hill, toward the north, and to climb its 1,800-foot summit. From that elevation, the view encompasses Grand Falls-Windsor and several surrounding lakes, and hikers often see moose and caribou, along with smaller animals and birds. Aspen Brook also has campsites along the river, with tent platforms.

■ **Aspenwood Hike and Bike Tours** in Springdale (☎ 709/673-4255) will take you on guided hiking trips to suit your energy level. Or, for a sampling of three outdoor sports, consider the triathlon adventure with a day each of hiking, canoeing and mountain bicycling, with rustic accommodations and meals included. Rates run from $20 per person for half-day tours to $85 on overnight trips. Springdale is just north of TransCanada-1 on Rte. 390.

■ On Wheels

Bicycling

Several sections of the former CN rail line have been reclaimed in this area as part of the TransCanada Trail. It crosses TransCanada-1 at Badger, and work is well underway to restore bridges around Grand Falls.

Bicycle Outfitters - Guided Tours

■ **Aspenwood Hike and Bike Tours** in Springdale (☎ 709/673-4255) offers mountain bike tours at rates ranging from $20 per person for half-day tours to $85 on overnight trips. Springdale is just north of TransCanada-1 on Rte. 390.

■ **Aspen Brook Adventures** in Aspen Brook, on TransCanada-1 west of Grand Falls (☎ 709/489-7675), offers mountain bike tours exploring the area around Hodge's Hill, to the north, with an elevation of 1,800 feet. Aspen Brook also rents mountain bikes to do your own exploring on the almost infinite woods roads and tracks that web the area. Bike rentals are $25 per day, $15 half-day; bikes are high-quality and helmets are included. Guided tours are $40 a day.

Driving

The route through the backcountry along Red Indian Lake is one of the rare car trips given special mention here, but it really is an adventure. Unless the weather has been very rainy, you can probably do this in your rented sedan (we say this at risk of being turned down for car rental in the future). Follow these directions very carefully, and try to get up-to-date information from a local person who uses the road. See the section on traveling woods roads in the introduction to Newfoundland, and be prepared to turn around and take the Trans-Canada Highway if the road deteriorates or a bridge is out.

TAKE NOTE: *On a map you will see what looks like a better road via Buchans on the north side of Red Indian Lake. As we write, this road is not passable except to high-wheeled vehicles (and often not to them). The new bridge over Lloyd's River at the end of the lake makes the southern route by far the best. You will be able to see the lake on your right often enough to give you confidence. We give distances in miles/km here, so however your odometer records your progress, you'll be with us.*

Why take this road, which provincial representatives in the tourist information centers will probably tell you is impassable? Because it's there (that's why we first took it) and to save repeating a long section of TC-1 if you are crossing the province twice (why we continue taking it). It is about 60 miles shorter, although the time is almost the same, but you certainly can't complain about the traffic. It's a good chance to see Newfoundland's outback, but it's not for those who get nervous when they drive for miles without seeing another car. The biggest hazard is that huge logging trucks use the road (and maintain it, so don't grumble at them), so in wet weather it can have wheel ruts deep enough to drown an Alpha Romeo.

Take an odometer reading in **Millertown**, which you reach from Badger on Rte. 370, and continue west along the southern shore of the lake, past Indian Lake Camping. You will come to a dam that you can't cross and must swing left to get around, then will cross a steel bridge with a wide road entering from the left just beyond it, at nine miles/15km from Millertown. Go straight, crossing several streams, for 24 miles/40 km, when a road will enter from uphill, on your left, and leave a short distance later on your right to go down to the lake. Somewhat later the road forks; keep to the right, and in about eight miles/13 km from the last mileage check you'll see cabins on the opposite shore of the lake. Very shortly you will go down a long hill and cross Lloyd's River. Go left after the second bridge and follow the river through a valley for 26 miles/44 km, when you will reach Rte. 480. A left turn will take you to the south coast and Burgeo, a right will take you, in 30 miles, to TransCanada-1, south of Corner Brook. Once you cross Lloyd's River, you will be on a maintained road.

■ On Water

Swimming

Thunder Brook Falls, six miles west of Grand Falls-Windsor, has a pool at the bottom that is a favorite swimming spot. **Botwood Municipal Park** has a supervised swimming beach.

Canoeing & Kayaking

The protected waters deep inside the **Bay of Exploits** and the mouth of the **Exploits River** are good for kayakers, who can paddle into the farthest reaches of its many long, narrow arms.

Kayak is clearly the best way to explore the islands of **Notre Dame Bay**. The outports that once thrived there are now ghost towns, some of the houses abandoned, others floated across the water to mainland resettlement sites. The shores are low and rocky, with little coves where the fishing stores once stood, and the inner waters are fairly protected. Icebergs drift into the outer waters in the summer, bringing a surrounding colony of plankton, which in turn attracts birds and whales. These islands are best explored with a guide who not only knows them, but knows how to paddle in the presence of whales and icebergs, both of which can be unpredictable and dangerous to kayakers. As you get to the outer islands, the sea becomes rougher and the wind stronger.

Canoe & Kayak Outfitters - Guided Tours

■ You can rent sea kayaks, river kayaks or canoes from **Ocean River Exploits**, 52 Commonwealth Dr. in Botwood, ☎ 709/257-4657 or 800/563-4657. They offer guided tours, too, of the area close to Botwood or of the fort at Phillip's Head, a World War II artillery emplacement north of Botwood. They also have two- and three-day kayak excursions.

■ **Gros Morne Adventure Guides** (PO Box 101, Pasadena, NF A0L 1K0, ☎ 709/458-2722, in winter 709/686-2241, Web site www.newcomm.net/gmag) does kayaking trips in Notre Dame Bay, and also provides guides for individuals and families. They will even meet you at Deer Lake Airport. Trips in Notre Dame Bay are not suitable for beginning paddlers, but do not require expert level, either. One week trips cost about $1,100, which includes equipment and meals. These trips average from seven to nine miles of paddling each day, with hikes around the islands to explore abandoned outports and lighthouses. The first and last nights are spent at B&Bs, with camping in between. Private guides are about $200 a day.

■ **Aspen Brook Adventures**, between Badger and Grand Falls-Windsor (☎ 709/489-7675, fax 709/489-5154), is a one-stop center for kayakers and canoeists, with rentals of both craft and guided trips on the Exploits River. A three- to four-hour mid-day tour includes canoe or kayak rental and return transportation, at $30 adult and $15 per child under 15. The five-hour evening tour includes a barbecue on an island ($40; $20 for children). They also guide overnight canoe and kayak tours, and have campsites along the river ($8).

■ **Red Indian Adventures** in Grand Falls-Windsor (☎ 709/486-0892) rents canoes; full day is $50, half-day $30. They also have several canoe trip options, and an instructor is available for special needs clients. A good introduction to canoeing is their Aspen Sunset Tour, on the calmer – but still very scenic – stretches of the Exploits River, through the grass-covered islands to a beach where you can swim and have dinner. The trip takes 6½ hours and includes canoe, equipment, and buffet dinner. Prices decrease with the number of people on the trip, from $50 each for eight people to $100 for one person. Their two-day Red Indian Falls Tour begins at the Millertown dam and ends in Badger. Experienced canoeists will enjoy the challenging rapids, which others can portage. The campsite for the night is below Red Indian Falls. The cost for this trip, which includes meals, tents and canoe equipment, is $130 each if eight people sign up, $180 for one person.

Red Indian Adventures also does excursions in 15-person voyager canoes, either on Rushy Pond for a sunset and moonlight still-water paddle with a weiner roast around a beach fire, or on Red Indian Lake for an overnight trip. Paddling a large canoe with 14 other people is a new experience for most canoeists; the evening trip is $25, the two-day trip from $130 to $180, depending upon how many are going.

■ **Aspen Brook Adventures**, between Badger and Grand Falls-Windsor, ☎ 709/489-7675, fax 709/489-5154, rents canoes and kayaks, at $30 a full day and $20 half-day for canoes and $25 full day and $15 half-day for kayaks.

■ **Aspenwood Hike and Bike Tours** in Springdale, ☎ 709/673-4255, also leads kayaking and canoe tours, but Tom couldn't fit everything into the business name. Tours, which can include accommodations and meals, run from $20 per person for half-day paddles to $85 on overnight trips. Springdale is just north of TransCanada-1 on Rte. 390, on Halls Bay.

River Rafting

Newfoundland's only rafting company is on the Exploits River (which is the province's largest). **Red Indian Adventures** in Grand Falls-Windsor, ☎ 709/486-0892, offers two trips daily, a two-hour run through a wild-water canyon or a five-hour trip with quiet waters interspersed with whitewater. The second includes a picnic lunch on the riverside, and is suitable for children; the first is only for age 14 or older. The canyon trip is $25, the longest one is $50-$100, depending on the number of participants.

Boat Tours & Ferries

Atlantic Blue Jay Tours at the end of Rte. 352 in Fortune Harbour, ☎ 709/257-2143 or 800/565-4782, use a stable catamaran for their three-hour tours through the islands to visit one of Canada's largest mussel farms, where, after a walk ashore to see the view, guests return to the boat for a feast of steamed mussels. Bald eagles returning to their nest in the cliff overhead are a bonus. The tour costs $25.

Icebergs, whales, seals and bald eagles are all in a day's work (or play) for **Iceberg Alley Ocean Adventures** in Baie Verte, ☎ 709/532-4502, fax 709/532-8092. Their daily 2½-hour tours on a 38-foot motor cruiser, leave at 8 am and 6 pm, June through October. The cost is $25 per person, half for those under age 16.

Oceanside Country Lodge, just north of Point Leamington on Western Arm in Notre Dame Bay, ☎ 709/483-2002, offers its guests daily boat tours from May through October. These can be as short as an hour buzz through the islands or overnight trips to farther reaches of the bay. They will take guests to **Rowsell's Island**, where they will see one of the area's three groups of **Newfoundland ponies**.

A five-minute ferry ride to **Long Island** begins on Pilley's Island east of Robert's Arm, operating hourly until 9 pm in the summer and until 6:30 pm in the winter. Service is suspended in the middle of the day on Tuesdays year-round and every day in the winter. The fare for vehicle and driver is $3.50 ($2.75 for seniors) and $1.75 for passengers (children and seniors, $1).

Little Bay Islands is an island town connected by a 45-minute ferry ride to Shoal Arm, north of Springdale via Rte. 392. The boat makes four or five crossings each day year-round, except on Wednesday in the summer, when there are fewer. The fare is $6.75 for vehicle and driver ($3.50 senior) and $2.25 for adult passengers ($1.25 for seniors and children).

Diving

Iceberg Alley Ocean Adventures in Baie Verte, ☎ 709/532-4502, fax 709/532-8092, offers scuba diving tours and courses.

Windsurfing

Rushy Pond in the former Beothuk Provincial Park, five minutes west of Grand Falls-Windsor on TransCanada-1, has good winds and a grassy rigging area. **Ocean River Exploits**, 52 Commonwealth Dr., in Botwood, ☎ 709/257-4657 or 800/563-4657, rents windsurfers by the day, weekend or week.

Fishing

The rivers and lakes south and west of Millertown are known for some of central Newfoundland's best fishing. Logging roads lead into this wilderness area, to **Granite, Meelpaeg and Lloyd's lakes**, or you can fish from the Exploits Dam or in Red Indian Lake, both just a few miles from Millertown. Four-pound trout are not rare here; neither are four-pound mosquitoes.

Guided Fishing Trips

- Salmon guide **Bill Lynch**, PO Box 556, Grand Falls-Windsor, NS A2A 2J9, ☎ 709/489-4662, can accommodate up to six people at Sandy Lake Lodge, a comfortable lodge with all the amenities and home-cooked meals. A week, with guide, transportation, licenses, meals and lodging is $1,000 (US funds).

■ On Snow

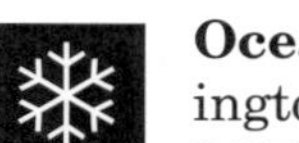

Oceanside Country Lodge, just north of Point Leamington on Western Arm on Notre Dame Bay, ☎ 709/483-2002, has a well-rounded program of winter sports available, along with lodging in its adjacent cabins. Guests can sign up for a winter package that includes all meals, at $60 per person per day. Snowshoes, cross-country skis and snowmobiles are available for rental at the lodge, and they also offer sleigh rides.

Skiing

King's Point has a network of about 15 miles of groomed cross-country ski trails off the east side of Rte. 391, about halfway between the town and TransCanada-1. Family membership is $10 for the whole season, but you're welcome to ski there free if you're in the area. They won't ask for a donation, but you should leave something to help buy gas for the grooming equipment. A rustic warm-up cabin has a stove where you can make hot drinks; bring your lunch, and meet some very nice local people there. For trail information, call Rob Toms, ☎ 709/673-3490.

The **Exploits Valley Ski Club**, ☎ 709/489-6703, close to TransCanada-1 on Rte. 410, has three trails of one to four miles in length.

The **Spruce Trails Cross Country Ski Club** is located two miles south of the Rte. 414 intersection on Rte. 410.

Oceanside Country Lodge, just north of Point Leamington on Western Arm, Notre Dame Bay, ☎ 709/483-2002, has cross-country ski trails and rentals, and can take you on guided ski tours, as well.

A small, but nicely maintained new downhill ski area has opened in at the far northern end of the peninsula. You can ski with an ocean view at **Copper Creek Mountain** in Baie Verte, ☎ 709/532-4338, fax 709/532-4374. Eight runs descend 1,100 feet of vertical drop to the shores of a long bay, and from the upper slopes you can see the open ocean. Full-day adult lift passes are $16 weekdays, $19 weekends, full equipment rentals are $17 a day, $30 for a weekend. They offer a ski school and learn-to-ski packages.

Snowmobiling

In less than two decades, **Buchans** (pronounced BUCK'ns) has changed from a closed "company town" owned lock, stock and barrel by a mining concern to the snowmobile capital of the central province.

Several sections of the former CN rail line have been reclaimed in this area as part of the TransCanada Trail. It crosses Trans-Canada-1 at Badger, and work is well underway to restore bridges around Grand Falls. This is used by snowmobilers, and promises to become a major snowmobile corridor once it is completed.

N.W. Gander Lodge, located south of Grand Falls, ☎ 709/754-5500 or 709/579-8055, offers winter coast-to-coast trips through the wilderness of central Newfoundland, from Notre Dame Bay all the way to Fortune Bay on the south coast. Ice fishing and wildlife-viewing on these trips is superb, but they traverse a rugged and wild backcountry, and are only for those who enjoy a real challenge and don't mind roughing it.

Oceanside Country Lodge, just north of Point Leamington on Western Arm, Notre Dame Bay, ☎ 709/483-2002, has direct access to trails and can take you on guided tours, as well. They rent snowmobiles at the lodge.

Sledding & Sleigh Rides

Flood's Stable and Carriage House, 181 Grenfell Heights, Grand Falls-Windsor, NF A2A 2J2, ☎ 709/489-7185, offers sleigh rides for guests at their inn or for others.

Oceanside Country Lodge at Point Leamington on Notre Dame Bay, ☎ 709/483-2002, will arrange sleigh rides for their guests.

On Horseback

Flood's Stable and Carriage House, 181 Grenfell Heights, Grand Falls-Windsor, NF A2A 2J2, ☎/fax 709/489-7185, has a vacation farm featuring an equestrian facility with indoor and outdoor arenas, and also offers carriage rides. For beginners, lessons can be packaged with lodging at the farm.

Cultural & Eco-Travel Experiences

The **Mary March Regional Museum** on St. Catherine St. (at Cromer Ave.) near TransCanada-1, Grand Falls-Windsor, ☎ 709/489-7331, tells the story of the Beothuk peoples, focusing on the natural history of the area, its aboriginal peoples, and the settlement of this area by Europeans. Mary March, the last surviving Beothuk (whose real name was Demasduit) has become a symbol of her people. A short film, *Lost Race*, is shown. This free museum is open Monday-Friday, 9 am to 5 pm, Saturday and Sunday, 2 to 5 pm.

Behind the museum is **Beothuk Village**, ☎ 709/489-3559, with replicas of mamateeks, the round Beothuk homes. Admission to the village is $2; it is open late May through early September

Archaeology

A hardly-known ledge at the tip of the Baie Verte Peninsula in **Fleur de Lys** is, we think, one of the most exciting archaeological sites in the province. In terms of what you actually see as a visitor, it is particularly rewarding, since it's all right there in front of you – no excavation site covered over, no artifacts in cases of an interpretation center. After a five-minute walk up a boardwalk you stand in front of a rock face pitted with round indentations carved from the gray soapstone. About 2,500 years ago, Dorset people, a late Paleoeskimo group from Labrador that hunted seals on this coast, began using this quarry for bowls and lamps. The larger round holes you see are the bowls, which were used to burn blubber for cooking, and the smaller are for lamps where blubber was burned for light.

■ Fauna & Flora

Rtes. 390 and 391 lead from TransCanada-1 to Kings Point, where a left turn takes you to the 400-foot **Rattling Brook Falls**, dropping in two streams and several stages from the top of the mountain in a thundering torrent during spring runoff, but impressive any time of year. It's about three miles from the Esso Station in King's Point. A 10-15-minute walk over a moss-covered forest floor of roots and talus, heady with balsam, brings you to the foot of the lower falls. In summer, you can probably scramble up the talus slope to see the upper part – but not in the spring, or if the weather is wet. At the trailhead by the road is a nice little picnic park beside the river.

A **waterfall** beside Rte. 410 in Baie Verte, as you drive north to Fleur de Lys on Rte.410, has a nice picnic area in woods beside it.

The **Salmonid Interpretation Centre** at the falls of the Exploits River in Grand Falls-Windsor, ☎ 709/489-7350, has displays telling about the salmon and the facility here, which is North America's largest salmon enhancement program. Viewing windows allow you to watch the salmon migrate upstream. Open daily, mid June through late September, from 8 am to dusk, with a nominal admission fee. It is wheelchair accessible.

Newfoundland's largest nursery for forest regeneration is in Grand Falls-Windsor: **Woodale Tree Nursery**, ☎ 709/489-3012. On a free tour you can see a tree seedline in operation, from the smallest seedlings to a new tree orchard.

Sightseeing

The town of **Fleur de Lys** is among most scenic fishing villages in the province, we think, and would be worth a trip even if it didn't have a remarkable archaeological site. The road drops into a series of steep streets above a harbor of

➲ **LOCAL LORE:** *And, in the curiosity department, we can't let these two go by unnoticed. In* ***Crescent Lake*** *near Robert's Arm, you can look for the local lake monster, Cressie. And, although we're not suggesting you can actually see Cressie, mind you, you can visit the spot – quite a big spot – where the world's largest recorded squid ran aground in November of 1878. At* ***Glover's Harbour****, which was then known as Thimble Tickles, the squid caused quite a stir, with tentacles 35 feet long, a body 20 feet long, and a weight of over two tons. What they did with all that calamari, we don't know.*

rocky hummocks. Small homes and fish stores are scattered about the rocks and skerries, wherever they can find a wide enough perch. The streets are no more than driveways winding between them. See *Archaeology*, page 563, for more information.

For a view over the bay to the open ocean, you can climb **Copper Creek Mountain**, or you can take the easy way up by riding the chairlift, which operates Saturday and Sunday, 2 to 4 pm in the summer. Adults pay $3, children $2.

Botwood Heritage Centre in Botwood, ☎ 709/257-3022, is in the former World War II airbase and tells the story of this small town's unique involvement in the war. You'll learn how the townspeople captured an enemy vessel (the first captured on this side of the Atlantic). Botwood's earlier aviation history, dating from 1919, is also featured. It's open daily, noon to 8 pm, mid-June through August. Admission is $2 adults, $1 student, $5 family.

The **John T. Upward Museum** in Harry's Harbour, ☎ 709/635-3865, is a privately owned museum created by a couple who enjoy sharing the history of this scenic area. It recreates the interior of the general store that once served the village, and shows the restored interior of the outport merchant's home. They also have a Newfoundland pony and a boat workshop.

Where To Stay & Eat

Near Grand Falls-Windsor

In the middle of TransCanada-1's 100-mile route through vast unsettled areas is the former rail outpost and logging community of Badger, with a most unexpected oasis, the **Woodland Kettle Bed & Breakfast and Tea Room**. Open May through September, it occupies a former convent, with the chapel transformed into a comfortable guest sitting room. Along with attractive decor, nice touches accent the rooms, including bathrobes, a thermos of hot tea and biscuits on arrival. As you would expect from a place with a tearoom, breakfasts feature home-baked breads. Afternoon tea for two, with cake, tarts and cream is $6. *19 Church St, Badger, NF A0H 1A0, ☎ 709/539-2588 or 888/539-2588 ($-$$).*

Oceanside Country Lodge is a full-service outdoor activity center, serving meals ($), renting sports equipment and offering guides and boat tours. *Just north of Point Leamington on Western Arm, Notre Dame Bay, ☎ 709/483-2002 ($).*

Exploits Valley Motel, at the intersection of TransCanada-1 and Rte. 360, has standard and housekeeping rooms and a good lunch counter (with generous chef salads). *PO Box 879, Bishop's Falls, NF A0H 1C0, ☎ 709/258-6665, fax 709/258-5785 ($).*

The **Salmonid Interpretation Centre** has a good restaurant and serves fresh salmon, which you'll find delicious, even if it is a bit disconcerting to lunch on one right after having looked its still-swimming cousin in the eye. *TransCanada-1, Grand Falls-Windsor, ☎ 709/489-7350 ($).*

The **Valley Restaurant** serves Newfoundland pea soup on Saturdays only; be there at noon to get it with dumplings. A big bowl of this thick, hearty soup made with yellow peas, carrots and ham is $1.90, $2.15 with dumplings. There's no sign for the mall, so look for Sobey's Supermarket. *Exploits Valley Mall, Harris Ave., half a mile from TransCanada-1 in Grand Falls-Windsor, ☎ 709/489-5961 ($).*

If you simply can't face another fish for dinner, try **Station Steak House**. It's open daily 2 pm to 1 am. *26 Station St., at TransCanada-1, Exit 22, Bishop's Falls, ☎ 709/258-5706 ($-$$).*

The **Badger Diner** serves home-style dishes seven days a week. *TransCanada-1 at Badger, ☎ 709/539-2625 ($).*

The Baie Verte Peninsula

Indian River Brook Bed & Breakfast has two rooms and a shop specializing in provincial tartans, plus a Newfoundland dog who's the hero of a book. *PO Box 664, Springdale, NF A0J 1T0, ☎ 709/673-3886 ($).*

Windamere Cabins are in Rattling Brook, a bit past the falls, to which you can walk on a hiking trail. New log cabins each have two bedrooms and a kitchen. *PO Box 154, King's Point, NF A0J 1H0, ☎ 709/268-3863 ($$).*

Budgell's Motel has an attractive restaurant with a bit more variety than most, and good lasagna ($4.99). In summer they serve lunch and dinner; in the winter they serve dinner only. The dining room is always open until midnight. *PO Box 76, King's Point, NF A0J 1H0, ☎ 709/268-3364 ($).*

Near South Brook, **Fort Birchy Tea Room** has a bakery and restaurant with homestyle local dishes, including baked beans, pea soup and partridgeberry pie. *TransCanada-1, ☎ 709/551-1318 ($).*

■ Camping

Fort Birchy Campgrounds has tent sites and RV spaces with hookups. If you don't feel like cooking breakfast you can walk to the homey restaurant. It's near South Brook. *TransCanada-1 (PO Box 1440), Springdale, NF A0J 1T0, ☎ 709/551-1318.*

Beothuk Park, a former provincial park, has 63 sites for tents and trailers, all at $9. It's on a swimming beach, with nature trails and a replica of a logging camp. Reservations accepted. *Exit 17, TransCanada-1, Grand Falls-Windsor, ☎ 709/489-9832.*

Bay d'Espoir & Fortune Bay

Most of the territory covered in this chapter is a vast wilderness, cut by only one road and a very few rough tracks. It includes the Bay du Nord and Middle Ridge Wilderness Reserves, and more wild areas covered in lakes and ponds. A single road connects the two clusters of ports on the central southern shore with the rest of Newfoundland. Most Newfoundlanders have never been to Harbour Breton. They've missed a spectacular part of their province.

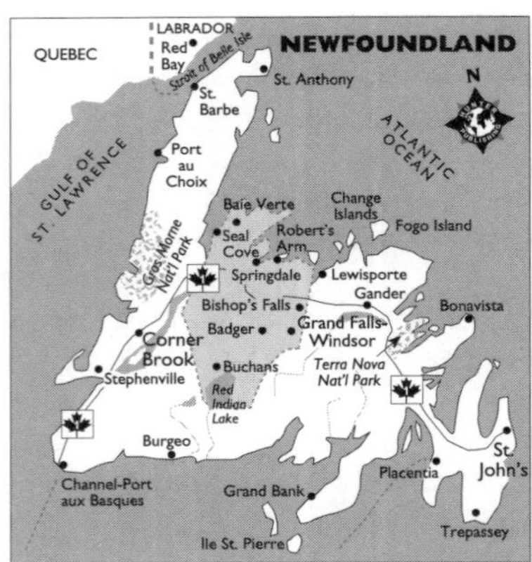

Geography & History

The wilderness through which you must travel to reach the towns along Fortune Bay and Bay d' Espoir cut off this part of the coast from overland contact until this century. Harbour Breton, the main community in the area, was settled by the French in the 1500s, and by the 1700s it was almost the sole province of the English firm of Newman & Company, the same Newman's of Port fame. The coastal towns made their living from the sea, mainly the fisheries, and their contact, like that of Grand Bank, was just as likely to be with New England and Nova Scotia as with Newfoundland.

The long arms of Bay d'Espoir (which is locally called Bay Despair, though not as a commentary) reach far into the land, to a town called Head of Bay. If you make the side trip to this area, don't be misled by its often low, gentle shoreline: it is no indication of what awaits you just below the intersection where you return to the main road. From there the land climbs steadily until it drops suddenly away on your right, and you are looking down – way down – into the narrow fjord of Hermitage Bay. It is not at all unusual to see clouds drifting between you and the water below.

Follow any of the roads that branch out like fingers to the harbor towns and, although the scenery of each will be stunningly different, the terrain will follow a familiar pattern: the road will climb or run along a high moorland ridge, then drop suddenly into a rockbound or cliff-enclosed cove or tiny bay, with a village clinging to its shore. Larger settlements climb the steep sides, smaller ones cluster at one edge or string along the water single-file. The scenery is indescribably beautiful. The life of every family in these villages revolves around the sea.

Getting Around

Rte. 360 drops like a plumb-bob out of Bishop's Falls, just east of Grand Falls-Windsor. Eighty miles later it intersects with the first

➲ **WARNING:** *We don't suggest traveling these roads in the rain. Most are in good condition, but the final approaches are frightfully steep, and some roads are not paved. Wet surfaces can be treacherous. And don't plan to travel after dark. If you find yourself lingering too long over the sunset in a particularly beautiful cove, ask anyone in the village if someone takes guests. Chances are very good that you will find a comfortable bed and a warm dinner right there, and can watch the sun rise over the opposite mountain shore in the morning.*

road. A rare dirt track may wander off into the scraggly woods, but no more. **Rte. 361** bears west to the towns around Bay d'Espoir, then **Rte. 362** goes east to Belleoram. A little later **Rte. 364** leaves to the west to follow a long peninsula, and 360 finally ends at the harbor in Harbour Breton. Planning your route is very easy: you simply follow the roads until they end.

If you love dramatic coastal scenery, and have a lot of film with you, we suggest you follow each of these three roads at the bottom, and each of the few little roads that branch from them. Very little a traveler does can compare to the discovery of a town appearing suddenly below, in a setting so grand.

If you can't face driving, these towns are connected, if infrequently, by **Bay d'Espoir Bus Line**, ☎ 709/533-3439.

Information Sources

Don't expect to find much information on this part of Newfoundland. Its attractions don't get listed in tourist brochures, though they are shown in pictures.

- This region is covered in the "Central Region" section of the annual *Newfoundland and Labrador Travel Guide*, available free from the **Department of Tourism, Culture and Recreation**, PO Box 8730, St. John's, NF A1B 4K2, ☎ 800/563-6353 or 709/729-2830.

- **Tourism Department**, Harbour Breton, NF A0H 1P0, ☎ 709/885-2425, fax 709/885-2095.

- **Fortune Bay North Shore Development Association**, PO Box 88, English Harbour West, Fortune Bay, NF A0H 1M0, ☎ 709/888-6521, fax 709/888-5101.

Adventures

On Foot

Get out and walk wherever you see a track too uncertain to drive, or a trail leading up a headland. Ask locally about other trails. Recreational walking hasn't really caught on here yet, and there are very few maintained trails.

Boxey, an area flatter than many harbor towns here, has walking trails, and the peninsula on the opposite side of its harbor, called **Stone's Head**, has rough trails for the ambitious.

English Harbour Mountain, in English Harbour West, on Rte. 363, is a rugged climb, but from its top you can see forever – or at least a fine view over Fortune Bay and the mountains.

At the end of the road in **Pool's Cove**, a trail leads up the great lump of red sandstone that punctuates the end of the land like a big exclamation point.

Guided Hiking Tours

■ For hiking and camping trips in the Middle Ridge Wildlife Reserve, west of the Bay du Nord Reserve, and elsewhere in this region, ask **Caribou Adventure Tours**, PO Box 284, Lewisporte, NF A0G 3A0, ☎ 709/535-8379.

PERMIT NEEDED: *The huge* ***Bay du Nord Wilderness Reserve*** *takes up an immense section of the land east of Rte. 360. In order to use the area you must obtain a free permit, which you can get, along with a map of the Reserve, from Parks Division, PO Box 8700, St. John's, NF A1B 4J6, ☎ 709/729-2431.*

On Water

Canoeing & Kayaking

The **Bay du Nord River** runs through the huge Bay du Nord Wilderness Reserve, and provides experienced canoeists with a real wilderness experience that, unlike most others of its caliber, can be done in five to seven days, instead of several weeks. The river flows through beautiful and varied countryside of bogs, heathland, forest, fens, lakes, and barrens, and patches of low stunted fir growing in a tangled mat known as tuckamore. It ends in a wooded area, with grassy marshes and alder swamps, both uncommon in Newfoundland. The Middle Range caribou herd, about 15,000 animals, calve here and spend the winter within the river's watershed. About two miles above the mouth is a valley that was formed by the-Dover-Hermitage Fault, the dividing line for the land left by the African plate after its collision with the North American plate.

The canoe route begins at the watershed between the Terra Nova and Bay du Nord rivers, with a put-in at Lake Kepenkeck, reached by a wilderness access road from the village of Terra Nova, on Rte. 301 from TransCanada-1 in Terra Nova National Park. It goes through a series of small lakes, then across Lake Kaegudeck and into Jubilee Lake. It then passes through two more good-sized lakes and into a channel of mixed rapids, waterfalls and widened lake-like stretches, which end with a portage around the 60-foot **Smokey Falls.** Below that the rapids increase in length and challenge until the river flows into the open views of Fortune Bay. The last two days of the trip are the most challenging, and you can do just this part if you go into Medonnegonix Lake by floatplane (see below).

The **Gander River** system begins on the west side of Rte. 360, which it crosses. The river has been a major transportation route since aboriginal times, and riverboats still ply some of its waters. You can access the Northwest Gander River from Rte. 360 for a trip of several days when the waters are high in the spring. This is for experienced paddlers only, with several rapids and an area filled with boulders. The river is quite deep in places. The most-canoed section of the river is from its crossing with Trans-Canada-1 in Glenwood to its mouth in Gander Bay; see Canoeing under the Gander Region.

Sea kayakers will find quiet coves in **Fortune Bay**, but the area is hard to reach and launching points are rare.

Canoe Outfitters & Guided Tours

- Local outfitters, such as **Gander River Guiding Services**, ☎ 709/676-2628, can advise you on the best shuttle arrangements to get you back to your car or get your car to you in Gander Bay.

- Floatplanes, which can carry canoeists, their canoes and gear into the reserve's lakes, are operated by **Pine Ridge Air Services**, ☎ 709/782-0979. They have bases in Gander and the village of Terra Nova, and are outfitters as well, so they can arrange for canoe guides, accommodations in a wilderness lodge, and full packages that include fishing.

- For canoeing and camping trips in the Middle Ridge Wildlife Reserve, west of the Bay du Nord Reserve, and elsewhere in the area, contact **Caribou Adventure Tours**, PO Box 284, Lewisporte, NF A0G 3A0, ☎ 709/535-8379.

> **FLOATPLANES:** *You will need floatplane access to do some of the other shorter rivers that flow into Fortune Bay: the Salmon, North East and North West rivers. The latter is far less strenuous than the others, a two-day trip through light woodlands, with only about two miles of challenging rapids and portages. The ponds that make up the route are shown in darker blue on the map in the* User's Guide to the Bay du Nord Wilderness Reserve, *available from the Parks Division, PO Box 8700, St. John's, NF A1B 4J6, ☎ 709/729-2431. Remember that you need an access permit to enter the reserve for any purpose.*

Boat Tours & Ferries

One of the best (and certainly cheapest) ways to see the coast of Fortune Bay is to take the ferries that connect these reaches, providing outside contact to towns with no land link to the rest of the province. These few remaining outports are filled with hospitable people and have a way of life that remains in very few places. The scenery is extraordinary, and the only way to see much of this shoreline is from the water.

The **ferry** from Pool's Cove to Rencontre East, ☎ 709/891-1050 or 709/466-7951, fax 709/891-2995, which in some seasons goes on to Bay d'Argent on the Burin Peninsula, makes enough trips each day between mid-June and mid-September that you can ride over and back for a day trip. If you choose to stop in Rencontre, without going to Bay d'Argent, you'll have about four hours to explore the town. All outport ferries stay overnight at the outport in case of emergency, so the first run of the morning is from Rencontre, and the last run at night is from Pool's Cove. The day fare is – are you ready? – $3 for adults and $1.50 for seniors and children. There is no ferry service on Wednesday. Ferries operate all year. This one is not shown on the provincial highway map, which marks the former ferry from English Harbour to Rencontre and Harbour Breton (this may change with a new map printing).

On the other side of the peninsula, off Rte. 364, you can take a ferry across Hermitage Bay from the village of **Hermitage-Sandyville** to **Galtois and McCallum**, ☎ 709/292-4300. Both of these destinations are outports with no other form of transport. The ferry shuttles back and forth across the bay, making two round-trips in the morning and two in the afternoon; at noon it leaves Galtois for McCallum, which takes about 1½ hours, returning to Hermitage at 2:15. This mid-day trip is a good way to see this part of the coast; the fare is $3 for adults, $1.50 for seniors and children.

This trip to McCallum does not run on Thursday, when the ***M/V Marine Voyager***, ☎ 709/635-4100 or 709/635-4127, the ferry connecting ports farther west, goes from Francois to McCallum and continues on to Hermitage. This is the only day you can connect to make the trip along the entire south coast. The fare from Hermitage to Francois is $5.25, $2.75 children and seniors.

Roti Bay near St. Albans is a major aquaculture center, and you can visit the pens, as well as outports and bald eagle nesting sites on a trip with **Eagle's Fjord Boat Tours and Charters**, in St. Albans, ☎ 709/538-3610. The bay is a scenic one, with hills on either side.

Fishing

For a description of the Bay du Nord River and the wilderness reserve, see *Canoeing*, above. This is prime salmon fishing country, and the best access is from the north, via roads from Trans-Canada-1 in Terra Nova National Park, or by air via floatplane.

Access to the lower waters of **Bay du Nord River** and the wilderness reserve is from Pool's Cove, a fishing village on an unpaved road, reached from Rte. 362. Rencontre East is one of the south coast's few remaining villages that is accessed only by ferry, and it lies at the outlet of some of the area's finest salmon waters, **Rencontre Lake** and **Long Harbour River.** From Wreck Cove, at the end of Rte. 363, it is a short boat ride to the **Salmonier River**, one of the finest for salmon fishing. **Taylor's Bay River** is close to Coomb Cove. Since these are scheduled rivers, you will need a guide unless you are a resident of Newfoundland.

The **Gander River** flows northeast across the northern part of this area, crossing Rte. 360 on its way. The lower (northern) reaches of the river are accessible by road from TransCanada-1,

FISHING TIP: *This is a good place to try the traditional Newfoundland technique of cod jigging, which is much more fun when you go out with a local fisherman on his boat than on a tourist cod-jigging party boat in a more touristed area. Ask your host, or just go to the wharves and ask around. You are almost certain to find someone going out. Talking with a local fisherman as you travel in his boat will be an experience, too.*

and several outfitters offer fishing trips by river boat or other means, traveling between camps by canoe.

Fishing Outfitters – Guided Trips

■ **Conne River Outfitters**, Bay d'Espoir, NF A0H 1J0, ☎ 709/882-2470, has camps on Lake Medonnegonix in the wilderness reserve, where you can stay during a completely catered fishing trip for salmon, landlocked salmon and brook trout. They provide access by air, guides (with a 1:1 ratio), canoes and all meals The outfitting company is operated by the Conne River band of Micmacs, who have a reserve there.

■ **Pine Ridge Lodge and Wilderness Tours**, ☎ 709/782-0979, also arranges complete packages, with plane access to lodges on waters adjoining the wilderness reserve. Weekly rates are $1,400 (US funds). To find other outfitters who have camps in this area, refer to the listing of licensed outfitters in the current *Hunting and Fishing Guide*, free from the tourism office.

■ **Gander River Tours** in Gander, ☎ 709/256-3252, has six-day packages to fish for brook trout, with guides (1:1 ratio) and all meals, accommodations, riverboat and canoe transport, at $1,200 (US funds). Salmon trips are $1,500.

■ **Gander River Guiding Services**, ☎ 709/676-2628, offers guides at $135 a day, as well as riverboat access and other packages that include airport pick-up, meals and accommodations.

Cultural & Eco-Travel Experiences

The culture of this area is rich in community life and solidarity, reflecting its long isolated history and the rigors of its climate and terrain. Local women, even more than elsewhere on the island, it seems, knit incessantly, and you should stop in the tiny craft shops here to look at their work. You will see an overwhelming variety of patterned sweaters, hats, mittens, gloves (and the useful, characteristic Newfie mittens, with one finger and thumb), baby wear, hiking socks, scarves and even kitchen towels knitted of cotton yarn. The prices will astonish you: a good pair of all-wool mittens for $8 (even less with the exchange rate) and no tax on local handcrafts.

> ➔ **SUPPORT THE LOCAL ECONOMY:** *This is not a heavily touristed area, and the gift you buy here puts much-needed money directly in the hands of families whose way of life and livelihood has been crushed by the closing of the fisheries. We outfitted every child on our gift list here and felt very good about it, too. Look for* ***Pool's Cove Crafts*** *in Pool's Cove for a particularly good selection of sweaters.*

The **bald eagle** population in this area is the highest in Canada, and we don't know anyone who's traveled here without seeing one. They literally fly past your windshield as you drive along Rte. 360. Stone's Head, opposite Boxey Harbor, is a nesting site for several bird species.

Caribou Adventure Tours, PO Box 284, Lewisporte, NF A0G 3A0, ☎ 709/535-8379, can take you into the Middle Ridge Wildlife Reserve, west of the Bay du Nord Reserve, to observe caribou, black bear and moose, accompanied by a local biologist, who not only knows where the animals are, but can tell you about their habits.

Sightseeing

The land itself, and the villages that sit in the shelter of its mountains and tiny coves, are the sights. Travel to the ends of the roads, especially to Belleoram, Pool's Cove (where you can take the ferry to Rencontre East and Bay d'Argent, on the Burin Peninsula – see *Boat Tours & Ferries* above), and English Harbour West.

Belleoram is a fishing town that was never meant to have access by road, but it does have one, which almost somersaults your car from the high headland into the harbor. Its cove is protected by a sandstone island, almost vertical cliffs on either side, and irregular lumps of mountain rising in between, along which the houses perch, propped up in places by pilings. The shore is lined with fishing sheds and wharves, from which kids are usually fishing. A huge Anglican church stands to one end, and from its cemetery is one of the best views on Fortune Bay.

English Harbour West sits in a deep protected harbor under moor-covered rocky slopes. Go to the right as you enter town, to the farthest end, until the pavement ends, then walk to the point, where you'll see an island rising like a mountain, a sloping moor on its top, dropping off in cut and convoluted cliffs.

Coombs Cove is almost enclosed by two headlands, with a waterfall dropping off the face to the left. **Furby's Cove**, with 21 homes to which the map shows no road at all, is now connected by an unsurfaced road that drops straight down to the waterfront at an alarming pitch.

Sunny Cottage Heritage Centre in Harbour Breton, ☎ 709/885-2425, is one of Newfoundland's largest Queen Anne houses. It's now a local museum, with each room displaying a different theme, from fisheries to the Newman & Company connection here. The makers of the famous Port had a major headquarters here in the early days. Another room tells the story of eight outport towns that were resettled in Harbour Breton; a tour takes 20 minutes with local guide, but you can stay to browse. It costs $3 and is open 10 am to 8 pm, Sunday-Friday, 6 to 8 pm on Saturday, or by appointment.

Cluett Heritage House in Belleoram, ☎ 709/881-3114, is a restored 1844 home, open in July and August, showing family and community life in a remote fishing village in the last century.

Where To Stay & Eat

Except for a few scattered hospitality homes, Harbour Breton is the center for tourist services. It's too big to be a cute little outport, but its setting is unbeatable, with houses strung in little clusters around the shore of a large inner harbor and along both sides of the channel leading into it.

If you plan to take the ferry trip from Pool's Cove to Rencontre or Bay d'Argent, it's convenient to spend the night in Pool's Cove at **By the Bay Hospitality Home**, a few steps from the little ferry dock. The engaging Williams family shares their tidy home on the harbor with travelers. They also serve meals. *Pool's Cove, NF A0H 2B0, ☎ 709/665-3176 ($).*

Sandyville Inn is a B&B in a modern home with a big front yard, close to the Sandyville beach. Turn left at the T (right goes to the ferry landing). *Hermitage-Sandyville, NF A0N 1R0, ☎ 709/883-2332 ($).*

To experience life in an island outport that's still connected by ferries, stay at the **Galtois Inn**. It has six comfortable rooms and a dining room that specializes in seafood. It's open all year round, as is the town's harbor, which allows a year-round fishery here. *PO Box 151, Galtois, NF A0H 1N0, ☎ 709/841-4141 ($-$$).*

Southern Point Hotel, just as you come into Harbour Breton, is the only act in town, with plain, but comfortable rooms, a little noisy when they're busy. The restaurant ($-$$) has warm, friendly service and can usually scout something up for late arrivals after they've closed. It's a pretty standard menu, with fried scallops, cod, shrimp, fish and chips, or pork chops. *Harbour Breton, NF A0H 1P0, ☎ 709/885-2283, fax 709/885-2579 ($$).*

Scott's Snack Bar and Restaurant, a bit farther along on the same road as Southern Point Hotel, is the only other place to eat in town except for a take-out at the far end of the right-hand side of the harbor (go straight instead of crossing the bridge into the center of town). *Harbour Breton, NF, no phone ($).*

Rainbow Restaurant is a pleasant, wheelchair-accessible restaurant serving properly-cooked seafood, not always fried. The steelhead dinner is excellent. They open at 9 am every day, and are open until 8 pm on weekdays, past midnight on weekends. *Main St., St. Albans, ☎ 709/538-3395 ($-$$).*

■ Camping

Jipujijkuei Kuespem Park is on Rte. 360 just south of the Rte. 361 intersection. A former provincial park, it is now operated by the Conne River Micmac Band. Campsite fees are $9 a night for up to two tents. Sites are separated from each other by trees, but all are close to the camp road; bring black-fly repellent. You can get information on the Wilderness Reserve here, including a map. *Conne River, NF A0H 1J0, ☎ 709/882-2470, fax 709/882-2292.*

Two miles north of intersection of Rtes. 360 and 364, on Rte. 360 is a **Municipal Park**, unattended and with somewhat overgrown but usable unserviced campsites. At the shore is a beach of tiny pink and blue pebbles worn smooth and round by the tides, and surprisingly warm water. Camping is free.

For camping trips in the Middle Ridge Wildlife Reserve, contact **Caribou Adventure Tours**. *PO Box 284, Lewisporte, NF A0G 3A0, ☎ 709/535-8379.*

The Great Northern Peninsula

No matter how many tourist brochure photographs you see of **Gros Morne National Park**, you are still not prepared for the beauty of the sheer wall of Western Brook Pond's fjord rising in front of you as you walk across the bog and through the forest. Gros Morne National Park also includes Bonne Bay, the fjord-cut coastline where the Appalachian Mountains end abruptly at the sea. This is a land of tall cliffs, deep valleys and fjords, long vistas and big icebergs drifting offshore.

Geography & History

The Great Northern Peninsula extends above the rest of Newfoundland, almost connecting it to southern Labrador, on the mainland. The two are separated by the Strait of Belle Isle, which you can cross on a ferry. At the southern part of the peninsula is Gros Morne National Park, nearly cut in two by the long East Arm of Bonne Bay.

In the smaller, southern part of the park is some of its best scenery, and the park's outstanding geological phenomenon, **Tablelands**, which gained the park its designation as a UNESCO World Heritage Site. This barren terra-cotta-colored landscape of crumbling rock is a section of the earth's mantle, usually a mile or more underground, forced to the surface here 450 million years ago as the European and African plates moved closer to the North American plate. Geologists come from all over the world to study this rare exposure of the earth's insides; Tablelands give geologists what the Galapagos Islands gave biologists studying evolution – a look back into the process. Interpretive signs and diagrams at **Tablelands Lookout** explain how this exposure came about.

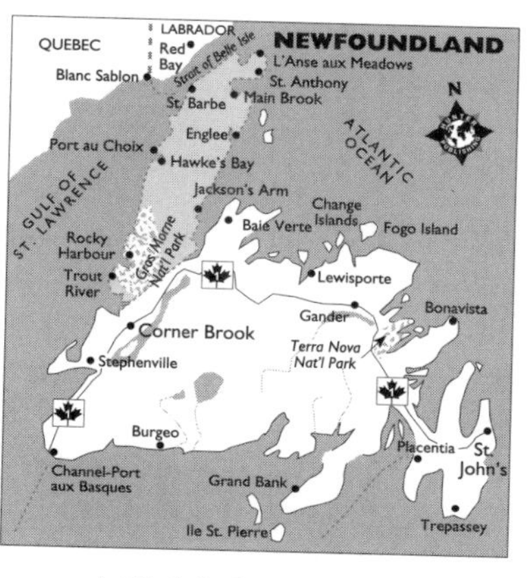

North of the park the land smooths out along the shore, rising inland to the spine of the Long Range Mountains. The Viking Trail hugs a coast where low headlands alternate with sandy coves and beaches. Small villages dot the shore, sometimes with icebergs almost literally in their backyards. Whales cavort and spout in the water, of which motorists have an almost steady view.

Just as the land in the southern part of the peninsula gives geologists valuable clues about the movement of the earth's crust, three sites along the northern route give archaeologists and historians valuable clues about human migrations. Although the best known of these is the Viking settlement at L'Anse aux Meadows near St. Anthony, graves and settlements uncovered at Port aux Choix and Bird Cove give valuable evidence of the southernmost Eskimo habitation in North America.

St. Anthony is the largest town. Located on a well-protected harbor, it grew as the last provisioning port for the Labrador fishing fleet. Follow any road (there aren't very many) until it ends at the sea to find stunning views from towering headland heights or a lovely little cove with bergy bits bouncing in its waters.

Getting Around

The small, new airport in Deer Lake has flights connecting to St. John and Halifax on **Air Nova**, the commuter partner of Air Canada (☎ 800/776-3000 in the US, ☎ 800/565-3940 in Maritime Canada, or ☎ 800/563-5151 in Newfoundland). Flying time from

Halifax is time is 1½ hours, less from St. John's; rental cars are available at the airport.

TransCanada-1 passes Deer Lake before reaching the town of the same name, where Rte. 430 leaves for Gros Morne National Park and the Great Northern Peninsula. **The Viking Trail** begins here, and you can follow its signs all the way to St. Anthony, at the northern tip.

At Wiltondale, 13 miles beyond on Rte. 430, a park sign points to Rte. 431 and the fishing villages of Woody Point and Trout River. Don't miss this southern section of the park, or Woody Point, which clings to the steep bank of the South Arm of Bonne Bay. A shorter diversion leads to Norris Point on the opposite side of Bonne Bay.

From this point, the only real road turning off is Rte. 432, to the peninsula's eastern shore, which leaves many miles later.

Shortly beyond, at St. Barbe, you can take a ferry across the Strait of Belle Isle to Labrador, via the border town of Blanc Sablon, Quebec. The ferry, operated by **Northern Cruiser, Ltd.**, ☎ 709/931-2309, makes two round-trips daily, May through December. The fee for passengers is $9; for automobiles, $18.50. No roads connect this southern coastal area to the rest of Labrador, so this is the best way to see it. In mid-summer you can make the round-trip in the same day and spend about five hours there.

At Eddie's Cove the **Viking Trail** turns sharply east, traveling over a wild barrens to the farthest tip of the peninsula, where the only thing between you and Greenland is icewater. Near St. Anthony, at the far end, a few short roads lead to tiny outports.

Rte. 430 is straight, traffic infrequent and services widely spaced for the 200 miles from Rocky Harbor to the top of the peninsula at St. Anthony. But it is a pleasant, undemanding drive. Do watch out for moose, however, especially late or early in the day.

Information Sources

■ Tourist Information on the Viking Trail is in the annual *Newfoundland and Labrador Travel Guide*, free from the **Department of Tourism, Culture and Recreation**, PO Box 8730, St. John's, NF A1B 4K2, ☎ 800/563-6353 or 709/729-2830, and from the Viking Trail Tourism Association, PO Box 430, St. Anthony, NF A0K 4S0, ☎ 709/454-8888. Pick up a free copy of *Where It's At* from any tourist office on the Viking Trail, for articles on places, events, and activities in the area.

■ In Deer Lake, the **Tourist Information Chalet,** on the TransCanada Highway, is open daily in the summer from 9 am to 9 pm, and May and September from 10 am to 5 pm, ☎ 709/635-2202.

■ You will pass the **Gros Morne Visitor's Centre** on Rte. 430 just before Rocky Harbour, ☎ 709/458-2066, open daily, 9 am to 10 pm from late June to early August, and 9 am to 4 pm daily the rest of the year. A **Tourist Chalet** at Torrent River Bridge, Hawke's Bay, NF A0K 3B0, ☎ 709/248-5344, 709/248-5225 (September through June), is open daily 10 am to 6 pm, July through August.

■ For information on the far north, contact the **Tourism Association**, Rte. 430 (PO Box 430), St. Anthony, NF A0K 4S0, ☎ 709/454-3077 (July through August), ☎ 709/454-8888 (September through June).

Adventures

At the entrance to Gros Morne National Park you will have to stop and buy a pass, unless you plan to go straight through without stopping for so much as a photo from a lookout point. Admission is $3 for one day, $9 for four days, family $6.50 and $19.50. Be sure to get a copy of the free publication called *Tuckamore* at the visitors center, listing current information on park facilities.

■ On Foot

Hiking

The best trails on the peninsula are in the national park, which has 50 miles of developed trails and another 20 of undeveloped trails for the highly experienced climber. The park trails are well marked and maintained, and the scenery just doesn't quit. You are almost certain to see wildlife as you use these trails, especially the more remote ones, including caribou and moose.

In the southern section of the park off Rte. 431, a trail leads to **Green Gardens**, over highland meadows and along the coast marked by sea stacks and caves. The visitors center has a bro-

➔ **TRAIL MAPS & INFORMATION:** *Pick up a copy of the* Tuckamore *(described above) for brief descriptions of the trails, their length and relative difficulty. The* Gros Morne National Park Trail Guide *is a waterproof map with trail descriptions, available at the visitors center for $10.*

chure on this trail, which has a map in it. You have two options, and two different trailheads to choose from, but we prefer the trailhead closest to Trout Brook, from which you can take either the long (8½ miles, about six hours) loop or the short (five-plus miles, two-plus hours) in-and-out trail. The second trailhead, with parking, is less than two miles beyond the first; both are marked Green Gardens.

The shorter trail is simply the first part of the longer one, leading to a beach with a number of attractions, where you will want to spend some time. Try to time your hike to arrive at the beach at low tide. The short trail has only one steep climb, which is the return from the beach to the highlands. The long loop trail has a lot of ups and downs, often steep, and fords a river twice. The riverbed is rocky and slippery, so a pair of water sandals are a good thing to throw in your pack. You'll want boots for the rest of the trail. Whichever trail option you take, follow the sign to the beach when the trail reaches the shore; for short-hikers, this is your destination. You'll find puffy blobs of pillow lava in the basalt hulk of the headland (formed by lava extruded and cooled suddenly underwater), and a sea cave on the other side (which you should not go to on a rising tide, only at low tide). In the other direction are sea stacks and a small waterfall.

The most difficult trail (other than multi-day trails traversing the mountain range) climbs **Gros Morne Mountain**. Again, get a copy of the trail brochure before starting. It's a 10-mile trip and takes six to eight hours, at least one of them spent scrambling up a steep gully filled with rocks. Save this trip for a nice day with a good weather forecast (and hope it's right). At the top of the mountain you walk along a trail overlooking the glacier-formed **Ten Mile Pond,** half a mile below. It's a boots, compass and survival equipment climb, and only for those in top condition. The view is grand, and the trail passes some nice glacial erratics, but it's mostly a day of rocks and tuckamore, the tightly tangled evergreen scrub that covers much of the park's upper landscape. (If you want our personal opinion, we'd choose Green Garden for its scenery and variety.)

An easy, level walk of less than two miles, much of it on boardwalk, leads to the park's scenic highlight (which is saying a lot here), **Western Brook Pond**. Even if such a prize didn't await at the end, the walk is a pleasant one, bordered in wild flowers, which change as the trail moves from pond shore to bog to woodlands. Interpretive signs explain how and when bogs were formed (and continue to form). But the scene so tantalizingly appearing ahead makes it hard to concentrate on the flora.

The trail leads to the shore of a lake so deep its temperature never rises far above freezing. But behind the lake, swallowing its narrow far end, is a straight wall just under half a mile high, split by a large vertical crack. What you can't see is the 500 more feet of sheer rock face under the waters of the lake. And from here you can't see the 10-mile-long tail of Western Brook Pond that extends between the ever-narrowing width of the land-locked fjord. To do that, you have to take the boat (see *Boat Tours*, below) that leaves from the dock in front of you. To get more fine views, follow the trail to your right around the pond shore. To stand directly under the cliffs, follow the trail to the left to Snug Harbour.

Very few places offer you quite such a view for so short and easy a walk, but this is by no means the end of the park's trails – or rewards at the end of them. **Bakers Brook Falls** is at the end of a three-mile trail, also easy. The trail begins from Berry Hill Campground, on the inland side of Rte. 430, just north of Rocky Harbour. The trail crosses bogs and woodsy areas, so be prepared for mosquitoes. The trail to the **Lookout** leaves from the Forest Management Station on Rte. 431, just past the road to Norris Point and, although it climbs steadily for more than a mile to a boggy meadow, it leads to a view over the South Arm and the main body of Bonne Bay and almost straight into Winter House Brook Canyon. On the way back down, you have a view back toward Birchy Head and the end of the arm, with mountains behind.

A longer hike along the shore of **Trout River Pond** in the southern segment of the park leaves from the picnic area, where the boat tours begin. It is a little over eight miles round-trip, and is rough and rocky in places, but the scenery is well worth it. As you travel through the low forest toward the barren slopes of Tablelands, where the rock composition prevents plants from growing, you begin to see bits of the rock from that mountain, then more and more, until finally the entire trail is covered. As you travel, the gray cliffs that border the fjord at its narrowest point loom closer, until you reach the narrows, when you can see the length of the inner, larger section of the fjord, gray cliffs on one wall and the reddish-yellow Tablelands on the other. The trail ends in this barren of peridotite, where most plants cannot survive.

Several hikes use portions of the cart path that once connected isolated outport fishing settlements. The trail to **Green Point** is a bit over six miles round-trip along this partly cobbled shore track. It begins just north of the point where Baker Brook crosses Rte. 430, north of Rocky Harbour; you can also start at Green Point Campground at the other end of the trail. On the south side of Baker Brook, you can walk along this old mail road from Baker Brook Picnic Area, past wreckage of a barge that ran aground here. Another section of the road leads north from **Shallow Bay** for about a mile.

At the park's northern end, a shore trail leads south to the old cemetery at **Sandy Cove**, and north to **Broom Point**, where an isolated fishing settlement has been restored and local fishermen discuss the fisheries with visitors.

Experienced hikers in top condition can backpack across the park, traversing the **Long Range Mountains** from Western Brook Pond (reached by boat), across the summit of Gros Morne Mountain and down to Rte. 430 near Norris Point. The route is unmarked, without trails for much of the way. It takes a minimum of three days and should only be attempted by groups. In three days, weather patterns can change drastically, so in addition to camping equipment and sufficient food and water, hikers will need emergency and survival gear. Just the climb out of the gorge at the end of Western Brook Pond is enough to exhaust the average climber, even without a full pack. In order to get permission to hike and camp this route, you must have an orientation session with park rangers.

With the plethora of good trails in the national park, it's easy to forget the other possibilities on the peninsula. Trails lead along the coast in many places, connecting former fishing settlements or simply leading to nice view points on the headlands. Ask your innkeeper how to find local ones.

At Port au Choix, a trail from **Port Ritchie Lighthouse** leads around the coast to the Phillips Garden archaeological site, about two miles one way. Until mid-July you are likely to see icebergs in the Gulf of St. Lawrence as they emerge from the Strait of Belle Isle.

Trails from the historic site at **L'Anse aux Meadows** lead along the coast to coves and to other bays and inland ponds. Another path goes from Great Brahat north to the abandoned site of **Little Brehat**, also north of St. Anthony. Trails circle **Fishing**

Point, at the far end of St. Anthony, along a dizzying height overlooking the open Atlantic and the harbor. Innkeepers at the Tickle Inn at **Cape Onion** can direct you to several others, some leading from their dooryard.

Hiking Outfitters & Guided Tours

■ A good way to take the Long Range Mountains/Western Brook Pond trip, especially if you are not highly experienced in finding your way with a compass, is with the area's resident experts, **Gros Morne Adventure Guides**, Rocky Harbour, NF A0L 1K0, ☎ 709/458-2722 or 800/685-GMAG (4624). Their six-day Great Caribou Campout follows this route, for $900 per person, which includes guides, camping equipment, meals and B&B accommodations the first and last nights. Gros Morne Adventure Guides also conducts week-long tours with day-hiking adventures in the park and accommodations in B&Bs. Participants walk about 10 miles a day, much of it climbing to explore the Tablelands and other elevations. Their guides are prepared to explain the area's unique geology and its wildlife. These trips cost $1,200 per person for the week.

■ **New Found Adventures, Ltd.**, ☎ 709/789-2809, also leads hiking and backpacking trips in Gros Morne National Park, with packages ranging from $125 to $1,200 per person.

■ On Wheels

RESTRICTED CYCLING AREAS: *Cycling is not allowed in some parts of Gros Morne National Park, so be sure to check with the visitors center.*

Bicycling Outfitters & Guided Tours

■ **Freewheeling Adventures** in Hubbards, Nova Scotia, ☎ 902/857-3600, fax 902/857-3612, offers cycling tours of Gros Morne and the peninsula, with lodging in inns. Tours begin at Deer Lake and end at L'Anse aux Meadows, van-supported. The trip costs $1,400 (including tax) per person, with $100 additional for bike rental if necessary.

This trip is scheduled so you can combine it with their cycling tour of Trinity, in central Newfoundland.

■ At the northernmost point on the peninsula, on Pistolet Bay, you can take tours by bicycle with **The North Atlantic Outfitting and Adventure Centre**, Parker's Brook, NF A0K 4S0, ☎ 709/551-0266. The scenery in this area, surrounded by water and bays dotted with tiny islands, is superb, with roads and trails running close to the shore, and whales a common sight.

■ On Water

Swimming

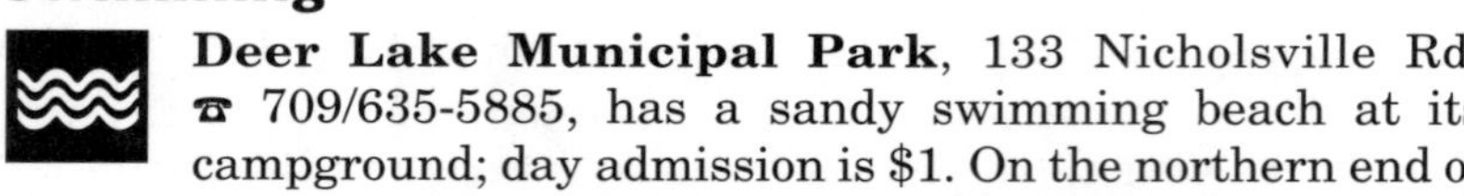

Deer Lake Municipal Park, 133 Nicholsville Rd, ☎ 709/635-5885, has a sandy swimming beach at its campground; day admission is $1. On the northern end of the peninsula, the municipally owned **Three Mile Lake Campground** in Plum Point, ☎ 709/247-2371, has a sandy beach, with waters shallow enough to be warmed by the summer sun. Admission is $2 per car.

Canoeing & Kayaking

When the winds are not too strong, the trip by kayak from Trout River to Woody Point is among the finest anywhere. The route has it all – towering cliffs, sea caves, beaches strewn with driftwood, basalt columns, mountains, whales – so many distractions it's hard to keep your attention on paddling. But this is the Gulf of St. Lawrence, not a protected arm, so don't go out alone, and choose your weather carefully. It's not for novice or weak paddlers, because of the danger of a sudden rise in wind.

Gros Morne's **Trout River Pond** is one of the most scenic places on the continent for stillwater canoeing. Launch from the park's day use area, where the boat tours leave, in Trout River.

At the other end of the canoeing spectrum is the **Main River**, which rises in the mountains of Gros Morne National Park and drops an adrenaline-pumping 1,500 feet in its 35-mile rush to the sea. Some of its canyons become Class IV and V rapids in the spring run-off, which is the only time you can canoe the whole river. Access to the headwaters is by floatplane from Deer Lake to Four Ponds Lake. Channels, boulders and rapids require lining or portages, and the river has to be scouted most of the way. This is only for experts, with well-honed skills and experience in technical waters. After you've survived four to seven days of this, you get to the hard part. The last dozen miles flows through The Canyon, where the river drops more than 65 feet per mile, with deep cliffs on either side and no shore to swim to. When the water is high, this becomes Class V.

You can reach the head of The Canyon by woods roads, from the town of Sop's Arm, off Rte. 420, which leaves TransCanada-1 about 30 miles east of Deer Lake. You can do the last part of the river, through The Canyon, in a day. This or any part of the Main is a trip only for experts; everyone in the group needs to be highly skilled. The Main runs through absolute wilderness, with no support or rescue in case of emergency. For more information on this trip, as well as suggestions for competent guides and floatplane pilots, contact **Newfoundland Canoeing Association**, PO Box 5961, St. John's, NF A1C 5X4.

The **Humber River**, north of Deer lake is a little more civilized. It's also easier to get to, with access from several woods roads off Rte. 420. A nice three- or four-day trip, accessible even in low water seasons, begins at Adies Pond, accessed from woods roads off Rte. 422. The river goes almost due north through wilderness to join the Humber, which you can follow through more wild land to Big Falls, in Squires Memorial Provincial Park. A short distance above Big Falls a series of Class II rapids can be portaged by less confident canoeists. From Little Falls south to Deer Lake, the Humber is deep, with a good current and some Class I rapids. It is a good one- or two-day trip, or you can do shorter segments, since road access is good and communities along the way offer take-out points.

On the Humber, you can rent canoes at **Squires Memorial Provincial Park**; the rental office is at the far left end of the campground, on the river.

Canoe & Kayak Outfitters - Guided Tours

■ To learn sea kayaking or to simply explore the sheltered waters of Bonne Bay's several welcoming arms, sign on for a 2½-hour or full-day trip with **Gros Morne Adventure Guides**, Rocky Harbour, ☎ 709/458-2722 or 800/685-GMAG (4624). These are designed for beginners, but more experienced paddlers often join the day excursions for a tour of the bay with a guide knowledgeable on local wildlife and history. Expect to pay $40 for a morning or evening trip, $90 for a full day. The short trip uses double kayaks.

■ **Discovery Outtripping Company**, 23 Dove's Road, Corner Brook, NF A2H 1M2, ☎ 709/634-6335, fax 709/634-2104, e-mail mtsang@thezone.net, provides guides for experienced canoeists interested in some of the more challenging rivers. They also rent a variety of outdoor equipment.

Boat Tours & Ferries

At Trout River you can learn about the unique geology that earned the park its UNESCO World Heritage site designation, on a boat tour into the land-locked fjord that separates this upthrust mountain from the cliffs of the neighboring mountain. **Tablelands Boat Tour** in Trout River, ☎ 709/451-2101, has tours daily at 9:30 am, 1 and 4 pm in July and August, 1 pm late June and early September. The cost is $30. The boat is wheelchair-accessible. From the boat, you can see more closely some of the geological evidence for plate tectonics, not to mention breathtaking scenery.

Explore Bonne Bay, where whales and eagles are often seen, on a cruise with **Gros Morne Boat Tours** in Norris Point, ☎ 709/458-2871. Tours run daily at 1 pm from late June through mid-September, for $25.

Western Brook I and *Western Brook II* take passengers into the 10-mile freshwater fjord at **Western Brook Pond** to see hanging valleys and long, ribbon-like waterfalls. Bring a wide-angle lens and a sweater to sail between these giant cliffs. There are several trips a day, weather willing, from late May to early October; they go in rain but not fog. It is important to make reservations as far ahead as possible. Hikers can leave at the end of the lake and be picked up by a later tour, but need to make firm arrangements and double-check them with the boat's captain. For reservations and information, call the **Ocean View Motel** in Rocky Harbour, ☎ 709/458-2730. Fares are $23 for adults, $6 for children eight to 16. Allow at least an hour to walk to the boat. There is no other access except along the trail.

North of Western Brook Pond, you can tour **St. Paul's Inlet**, where seals sunbathe on the rocks and terns and eagles are common, with **Seal Island Boat Tours**, PO Box 11, St. Pauls, ☎ 709/243-2376 or 2278, daily 10 am, 1, 4, and 7 pm, mid-June through September, 10 am, 1 pm, late May through mid-June; the fare is $20, $10 for children.

The waters between Cape Onion and L'Anse aux Meadows are filled with scenic rocky islands and headlands, icebergs, whales, even a wrecked ship lying ashore, and the best vantage is from an authentic replica Viking ship operated by **Viking Boat Tours**, PO Box 45, St. Lunaire, NF A0K 2X0, ☎ 709/623-2100, fax 709/623-2098. You'll get a Viking's-eye view of Leif Ericson's colony at L'Anse aux Meadows from ***The Viking Saga***, a carefully reproduced *knaar*, a working ship used by the Vikings to carry cargo. Knaars would have brought the first Norse settlers to L'Anse aux Meadows. A rare example of this vessel was recovered from Roskilde Fjord, in Denmark, where it sank in water that preserved it, and the builders of *The Viking Saga* traveled to Denmark to replicate it exactly. They've added safety features and the engine required by the Canadian Coast Guard for passenger boats.

Although the Coast Guard says they can't carry passengers under sail, they demonstrate the use of the sail before each cruise and explain all the boat's construction details. The attention to detail is minute: blocks with no moving parts, ropes of real Manila hemp, and a linseed oil finish. The crew explains the wildlife as you see it (and you will), along with the history and the handling of these Viking craft. The trip includes a close-up visit to the shipwreck, a sea view of the Viking settlement, and close-ups with whales and icebergs. Four daily trips (three daily in May, early June and September) cost $26 for adults, $13 for ages five-12. You'll pass their dock on the way to the Viking site.

The southern coast of Labrador is only a few miles away from St. Barbe, where you can cross the Strait of Belle Isle on a ferry operated by **Northern Cruiser, Ltd.**, ☎ 709/931-2309. It makes two round-trips daily, May through December; passengers pay $9, automobiles $18.50. You will arrive in Quebec, minutes from the Labrador border, and can easily drive to the end of the road and back for the return ferry later in the day, if you schedule it in summer when they make two trips. Roads don't connect this coastal area to the rest of Labrador, so this is the best way to see it. (See *Sightseeing* below for suggestions on what to see there.)

A ferry connects the province's most isolated town, **Great Harbour Deep**, on the eastern shore of the peninsula, to Jackson's Arm at the end of Rte. 420. The ferry operates five days a week in the summer and four days a week September through January 3, at $4.75 or $2.50 for seniors, ☎ 709/459-9109. The trip along the coast is beautiful, but the entrance to Harbour Deep, with its steep mountains almost pushing it into the sea, is even more so. Because the ferry turns right around and returns, you'll have to stay over to see anything of the area or hike its trails.

Windsurfing

Deer Lake Municipal Park on TransCanada-1, 133 Nicholsville Rd, ☎ 709/635-5885, has a sandy beach with shallow water, and campground; day admission is $1.

Shallow Bay, on the north end of Gros Morne National Park, has three miles of white sand beach, with an adjacent campground. The surf is big anytime, but the winds are most consistent from mid-August to mid-September (which is when the water's the warmest, too). To use the beach you must have a park entry permit; it's $3 for one day, $9 for four days. Ten miles north of the park boundary at Parson's Pond is **Summer Fun Boat Park**, ☎ 709/243-2505, on Moulting Pond. It's a municipal recreation area with board rentals.

Fishing

River of Ponds Park south of Port au Choix has picnic and swimming areas. One of the premier fishing areas in the province, trout here grow to more than three pounds.

The **Humber River**, which has headwaters east of Gros Morne National Park, is known for its fishing. Until regulations on salmon fishing were instituted, it was not uncommon for anglers to catch 30 salmon there per season. **Big Falls** has a worldwide reputation for salmon, but trout is also plentiful. The Humber between Squires Memorial Provincial Park and Deer Lake, has some world-famous salmon pools, too. You can rent both canoes and dories in the park.

For a fishing experience that will provide you with years of campfire stories, take the ferry to **Harbour Deep**, Newfoundland's most isolated community, a three-hour ferry ride from the nearest road, and accessible by boat only in the summer. Unlike wilderness fishing camps, this experience includes living in a very traditional Newfoundland town, where you will meet and fish with locals (who know the waters inside out and will vie with each other to be the most hospitable and show you their favorite pool). Little Harbour Deep River and Soufflets River flow into their respective arms of Orange Bay, which is surrounded by steep mountainsides; both are prime trout and salmon rivers. For lodging and the requisite guide, contact **The Danny Corcoran Lodge,** Great Harbour Deep, White Bay, NF A0K 2Z0, ☎ 709/843-2112, fax

709/843-3106 ($). The ferry operates five days a week in the summer at $4.75 or $2.50 for seniors, ☎ 709/459-9109.

Northern rivers known for their salmon include **Torrent River, St. Genevieve River, Castor River** and **Ten Mile Lake**, all north of Hawke's Bay. **Three Mile Lake** and **All Hands Brook**, in Plum Point, are good for trout fishing. **Portland Creek River** is well-known to anglers, having been made famous by fishing great, Lee Wulff.

Fishing Outfitters - Guided Tours

■ Highly recommended guides to the Upper Humber are Mark and Jonathan Tsang of **Discovery Outtripping Company**, 23 Dove's Road, Corner Brook, NF A2H 1M2, ☎ 709/634-6335, fax 709/634-2104, e-mail mtsang@thezone.net. Discovery Outtripping works all the rivers in the area, taking clients where the fish are. Their service includes pick-up and drop-off at the airport, and rates are about $150 a day. These are the guides the guides recommend. (Thanks to Sara Godwin and Charles James for this tip.)

■ **Cow Head Outfitters** at the northern end of Gros Morne National Park, PO Box 61, Cow Head, NF A0A 2A0, ☎ 709/243-2258, has camps on Taylor's Brook and Caribou Lake, both reached by floatplane. They offer packages that include guides, transportation, meals and lodging on these excellent salmon and brook trout waters.

On Snow

Green Point Campground in Gros Morne National Park is open year-round, but the water is shut off and the access road may not be plowed in the winter. They do clear a small parking area on Rte. 430.

Dogsledding

If your idea of what Newfoundland should look like in the winter includes the curled tails of a team of excited huskies in the foreground (as ours does), contact **Terra Nova Adventure Tours**, PO Box 368, Port-Au-Choix, NF A0K 4C0, ☎ 709/861-3015.

Cross-Country Skiing

Gros Morne National Park grooms and tracks nearly 20 miles of trails in the winter, or you can roam the coastal lowlands and backcountry. Two backcountry ski huts have been added recently, one on the eastern end of the Tablelands, and another near Bakers Brook Pond. The Gros Morne National Park Visitors Centre has a map of the ski trails, with hut locations marked, and they can give you advice on good backcountry areas. Most of the trails are for novice and intermediate skiers. Backcountry skiing is only for advanced to expert skiers.

A scenic (albeit windy) trail especially good for novice skiers runs along the coast, following the old mail road north from **Shallow Bay**, a round-trip of about three miles, with a shelter in the campground. At **Berry Hill**, a series of stacked loops offers four- , six- and 10-mile trails, with a shelter. You can ski to the frozen cascades of **Baker's Brook Falls**, one of the most scenic destinations of any trail in the park. **Trout River** has forest trails in stacked loops of one, two and three miles respectively, with a shelter.

The **Wigwam-Stuckles Trail** has a hut, and is seven miles one-way, intermediate except for one hill, which can only be described as advanced. It leads from Rte. 430 to Rte. 431.

At the Gros Morne National Park **Visitors Centre**, which has a warming and waxing facility, six groomed trails vary in length from less than a mile to five miles; a one-mile intermediate trail is lighted for night skiing.

Outside the park, local cross-country clubs maintain trails. At Plum Point near St. Barbe, the **Mount St. Margaret Club**, ☎ 709/247-2651, has three miles of trails, groomed and lighted for night skiing. They also offer lessons and have a warm-up cabin. Also in the St. Barbe area at Flowers Cove, the **Deep Cove Club**, ☎ 709/456-2569, maintains six miles of trails, of which four are groomed. They have a cabin.

St. Anthony's Aurora Nordic Club, ☎ 709/454-3108, has seven miles of ungroomed trails. At Main Brook, an almost-outport connected to Rte. 420 via Rte. 432, unpaved for the last several miles, the **Belvy Bay Club**, ☎ 709/865-4501, has 15 miles of ski trails, of which three are groomed. They also have a warm-up cabin and offer lessons.

Ski Outfitters – Guided Tours

■ Also in Main Brook, cross-country skiers can sample other winter sports at **Tuckamore Wilderness Lodge and Outfitters**, PO Box 100, Main Brook, NF A0K 3N0, ☎ 709/865-6361, fax 709/865-2112. Along with cross-country ski tours, they offer snowshoeing, ice fishing and snowmobile trips.

■ Guided backcountry ski trips are available in Gross Morne and the Long Range mountains with **Gros Morne Adventure Guides**, Rocky Harbour, NF A0L 1K0, ☎ 709/458-2722, 800/685-4624. Trips can range from one day to a week, on as much as 20 feet of snow in protected valleys backed by snow-covered dramatic scenery, or on the open bare slopes of tablelands. Both telemark and cross-country itineraries are available, with lodgings in a cozy log cabin. Day trips cost about $100 and a week-long ski adventure is $1,000 (taxes included).

■ **New Found Adventures, Ltd.**, Frenchman's Cove, NF A0L 1E0, ☎ 709/789-2809, offers guided ski trips in Gros Morne National Park, with packages ranging from $125 to $1,200.

Snowmobiling

In the winter, more miles are covered in any given week by snowmobile than by car throughout most of the Great Northern Peninsula, especially in the north. "Skidoos," as they call all snow machines, are a way of life in the winter here, as they are in the rest of far northern Canada. Trails follow old woods roads, frozen rivers and hiking trails, and they criss-cross bogs and ponds not traversable in the summer.

Snowmobile Outfitters – Guided Tours

■ **Frontier Cottages** in Wiltondale, ☎ 709/453-2520 or 800/668-2520, does guided snowmobile trips, either day or overnight adventures in Gros Morne National Park or into the Long Range Mountains.

■ You can arrange a complete winter experience in remote Main Brook with **Tuckamore Wilderness Lodge and Outfitters**, PO Box 100, Main Brook, NF A0K 3N0, ☎ 709/865-6361, fax 709/865-2112. They lead snowmobile tours and offer snowshoes so their guests can explore this ultra-scenic region on Hare Bay.

■ Even more remote is **Harbour Deep**, which has no road access, and in the winter no sea access, either. You can arrive by regularly scheduled flights, twice a week, and enjoy the hospitality of a local family, who will find you a snowmobile to use (everybody has them) and feed you hearty Newfoundland dishes. To find the family for you, contact **Pamela Ropson**, ☎ 709/843-4120, or **Crystal Smith**, ☎ 709/843-4132. Either may be contacted by mail at General Delivery, Great Harbour Deep, NF A0K 2Z0.

■ For more traditional accommodations in Harbour Deep, book into a motel or B&B room at **The Danny Corcoran Lodge,** Great Harbour Deep, White Bay, NF A0K 2Z0, ☎ 709/843-2112, fax 709/843-3106, where they will arrange snowmobiling trips for you.

■ Or join a snowmobile trip to Harbour Deep with **Northern Tours** in Port au Choix, ☎ 709/861-3739, which stops at Middle Gulch Camp where the caribou and moose herds winter. Northern Tours offers other snowmobile trips as well.

■ At the top of the peninsula on Pistolet Bay, snowmobile tours are offered by **The North Atlantic Outfitting and Adventure Centre** in Parker's Brook, NF A0K 4S0, ☎ 709/551-0266. This region, with an irregular coast of tiny coves and islands, is beautiful in the winter, with long white vistas ending at the sea. You can combine winter camping and snowshoe treks with your snowmobile adventure.

On Horseback

Cache Rapids Stable on the main road in Reidville, ☎ 709/635-5224, offers Western riding with trail rides, including overnight rides. One of their trails leads along the Cache Rapids of the Humber River, one of its most scenic spots. They also have pony rides, wagon rides and, in the winter, sleigh rides, plus miniature horses, a Shetland pony and a Newfoundland pony. The stable is open year-round, but you'll need reservations between October and April. To get to Reidville, turn east off Rte. 430, shortly after leaving TransCanada-1.

Trails at **Gros Morne Riding Stables** in Rocky Harbour, ☎ 709/675-2073, have views of the rocky summit of the mountain. The stable offers Western riding, with trail rides as short as half an hour or overnight rides. They are open from late May to October.

Cultural & Eco-Travel Experiences

Each shore community, where families have depended on the sea for their livelihood, has made adjustments to survive the moratorium on cod fisheries. Not all have been as successful as Port au Choix, just off Rte. 430 on Ingornachoix Bay. The town is the home port of the northern shrimp fleet, and in mid-July they celebrate at a **Shrimp Festival and Blessing of the Fleet**, ☎ 709/861-3911. You can watch the boats come in around dusk each evening from May through July, when the docks hum with activity as the catch is unloaded.

Gros Morne National Park has a very good interpretive program in the summer, which includes naturalist walks to the geologic highlights at Tablelands and Green Point, evening programs on the glaciers, marine life, Arctic plants in the park, bears, and campfire programs that highlight life in the isolated outports. These programs are free to anyone with a park entry permit. Special programs, which include kayak explorations, are by reservation and involve a fee. You can pick up a copy of each month's schedule at the visitor center.

■ Archaeology

Finds in three ancient cemeteries excavated at Port aux Choix (pronounced porta SHWAW), remains of the Maritime Archaic people who lived here over 4,000 years ago, provide evidence of the southernmost known Eskimo habitation in North America. Tools, weapons and ornaments, as well as the skeletons, provide archaeologists with new information on the lives and even the intellectual and social development of these early people. Superimposed on their community are the remains of much later Dorset and Groswater Paleoeskimo cultures. Since the last burials are about

3,000 years old, what became of these people is unknown; the fact that remains of later cultures are found in the same place, may suggest that the Dorset and Groswater assimilated them, but they may have become extinct. Very well-done displays in the **Port au Choix National Historic Site Visitor Reception Center**, ☎ 709/861-3522 summer, 709/623-2608 winter, show artifacts and explain how they reveal important information. It is open daily, 9 am to 6 pm, from mid-June to Labor Day; admission is $1 for adults, 50¢ for children.

From the visitor center, follow the road to its end, then walk along the trail to tour the archaeological dig overlooking the sea at **Phillips Garden**. This site was once at the edge of the water, but rising land and falling sea levels in the past millennia have combined to raise it to this moderate elevation. The highly acid environment of the peat bed in which they were buried helped preserve the artifacts found here. Phillips Garden is often enveloped in fog the consistency of Newfoundland pea soup, which makes it dangerous to explore; if the day is murky, ask about conditions while you are in the visitor center.

With such a variety of peoples settled at Port au Choix, archaeologists believed that other aboriginal sites must surely exist nearby. These had eluded them until recently, when finds at **Bird Cove**, 35 miles north, began to prove them right. Visitors are welcome at the dig on Dog Peninsula, and can ponder the recovered artifacts at the **Bird Cove Museum**, 67 Michael's Drive, ☎ 709/247-2256. Artifacts from several other local digs are here, too, showing settlements by Beothuk, Maritime Archaic and Dorset peoples, as well as early Europeans and some puzzling finds of unknown origin.

Somewhat more recent settlements interest archaeologists at **Old Ferolle Island** near Bird Cove. Here they are investigating the site of a Basque fishing settlement, possibly an offshoot of the 16th-century Basque whaling station at Red Bay, across the Strait of Belle Isle in Labrador.

You can take a guided tour of these locations and the **Basque whaling station** site with a knowledgeable guide for $20 (two hours) or $50 (five hours). To arrange for a tour, stop at or call the **Plum Point Motel**, ☎ 709/247-2533, or the **Town Hall**, ☎ 709/247-2256.

The historical importance of **L'Anse aux Meadows National Historic Site** on Rte. 436 in L'Anse aux Meadows, ☎ 709/623-2608, is best illustrated by the fact that it was the first UNESCO World Heritage Site. This status depends not so much on whether it was the gateway to Leif Ericson's Vineland (which was a land, not a particular site), but on the undisputed fact that it is the earliest evidence of European settlement and industry in the New World. Artifacts recovered, the shape of the houses, and – most telling of all – the discovery of iron rivets used in Norse boat building, show it to have been a Norse settlement from about the year 1000 AD. Iron was smelted and forged here, timber cut and prepared for shipping to Greenland, boats repaired and built. Domestic tasks, including sewing, spinning and cooking were carried on here. The site has three main components. An outstanding museum and interpretive center shows how the Viking adventurers lived here, what their boats looked like, how they navigated and how we know this from the artifacts recovered (many of which are displayed here). A walk to the village gives an overview of the protected cove and house sites, which show as the mounds that first attracted the attention of archaeologists. You can walk among these, covered over and returned to their pre-dig appearance. Beside the village is a reconstruction of a peat dwelling, complete with cooking fire (and its smoke). L'Anse aux Meadows should be a model for interpreting ancient sites to the modern public. The site is open daily, 9 am to 8 pm, mid-June to early September, sometimes into October. Admission is $2.50; seniors $2, youths $1.25.

Geology

The Appalachian Mountains end at the sea in The Great Northern Peninsula (or the part that remain in North America do – the rest are in Scotland and Norway). But the mountains you see are only part of what was once here. Glaciers have scoured their summits clean, ground them down and gouged deep slashes of fjords between them. Before that – about 500 million years ago – a piece of the earth's mantle was forced to the surface as continental plates collided, leaving a barren mountain on which few plants will grow.

This crumbling mass of reddish rock at **Tablelands** is the only place where geologists can study a piece of our planet that is normally more than a mile below the surface. The segment of mantle that earned the park its UNESCO kudos is easy to see; you drive along it on Rte. 431 to Trout River, and can inspect it more closely from a boat trip up the long fjord beside it (see *Boat Tours*, above).

Other geologic phenomena are visible at **Green Point**, where layers of ancient sediment that solidified in a long ago seabed have been turned sidewise, standing almost on end so scientists (and you) can study the sequence of fossils between the Cambrian and Ordovician periods.

At **Western Brook Pond** you can examine the walls of a land-locked fjord cut by glaciers, and see the dikes created 600 million years ago when these rocks were broken by the shifting of plates, and hot lava was thrust into the cracks. (But the sheer majesty of this fjord will distract you from such details.)

On the shore at **Green Gardens** you can see the reddish and gray basalt and pillow lava formed by the cooling of lavas similar to those found in Hawaii.

Beyond the park boundary to the north is a small Provincial Park at **The Arches**, a large rock formation of two arches cut under a huge outcrop of dolomite. This was formed under the sea, and now stands just offshore, with bright blue sea visible through the white arches. The relentless waves that carved the arches still beat at their base.

> **RECOMMENDED READING:** *To better understand the geological sights in Gros Morne National Park, and the forces that shaped them, get a copy of* **Rocks Adrift: The Geology of Gros Morne National Park**, *which you can buy at the Gros Morne Visitors Centre. Good color photographs of geological phenomena in the park show exactly where to go and what you'll see there.*

■ Wildlife-Watching

Whales and seabirds may have become a familiar theme by now, but the Great Western Peninsula is a prime site for seeing both.

If you are traveling here in June or July you are almost certain to see whales, with 20 species breaching and spouting in coves and in the deeper waters offshore. You will probably see them as you drive along the Viking Trail north of Gros Morne National Park. Look for them from Fishing Point in **St. Anthony** at the tip of the Northern Peninsula, where you can watch whales out the windows as you dine at the Lighthouse Café.

In the fascinating outport of **Harbour Deep**, pods of whales come to feed in the harbor in August and September. As you stand on one of the community's many wharves, you may see 10 or 15 whales spouting at once, and as you arrive and leave by the ferry (no roads connect this town) you are sure to see more.

More of Newfoundland's world-class bird islands are off the town of Main Brook and included in the **Hare Bay Ecological Reserve**. This group of islands has large colonies of Arctic and common terns, several gull varieties, and hundreds of eider ducks. It is the best place in the province to see these, especially when the young ducklings are out on the ocean early in the summer. **Tuckamore Wilderness Lodge and Outfitters**, PO Box 100, Main Brook, NF A0K 3N0, ☎ 709/865-6361, fax 709/865-2112, offers birding and whale-watching trips to these islands in the summer, or you can always find a local boat going out.

You can watch salmon jump ladders constructed to make the upper reaches of the Humber and Torrent rivers accessible for spawning. At **Big Falls**, in the Squires Memorial Provincial Park, you can drive almost to the falls, while **Torrent River Nature Park**, in Hawke's Bay, provides a boardwalk and stairs through bogs and woodlands, past the rapids and gorges to the waterfall. Before the ladder, salmon were unable to jump the falls. The trail into the park begins at the Tourist Chalet.

Sightseeing

Before turning off TransCanada-1 to follow the Viking Trail, stop at the **Roy Whalen Regional Heritage Center**, ☎ 709/635-4440, next to the Tourist Chalet. Its exhibits show life from the early settlement of the Humber Valley, and a shop, Valley Crafts, sells handknit sweaters and mittens, moosehide slippers, woodcarvings and other local crafts. Both are open from 9 am to 9 pm, mid-June through mid-September; admission $2.

Just south of the entrance to the national park, stop at **Wiltondale Pioneer Village**, on Rte. 430, ☎ 709/453-2464. It reconstructs a town from the early 20th century: a home, school, general store, church and tearoom. The complex is open daily, 10 am to 6 pm, mid-June to mid-September. Admission is $3, family $6.

On the north end of the park you can tour the free **Cow Head Lighthouse** at Cow Head, ☎ 709/243-2446. Nearby, **Tete de Vache Museum and Craft Shop**, ☎ 709/243-2023, is open daily from 10 am to 5 pm, late June through September. Admission is free, but donations are welcome at this small community museum. Mittens and other locally made crafts fill its shop.

On the way to the dig at Port au Choix, stop to see the whale skeleton at **Studio Gargamelle**, ☎ 709/861-3280, where a local craftsman creates sculptures of whales, seals, dolphin and other marine creatures that share the neighborhood, using materials found locally: stone, wood, whale bone, driftwood and shells.

To appreciate how much difference one determined person can make, visit **Grenfell House**, Rte. 430, St. Anthony, ☎ 709/454-3333. In 1894, Wilfred Grenfell observed that fishing settlements in Labrador were without medical care and established the Grenfell Medical Mission, with headquarters in St. Anthony. He realized that in order to keep going, the mission would have to be self-supporting, so he founded Grenfell Crafts, which made high-quality weatherproof parkas from a specially made material, decorated with hand embroidery of local scenes and animals. This employed local people and the profits paid for nursing stations, hospitals and orphanages in remote settlements.

The Grenfells' home and a museum in the restored dockhouse, demonstrate life and work in a late 19th-century fisheries port. At the shop (the project is still operating) you can buy handmade coats, jackets and snowsuits at prices beginning under $100, without tax since they are local handcrafts. The shop is open Monday to Friday, 9 am to 9 pm; Saturday, 9 am to 6 pm; Sunday, 1-6 pm. Admission to the house and museum is $2; for seniors and children, $1.

A little-known relic of enemy submarine activity in the waters off Newfoundland lies on the shore at **Big Brook**, at the end of an unpaved road branching off Rte. 435, west of St. Anthony. Here lie the remains of a freighter torpedoed by the Germans during World War II.

Across the Strait in Labrador

The ferry from St. Barbe lands in Blanc Sablon, Quebec, just over the border from **L'Anse-au-Clair** in Labrador, where you will find a **Visitors Information Centre**.

Twelve miles north of there in L'Anse Amour is the **Labrador Straits Museum**, ☎ 313/271-1620, with exhibits on the first nonstop east transatlantic flight in 1928, which landed on nearby Greely Island. Other exhibits examine the role of women in the history of this coast.

Point Amour Lighthouse, built in 1857, is the tallest lighthouse in Atlantic Canada and the second tallest in all Canada at 109 feet. Its walls are more than six feet thick at the base, and you can climb to the top. It is still in use, and the interpretive center will tell you about the light's history. It's open June to mid-October from 8 am to 5 pm daily, ☎ 709/927-5826.

L'Anse Amour is also the site of the oldest **burial mound** in North America, and its location on the road to the lighthouse has a monument. The remains of a Maritime Archaic Indian child buried a 7000 B.C. were unearthed.

The road farther north parallels the Pinware River, along which are glacial erratics, large boulders left there by melting glaciers. When its waters are in sight, you can see pieces of modern-day glaciers float by in the Strait.

You can drive only to **Red Bay,** where the road ends, and where you will find another **Visitor Centre**, ☎ 709/920-2197, and the Interpretation Centre for **Saddle Island**. On this island, in the 1500s, Basque whalers had a full-scale whaling station. Transportation to archaeological sites on the island is free, Monday through Saturday from 9 am to 4 pm in the summer. Exhibits in the Interpretive Centre relate how the Basques arrived as early as the 11th century, and include models of a cooperage and try-works, where blubber became lamp oil.

Where To Stay & Eat

This region, like most of the province, is blessedly uncrowded, although it is one place where you probably should make room reservations ahead of time, since facilities close to the park are somewhat limited. Because this route is linear, we've mixed the lodging and dining and given them in geographical order from south to north.

Near Gros Morne

Throughout the park are scattered towns, which is fortunate for travelers, since there are no accommodations other than campgrounds on park land.

Deer Lake Motel is a modern hotel, with room service, coffee-makers, snack bar with take-out, even in-room movies. The **Cormack Dining Room** ($$) serves a standard Newfoundland menu of seafood and a few meat entrées. *TransCanada-1 (PO Box 820), Deer Lake, NF, A0K 2E0, ☎ 709/635-2108, fax 709/635-3842 ($$).*

Frontier Cottages are new log cabins, suitable for one or two couples. They have kitchens, and a convenience store is adjacent. They are open year-round, with snowmobile trails leading from the door. *Wiltondale (PO Box 172, Rocky Harbour), NF A0K 4N0, ☎ 709/453-2520 or 800/668-2520 ($).*

Victorian Manor offers hospitable inn rooms and housekeeping units with complete kitchens. They also have two other bed and breakfast homes in Woody Point, a scenic town perched on a slope overlooking beautiful views of the arm and mountains rising from its shore. *Main St. (PO Box 165), Woody Point, NF A0K 1P0, ☎ 709/453-2485 ($$).*

At **Crockers Bed and Breakfast** you'll be staying in a warm family home, with a kitchen you're welcome to use. *PO Box 165, Woody Point, NF A0K 1P0, ☎ 709/451-451-5220 ($$).*

Aunt Nellie's Tea Room and Bakery at the Wiltondale Pioneer Village serves several traditional Newfoundland dishes, including fish cakes served with partridgeberries, toutons (deep-fried bread dough) as well as pastries and tea or rhubarb punch. *In Wiltondale, ☎ 709/453-2464 ($).*

Surrounded by the southern section of the park, **Seaside Restaurant** overlooks the beach, serving, of course, fresh fish. If they are in season, ask for the capelin, which are perfectly cooked, but you can't go wrong here as long as you stick to fish. *Trout River, ☎ 709/451-3461 ($$).*

Across Bonne Bay, **Sugar Hill Inn** is tonier than most in the area, with hot tub and sauna, fluffy down comforters and a dining room that serves a full-course dinner in the $30-plus range (by reservation). Breakfast is extra. *PO Box 100, Norris Point, NF, A0K 3V0, ☎ 709/458-2147, fax 709/458-2147 ($$-$$$).*

Gros Morne Cabins are roomy, self-catering log cabins, with TVs and full-sized kitchens with dining tables. Picnic tables and grill on the lawn overlook the water. The whole property, including the cabins, is scrupulously maintained. *PO Box 151, Rocky Harbour, NF, A0K 4N0, ☎ 709/458-2020, fax 709/458-2882, off season reservations 709/458-2525 ($$).*

For a homey B&B at prices you can't beat, try **Violet Major's Hospitality Home**. You'll find private baths, in-room TV and homemade breads at breakfast. *Pond Rd., Rocky Harbour, NF A0K 4N0, ☎ 709/458-2537 or 800/999-2537 ($).*

Ocean View Motel in Rocky Harbour is in the town's busy center along the harbor (don't get the wrong idea – you won't be kept awake by the activity in this little resort town). Its **Ocean Room** ($$) serves three good meals daily, but service can be slow when a tour group descends. *Rte. 430 (PO Box 129), Rocky Harbour, NF A0K 4N0, ☎ 709/458-2730, fax 709/458-2841 ($$).*

Next door to the Ocean View Motel is **Fisherman's Landing,** which serves three meals daily year-round; open to 11 pm in the summer. Early-bird breakfast costs $2.99 before 7 am; the menu offers alternatives to deep-fried food, a welcome sight. *Rte. 430, Rocky Harbour, ☎ 709/458-2060 ($$).*

Up Rte. 430, the only reason you'd notice Sally's Cove is **Aunt Polly's** bakery. It has only two tables, but the scones are worth standing up to eat. Auntie sells fresh breads and other goodies daily from 8 am to midnight.

In The North

At the northern edge of the park, there's a small town surrounded by parkland, where you can stay at **Shallow Bay Motel and Cabins**. *PO Box 44, Cow Head, NF A0K 2A0, ☎ 709/243-2471 or 800/563-1946, fax 709/243-2816 ($$).*

Maynard's Motel has tidy rooms, housekeeping units and a restaurant. *Rte. 430 (PO Box 59), Hawke's Bay, NF A0K 3B0, ☎ 709/248-5225 or 800/563-8811, fax 709/248-5363 ($$).*

Point Richie Inn overlooks the sea on the road to the lighthouse. Breakfast here will last you until teatime. *32 Pt. Richie Road, Port au Choix, NF A0K 4C0, ☎ 709/861-3773 or 861-2112 ($).*

Sea Echo Motel has standard motel-style rooms and a kitchenette for guests to use. Their **Anchor Café**, 709/861-3665, serves three meals daily and is open until midnight. The menu will please travelers tiring of seafood, with Italian, vegetarian and low-fat choices added. *PO Box 179, Port au Choix, NF A0K 4C0, ☎ 709/861-3777 ($-$$).*

Plum Point Motel is a good base for seeing the newly found archaeological sites farther north, or for a long day-trip to the east coast, less than two hours away. It has a dining room. *PO Box 106, Plum Point, NF A0K 4A0, ☎ 709/247-2533, fax 709/247-2327.*

To spend more time in the hardly-ever-visited communities reached by Rte. 432, stay at **Reeve's Oceanview B&B** in Englee. Two rooms with private baths overlook waters where you're likely to see icebergs and whales. Englee is the end of the road. *69 Church Rd., Englee, NF A0K 2J0, ☎ 709/866-2531 ($).*

If you follow Rte. 432 to its end you'll find **Tuckamore Wilderness Lodge and Outfitters**, open all year, offering birding and whale-watching trips in the summer and a full range of outdoor sports in the winter. *PO Box 100, Main Brook, NF A0K 3N0, ☎ 709/865-6361, fax 709/865-2112 ($$).*

Those exploring the eastern shore by ferry or air to **Harbour Deep**, which has no road access, can enjoy the hospitality of a local family, who will tell you all about life in such a far-flung port and feed you hearty Newfoundland favorites, like their orange-colored pea soup with dumplings or vinegar tarts baked in a molasses crust. *To find a home there, contact **Pamela Ropson**, General Delivery, Great Harbour Deep, NF A0K 2Z0, ☎ 709/843-4120, or **Crystal Smith**, General Delivery, Great Harbour Deep, NF A0K 2Z0, ☎ 709/843-4132.*

Or stay in a motel or B&B room at **The Danny Corcoran Lodge**, a sporting lodge where they will help you arrange fishing or snowmobile trips. *Great Harbour Deep, White Bay, NF A0K 2Z0, ☎ 709/843-2112, fax 709/843-3106.*

Marilyn's Hospitality Home is a mile's walk from the Viking settlement and boat trips. Full breakfast is included in this pleasant family home, and Marilyn will serve you other meals if you reserve ahead. *PO Box 5, Hay Cove, NF A0K 2X0, ☎ 709/623-2811 ($).*

St. Anthony Haven Inn, located on a hill close to the center of town, has well-decorated rooms and suites, plus a dining room. *Goose Bay Rd (PO Box 419), St. Anthony, NF A0K 4S0, ☎ 709/454-1900, fax 709/454-2270 ($$).*

When we're in the St. Anthony area, we can think of dozens of reasons to stay at **Tickle Inn**. Start with the setting, in a cove between two headlands. Add whales, which cavort in the water below your bedroom window. Then there's dinner (by reservation) with local food specialties, including Atlantic char and wild berries. The owner is the fourth generation of his family to live here, and his restorations have kept the historic qualities while adding some luxuries and a comfortably stylish decor. Plan to be there in the evening, when guests gather to learn more about the area from their good-humored host. *RR 1 (Box 62), Cape Onion, NF, A0K 4J0, ☎ 709/452-4321 (June through September) or 709/739-5503 (October-May) ($-$$).*

Daylight lingers long into the summer evening this far north, so you can watch whales and icebergs over a fashionably late dinner at **The Lightkeeper's Café**. Or you can have their hot muffins for breakfast or their excellent seafood chowder at lunch, since the café serves three meals daily. The cliff-top location and view make dinner reservations wise. *Fishing Point, St. Anthony, ☎ 709/454-4900 ($-$$).*

A local institution and a haven for travelers on a low budget, **Smith's Restaurant** serves traditional local dishes, including wild berry pies. They are open daily until midnight. *Rte. 436, St. Lunaire-Griquet, ☎ 709/623-2539 ($).*

Valhalla Bed & Breakfast has rooms furnished in Scandinavian pine overlooking the water. Their nearby **Norsemen Gallery and Café**, on the harbor in L'Anse aux Meadows, ☎ 709/623-2018 ($$), serves updated Newfoundland specialties, surrounded by local art, all of it for sale. *PO Box 10, Gunner's Cove, NF A0K 2X0, ☎ 709/623-2018 ($$).*

In Labrador

Northern Light Inn is a large (by local standards) inn, with rooms and housekeeping units. The coffee shop ($) is open all day, with sandwiches and full entrées, and the Basque Dining Room ($$) serves seafood. *L'Anse-au-Clair, LB, A0K 3K0, ☎ 709/931-2332, fax 709/931-2708 ($$).*

Seaview Motel has two motel rooms and two efficiency units, along with a family-style restaurant, eight miles from L'Anse-au-Clair. Seafood reins supreme. *35 Main St., Forteau, ☎ 709/931-2840 ($$).*

Grenfell Louis A. Hall is in the former nursing station built by the Grenfell Association (see *Sightseeing* in St. Anthony), and now has five rooms and a restaurant ($-$$). *3 Willow Ave. (PO Box 137, Forteau, LB A0K 2PO, ☎ 709/931-2916 ($).*

Davis Hospitality Home has three comfortable rooms overlooking the water. Seafood suppers are not included in the modest rate, but your hosts can serve them by reservation. You can walk to Point Amour Lighthouse by a shore trail from here. *L'Anse-Amour, Labrador, A0K 3J0, ☎ 709/927-5690 ($).*

■ Camping

Deer Lake Municipal Park has lakefront tent sites and a sandy swimming beach. *133 Nicholsville Rd, ☎ 709/635-5885.*

The private **Juniper Campground** has 54 tent sites , some with semi-hookup, and hot showers. Daily fees are $9 to $11, and it's open from late May to mid-September. *Pond Road, Rocky Harbour, NF A0K 4NO, ☎ 709/458-2917.*

North of Gros Morne National Park, **River of Ponds Provincial Park** has unserviced wooded campsites with outhouses; no showers or electricity. Open from June through early September. *No phone.*

On the northern end of the peninsula near St. Barbe, the municipally owned **Three Mile Lake Campground** has 32 sites ($8) with water hook-ups, a sandy beach, and a good fishing brook. *PO Box 120, Plum Point, NF A0K 4A0, ☎ 709/247-2371.*

Gros Morne National Park

Inside Gros Morne National Park the major campgrounds are **Berry Hill**, **Trout River**, **Green Point**, and **Shallow Bay**. All have tent and trailer sites, but no electrical hookups. No reservations for campsites, which cost $10-$14.

Our favorite campsite is **Trout River Campground**, overlooking the lake, with nicely separated wooded sites and close to

> ➲ **GROS MORNE CAMPING:** *Permits for backcountry camping in Gros Morne National Park are free and available at the Visitor Center.*

some of our favorite trails. None of the campgrounds has a telephone, but the Woody Point Visitors Center has radio contact. Their phone number is ☎ 709/458-2417 in case you want to call for availability of sites. Our experience is that this one is rarely more than half-full.

Southwest Newfoundland

Geography & History

Channel-Port aux Basques is the first sight many travelers have of Newfoundland, as the Marine Atlantic ferry approaches from North Sydney, Nova Scotia. Parallel to the western coast is the long chain of the Appalachians, the last portion of this range that begins in Georgia. Some portion of these mountains are visible throughout the southwest: first flat Table Mountain, visible from the ferry, then the Long Range, with the Anguilles to their west at the edge of the sea and the Annieopsquotch (somehow these are easier to remember as Annie-hop-scotch) to the east. To the north, the Lewis Hills, squeezed into the narrow land between St. George's Bay and the Bay of Islands, rise to more than 2,600 feet before they drop suddenly into the sea.

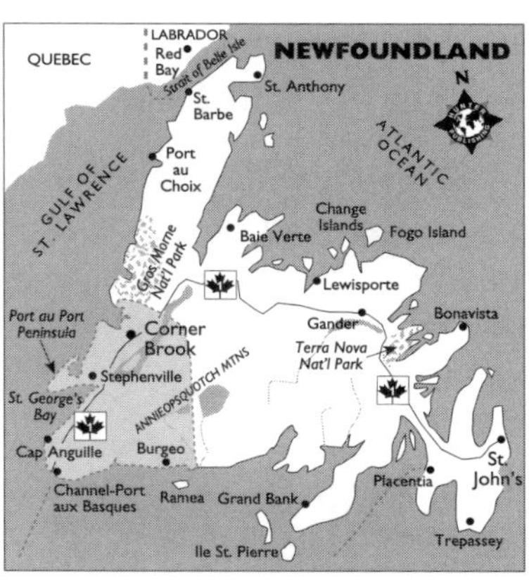

Newfoundland's second largest city, **Corner Brook**, sits at the end of the Humber Arm of the Bay of Islands, where the Humber River meets salt water. Its streets all seem to climb the slopes of the Blow Me Down Mountains, which form its backdrop and extend along the south coast of the bay.

Jutting westward below Corner Brook and the Lewis Hills, its shape looking like the head of some prehistoric bird, is the Port au Port Peninsula, which narrowly misses being cut adrift as an island. It, too, rises to a headland of dramatic cliffs, and drops to long low beaches.

The south coast is virtual wilderness, its fishing settlements too widely spread and its long bays too deep and wide to make a connecting road feasible. Villages are connected instead by the tenuous thread of ferry service, which grows less frequent as each decade passes. Burgeo is the only town here with a road connection to the rest of Newfoundland.

Long after the rest of Newfoundland was firmly in British hands, the French retained fishing rights to the western coast, and maintained seasonal settlements into the mid 1800s. The first real settlers were the Acadians, who resettled here after being expelled from Nova Scotia in the 1750s. The French influence was later augmented by arrivals from St. Pierre, Cape Breton and Brittany.

Getting Around

If you are arriving in Newfoundland by ferry, you will probably arrive in Channel-Port aux Basques, where you will drive off the ramp and find yourself on TransCanada-1. You will, in fact never have left it, since the agreement by which Newfoundland became part of Canada in the late 1940s stipulates that the ferry be officially part of TransCanada-1.

Marine Atlantic ferries depart from North Sydney on Cape Breton Island in Nova Scotia every day all year round, several times a day in the summer. The crossing takes five hours. The fare is about $60 for automobiles (including pickup trucks), $20 for adult passengers, $9.50 for children. If you cross at night you can catch a few winks in a dormitory sleeper for $7-$13, depending on which boat you travel on. Cabins add another $50-$100 to your fare. You should make advance reservations for your car, and must arrive one hour before departure to claim that reservation. To reserve, call ☎ 800/341-7981; in North Sydney, ☎ 902/794-5814; in Port aux Basques, ☎ 709/695-2124.

TransCanada-1 travels southwest/northeast between Corner Brook and Channel-Port aux Basques, much of the way along the Codroy Valley, between mountain slopes where snow patches still glisten in mid-summer. The road bypasses Stephenville, at the beginning of the Port au Port Peninsula, less than an hour south of Corner Brook.

From Stephenville to Channel-Port aux Basques is about a two-hour drive (unless, of course, you're hurrying to catch the ferry, in which case it will certainly take longer). On the way, two short webs of roads lead to the shore, the northernmost one connecting along the shore to make a pleasant loop sidetrack. The southern one leads to Cape Anguille.

Exploring the south coast is more difficult. Rte. 480 leads to the coast's only town between Fortune Bay and Channel-Port aux-Basques that is connected by roads to the rest of Newfoundland. It's a lonely road, with little traffic and almost no settlement, traversing a wild landscape with lake and mountain views as it climbs over the low shoulders of two ranges. About a third of the way from TransCanada-1, the road to Red Indian Lake heads east (see *Driving*, page 556). It takes about 90 minutes to get from TransCanada-1 to Burgeo.

The only way to see the rest of the coast, and the outports that lie like unevenly strung beads along its rim, is by ferry. Although you cannot do it in one continuous trip, you can cover much of the way from Channel-Port aux Basques to the Harbour Deep region by boat. The fares are very cheap (and half-price for seniors), but you cannot take a car most of the way, so you will have to arrange transportation at either end. Irregular schedules require that you make several stopovers. In fact. the schedules seem to have been planned purposely to discourage travelers from trying to visit the entire coast. For ferry information, ☎ 709/635-2162.

Information Sources

- Information on the entire route is in the annual *Newfoundland and Labrador Travel Guide* from the Department of Tourism, Culture and Recreation, PO Box 8730, St. John's, NF A1B 4K2, ☎ 800/563-6353 or 709/729-2830.

- For information on the Humber Valley, stop by or contact the **Tourist Chalet**, West Valley Rd. (just off Trans-Canada-1, Corner Brook, NF A2H 6E6, ☎ 709/639-9792, open daily from 9 am to 8 pm.

- You can learn about the southern shore at **Port aux Basques Information Centre** on TransCanada-1 just north of town in Port au Basques, NF A0N 1K0, ☎ 709/695-2262, open Monday, Tuesday, Thursday and Saturday, 6 am to 11 pm; Wednesday, Friday and Sunday,

6 am to 9:30 pm, June through October. Opening times are governed by each day's last boat departure.

■ For information on Burgeo, contact **Burgeo Tourism Association**, ☎ 709/886-2544.

Adventures

■ On Foot

Nature Trails

Pasadena Nature Trail follows a cross-country ski trail system, adding more than 100 numbered stops which are keyed to a 143-page nature guide to the trail. It is one of the most detailed and longest interpretive nature trails we have seen anywhere, covering more than three miles. Shorter loops are possible. The booklet, which you can take as you enter and drop off as you leave, discusses animal and plant life in terms of the whole environment of the forest. Guided tours leave from the parking area at 2 pm on Mondays, Wednesdays and Fridays in the summer. The trail access is off TransCanada-1 in Pasadena, east of Corner Brook. Turn south on Fourth Ave., then right on Midland Row, left on Carroll and Castlewood and park at the ski club lot. The trails begin at the club's cabin on Snowflake Lane, a short walk away.

Another good nature trail, about a mile long, winds through the **Bottom Brook Arboretum**, south of Stephenville at the Hydro Substation on TransCanada-1. The arboretum is to the left. An interpretive booklet describes the trees. and other wildlife. The trail is being expanded, and will eventually reach a large plantation of spruce, and a pond.

Blow Me Down Provincial Park at the far end of Rte. 450, west of Corner Brook, has a trail to the top of a lookout point, with a tower from which you can see the mouth of the Humber Arm and the many islands that give Bay of Islands its name. Known as **Governor's Staircase**, it takes about an hour round-trip. Or you can continue to **Tortoise Point**, a four-mile round-trip over three hills that form the plateau-like peninsula, each with more fine views. See *Geology*, below, for more descriptions of the trails, which begin from the entrance of the day-use area.

This little peninsula at the entrance to Bay of Islands has several trails leading to lookout points, a lighthouse at Little Port

Head, the driftwood-strewn beach at Cedar Cove and to a marine communications beacon. In York Harbour, you can walk across the marshes to Wild Cove Pond (enter through the woods at the end of Snook's Lane).

We Care Nature Trail in Stephenville is less than a mile long, but travels through several different habitats: a wildflower meadow, a marshy area, a mature boreal forest, alder and birch/balsam thickets, a bog and different kinds of peatlands. The trail is in the eastern part of town, reached from the east end of Main Street, between the river and Georgia Drive. You can begin at the Kindale Library, where there is an interpretation center. Here you can get trail maps with information on the various habitats.

Hiking

Cape St. George lies at the very tip of the Port au Port Peninsula, at the end of Rte. 460. Even if you don't plan to hike the trail, walk out to the point to see the cliffs that drop straight into the sea. You can get a dizzying view of them by climbing the trail to the top of the headland. This is not a place for people with vertigo. The trail along the headland begins farther back, at the end of the settlement near the Boutte du Cap Parc. The trail crosses the headland at some distance from the shore, along a high ridge. At the far end, it drops into the town of Mainland, with a large island of red bluffs and green moor prominent off its shore. The hike is a little over six miles one way, with no shortcuts back to the road, and no source of water.

The day to be here is June 24, St. John the Baptist Day, when the people of Mainland and those of Cape St. George walk the trail between the villages. It's a joyful local festival with little outside notice, but anyone is welcome to join.

In **Barachois Pond Provincial Park**, climb **Erin Mountain** for a panoramic view into the interior and of St. George's Bay and the Gulf of St. Lawrence. The entire climb and return will take less than three hours, but the trail gives you a look at several environments, bog to sub-alpine vegetation to rock-strewn barren summit, all in a climb of little more than 1,000 feet. This gentle climb, with a lookout point halfway, makes a good non-boot hike. Near the beginning of the trail, a short self-guided nature trail diverges to the left, rejoining the main trail a bit farther on. A wilderness campsite is located not far from the summit, between two ponds. To use it, you must have a permit from the park office, which you can get when you pay your park entry fee. The trail is well-marked, and leaves from the bridge at the narrows, past the campground.

South of Stephenville and connected to TransCanada-1 by a short road, the town of St. George's gives access by boat to the island of **Sandy Point**, which really was a point before the tides washed away the linking sandbar. Once home to hundreds of people, it is now home to piping plover and other birds. A spider's web of trails wander about the island, connecting former homesites, cemeteries, foundations and the striped lighthouse, passing bogs and small lakes as they cross the interior. Bring water and a lunch, and go to the St. George's wharf to catch the boat operated by **Sandy Point Tours**, ☎ 709/647-3383, 709/647-3553 or 800/563-9500, leaving at 10 am, 1 pm and 5 pm, Wednesday through Sunday.

Table Mountain is a must-climb for World War II buffs. Just north of Channel-Port aux Basques, and right alongside TransCanada-1, it is one of the most accessible of mountains, and the view from its huge flat 1,600-foot summit is sweeping. To climb it takes three-four hours, which gives you time to make a circle of the top and investigate the remains of the US radar station and airstrip. The radar station was on a separate summit, where you will find yellow lady slippers growing in the early summer. The hike up Table Mountain isn't as inspiring as the view, but it's easy walking along a gravel road. To access it, follow the road and park at the barway. The top of the mountain is tundra, an interesting environment with a number of tiny plants that you don't often see.

The **Cormack Trail** leads from the Grand Bay West section of Channel-Port aux Basques, along the shore to **J.T. Cheeseman Provincial Park**, a distance of about six miles. Most of it is along beaches, and since it passes through several piping plover nesting areas, it is important to walk right at the water's edge and not take your dog to walk with you. At either end of the trail are centers from which occasional guided interpretive walks begin. You can reach the beginning of the trail at Grand Bay West from Grand Bay Road, which runs from TransCanada-1, near the Mounted Police (RCMP) building north of town, to the downtown area; you can access it from either side. Parking is available here and at the provincial park. You can re-

➲ **MAPS:** *Topographical maps of southwestern Newfoundland are sold at* ***Barnes Sporting Goods,*** *16 Humber Rd., Corner Brook,* ☎ *709/634-2291.*

turn to Channel-Port aux Basques the same way, or along the old railway right-of-way, which is being developed as part of the TransCanada Trails network. From Big Barachois to the park, the last third of the route, the Cormack Trail follows the rail trail.

The Cormack Trail will eventually extend north along most of this coast, and sections are completed in several places. From Cape Ray, where the provincial park is located, to Red Rocks, a short distance north, the trail is marked and dry.

Sandbanks Provincial Park in Burgeo has a four-mile beach of fine white sand, where walkers will see shore birds in the shallow water. Inland trails travel through forests and a bog, and to a lookout point at Cow Hill, with good views. The park brochure has a full trail map, although it has few identifying labels. The trails themselves are better marked.

On the island of **Ramea**, a 70-minute ferry trip from Burgeo, you can walk to the old lighthouse – about a half-hour each way – and explore the rock formations at its base.

The **Lewis Hills** run along the coast between Corner Brook and the Port au Port Peninsula, and are Newfoundland's highest elevation at over 2,600 feet. Snowfields remain through the summer, and their meltwaters form long ribbons of waterfalls that drop into canyons hundreds of feet deep. Like the Tablelands of Gros Morne park, the hills are formed of a segment of the earth's mantle, mainly peridotite, filled with levels of minerals toxic to most plant growth. But close inspection reveals a few species that can tolerate the hostile environment of these otherwise barren slopes. Trails don't exist here, so to explore this wilderness you will need a guide.

Guided Hiking Trips

- **Cormack Expeditions**, 1 Pleasant Ave., Stephenville, NF A2N 1R9, ☎ 709/643-9057, specializes entirely in guided hiking trips in the Lewis Hills and other mountains on the southwest shore. A full-day trip is $75 per person. They do overnight backpacking trips, as well, at $50 per person per day.

- **Grand River Hiking Tours** in Searston (Box 437, Doyles, NF A0N 1J0), ☎ 709/955-2016, leads walking trips of one to three days in the beautiful Codroy Valley, not far north of Channel-Port aux Basques. The area is on the migratory routes of dozens of bird species, and hikers on these trips are bound to see many of them.

■ For guided hiking adventures of two to five days, contact **Great Out Tours Company**, PO Box 283, Corner Brook, NF A2H 6C9, ☎ 709/634-0064, fax 634-0064, e-mail adamsb&b@newcomm.net.

■ **New Found Adventures, Ltd.**, Frenchman's Cove, NF A0L 1E0, ☎ 709/789-2809, leads hiking and backpacking trips in the Lewis Hills and Blow Me Down Mountains, with packages from $125 per person.

On Wheels

Road Biking

One of the most scenic routes in the Corner Brook area follows two gravel roads leading from TransCanada-1 to Corner Brook Lake, southeast of town. The 12-mile route begins about two miles south of the Confederation Drive exit, and follows 12 Mile Dam Rd. A large parking area is at the barred entrance to the road. The directions are easy: take all right turns onto "main" roads (avoiding only the tiny woods tracks that wander off to a favorite fishing hole) until you reach the bridge near the dam, at the halfway point. Follow the same directions on the way back and you will come to TransCanada-1 via Lady Slipper Rd., about a mile south of your entry point.

Another scenic trip near Corner Brook takes you to **Old Man's Pond**, northwest of the city, but it doesn't provide the handy loop route of 12 Mile Dam. Drive on Rte. 440 toward Cox's Cove, turning north at Hughes Brook, about seven miles from Corner Brook. In another seven miles of gravel road, you will come to Old Man's Pond, and a small parking area near the junction of a rough, unsurfaced road from your left. This is your route, easy to follow (although a tough climb of about 600 feet in elevation at the beginning). After that, the road levels out and you get good views of the mountains and sea as you travel west. In about six miles, you will reach the other end of Old Man's Pond, a nice place to rest beside the brook before returning. The climb on the way back isn't as steep.

Mountain Biking

The island of **Ramea**, a 70-minute ferry ride from Burgeo, is a good place to explore by mountain bike.

Marble Mountain has become a center for competitive mountain biking, and even the professionals find its vertical ascent and drop challenging. The new service road offers the gentlest climb and the old service road the easiest descent. The total distance is about six miles, but the vertical is 1,700 feet, so no matter how you tackle it you'll get a workout. So will your brakes, which you should check first.

Bicycle Rentals

- You can rent mountain bikes at the base of Marble Mountain from **George's Ski World**, ☎ 709/639-8168.
- In Corner Brook, rentals are available from **T & T Cycles**, 166A Humber Rd., ☎ 709/634-6799, which offers free pick-up and delivery of bikes. You can also get a free mountain biking brochure that describes several routes.

➲ **BIKING TIP:** *You should always take a topographical map when you travel by bicycle on the woods roads. These are sold at* ***Barnes Sporting Goods****, 16 Humber Rd., Corner Brook,* ☎ *709/634-2291.*

- Near Stephenville, you can rent bikes at **Barachois Pond Provincial Park**, ☎ 709/646-2366.

■ On Water

Swimming

The best swimming in the area (and one of the best beaches in the province) is at **J.T. Cheeseman Provincial Park**, where the waters are an almost electric blue. The beach is a long sandy barachois, a sandbar thrown up by the sea, providing a barrier between the cold, tidal ocean waters and the warmer, smooth waters of the lagoon. **Parc Regional Picadilly Head** on the Port au Port Peninsula has a nice sandy beach, with a day-use fee of $2. **Margaret Bowater Park** in the heart of Corner Brook has a nice river beach with supervised swimming, changing facilities and picnic area.

Canoeing & Kayaking

The lower **Humber River**, from Deer Lake to Corner Brook, is good for canoeing. It stretches 12 scenic miles with steep hills rising on both sides, often thick with forest. You'll be paddling a route used by Captain James Cook when he explored the river as far as Deer Lake. Rapids and a canyon enliven the last stretch, between Shellbird Island and the tidal zone. Moose, bald eagles, salmon and ducks may keep you company along the river. Enter the lake from South Brook Park, off TransCanada-1.

> **CAUTION:** *The current in this part of the Humber River is fast and can be dangerous. It is best to go with a guide or group that knows the river.*

If you took our advice and traveled the remote Badger-to-Rte. 480 road past Red Indian Lake, you've already seen **Lloyd's River** as it flows past the Annieopsquotch Mountains. It's one of our favorite canoe routes in the early summer (later in the season you can too easily drag bottom in the shallows), with good campsites along the way. Several areas are Class 1 or 2 rapids, so it's not a ho-hum paddle, but they are separated by pleasant rests of flatwater. About six miles of it is along the length of Lloyd's Lake. For a several-day trip, put in on the Burgeo Road (Rte. 480), about four miles south of the road to Red Indian Lake. The best take-out is at the second bridge, just before the river empties into Red Indian Lake, reached by the road you passed before the put-in. For a very long trip, you can paddle the length of the lake and then into the Exploits River. For any part of this trip, you will need topographical maps and a good talk with someone locally who knows the river and its water levels at the time.

Less confident canoeists can find a flatwater route along the **Grand Codroy River** in Grand Codroy Provincial Park, just a short drive from Port aux Basques. Access to upper regions is easy from several points along TransCanada-1, which runs close to the river, but mostly out of sight. Both branches cross the highway, at the towns of North Branch and Coal Brook, respectively. The river is fairly shallow, the views are good, and the pace leisurely here. In spring high water, the North Branch provides an exciting trip with a put-in at the town of North Branch and a take-out near South Branch, where the two rivers join. An 18-mile paddle from South Branch to the mouth of the Grand Codroy at Searston, is a long day's trip.

It's hard for sea kayakers to beat the scenery from the waters of the **Bay of Islands**; no matter which way you turn there's either the Blow Me Down range or the mountains of Gros Morne Park, or one of the dramatic islands that give the bay its name. The protected waters inside the bay are bounded by a rugged shore filled with little coves and crannies to explore. Early morning is the best time for calm waters, before the winds rise. In a wind, the south shore is more protected, and has more places to land. The northern shore is better for highly experienced paddlers, more isolated, fewer landings and more exposure to the prevailing winds.

To kayak the island's south coast is to see Newfoundland as it looked to the first European explorers, miles of rock-bound coastline cut by coves and fjords, with long narrow bays where rivers flow into the sea. Towns are rare, and the few that exist are reached only by water. You share the sea with marine life, a few fishing boats and a ferry on its way from Rose Blanche to Burgeo once a week.

Canoe & Kayak Outfitters - Guided Tours

■ Joe Dicks at **Marble Mountain Cabins** in Steady Brook (PO Box 63), Corner Brook, NF A2H 6C3, ☎ 709/634-2237, fax 709/639-1592, is "Mr. Adventure" in the Corner Brook area. He leads kayaking trips along this remote coast, from Burgeo to Channel-Port aux Basques. Trips begin with a day of training for warm-up and to bring participants up to a level-3 competency, since some days they may be paddling 12-15 miles. Marble Mountain Cabins also offers a unique kayaking experience for those who enjoy fishing, combining the two sports in one river kayaking trip. Or, they will guide you on day trips in the scenic Bay of Islands. Marble Mountain rents kayaks and canoes and gives full courses or short lessons, with practice in their heated pool. While there, pick up a copy of the yellow *Canoeing Guide and Map*, which describes several rivers of varying skill levels.

■ **Discovery Outtripping Company**, 23 Dove's Road, Corner Brook, NF A2H 1M2, ☎ 709/634-6335, fax 709/634-2104, e-mail mtsang@thezone.net, does backcountry canoe trips on several rivers in the area and will pickup and dropoff at the airport. Rates are about $150 a day.

■ **New Found Adventures, Ltd.**, Frenchman's Cove, NF A0L 1E0, ☎ 709/789-2809, offer canoe excursions tailored to individual skills and interests, which may include wildlife-watching and/or photography.

■ **Backwoods Enterprizes**, 7 MacGregor Place, Corner Brook, NF A2H 7B7, ☎ 709/634-6124, fax 709/634-1418, e-mail vbelbin@calvin.stemnet.nf.ca, also emphasizes wildlife viewing and photography, with canoe trips on the Humber in areas known for caribou, moose, Canada geese, Arctic hare, beaver, muskrat and otter. They also rent canoes.

■ **Outside Expeditions**, PO Box 2336, Charlottetown, PEI C1A 8C1, ☎ 902/892-5425 or 800/207-3899, fax 902/829-5425, e-mail kayak@getoutside.com, Web site www.getoutside.com. They lead full-week kayaking and hiking expeditions along the remote south coast. Tours visit remote outports whose only contact with the rest of the world is by boat.

Boat Tours & Ferries

If paddling down the Humber in a canoe doesn't appeal to you, but you'd still like to see this beautiful stretch of river that Captain Cook explored, take a tour of the river in a small power boat with **Humber River Boat Tours**, Steady Brook, ☎ 709/634-8140. Rates for a two-hour cruise that covers 15 miles are $20 adults, $12 for children. Waterfowl, raptors and moose are often seen along the riverbanks.

It would be a shame to waste the steady winds that riffle the waters of Bay of Islands, and you can take full advantage of them on board the 26-foot Contessa ***Sohesten***, ☎ 709/643-6965. The boat is certified to carry three passengers, and you can either go for a ride or help sail. Leaving from the Yacht Club Marina, it's your choice whether the *Sohesten* sails into Corner Brook or west into the waters of the outer bay. The cost is $15 per hour for adults, $12 for children.

Sandy Point in St. George's Bay is really an island. Once a thriving community, it's now an abandoned rise of bogs and ponds, surrounded by beaches where plover nest. A boat operated by **Sandy Point Tours**, ☎ 709/647-3383 or 709/647-3553, leaves the wharf in St. George's at 10 am, 1 pm and 5 pm, Wednesday through Sunday, and you can just go for the ride, stay a few hours or take your camping gear and stay a few days (be sure to bring enough water).

The **ferries** that connect the towns along the southern coast are infrequent and scheduled so as not to encourage through traffic. In addition, you can't take cars on most of them, so when you arrive at the other end you will need to take a local bus or have someone meet you with a car. You can take a car from Burgeo to the island of **Ramea**, a 70-minute ride costing $7.50 for vehicle and driver; $3.75 if the driver is a senior. Passenger fare is $2.50. From Ramea, you can continue on by ferry to the tiny outport of **Grey River** on Tuesdays and Thursdays; car and driver costs $12 ($6 seniors), passengers pay $4 ($2 seniors). For ferry information and schedules, call ☎ 709/635-4100 or 709/635-4127. For information on the Ramea ferry, call ☎ 709/635-2167.

To reach **Burgeo** by boat from Channel-Port aux Basques, you can drive to Rose Blanche on Rte. 470, and take a ferry to La Poile and on to Grand Bruit, where you must stay overnight before going on to Burgeo. Bear in mind that these schedules change, and that it is very important to get the exact schedule for the dates you plan to travel. For information on ferries from Rose Blanche to Grand Bruit, ☎ 709/635-4100. The fare from Rose Blanche to Burgeo is $7.75, $4 seniors.

Diving

Pro Sport Diving, 147 Main St., Stephenville, NF A2N 1J5, ☎ 709/643-9260, is a full-service dive center, operating diving trips to offshore reefs around the Port au Port Peninsula as well as short dives to see the region's plentiful marine life. They stock a complete line of rental gear, and have equipment for underwater video and photography.

Northern Arm Adventure Sports, ☎ 709/783-2712, fax 709/634-3810, operating out of Cox's Cove north of Corner Brook, provides transportation and guides for divers.

Burgeo Diving Tours, PO Box 428, Burgeo, NF A0M 1A0, ☎ 709/886-2122, explores shipwrecks off the south coast, some dating to the mid-1800s. Visibility in these waters is often compared to that of Caribbean dive sites. Marine life is plentiful, too. Wrecks are readily accessible, within decompression limits.

Windsurfing

On TransCanada-1 near Pasadena between Deer Lake and Corner Brook, you can surf from a sandy beach in the deep, cool waters of

Deer Lake at **South Brook Park**. On the other side of Corner Brook on Rte. 450, **York Harbour** has a pebble beach where the mountain drops to the waters of Bay of Islands.

The sandy beach at **Black Bank** in Stephenville Crossing has high winds and big surf. **Barachois Pond Provincial Park**, nearby on TransCanada-1, has two beaches on a long pond. **Cheeseman Provincial Park,** close to Channel-Port aux Basques, has a sandy beach, good waves and strong winds.

Windjammer Boardsailing Club in Corner Brook has weekend activities and a number of special events during the summer. You can find out who the current president is from **Freedom Sports**, ☎ 709/634-0864, where you can also rent boards and take lessons. For access by boat to some of the more remote surfing beaches, contact **Northern Arm Adventure Sports**, ☎ 709/783-2712, fax 709/634-3810, operating out of Cox's Cove, north of Corner Brook.

Fishing

The southwest corner of this region alone, from Cape Anguille to Rose Blanche (a distance of 60 miles by road), has nine licensed salmon rivers. Within a 30-minute drive of Stephenville are nine more. Near Burgeo, **Grandy's River**, just north of Sandbanks Provincial Park, is known as one of the province's best salmon rivers.

Fishing Outfitters - Guided Tours

■ **Humber River Boat Tours** in Steady Brook, ☎ 709/634-8140, will take you for a half-day excursion or a longer trip and can supply all equipment if you need it. Owner Todd Neil claims that the Humber has salmon weighing in at 60 pounds; he doesn't promise you'll catch one of those, but does promise you a good time trying.

■ Tucked under the Blow Me Down Mountains on the north shore of Serpentine Lake is **Serpentine Valley Wilderness Lodge**, ☎ 709/639-1968 or 709/789-2935, e-mail daled@atcon.com. It's about as wilderness as you can get and still arrive on wheels (their 4X4 will meet you in Corner Brook or at the airport). An hour outboard ride downstream brings you to pools where 20-pound salmon and five-pound sea-run trout swim. It's a rustic lodge atmosphere, as you would expect, with all meals, fishing guides, boats and comfortable lodging for $1,100 a week.

➲ **SERPENTINE LAKE:** *When fly-fishing legend Lee Wulff wasn't waxing eloquent about Portland Creek on the Great Northern Peninsula, he was describing the charms of the Serpentine. He was right; it* ***is*** *spectacular fishing.*

Guides will take you on hiking expeditions, too, if you can tear yourself away from the fishing.

■ For a fishing guide in the Stephenville area, contact **Byrne's Guiding and Referral Service**, 37 Valley Rd., Stephenville, NF A2N 2R3, ☎ 709/643-2075, fax 709/643-5367.

SPORTFISHING AT STRAWBERRY HILL RESORT

At the high end of sport fishing is **Strawberry Hill Resort** on TransCanada-1 in Little Rapids (mailing address: PO Box 296, Station C, St. John's, NF A1C 5J2), ☎ 709/754-1174 or 709/634-0066, fax 709/754-4606, e-mail newfound@nfld.com. Built by Sir Eric Bowater as an elegant private estate on 22 acres fronting the Humber River, Strawberry Hill has hosted Queen Elizabeth, among other distinguished guests. This is fishing at its most luxurious.

Strawberry Hill's fishing program is run by Rob Solo, who is without question Newfoundland's guide and raconteur par excellence. The dining room has a magnificent view over the grounds and the Lower Humber, and the food here is the finest. Strawberry Hill Resort is 20 minutes from Deer Lake Airport (free guest pick-up can be arranged) and 15 minutes from the town of Corner Brook. Rates are $550 per day, including private room with bath, three meals, boat, guide, and license. Bring your own tackle and gear: rods, reels, lines, flies, fishing vest, and waders. The resort can supply some tackle, flies, and gear. (Solo is internationally famous for his unique hand-tied fly patterns.)

Strawberry Hill offers other summer activities in addition to salmon fishing: hiking, rock climbing, cave exploring, wildlife tours, sea kayaking, canoeing, and golf. – *Sara Godwin and Charles James*

On Snow

Special Events

Corner Brook bills their **Winter Carnival** (☎ 709/637-1500) as the biggest in Atlantic Canada. Held in mid-February, it lasts for 10 activity-filled days and nights. Anything that's fun and can be done outdoors in the winter is probably on the program, which includes snow sculpture, Viking games, skiing, fireworks, a torchlight parade, cross-country events, and plenty of Newfie food and drink.

Downhill Skiing

Marble Mountain in Steady Brook (PO Box 394, Corner Brook, NF A2H 2N2, ☎ 709/639-8531) is a growing alpine ski resort, with a 1,600-foot vertical (often very vertical) drop to challenge skiers. New trails and facilities are added every year. The snowfall is the highest of any ski area in eastern North America, with an average 16 feet of snow. The base lodge is roomy and shuttle buses connect skiers to Corner Brook hotels. Lift rates are low and beginners use the two T-bars free, as do children. These perks, combined with dollar-saving packages (such as free lift tickets with your car rental) make it an outstanding value. A village of tidy cabins and other services is growing at its feet along TransCanada-1.

Cross-Country Skiing

Pasadena Nordic Ski Club between Corner Brook and Deer Lake, ☎ 709/686-5212, has four miles of groomed trails, with lessons and ski chalet. Access is off TransCanada-1 in Pasadena: turn south on Fourth Ave., then right on Midland Row, left on Carroll and again on Castlewood.

Blow Me Down Cross Country Ski Club, ☎ 709/639-2754, maintains more than 20 miles of groomed trails suitable for gliding and skating styles, with racing trails built to accommodate the Canadian Winter Games. They groom 25 miles of trails, on which accumulates the highest annual snowfall of any community in Canada. Some trails are lighted for night skiing; the club offers lessons and has a lodge with a cafeteria and a warming hut on the trails. Follow Lewin Parkway to Lundrigan Drive, where you'll find signs. rates are $10 weekend and $8 midweek adults, half-price for children. Night skiing is $5.

Whaleback Nordic Ski Club, ☎ 709/643-3259, has 13 miles of groomed trails that begin near White's Rd. and Cold Brook. Some are lighted for night skiing and they have a warming cabin. In the Stevensville area as a whole, you'll find about 50 miles of trails, and a dependably good snowcover.

Ski Outfitters – Guided Tours

- **New Found Adventures, Ltd.**, Frenchman's Cove, NF A0L 1E0, ☎ 709/789-2809, does hut-to-hut ski touring trips in the Lewis Hills and Blow Me Down Mountains, with packages from $125 per person. Guided backcountry ski excursions in the Long Range and Blow Me Down mountains are led by Gros Morne Adventure Guides, ☎ 709/686-2241.

- Snow fields cover the treeless tops and upper slopes of the Long Range Mountains, which you can reach in a heated 10-passenger snow-cat with **Blomiden Cat Skiing**, ☎ 709/783-2712, fax 709/634-3810. The ride, which is as exciting as the skiing itself, begins at Benoit's Cove, 20 minutes from Corner Brook (where they will pick you up by bus). You can make four runs in the morning, enjoy the included lunch, and make four more afternoon runs, all across powder-covered fields that range from intermediate to expert-plus. Guides are radio-equipped for emergencies and all skiers carry electronic tracers. This is an experience for advanced intermediate skiers, at the least. A day of alpine skiing, with shuttle from Corner Brook or Marble Mountain, guides, lunch and snacks, is $150. A single ride up for access to higher altitude cross-country skiing is $25.

Snowmobiling

The entire area around Corner Brook is covered with woods roads and trails used by snowmobilers in the winter. In addition, miles of backcountry are cut by impromptu tracks.

Guided Snowmobile Tours

- At **Marble Mountain Cabins** in Steady Brook, ☎ 709/634-2237, fax 709/639-1592, you can join a day excursion into the Lewis Hills by snowmobile, or you can take a two-day trip inland to Buchans, near Red Indian Lake. For the biggest thrill in the shortest time, join their trip into Gros Morne National Park, where in only two hours you can be on the mountain overlooking the fjord far below.

■ **New Found Adventures, Ltd.**, Frenchman's Cove, NF A0L 1E0, ☎ 709/789-2809, leads guided snowmobile adventures in the Lewis Hills and Blow Me Down Mountains.

On Horseback

Mountain Meadow Farm on Tower Rd. (off Lewin Parkway) in Corner Brook, ☎ 709/634-9977 or 709/639-9626, has horse and pony rides for adults and children, 10 am to 9 pm daily. Ring rides are $2, practice rides $5 and trail rides $15 per hour. Children will enjoy seeing the array of farm animals and birds, from Newfoundland ponies and miniature rabbits to peacocks.

Double C Ranch in Flat Bay, ☎ 709/647-3130, offers trail rides, and **Steve's Horse Rides**, ☎ 709/695-3920, will take you riding on the beaches at Grand Bay West in Channel-Port aux Basques.

Cultural & Eco-Travel Experiences

Port au Port Peninsula is the center of the province's French community, just as Avalon is the heart of Irish Newfoundland. Settled by Nova Scotia Acadians and French from Brittany over 100 years ago, when the French held fishing rights to Newfoundland's western coast, it has remained largely French. On the first weekend in August is **Une Longue Vieille**, a French music festival.

Geology

Governor's Staircase, a half-hour climb from Blow Me Down Provincial Park at the far end of Rte. 450 west of Corner Brook, travels through and over rocks formed 450 million years ago. The agglomerate is formed from pieces of volcanic rock mixed with a dense quartz-like rock. In places you can see swirls that give you a picture of what it looked like in its molten state.

THE DAILY NEWS FROM CORNER BROOK

If you live in Dallas or Miami, or a number of smaller US cities, when you read your daily newspaper you may be holding paper made in Corner Brook. Kruger, Inc., successor to the Bowater Paper Corporation, is one of the largest paper mills in the world and produces more than 300,000 tons of paper a year. They provide newsprint to newspapers throughout North America and Europe. The trees that become pulp for their paper come from all over western, central and northern Newfoundland, and it is quite likely that the logging trucks and log piles you see in the area are headed for the Kruger plant in downtown Corner Brook. You can thank Kruger for many of the back roads and woods tracks you follow in your adventures.

On its way to the Bay of Islands, the Corner Brook Stream has cut its way through the limestone to provide entrances to a **large cave system**, with a sinkhole, subterranean waterfall and a single cavern 1,500 feet long. But the stream that exposes its entrance also floods a good part of it, making some areas quite dangerous without proper equipment and a guide who knows the cave system well. It's not a place to go poking about alone, but if you are a serious spelunker, Joe Dicks at **Marble Mountain Cabins** in Steady Brook, ☎ 709/634-2237, fax 709/639-1592, will take you there. He's an experienced spelunker and knows the caves well. For a more casual tour of the caves, which are fascinating even without exploring their nethermost reaches, call Joe. He can also tell you the names of several other guides who will take you there safely and who know how to find the hidden entrances.

This being a limestone region, it is rich in fossils. **Aquathuna**, just west of Port au Port, is a world-class fossil area where you can see ammonoids, graptolites and clam burial sites. Two limestone quarries operated here until 1965. There is also a waterfall in Aquathuna.

For the granddaddy of waterfalls, look up as you drive east on TransCanada-1, just to the left of the Marble Mountain ski slopes. You'll see only part of **Steady Brook Falls**. To see the rest of it, follow the trail from the base lodge, about half a mile to the falls. There are no railings, only a dizzying drop filled with thundering water, so be careful, don't get too close to the edge – and hang onto the kids.

■ Wildlife-Watching

Whales

Whales are the biggest wildlife to watch, as they follow the capelin schools into the Gulf of St. Lawrence. In May and June the minkes arrive in the Bay of Islands, followed by the pilot whales, pods of which you're more likely to see in July and August. Humpbacks arrive in late May and stay through August, usually best seen farther out among the outer islands and off the lower coast. Killer whales, although rare, have been seen off this coast. The rare blue whale, the largest animal on earth, appear in late winter along the southwest coast, and can be seen there for several months; a few hundred of them summer in the Gulf of St. Lawrence.

The best place to spot whales is off **Cape Ray**. In the Bay of Islands, the best locations for whale viewing are at **Frenchman's Cove**, on its southern shore, and **Cox's Cove**, at the end of Rte. 440 on the northern shore of the Humber Arm.

Birds

Because it is on major migration routes, this region is excellent for birding. Its miles of sandy beaches and dunes make it an important habitat for shorebirds, especially the endangered piping plover. Beaches at **J.T. Cheeseman Provincial Park** and at **Sandbanks Provincial Park** in Burgeo have ideal environments for them, with soft sand for nests, wet sand for invertebrate foods, and few people to disturb them.

Sandy Point is a nesting site for the rare blackhead gull, as well as more plover. Eagles and osprey nest along the cliffs above the lower Humber. Waterfowl, including ducks and geese, thrive in the intertidal areas.

J.T. Cheeseman Provincial Park is a habitat or migration stop for great blue herons, American bitterns, great and snowy egrets, and yellow crowned night herons, four species of plover, six of sandpiper, sanderlings and dotterels.

ATVS 10, PIPING PLOVER NOTHING

Piping plover, already threatened by gulls and by increasing development of areas close to their beach nesting spots, are threatened in Newfoundland, as elsewhere, by ATVs racing up and down the beaches. The threat is many-pronged. First, the eggs, in nests camouflaged in the sand, are crushed as vehicles drive over them. Second, the ATVs destroy the invertebrate life closer to the water line, the plover's main food source, by driving over them. Third, ATVs destroy the dunes and dune grass that protects the plovers' beach nesting sites. When the dune grass is gone, there is nothing to hold the dunes in place, and no sand for the plover to build a nest in. The noise of the vehicles, and the increased human presence they bring to more remote beaches previously used only by a few non-intrusive walkers, causes alarmed plover to abandon nests. At the last census, the entire population in North America, the only place these birds are found, was about 5,000, and decreasing by more than 20% a decade.

Sightseeing

Much of this area's attraction is in its scenery, which varies from mountainsides with snow patches in July and long waterfalls dropping through their ravines, to long stretches of beach and barachois separated by high headlands. One of the most scenic of all these is at the tip of Cape Anguille, where a lighthouse sits below a steep hill. You can navigate the rutted track by car if the weather has not been too wet. It's okay to open the cattle bar to drive through; just be sure to close it promptly. At the top, walk beyond the end of the road to see magnificent cliffs drop straight into the sea. More headlands drop to the north. The strong westerly wind that blows steadily here seems to be trying to keep you from falling off the edge.

Stop also in **St. Andrew's** for the dramatic view of mountains, with their rounded tops joining in a plateau, their sides scooped and dropping off in a series of narrow ravines. Go to the end of the town's road, where there is a small beach with views over the channel and across the downs to Table Mountain.

Between Channel-Port aux Basques and Corner Brook, the Port au Port Peninsula juts into the Gulf of St. Lawrence, ending at the sharp point of **Cape St. George** on the west and the well-named needle-like **Long Point** on the north almost enclosing Port au Port Bay. Plan at least half a day to circle this scenic peninsula, following Rte. 460 along the moderate cliffs on the southern shore, where towns perch on their rims in a string, backyards dropping off into the sea. Little streams at the settlement of Sheaves become waterfalls at the cliff-edge. At Cape St. George, **Boutte du Cap Parc** has picnic sites tucked into a protected lee; go all the way to the top for a view of layer after layer of headlands. Rte. 463 climbs over these, with good views looking back over the bay and ahead, where the whole coast to Gros Morne is spread before you. The Port au Port Peninsula is not a sandspit, as it looks on the map, but a long series of high headlands. At the tip of Long Point is a seasonal fishing settlement reminiscent of the old outport days.

One of the most scenic enclosed fishing coves in this region is **Bottle Cove,** close to Corner Brook at the end of Rte. 450, which is a view-packed drive along the southern shore of the Humber Arm. Rocky promontories jut straight up on both sides of the cove, forming a ring that almost completely encircles the harbor. At low tide you can visit a sea cave on the western side of the cove.

The Gulf Museum, 118 Main St in Port Aux Basques, ☎ 709/695-3408, has Dorset and maritime artifacts, including an astrolabe dating from the 1600s found on the shore nearby. Old tools, a century-old diving suit, ship models and a working print shop are also here. The museum is open daily 10 am to 6 pm, June through August; admission is $2, $1 for children.

Our Lady of Mercy Church in Port au Port West was begun by the local faithful in 1914, and completed – completely by volunteer labor – in 1925. The church is the largest all-wooden structure in Newfoundland, one of the largest wooden churches in Atlantic Canada. Inside, the woodwork in its ornate domes, altar rail and other embellishments are all the work of local volunteers, and the marble stations of the cross are from Italy. The 1,200-member parish is busy restoring and preserving this monumental structure. Read the brochure to learn the several incidents connected to the statue of St. Theresa. Next door is a small museum with a collection of historical toys and dolls, fossils from nearby Aguathuna, and local and religious artifacts. A craft shop at the museum features locally made quilts, knitwear and woodenware. The museum and shop are open June through September.

Where To Stay & Eat

Near Corner Brook

Glynmill Inn is in the middle of downtown but seems miles away, separated by a row of trees, surrounded by gardens and overlooking a ravine and pond. It's a gracious hotel, with guest service and hotel amenities, but the friendly warmth of an inn. Rooms are stylishly decorated and suites on the first floor are lush. The **Carriage Room** ($-$$$) has the ambiance and menu of a resort hotel dining room and **The Wine Cellar** ($$) is a cozy steakhouse with stone-lined walls. *1 Cobb Lane (PO Box 550), Corner Brook, NF A2H 6E6, ☎ 709/634-5181 or 800/563-4400, fax 709/634-5106; $$).*

Mamateek Inn is a modern hotel on the highway, overlooking the town and the bay. Rooms are spacious; some have sitting areas. Their **Beothuk Dining Room** ($$-$$$) is surrounded by glass to take advantage of the view, and serves a surprisingly eclectic menu. *64 Maple Valley Rd. (PO Box 787), Corner Brook, NF A2H 6G7, ☎ 709/639-8901 or 800/563-8600, fax 709/639-7567 ($$).*

Marble Mountain Cabins in Steady Brook, are so well known as the area's adventure center that it's easy to forget that their attractive, well-kept cabins are what started it all. Some cabins have been enlarged to have three and four bedrooms, designed for several couples traveling together. Kitchens in both the cabins and efficiency units allow you to buy seafood from the fishermen along the Humber Arm and dine at home. *PO Box 63, Corner Brook, NF A2H 6C3, ☎ 709/634-2237, fax 709/639-1592 ($-$$).*

Kindlewood Chalets, Little Rapids, offers modern chalets with big windows, cathedral ceilings and sleeping lofts, in addition to full bedrooms. Little Rapids is near Steady Brook, a mile east of Marble Mountain ski area. Cottages sleep six, but a $15 charge is added for each additional person, making them a bit pricey, we think, but they are nice. *PO Box 2110, Station Main, Corner Brook, NS A2H 2N2, ☎ 709/634-9555, fax 709/634-9556 ($$$-$$$$).*

Our choice for dining in Corner Brook is the European-style **Thirteen West**, serving an innovative menu of seafood and other dishes with an Italian touch. The chowder is wonderful, prepared with fresh and smoked fish, and the pork tenderloin with port and caramelized pears is a nice break from seafood. *13 West Street, Corner Brook, ☎ 709/634-1300 ($$).*

Gilbert's Restaurant serves a home-style menu with a number of lunch options, daily from noon until 7:30 pm. *On Rte. 450 between Blow Me Down Provincial Park and Bottle Cove, ☎ 709/681-2679 ($-$$).*

Lynn's Café offers traditional Newfoundland dishes not easily found in restaurants. *37 Broadway, Corner Brook, ☎ 709/634-2330 ($).*

St. George's Bay & South

Spruce Pine Acres sits right over water, on mowed, tidy grounds. It has a rustic lodge look, but the rooms are nicely decorated, and there is a hot tub and sauna. *PO Box 219, Port au Port, NF A0N 1T0, ☎ 709/648-9600, fax 709/648-9600 ($$).*

Tomkins Tourist Home and Cabins is a well-kept home just at the Doyles turn-off. *Box 1, Doyles, NF A0N 1J0, ☎ 709/955-2901. Rooms with shared bath are $20, motel rooms $30 ($).*

Heritage Home is a homey B&B within a short walk of the ferry terminal. *11 Caribou Road, PO Box 1187, Port aux Basques, NF A0M 1C0, ☎ 709/695-3240 ($-$$).*

St. Christopher's Hotel, also on Caribou Road, is a two-story motel-style property with modern rooms, about half a mile from the ferry landing. *PO Box 2049, Port aux Basques, NF A0M 1C0, ☎ 709/695-7034, fax 709/695-9841 ($$).*

Burgeo Haven B&B is in an historic waterfront home, with hosts that can direct you to hiking trails, the best birding sites and other activities. *63 Reach Rd., PO Box 414, Burgeo, NF A0M 1A0, ☎ 709/886-2544, fax 709/886-2544 ($-$$).*

Chignic Lodge is about 35 miles from Channel-Port aux Basques. Don't be put off by its roadhouse looks; inside it is bright and very hospitable, and the food is good. It's hard to find a breakfast or lunch entrée over $5 or a dinner entrée for more than $8, including shrimp or scallops. They have cabins and motel rooms ($) which are basic but clean. *TransCanada-1, Doyles, NF A0N 1J0, ☎ 709/955-2880, fax 709/955-2306 ($).*

Hexagon Restaurant is plain, with fried fish, sandwiches and casual service, open until 11 pm. We were eating dinner here one evening when a double rainbow appeared over and dropped into the bay. Everyone in the restaurant – cook, bottle-washer, waitress, local kids crowded into a booth and all of us in mid-dinner – rushed out to the parking lot and stood watching it until it faded away. That's what we like about Newfoundland: they haven't lost the wonder of their beautiful land and will take time to enjoy it, even if it means a cold dinner. *In Piccadilly, on the Port au Port Peninsula, ☎ 709/642-5830 ($).*

Our Lady of Mercy Church in Port au Port West has a tearoom in the adjoining museum, formerly the rectory.

■ Camping

J.T. Cheeseman Provincial Park, eight miles north of Channel-Port aux Basques on TransCanada-1, has 101 campsites, three of which are wheelchair accessible. They have a fine swimming beach in a protected bay and miles of walking trails along the shore. *To reserve a site, call ☎ 709/695-7222 or 800/866-CAMP (mid-May through August).*

Blow Me Down Provincial Park, open mid-May through August, has tent and trailer sites for $11 a night. The park has trails along the mountains and to Bottle Cove. *Lark Harbour, ☎ 709/570-7573 or 800/866-CAMP.*

The former Picadilly Head Provincial Park is now **Parc Regional Picadilly Head**, and privately operated by energetic young management that maintains the campsites well and hopes to expand the park's facilities. Sites, some with tent platforms, all without hookups, are $8 a night, $40 a week. Site 16 has a sea view, and the entire campground seems to have a lower population of carnivorous insects than is normal for Newfoundland. *Rte. 463, Picadilly, NF A2N 3B5, ☎ 709/642-5067.*

Index

A

B

D

G

H

N

Index

T

U

V

W

Index

Y

Z

Adventure Guides from Hunter Publishing

This signature Hunter series targets travelers eager to explore the destination. Extensively researched and offering the very latest information, Adventure Guides are written by knowledgeable, experienced authors. The focus is on outdoor activities – hiking, biking, rock climbing, horseback riding, downhill skiing, parasailing, scuba diving, backpacking, and waterskiing, among others - and these user-friendly books provide all the details you need, including prices. The best local outfitters are listed, along with contact numbers, addresses, e-mail and Web site information, and recommendations. A comprehensive introductory section provides background on history, geography, climate, culture, when to go, transportation and planning. These very readable guides then take a region-by-region approach, plunging into the very heart of each area and the adventures offered, giving a full range of accommodations, shopping, restaurants for every budget, and festivals. All books have town and regional maps; some have color photos. Fully indexed.

ALASKA HIGHWAY

2nd Edition, Ed & Lynn Readicker-Henderson

"A comprehensive guide.... Plenty of background history and extensive bibliography."
Travel Reference Library on-line

The fascinating highway that passes settlements of the Tlingit and the Haida Indians, with stops at Anchorage, Tok, Skagway, Valdez, Denali National Park and more. Sidetrips and attractions en route, plus details on the Alaska Marine Hwy, Klondike Hwy, Top-of-the-World Hwy. Color photos.

400 pp, $16.95, 1-55650-824-7

BAHAMAS

2nd Edition, Blair Howard

Fully updated reports for Grand Bahama, Freeport, Eleuthera, Bimini, Andros, the Exumas, Nassau, New Providence Island, plus new sections on San Salvador, Long Island, Cat Island, the Acklins, the Inaguas and the Berry Islands. Mailboat schedules, package vacations and snorkeling trips by Jean-Michel Cousteau.

280 pp, $15.95, 1-55650-852-2

EXPLORE BELIZE

4th Edition, Harry S. Pariser

"Down-to-earth advice.... An excellent travel guide." – *Library Journal*

Extensive coverage of the country's political, social and economic history, along with the plant and animal life. Encouraging you to mingle with the locals, Pariser entices you with descriptions of local dishes and festivals. Maps, color photos.

400 pp, $16.95, 1-55650-785-2

CANADA'S ATLANTIC PROVINCES

Barbara Radcliffe Rogers & Stillman Rogers

Pristine waters, rugged slopes, breathtaking seascapes, remote wilderness, sophisticated cities, and quaint, historic towns. Year-round adventures on the Fundy Coast, Acadian Peninsula, fjords of Gros Morne, Viking Trail & Vineland, Saint John River, Lord Baltimore's lost colony. Photos.

672 pp, $19.95, 1-55650-819-0

CAYMAN ISLANDS

Paris Permenter & John Bigley

The only comprehensive guidebook to Grand Cayman, Cayman Brac and Little Cayman. Encyclopedic listings of dive/snorkel operators, along with the best sites. Enjoy nighttime pony rides on a glorious beach, visit the turtle farms, prepare to get wet at staggering blowholes or just laze on a white sand beach. Color photos.

224 pp, $16.95, 1-55650-786-0

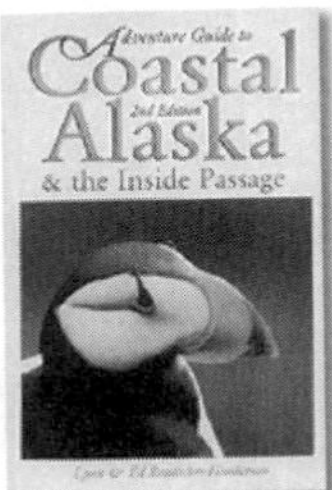

COASTAL ALASKA & THE INSIDE PASSAGE

3rd Edition, Lynn & Ed Readicker-Henderson

"A highly useful book." – *Travel Books Review*

Using the Alaska Marine Highway to visit Ketchikan, Bellingham, the Aleutians, Kodiak, Seldovia, Valdez, Seward, Homer, Cordova, Prince of Wales Island, Juneau, Gustavas, Sitka, Haines, Skagway. Glacier Bay, Tenakee. US and Canadian gateway cities profiled.

400 pp, $16.95, 1-55650-859-X

COLORADO

Steve Cohen

Adventures in the San Juan National Forest, Aspen, Vail, Mesa Verde National Park, The Sangre de Cristo Mountains, Denver, Boulder, Telluride, Colorado Springs and Durango, plus scores of smaller towns and attractions. Resident-author Cohen knows the state intimately.

296 pp, $15.95, 1-55680-724-0

COSTA RICA

3rd Edition, Harry S. Pariser

"... most comprehensive... Excellent sections on national parks, flora, fauna & history."
– *CompuServe Travel Forum*

Incredible detail on culture, plants, animals, where to stay & eat, as well as practicalities of travel. E-mail and Web site directory.

560 pp, $16.95, 1-55650-722-4

EXPLORE THE DOMINICAN REPUBLIC

3rd Edition, Harry S. Pariser

Virgin beaches, 16th-century Spanish ruins, the Caribbean's highest mountain, exotic wildlife, vast forests. Visit Santa Domingo, revel in Sosúa's European sophistication or explore the Samaná Peninsula's jungle. Color.

340 pp, $15.95, 1-55650-814-X

FLORIDA KEYS & EVERGLADES

2nd Edition, Joyce & Jon Huber

"... vastly informative, absolutely user-friendly, chock full of information..." – Dr. Susan Cropper

"... practical & easy to use." – *Wilderness Southeast*

Canoe trails, airboat rides, nature hikes, Key West, diving, sailing, fishing. Color.

224 pp, $14.95, 1-55650-745-3

FLORIDA'S WEST COAST

Chelle Koster Walton

A guide to all the cities, towns, nature preserves, wilderness areas and sandy beaches that grace the Sunshine State's western shore. From Tampa Bay to Naples and Everglades National Park to Sanibel Island.

224 pp, $14.95, 1-55650-787-9

GEORGIA

Blair Howard

"Packed full of information on everything there is to see and do." – *Chattanooga Free Press*

From Atlanta to Savannah to Cumberland Island, this book walks you through antique-filled stores, around a five-story science museum and leads you on tours of old Southern plantations.

296 pp, $15.95, 1-55650-782-8

GEORGIA & CAROLINA COASTS

Blair Howard

"Provides details often omitted... geared to exploring the wild dunes, the historic districts, the joys... "
– *Amazon.com Travel Expert*

Beaufort, Myrtle Beach, New Bern, Savannah, the Sea Islands, Hilton Head and Charleston.

288 pp, $15.95, 1-55650-747-X

GREAT SMOKY MOUNTAINS

Blair Howard

"The take-along guide." – *Bookwatch*

Includes overlapping Tennessee, Georgia, Virginia and N. Carolina, the Cherokee and Pisgah National Forests, Chattanooga and Knoxville. Scenic fall drives on the Blue Ridge Parkway.

288 pp, $15.95, 1-55650-720-8

HAWAII

John Penisten

Maui, Molokai, Lanai, Hawaii, Kauai and Oahu are explored in detail, along with many of the smaller, less-visited islands. Full coverage of the best diving, trekking, cruising, kayaking, shopping and more from a Hawaii resident.

420 pp, $16.95, 1-55650-841-7

HIGH SOUTHWEST

2nd Edition, Steve Cohen

"Exhaustive detail... [A] hefty, extremely thorough & very informative book." – *QuickTrips Newsletter*

"Plenty of maps/detail – an excellent guide." – *Bookwatch*

Four Corners of NW New Mexico, SW Colorado, S Utah, N Arizona. Encyclopedic coverage.

376 pp, $15.95, 1-55650-723-2

IDAHO

Genevieve Rowles

Snake River Plain, the Owyhee Mountains, Sawtooth National Recreation Area, the Lost River Range and the Salmon River Mountains. Comprehensive coverage of ski areas, as well as gold-panning excursions and activities for kids, all written by an author with a passion for Idaho.

352 pp, $16.95, 1-55650-789-5

THE LEEWARD ISLANDS

Antigua, St. Martin, St. Barts, St. Kitts, Nevis, Antigua, Barbuda

Paris Permenter & John Bigley

Far outdistances other guides. Recommended operators for day sails, island-hopping excursions, scuba dives, unique rainforest treks on verdant mountain slopes, and rugged four-wheel-drive trails.

248 pp, $14.95, 1-55650-788-7

NEW HAMPSHIRE

Elizabeth L. Dugger

The Great North Woods, White Mountains, the Lakes Region, Dartmouth & Lake Sunapee, the Monadnock region, Merrimack Valley and the Seacoast Region. Beth Dugger finds the roads less traveled.

360 pp, $15.95, 1-55650-822-0

NORTHERN FLORIDA & THE PANHANDLE

Jim & Cynthia Tunstall

From the Georgia border south to Ocala National Forest and through the Panhandle. Swimming with dolphins and spelunking, plus Rails to Trails, a 47-mile hiking/biking path made of recycled rubber.

320 pp, $15.95, 1-55650-769-0

ORLANDO & CENTRAL FLORIDA

Including Disney World, the Space Coast, Tampa & Daytona

Jim & Cynthia Tunstall

Takes you to parts of Central Florida you never knew existed. Tips about becoming an astronaut (the real way and the smart way) and the hazards of taking a nude vacation. Photos.

300 pp, $15.95, 1-55650-825-5

MICHIGAN

Kevin & Laurie Hillstrom

Year-round activities, all detailed here by resident authors. Port Huron-to-Mackinac Island Sailboat Race, Isle Royale National Park, Tour de Michigan cycling marathon. Also: canoeing, dogsledding and urban adventures.

360 pp, $16.95, 1-55650-820-4

NEVADA

Matt Purdue

Adventures throughout the state, from Winnemucca to Great Basin National Park, Ruby Mountain Wilderness to Angel Lake, from Cathedral Gorge State Park to the Las Vegas strip. Take your pick!

256 pp, $15.95, 1-55650-842-5

NORTHERN CALIFORNIA

Lee Foster & Mary Lou Janson

Waves lure surfers to Santa Cruz; heavy snowfall attracts skiers to Lake Tahoe; scuba divers relish Monterey Bay; horseback riders explore trails at Mammoth Lake. Travel the Big Sur and Monterey coasts, enjoy views of Yosemite and savor Wine Country. Resident authors.

360 pp, $15.95, 1-55650-821-2

OKLAHOMA

Lynne Sullivan

The only full-sized comprehensive guidebook covering Oklahoma from tip to toe. Explore the rich history of the state's 250,000 Native American residents, their lands and culture, with details on pow-wows, historical reenactments, and celebrations. The author also tells where, when and how to bike, hike, float, fish, climb, ride and explore, with full information on outfitters and guides. Photos.

300 pages, $15.95, 1-55650-843-3

PACIFIC NORTHWEST

Don & Marjorie Young

Oregon, Washington, Victoria and Vancouver in British Columbia, and California north of Eureka. This region offers unlimited opportunities for the adventure traveler. And this book tells you where to find the best of them.

6 x 9 pbk, 360 pp, $16.95, 1-55650-844-1

PUERTO RICO

3rd Edition, Harry S. Pariser

"A quality book that covers all aspects... it's all here & well done." – *The San Diego Tribune*

"... well researched. They include helpful facts... filled with insightful tips." – *The Shoestring Traveler*

Crumbling watchtowers and fascinating folklore enchant visitors. Color photos.

344 pp, $15.95, 1-55650-749-6

SIERRA NEVADA

Wilbur H. Morrison & Matt Purdue

California's magnificent Sierra Nevada mountain range. The Pacific Crest Trail, Yosemite, Lake Tahoe, Mount Whitney, Mammoth Lakes, the John Muir Trail, King's Canyon and Sequoia – all are explored. Plus, excellent historical sections. An adventurer's playground awaits!

300 pp, $15.95, 1-55650-845-X

SOUTHEAST FLORIDA

Sharon Spence

Get soaked by crashing waves at twilight; canoe through mangroves; reel in a six-foot sailfish; or watch as a yellow-bellied turtle snuggles up to a gator. Interviews with the experts – scuba divers, sky divers, pilots, fishermen, bikers, balloonists, and park rangers. Color photos.

256 pp, $15.95, 1-55650-811-5

SOUTHERN CALIFORNIA

Don & Marge Young

Browse an art festival, peoplewatch at the beach, sportfish near offshore islands and see world-class performances by street entertainers. The Sierras offer a different adventure, with cable cars ready to whisk you to their peaks. A special section covers daytrips to Mexico.

400 pp, $16.95, 1-55650-791-7

TEXAS

Kimberly Young

Explore Austin, Houston, Dallas/Ft. Worth, San Antonio, Waco and all the places in-between, from Dripping Springs to Marble Falls. Angle for "the big one" at Highland Lakes, or try some offshore fishing. Tramp through the Big Thicket or paddle on Lake Texoma. Photos throughout.

380 pp, $15.95, 1-55650-812-3

VIRGIN ISLANDS

4th Edition, Harry S. Pariser

"Plenty of outdoor options.... All budgets are considered in a fine coverage that appeals to readers."
– *Reviewer's Bookwatch*

Every island in the Virgins. Valuable, candid opinions. St. Croix, St. John, St. Thomas, Tortola, Virgin Gorda, Anegada. Color.

368 pp, $16.95, 1-55650-746-1

VIRGINIA

Leonard M. Adkins

The Appalachian Trail winds over the state's eastern mountains. The Great Dismal Swamp offers biking, hiking and canoeing trails, and spectacular wildlife. Skyline Drive and the Blue Ridge Parkway – popular drives in spring and summer. Photos.

420 pp, $16.95, 1-55650-816-6

THE YUCATAN
Including Cancún & Cozumel

Bruce & June Conord

"... Honest evaluations. This book is the one not to leave home without." – *Time Off Magazine*

"... opens the doors to our enchanted Yucatán."
– Mexico Ministry of Tourism

Maya ruins, Spanish splendor. Deserted beaches, festivals, culinary delights.

376 pp, $15.95, 1-55650-792-5

All Hunter titles are available at bookstores nationwide or from the publisher. To order direct, send a check for the total of the book(s) ordered plus $3 shipping and handling to Hunter Publishing, 130 Campus Drive, Edison NJ 08818. Secure credit card orders may be made at the Hunter Web site, where you will also find in-depth descriptions of the hundreds of travel guides we offer.

www.hunterpublishing.com

ORDER FORM				
Yes! Send the following *Adventure Guides*:				
TITLE	ISBN #	PRICE	QUANTITY	TOTAL
SUBTOTAL				
SHIPPING & HANDLING (United States only) (1-2 books, $3; 3-5 books, $5; 6-10 books, $8)				
ENCLOSED IS MY CHECK FOR				

NAME:		
ADDRESS:		
CITY:	STATE:	ZIP:
PHONE:		

Make checks payable to Hunter Publishing, Inc., and mail with order form to:

HUNTER PUBLISHING, INC.
239 SOUTH BEACH RD
HOBE SOUND FL 33455
561 546 7986 / FAX 561 546 8040